THE BRIDGE

The Life and Rise
of Barack Obama

David Remnick

PICADOR

First published 2010, as a Borzoi Book by Alfred A. Knopf,
a division of Random House, Inc., New York

First published in Great Britain 2010 by Picador
an imprint of Pan Macmillan, a division of Macmillan Publishers Limited
Pan Macmillan, 20 New Wharf Road, London N1 9RR
Basingstoke and Oxford
Associated companies throughout the world
www.panmacmillan.com

ISBN 978-0-330-50994-7 HB
ISBN 978-0-330-51998-4 TPB

A portion of this work originally appeared in slightly different form in
The New Yorker.

Grateful acknowledgment is made to the following for permission to
reprint previously published material:

Alfred Publishing Co., Inc., and Harry Revel Music Co.: Excerpt
from "Underneath the Harlem Moon" by Mack Gordon and Harry Revel,
copyright © 1932 (renewed) by WB Music Corp. (ASCAP) & Harry
Revel Music Corp. (ASCAP). All rights reserved. Reprinted by
permission of Alfred Publishing Co., Inc., and Harry Revel Music Co.

Simon & Schuster, Inc.: Excerpts from *Walking with the Wind:
A Memoir of the Movement* by John Lewis with Michael D'Orso,
copyright © 1998 by John Lewis. Reprinted by permission of
Simon & Schuster, Inc.

9 8 7 6 5 4 3 2 1

A CIP catalogue record for this book is available from
the British Library.

Printed by CPI Mackays, Chatham ME5 8TD

Visit **www.picador.com** to read more about all our books
and to buy them. You will also find features, author interviews and
news of any author events, and you can sign up for e-newsletters
so that you're always first to hear about our new releases.

To Esther

*There's no question that in the next thirty or forty years,
a Negro can also achieve the same position that my brother has
as President of the United States.*

—Robert F. Kennedy, May 27, 1961, Voice of America

*I remember when the ex-Attorney General, Mr. Robert Kennedy,
said it was conceivable that in forty years in America we might
have a Negro President. That sounded like a very emancipated
statement to white people. They were not in Harlem when this
statement was first heard. They did not hear the laughter and
bitterness and scorn with which this statement was greeted. From
the point of view of the man in the Harlem barbershop, Bobby
Kennedy only got here yesterday and now he is already on his way
to the Presidency. We were here for four hundred years and now
he tells us that maybe in forty years, if you are good, we may let
you become President.*

—James Baldwin, *The American Dream and the American
Negro* (1965)

Barack Obama is what comes at the end of that bridge in Selma.

—John Lewis, Washington, D.C., January 19, 2009

Contents

Contents / x

THE BRIDGE

Prologue

The Joshua Generation

Brown Chapel
Selma, Alabama

This is how it began, the telling of a story that changed America.

At midday on March 4, 2007, Barack Obama, the junior senator from Illinois, was scheduled to speak at Brown Chapel, in Selma, Alabama. His campaign for President was barely a month old, and he had come South prepared to confront, for the first time, the Democratic frontrunner, Hillary Clinton. He planned to discuss in public what so many believed would ultimately be his undoing—his race, his youth, his "exotic" background. "Who is Barack Obama?" Barack *Hussein* Obama? From now until Election Day, his opponents, Democratic and Republican, would ask the question on public platforms, in television and radio commercials, often insinuating a disqualifying otherness about the man: his childhood in Hawaii and Indonesia; his Kenyan father; his Kansas-born, yet cosmopolitan, mother.

Obama's answer to that question helped form the language and distinctiveness of his campaign. Two years out of the Illinois State Senate and barely free of his college loans, Obama entered the Presidential race with a serious, yet unexceptional, set of center-left policy positions. They were not radically different from Clinton's, save on the crucial question of the Iraq war. Nor did he possess an impressive résumé of executive experience or legislative accomplishment. But who Obama was, where he came from, how he came to understand himself, and, ultimately, how he managed to project his own temperament and personality as a reflection of American ambitions and hopes would be at the center of his rhetoric and appeal. In addition to his political views, what Obama proposed as the core of his candidacy was a self—a complex, cautious, intelligent, shrewd, young

African-American man. He was not a great man yet by any means, but he was the promise of greatness. There, in large measure, was the wellspring of his candidacy, its historical dimension and conceit, and there was no escaping its gall. Obama himself used words like "presumptuous" and "audacious."

In Selma, Obama prepared to nominate himself as the inheritor of the most painful of all American struggles, the struggle of race: not race as invoked by his predecessors in electoral politics or in the civil-rights movement, not race as an insistence on ethnicity or redress; rather, Obama would make his biracial ancestry a metaphor for his ambition to create a broad coalition of support, to rally Americans behind a narrative of moral and political progress. He was not necessarily the hero of that narrative, but he just might be its culmination. In the months to come, Obama borrowed brazenly from the language and imagery of an epochal American movement and applied it to a campaign for the Presidency.

The city of Selma clusters around the murky waters of the Alabama River. Selma had been a prosperous manufacturing center and an arsenal for the Confederate Army. Now it is a forlorn place of twenty thousand souls. Broad Street ordinarily lacks all but the most listless human traffic. African-Americans live mostly in modest houses, shotgun shacks, and projects on the east side of town; whites tend to live, more prosperously, on the west side.

Selma's economy experiences a burst of vitality during the annual flowerings of historical memory. The surviving antebellum plantation houses are, for the most part, kept up for the few tourists who still come. In mid-April, Civil War buffs arrive in town to commemorate the Confederate dead in a re-enactment of the Battle of Selma, where, in 1865, a Confederate general, a particularly sadistic racist named Nathan Bedford Forrest, suffered defeat. The blacks in town do not share in the mood of Confederate nostalgia. An almost entirely black housing project just outside of town was, for decades, named for General Forrest, who had traded slaves and became Grand Wizard of the Ku Klux Klan.

After the Civil War, black students came to Selma University, a small Bible college, and the town—a town of churches—became renowned as a center of African-American preaching. Selma, Ralph Abernathy wrote in his memoirs, "was to many of us the 'Capital of the Black Belt,' a place where intelligent young people and learned elders gathered." At the same time, because of the grip of Jim Crow, Selma was, as late as the nineteen-sixties, a place of literacy tests and poll taxes; almost no blacks were able to register to vote. Surrounded by disdainful white registrars, they were made to answer questions like "How many bubbles are there in a bar of soap?"

The local sheriff, Jim Clark, was in the grotesque folkloric mold of Birmingham's Bull Connor; he wore a button reading "Never" on his uniform and could be relied upon to take the most brutal measures against any sign of anti-segregationist protest—which is why, as the civil-rights movement developed, the grassroots leaders of the Southern Christian Leadership Conference (S.C.L.C.) made Selma a test case in the struggle for voting rights.

On January 2, 1965, Martin Luther King, Jr., came to Brown Chapel, a brick citadel of the African Methodist Episcopal Church, and told the congregation that Selma had become a "symbol of bitter-end resistance to the civil-rights movement in the Deep South." Just as Montgomery had been the focus of the first bus boycotts and the struggle for civil rights and equal access to public facilities, Selma, King and his comrades decided, would be the battleground for voting rights.

Barack Obama had been invited to Selma more than a month before the anniversary event by his friend John Lewis, a veteran congressman from Atlanta. In his late sixties, portly and bald, Lewis was known around Capitol Hill and in the African-American community less as a legislator than as a popularly elected *griot*, a moral exemplar and a wizened truth-teller of the civil-rights movement. During the long "conservative darkness," from the first Reagan inaugural onward, Lewis said, it was especially "hard and essential" to keep progressive politics alive. "And the only way to do that was to keep telling the story," he said. While King was organizing for the S.C.L.C. in Alabama, Lewis had been the chairman of the Student Nonviolent Coordinating Committee (SNCC). Lewis was present at nearly every important march. He was at King's side at the front of countless demonstrations and in meetings with John Kennedy and Lyndon Johnson in the Oval Office. He was the youngest—and most militant—of the many speakers at the March on Washington in 1963; now he was the only one among them still alive. People called John Lewis a hero every day of his life, but now he was feeling quite unheroic, unsure whom to support: the Clintons, who had "never disappointed" him over the years, or a young and talented man who had introduced himself to the country with a thrilling speech at the 2004 Democratic Convention in Boston. At first, Lewis signaled to Obama that he would be with him, but the Clintons and their circle were appealing to his sense of friendship and loyalty—and they were almost as hard to resist as the lure of history. Feeling acute pressure, Lewis promised both the Clintons and Obama that he would soon have "an executive session with myself" and decide.

For Lewis, growing up in Pike County, Alabama, Jim Crow was like a familiar but ominous neighbor. As a boy, he wanted to leave so badly that he dreamed of making a wooden bus out of the pine trees that surrounded his family's house and riding it all the way to California. His parents were sharecroppers and he was one of ten children. He wanted to be a preacher, and, to practice, he declaimed sermons to the chickens in the coop in the backyard. He preached to them weekdays and Sundays alike, marrying the roosters and hens, presiding over funerals for the dead. ("There was something magical, almost mystical, about that moment when those dozens and dozens of chickens, all wide awake, were looking straight at me, and I was looking back at them, all of us in total, utter silence. It felt very spiritual, almost religious.")

In 1955, Lewis listened on the radio to a young preacher from Atlanta giving a sermon called "Paul's Letter to the American Christians." The preacher, Martin Luther King, Jr., spoke in the voice of the apostle Paul addressing Christians, white Christians, condemning them for a lack of compassion toward their black brothers and sisters. As he listened to the sermon, Lewis wanted to become a minister like Dr. King. Later that year, he joined a movement that started when a department store clerk in Montgomery named Rosa Parks was arrested after she refused to change her seat on the Cleveland Avenue bus. As a seminarian at Troy State, Lewis took workshops in nonviolent resistance and joined the drive to integrate lunch counters and bus-station waiting rooms in Nashville and other Southern towns and cities. He passed out the axioms of Jesus, Gandhi, Thoreau, and King to his fellow demonstrators even as he was being taunted as an agitator, a "nigger," a "coon," as teenaged thugs flicked lighted cigarettes at his neck. As a Freedom Rider, Lewis was nearly killed at the Greyhound station in Rock Hill, South Carolina. Getting beaten, arrested, and jailed became a kind of routine, his regular service, and, after each incident, he would rest a little, as if all he had done was to put in a decent day's labor:

> Some of the deepest, most delicious moments of my life were getting out of jail in a place like Americus, or Hattiesburg, or Selma—especially Selma—and finding my way to the nearest Freedom House, taking a good long shower, putting on a pair of jeans and a fresh shirt and going to some little Dew Drop Inn, some little side-of-the-road juke joint where I'd order a hamburger or cheese sandwich and a cold

soda and walk over to that jukebox and stand there with a quarter in my hand, and look over every song on that box because this choice had to be *just* right. . . . and then I would finally drop that quarter in and punch up Marvin Gaye or Curtis Mayfield or Aretha, and I would sit down with my sandwich, and I would let that music wash over me, just wash right *through* me. I don't know if I've ever felt anything so sweet.

John Lewis knew Selma, knew all its little streets, the churches, the cafés, the Hotel Albert, the paved roads in the white parts of town, the shanties and the George Washington Carver projects where the blacks lived. He knew Jim Clark, the sheriff, of course, and the mayor, Joe Smitherman, who, although less virulent than Clark, slipped and spoke of "Martin Luther Coon." Even after the Civil Rights Act of 1964, there were few places in Selma where black people could meet safely, especially if it was known that they were meeting for political purposes. They got together at a couple of modest restaurants—Clay & Liston's, Walker's Café sometimes—but mostly they gathered at Brown Chapel and at the First Baptist Church, just down the street.

At the rallies and services at Brown Chapel, most of the speakers were from the S.C.L.C. or SNCC, the Urban League or the N.A.A.C.P.—the mainstream groups of the civil-rights movement—but Malcolm X, too, had his turn in the pulpit. In early February, 1965, while King sat in a Selma jail cell, Malcolm spoke in Selma, warning, "I think the people in this part of the world would do well to listen to Dr. Martin Luther King and give him what he's asking for and give it to him fast, before some other factions come along and try to do it another way."

King had received the Nobel Prize for Peace in December, and he described the "creative battle" that "twenty-two million Negroes" were waging against "the starless midnight of racism." Now, in early February, he wrote a letter from his Selma jail cell that ran as an advertisement in the New York *Times:*

Dear Friends,
 When the King of Norway participated in awarding the Nobel Peace Prize to me he surely did not think that in less than sixty days I would be in jail . . . By jailing hundreds of Negroes, the city of Selma, Alabama, has revealed the persisting ugliness of segregation to the nation and the world. When the Civil Rights Act of 1964 was passed many decent Americans were lulled into complacency because they thought the day of difficult struggle was over.
 Why are we in jail? Have you ever been required to answer 100

questions on government, some abstruse even to a political science specialist, merely to vote? Have you ever stood in line with over a hundred others and after waiting an entire day seen less than ten given the qualifying test?

THIS IS SELMA, ALABAMA. THERE ARE MORE NEGROES IN JAIL WITH ME THAN THERE ARE ON THE VOTING ROLLS.

But apart from voting rights, merely to be a person in Selma is not easy. When reporters asked Sheriff Clark if a woman defendant was married, he replied, "She's a nigger woman and she hasn't got a Miss or Mrs. in front of her name."

This is the U.S.A. in 1965. We are in jail simply because we cannot tolerate these conditions for ourselves or our nation . . .

Sincerely,

Martin Luther King, Jr.

King was released soon afterward, but Sheriff Clark and his men went on attacking the voting-rights protesters in town, shocking them with cattle prods, throwing them in jail. Since the day King arrived in Selma, Clark's men had jailed four thousand men and women. Lewis gave a handwritten statement to reporters in Selma saying that Clark had proved himself "basically no different from a Gestapo officer during the Fascist slaughter of the Jews." At a confrontation on the steps of the Selma courthouse, he punched one of King's allies, the Reverend C. T. Vivian, in the mouth so hard that he broke a finger. Then he arrested Vivian. "Would a fiction writer," King wrote a few weeks later in the New York *Times*, "have the temerity to invent a character wearing a sheriff's badge at the head of a helmeted posse who punched a clergyman in the mouth and then proudly boasted: 'If I hit him, I don't know it.' "

At a nighttime rally in the nearby town of Marion, a state trooper shot a young Army veteran and pulpwood worker named Jimmie Lee Jackson twice in the stomach. (Jackson had attempted to register to vote five times.) In the same skirmish, Jackson's mother, Viola, was beaten, and his eighty-two-year-old grandfather, Cager Lee, was injured, too, but declared himself ready for the next demonstration. Jackson lingered for several days, then died.

At the funeral, in Brown Chapel, King declared, "Jimmie Lee Jackson is speaking to us from the casket and he is saying to us that we must substitute courage for caution. . . . We must not be bitter, and we must not harbor ideas of retaliating with violence." James Bevel, one of the youngest leaders of SNCC, suggested that the movement lead a march, from Selma to the capital, Montgomery, place Jimmie Lee Jackson's casket on the steps of the capitol, and demand justice from the governor, George C. Wallace. Earlier that month, Bevel had been beaten with a nightstick by Sheriff Clark, thrown into a jail cell, and pummeled with cold water from a hose.

When Governor Wallace heard reports about what King and the others were planning, he told his aides, "I'm not gonna have a bunch of niggers walking along a highway in this state as long as I'm governor."

Over the years, Lewis has told the story of the afternoon of March 7, 1965—"Bloody Sunday"—hundreds of times. He tells it best in his memoir, *Walking with the Wind:*

> I can't count the number of marches I have participated in in my lifetime, but there was something peculiar about this one. It was more than disciplined. It was somber and subdued, almost like a funeral procession. . . .
>
> There was no singing, no shouting—just the sound of scuffling feet. There was something holy about it, as if we were walking down a sacred path. It reminded me of Gandhi's march to the sea. Dr. King used to say there is nothing more powerful than the rhythm of marching feet, and that was what this was, the marching feet of a determined people. That was the only sound you could hear.

Lewis and a young comrade from the S.C.L.C., Hosea Williams, led the march—a huge, double-file line of six hundred people. Lewis was twenty-five at the time, a slight, shy, yet determined figure in a tan raincoat with a knapsack on his back containing a book, a toothbrush, and a couple of pieces of fruit ("in case I got hungry in jail"). Lewis and Williams led the crowd from Brown Chapel, past a housing project, and toward the arching span of the Edmund Pettus Bridge. (Pettus was the last Confederate general to serve in the U.S. Senate.) At the crest of the bridge, Lewis and Williams came to a halt. Six hundred men, women, and children stopped behind them.

> There facing us at the bottom of the other side, stood a sea of blue-helmeted, blue-uniformed Alabama state troopers, line after line of them, dozens of battle-ready lawmen stretched from one side of U.S.

Highway 80 to the other. . . . On one side of the road I could see a crowd of about a hundred whites, laughing and hollering, waving Confederate flags.

Hosea Williams looked down into the water and asked Lewis, "Can you swim?" He could not.

Again, they started forward. As Lewis recalled, "The only sounds were our footsteps on the bridge and the snorting of a horse ahead of us." The troopers slipped gas masks over their heads. Behind them were many more white men; Clark had deputized volunteers from around Dallas County, a posse armed with whips and nightsticks. One even brandished a rubber hose wrapped with barbed wire.

The officer in charge, Major John Cloud, told Lewis that the protesters made up an "unlawful assembly" that was "not conducive to the public safety." Cloud ordered Lewis and Williams to turn around and "go back to your church or to your homes."

"May we have a word with the Major?" Williams asked.

"There is no word to be had," Cloud said and gave them two minutes to disperse.

Lewis knew that to advance would be too aggressive, to retreat impossible. And so he said to Hosea Williams, "We should kneel and pray."

They turned around and passed the word. Hundreds got to their knees.

But within sixty or seventy seconds of the order to disperse, Cloud lost his patience and ordered his men, "Troopers, advance!"

Lewis remembered the terrible sound of the troopers approaching:

The clunk of the troopers' heavy boots, the whoops of rebel yells from the white onlookers, the clip-clop of horses' hooves hitting the hard asphalt of the highway, the voice of a woman shouting, "Get 'em! *Get the niggers!*"

And then they were upon us. The first of the troopers came over me, a large, husky man. Without a word, he swung his club against the left side of my head. I didn't feel any pain, just the thud of the blow, and my legs giving way. I raised an arm—a reflex motion—as I curled up in the "prayer for protection" position. And then the same trooper hit me again. And everything started to spin.

I heard something that sounded like gunshots. And then a cloud of smoke rose all around us.

Tear gas.

I'd never experienced tear gas before. This, I would learn later, was a particularly toxic form called C-4, made to induce nausea.

I began choking, coughing. I couldn't get air into my lungs. I felt as if I was taking my last breath. If there was ever a time in my life for me to panic, it should have been then. But I didn't. I remember how strangely calm I felt as I thought, This is it. People are going to die here. *I'm* going to die here.

Dozens of demonstrators were carried off to Good Samaritan Hospital, the biggest black hospital in Selma. The rest retreated to Brown Chapel, running, stumbling, gasping for breath. Some stopped and tried to flush out their stinging eyes with water from puddles in the street. The police and the vigilantes kept chase until—and sometimes past—the church door. At First Baptist, a vigilante threw a teenaged protester through a church window. At Brown Chapel, the pews were filled with bleeding, weeping people.

John Lewis had a fractured skull. His raincoat was splattered with mud and his own blood. But he was still conscious, and somehow moving. He refused to go to Good Samaritan and headed for Brown Chapel instead. Once inside, he stepped to the pulpit and said to his fellow demonstrators, "I don't know how President Johnson can send troops to Vietnam. I don't see how he can send troops to the Congo. I don't see how he can send troops to *Africa*, and he can't send troops to Selma, Alabama."

"Tell it!" the marchers shouted. "Go on!"

"Next time we march," Lewis declared, "we may have to keep going when we get to Montgomery. We may have to go on to *Washington*."

That night, at around 9 P.M. on the East Coast, ABC television broke into its broadcast of the film "Judgment at Nuremberg," for what the announcer called "a long film report of the assault on Highway 80." The ABC audience that night was huge—around forty-eight million—and the newscast lasted fifteen minutes before the film resumed.

Bloody Sunday was likely the most important act of nonviolent resistance since 1930, when Mahatma Gandhi led seventy-eight other *satyagrahis* (truth-force activists) in a twenty-three-day march from his ashram to the coastal town of Dandi in protest against the British government and the colonial tax on salt. For millions of Americans, the sight of peaceful protesters being clubbed and gassed in Selma disturbed the foundations of American indifference no less than Gandhi inspired Indians and unnerved the British.

On March 15th, before a joint session of Congress, President Johnson delivered the most ringing endorsement of civil rights ever by a sitting President. In his first twenty years in the House and Senate, from 1937 to 1957, Johnson had voted against all kinds of bills proposing to help blacks, including anti-lynching measures. As Robert Caro makes clear in his multivolume biography of Johnson, L.B.J. had been profoundly affected by his experience as a young man in Cotulla, Texas, teaching poor Mexican-American children, but it was only in the mid-fifties—when, as Caro writes, his "ambition and compassion were finally pointing in the same direction"—that he allowed himself to start working in behalf of civil rights. By 1965, the white supremacists in Congress were weak; Johnson had crushed Barry Goldwater in the 1964 election; the balance of power was shifting, making a bill possible. That night, Johnson said, "At times, history and fate meet at a single time in a single place to shape a turning point in man's unending search for freedom. So it was at Lexington and Concord. So it was a century ago at Appomattox. So it was last week in Selma, Alabama." Johnson's Justice Department had drafted a bill two days before Bloody Sunday. He said that, even if the country could double its wealth and "conquer the stars," if it proved "unequal to this issue, then we will have failed as a people and as a nation." The voting-rights act that he was introducing, he said, would prove insufficient if it allowed the country to relax in its pursuit of justice for the men and women whose forebears had come to America in slave ships:

> What happened in Selma is part of a far larger movement, which reaches into every section and state of America. It is the effort of American Negroes to secure for themselves the full blessings of American life.
>
> Their cause must be our cause, too. Because it is not just Negroes, but really it is all of us who must overcome the crippling legacy of bigotry and injustice. And we *shall* overcome.

Watching Johnson that night on television in Selma, King wept. Six days later, on March 21st, King, Lewis, and thousands of others set out from Brown Chapel on a peaceful march to Montgomery, the "Cradle of the Confederacy." When, five days later, they reached the capital and its government square, King spoke to the crowd as Governor Wallace peeked through the blinds of his office. King declared that segregation was "on its deathbed." Bombings, church fires, or the beating of clergymen would not deter them. "We are on the move now!" King said. And his aim, "our aim," was not to defeat or humiliate the white man, but, rather, to "win his friendship and understanding" and achieve a society "that can live with its conscience":

> I know you are asking today, "How long will it take?" . . . I come to say to you this afternoon, however difficult the moment, however frustrating the hour, it will not be long because truth pressed to the earth will rise again.
> How long? Not long, because no lie can live forever.
> How long? Not long, because you shall reap what you sow. . . .
> How long? Not long, because the arc of the moral universe is long but it bends toward justice.

This last refrain became Barack Obama's favorite quotation. He was three when it was uttered. Over the years, Obama read the leading texts of the black liberation movement: the slave narratives; the speeches of Frederick Douglass, Sojourner Truth, Marcus Garvey, Martin Luther King, Fannie Lou Hamer, Ella Baker, and Malcolm X; the crucial court opinions of desegregation; John Lewis's memoir. Scenes of the movement's most terrifying and triumphant moments—dogs tearing at marchers, King on the steps of the Lincoln Memorial, his assassination on the balcony of the Lorraine Motel, in Memphis—unspooled in his mind in "black and white," he said, exciting his imagination and deepening his longing for a firm identification with African-American community and history and for a sense of purpose in his life. Obama's racial identity was both provided and chosen; he pursued it, learned it. Surrounded by a loving white mother and sympathetic white grandparents, and raised mainly on a multicultural island where the one missing hue was his own, Obama had to claim that identity after willful study, observation, even presumption. On a visit to Chicago during law school, Obama, a friend noticed, was reading *Parting the Waters*, the first volume of Taylor Branch's magnificent history of the civil-rights movement. Only a few years earlier, he had endured a tumultuous inner struggle about his identity, but Obama nodded at the book and said with absolute confidence, "Yes, it's *my* story."

In January, 2007, a month before Obama formally declared his candidacy for President, the polls indicated that Hillary Clinton had a firm hold on the African-American vote. At that time, not all African-Americans knew who Obama was; among those who did, many were either wary of

THE BRIDGE / 14

another symbolic black candidacy, another Shirley Chisholm or Jesse Jackson, or loyal to the Clintons.

African-Americans know that their votes are especially crucial in the nominating process. "The Negro potential for political power is now substantial," Dr. King wrote in 1963, in *Why We Can't Wait*. "In South Carolina, for example, the 10,000-vote margin that gave President Kennedy his victory in 1960 was the Negro vote. . . . Consider the political power that would be generated if the million Americans who marched in 1963 also put their energy directly into the electoral process." King's prediction, which preceded passage of the Voting Rights Act and the registration of many hundreds of thousands more black voters, became an axiom of Democratic Party politics.

No one knew this calculus better than Bill Clinton. A white Southerner, Clinton had read black writers and had black friends—a sharp difference from nearly all of his predecessors. The syndicated black radio host Tom Joyner recalled how Clinton awarded Rosa Parks the Congressional Medal of Freedom in 1996, and, at the ceremony, Jessye Norman led the audience in "Lift Every Voice and Sing," the James Weldon Johnson hymn commonly known as the Negro national anthem. "Every living black dignitary was in the audience that great day and everyone stood and sang the first verse loudly and proudly," Joyner recalled. "As we got to the second verse, the singing got faint. Most of us left it up to Miss Norman, who had the words in front of her. The only person in the room who sang every word of every verse by heart was Bill Clinton. By the third verse, he and Jessye Norman were doing a duet."

Writing in *The New Yorker* in 1998, in the midst of the Monica Lewinsky scandal and the sanctimony parade that followed, Toni Morrison remarked that Bill Clinton, "white skin notwithstanding," had been the "first black president," a Southerner born poor, a "saxophone-playing, McDonald's-and-junk-food-loving boy," the first national leader to have a real affinity for and ease with African-American friends, churches, and communities.

In January, according to a Washington *Post*/ABC poll, Hillary Clinton was ahead among African-Americans three to one. Obama had failed so far to win support from civil-rights leaders. There was a constant stream of negative talk in public forums and on the Internet, trash talk about his patriotism, his left-wing associations, how he'd been schooled and indoctrinated at an Indonesian madrassa. Some civil-rights leaders of the older generation, like Jackson and the Reverend Al Sharpton, who were worried about being surpassed by a new generation, betrayed their anxieties by trying to instruct Barack Obama on the question of genuine blackness. "Just because you are our color doesn't make you our kind," Sharpton said.

Obama and his closest aides recalled that he had been in a similar position at the start of the Illinois Senate race in 2004, with many urban blacks more comfortable, at first, with machine politicians and many whites more comfortable with just about anyone but a black man with a foreign-sounding name that rhymed with the first name of the most notorious terrorist in the world. "We'd been in the same place before," David Axelrod, Obama's chief strategist, recalled. "But one of the most important things you face in a Presidential campaign is the fact that there is almost a year between the announcement and the first real contest, in the Iowa caucuses, and so you have a whole series of surrogate contests in the interim." Selma was the first of those surrogate contests.

One week before the event, the Clinton campaign learned that Obama was speaking at Brown Chapel. They hurriedly made arrangements for Hillary Clinton to speak three blocks down the street, at First Baptist Church. Artur Davis, an African-American congressman from Alabama and a friend of Obama's, said that Hillary Clinton knew she had to come to Selma: "There was no better place than this stage to make a statement about her seriousness in contesting the black vote." The former President would come, too, and be inducted into the National Voting Rights Museum's "hall of fame."

Bill Clinton was wise enough to know that in Selma Hillary could emerge from the day's news cycle with, at best, an undramatic, gaffe-less draw. He had been counseled to keep his remarks to a minimum in Selma lest he draw attention from his wife. When he and Hillary spoke side by side at the funeral of Coretta Scott King, in February, 2006, he had been masterly, heartfelt, as good, many felt, as any of the best black preachers in the pulpit that day. By comparison, Hillary, speaking just after him, was stiff, awkward, routine. When Bill Clinton read the comparative accounts of their speeches, he told me that he said to Hillary, "If we both spoke at the Wellesley reunion, you'd probably get a better reception. You can't pay any attention to this. This is my life. I grew up in these churches. I knew more people by their first name in that church than at the end of my freshman year. This is my life. You don't have to be better at this than me. You got to be better than *whoever*."

At First Baptist, Hillary Clinton spoke earnestly and well. (Her husband did not attend the speech.) Her goal was to project the movement forward and to place herself within its mainstream. "After all the hard work getting rid of literacy tests and poll taxes, we've got to stay awake because we've got a march to continue," she said in her speech. "How can we rest while poverty and inequality continue to rise?"

Clinton tied the history of Selma and civil rights to a narrative of American emancipation, generalizing its lessons and implications to include herself. The Voting Rights Act, she insisted, was a triumph for all men and women. "Today it is giving Senator Obama the chance to run for President," she said. "And, by its logic and spirit, it is giving the same chance to Governor Bill Richardson to run as a Hispanic. And, yes, it is giving me that chance, too." The writing was, at times, more convincing than the delivery, especially when Clinton, a daughter of northern Illinois, began dropping her "g"s and channeling her inner Blanche DuBois. Where had that accent come from? Some of Obama's black critics, especially those steeped in the church and the lineage of civil-rights-era speakers, said that he did not have a natural gift for the pulpit, either, that his attempts at combining the rhetoric of the sacred and the street—a traditional language of liberation and exhortation—sometimes sounded forced. But it took no expert to hear the extra effort in Clinton's voice. She was sincere, she was trying, but she did not win the day in Selma.

At Brown Chapel, the pews were crammed with men and women who had either been present at Bloody Sunday or had arrived later to set out with Dr. King for Montgomery. Three of King's leading colleagues—John Lewis, C. T. Vivian, and Joseph Lowery—were there, sitting behind Obama. The Reverend Lowery, who was now eighty-five, and a reigning figure in the black churches of Atlanta, saw Obama as a kind of miracle. It could only be a miracle that white Americans, even white Southerners, were prepared at last to vote for a black man. How could he turn away from him? Lowery had also been an ardent supporter of Bill Clinton, in the nineties, but this political moment was different. Lowery had lived through too much to hesitate when it came to Obama. In 1963, Lowery barely escaped the bombing of his hotel room in Birmingham. In 1979, Klansmen opened fire on him in Decatur, Alabama, when he was protesting the jailing of a black mentally retarded man who had been charged with raping a white woman. In Selma, he decided, "I had a candidate."

The trouble was, Lowery damn near knocked that candidate off the stage at Brown Chapel. He came to the pulpit following Lewis's more stolid welcome; he walked gingerly, his voice was scratchy and strained, but he was wily, energized, his eyes full of mischief. In a way that seemed scattered at first, like the opening bars of a piece of avant-garde music that defy resolution, Lowery started talking about all the "crazy" things that had been happening lately—the craziness of him, a Methodist preacher, being in a Catholic church not long before, praying for the health of a Muslim preacher; the "craziness" of a Muslim congressman in church singing Christian hymns. Then the music, and the idea behind it, began to cohere:

> When Harriet Tubman would run up and down the underground, she was as crazy as she could be—but it was a *good* crazy. And when Paul preached to Agrippa, Agrippa said, "Paul, you're crazy." But it was a *good* crazy.
>
> And I'm saying today we need more folks in this country who've got a good crazy. You can't tell what will happen when you have the good crazy folks going to the polls to vote. . . .
>
> Let me tell you what *good* crazy can do. The other day in New York, a man on the platform of the subway had a good crazy. He looked down between the tracks and saw a brother, prostrate, doomed by an oncoming train. And he jumped down in the middle of the tracks. And I asked a friend of mine, I said, Go out there and measure how deep it is. The deepest measurement they've given me is twenty-six inches. Ain't no way in the world for one man to get on top of the other in twenty-six inches, and the train go over, and the only thing it touched, left a little grease on his cap . . .
>
> That *same* God is here today. Something crazy may happen in this country. Oh Lord!

Through most of Lowery's five-minute speech, Obama had a faraway look, but as Lowery started waving his hands, as his homily went into overdrive, as it got funnier, as it became clearer that the really "good crazy" notion behind it all was the possible election of a black man to the Presidency, Obama started laughing and clapping like everyone else. As Lowery stalked away, with the laughter and applause still booming, Obama's face split into an enormous grin. The stage was not merely set; it was as if Lowery had set it ablaze. "Barack told me I stole the show," Lowery said later, "but, I swear, I didn't mean to."

Long before the speech that brought Obama to national attention—the keynote address at the Democratic National Convention in August, 2004, when he was still a state senator—Obama had been speaking to audiences all over Illinois, telling his own story: his family background, his growth as an organizer and as a student, his gratitude to earlier generations, his evolution as a public servant. He learned to make it an emblematic story: my story is *your* story, an *American* story. Obama was not suggesting that he was unique; there are many millions of Americans with complex backgrounds and identities, criss-crossing races, nationalities, origins. But Obama proposed to be the first President who represented the variousness of American life.

Obama could change styles without relinquishing his genuineness. He subtly shifted accent and cadences depending on the audience: a more straight-up delivery for a luncheon of businesspeople in the Loop; a folksier approach at a downstate V.F.W.; echoes of the pastors of the black church when he was in one. Obama is multilingual, a shape-shifter. This is not a cynical gift, nor is it racist to take note of it. The greatest of all American speakers, Martin Luther King, Jr., did the same, shifting from one cadence and set of metaphors and frame of reference when speaking in Ebenezer Baptist to quite another as he spoke to a national, multiracial audience on the steps of the Lincoln Memorial. There was, for King and for other preachers, a time to quote Tillich and a time to quote the blues, a time to invoke Keats and Carlyle, a time to speak of the Prophets. Obama was nowhere near this level of rhetorical magic and fluidity, but, as a politician, he had real gifts. Like the child of immigrants who can speak one language at home, another at school, and another with his friends— and still be himself—Obama crafted his speech to fit the moment. It was a skill that had taken years to develop.

Obama's speech in Selma had the structure of a Sunday sermon. It began with an expression of gratitude to the elders in the room: Lowery, Vivian, Lewis, and the spirit of Dr. King. Then came the ritual acknowledgment of his own "presumptuousness" in running for President after spending such a short time in Washington. Then, by way of invoking the endorsement of an unimpeachable authority, Obama mentioned a preacher known to all in Brown Chapel—the Reverend Otis Moss, Jr., of Cleveland, an important figure in the black church, a trustee of Morehouse College, a former co-pastor, with Martin Luther King, Sr., at Ebenezer Baptist Church in Atlanta—who, he said, had sent him a letter saying, "If there's some folks out there who are questioning whether or not you should run, just tell them to look at the story of Joshua, because you're part of the Joshua generation." In other words, Obama was ascending the pulpit with a message blessed by a spiritual father of the civil-rights movement. And there was another link: Moss's son, Otis Moss III, would soon replace Obama's own pastor, the Reverend Jeremiah Wright, at Trinity United Church of Christ on the South Side of Chicago.

From the early black church through the civil-rights movement, preachers used the trope of Moses and Joshua as a parable of struggle and liberation, making the explicit comparison between the Jewish slaves in Pharaoh's Egypt and the black American slaves on Southern plantations. In *Moses, Man of the Mountain*, Zora Neale Hurston wrote of a fictional Moses who was a figure of both authority and confrontation before the forbidding pharaoh. When Hurston's Moses wins the liberty of the Israelites, he prefigures another Mosaic figure, Martin Luther King, Jr., and a cry goes up, "Free at last! Free at last! Thank God Almighty, I'm free at last!" God's promise to the "children of Israel" was, in the terms of preachers like King, like the promise of equality inscribed in the Declaration of Independence and the Emancipation Proclamation. King asserted his role as the Moses-like standard-bearer for the millions of black men and women "who dreamed that someday they might be able to cross the Red Sea of injustice and find their way to the promised land of integration and freedom." And, as everyone in Brown Chapel knew, King, like Moses, had failed to complete his mission. Indeed, King had had a premonition of his own martyrdom:

> I just want to do God's will. And He's allowed me to go up to the mountain. And I've looked over, and I've seen the Promised Land. I may not get there with you. But I want you to know tonight, that we, as a people, will get to the Promised Land.

Forty years later, forty years of wandering in the desert after the murder of King, Obama paid tribute to the other "Moses" figures in the room—not only the famous ones but also the foot soldiers and the dead. And to universalize his message, to bring it beyond race, beyond Selma, he emphasized that those Moses figures had battled against "Pharaoh" "not just on behalf of African-Americans but on behalf of all of America." Echoing Lincoln at Gettysburg, Obama said that these were people who not only endured taunts and humiliation but "in some cases gave the full measure of their devotion."

Obama had grown up with a secular mother and grandparents, but, since his twenties, he had spent countless hours in black churches, first as an organizer, then as a parishioner, and, like the first preachers of the early black church—underground churches hidden from Southern slave masters—he adapted the emblematic Biblical story of bondage and emancipation to describe a circumstance that was, at once, personal ("*my story*"), tribal, national, and universal. He began by relating that Biblical story to the struggle of the elders of civil rights:

> They took them across the sea that folks thought could not be parted. They wandered through a desert but always knowing that God was with them and that, if they maintained that trust in God, that they would be all right. And it's because they marched that the next generation hasn't been bloodied so much. . . .

Then Obama brought himself into the narrative of civil rights and, as he explained the particularity of his background, insisted on his place in the story:

> My very existence might not have been possible had it not been for some of the folks here today . . . You see, my grandfather was a cook to the British in Kenya. Grew up in a small village and all his life, that's all he was—a cook and a house-boy. And that's what they called him, even when he was sixty years old. They called him a house-boy. They wouldn't call him by his last name. Call him by his first name. Sound familiar?

Obama was making the claim that his grandfather's experience in Africa was not so different from the experience of so many grandparents of the people in the chapel. Racism is racism, suffering is suffering, and they were all provided the same moral and historical moment of possibility:

> Something happened back here in Selma, Alabama. Something happened in Birmingham that sent out what Bobby Kennedy called, "ripples of hope all around the world." Something happened when a bunch of women decided we're going to walk instead of ride the bus after a long day of doing somebody else's laundry, looking after somebody else's children. When men who had Ph.D.s were working as Pullman porters decided that's enough and we're going to stand up, despite the risks, for our dignity.

In Obama's telling, the American moment of uprising and empowerment should be understood as a universal one:

[It] sent a shout across oceans so that my grandfather began to imagine something different for his son. And his son, who grew up herding goats in a small village in Africa, could suddenly set his sights a little higher and suddenly believe that maybe a black man in this world had a chance.

What happened in Selma, Alabama, and Birmingham also stirred the conscience of the nation. It worried folks in the White House who said, "You know, we're battling Communism. How are we going to win the hearts and minds all across the world if right here in our own country, John, we're not observing the ideals that are set forth in our Constitution. We might be accused of being hypocrites." So the Kennedys decided we're going to do an airlift. We're going to go to Africa and start bringing young Africans over to this country and give them scholarships to study so that they can learn what a wonderful country America is.

This young man named Barack Obama got one of those tickets and came over to this country. And he met this woman whose great-great-great-great-grandfather had owned slaves; but she had a different idea, there's some good craziness going on, because they looked at each other and they decided that we know that in the world as it has been it might not be possible for us to get together and have a child. But something's stirring across the country because of what happened in Selma, Alabama, because some folks are willing to march across a bridge. So they got together and Barack Obama, Jr., was born. So don't tell me I don't have a claim on Selma, Alabama. Don't tell me I'm not coming home when I come to Selma, Alabama.

I'm here because somebody marched. I'm here because y'all sacrificed for me. I stand on the shoulders of giants.

Never mind that Obama was born four years before Bloody Sunday. Obama did not stop at his romantic (and partly romanticized) assertion of heroic continuity. He moved on to the new generation's responsibilities, criticized it for its disappointing fecklessness. In its self-regard, its obsession with money, the new generation was not fulfilling its obligations to the tradition of struggle and humanity itself. In Selma, this seemed a message confined to African-Americans; in the days and months that followed, it widened to include people of all races and creeds.

"I worry sometimes that the Joshua generation in its success forgets where it came from," Obama said in Selma. "It thinks it doesn't have to make as many sacrifices. Thinks that the very height of ambition make as much money as you can, to drive the biggest car and have the biggest house and wear a Rolex watch and get your own private jet, get some of that Oprah money." Not that he was against capitalism—"There's nothing wrong with making money"—but focusing on the accumulation of wealth alone led to a "certain poverty of ambition."

Voting for a candidate, even an African-American candidate, was insufficient; it was just another step in a battle against the poverty and inequality that still existed:

> Blacks are less likely in their schools to have adequate funding. We have less-qualified teachers in those schools. We have fewer textbooks in those schools. We got in some schools rats outnumbering computers. That's called the achievement gap. You've got a health care gap and you've got an achievement gap. You've got Katrina still undone.

Even before he announced his candidacy, Obama was selective in talking about race. As the only African-American in the Senate, it would have been natural for him to be the most constant voice on "black issues": structural inequality, affirmative action, poverty, drug laws. But he was determined to be an individual with a black identity but a politician with a broad outlook and purpose. After Hurricane Katrina, an event that reawakened many Americans to the persistent problems of race, Jesse Jackson, Sr., expressed his fury about the treatment of poor blacks in New Orleans, saying that the devastation resembled "the hull of a slaveship." Obama approached the problem with less racially charged language. But now, in Selma, his language was one of cool outrage. It was the language of King in his later years, in the years of the Poor People's Campaign. Obama insisted that the legacy of injustice had continued long past the Civil Rights Act of 1964 and the Voting Rights Act of 1965.

But Obama did not stop at protest. In a sentence that echoed the most famous moment in Kennedy's inaugural address, he wondered if the Joshua generation had lost some of the "discipline and fortitude" instilled in the marchers of a half-century ago as they tried to "win over the conscience of the nation." The new generation's responsibility was both at the kitchen table and in the larger social arena; there was a pressing need to "turn off the television set when the child comes home from school and make sure they sit down and do their homework," to instill the sense that educational achievement is not "something white."

Obama was saying things that a thousand black preachers had said before him, but as a Presidential candidate he was talking not just to the audience in the room but to the cameras, to the rest of the country:

I also know that, if cousin Pookie would vote, get off the couch and register some folks and go to the polls, we might have a different kind of politics. That's what the Moses generation teaches us. Take off your bedroom slippers. Put on your marching shoes. Go do some politics. Change this country! That's what we need. We have too many children in poverty in this country and everybody should be ashamed, but don't tell me it doesn't have a little to do with the fact that we got too many daddies not acting like daddies. Don't think that fatherhood ends at conception. I know something about that because my father wasn't around when I was young and I struggled. . . .

If you want to change the world, the change has to happen with you first. . . . Joshua said, "You know, I'm scared. I'm not sure that I am up to the challenge." The Lord said to him, "Every place that the sole of your foot will tread upon, I have given you. Be strong and have courage, for I am with you wherever you go." Be strong and have courage. It's a prayer for a journey. A prayer that kept a woman in her seat when the bus driver told her to get up, a prayer that led nine children through the doors of the Little Rock school, a prayer that carried our brothers and sisters over a bridge right here in Selma, Alabama. Be strong and have courage. . . .

That bridge outside was crossed by blacks and whites, northerners and southerners, teenagers and children, the beloved community of God's children. They wanted to take those steps together, but it was left to the Joshuas to finish the journey Moses had begun, and today we're called to be the Joshuas of our time, to be the generation that finds our way across this river.

It was a fascinating rhetorical performance. At his announcement speech in Springfield, Obama had recounted his past and then tied it to a larger, common purpose, using the phrase "Let's be the generation . . .": "Let's be the generation that ends poverty in America," "Let's be the generation that finally, after all these years, tackles our health-care crisis." The metaphor that day was Lincoln—the man of scant experience and potential greatness facing a nation on the brink. Obama's address in Springfield was to everyone, not African-Americans in particular. In Selma, he addressed African-Americans, especially, directly, praising elders and both mobilizing and placing demands on the younger generation, the Joshua generation. His rhetoric created a parallel between the particularities of a candidate's life and a political struggle; put forth the self-appointment of a young man to continue and develop a national movement; and delivered it all in the rhetoric of the traditional black church—the first liberated space among the slaves and still the essential black institution. In Selma, Obama evoked not Lincoln but King; he adopted the gestures, rhythms, and symbols of the prophetic voice for the purposes of electoral politics.

There was no question that he won the approval of his elders. "He was baring his soul and I liked what I saw," the Reverend Lowery said. "People were talking that nonsense about was he black enough, but, to me, it's always a question of how you see the movement, where you see yourself in the movement. And he came through."

"Barack was putting matters into the context of church history, which is so important to black Americans," the Reverend C. T. Vivian said. "To black people, Barack was right on base. Martin Luther King was our prophet—in Biblical terms, the prophet of our age. The politician of our age, who comes along to follow that prophet, is Barack Obama. Martin laid the moral and spiritual base for the political reality to follow. And this is a transformative time in our history. It is no *ordinary* time."

In the months that followed, there was much talk about Obama's early distance from the centers of African-American life, the fact that he grew up in a white family, with the black father almost entirely absent. "Oh, please," Reverend Vivian said. "Any time you decide to be black in America, it will give you all the pain you need."

Ever since the assassination of King, in April, 1968, and of Robert Kennedy, two months later, the liberal constituencies of America had been waiting for a savior figure. Barack Obama proposed himself. In the eyes of his supporters, he was a promise in a bleak landscape; he possessed an inspirational intelligence and an evident competence when the country had despaired of a reckless and aggressively incurious President; he possessed a worldliness at a time when Americans could sense so many rejecting, even hating, them; he was an embodiment of multi-ethnic inclusion when the country was becoming no longer white in its majority. This was the promise of his campaign, its reality or vain romance, depending on your view.

Obama also proposed a scenario for improbable victory. He had taken an antiwar position on Iraq before the invasion—not an act of overwhelming courage for a state senator from Hyde Park, perhaps, but hardly risk-free, and enough to distinguish him from his Democratic opponents. It would attract younger voters and the liberal wing of the Party. And it was just possible that race—especially as he projected it—would help him far more than it would hurt him.

.   .   .

The final event of the day in Selma was the ritual crossing of the Edmund Pettus Bridge. On the far end of the bridge there was a billboard thanking visitors for supporting local Civil War tourist spots; it featured a huge portrait of General Forrest. "To visit Selma today is to remember that America still hasn't lived up to its promises," C. T. Vivian said. "But black folks know that, step by step, we are winning. The forces of evil are being defeated."

Unlike the ritual re-enactments of the Battle of Selma, the re-enactment of the crossing of the Pettus Bridge involved no mock violence. The skirmishes were limited to the jostling of photographers trying to get a picture of the Clintons and Obama. Would they stand together and link arms? They would not. But they did share the front row with Lewis and Lowery and younger politicians, like Artur Davis. Along the way, Obama encountered the Reverend Fred Shuttlesworth, a civil-rights icon in his mid-eighties, who had battled Bull Connor in Birmingham and survived beatings, bombings, and years of slanderous attack. Shuttlesworth had recently had a brain tumor removed, but he refused to miss the commemoration. On the bridge, he chatted awhile with Obama. And then Obama, who had read so much about the movement, who had dreamed about it, took off his jacket, rolled up his sleeves, popped a piece of Nicorette gum in his mouth, and helped push the wheelchair of Fred Shuttlesworth, a leader of the Moses generation, across the bridge and over to the other side.

Part One

You have to leave home to find home

—Ralph Ellison, marginal note in an unfinished manuscript

Chapter One

A Complex Fate

It is an ordinary day, 1951, downtown Nairobi. A city sanitary inspector sits alone in his office. He is moon-faced, with wide-set features, an intelligent young African of twenty-one, stifled in his ambitions at a time of political turmoil. He is testing milk samples for the local health department. The colonial government has initiated a crackdown on the Kenyan independence movement that began to flourish after the end of the Second World War. By 1952, the British will institute a state of emergency and carry out a systematic campaign of arrests, detentions, torture, and killing to quell the Kikuyu nationalist movement they've come to call "the Mau Mau rebellion."

The door opens: a white woman steps through carrying a bottle of milk. Farming families, Europeans and Africans, come to the office all the time to have food products examined and to make sure they are free of disease before taking them to market.

The young man offers to help. Being a trained functionary in the sanitation bureaucracy is considered a decent job. He grew up in eastern Kenya, on Kilimambogo, a vast sisal farm owned by Sir William Northrup McMillan, a Great White Hunter sort. The farm was in the "white highlands," near Thika, where Europeans owned all the land. His farm manager carried a *kiboko*, a whip made of the hide of a hippopotamus, and was not reluctant to use it. The health inspector's father was illiterate, but he held a relatively privileged job as a kind of foreman on the estate. The family lived in a mud-and-wattle hut with no plumbing or electricity, but he made seven dollars a month, enough to send his son to missionary schools. At Holy Ghost College, a secondary school in the town of Mangu, the young man studied English and learned about Abraham Lincoln and Booker T. Washington. Soon, however, he was at a dead end. There was only so much he could learn in schools where there were no textbooks and students sometimes wrote their lessons in the sand. There were no universities in Kenya. The children of Europeans went "home" to study and the few blacks who could afford college went elsewhere in East Africa. He thought about studying for the priesthood, but, as he said later, the white missionaries in Kenya were "among those who constantly told the African he was not ready for various advances, that he must be patient and believe in God and wait for the day when he might advance sufficiently." And so the young man studied instead on scholarship at the Royal Sanitary Institute's training school for sanitary inspectors.

The European woman regards the young man coolly. His name is Thomas Joseph Mboya, though the woman seems to have no desire to learn that.

"Is *nobody* here?" she says, looking straight at Tom Mboya.

When Tom was still living on Sir William's farm, his father used to tell him, "Do not set yourself against the white man." But Tom couldn't bear the manager of the estate, with his whip, his entitled swagger; he couldn't bear the fact that his white colleagues in the inspection bureaucracy made five times as much as he; and now, on this ordinary day, he cannot bear this impertinent white woman making so determined an effort to stare right through him, to will him into invisibility.

"Madam," he says, "something is wrong with your eyes."

The woman stalks out of the inspection lab.

"I must have my work done by Europeans," she says. "This boy is very rude."

Like thousands of other Kenyans at the time, Tom Mboya was listening to the speeches of Jomo Kenyatta, known as the Burning Spear, the elder statesman and leading voice of the Kenyan independence movement. Anti-colonialist movements were gaining strength throughout Africa: in Nigeria, Congo, Cameroon, the Gold Coast, Togo, the Mali Federation of Senegal and French Sudan, Somalia, Madagascar.

In 1955, when he was twenty-five, Mboya won a rare scholarship to study for a year at Ruskin College, in Oxford, where he read widely in politics and economics, joined the Labour Club and the Socialist Club, and discovered a circle of liberal, anti-colonial professors. For Mboya, who had no prior university experience, the year at Ruskin prodded him to think of what other Kenyans could gain from a higher education abroad.

When Mboya returned to Nairobi, the next year, he began to make a name for himself as an activist and labor organizer. With Jomo Kenyatta in jail for nearly all of the last decade of colonial rule, people began to speak of charismatic young Tom Mboya, a member of the minority Luo tribe, as a future leader of post-colonial Kenya and a politician of a new kind. Kenyatta was the singular Kenyan hero, but he was a traditional anti-colonial fighter surrounded mainly by loyal Kikuyu. Mboya hoped that Kenya would look beyond tribal divisions and toward an integrationist conception of democratic self-rule and liberal economic development.

In 1957, after the British made concessions concerning the number of Africans permitted to sit on Kenya's Legislative Council, Mboya, at twenty-six, won a seat representing Nairobi, a predominantly Kikuyu-speaking constituency. Mboya's Luo tribe came mainly from the areas near Lake Victoria, in the western part of Kenya. Soon he became the secretary-general of both the Kenya African National Union, the leading independence party, and the Kenya Federation of Labor. He was an electrifying speaker and an effective diplomat. Well before he turned thirty, Mboya was an international symbol of anti-colonialism and civil rights. In the U.S., he met with Eleanor Roosevelt, Richard Nixon, Thurgood Marshall, and Roy Wilkins and even shared a stage with Martin Luther King, Jr., at a civil-rights rally. In Kenyatta's absence, he led delegations to Lancaster House, in London, to negotiate the final arrangements for Kenyan independence. In March, 1960, the editors of *Time* put Mboya on their cover as an exemplar of independence movements across the continent.

One of the movement's frustrations was that there was no easy way to develop the intellectual potential of young Kenyans. Kenyatta and Mboya could more easily envisage the end of colonialism than they could a sufficiently educated cadre of Africans to run the country. "Too often during the nationalist struggle," Mboya wrote, "our critics informed us the African people were not ready for independence because they would not have enough doctors and engineers and administrators to take over the machinery of government when the colonial power was gone. This criticism has never been justified. At no time has a colonial power deliberately educated the mass of the people for the day of independence." The Kenyans would have to do it themselves.

Mboya tried to persuade the British to provide some of the most promising young Kenyans with scholarship money to study abroad. He came up with the notion of an "airlift" to foreign universities. He worked closely with a number of wealthy liberal Americans on the idea, particularly the industrialist William X. Scheinman. For the Americans, the airlift had a Cold War motivation: as African countries became independent, they might tie themselves more closely to the West, rather than to the Soviet Union, if their young élites went to universities in the United States and Western Europe. In 1958, as Mboya was developing the idea, the total number of black Kenyans in college amounted to a few hundred in African schools, seventy-four in Great Britain, and seventy-five in India and Pakistan. Albert Sims, a former State Department and Peace Corps educational expert, estimated that, in sub-Saharan Africa, only one child in three thousand attended secondary school and one in eighty-four thousand went to college "of any sort." That was certainly part of the reason that a colony of sixty-five thousand Europeans had been able to retain power for so long over more than six million Africans.

The colonial administration rejected Mboya's airlift proposal, telling him that his "crash" educational program was more political than educational and that most of the students were under-prepared, ill-financed, and bound to fail out of American colleges.

The U.S. State Department was not eager to defy the British by sending Mboya money. Instead, Mboya came to the United States to raise money privately. For six weeks, he gave as many as six speeches a day on college campuses in the hope of arousing interest in the program and in collecting promises for scholarships. He obtained promises of cooperation from a range of schools, especially historically black colleges like Tuskegee, Philander Smith, and Howard and religious-based colleges like Moravian College, in Pennsylvania, and St. Francis Xavier University, in Nova Scotia.

Along with his new American friends, Mboya helped found the African-American Students Foundation to increase fund-raising. And, in the fall of 1959, with the support of the A.A.S.F. and dozens of American universities, the airlift began. Among the eight thousand donors were black celebrities such as Jackie Robinson, Sidney Poitier, Mrs. Ralph Bunche, and Harry Belafonte and white liberals like Cora Weiss and William X. Scheinman.

Back in Nairobi, Mboya didn't have much time to review applications. Hundreds of people lined up outside his door every day, petitioning him about health care, divorce decrees, dowries, land disputes. Mboya studied the stacks of files of young Kenyan men and women who had worked hard in secondary school and were now in dull or menial jobs far below their potential. The students' applications were sincere and patriotic. Their ambitions were not of emigration and escape but of education and return, of service to an independent Kenya.

The airlifts, which continued until 1963, had a profound effect, and the program soon expanded to other African countries. "My father was one of the few Kenyan politicians who was equally at home in a village and Buckingham Palace," Mboya's daughter Susan said. "Africa is a very complex society, and you need people who are educated and worldly enough to translate those worlds to each other. Without it, you are lost. The airlift provided a pool of people like that for Kenya's future."

The airlift was a signal event in the history of Kenya as it approached independence. According to a report conducted by the University of Nairobi, seventy per cent of the upper-echelon posts in the post-colonial government were staffed by graduates of the airlift. Among them was the environmentalist Wangari Maathai, the first African woman to win the Nobel Peace Prize. Another was a Luo from a village near Lake Victoria, an aspiring economist with a rich, musical voice and a confident manner. His name was Barack Hussein Obama.

In Selma, Barack Obama, Jr., had said that he could trace his "very existence" to the Kennedy family because the Kennedys had donated money to Tom Mboya's educational program for young Kenyans. Factually and poetically, Obama had overreached. The Kennedys did not contribute to the first airlift that, in September, 1959, brought Obama's father and eighty others from Nairobi to the United States. As the Washington *Post* reported a year after the Selma speech, Mboya approached Kennedy at the family compound in Hyannisport in July, 1960, *after* the first airlift and in the hope of funding the second. At the time, Kennedy was chairman of a Senate subcommittee on Africa and was running for President. He listened to Mboya's proposal and then gave him a hundred thousand dollars from a family foundation named for his brother Joseph, who was killed in the Second World War. Vice-President Richard Nixon, who was running against Kennedy that year and was also eager to win black votes, had earlier tried to get support for the plan from the Eisenhower Administration but failed. This, and the prospect of Kennedy's getting to advertise his largesse, deeply frustrated him. A Nixon ally, Senator Hugh Scott, accused Kennedy of making the donation from a tax-exempt foundation for political purposes—a charge that Kennedy called "the most unfair, distorted, and malignant attack I have heard in fourteen years in politics."

One of Obama's campaign spokesmen, Bill Burton, belatedly apologized for the error in the Joshua generation speech, yet the thrust of Obama's narrative in Selma was hardly a hoax. The Kenyan side of his family had not escaped history. His father was a member of a transitional generation, making the leap from colonialism to independence, from enforced isolation to the beginnings of worldly opportunity. And Obama himself was proposing not only to be the first African-American elected to the White House but to do it as a man whose family was one generation removed from a rural life, an oppressed life, under colonial rule.

When Obama was running for senator in 2003 and 2004, he said that his father had "leapfrogged from the eighteenth century to the twentieth century in just a few years. He went from being a goat herder in a small village in Africa to getting a scholarship to the University of Hawaii to going to Harvard." The notion that Obama's father or grandfather was a mere "goat herder" is also a form of romantic overreach. Manual work was never their destiny or occupation; goat herding was something that all villagers did, even distinguished elders, like the Obama men. "All of us who grew up in the countryside were part-time herdsmen," Olara Otunnu, a Luo and a former foreign minister of Uganda, who was a close friend of Obama's father, said. "It was absolutely of no consequence. It's just something you did while you were in school. Obama's grandfather was, by African standards, middle or upper middle class. He brought china and glassware to the home! The earnings he made as a cook for the British were a pittance by Western standards, but it was cash in hand. He was exalted in his village. And Obama's father grew up with all of that and, of course, surpassed it. Look at the cover of *Dreams from My Father*. Look at the photograph on the left of Obama's father in his mother's lap. He is wearing Western clothes. A true 'goat herder' would be in a loincloth. Clearly, the grandfather was far more Westernized than most and it went on from there."

Barack Obama, Sr.,'s father, Onyango Obama, was born in 1895 in western Kenya. He was impatient with village life. "It is said of him that he had ants up his anus," his third wife, Sarah Ogwel, once said. He learned to read and write English, then made the two-week trek to Nairobi, where he found work as a cook for white Britons. A "domestic servant's pocket register" that Obama saw when he visited Kogelo, shows that, in 1928, when Onyango was thirty-three, he worked as a "personal boy," and there are short remarks of evaluation in the register from a Mr. Dickson, a Captain C. Harford, a Dr. H. H. Sherry, and a Mr. Arthur W. H. Cole, of the East Africa Survey Group. Mr. Dickson praised Onyango's food ("His pastries are excellent"), but Mr. Cole declared him "unsuitable and certainly not worth 60 shillings per month."

After Onyango's first wife, Helima, discovered that she could not conceive, he outbid another man for a young woman named Akumu Nyanjoga, paying a dowry of fifteen head of cattle. In 1936, Akumu bore a son, Barack. Soon afterward, Onyango Obama met and married Sarah Ogwel. Akumu found her husband to be imperious and demanding. She left him with two children. Barack considered both Akumu and Sarah to be his mother. (And, today, Barack, Jr., calls Ogwel, who is in her late eighties and still lives in the village of Kogelo, "Granny" or "Mama Sarah.") Sarah recounted to her grandson tales of her husband's mythological adventures—how Onyango, on his trek to Nairobi, fought off leopards with his *panga*, climbed a tree, and stayed in the branches for two days to avoid a rampaging water buffalo, and how he found a snake inside a drum.

Onyango was an herbalist, a healer, a well-respected farmer, and a prominent man in his village. He was also, like most Luo men, a stern father, demanding that his children behave like the obedient little boys and girls he had seen when working for the British colonials. "Wow, that guy was *mean*!" Obama quotes his half brother Abongo as saying. "He would make you sit at the table for dinner, and served the food on china, like an Englishman. If you said one wrong thing, or used the wrong fork—pow! He would hit you with his stick. Sometimes when he hit you, you wouldn't even know why until the next day." Before Barack, Sr., was born, Onyango lived for a while in Zanzibar and converted to Islam. Well over ninety per cent of the Luo were Christians; the decision to convert was highly unusual and the reasons were vague. Onyango added "Hussein" to his name and gave it to Barack when he was born.

During the Second World War, Onyango served as a cook in the British Army in Burma. He was likely attached to the King's African Rifles, a colonial regiment that drew on British-controlled lands on the African continent. He was called "boy" by the British officers and soldiers and suffered all the other indignities of a black African in such a situation. The work itself was an indignity: in Luo society, men do not cook. "So here is a grand village elder, the head of an important clan, doing women's work for the white man: he has to psychologically adapt," Olara Otunnu, Obama's Ugandan friend, said. "The colonials treated their servants very badly. They were rude and disrespectful. It would hurt anyone to be a 'coolie,' to use the old colonial term, but especially a village leader like Onyango."

Onyango had also come to sympathize with the independence movement. Working for the British, he had earned cash in the new money economy, but he had also accumulated a well of resentment. "He did not like the way the British soldiers and colonialists were treating Africans, especially members of the Kikuyu Central Association, who at the time were believed to be secretly taking oaths which included promises to kill the white settlers and colonialists," Sarah Ogwel said.

In the nineteen-fifties, the colonial government tried to smash African uprisings by any means necessary—land confiscation, midnight roundups, forced marches, mass arrests, detention, forced labor, food and sleep deprivation, rape, torture, and executions. The government fed the British and the world press lurid tales of savage Mau Maus, rebel gangsters, led by the anti-colonialist fighter Dedan Kimathi, taking wild occultist oaths to slaughter Europeans, who, after all, had come to the "Dark Continent" in the nineteenth century with nothing more than a "civilizing mission" in mind. Except in the most liberal and left-wing circles, very little was said against the anti–Mau Mau campaign, or against colonialism as it was actually practiced. The rebel Kenyans, the colonial British charged, had not taken an oath of *ithaka na wiyathi*, land and freedom, as they had claimed, but, rather, a "black-magic" vow to kill.

The colonial government set in motion an elaborate system of exaggeration and repetition that spawned stories all over the world about bloodthirsty Africans and the noble civil servants and soldiers fighting to prevent the collapse of civilization. Those stories—in British newspapers, on the radio, in *Life* magazine—tilled the emotional ground and provided the political pretext for a campaign of vicious retribution. The colonial government established many detention centers—Langata, Kamiti, Embakasi, Gatundu, Mweru, Athi River, Manyani, Mackinnon Road— that historians, such as Caroline Elkins, later termed the "Kenyan gulag." The British claimed that these detention camps held only a few thousand Kikuyu temporarily and were merely a tool of re-education, rehab centers where classes in elementary civics and handicrafts were taught. In fact, when the colonial administration declared a state of emergency, in 1952, it went on a campaign of "pacification" reminiscent of the worst state terror rampages in history. The campaign of mass arrests only increased in its virulence with the commencement, in April 1954, of Operation Anvil, as Britain's soldiers, under General Sir George Erskine, sought to purge Nairobi of all Kikuyu. In the years of the Mau Mau rebellion, fewer than a hundred Europeans were killed; the British killed tens, if not hundreds, of thousands of Africans. The Mau Mau leader, Dedan Kimathi, was arrested in 1956, hanged, and buried in an unmarked grave.

"During the Emergency," Mboya wrote in his memoir, *Freedom and After*, "most publicity was centered around what the Mau Mau did and very little was concerned with what the security forces did. The many Africans who disappeared never to be seen again, the many people arrested in the night who never came back, the fact that some security forces were reportedly paid so many shillings for each person they shot—these were atrocities that came out only in part during court hearings at the time. It is unlikely that the full story will ever come out, because at most district headquarters there have been bonfires of documents relating to the Emergency period, but there are many facts which cannot be burned into oblivion."

The full story did not emerge until the twenty-first century, but when it did the evidence was overwhelming. After spending years combing the British and African archives, the historian Caroline Elkins concluded that the camps held well over a million Kenyans. Prisoners were often subjected to hideous methods of torture, which had been employed in British Malaya and in other imperial outposts. For her book *Imperial Reckoning*, Elkins interviewed hundreds of Kenyans who had survived the depredations of the period, including a Kikuyu woman named Margaret Nyaruai, who was questioned by a British officer. Nyaruai was asked:

> Questions like the number of oaths I had taken, where my husband went, where two of my stepbrothers had gone (they had gone into the forest). I was badly whipped, while naked. They didn't care that I had just given birth. In fact, I think my baby was lucky it was not killed like the rest. . . . Apart from beatings, women used to have banana leaves and flowers inserted into their vaginas and rectums, as well as have their breasts squeezed with a pair of pliers; after which, a woman would say everything because of the pain. . . . Even the men had their testicles squeezed with pliers to make them confess! After such things were done to me, I told them everything. I survived after the torture, but I still have a lot of pain in my body even today from it.

The cruelty, Elkins writes, was limited only by the "sadistic imagination of its perpetrators." One woman she interviewed, Salome Maina, told her that members of the colonial forces beat her, kicked her, bashed heads together, shoved a concoction of paprika pepper and water into her "birth canal"—all in an attempt to force a confession of complicity with the Mau Mau. After she recovered from those humiliations, she said, she was subjected to electric shock:

> The small conductor was either placed on the tongue, on the arm, or anywhere else they desired. At first, I was made to hold it in my hands, and it swirled me around until I found myself hitting the wall. When it

was placed on your tongue, held in place with some kind of wire, it would shake you until you wouldn't even realize when it was removed.

Although some critics charged Elkins with minimizing the violence of Africans against Europeans, most of their charges seem to be the result of historical disbelief, of having to accommodate a murderous colonial legacy that had been talked about so rarely, and with so little understanding, in both Africa and in the West. This was the Kenya of Barack Obama, Sr.,'s memory, of his youth and early manhood.

During the 2008 American Presidential campaign, many foreign reporters called on Sarah Ogwel, in the village of Kogelo, and, with each visiting television truck and satellite dish, she sat dutifully under her mango tree or in her house and submitted to questions about her husband, her stepson, her grandson. According to an interview Ogwel gave to the *Times* of London, a white employer had denounced Onyango to the colonial authorities in 1949 and he was arrested, suspected of consorting with "troublemakers." The Mau Mau movement was recognized by colonial authorities in their documents only the following year, 1950; Hussein Onyango Obama was a Luo, not a Kikuyu; and yet it is entirely possible that the British determined that he was sympathetic to the anti-colonial movement. It was not the detention that made news around the world—Obama mentions it in *Dreams from My Father*—but, rather, Sarah Ogwel's detailed description of his treatment in prison.

"The African warders were instructed by the white soldiers to whip him every morning and evening till he confessed," the *Times* reported Sarah Ogwel as saying. She said that "white soldiers" visited the prison every few days to carry out "disciplinary action" on the inmates. "He said they would sometimes squeeze his testicles with parallel metallic rods. They also pierced his nails and buttocks with a sharp pin, with his hands and legs tied together with his head facing down." Ogwel said she was not able to visit or send food. He was beaten until he promised "never to rejoin any groupings opposed to the white man's rule." Some of Onyango's fellow prisoners, she said, died from the torture they experienced in prison.

As a young man, Onyango had not disdained the British. He was the first in his village to wear a shirt and trousers and he had sought out employment with the British as a cook. But now, coming home from detention, he was embittered. "That was the time we realized that the British were actually not friends but, instead, enemies," Sarah Ogwel said. "My husband had worked so diligently for them, only to be arrested and detained."

Onyango's fate, and Sarah's description of it in the *Times*, is plausible, if undocumented. Even though the colonial authorities began "systematic" torture only in 1952, Africans suspected of political disloyalty were sometimes arrested before that and were badly treated. In *Dreams from My Father*, Obama writes that his grandfather was detained for six months and came home looking old, thin, dirty—too traumatized, at first, to say much about his experience. "He had difficulty walking," Obama writes, "and his head was full of lice." Scholars also say that at the time of Ogwel's interview, the political atmosphere in Kenya was tense and was playing havoc with issues of historical memory and accounting. After decades of silence, shame, and ignorance, the air was filled with claims that are not always easy to verify in every detail. Onyango was almost certainly mistreated in a miserable jail, but the details remain imprecise.

Barack Obama, Sr., was no less headstrong than his father, and a great deal more educated. When he was a child, he refused to go to the school closest to his home, where the teacher was a woman. "When the pupils were naughty, they would get spanked," Sarah Ogwel recalled. "He told me, 'I'm not going to be spanked by a woman.'" Instead, she enrolled Barack in a primary school six miles away, and he either walked or she rode him there on her bicycle. He was hardworking and prideful. "I got the best grades today," he would tell Ogwel when he came home from school. "I am the cleverest boy." Barack attended the Gendia Primary School, the Ng'iya Intermediate School, and, from 1950 to 1953, the Maseno National School, run by the Anglican Church. Like Tom Mboya, Obama did well in his exams and got outstanding grades, but he was expelled, for all kinds of infractions: sneaking into the girls' dormitory, stealing chickens from a nearby farm. He left Maseno without a certificate of graduation. When Barack was expelled from school Onyango beat him with a stick until his back was a bloody mess.

In 1956, Barack moved to Nairobi to work as a clerk. While he was in Luoland, he met a girl named Kezia at a village dance party. She was sixteen. "He asked to dance with me during the party and I could not turn him down," she said. "He picked me from several girls present. A few days later, I married him. He paid fourteen cows as dowry, which were delivered in two batches. This was because he loved me greatly."

Barack, like most young educated Africans, admired Kenyatta and the anti-colonial movement. He was even detained for a few days for the crime of attending a meeting in Nairobi of K.A.N.U., the Kenya African National Union.

Obama was stuck. He could get nowhere without a formal education and a degree. Some of his friends from Maseno won spots at Makarere University, in Uganda. Others went on from Makarere to study in England. In his spare time, with the encouragement of two American teachers working in Nairobi—Helen Roberts, of Palo Alto, and Elizabeth Mooney Kirk, of Maryland—Obama took correspondence courses to get his secondary-school equivalence certificate. He took a kind of college application exam at the American Embassy and scored well. He wrote dozens of letters to American universities—the historically black college Morgan State, Santa Barbara Junior College, San Francisco State among them—and was finally accepted by the University of Hawaii, a modest school in a fledgling Pacific outpost of America. Tom Mboya's airlift program would bring him there. Elizabeth Mooney Kirk underwrote some of Obama's expenses in Hawaii.

"My father was very impressed by Obama's intelligence," Mboya's daughter Susan said. "My father was not much older than Obama, but he developed a paternal relationship with him and hoped his studies would lead him somewhere great, and somewhere useful for Kenya."

In September, 1959, Obama prepared to leave for the United States. He and Kezia already had a son, named Roy, and Kezia was three months pregnant with a girl they named Auma. Obama told his wife that he would surely return, that she should wait for him. Few would deny him the chance to make the journey. A brazenly confident young man, Obama boasted to his friends that after he had studied economics abroad he would return home to "shape the destiny of Africa."

"Tom Mboya, what he did for me and Obama and the others, is more than we could ever have expressed," Frederick Okatcha, who went to Michigan State to study educational psychology, said. "The airlift saved us! We took off from Nairobi and none of us had ever been anywhere. We'd never flown in a plane. When we landed in Khartoum a little while later to refuel, we all thought we had reached America! I grew up about fifteen miles from Obama. For years I never wore shoes. We had things like witchcraft, which is embedded in traditional society. My maternal grandfather worried that jealous witch doctors would bewitch our flight to America. Those were things people believed in. Obama, by the time he finished high school, had attended British-influenced schools so the shock was not so severe. But all of our lives would change forever, so completely."

"There was so much excitement during that time," Pamela Mboya, the wife of Tom Mboya, said. As a young woman she had gone to college in

Ohio on the first airlift. "We were going to the U.S. to be educated so we could come back and take over—and that's exactly what we did."

A couple of months into Obama's Presidency, a writer asked Bob Dylan about reading *Dreams from My Father*. Dylan, who had been uncharacteristically swept up in the campaign ("We've got this guy out there now who is redefining the nature of politics from the ground up"), said that he had been struck by Obama's complicated background: "He's like a fictional character, but he's real." Dylan comes from the long American tradition of self-summoned men and women: in his case, a Jew from the Minnesota Iron Range, who braided together various roots from the national ground—Woody Guthrie, the Delta blues, Hank Williams, the Beats, Elvis Presley—to create a unique voice of his own. Dylan read about Obama's parents, Ann Dunham and Barack Obama, Sr., and recognized what a unique set of influences, maps, histories, and genetic codes they contained for their unborn son: "First off, his mother was a Kansas girl. Never lived in Kansas, though, but with deep roots. You know, like Kansas bloody Kansas. John Brown the insurrectionist. Jesse James and Quantrill. Bushwhackers. Guerrillas. 'Wizard of Oz' Kansas. I think Barack has Jefferson Davis back there in his ancestry someplace. And then his father. An African intellectual. Bantu, Masai, Griot-type heritage—cattle raiders, lion killers. I mean, it's just so incongruous that these two people would meet and fall in love." For Dylan, whose mind races to the mythopoetic, if not to the strictly accurate, the story of Obama's origins and identity is "like an odyssey except in reverse."

What does Dylan mean by that? "First of all, Barack is born in Hawaii," he said. "Most of us think of Hawaii as paradise—so I guess you could say that he was born in paradise." He was also born with an endlessly complicated family legacy, one that stretched from the shores of Lake Victoria to the American plains. Obama's grandmother could recite, as if in a Homeric song, the generations of Luo on his father's side. And as a genealogist at the Library of Congress, William Addams Reitwiesner, discovered, Obama's ancestors included Jesse Payne, of Monongalia County, West Virginia, who, in the first half of the nineteenth century, owned slaves named Moriah, Isaac, Sarah, Selah, Old Violet, Young Violet, and Little William. A great-great-great-grandfather, Christopher Columbus Clark, fought for the Union Army.

In his speeches, Obama usually alluded to Kansas as a kind of counterpoint to faraway Kenya, a locus of Midwestern familiarity—the opposite of (that dubious word) "exotic." But Kansas, for him, is something deeper, more resonant, the crossroads of the Confederacy and the Union, the nexus of the battle between pro-slavery forces and abolitionist insurrection; it is the site of Brown v. Board of Education; and it is, for his grandparents, Stanley and Madelyn, a place of soul-defeating dullness. Kansas was the "dab-smack, landlocked center of the country, a place where decency and endurance and the pioneer spirit were joined at the hip with conformity and suspicion and the potential for unblinking cruelty."

It took a long time for Obama to learn to negotiate between the restlessness in his parents' makeup and a rooted worldliness that he could live with. His mother, Stanley Ann Dunham, spent her life in constant motion, as much at home in a Javanese village as she ever was in El Dorado, Kansas, where she went to grade school. Everywhere she landed, in a rural outpost in Pakistan or a densely populated Indonesian city, she looked around and said wryly, "Gee, Toto, I don't think we're in Kansas anymore."

Once, after a campaign stop in Kansas, a reporter on the plane asked Obama about his family's legacy of wanderlust, and, from his answer, it was evident that he viewed all the movement—his grandparents' constant flight, his mother's yearning to stay in motion—as something he wanted to avoid for himself. "Part of me settling in Chicago and marrying Michelle was a conscious decision to root myself," he said. "There's a glamour, there's a romance to that kind of life and there's a part of that still in me. But there's a curse to it as well. You need a frame for the canvas, because too much freedom's not freedom." Then he laughed and said, "I'm waxing too poetic here."

Stanley Armour Dunham's parents, Ralph Waldo Emerson Dunham, Sr., and Ruth Lucille Armour, were stolid Baptists, and when they were young parents they opened a modest restaurant, the Travellers Café, next to an old firehouse on William Street in downtown Wichita. Their promise as a young family did not last. Ruth Dunham killed herself, and Stanley, who was eight years old, found her body. The date was November 26, 1926. In his memoir, Obama alludes to his great-grandfather's "philandering" as a possible reason for Ruth's suicide. (The local press obituaries ascribe the death to ptomaine poisoning, Washington *Post* reporter David Maraniss discovered.) Not long after his wife's death, Ralph Dunham ran off, leaving Stanley and his brother, Ralph, Jr., to be raised by their maternal grandparents in El Dorado, the county seat of Butler County.

In 1918, the year Stanley was born, El Dorado had been an oil-boom town for a few years; through the nineteen-twenties, the region was responsible for nine per cent of the oil in the world. The Depression snuffed out the boom. El Dorado suffered foreclosures and unemployment. Stanley did not usually seem devastated by his bleak beginnings. As he grew up, he became a gregarious, argumentative kid. Sometimes, he betrayed a sense of fury and outrage. In high school, he managed to get suspended for punching the principal in the face. Later, he spent a few years riding rail cars cross-country and working odd jobs. For a while, at least, he seemed like someone aspiring to a role in "Bound for Glory."

When Stanley returned to Wichita, he met a smart, rather quiet girl named Madelyn Lee Payne. Her parents, Rolla Charles (R.C.) Payne and Leona Bell Payne, were Methodists. "They read the Bible," Obama writes, "but generally shunned the tent-revival circuit, preferring a straight-backed form of Methodism that valued reason over passion and temperance over both." Her circumstances were more comfortable than Stanley's and her childhood was far less traumatic. Born in Peru, Kansas, in 1922, Madelyn grew up in the nearby town of Augusta. She was a studious girl and spent her spare time with friends at the drugstores and soda fountains in town: Cooper's, Carr's, Grant's. When they wanted air-conditioning in the summer they went to the movies. Nearly all five thousand people in the town were white. "There were only two black families in Augusta," her friend Francine Pummill recalled. The population was solidly Republican, Madelyn's parents very much included. R.C. worked as a clerk on an oil pipeline and the family lived in a small company house. Despite the family's adherence to strict Methodist rules—no drinking, no dancing, no card-playing—Madelyn used to sneak off to Wichita with her friends to go to the Blue Moon Club and hear the big bands that were passing through: Benny Goodman, Glenn Miller, Tommy Dorsey. Kansas was dry but at the Blue Moon you could get a drink, even if you were under-age.

During her senior year at Augusta High, Madelyn met Stanley Dunham and they married in secret. Madelyn told her parents that she was married only after she had a diploma in hand. No one in the family approved of the marriage. Charles Payne, Madelyn's younger brother, said their parents were "shocked" when they learned that their daughter had married Stanley Dunham and hardly thought he was an "appropriate choice."

Some of Madelyn's friends didn't much like Stanley, either. He seemed too loud and cocky. "Stan was a smart-aleck. He was really king of the castle," Pummill said. "He looked like a greasy spoon, with his dark hair slicked down with something. None of the other fellas in Augusta did that then." He also had unconventional tastes: he wrote poetry and listened to jazz records. He was sarcastic, much louder than Madelyn.

The couple moved to California for a while, but after Pearl Harbor they returned to Kansas and Stanley enlisted in the Army. He was inducted on January 15, 1942, at Fort Leavenworth. "He was really gung-ho," his brother Ralph said. "He didn't have to go, because he was married. He could have held off."

The Dunhams' daughter, Stanley Ann, was born at Fort Leavenworth, in November, 1942.

In October, 1943, after a year stationed at various U.S. bases, Dunham sailed for England on the H.M.S. Mauritania. He was an Army supply sergeant, and on D-Day he was serving at an Allied airfield near Southampton called Stoney Cross with the 1830th Ordnance Supply and Maintenance Company, which helped support the Ninth Air Force before it set out for Normandy. To guard against German aerial attack, the company dug foxholes at Stoney Cross, but the retaliation never came. Dunham helped put together a celebration at a local gym. Six weeks after D-Day, the company, with about seventy-five men, landed at Omaha Beach, in Normandy, and worked at Allied airfields across France: in Cricqueville, Saint-Jean-de-Daye, Saint-Dizier, and others. In February, 1945, Dunham's unit was attached to George Patton's Third Army for three months. Dunham's record was solid. "Sgt. Dunham has been doing a good job as Special Service noncom," his commanding officer, First Lieutenant Frederick Maloof, recorded in one of his weekly reports, from September, 1944. The company documents, uncovered by Nancy Benac of the Associated Press, also record the daily activities of Dunham and his men—the hikes, the lectures on tactics and weapons, the drills, the lectures on "sex morality," and, in October, 1944, a talk on "What to Expect When Stationed in Germany." On April 7, 1945, just as the German Army was disintegrating and three weeks before Hitler's suicide, Dunham was transferred to Tidworth, England, where he was to train as a reinforcement for American infantry; soon afterward, he was transferred back to the States. Like many soldiers returning from Europe, Dunham waited anxiously to see if he would be shipped off to the war in the Pacific, but, with the dropping of atomic bombs on Hiroshima and Nagasaki, the call never came.

Madelyn Dunham, even with a baby at home and her husband fighting in Europe, worked full-time, taking a job at the Boeing assembly line in Wichita, one of the most famous munitions projects of the war. Henry

(Hap) Arnold, a five-star general who had learned his flying at the Wright Brothers school and then went on to command the U.S. Air Force during the war, designed an aerial strategy that called for a huge output of heavy bombers. Designers came up with what was known as the Superfortress, a plane instrumental in the bombing of Pacific targets. The rapid design and construction plan was known as the Battle of Kansas—sometimes the Battle of Wichita. Women like Madelyn Dunham were called on to work long, sometimes double, shifts, to keep the assembly line in Wichita running at the pace that Hap Arnold demanded.

When Stanley Dunham came home from Europe, he briefly tried going to Berkeley on the G.I. Bill, but, as his grandson put it, "the classroom couldn't contain his ambitions, his restlessness." He was nearly as restless as he had been as a teenager riding the rails. He still had a need to keep moving, but now he did it wearing proper clothes and with a wife and daughter in tow. Barack Obama writes about the way Stanley Dunham infected Madelyn, his grandmother, a home-economics major "fresh out of high school and tired of respectability," with "the great peripatetic itch" to escape the "dust-ridden plains, where big plans mean a job as a bank manager and entertainment means an ice-cream soda and a Sunday matinee, where fear and lack of imagination choke your dreams." They moved constantly: from Kansas to Berkeley and Ponca City, Oklahoma; from Wichita Falls, Texas, to El Dorado, Kansas, and, in 1955, to the state of Washington. In Ponca City, Francine Pummill recalled, Madelyn had a miscarriage and a hysterectomy. The Dunhams' daughter remained an only child.

Even as a small girl, Stanley Ann Dunham proved witty and curious. She was unapologetic about her odd name, a relic of her father's initial disappointment at failing to sire a son. During her childhood and adolescence, as the family moved from state to state, she introduced herself to new friends, saying, "Hi, I'm Stanley. My dad wanted a boy." It would take a while before friends started calling her Ann. (I'll do it hereafter, though, to avoid confusion.)

Stan Dunham became a furniture salesman. He enjoyed his job. Friends who worked with him over the years said that as a salesman, he could "charm the legs off a couch." "He was a good salesman, very sharp," Bob Casey, who worked with him at J. G. Paris's furniture store in Ponca City, said. "He was a forward-thinker, one of the first to incorporate room design and a decorating approach to the sale of furniture."

When, in 1955, the family moved to Seattle, Stanley found work selling furniture downtown, first at Standard-Grunbaum at the corner of Second Avenue and Pine Street, and, a few years later, at Doces Majestic Furniture. In the meantime, Madelyn worked as an escrow officer in the nearby town of Bellevue. The post-war Eisenhower-era boom was well under way. Builders were expanding the suburbs, which meant that new homeowners were taking out loans and buying furniture. In their first year in Seattle, the Dunhams lived at an apartment on Thirty-ninth Avenue N.E. and Ann went to eighth grade at the Eckstein Middle School. But the Dunhams decided that they could do better and rented an apartment at the new Shorewood development on Mercer Island, an island in Lake Washington connected to the city by a mile-long floating bridge. Many years later, after the tech boom and the rise of Microsoft, executives built mansions on Mercer Island, but in the fifties it was a middle-class, if expanding, suburb of Seattle. On the island, the Dunhams had a view of the Cascades, and, more important, their apartment was close to a new, and well-regarded, high school where they intended to send their daughter.

The culture at Mercer Island High School was, for most kids, one of sock-hops, basketball games, pep rallies, sleepover parties, Elvis records. But those were not the limits of Ann's frame of reference. An intelligent, even intellectual girl, she had budding bohemian tastes: a love of jazz, an Adlai Stevenson for President button, afternoons at the Encore coffee shop in the University District, foreign films at the Ridgemont theater, on Greenwood Avenue, in Seattle. Ann's crowd was not socially fast, but they were engaged, political, liberal, hungry to read and learn about the world. The first signs of a civil-rights movement, the first discussions about equal rights for women, one of her closest friends, Susan Botkin, said, were what "shaped our values for the future." At school, Ann and her friends took honors courses from a couple of progressive teachers, Jim Wichterman and Val Foubert, who outraged some of the parents by teaching things like the essays of Karl Marx, Margaret Mead's anthropological work on culture and homosexuality, William Whyte's *The Organization Man*, and David Riesman's *The Lonely Crowd*. (Ann's friends jokingly dubbed the length of hallway between those two classrooms Anarchy Alley.) Wichterman, especially, drew the wrath of some parents when he had the class talk about God—and theories of His nonexistence. "This was the Eisenhower era— that was really unusual," another friend, Chip Wall, recalled. Wichterman said that when parents came to the school in an effort to fire him, Foubert, and another teacher, Clara Hayward, they referred to the group as The Mothers' March. Ann Dunham, Wichterman recalled, was a studious young woman who was "not your typical high-school student. She just wasn't all that interested in the things high-school students take an interest in, like who's dating whom and things like that."

Ann was getting some ideas about what she would like to do with her life. She told Susan Botkin that she wanted to study anthropology, possibly even make a career of it. "I had to look up what anthropology was in the dictionary when she told me that!" Botkin said.

Although Ann's parents had church-going Republican backgrounds, the atmosphere at home was, by the standards of the time and Mercer Island, liberal and secular. The Dunhams sometimes attended the East Shore Unitarian Church, which was jokingly known around town as "the Little Red Church on the Hill." But religion was hardly paramount in the Dunham household. Ann usually spoke of herself as an atheist.

The family was also in the minority when it came to politics. "There weren't too many families who were Democrats in our community," Marylyn Prosser Pauley, a friend of Ann's, said. "There were a few of us, though, and we felt a kinship about that. Stanley's family and my family were on the Adlai Stevenson side of things."

There was one disturbing local issue—an outgrowth of McCarthyism—that haunted Mercer Island. In 1955, the House Subcommittee on Un-American Activities summoned John Stenhouse, the chairman of the Mercer Island school board, to testify. Stenhouse was one of the most popular men in town: friendly, intelligent, civic-minded. In 1951, he had moved to Mercer Island with his family (including a daughter whom Ann came to know well) and gone to work for Prudential Insurance. But, four years later, investigators started showing up at his house, and at his neighbors' houses, to ask questions. "I remember two F.B.I. agents coming to our garden to talk to my mother," Marylyn Prosser Pauley said. "My mother was literally kneeling over her gardening when they came on her. They were polite but they were clearly there to ferret out how bad a Communist Jack Stenhouse must have been. Those were the times."

Stenhouse was born in Chungking, China. His father was a trader, and he worked in the family business until the family left China, for Los Angeles, on the eve of the Second World War. During the war, he became a machinist in a weapons factory. His union was the United Auto Workers. Stenhouse began to join left-wing discussion groups. He signed a Communist Party card, attended a few more meetings, and then quit the Party, in 1946. "The changing time was impressing itself on me," he told *Time* in 1955, "and I felt those people were going off on entirely the wrong track, excusing the Soviet Union and criticizing the U.S."

But Stenhouse paid a humiliating price for his brief encounter with the Party, becoming the focus of small-town gossip and outrage. When the story of the House investigation broke, three of his four fellow school board members demanded that he resign the chairmanship. A town meeting was called, at the Mercer Crest School, and two hundred and fifty people from town gathered to debate the fate of John Stenhouse.

"Let's rise on our hind legs and throw him out!" one said.

And yet most of the people at the meeting, including the county spokesman for the Young Republicans, said that, while Stenhouse had made a mistake, he had also confessed to it and ought to be allowed to stay on the board. "I realize I made a mistake," he said at the meeting. "I believe we have the power to show people throughout the world that we have a better way than the Communists." "At the time it was a subject that we girls talked about only among our liberal friends," Marylyn Prosser Pauley said. "This was the first time that we all realized that our government wasn't always all for the good. We had been so idealistic about our wonderful government and our wonderful country until then. It was quite a wake-up call."

"There were times when my father really suffered from all of this," Ann's friend Iona Stenhouse recalled. "I applied for the Peace Corps after I graduated from the University of Washington, in 1965, and was accepted, but when I went for training I was delayed. My security clearance hadn't come through and my father knew why."

Ann was liberal, but she was hardly at the ramparts. She wore pleated skirts and twinsets, joined the French and biology clubs, and worked on the high-school yearbook. "She was a rebel in that she made decisions and she played that through and accepted the consequences when she ran afoul of her parents," Susan Botkin said.

"We were critiquing America in those days in the same way we are today: the press is dumbed down, education is dumbed down, people don't know anything about geography or the rest of the world," Ann's classmate Chip Wall, a retired teacher, said. "She was not a standard-issue girl. You don't start out life as a girl with a name like 'Stanley' without some sense you are not ordinary."

"We could see Stanley, with her good grades and intelligence, going to college, but not marrying and having a baby right away," Maxine Box, another friend from Mercer Island, said.

In Ann's senior year of high school, her father announced that he wanted to move the family yet again—this time to the newest and farthest edge of the American imperium, Hawaii. They would move, he said, a few days after Ann's high-school graduation, in June, 1960. He had heard that speculators and contractors were beginning to build apartment buildings and houses in every mossy crenellation of Oahu. Hotels were sprouting, the military bases sprawling; rows of tract houses were going up. It was another land of promise, especially for a furniture salesman.

Ann was not pleased. She wanted to stay on the mainland for college—she had already been accepted at the University of Washington and the University of Chicago—but the Dunhams said no, they would not allow their daughter, their only child, to live thousands of miles away. And so she reluctantly applied to, and was accepted at, the University of Hawaii.

Father and daughter had a complicated relationship by this time. Ann could not abide her father's rough manners and sometimes explosive temper, and Stanley was still intent on reining in his headstrong daughter. Through the prism of time and recollection, Barack, Jr., saw the family's move to Hawaii as part of Stanley's desire to "obliterate the past," to remake the world. Despite the differences between father and daughter, they shared that restlessness—a kind of patrimony.

Most of the eighty-one members of the 1959 airlift class from Kenya came together on a single charter flight from Nairobi to New York, with fuelling stops along the way. Because the plane was full, Obama took a different flight. "But he certainly is considered part of that contingent," Cora Weiss, the executive director of the program, said. "Hawaii was off the beaten path—statehood had just happened—but they took him. And we wrote checks for his tuition, books, and clothes."

Within weeks of arriving in Honolulu, Obama came to see Hawaii as a refuge from Kenya's tensions and hardships, a remote enclave of racial understanding. The local press took a keen interest in the arrival of a black African who had come there to study. Interviewed by the Honolulu *Star-Bulletin*, Obama described his background as a Luo growing up in western Kenya and how, as a young man in Nairobi, he had learned about Hawaii's atmosphere of racial tolerance "in an American magazine." (The struggles of native Hawaiians seemed lost on him.) He said that he had enough money to stay for a year and then, after getting a background in business administration, he would return home to help build a stable, independent Kenya.

Obama was welcomed as an emissary from a distant world. He was invited to speak about "the African situation" in front of church groups and other community organizations. Like Tom Mboya, Obama told those audiences that he feared that tribal divisions were the greatest threat to an independent Kenya. He was not always patient with the fact-starved opinions of others. When a Honolulu paper published what he thought was a wrong-headed editorial on the Congo, he wrote a stern letter suggesting that "maybe you needed more first hand information."

And yet Obama was almost always inclined to be the pleasantly surprised new arrival. "When I first came here, I expected to find a lot of Hawaiians all dressed in native clothing and I expected native dancing and that sort of thing," he said, "but I was surprised to find such a mixture of races."

The Hawaiian Islands, which had become the fiftieth American state in August, 1959, had a remarkably various population of native Hawaiians, Chinese, Japanese, Filipinos, Samoans, Okinawans, Portuguese, and whites from the mainland of various origins. There were few blacks in evidence at the University of Hawaii, or anywhere else on the islands. The black population was under one per cent, mostly soldiers and sailors living on various bases.

Coincidentally, with statehood, came the arrival at Honolulu airport of the first passenger jets. Until then, it had been a thirteen-hour flight by propeller plane from Los Angeles or San Francisco—far too tedious and grueling a trip for most tourists. The five-hour flight from the mainland transformed Hawaii into an accessible paradise for Americans and, eventually, Japanese and other Asians. And with the rise of mass tourism came a demand for hotels, resorts, shopping centers, freeways, high-rise apartment buildings. Until statehood, the Republican Party, the party of the white plantation-owning élite, had dominated the Hawaiian territory. But as returning Asian veterans got their education under the G.I. Bill, they moved into the mainstream and built up the Democratic Party.

Obama's cheerful first impressions of multicultural Hawaii were the impressions of many sociologists, too. Since the nineteen-twenties, scholars have been referring to Hawaii as a kind of racial Eden. There were no laws against marriage between the races or ethnic groups as there were in so many American states. (It wasn't until the case of Loving v. Virginia, in 1967, that state mandates criminalizing intermarriage—some of the oldest laws in the history of American jurisprudence—were finally ruled unconstitutional by the Supreme Court.) Scholars could be as misty-eyed as poets or politicians when they envisioned the Hawaiian future. The sociologist Romanzo Adams wrote in *The Peoples of Hawaii* (1925) that there was "abundant evidence that the peoples of Hawaii are in a process of becoming one people. After a time the terms now commonly used to designate the various groups according to the country of birth or ancestry will be forgotten. There will be no Portuguese, no Chinese, no Japanese— only American." Lawrence Fuchs, writing four decades later, in his social history *Hawaii Pono*, lauded Hawaii's "revolutionary message of equality." This was 1961. While the American mainland was undergoing a nonviolent revolution against Jim Crow racial laws in the South, Hawaii exuded a forward-looking, laid-back multiculturalism popularized as the "aloha spirit." Sociologists and scholars of race relations, such as Robert Park, Herbert Blumer, and E. Franklin Frazier, attended conferences or went on sabbatical leaves to come to Hawaii to study the racial situation.

Obama lived at a Y.M.C.A. near campus and fell easily into a range of friendships with fellow students and Honolulu bohemians, among them Neil Abercrombie, a native of Buffalo who went to Honolulu as a graduate student in sociology and stayed in Hawaii, eventually becoming a Democratic congressman; Andrew (Pake) Zane, a Chinese-American student and traveler who eventually settled down to run an antiques and collectibles store near Waikiki; and Chet Gorman, who became a prominent anthropologist and archeologist studying Southeast Asia.

In those days, the university was small, the atmosphere casual. You could rent a cottage for fifty dollars a month. Neil Abercrombie, who had come straight from the frozen campus of Union College, in Schenectady, New York, thought he had arrived in heaven. At night, the stars came out, "as if God had hurled them across the sky," and the smell of flowers was so rich as you walked down the street that "you thought the very atmosphere was perfumed."

One day after class, Abercrombie recalled, he headed for lunch to the university snack bar, a simple wooden building with benches, picnic tables, and cheap food, "and as everyone is talking this black guy, a *popolo*, comes in." *Popolo*—Hawaiian for the black nightshade, a weed with dark berries—was not quite as bad as "nigger," but, said with a certain intonation, it was bad enough and certainly carried the connotation of separateness, of otherness. "So here was this coal-black guy, and there was this absolutely dynamic aura about him," Abercrombie went on. "A big smile. Easy to meet. Incredibly smart. And he was exotic in the land of the exotic. He was somebody new. In this world of the incredible spectrum of color and eye shapes and physiognomy, he stood out from even that mélange. And he had this electric vitality. We were what passed for the academic free-spirit world—drinking beer and eating pizza and talking through the night about politics and ideas. Drugs and marijuana and the Beatles—all that came later. It was jazz artists and folk artists—Jimmy Reed and Leadbelly and Sonny Terry and Brownie McGhee. And so Barack immediately got immersed in this little world of ours. He became part of us, our unlikely crowd."

Obama's new friends knew him as "*Bear*-ick"—not "Buh-*rock*"—and they were impressed by the great rumble of his voice, his elegant pipe, his black-rimmed glasses, and the way he held forth, hour after hour, over dollar-fifty pitchers of beer at local dives like George's Inn and the Stardust Lounge. They'd talk sometimes about cultural things, about the Beat poets and Jack Kerouac, about the latest albums they'd heard, but usually Obama steered the conversation to politics, particularly to the anticolonial wave in Africa. No one minded when he held forth. Everyone found him wonderfully intelligent and spectacularly self-absorbed. "Everything was oratory with him, that huge James Earl Jones voice," Abercrombie said. With enough beer in him, Obama could cross into the slightly insufferable zone. His ego was outsized. And yet he never ceased to fascinate his friends. He was never dull. If he raised the subject of a book, he'd read it, absorbed it.

"He had a lot to say," Pake Zane said. "Barack was an impressive fellow. He was the blackest man I had ever met in my life, with that mesmerizing low voice. He spoke with a Kenyan British accent, with a slight touch of Oxford arrogance. But he was real smart. He liked jazz music, dancing, and drinking beer. I could listen to him for hours. And did."

Obama told his friends that Kenya would soon be independent and that Jomo Kenyatta would be its leader, but he feared the inevitable rise of a coterie of hustlers in the leadership. "He was afraid that Tom Mboya would not be accepted, not only because he was a Luo but also because he was brilliant and eclectic and could talk to white people and was not intimidated by them," Abercrombie recalled. "He told us that Mboya was so self-confident that he didn't need to prove himself the tough black revolutionary. But Barack feared that meant he would be perceived as a rival. He knew there was trouble ahead."

Obama also informed his new friends that he had much to offer his country—and that everyone back home would surely recognize that. "Beneath the braggadocio," Abercrombie said, "he feared that he would be overlooked, ignored. He couldn't bring himself to finesse people. He had to tell them exactly what he thought and what he thought of them. He had to offend them. When he got back to Kenya, he behaved in the exact opposite way his son would one day. Maybe it's not fair to be an armchair psychoanalyst, but it's not outrageous to think that a lot of the way Barack, the son, is today—cool, rooted, polite, always listening—is a way of not being like his father."

In that first year of his studies at Hawaii, Obama took a Russian-language course and met a younger student, an intelligent girl, slightly plump, with large brown eyes, a pointed chin, and chalk-white skin. ("She was no beach bunny, that's for sure," Abercrombie recalled. "Ann was Kansas white.") Ann Dunham was seventeen. They struck up an acquaintance. One day Obama asked her to meet him at one o'clock in the afternoon near the main library. She agreed. She waited awhile and, because it was a sunny day, she lay down on one of the benches. "An hour later," she told her son, "he shows up with a couple of his friends. I woke up and the three of them were standing over me, and I heard your father saying, serious as can be, 'You see, gentlemen, I told you that she was a fine girl, and that she would wait for me.' "

Not long afterward, Ann wrote to her friend Susan Botkin, telling her that she was adjusting well to Hawaii, enjoying her classes, and dating a Kenyan man whom she'd met in her Russian class. At first, Botkin said, "I was more interested that she was taking Russian than dating a Kenyan, to tell you the truth."

Obama began bringing Ann to his evenings out with Neil Abercrombie and his other friends, though she was shy about talking in front of the others. Obama didn't seem to care much, as he tended to dominate any discussion and treated women in a way that one could politely call traditional. "She was so young and quiet, almost ephemeral in those days," Abercrombie said. "But he was the dominant voice in every conversation he was in. She was a girl. He was the center of the universe. She was listening and learning."

As a grown man, Barack Obama, Jr., wrote skeptically not only about his father but about his mother's youthful romanticism. He is not entirely easy on his teenaged mother, but ultimately reconciled to her innocence and good intentions—and her love for him. Ann was a romantic idealist about nearly everything, including race and her own possibilities. She "was that girl with the movie of beautiful black people in her head, flattered by my father's attention, confused and alone, trying to break out of the grip of her own parents' lives," he wrote. "The innocence she carried that day, waiting for my father, had been tinged with misconceptions, her own needs, but it was a guileless need, one without self-consciousness, and perhaps that's how any love begins." A fascinating moment of a son judging his mother in her youth as he imagines it, struggling to see her clearly: until the final phrase, he is part censorious, part sympathetic.

Ann's lover was not so guileless. He failed to tell her that he had a wife in Kenya with a son and another child on the way. (Nor did he tell his friends.) He lied to Ann, telling her he was divorced. In the years that followed, he carried on overlapping relationships and marriages. If Obama felt any guilt about his cavalier attitude toward his wives and children, he concealed it. Kezia told a Kenyan reporter that she did not object to her husband taking a second wife, that it was not out of keeping with Luo customs, and that "he used to send me gifts, money, and clothes through the post office. Many people envied me."

By December, Ann was pregnant, and, in early February, telling no one, she and Barack flew to the island of Maui and got married.

"At Christmastime, she said she was in love with the African, and that her folks were dealing with it *reasonably* well," Susan Botkin recalled. "In the spring, she said she was married to the African and expecting a baby, and that her parents were coping *reasonably* well." Until then, Ann had seemed more interested in almost anything other than having, and rearing, a child. "It was such a surprise to me, because I had little brothers, and she would look at them and say, 'Aren't they cute—won't they go away?'" Botkin said. "She was never particularly interested in them. It was fascinating to me that she opted for matrimony and motherhood early in life. She was head over heels in love with this man."

Ann's parents found Obama smooth, smart, even charming, but not entirely familiar or trustworthy. (Toward the end of her life, Madelyn Dunham said of Obama, Sr., "He was *straaaaange*.") Although the Dunhams thought of themselves as tolerant, they had a hard time adjusting to the thought of their daughter married so young to *anyone*, much less to an African with a murky past and an uncertain future. "Stan worked hard at accepting Barack, Sr.," Abercrombie said, "and he had an instinctive reaction that life would be hard for Barack, Jr. But he came to adore that child like nothing else."

"Guess Who's Coming to Dinner," Stanley Kramer's popular film about the marriage of a brilliant black doctor to an idealistic young white woman and the reaction of the girl's parents, did not come out until 1967. But, after it did, Stanley Dunham had no compunction about likening his initial reaction to his new son-in-law to Spencer Tracy's shock at encountering Sidney Poitier. He was suspicious, angry, confused, protective, and bewildered by the difference between what he thought he believed about race and what he actually felt. Stanley Dunham, who died in 1992, did not live to enjoy the prescience of one particular detail of Kramer's film. In one scene, Tracy wonders how the young couple plan to rear their biracial children. Poitier says of his fiancée, "She feels that every single one of our children will be President of the United States. And they'll have colorful administrations." As for himself: "Frankly, I think your daughter is a bit optimistic. I'd settle for Secretary of State."

It sounds very much like the boundless idealism and sense of promise that Ann Dunham carried around in her head. It was a racial idealism uncomplicated by all the trials and historical turns to come—the assassinations, the rise of Black Power, the lure of separatism. "She was very much of the early Dr. King era," her son has said. "She believed that people were all basically the same under their skin, that bigotry of any sort was wrong, and that the goal was then to treat everybody as unique individuals."

The family news from Kenya was not particularly welcoming, either. Hussein Onyango Obama wrote a barbed letter to his son saying that he deeply disapproved of the marriage, not because it meant a second wife but because a *mzungu*, a white woman, would sully the Obama bloodlines. "What can you say when your son announces he's going to marry a *mzungu*?" Sarah Ogwel recalled.

Barack Hussein Obama, Jr., was born at 7:24 P.M. on August 4, 1961, at Kapi'olani Medical Center, in Honolulu, not far from Waikiki. On the birth certificate, the mother's race is listed as "Caucasian," the father's as "African."

Ann dropped out of school to care for her infant son. She never expected to be in such a traditionally domestic spot so soon: home alone with Barack, Jr., while Barack, Sr., was in classes, studying at the library, out drinking with his friends. Yet her friends don't recall her being resentful or depressed. As a young mother, and later, too, when she matured into an accomplished anthropologist, based in Indonesia and other countries, she was a take-life-as-it-comes optimist. The last thing on her mind was what people might say as they saw her, a white woman, walking down the street holding a black child. Alice Dewey, an anthropologist at the university who became Ann's academic mentor and one of her closest friends, said, "They say she was so 'unusual,' but growing up in Hawaii it doesn't seem that unusual that she would have married an African. It's not breaking the rules in Hawaii. It didn't seem totally strange. If she had been growing up in Kansas, it would have been mind-boggling. In Hawaii, there's that mixture, a meeting point of different cultures."

In June, 1962, Obama, Sr., graduated from the University of Hawaii Phi Beta Kappa. He had a choice between staying in Hawaii for graduate school, going to graduate school at the New School, in New York, on a full scholarship, with a stipend capable of supporting the three of them— or going to Harvard. For him, the choice was easy: "How can I refuse the best education?" Ambition always came before anything else, particularly women and children. He informed Ann that he was going to Cambridge to be a graduate student in econometrics. The Honolulu *Advertiser* marked his departure, in late June, without mentioning Ann or Barack, Jr. Obama promised his wife that he would retrieve the family when the time was right, but he was no more truthful about that than he had been about his first marriage.

"Stanley was disappointed that Barack had left his daughter, but not *too* disappointed," Neil Abercrombie said. "He figured that the marriage was going to fail sooner or later and so it might as well not go on so long that it would hurt Little Barry, as he always called him. If he was going to play the father figure in the boy's life, he felt, he might as well start."

That fall, Ann went with the baby to Cambridge briefly to visit her husband, but the trip was a failure and she returned to Hawaii. Barack, Sr., did not see Ann or their son again for nearly a decade and he did not advertise the fact that he had a family in Hawaii. He used to meet Frederick Okatcha, a friend from the airlift, in New York, at the West End bar, near Columbia, and they talked about almost everything—politics, economics, tribal problems, and nepotism in Kenya, and the way they would help shape the new Nairobi when they returned. "The one thing Obama never talked about was his family," Okatcha, who was studying psychology at Yale, said. "I didn't even know he had married. I never knew he had a son. Not then, anyway."

Ann Dunham was twenty years old, and a single mother. All the early promises of adventure now seemed unlikely. "It was sad to me when her marriage disintegrated," her old friend Susan Botkin said. "I was so impressed by how relaxed and calm she was when she had Barack—she was excited about going to Africa—and how in love she was, how her husband was going to take a serious role in government. It was a great disappointment to her that Barack, Sr.,'s father wrote and said, Don't bring your white wife and your half-breed child, they will not be welcome. There were Mau Mau uprisings, they were beheading white women, and doing unspeakable things. Ann's parents were very worried when they heard that."

According to the registrar at the University of Washington, Ann registered for an extension course in the winter of 1961 and enrolled as a regular student in the spring of 1962. She moved to Seattle with Barack, Jr., rented an apartment at the Villa Ria development in the Capitol Hill neighborhood of Seattle, and reconnected with some of her old high-school friends. One thing Ann's friends noticed was that she was not at all reluctant to show off her baby. When she wasn't studying, she pushed

Barack around the streets of Seattle in a stroller—a somewhat startling sight for some. "It was very different at that time for a black man and a white woman to marry," Ann's friend Maxine Box said. "She was not shy about the fact that she'd married a black man at all."

But trying to keep up with her studies and taking care of Barack was difficult, and, after a year, she decided to return to Honolulu, move in with her parents, and go to the University of Hawaii. To help make this work, she applied for, and received, food stamps for several months.

There was little word from Cambridge. Barack, Sr., was studying econometrics, drinking with a new set of friends, and soon had a girlfriend to add to his two marriages. "But by then Ann was under no illusions," Neil Abercrombie said. "He was a man of his time from a very patriarchal society."

Stanley Dunham, who had struggled with the idea of his daughter marrying so young and to such a complicated man, now became a doting grandfather, taking the boy to the beach, playing with him in the park. "Stanley loved that boy," Abercrombie recalled. "In the absence of his father, there was not a kinder, more understanding man than Stanley Dunham. He was loving and generous."

In January, 1964, Ann filed for divorce, citing "grievous mental suffering." In Cambridge, Obama signed the papers without protest.

Ann may have been wounded by Barack's abandonment, but she certainly had no hesitation about, once again, dating a man of color. A couple of years after Obama left for Harvard and then returned home to Kenya (with yet another woman, an American teacher named Ruth Nidesand, whom he had met in Cambridge), she began dating an Indonesian geologist, Lolo Soetoro, who was studying at the University of Hawaii. Lolo was a more modest, less aggressively ambitious man than Obama, and Ann's parents were far more at ease with him.

Soetoro, born in the city of Bandung, had grown up in a landscape of violence and upheaval—Dutch colonialism, Japanese occupation, revolution—and his family had not escaped the worst. His father and eldest brother were killed during Indonesia's revolt in the late nineteen-forties against the Dutch, who were vainly trying to repossess the country. The Dutch burned the Soetoros' house to the ground and the family fled to the countryside to wait out the conflict. To survive, Lolo's mother sold off her jewelry, one piece at a time, until the war finally ended. Eventually the family resettled near their old home and Soetoro got his undergraduate degree in geology at Gadjah Mada University, a prestigious school in Yogyakarta in central Java.

In Hawaii, Soetoro pursued his master's degree—and Ann Dunham—at a time when his country was enduring a horrific civil war. After Lolo and Ann married, in 1965, the Indonesian government called on all students studying abroad, Soetoro included, to return home to prove their loyalty and help "repair the country."

In 1967, Ann and Barry, who was now six years old and ready for first grade, flew to Japan, where they stayed for a few days to see the sights in Tokyo and Kamakura, and then went on to Jakarta to live with Lolo, who had taken a job as an army geologist, surveying roads and tunnels. Arriving in Indonesia in 1967 was like arriving on a battlefield where the ground was still strewn with the detritus of war and with fresh graves. For two decades, from 1945 to 1967, Sukarno was Indonesia's post-colonial ruler, its Father of the Nation, the great *dalang*, the puppet-master, manipulating factions and challengers, crushing or co-opting enemies, shifting from nationalism to "guided democracy" to autocratic rule as he deemed necessary. He had been master of the most complex of nations: seventeen thousand five hundred islands; three hundred languages; a culture shaped by Islam, Buddhism, Hinduism, the Dutch, and the British. He managed by forging a delicate alliance drawn from the military, Communists, nationalists, and Islamists.

On the night of September 30, 1965, a group of Sukarno's generals were murdered by rival officers, a faction called the 30 September Movement. Within days, Major General Suharto forced Sukarno to yield effective power. The conflict came in a period of economic crisis—hyperinflation and, in many regions, famine. Suharto claimed that the violence had been initiated by leftists and he went about crushing the Indonesian Communist Party, the P.K.I., giving rise to a prolonged period of political imprisonments, purges, and suppression of the political left. In the months that followed, hundreds of thousands of people were killed.

For decades after the bloody events of the mid-sixties, Indonesians debated who was to blame for the violence. The growth of the P.K.I. under the Sukarno government had infuriated the military and the United States. Sukarno had also angered Western investors by nationalizing major industries, including oil. Most historians agree that one of Suharto's essential allies in the overthrow of Sukarno was the C.I.A.

The Soetoros lived in a crowded middle-class neighborhood, in a stucco house on Haji Ramli Street, a dirt lane that turned to mud in the rainy season. Ann's and Barry's early impressions of Jakarta were of heat and glare, poverty in the streets, beggars, the smell of diesel fuel, the din of traffic and hawkers. Thanks to his stepfather's playful munificence, Barry had a backyard menagerie: chickens and roosters pecking around a coop, crocodiles, birds of paradise, a cockatoo, and an ape from New Guinea named Tata. One day, Lolo mentioned that one of the crocodiles had escaped, crawled into a neighboring rice field and eaten the owner's ducks. Just as Ann was Barry's teacher in high-minded matters—liberal, humanist values; the need to remember that they, and not the Indonesians, were the "foreigners"; the beauty of Mahalia Jackson's singing and Martin Luther King's preaching—Lolo was his instructor in the rude and practical skills of middle-class Indonesian life. Lolo taught him how farm animals were killed for eating; how to box and defend himself, just in case; how to treat servants; how to ignore street beggars and keep enough for yourself; how the weak perish and the strong survive.

Before they left for Indonesia, Madelyn Dunham had called the State Department, asking about the perils of Jakarta—the political struggles, the strange foods. She could do nothing about the politics, but she did pack a couple of trunks of American packaged foods. "You never know what these people will eat," she said. She was right; soon, Barry sampled dog, snake, and roasted grasshopper. He took part in competitive battles with Indonesian kites, chased crickets, gaped at the poor in the streets— some of them missing a limb, an eye, a nose—and befriended all kinds of kids in the neighborhood: the children of government bureaucrats, the children of workers and farmers.

At home, Soetoro, who had always been cheerful back in Hawaii, wrestling and playing with Barry, was moodier, harder to talk to. In Hawaii, he had seemed liberated; in Jakarta, Obama recalled him "wandering through the house with a bottle of imported whiskey, nursing his secrets."

Ann also sensed the hauntedness of Jakarta. On one of her expeditions near the city, she came across a field of unmarked graves. She tentatively asked Lolo what had happened with the coup and the counter-coup, the scouring of the countryside for suspected Communists and the innumerable killings, the mass arrests, but most Indonesians, Lolo included, were extremely reluctant to talk about the horrors of the mid-sixties.

In 1970, Ann gave birth to a daughter named Maya. Maya developed a keen sense of her mother's attachment to the country. "There is a phrase in Indonesian, *diam dalam seribu bahasa*, that means 'to be silent in a thousand languages.' It's a very fitting phrase for the country," Maya said. "There are so many ways to be silent. Sometimes it's in the constant cheerfulness or the space between words. Indonesia became more interesting to her. And it was a challenge. I'm sure this girl from Kansas, having to navigate through this complex culture that was so remote from what she grew up with, accepted it gracefully and with great strength and affability. She didn't ever feel afraid or alone. She simply made friends with those she encountered and worked to understand their lives as best she could."

One friend, Julia Suryakusuma, a well-known feminist and journalist, recalled that when Ann arrived in Indonesia she was "ensnared and enchanted" by the culture. "You know, Ann was really, really white," she said, "even though she told me she had some Cherokee blood in her. I think she just loved people of a different skin color, brown people."

Barry was doing his best to fit in at school. As an African-American, of course, he stood out. "At first, everybody felt it was weird to have him here," said one of his teachers at St. Francis, Israella Dharmawan. "But also they were curious about him, so wherever he went, the kids were following him." Kids at school often called him "Negro," which they didn't consider a slur, though it certainly upset Barry.

Obama was the one foreign child in his immediate neighborhood, and the only one enrolled in St. Francis. Most of the children in the area were Betawis, tribal Jakaratans, and traditional Muslims. Cecilia Sugini Hananto, who taught Obama in second grade, told the Chicago *Tribune* that some of the Betawi kids threw rocks at the open windows of the Catholic classrooms. Barry learned a lot of Indonesian quickly. He was never fluent, but he more than managed to navigate school. He'd yell "*Curang! Curang!*"—Cheater! Cheater!—when he was teased. Zulfan Adi, one of those who teased him, recalled a time when Barack followed his gang to a swamp: "They held his hands and feet and said, 'One, two, three,' and threw him in the swamp. Luckily, he could swim. They only did it to Barry." Obama, though, was husky and not easy to intimidate. "He was built like a bull, so we'd get three kids together to fight him," a former classmate, Yunaldi Askiar, said. "But it was only playing."

After Maya was born, the Soetoros moved three miles west, into a better neighborhood, where the old Dutch élite lived. Lolo now worked as a liaison with the government for Union Oil. With the new job came new acquaintances and colleagues; some were the sort of foreigners who complained about the "locals" and the servants. The Soetoros were surrounded by diplomats and Indonesian businessmen who lived in gated houses. Barry's new school, Model Primary School Menteng 1, was, like almost all schools in Indonesia, mainly Muslim. Israella Dharmawan inadvertently helped feed a campaign sensation—mainly on the Internet and cable news—when she told the Los Angeles *Times*, in March, 2007, that "Barry was a Muslim. . . . He was registered as a Muslim because his father, Lolo Soetoro, was Muslim." A third-grade teacher named Effendi and the vice-principal, Tine Hahiyari, also told the *Times* that Barry was registered as a Muslim. No matter what the registry said, this was untrue. Ann remained a religious skeptic and did not consider herself or her son a Muslim. Lolo was not a practicing Muslim. "My father saw Islam as a way to connect with the community," Maya said. "He never went to prayer services except for big communal events."

Obama doesn't remember taking the religious component of either school in Indonesia very seriously. "In the Muslim school, the teacher wrote to tell my mother that I made faces during Koranic studies," he writes. "My mother wasn't overly concerned. 'Be respectful,' she'd said. In the Catholic school, when it came time to pray, I would pretend to close my eyes, then peek around the room. Nothing happened. No angels descended. Just a parched old nun and thirty brown children, muttering words."

Ann and Lolo had a comfortable life in Jakarta: because of the cheap price of labor, they had someone to market and cook, someone to tend the house. But Ann still couldn't afford to send Barry to the international school. Although she spent a full day teaching English at the American Embassy, she woke Barry at 4 A.M. every weekday in order to deepen his knowledge of English, history, and other subjects. It was something he resented—what young boy wouldn't?—but she was preparing him for the moment when he would go back to America to continue his education.

Ann was thriving, immersing herself in the local arts and handicrafts, learning the language, acquainting herself with the way people lived, traveling to Bali and villages in central Java. At the same time, Lolo was becoming more like his oilmen friends at the office. He played golf at Union Oil's club, and, what was worse as far as Ann was concerned, he *talked* about golf. He seemed so eager to assimilate into the world of his employers. "Step by step, Lolo became an American oilman and Ann was—O.K., to an *extent*—becoming a Javanese villager," Ann's close friend Alice Dewey said. "He was playing golf and tennis with the oil people and Ann was riding on the back of motorcycles in villages, learning."

Maya Soetoro (now Soetoro-Ng) had been born when Barry was nine. Ann surrounded her with dolls of all ethnicities: black, Inuit, Dutch. "It was like the United Nations," she says. Not long after Maya's birth Ann and Lolo could feel the marriage really begin to unravel. "She started feeling competent, perhaps," Maya Soetoro-Ng says. "She acquired numerous languages after that. Not just Indonesian but her professional language and her feminist language. And I think she really got a voice. So it's perfectly natural that she started to demand more of those who were near her, including my father. And suddenly his sweetness wasn't enough to satisfy her needs."

Barack Obama, Sr., wrote occasional letters to Ann and Barry, but for the most part he was out of sight. The disappointments of his life were barely known to them. The story of his return to Africa was one of bitter decline. When he arrived in Nairobi from Harvard in 1965 with his master's degree in economics, Obama split his personal life between his third wife and his first, between Ruth Nidesand and Kezia Obama. He would have two more children with Kezia (for a total of four) and two with Ruth, before she ended the marriage.

"Like many men of his generation who had the chance to go abroad for an education, Obama suffered the schizophrenia of one who is both a Luo man and a Western man," his friend Olara Otunnu said. "He absorbed the mindset and framework both of his home and of the West and he was always wrestling with trying to reconcile them. So when he marries several women and tries to keep them separate and fails miserably to do so, this is a symptom of the schizophrenia."

Obama's "schizophrenia"—the schizophrenia of the "been-to" generation of African élites who studied in the West in the nineteen-fifties and sixties and then returned home—is described by the Ghanaian writer Ayi Kwei Armah in his novel *Why Are We So Blest?* Armah, who was sent abroad to study at Groton and Harvard, depicts the disillusion and downfall of a young man named Modin Dofu, who has left Harvard and winds up back in Africa, a destroyed man.

Obama, Jr., has called his father a "womanizer." The reality was grimmer. Obama, Sr., not only married four times and had many affairs; he didn't seem to care with any consistency about any of his wives or children. Philip Ochieng, a prominent Luo journalist and a friend of Obama, Sr.,'s, wrote a lighthearted article in the *Daily Nation* saying that the Luo "shared with the ancient Hellenes the habit of waylaying foreign women and literally pulling them into bed as wives":

> So for Senior to grab wives from as far away as Hawaii and Massachusetts—and Caucasian ones to boot—was no big deal. Given time, he might even have grabbed an Afghan, a Cherokee, an Eskimo,

a Fijian, an Iraqi, a Lithuanian, a Mongolian, a Pole, a Shona, a Vietnamese, a Wolof, a Yoruba, and a Zaramo—not to mention hundreds
from Luoland, apart from Kezia. The Luo would have noted his "he-
man-ship" with complete approval.

"Where Obama comes from, a man can have many wives," Ochieng
said. "If you have only one wife, like I do, you are not yet a man! The
deeper question was how he treated the family."

For the affected family members, Obama's wandering and his indifference were painful. When Barack, Jr., visited Nairobi as a U.S. senator, he
said of his father that "he related to women as his father had, expecting
them to obey him no matter what he did." But there was more to it than
cultural differences. Obama had been a miserable husband. Mark Ndesandjo, Obama's son by Ruth Nidesand, says that Obama beat him and his
mother. "You just don't do that," he said. "I shut those thoughts in the
back of my mind for many years. . . . I remember times in my house when
I would hear the screams, and I would hear my mother's pain. I was a
child . . . I could not protect her." Ndesandjo dropped his father's name
and, since 2001, he has lived in Shenzhen, China, and has worked in the
export trade. "At a certain point, I made the decision not to think about
who my real father was," he said. "He was dead to me even when he was
still alive. I knew that he was a drunk and showed no concern for his wife
and children. That was enough."

Obama, Sr.,'s political mentor, Tom Mboya, made sure that he had
decent jobs—as an economist for BP/Shell and then for both the Ministry
of Economic Planning and Development and the Ministry of Tourism.
From the moment of his return from America, Obama, Sr., was dissatis-
fied with the direction the government was taking. Little more than a year
after independence, in July, 1965, he published an article in the *East Africa
Journal* entitled "Problems Facing Our Socialism." The article was a critique of the government's working development plan known as "Sessional
Paper No. 10," which had been issued in April, 1965.

The lead author of Sessional Paper No. 10 was Tom Mboya, who had
been called on by the Kenyatta government to answer the Soviet-oriented
development plans conceived at the Lumumba Institute by leading leftist
politicians like Oginga Odinga. As an ideologist of Kenyan independence,
Mboya was a moderate; he considered himself a "Socialist at heart and a
believer in democracy." "The Kenya Question: An African Answer," a
pamphlet he wrote in 1956, before independence, when he was just
twenty-six, was an important document in the anti-colonial movement—
so important in its call for representative democracy and the development

of strong trade unions that the white Nairobi government banned it from certain Kenyan bookstores. Indeed, Mboya's paper was instrumental in spreading his reputation in the United States among politicians and labor leaders; as a result it helped win support for the airlift. Sessional Paper No. 10 is a far different sort of document, a more technical and prescriptive plan for Kenyan economic development. Unlike the Lumumba Institute plan, it was extremely wary of the nationalization of industries.

Even though Obama himself had likely had a hand in the conception of the paper and was an ally of Mboya, he did not hesitate to criticize it under his own name. Obama's article cautions against a national policy that ignores poverty and inequality and is based on outsized expectations of rapid economic growth. It poses a central question of a country exiting a colonial system and entering independence: "How are we going to remove the disparities in our country, such as the concentration of economic power in Asian and European hands, while not destroying what has already been achieved?" Post-colonial Kenya, Obama argued, must not re-create yet another economic scheme that produces a small, super-wealthy ruling class and a mass of poor—in other words, a repetition of the old system, without a white ruling and bureaucratic class. Obama supported the redistribution of land to both individuals and tribes. One Kenya scholar, David William Cohen, of the University of Michigan, calls it an "improbable yet extraordinary rehearsal" of the best critiques of "unregulated capital" that came only a quarter of a century later. It navigates the differences among the leading figures in Kenyan politics—Kenyatta, who was pro-Western, and his left-wing vice-president, a Luo, Oginga Odinga, and Mboya, who was also a Luo but ideologically closer to Kenyatta. "It was very much like Obama to feel free to critique aspects of a paper he'd been part of," Olara Otunnu said. "He was a rarity in Kenya. Most people in the political class were respectful, to a fault, of the leadership. Not Obama. He felt free to speak his mind, and loudly." In his article, Obama made a case for progressive taxation and the regulation of private investment. The article warns against the dangers of continued foreign ownership and excessive privatization of commonly held resources and goods. Obama wrote:

One need not be a Kenyan to note that nearly all commercial enterprises from small shops in River Road to big shops in Government Road and industries in the Industrial Areas of Nairobi are mostly owned by Asians and Europeans. . . . For whom do we want to grow? Is it the African who owns this country? . . . It is mainly in this country that one finds almost everything owned by the non-indigenous populace.

In all, Mboya was pleased with Obama's paper and hired him at the Ministry of Economic Planning and Development. But what came next in Kenya was political chaos—a chaos that engulfed Barack Obama, Sr.

In 1966, Odinga resigned from Kenyatta's government and established a left-wing opposition party. At first, this seemed a purely ideological divide between Odinga, who pressed for Kenya to lean closer to the Eastern Bloc and a socialist economic system, and Kenyatta, who was more oriented toward the United States and Western Europe. But, in the months to come, the divide, especially among their followers, took on an ugly tribal cast.

In 1967, Pake Zane and Neil Abercrombie set off on a trip around the world that eventually brought them to the doorstep of their old friend in Nairobi. By then, Obama was living in a pleasant government-owned cottage with a small lawn, but he was hardly taking care of himself. He chain-smoked—local brands, 555s and Rex—and, calling beer "a child's drink," he now drank quadruple shots of Vat 69 or Johnnie Walker.

"He was aloof toward his family," Abercrombie said. "He wasn't quite a complete mess yet. That would come later. But I remember thinking, They are never going to give him a chance. He was just so discouraged. . . . When I saw him there, I thought, This is hopeless. Daniel Arap Moi was already on the scene"—Arap Moi was Kenyatta's vice-president and, in 1978, became President and was known for corruption and human-rights abuses. "Arap Moi was a power-mongering bastard, a thief. And Arap Moi was every fear that Barack had ever had come true." At the Ministry, Obama constantly got in fights with his superiors and embarrassed them by trying to expose instances of bribery and fraud.

Obama's decline, his old friends say now, was at least partly related to the disappointed belief that the best would rise to the top. He would never be able to overcome tribalism, cronyism, and corruption. "To that extent, he was naïve," Peter Aringo, a friend and a member of parliament from Obama's village, said. "He thought he could fight the system from outside. He thought he could bring it down."

"Obama, Sr., was very concerned about corruption at home, which still stands in the way of development," Frederick Okatcha, a professor of educational psychology at Kenyatta University, said. "He so much wanted to do good for his people, but, after being in America, we had learned new values and ways of speaking and behaving, and we saw corruption, nepotism. It is hard when you see that your bosses don't have half the education you do. You could see how frustrated he was. He was very brilliant and now he had to report to people who knew so much less than he did. That would drive anyone to the bottle."

Obama's most perilous habit was his tendency to drink and drive. "You remember the character Mr. Toad from *The Wind and the Willows*? He was a crazy driver, and Obama was like Mr. Toad," the journalist Philip Ochieng said. "He once drove me from Nairobi to Kisumu, and it was very scary. Terrifying! And he wasn't even drinking."

In 1965, Obama was behind the wheel when he had an accident that killed a passenger, a postal worker from his home town. The accident left Obama with a terrible limp. "Barack never really recovered from that," a friend of his, Leo Odera Omolo, told Edmund Sanders of the Los Angeles *Times*. His outspokenness and arrogance had lost their charm. He had become melancholy, argumentative, and convinced, with good reason, of his own marginalization. He was drinking more and more, introducing himself as "Dr. Obama" when he had not, in fact, completed a doctorate. A man who had been one of Kenya's most promising young minds was now a source of gossip and derision. Walgio Orwa, a professor at Great Lakes University, in Kisumu, said, "Before, he was everyone's role model. With that big beautiful voice, we all wanted to be like him. Later, everybody was asking what happened."

On July 5, 1969, a quiet Saturday afternoon, Tom Mboya returned from an official trip to Ethiopia and, at around 1 P.M., stopped by a pharmacy on Government Road. As he came out of the pharmacy, a young Kikuyu named Nahashon Isaac Njenga Njoroge, wearing a suit and carrying a briefcase, pulled a revolver out of his pocket. He fired twice, hitting Mboya both times in the chest. He died almost immediately.

As news of Mboya's death spread, there were large demonstrations of outrage in both Nairobi and the cities and villages of Luoland, in western Kenya. Luos had seen the government crush the leftist Oginga Odinga; now they suspected that Kenyatta's inner circle was behind the death of the most popular Luo politician of all. The government conducted an investigation that was anything but transparent. The gunman, Njenga, was known around Nairobi for shaking down businesses and threatening them with his connections to high-ranking government officials. He was locked up in Kamiti prison and was tried in September. Only a few journalists loyal to the government were allowed to attend the ten-day trial, and the national archives do not possess a decent record of the proceedings. Police said they found Njenga's gun on the roof of his house, at Ofafa Jericho Estate. According to Njenga's lawyer, Samuel Njoroge Waruhiu, his client did not protest his innocence and appeared serene about his fate, seeming confident that eventually he would be spirited to safety in a far-off country. "It was hard dealing with him," Waruhiu said. "Here I was, trying to get information so that I could arm myself with a tangible defense. But here was a client who was keen to hide as much as possible." Njenga told his lawyer that Mboya had got what he deserved for "selling us to the Americans."

Njenga did not give a final statement in court and was condemned to death. According to a government announcement, he was executed by hanging on November 8th. He was reported to have said earlier, "Why do you pick on me? Why not the big man?" He declined, however, to say who "the big man" was, and his enigmatic question lingered on in the Kenyan political imagination for decades to come.

"There is pretty convincing talk that the execution was never carried out," David William Cohen says. "The Kenyatta government *announced* that he was executed and yet there were reports that the condemned man was seen in Bulgaria, Ethiopia, and Kenya. A lot of people believe that it was all part of a plot to do the killing, and then the powers that be set him free and let him leave the country."

According to Pake Zane, who visited Obama in 1968 and 1974, Obama claimed that he knew the inside story of Mboya's assassination and even claimed to have seen Mboya on the morning of the killing. The Mboya assassination remains an abiding mystery of Kenyan political history. Most people who are not in the government power élite say they are sure that the killer acted at the behest of one of Mboya's opponents—people around Kenyatta and Daniel Arap Moi. No one has offered conclusive evidence. But the suspicions about Kenyatta and his circle persist, particularly in Luoland. When Kenyatta came to campaign for re-election in Kisumu, a Luo city close to where Barack Obama grew up, the local people jeered, saying, "Where's Tom? Where's Tom?"

Obama, for his part, was enraged about the murder and vocal about it. He demanded an explanation for the killing. ("I was with Tom only last week. Can the Government tell me where he is?") Mboya's execution was the effective end of Obama's public life. He had lost the one real mentor and benefactor he had ever had. They had not agreed on everything—Obama's views on development were more to the left—but Mboya had looked out for him, provided jobs for him in the state bureaucracy, kept him connected to the Nairobi political class. He was fired from the government and never returned.

Three months after Mboya's murder, the tension in Kenya deepened. In late October, 1969, Kenyatta went to Kisumu to dedicate a hospital for which Odinga had arranged Soviet funding. Hundreds of Luo men heckled Kenyatta. The President was not prepared to be shamed. He declared that Odinga's party, the Kenya People's Union, "is only engaged in dirty divisive words. Odinga is my friend, but he has been misled and he in turn continues to mislead the people of this area." Then he warned Odinga and his followers, "We are going to crush you into flour. Anybody who toys with our progress will be crushed like locusts. Do not say later that I did not warn you publicly." Kenyatta's car left Kisumu under a hail of stones, and the police turned their guns on the crowd, killing at least nine people and wounding seventy.

Two days later, Kenyatta made good on his ominous warning, arresting Odinga and most of the leadership of the K.P.U., charging them with trying to overthrow the government. Odinga remained in prison for two years and every Luo intellectual and civil servant felt the pressure.

After the events of 1969, Obama began drinking himself into a stupor nearly every night and driving, perilously, home. "He would pass out on the doorstep," Leo Odera Omolo said. Sebastian Peter Okoda, a former senior government official who shared his apartment with Obama in the mid-seventies, recalled that Obama kept drinking the best whiskies at hangouts like the Serena Hotel and the Hotel Boulevard. He complained to Okoda, "*Pesa michula en pesa ma ahingo*": "I'm being paid peanuts."

In 1974, Pake Zane and his wife came through Nairobi. They were camping at Nairobi City Park. "At one point Barack came out and said, 'Come stay with me.' There was a problem with gangs. So we went to stay with Barack, and he was drinking more heavily and he was limping. I asked him what happened, and at that time I heard the story, 'They tried to kill me.' He told me the story of being a witness. He said he knew who [Mboya's] assassins were, and 'I do know, they will kill me.' He got very drunk and very angry those nights—angry at life. Here he was, a very smart man, and he was prevented from revealing who the assassin was. He said there was no real work for him in Kenya. These things added up to a frustrated, angry young man.

"It got real scary after a while, he was so angry, so arrogant, and getting dangerous, calling out against the government to whoever would listen," Zane went on.

In his sober moments, Obama could recognize his own disappointments, the unraveling of his ambition, and he would say, "I want to do my things to the best of my ability. Even when death comes, I want to die thoroughly."

Chapter Two

Surface and Undertow

Barack Obama's family, broadly defined, is vast. It's multi-confessional, multiracial, multilingual, and multicontinental. He has a Kenyan step-grandmother in a village near Lake Victoria who speaks only Luo and Swahili; a biracial half brother who speaks fluent Mandarin and trades in southern China; a cousin-by-marriage who is an African-American rabbi in Chicago determined to forge closer relations among Jews, Muslims, and Christians on the South Side. As Obama has put it, he has some relatives who look like Bernie Mac and some who look like Margaret Thatcher. He has relatives who have been educated in the finest universities in the world, others who live in remote Kenyan towns, another who has lived in a Nairobi slum, yet another, an African half sister, who wound up in a Boston housing-project with immigration problems. The Obama family tree is as vast and intricate as one of those ancient banyan trees near the beach at Waikiki. As a politician, Obama would make use of that family, asking voters to imagine it—and him—as a metaphor for American diversity.

But as a child, Obama experienced his family as a small unit dominated not so much by the absence of his African father as by the presence of his mother, Ann Dunham. She was now twenty-nine. Her second marriage was all but over. She was faced with trying to find a way to nourish her growing interest in the economic and social anthropology of Indonesia and her overall sense of idealism, and, at the same time, support her ten-year-old son and year-old daughter. She could not go on tutoring Barry before dawn indefinitely; she started thinking about a way to get him an education in the United States.

Dunham's own ambitions were uncertain. Money did not much interest her. "I don't know what she wanted," Barack's sister, Maya Soetoro-Ng, said, "beyond what any of us wants—some measure of satisfaction that we have contributed positively to the lives of others and enriched our own understanding of the world around us and taken full measure of our own place in this life and world."

Ann had arrived in Indonesia in the aftermath of political upheaval, but it was not her way to get involved with politics directly. "She was interested in what was happening at the grassroots level, and she understood that better," Maya continued. "She was not an unthinking woman, she wasn't a stick-your-head-in-the-sand Pollyanna, but she really did believe that all this fighting was silly and unnecessary and why can't we all get along?" Was Ann politically naïve? "Sometimes perhaps, but more about [America] than about Indonesia," she said. "In part, that was because she came to Hawaii when she was seventeen and didn't really see or feel the full impact of the civil-rights movement on the mainland. We always have to be hopeful about home, and so she always felt we made a lot of progress. Some could interpret it as naïve. You could say optimistic. She saw the corruption elsewhere a little more clearly. It's not that she wished to ignore it or didn't see it, but her focus was more on socioeconomic realities on the grassroots level. She was deeply impacted by all of it, by the sharp contrast between the haves and have-nots, by the extremes of poverty and abuse, but also by the fact that there was so much beauty that resided behind it and beneath it and around it. She didn't simply see the challenges; she always saw the beauty."

Ann started to roam the markets of Jakarta and make trips around the country, learning more about Indonesian culture and handicrafts. "She loved batik and Indonesian art and music and all of the human creation that in her estimation elevated the spirit," Maya said. "She saw the beauty of community and kinship, the power of cultural collision and connection. She thought that all of her encounters were delightful—in Indonesia and elsewhere. She was just *happy*. She enjoyed herself immensely. Although she was aware of struggle and grappled with it, she did so cheerfully and with great optimism and belief that things could get better. Why mourn reality?"

After Barry finished the fourth grade in Jakarta, Ann Dunham put him on a flight to Hawaii to stay with his grandparents for the summer. Obama recalls this moment of re-entry into Hawaiian life with mixed emotions. There was the thrill of returning to America—air-conditioning, fast-food restaurants, and familiar sports—yet there was also the dreariness of staying with grandparents he hardly knew.

Stanley and Madelyn Dunham lived in a two-bedroom apartment in a ten-story high-rise on South Beretania Street, in Honolulu. The building faces a large green and one of the oldest Protestant churches in the city. Stanley, who had switched from the furniture business to selling insurance, was struggling in his work, frustrated with his bosses and with elusive would-be customers. Madelyn was a banking executive—a considerable achievement for a woman with no connections or college degree. The banks in Hawaii then were run by a coterie of wealthy families who were not inclined to treat women and men equally. "They didn't pay someone like Madelyn very much, even as she rose in the ranks. There was still a lot of gender bias," Neil Abercrombie said. "The Dunhams didn't live in that apartment out of some philosophical rejection of materialism. They were renters."

Madelyn Dunham took pride in her advancement and made sure to get to the office before seven each morning. Years later, she confided to her grandson that what she had really wanted all along was "a house with a white picket fence, days spent baking or playing bridge or volunteering at the local library."

One gift that his grandparents could provide Barry was a connection to Punahou, the finest private school in Hawaii and the oldest west of the Mississippi River. Punahou, a seventy-six-acre island of lush greenery and distinguished architecture, was a ten-minute walk from their apartment—a pleasant stroll past a church, over the bridge spanning the H-1 freeway, and you were there. The waiting list was long and the academic requirements considerable, but Stanley's boss at the insurance company, an alumnus, helped Barry get into Punahou. "My first experience with affirmative action, it seems, had little to do with race," Obama writes, winking at a fact that looms so large at élite American prep schools and Ivy League colleges: that affirmative action for alumni children and the well-connected is far more pervasive than any breaks extended on the basis of ethnic background. By the fall, Ann and Maya had returned to Honolulu and reunited with Barry as he started in his new school. Ann began taking graduate courses in anthropology at the University of Hawaii.

Punahou's overall effect is of Phillips Exeter Academy-*sur-Mer*. Students walk around the campus as if dressed for the beach. Everywhere you go are spreading palms and monkey-pod trees, springy close-cropped lawns, lava-rock walls covered with otherworldly vines of night-blooming cereus flowers that were imported from Mexico and given to the school's founders. No interest is left unindulged. There is an arts and athletic center the size of an airplane hangar; a glass-blowing shed; a vast outdoor pool that glitters in the sunshine. The centerpiece of the campus is Thurston Chapel, a modernist building designed by an émigré architect named Vladimir Ossipoff and surrounded by a lily pond stocked with koi and tilapia.

If Hawaiians of any ethnic background meet each other on the mainland they tend not to begin the conversation with what town they come from. Instead, speaking pidgin, they will ask, "What school you wen grad?" The most exalted answer is Punahou. Happily, Obama was accepted and he got some scholarship money to help with the nineteen-hundred-dollar tuition fees.

In 1829, the Hawaiian queen, Ka'ahumanu, urged the local governor to give a large tract of land to Hiram Bingham, one of the first Christian missionaries on the islands. Bingham hoped to build a school that would equal the best in his native New England. Punahou was founded in 1841; it was devoted at first to educating the children of missionaries and to raising indigenous Hawaiian students "to an elevated state of Christian civilization." One of the early students included Bingham's grandson, Hiram III, who helped discover the lost city of Machu Picchu and became a model for Indiana Jones.

When Barry Obama arrived at Punahou, he was in fifth grade. He had two homeroom teachers, a history teacher from New York named Mabel Hefty and a math and science teacher named Pal Eldredge. Barry was a chunky, laid-back boy, still wearing the leather sandals he'd brought from Indonesia. The novelist Allegra Goodman, who was six years behind Obama at Punahou, describes Mabel Hefty, who died in 1995, as "old-fashioned, Christian, strict." She did not tolerate anyone speaking pidgin. Her classroom, on the third floor of Castle Hall, still had blackout curtains left over from the Second World War.

The first weeks of school were a misery. When roll was called—"*Ba–rack* Obama"—the kids laughed at the strangeness of the boy's name.

"Would you prefer if we called you 'Barry'?" Miss Hefty asked. "Barack is such a beautiful name. Your grandfather tells me your father is Kenyan. I used to live in Kenya. . . ."

Mabel Hefty was an earnest traveler. She had spent the previous year in Africa teaching in a village primary school. But when she tried to engage Barry in a high-minded conversation about his Kenyan background ("Do you know what tribe your father is from?"), Obama went silent. One kid made monkey sounds. One classmate asked if his father was a cannibal; another asked if she could just touch his hair. He was a curiosity, a source of giddy fascination—the last thing a child wants to be. Barack preferred "Barry."

Of the more than thirty-five hundred students at Punahou when Obama arrived, only three or four were black. Obama kept the miseries he felt that autumn neatly submerged. "One of the challenges for a ten-year-old boy coming to a new place is to figure out how you fit in," Obama said in a speech in 2004 on the campus. "And it was a challenge for me, partly because I was one of the few African-Americans in the school, partly because I was new and a lot of the students had been together since kindergarten."

Before Obama arrived, perhaps the loneliest child in Punahou was Joella Edwards. (Obama calls her "Coretta" in his memoir.) The daughter of a doctor, Joella suffered mightily at Punahou. "Some kids—not all of them, but enough—called me 'jello,' 'pepper,' 'Aunt Jemima,' 'burnt toast with guava jelly,' " she said. "And they'd use that local term, *popolo*. They could be brutal. Back then, it was a different time and space, it was the sixties and early seventies, and America as a whole didn't talk about race. I remember cringing at the word 'black.' Black was a color in the crayon box. Because of that, you couldn't really say what you wanted to say.

"If I had been on the mainland with other blacks as peers, it would have been a lot different," Edwards continued. "The only other peer I had was Barry. When we met, we were ten—it's so crazy! He came to school and I was so excited! This kid had my same coloring. He *looked* like me. He was just *like* me. We didn't avoid each other. We were drawn to each other. But we had to keep a distance." Edwards and Obama both remember that, any time they drifted together, someone was sure to mock them as a couple—the two black kids. *Barry and Joella sittin' in a tree. . . K-i-s-s-i-n-g. . . .* And yet Barry never rejected Joella. "He was my knight in shining armor," said Edwards, who lives now in Florida. "He was me—except with different anatomy."

Joella came home crying on a regular basis. When she tried to raise her grades and started studying harder, her teacher accused her of cheating on a paper. Only when she re-did a paper in the presence of the teacher did anyone believe she had done her own work. After ninth grade, rather than endure more humiliation, she dropped out and enrolled in a public school. "I was a basket case for years," she said.

Barry's discomfort at Punahou only increased that first year. For months he had told small, childhood fibs to his classmates. His father was an African prince, he told them, the son of a tribal chief. In truth, he knew little about his father—mainly "scraps of information I'd picked up from my mother." But now, in 1971, Barack Obama, Sr., was coming to Honolulu for a month-long stay. He had not seen Barry since he was a toddler. When Obama arrived in Oahu, his son was surprised at how diminished

he looked, compared with the old pictures. He was fragile—oddly cautious "when he lit a cigarette or reached for his beer"—and his eyes had a yellow, malarial tint.

Obama tells the story of his father's visit with clarity that makes the reader wince: the old man trying to reassert his authority ten years too late; the mysterious renewed intimacy between his father and mother; Stanley Dunham declaring that this was his house and no one was going to boss anyone around; Ann trying vainly to keep the peace; the boy's sad confusion when his father commands him to work harder and forbids him to watch "How the Grinch Stole Christmas" on television. "We all stood accused," he wrote a quarter-century later. "I felt as if something had cracked open between all of us, goblins rushing out of some old, sealed-off lair." There were some good times—Obama took Barry to a Dave Brubeck concert in Honolulu that helped make him a lifelong jazz fan— but it was a complicated visit, fraught with the boy's knowledge that it could not last.

Barry started counting off the days in his mind until his father left for Africa, but before the ordeal came to its natural end, he had to endure one last trial: Miss Hefty had invited Obama, Sr., to speak to a combined class with Barry's math teacher, Pal Eldredge. Obama describes the agony of anticipating the event, imagining the exposure of his lies and the mockery that would follow. He remembers that the next day his father spoke of tribes that had their young men kill lions in order to prove their manhood, of Kenya's struggle for independence, and of "the deep gash in the earth where mankind had first appeared."

Pal Eldredge remembers a more prosaic, uneventful, even pleasant presentation: "The whole thing about Barack is that at that time we didn't have a lot of black kids or half-black kids. It was my second year teaching, so I remembered his father and what he talked about. He talked about education and what life was like where he was from."

Mabel Hefty and Pal Eldredge were delighted and, at the conclusion of the presentation, thanked Barack Obama profusely and congratulated Barry for having such a fascinating father. No one said anything about Barry's "lies." To the contrary, the boy who had asked about cannibalism in the first weeks of school said, "Your dad is pretty cool." It was hard for Barry to see it that way. By now, he was aware that he could expect nothing from his father. He was there to check in, to salve his conscience, perhaps, but soon he was gone. He never saw his son again.

. . .

Any reader of Obama's memoir, anyone familiar with his campaign speeches, knows the touchstones of his life and family that he chooses to emphasize: the idealist, who, as a single mother, went on food stamps for a while and struggled with medical-insurance forms as, in her early fifties, she lay dying of cancer; the plainspoken Midwestern grandparents and their warm embrace and quiet desperations; the internal struggle with race and identity as a teenager and a young man; the career as a community organizer on the South Side of Chicago. He places less emphasis on an equally crucial part of his background: the élite institutions that also formed him—Punahou School, Occidental College, Columbia University, Harvard Law School, and the University of Chicago Law School.

Obama received a liberal education in the most rounded sense of the term. He was too young for the sixties; rather, his teachers were products of the period and brought new values and historical narratives to the classroom and lecture hall: the antiwar movement, civil rights, gay and women's liberation, ethnic diversity. These were not the struggles of Obama's youth; they were the givens, the environment. This was evident even as early as the mid- and late-seventies at Punahou.

The only trace of Punahou's Congregationalist past was weekly chapel. At Thurston Chapel in the nineteen-seventies, the students heard readings from the Bible, recited secular poetry, listened to renditions of "The Sounds of Silence," "Blowin' in the Wind," and "The Rose." It was the kind of chapel that Ann Dunham, who spoke of a "higher power" and read to her children from religious texts of all kinds, but never joined a church, could easily abide. "We all gathered as a group, mostly to contemplate philosophical and/or spiritual aspects of the world around us, but also to enjoy a bit of community singing, laughing and emotional rekindling of a certain sense of harmony and well-being," Constance Ramos, a classmate of Obama's, wrote in an album of remembrances by the Class of 1979. "The focus was not on any formal religion *per se*, but, rather, on giving us an appreciation for quiet contemplation about our place in the Universe and the inherent joy that accompanies being a member of a community.

"In the eighth grade," Ramos went on, "we were also required to attend a weekly class called Christian Ethics. We'd lie around on floor cushions and talk freely about various ideas—the meaning of 'friendship,' for example—or what we thought about life in general. We'd listen to Simon and Garfunkel's album *Bridge Over Troubled Water,* over and over again. . . . In retrospect, some might say that Christian Ethics was more like a teenage group-therapy session than anything else."

Barry Obama was never the top student in his class or the hardest worker—a pattern that persisted from fifth grade to the end of high school. ("He was a B student," Eric Kusunoki, Obama's homeroom teacher in high school, said. "I never bugged him about not working harder. Some kids suffer from too much pressure and work their brains out.") The curriculum was more rigorous and multicultural than what he had experienced at his two schools in Indonesia. The sixth-grade curriculum included topics in world cultures and field trips to a local synagogue and a Buddhist temple. Later, in history classes, students read about American failures of policy and moral direction in Dee Brown's *Bury My Heart at Wounded Knee*, Jeanne Wakatsuki Houston and James D. Houston's *Farewell to Manzanar*, about the internment of the Japanese-Americans during the Second World War, and Gavan Daws's history of the Hawaiian Islands, *Shoal of Time*. To learn about the Holocaust they watched Alain Resnais's documentary "Night and Fog." For "Ideas in Western Literature," a popular course in the high school, students read Sartre, Camus, Borges, Hesse, and Kafka.

And yet so cheerful was the general atmosphere at Punahou that it was not always easy for some students to imagine the catastrophes of history or the troubled inner lives of literary characters. Jonathan Selinger, who is now a professor of chemical physics at Kent State University, recalled one teacher who had just moved to Hawaii and complained about how hard it was to teach literature at Punahou. "On the mainland, he said, students could relate to literature because so many were depressed or had even considered suicide," Selinger recalled. "In Hawaii, students were just too happy to appreciate great literature."

Barry Obama did not always share that light spirit. He suffered his share of loneliness and confusion in high school. His mother, after three years at the University of Hawaii studying for a master's degree in anthropology, decided that she needed to move back to Indonesia. There she would do the fieldwork for her doctorate, live more cheaply, and satisfy her restless need to explore the world. She was determined to go, but Barry was determined to make his way at Punahou, even if it meant living with his grandparents in the apartment on Beretania Street.

"When she first came back to Hawaii, in the early seventies," Obama's sister, Maya, said, "she never planned on leaving Barack. But she returned [to Indonesia], thinking, Let me work on my marriage and career. Barack had already spent three years at Punahou and he wanted to stay. She felt that was probably the best temporary solution. Still, it was hard. She missed him very much and wrote lots of letters to him and he wrote some back and there were frequent calls and summers and Christmases together. But it was painful not to have him there. The idea of taking him away from all that and thrusting him back into another country was hard. You change so much in three years in adolescence, and it was sort of impossible for him to go back to Indonesia."

Barry was now without a father and, for most of the year, without his mother. At about that time he began what he later called his "fitful interior struggle."

Hawaii does not much resist the image of paradise: the physical beauty, the isolation from the mainland (from *everywhere*), the languid pace of life, the self-marketing as the "Aloha State," the ultimate vacation spot, are intoxicating. Even in the capital, Honolulu, which can be as over-developed as Hong Kong, the mountains and the beach are visible from nearly everywhere. Obama spent plenty of time with his friends having fun: body-surfing at Sandy Beach, camping and hiking in the Mokule'ia Forest Reserve and Peacock Flats, seeing movies at the old Cinerama Theater, hanging out at the Mr. Burger Drive-In near the university or at Zippy's, for the chili with rice. To say nothing of sampling, in time, the ubiquitous brands of marijuana: Maui Wowie, Kaua'i Electric, Puna But-ter, Kona Gold. When Barry was in school, the legal driving age was fif-teen. Punahou was like a paradise as conceived by well-to-do American teenagers.

Barry was known on campus as a smart, engaging, friendly kid, an obsessive basketball player, tight with the jocks, friendly with the artier types, able to negotiate just about any clique. Unlike some adolescents, he bore his confusions privately, without self-dramatizing. To most kids, he was cheerful—and game. He wrote poems for *Ka Wai Ola*, the campus lit-erary magazine. He sang in the chorus. He took part in high-school goofs, once helping make a film called "Narc Squad," based on the ABC police drama "The Mod Squad." ("One White, One Black, One Blond" went the "Mod Squad" promo, and, of the three young undercover cops, Barry played the dashiki-wearing character. He peeled it off for the pool party scene.)

But negotiating his identity was far more complicated than anyone could sense. Punahou teachers and graduates tend to view ethnicity as one more element in their rosy view of the school and of Hawaii itself. Obama's self-portrayal in his memoir as a troubled kid trying to cope with race and racism came as a shock to some of his old teachers and classmates. His teacher Eric Kusunoki was surprised by the book. "In Hawaii, ethnicity is blurred. I like to think of kids not in terms of black and white—it's more like a golden brown," he said. "Everyone is mixed and everyone is different. So when I read his book it was kind of a surprise to me. I had him in homeroom every day for four years. He expressed himself quite well and was never upset or lost his cool. He always had a big smile and could negotiate his way through the school."

Constance Ramos, whose background is Filipino-Hungarian, wrote, "I never once thought of Barry as 'Black.' I still don't. On a very deep, emotional level, I honestly don't know what 'Black' means: Why is Barry supposed to fall into that 'color' category, when his skin tone is just about the same as mine? Nobody would call me 'black.' It remains unclear to me why skin color is so important to so many people." She said she felt "betrayed" by Obama's angst-ridden self-portrayal.

There are very few writers and observers about the Punahou scene who allow even a tinge of anxiety, an element of darkness, to cloud the sunny self-regard. The novelist Allegra Goodman is an exception, describing a place where the walls of privilege were manned at all times and nearly impregnable:

> The lovely tropical home of so many diverse people is not beyond distinctions—it is all about them. Tensions simmer between native Hawaiians and newcomers. The rich layered cultures of Polynesia, Asia, and America bump up against bigotry and ignorance, often voiced in racist jokes and sometimes expressed in physical violence. Punahou's student body is multicultural, and its financial aid generous. But, for some, Punahou symbolizes exclusive privilege. More than once when I was a student there, rough kids from outside breached the walls. Teachers sounded the alarm: "The mokes are on campus again"—the word "mokes" designating kids who were native and poor.

In high school, Barry eventually stopped writing letters to his father. His effort to understand himself was a lonely one. Touchingly, awkwardly, he was giving himself instruction on how to be black. According to his math and science teacher, Pal Eldredge, the way Barry carried himself changed. "His gait, the way he walked, changed," he said. "And I wasn't the only one who noticed." Step by step he began immersing himself in an African-American culture that seemed to live thousands of miles from where he was. He listened to Marvin Gaye and Stevie Wonder, Grover Washington and Miles Davis; he watched "Soul Train" and Richard Pryor on television. On his own he read Richard Wright's *Native Son*, the poems of Langston Hughes, *The Autobiography of Malcolm X*, *The Souls of Black Folk*, the essays of James Baldwin, Ralph Ellison's *Invisible Man*.

Obama could not, and did not, pretend to be starting his journey from the neighborhood. Honolulu was hardly Detroit or Lansing, the South Side or Harlem—much less the hamlets of the Mississippi Delta—but he did not escape moments of real racial humiliation. He fleetingly mentions one incident, when he was eleven or twelve, that one white classmate, Kristen Caldwell, recounted many years later in far greater detail:

> When I started reading more about Barack Obama's early years at Punahou, my first instinct was that the racial issues were exaggerated. Then I realized that I really would have had no way of knowing what his experience, his perception had been—just as he wouldn't be aware of mine. I did remember one incident very vividly: We were standing on the *lanai* (patio) looking at the draw sheets that had just been posted for a tennis tournament . . .
>
> Everyone does the same thing: You look for your name, and then run your finger across the draw to see whom you might play as you advance into later rounds of the tournament . . .
>
> Barry was doing what we all did, completely normal behavior. But Tom M. came over and told him not to touch the draw sheet because he would get it dirty. He singled him out, and the implication was absolutely clear: Barry's hands weren't grubby; the message was that his darker skin would somehow soil the draw. Those of us standing there were agape, horrified, disbelieving . . .
>
> Barry handled it beautifully, with just the right amount of cold burn without becoming disrespectful. "What do you mean by that?" he asked firmly. I could see in his eyes that Tom realized he had gone too far—his remark was uncalled for; he had crossed a line—and there were witnesses. He fumbled in his response, ultimately claiming that he had only been joking. But we all knew it had been no joke, and it wasn't even remotely funny.
>
> Some of our innocence was gone: That was the price of an ugly remark, one I've never forgotten.

It wasn't a singular incident. In the ninth grade, classmate Ronald Loui recalled, a physical-education teacher advised the students to change their style of running. "You should try to run like a black man," the teacher said. "Not so straight up, tilt your pelvis!" Obama, the only black kid in the class, "was really embarrassed but, in part to get away from the uncomfortable situation, he took off running," Loui said.

In high school, Obama found a few older black friends to talk with. He spent some time with Keith Kakugawa—"Ray" in the memoir—but Keith's bitter monologues about "the white man" seemed to do little but stoke Obama's anger and confusion. (As an adult, Kakugawa spent seven years in prison on drug and auto-theft charges. When he started making trouble for the Obama campaign—telling reporters that *Dreams* was inaccurate and asking for money—one spokesman, Bill Burton, said, "There's no doubt that Keith's story is tragic and sad.")

But while Obama's most constant comrades—Greg Orme, Bobby Titcomb, and Mike Ramos—were not black, he had valuable friendships with two older African-American Punahou students: Rik Smith, who is now a physician, and Tony Peterson, who works for the United Methodist Church. The three of them would gather weekly outside Cooke Hall for what they jokingly called Ethnic Corner. They talked about classes, philosophy, race—and not least how race affected their ability to date Punahou girls, who were nearly all either white, Asian, or mixed race. They asked each other what it meant to "act white" or "act black." They even discussed whether there would be a black President in their lifetime—and they decided that it wasn't possible.

Often they just talked about the same mysteries that bewitch anyone at that age. In the spring of 1976, Tony tape-recorded one session of the Ethnic Corner because he had to write a school essay on the subject of time; he thought he might collect some material from the others:

RIK: Have you guys ever thought about time?
BARRY: Yeah.
TONY: I thought about it.
RIK: Think about time, okay. What is it? What is time?
TONY: I don't know.
BARRY: Eh. Time is just a collection of human. . . . listen, this is gonna sound good, boy! See, time is just a collection of human experiences combined so that they make a long, flowing stream of thought.

The dialogue is "No Exit" meets "Fast Times at Ridgemont High." "We were three black guys trying to impress each other with how smart we were," Peterson said, laughing. "We weren't screwing around, we weren't playing the dozens. We were challenging each other."

They also formed a means of protection for each other, Rik Smith said. Punahou thought of itself as an exemplar of multicultural comity, but Smith, who was two years older than Obama, described a Halloween celebration at Punahou where a couple of students came in blackface and tattered clothing—"minstrel stuff." The kids who had dressed up had no idea that they had done anything racist. In fact, they were offended that Rik took offense. How could they be racist when their hearts were pure? Nearly all teenagers tend to think of themselves as outsiders—there is solace in it, loneliness is transformed into a variety of glamour—but Obama, Smith, and Peterson were always talking among themselves about whether or not they were black first or individuals first. The answers provided by the Punahou School were confusing.

"Barack's experience was my experience," Smith said. "I talk to my kids about this and my kids can't imagine it in California. As a child in Seattle, I couldn't play at recess because the kids wouldn't let me play baseball. One of the funny stories that I recall is that a *haole* girl that I liked, a nice individual, would never go out with me. It was weird because I would go sneak into her room at home past midnight and then I would go. But she wouldn't talk to me in school. It was an *interesting* activity."

The subjects of the Ethnic Corner were hardly ephemeral. "When Barry gave the speech at the Democratic Convention in 2004 and talked about wanting to eradicate the idea that if a black kid has a book he's acting white—that was a huge part of what we were talking about back in high school," Tony Peterson said. "Kids wrestle with their identities. And if you are biracial and look black and grow up in a white family, the issues are deep."

Ronald Loui, who is Chinese-American, said, "People in Hawaii have no real access to an understanding of the black-white divide. So many of the icons of that era were black. We were all listening to Earth, Wind & Fire and we all pretended that we were Dr. J on the basketball court, and yet there were parents who were telling their kids to watch out for black people."

Barry's mother visited Honolulu when she could or brought him to Indonesia during school breaks when she could afford it, but Barry was growing up on the margins of her vision. He could still appreciate her energy, her sweetness, and her intelligence, but she had little to offer now about what troubled him most. When she naïvely tried to find common ground with her son—"You know, I don't *feel* white!"—he only got disgusted at her attempt. Living in Indonesia, Ann Dunham had become fixed on the axioms, the hopes, and the mood of the early civil-rights days;

she had precious little feel for what had come after: the mutual resentments, Black Power, the Panthers, the clashes over busing and affirmative action. "I remember her feeling saddened by the anger that she sensed in parts of the African-American community," Obama said.

How could Ann possibly know what it was to be a black man in America—and who, besides a few teenagers no less confused than he, was around to help? "Some of the problems of adolescent rebellion and hormones were compounded by the fact that I didn't have a father," Obama said. "So what I fell into were the exaggerated stereotypes of black male behavior—not focusing on my books, finding respectability, playing a lot of sports."

"We were all a little *untethered,*" Maya Soetoro-Ng says. Maya, who lived with Ann in Indonesia while Barry attended Punahou, said that she and her older brother struggled with their rootlessness in different ways. "We went to a lot of places—four, five months at a time," including Pakistan, Thailand, India, she said. "Long enough to get a sense of the textures of the place and really know it a bit. I have tremendous wanderlust. Until 2004, when I became a mother, at age thirty-four, the wanderlust eased but it didn't go away. Now its voice is very soft. I think Barack was less in love with it. He had greater examples, in our grandparents and elsewhere, of the beauty of claiming community, of being grounded, of being loyal, of being in one place and really working on the relationship with that place and the people in it. I think that became very desirable to him. I can't speak for him but probably some of our mother's decisions may have looked selfish in comparison."

As an adult, Obama always expressed deep love for his mother—he readily acknowledged her influence as the most powerful in his young life—but he could also step back and evaluate critically the choices she made as a young woman. "When I think about my mother," he said during the campaign, "I think there was a certain combination of being very grounded in who she was, what she believed in. But also a certain recklessness. I think she was always searching for something. She wasn't comfortable seeing her life confined to a certain box."

Maya doesn't believe her mother was aware of her son's crisis of identity as he navigated Punahou. "I'm sure part of our mother's optimism was a constant reminder to both of us that we were special because we came from more than one world and we could access many worlds easily," she says. "When we struggled with not feeling entirely at home here or there, I think that she would push an optimistic perspective of things. My brother has never been one to air his grievances or talk about things that were troubling him. He is one of these people who work things out in their own solitary way. He works it out by walking and thinking. He has never been neurotic."

During Barry's last three years at Punahou, Ann worked in Jakarta doing the fieldwork for her doctoral dissertation in anthropology. Once she finished her master's, however, her interest was more in gaining the knowledge and expertise needed to work in the field of international development. She did not complete the dissertation until 1992, when she was fifty. In the meantime, as she did research and wrote, she worked in development jobs for the Ford Foundation and the World Bank, and as research coordinator for Bank Rakyat, a leading Indonesian bank.

A disarmingly gregarious personality, Ann knew many foreign diplomats, business people, and development officers, but more and more she came to immerse herself in the life of Indonesians—in Jakarta and in the provinces. Her marriage was strained. Lolo moved increasingly into the international oil business, with its office meetings and golf games and cocktail parties. Ann was repelled by the wealthy, entitled foreigners in their midst who spent their time complaining about the servants, "the locals," and maximizing the ways they could make Jakarta more like "home." Ann's Indonesian was fluent. She invited interesting people to the house for dinner: artists, writers, development officers. She started making frequent trips out of the capital to the regional centers, especially the villages of central Java near Yogyakarta.

"She home-schooled me and took me to the villages," Maya said. "Blacksmith villages, tile factories, clove cigarette factories, ceramic villages, basket-weaving villages—all manner of textiles and cottage industries." It was an interesting, engaged life, but it did have one distinct cost. Obama admits that, much as he tried to deny it at the time, the separations from his mother took their toll. "I didn't feel [her absence] as a deprivation," he said. "But when I think about the fact that I was separated from her, I suspect it had more of an impact than I know."

The disconnection—and time—had a way of catching them all by surprise. When he was in high school, Barry arrived alone at the airport in Jakarta for a summer stay with Ann and Maya. Ann had a panicky feeling as she searched the arrivals area for her son. Somehow, in her mind, Barry was still chubby-cheeked, stocky, not especially tall, and now he was nowhere to be found. Had he slipped by her and wandered off somewhere in the airport? Not likely. Had he missed the plane?

"And then comes this . . . figure! Tall and handsome—another *person*!" Ann's friend and academic adviser, Alice Dewey, recalled. "Suddenly he was towering over her and speaking in this very low newly-acquired man's voice. The voice that everyone knows nowadays!"

From the mid-seventies on, Alice Dewey was Ann's "mother hen," both an intimate friend and her academic mentor. When Alice visited Jakarta or, later, Yogyakarta, she often stayed with Ann. Alice Dewey is the granddaughter of the American philosopher John Dewey. Her office, in Saunders Hall, at the University of Hawaii, is small, the sort of alarmingly cluttered warren that always seems one piece of paper away from crashing down and crushing its inhabitant to death. A friendly woman with a white corona of curls and a sharp smile, Dewey sits in a creaky desk chair surrounded by stacks of ancient memos, bulging files, dusty dissertations, each teeteringly perched on the next. Like so many of Ann's friends and acquaintances, she remembers her as restless, curious, funny, tirelessly idealistic. Dewey was angry at the occasional depiction of Dunham during the campaign as a flighty idealist who "ignored" her son to pursue her own muses. "She *adored* that child," she said, "and they were in constant touch. And he *adored* her."

It pained Ann to be apart from Barry for such long stretches, Alice Dewey said, but Ann really believed that it was possible to live an unconventional life and still find a way for her children to grow up into whole, independent people. She struck Alice Dewey as a mature student, somebody with a sense of intellectual penetration long before she even embarked on her dissertation. "She was one of those students that you think, 'Why don't I let her lecture?' "

Both Dewey and Dunham were deeply interested in the lives and the futures of the craftsmen of central Java. They studied not only their art, but also the effect of modernization on their way of life. Would village craftsmen disappear? Dunham's research and her point of view was a kind of implicit argument with Clifford Geertz and other anthropologists, who believed that village craftsmen were, for various cultural reasons, destined for extinction. Where Geertz saw dispirited, tradition-bound irrationality among villagers, Dunham saw potential vitality. She was convinced that, with the help of modest financing from banks and non-governmental organizations, cottage industries in rural Indonesia could not only sustain ancient crafts and traditions but also provide a strong alternative economy to agriculture. Her mode of work—socially engaged, policy-directed— was hardly fashionable when she was doing her research, yet her conclusions proved prescient. Blacksmithing was just one of the Javanese crafts that began to expand in the nineteen-eighties. The idea of providing microcredits to craftsmen and to small, rural enterprises is common currency in the twenty-first century; it was a fairly radical and unconventional idea when Dunham championed it.

At first, Ann studied a wide range of crafts—weaving, batik, leatherwork, puppetry, ironwork, ceramics, sculpture—and she wanted to include all of these crafts in her dissertation. She examined everything from the way motifs from the Hindu epics were applied to resist-dye batiks to the intricate construction of bamboo birdcages. She tried to cover vast scholarly territory and numerous villages in central Java. "When she came to write her proposal for her dissertation, we told her, for God's sake, choose one," Dewey recalled. "She chose blacksmithing. Iron lives in the ground and so you can talk about the mythological dimensions of the craft, too." Javanese blacksmithing is an art with a history that is more than a thousand years old, and Dunham was entranced by both the objects themselves and the lives of the craftsmen.

To do her research, Dunham had to insinuate her way into the smithies of Kajar, a village in Gunung Kidul, a region of central Java. When she first started visiting there in the late nineteen-seventies, the village had to be approached by foot for the last mile; electricity did not arrive in Kajar for another decade. The blacksmith's workshop, in Javanese tradition, is sacred and mostly barred to women. The craftsmen think of their work as a spiritual endeavor, their products as sacred as a crucifix or Torah scroll. Offerings are draped on the anvil. Dunham's work was, in many ways, economic anthropology, but she also had the requisite skill of a social anthropologist: the capacity to gain access. She persuaded these craftsmen to let her inside the smithy, observe their work, and interview them at length. She had a capacity to get these craftsmen to reveal even their innermost thoughts; in one passage, Pak Sastro, the head of the blacksmithing cooperative in Kajar, describes a dream he had before being visited by the regional sultan. Because Dunham was American, she was regarded, above all, as a foreign guest and able to transcend, somehow, her status as a woman among men.

"She really earned their trust," Maya Soetoro-Ng said. "She knew their extended families and their children and grandchildren."

"The fact that she worked so closely with blacksmiths is proof of her subtlety as a person," Bronwen Solyom, a friend and expert in Indonesian art, said. "If she hadn't been so congenial, she wouldn't have been able to gain access to those men and their venerable skills."

Even though Dunham narrowed her topic to the smiths of central

Java, her dissertation, "Peasant Blacksmithing in Indonesia: Surviving and Thriving Against All Odds," was over a thousand pages long in manuscript. (In 2009, Duke University Press published a condensed version edited by Alice Dewey and another of Dunham's colleagues, Nancy I. Cooper.) Dunham was an indefatigable researcher. Some passages are so detailed and arcane that they nearly reach the level of parody, yet the dissertation reveals, in its study of a single village, the dense textures of culture inherent in any one place. To read it is to learn the history, beliefs, and skill of nearly every inhabitant of the village; its intricate and evolving social, religious, and class structures; its cultural formation through centuries of foreign and indigenous influence. At times it seems that the reader learns more here about the Indonesian *keris*, the daggers made by the smiths—about iron forging, iron casting, silver and gold smithing— than about the fall of Rome in Gibbon. But one cannot help admiring both the complexity of Kajar and the industry of Ann Dunham. It's clear from the text that Dunham became intimate friends with everyone there: Pak Paeran, the village headman; Pak Sastrosuyono, the leading blacksmithing entrepreneur; the artisans; the bureaucrats. There is an evident affection for the people she writes about and an obvious hope that the Indonesian government, along with international aid and development institutions, will help insure the continuing health of small handicraft industries, as an element both of cultural continuity and of economic diversity. Dunham's text seems directed as much to the agencies and bureaucracies that might help the people of Kajar and other Indonesian villagers as to her fellow scholars. "There is a balance there of intimacy and objectivity," Maya Soetoro-Ng said. "She tried to combat others who were simplistic or patronizing to the craftsmen. She emphasized applied anthropology, the idea that this work should be about making lives better."

In her letters to Dewey, Ann Dunham wrote about her encounters; she wrote with news about her assistants and sources, academic gossip, even updates on the latest Dorothy Sayers mysteries that she was reading as a diversion. On July 28, 1978, while Barry was a junior at Punahou, Dunham wrote to Dewey from Indonesia:

Dear Alice,

    I finally got back to Gunung Kidul, finishing up our work last week, exhausted but quite satisfied with the results. Kajar is certainly an interesting village from several points of view, not the least of which is political. I can envision a little article someday with a model of the balance of power there and the shifts affected by various styles of tinkering from outside. . . .

We stayed at the house of Pak Rianto . . . [who] in turn rents part of the house of a man called Pak Harjo Bodong (Roughly translated "Father Harjo with the Long Belly Button," though I never had the courage to really ask why.) Pak Harjo Bodong used to be the most famous [smith] in the Wonosari area. He also used to be a famous thief and was in jail four times when he was young. . . . Lives there with his twelfth wife (he is her tenth husband). They are both in their seventies and quite a sketch. . . .

We arrived in Kajar just at the time of the peanut harvest. This meant that at every house we surveyed we were given large glasses of sticky tea, refilled at least 3 times despite all my "sampuns," and big plates of peanuts in the shell to consume . . . [I won't] ever be able to look a peanut in the face again (yes, peanuts *do* have faces—smirky, nasty little faces, in fact). . . .

I forgot to mention that we grew very fond of Pak Atmo Sadiman dukoh of Kajar. . . . He was giving me a new Javanese name, "Sri Lestari." I gather it means "Forever Beautiful," and wasn't that gallant of him. Thank God for nice comfortable middle-aged men who don't give you any complexes. Amen! . . .

Reading over this letter it sounds rather flippant. It's the influence, I think, of Lord Peter Wimsey who kept me sane all through my weeks in Gunung Kidul. Especially liked *Gaudy Night. Unnatural Death* was fun but less padded out with good tidbits. . . .

I haven't seen a newspaper or a magazine for the last month, so if anything exciting has happened you might let me know. . . .

Aloha,

Ann

Dunham decorated her house with *keris*, puppets, prints, and paintings. "Ann loved beautiful things, but not as a connoisseur," Solyom said. "She was a supporter of all kinds of craftsmen, and she collected the things people she knew made." When, years later, Michelle and Barack Obama set up house in Chicago, their decorations included Indonesian prints.

In order to be close to the villages that she was studying, Ann stayed in Yogyakarta and made trips to the villages on the arid plateau of south central Java. Lolo visited frequently, but he continued to work in Jakarta. Ann's three-bedroom house was on the grounds of the sultan's pleasure palace, a landscape of reflecting pools and gardens, ruins and towers, batik sellers and the old bird market. According to Maya, Lolo's aged mother had royal blood and lived with them in Yogyakarta. "She spoke fluent Dutch and Javanese," Maya recalled. "She was a tiny woman. She must have weighed, perhaps, ninety pounds and she birthed fourteen children. She chewed betel nut and spit into a silver spittoon. She was very much the lady, just like our Kansan grandmother, though they were worlds apart. She was very discreet. I would guess in Indonesia we would call it *halus*—sort of refined, very aware of her language." Dewey said that when Barry came to visit, Ann had to rent a house outside the pleasure palace grounds. The presence of one foreigner was an event; the presence of a teenager with no royal blood at all would have been "too much."

Ann's eventual separation from Lolo was undramatic and relatively free of rancor. After a long time apart, they were finally divorced in 1980. Ann never asked for or received regular alimony or child support, according to the divorce records.

Politically, Dunham was a "garden-variety Democrat," Dewey recalled, but her mind was inclined not so much toward politics as it was toward a kind of engaged service. She joked that she wanted equal pay but wouldn't stop shaving her legs. "She wasn't ideological," Obama says. "I inherited that, I think, from her. She was suspicious of cant."

Mary Zurbuchen, who worked for the Ford Foundation, got to know Dunham when she was working at the foundation in the nineteen-eighties. Although Dunham was always trying to keep her dissertation moving forward, she earned her living, and made her greatest impact, as a development officer. "She was really concerned about women's rights and their livelihoods," Zurbuchen said. Women in Java were often central to the household economy but had no access to credit. Factory jobs were opening for young women, yet there was little talk about improving labor conditions. To raise issues of labor rights or human rights was risky, even for an established foundation like Ford. Dunham opened contact with labor activists. She helped start a consumers' rights organization. "It sounds anodyne now," Zurbuchen said, "but in those days a consumer organization raising questions about additives in food or the marketing of fake drugs—this was a cutting-edge civil-society activity.

"In the expat community, the things she was interested in and that Ford was pushing were not conventional," Zurbuchen went on. "The Indonesian government and the military pushed back. The economic interests, allied with the military, pushed back. If you worked on forestry, it wasn't long before you ran into the military-backed companies who were exploiting the forests. Ann faced pushback on labor-rights issues. She was also interested in family law and inheritance of property rights for women.

Women who wanted to ban polygamy and to get their legal rights in the family were also her concern. There has been progress, but it came slowly."

Ann wrote to Alice Dewey in 1984 while she was working for the Ford Foundation and teaching at provincial colleges; back home, her son had graduated from Columbia and was writing business reports for a firm in New York. The letter is filled with details of her frenetic efforts on behalf of women all over Southeast Asia:

> Dearest Alice,
>
> Apa kabar? I hope this letter finds you and all the canine, feline and hominid members of your household doing well. . . .
>
> Other than worrying about plans for fall, life is good here. Maybe you remember that I am handling projects for Ford in the areas of women, employment, and industry (small and large). . . . This year I have major projects for women on plantations in West Java and North Sumatra; for women in kretek factories in Central and East Java; for street-food sellers and scavengers in the cities of Jakarta, Jogja and Bandung; for women in credit cooperatives in East Java; for women in electronics factories, mainly in the Jakarta-Bogor area; for women in cottage industry cooperatives in the district of Klaten; for hand-loom weavers in West Timor; . . . for street food sellers in Thailand (with Cristina Szanton as the project leader); etc. In addition I am still team-teaching the Sociology of the Family course with Pujiwati Sayogo at Bogor Agricultural Univ., and I am project specialist on a research project that she is coordinating on The Roles of Rural Women on the Outer Islands of Indonesia. . . . In April the Foundation is sending me to Bangla Desh for an employment conference. I am hoping to take Maya with me (in lieu of home leave this year) and stop off in Thailand on the way there and Delhi on the way back . . .
>
> Maya is enjoying life as an 8th grader at the International School, and she seems to be turning into a people right on schedule. She hates me to brag, but I am forced to mention that she made high honors this term. . . .
>
> Much love,
> Ann

When Obama describes his mother as a singular influence, someone directed toward public service and the improvement of the lives of the poor but without an emphasis on ideology, this was the sort of work he is referring to. "He became the kind of person Ann was, the maverick who really wanted to bring change to the world," the Indonesian jounalist Julia Suryakusuma said.

Dunham may have been unable to help her son in all the ways that she had hoped or that he needed, but, in her own way, she did what she could. Obama remembers that even when he was very young she would give him books, record albums, and tape recordings of the great voices of African-American history. Obama teased his mother, saying that she had been a pioneer in Afrocentric education. Similarly, Ann made sure that Maya learned Indonesian. Maya went on to study Javanese dance and got a Ph.D. in education; Alice Dewey was on her dissertation committee. Her husband, Konrad Ng, teaches media studies at the University of Hawaii and has written articles such as "Policing Cultural Traffic: Charlie Chan and Hawaii Detective Fiction."

Ann was able to do what her first husband could not. She was able to negotiate the distances between worlds and cultures and remain whole; the passage enriched her even when it caused complications in her role as a mother to her son. Dunham might not have been the most conventional mother, but she cannot be faulted for stifling her son's ambitions. "I do remember Mom and I making jokes about, 'Oh yeah, you're going to be the first black President,' " Maya said. "I don't know why we would make those jokes. I can only assume it was because he was always right. He was one of those people who even as a young man was like an old man, you know?

"When he went to college," Maya continued, "I would have been nine, ten, eleven, twelve, and we would joke about this, but I think on the one hand we were teasing him, but behind the joke there was the sense that he was going to do something important. I always felt that way about him, and my mother felt pretty early on that he belonged to something bigger."

At Punahou, however, he was not the student-politician sort. Barry Obama was a basketball fanatic, the kid you saw walking down the street to school, to the grocery store, to visit friends, always dribbling a ball slick with wear. On weekends, he played full-court runs at Punahou. In the early mornings before class and after school until dark, he played with schoolmates on the outdoor courts at Punahou. In Tony Peterson's year-book, he wrote:

> Tony, man, I sure am glad I got to know you before you left. All those
> Ethnic Corner trips to the snack bar and playing ball made the year a

lot more enjoyable, even though the snack bar trips cost me a fortune. Anyway, great knowing you and I hope we keep in touch. Good luck in everything you do, and get that law degree. Some day when I am a pro basketballer, and I want to sue my team for more money, I'll call you.

Barry made the junior varsity team in tenth grade and varsity the next year. The basketball court was a circumscribed area of life where Obama felt comfortable and, sometimes, where he encountered a world beyond Punahou. Some of the black soldiers on the island played on the courts near his building and Barry was happy not only to play with them but also to pick up on their language, their manners and style on the court—something that watching N.B.A. games on television did not provide. "He didn't know who he was until he found basketball," his future brother-in-law Craig Robinson said. "It was the first time he really met black people." This was an exaggeration, but not by much.

On the varsity team, Barry played under Chris McLachlin, a locally celebrated coach with a sympathetic manner and a distinctly old-school approach to the game. McLachlin's emphasis on disciplined teamwork and stalwart defense did not encourage the flamboyance of Obama's hero, the Philadelphia 76ers star Julius Erving. McLachlin's teams were successful playing the sort of full-court, maximum-pressure defensive press that Dean Smith used at North Carolina and employing many of the disciplined offensive plays that John Wooden ran at U.C.L.A.

Obama hustled in practice, and he impressed his teammates with his fluidity and an odd, but effective, double-pump jump shot that he took in the lane off the dribble. He had skill and drive, but because the team was so packed with exceptional talent—three players on the starting five in his senior year went on to play serious college ball, and one forward, John Kamana, went on to a career in professional football—Obama did not get nearly as much playing time as he wanted. He groused about that to his friends, but he kept playing.

"Basketball was a good way for me to channel my energy," Obama said during the Presidential race. "It did parallel some of the broader struggles I was going through, because there were some issues in terms of racial identity that played themselves out on the basketball court. You know, I had an overtly black game, behind-the-back passes, and wasn't particularly concerned about fundamentals, whereas our coach was this Bobby Knight guy, and he was all about fundamentals—you know, bounce passes, and four passes before you shoot, and that sort of thing. So we had this little conflict that landed me on the bench when I argued. The truth was, on the playground, I could beat a lot of the guys who were starters, and I think he thought it was useful to have me there in practice."

"We had our clash between his playground style and our very deliberate style," McLachlin said. "He argued for more playing time, even called a meeting for him and a couple of others. He respectfully lobbied for their cause, and rightfully so. . . . He would have started for anyone else in the state." In his senior year, Obama had a few good games and his grandfather was pleased to hear him complimented on the local radio broadcasts. "It was good to get a few props late in life," Obama joked many years after.

In Barry's senior year, Punahou overpowered Moanalua High School, 60–28, to win the state championship. As he had all season, Obama played a secondary role. "It's never easy when you're young to realize you're never going to be the best at something you love," Larry Tavares said. "Barry had to realize he was going to have to look in other directions."

In 1999, Obama, writing an article for the *Punahou Bulletin* in the avuncular mode of a successful alumnus, said, "By the time I moved back to Hawaii, and started school at Punahou, I had come to recognize that Hawaii was not immune to issues of race and class, issues that manifested themselves in the poverty among so many native Hawaiian families, and the glaring differences between the facilities we at Punahou enjoyed and the crumbling public schools that so many of our peers were forced to endure. My budding awareness of life's unfairness made for a more turbulent adolescence than perhaps some of my classmates' experiences. As an African-American teenager in a school with few African-Americans, I probably questioned my identity a bit harder than most. As a kid from a broken home and family of relatively modest means, I nursed more resentments than my circumstances justified, and didn't always channel those resentments in particularly constructive ways.

"And yet," he concluded optimistically, "when I look back on my years in Hawaii, I realize how truly lucky I was to have been raised there. Hawaii's spirit of tolerance might not have been perfect or complete, but it was—and is—real. The opportunity that Hawaii offered—to experience a variety of cultures in a climate of mutual respect—became an integral part of my world view, and a basis for the values that I hold most dear."

But, as the author of his own past, Obama cast a far harsher light on his Punahou years. In his memoir, he writes of occasional internal rages, of confusion, of the drugs that provided momentary escape. Exhausted in his attempt to "untangle a mess that wasn't of [his] making"—the mess that was his non-relationship with his father—he stopped caring, or tried to. In what may be the most famous passage in the book, Obama writes, "Pot had helped, and booze, maybe a little blow when you could afford it." When I interviewed Obama in 2006, he denied none of it and made no coy remarks about not inhaling or about being young and foolish. These were the dodges of his two predecessors—Clinton and Bush. Had he inhaled?

"That was the point, wasn't it?" he said with a broad smile.

Indeed it was. "It was Hawaii in the seventies—everywhere you looked there were posters of marijuana leaves," a classmate, Kelli Furushima, said. "It was kind of like the sixties were lingering on and so it was totally party, recreational. It wasn't some sort of deep, dark getaway from society. It was palm trees are swaying, blue skies, waves lapping on the ocean, just part of island life in paradise."

Obama did get high with some frequency, and he was not especially reluctant to advertise the fact. His yearbook, *The Oahuan*, includes not just a standard senior-year portrait of him in a seventies white leisure suit but also a still-life photograph of a beer bottle and Zig Zag rolling papers. In the caption, Obama wrote thanks to "Tut and Gramps" and the "Choom Gang." "Chooming," in Hawaiian slang, means smoking marijuana.

"I'm sure if my mother had had any clue what that was," Obama said, "she would not have been pleased."

In a letter from Indonesia, Ann tried to prod Barry during his senior year about his grades and college: "It is a shame we have to worry so much about [grade point average], but you know what the college entrance competition is these days. Did you know that in Thomas Jefferson's day, and right up through the 1930s, anybody who had the price of tuition could go to Harvard? . . . I don't see that we are producing many Thomas Jeffersons nowadays. Instead we are producing Richard Nixons." Obama had the capacity to be an A student, but his overall aimlessness, the partying, his lack of direction, held him back. Obama admits, "I probably could've been a better ball player and a better student if I hadn't been goofing off so much." Recalling not only the drugs he did take, but also the heroin that was offered to him (and rejected), Obama wonders, in a searching, self-dramatizing moment, if he hadn't been in danger of taking a far more desperate road than that of the typical high-school partier:

Junkie. Pothead. That's where I'd been headed: the final, fatal role of the young would-be black man. Except the highs hadn't been about that, me trying to prove what a down brother I was. Not by then, anyway. I got high for just the opposite effect, something that could push questions of who I was out of my mind, something that could flatten out the landscape of my heart, blur the edges of my memory.

On one of her trips home during Obama's senior year, Ann Dunham heard about the drug arrest of one of Barry's friends and barged into his room wanting to know about it. She tried to express her concern about his declining grades, his lack of initiative in filling out college applications. Barry flashed his mother the sort of reassuring smile that had been so effective in the past. Barry knew he was adrift. Rage, drugs, disaffection, racial fury—he trusted none of them. "At best, these things were a refuge; at worst, a trap," he wrote. "Following this maddening logic, the only thing you could choose as your own was withdrawal into a smaller and smaller coil of rage, until being black meant only the knowledge of your own powerlessness, of your own defeat. And the final irony: Should you refuse this defeat and lash out at your captors, they would have a name for that, too, a name that could cage you just as good. Paranoid. Militant. Violent. Nigger."

Barry was so *far* from "black America." The closest center of African-American life was Los Angeles, a five-hour flight away. One of the more thoughtful and consequential things Stanley Dunham did in his role as a surrogate father was to take his grandson to one of his African-American friends in the neighborhood known as the Jungle, in Waikiki. A kind of bohemian beach community of narrow lanes, cheap hotels, rooming houses, students, travelers, and surfer-bums, the Jungle was home to an aging poet, and journalist, named Frank Marshall Davis.

Davis lived at the Koa Cottages on Kuhio Avenue. He wore an aloha shirt and cut-offs. People dropped in on him all the time to drink, maybe smoke a joint, talk, play Scrabble or bridge. His bungalow was like a non-stop salon: literary, political, and relaxed. Frank Davis was one of the more interesting men in Honolulu and Stanley Dunham was one of his regular visitors.

Like Stanley, Frank Marshall Davis was from Kansas. He grew up in Arkansas City, "a yawn town," he called it, fifty miles south of Wichita. In his memoir, *Livin' the Blues*, Davis writes, "Like virtually all Afro-Americans—and a high percentage of whites—I am ethnic hash"—African mainly, an eighth Mexican, and "I have no idea what." Frank's

Kansas was not much like Stanley's—his was a land of lynchings and frontier racism—but they became friends. Frank Davis was a raconteur, capable of expounding on everything from the Harlem Renaissance to the various charms of the surfer girls in Waikiki. He spoke in a fantastically deep Barry White voice and he tended to dominate the discussion, telling stories for hours about his grandmother, who had been a slave; the indignities of being black in Arkansas City, including nearly being lynched when he was five years old; his distinguished career as a columnist and editor in the world of the black press in Chicago, Gary, and Atlanta; his friendships with Richard Wright and Paul Robeson. In the nineteen-thirties and forties, Davis wrote four collections of poems about black life—*Black Man's Verse, I Am the American Negro, Through Sepia Eyes,* and *47th Street*—and won the praise of distinguished critics like Alain Locke, who believed that Davis would help fulfill the promise of a New Negro Renaissance in poetry.

In 1948, Paul Robeson came to Hawaii on a concert tour sponsored by the International Longshore and Warehouse Union, a left-wing union. Robeson was so enamored of the atmosphere on the islands that he told reporters, "It would be a tremendous impact on the United States if Hawaii is admitted as a state. Americans wouldn't believe the racial harmony that exists here. It could speed democracy in the United States." In 1946, Davis had married a much younger woman, a white Chicago socialite named Helen Canfield. Robeson extolled Hawaii to such a degree that Helen read more about the islands, and she and Frank Davis decided to move for a while to Honolulu, thinking that they would stay for the winter. They divorced in 1970, but Davis never left. "I am not too fond of what I read about the current mainland scene, so I prefer staying here," Davis told the newspaper *Black World* in 1974. "Since we do not have the confrontations that exist between white and Black in so many parts of the mainland, living here has been a relief."

In Honolulu, Davis ran a paper company, but that soon burned to the ground. He also worked with the I.L.W.U. and wrote for its weekly newspaper, the Honolulu *Record,* which lasted from 1948 to 1958. Some of his "fellow freedom fighters" back in Chicago accused him of "deserting the battle," he wrote, but in Hawaii he was less angry than he had been on the mainland, more at ease, though he never gave up his political views. He wrote fierce columns about the suppression of unions, conditions on the plantations, the power of the oligarchic Hawaiian families, race relations. He was one of many leftists who, in the nineteen-fifties, were investigated, and tainted, by the House Un-American Activities Committee. In Hawaii he could put many thousands of miles between himself and his would-be tormentors.

"Virtually from the start I had a sense of human dignity," Davis writes in *Livin' the Blues*. "On the mainland, whites acted as if dignity were their exclusive possession, something to be awarded only as they saw fit. Yet dignity is a human right, earned by being born. In Hawaii I had at last come into ownership of this birthright, stolen by the white power structure as a penalty of being black. Even on the Chicago South Side, where I was but another drop in a black pool, I was painfully conscious we had been baled, like cotton, into this area because whitey so decreed. It was a relief to soar at last with no wings clipped by the scissors of color." Davis was well aware that "under the placid surface of aloha was an undertow of racism," and he knew that he had given up the pleasures of the South Side. "Hawaii is not for those who can be happy only in Soul City," he warned. "This is no place for those who can identify only with Afro-America. 'Little Harlem' is only a couple of blocks of bars, barbershops, and a soul food restaurant or two."

Dawna Weatherly-Williams, a close friend who lived next door—she called Frank Davis "Daddy"—remembers that Stanley Dunham came by to visit with his grandson sometime in the early nineteen-seventies. "Daddy had his feet propped up and he saw them and called out, 'Hey, Stan! Oh, is this him?' " she recalled. "Stan had been promising to bring Barry by because we all had that in common—Frank's kids were half white, Stan's grandson was half black and my son was half black. Barry was well dressed, in a blazer, I think. He was tired and he was hungry. He had a full face—it wasn't pointed like it is now. We were all grinning like idiots, me and Frank and Stan, because we were thinking that we know this secret about life and we were going to share it with Barry. He hadn't seen anyone that looked like him before.

"Frank was also a great listener, which may be why Barack liked him, too. I am sure he influenced Barack more than Barack is saying. About social justice, about finding out more about life, about what's important, about how to use your heart and your mind. It's probably good that it wasn't a big thing, that he didn't make too big a thing of it all, because he was way ahead of his time."

As a teenager, Obama called on Davis on his own, driving along the Ala Wai Canal to the Jungle. One night, Frank gave him some insight into Stanley, telling him a story about how many years before the Dunhams had hired a young black woman to help care for Ann.

"A preacher's daughter, I think it was. Told me how she became a regular part of the family."

A regular part of the family—the language that earnest middle-class white people use to soothe their guilt about hiring blacks to clean their houses, to be nannies for their children.

Barry had told Frank about his grandmother's anxiety at encountering a scary-seeming black man on the street. Everything about the incident was confusing—his grandmother's fears, Stanley's shame—but Frank, who considered himself friends with the family, seemed to understand it all. He explained that even the most sympathetic white people could never fully comprehend a black man's pain. ("He's basically a good man. But he doesn't *know* me. Any more than he knew that girl that looked after your mother. He *can't* know me, not the way I know him.") Why was it, after all, that Stanley could visit, drink Frank's whiskey, fall asleep in his chair, and yet Frank couldn't do the same in his house?

"What I'm trying to tell you is," Frank Davis said, "your grandma's right to be scared. She's at least as right as Stanley is. She understands that black people have a reason to hate. That's just how it is. For your sake, I wish it were otherwise. But it's not. So you might as well get used to it."

When Obama was running for President, the right-wing blogosphere attacked Frank Marshall Davis. He was, by turns, a card-carrying Communist, a pornographer, a pernicious influence. The attacks were loud and unrelenting. For them, an acquaintanceship with Frank Marshall Davis was all part of an ominous picture of radical associations. And yet, while that relationship was neither constant nor lasting, certainly of no great ideological importance, Davis, by Obama's own accounting, made the young man feel something deep and disorienting. That night in the Jungle in Waikiki, he felt completely alone. To make some sense of himself, he would have to leave Hawaii for another country.

Chapter Three

Nobody Knows My Name

Obama's academic performance at Punahou was unremarkable, but even though he was a B-student his college prospects were promising. Like the best New England prep schools, Punahou routinely sent its top-tier students to the best colleges and universities in the country—and the second-tier students, Obama included, did almost as well. Along with most of his classmates, Obama had developed a case of "rock fever." He was eager to get off the island. From a girl he met in Hawaii, he heard about Occidental, a small, highly regarded school of about sixteen hundred undergraduates in Eagle Rock, California, near Pasadena. Accepted at several colleges, Obama took a flyer: he chose Occidental.

Obama writes that just before leaving for the mainland and his freshman year, he paid a last visit to Frank Marshall Davis. As he always did, the old man welcomed Obama warmly—and then challenged him. Rattling Obama was his way of giving counsel. He had told Obama that black kids lucky enough to go to college invariably emerge into the world with "an advanced degree in compromise." Now he was telling Obama that no one was telling him the truth about "the real price of admission" to college.

And what was that? Obama asked.

"Leaving your race at the door," Davis said. "Leaving your people behind."

A place like Occidental wouldn't give Obama a real education, Davis insisted, so much as "train" him. "They'll train you so good, you'll start believing what they tell you about equal opportunity and the American way and all that shit. They'll give you a corner office and invite you to fancy dinners, and tell you you're a credit to your race. Until you want to actually start running things, and then they'll yank on your chain and let you know that you may be a well-trained, well-paid nigger, but you're a nigger just the same." Go to college, Davis said, but "keep your eyes open."

Obama thought of Davis much the way he thought of his mother—as a product of his time. And yet he couldn't dismiss him. Even before Obama joined the swim of African-American life, he had been warned about the perils of selling out, of tokenism and the limits of white tolerance. Obama soon discovered that the political and internal wariness that Davis prescribed was not so easy to uphold at Occidental. With Spanish Revival architecture and unfailing weather, Occidental was a favorite of Hollywood; in films from the Marx Brothers to "Clueless," Occidental was the generic California campus. The college was surrounded by a working-class Hispanic neighborhood, but students seldom got much beyond campus; when they did, it was usually to go roller-skating on the boardwalk at Venice Beach, body-surfing at Newport Beach, or to a concert downtown. Everyone knew everyone. "Oxy is like Peyton Place, it's so small," Obama's classmate and friend Phil Boerner said.

In September, 1979, Obama moved into a single-room triple in a dormitory known as Haines Hall Annex. He shared Room A104 with a Pakistani named Imad Husain, who is now a banker in Boston, and Paul Carpenter, now a mortgage banker in Los Angeles. His roommates and dorm mates were friendly and inviting. The hallway was unusually diverse for Occidental: there were African-Americans, Asians, Hispanics, Arabs. Occidental draws heavily on middle- and upper-middle-class kids from California, but Obama seemed at ease. Although he was getting financial aid, no one saw him as particularly disadvantaged.

Occidental required undergraduates to take a core curriculum. The year before Obama arrived, the multicultural movement had exerted some influence on Occidental; reading lists now included more texts from Asia, Africa, the Middle East, and Latin America, as well as from the United States and Europe. Obama took courses mainly in politics, history, and literature, and a minimum of science. From the start, one of his favorite professors was Roger Boesche, a Tocqueville scholar, who taught American and European political thought. As a freshman, Obama took a survey course in American politics with Boesche, which covered the British and American liberal theorists of the seventeenth and eighteenth centuries, and *The Federalist Papers*. The following year he took Boesche's political theory course, in which he read excerpts from Nietzsche, Tocqueville, Sartre, Marcuse, and Habermas. Boesche was an outspoken liberal on the political issues of the day—the upcoming election between Reagan and Carter; the 1979 Soviet invasion of Afghanistan; the potential reinstatement of the draft—and Obama was sympathetic.

Obama studied regularly, but he also did plenty of hanging out at The Cooler, a ramshackle student center that was a favorite of the crowd he most identified with. As he put it, "The more politically active black students. The foreign students. The Chicanos. The Marxist professors and structural feminists and punk-rock performance poets. We smoked cigarettes and wore leather jackets. At night, in the dorms, we discussed neocolonialism, Frantz Fanon, Eurocentrism, and patriarchy. When we ground out our cigarettes in the hallway carpet or set our stereos so loud that the walls began to shake, we were resisting bourgeois society's stifling constraints." As a memoirist, Obama winks at his own undergraduate pretensions, but he also spent time on more demotic pursuits. He and his friends were big fans of the Lakers and they watched games on TV at a local pizza joint. He also became very disciplined about exercise. Obama took long morning runs and played basketball and tennis.

At the start, Obama went by either Barry or Obama. Some teachers, seeing his real name on their rolls, tried to call him Barack but they were soon asked to call him Barry. When he did talk about his background, it was with a minimum of anguish or revelation. "I don't see him as tortured," Phil Boerner said. "He seemed pretty happy, even if reserved at times. Some of the things I later discovered about his early life, he really didn't mention. We were living in the moment."

The bands pounding out of the stereo in Obama's room and the rooms along the dorm hallway included the B-52s, The Specials, Talking Heads, Roxy Music, UB40, Jimi Hendrix, Stevie Wonder, Earth, Wind & Fire, Bob Marley, Black Uhuru, The Flying Lizards. Obama also had a taste for jazz, for Miles Davis, John Coltrane, and Billie Holiday, along with middle-brow contemporaries like Grover Washington, Jr. Obama's accustomed uniform was shorts or jeans, T-shirt or Hawaiian aloha shirt, and flip-flops. Part of his getup was also a Marlboro dangling from his lips. ("I smoke like this because I want to keep my weight down," Obama told one friend. "After I get married, I'll stop and just get real fat.") By the standards of the time and place, he was hardly heroic in his drug use. Marijuana and hash were almost as common as beer at the Haines dorm parties, and Obama was not reluctant to join in the fun. The second semester of his sophomore year was known to some in his circle as "the spring of powdered cocaine," and Obama has never denied his acquaintance with "a little blow," either. It wasn't until his junior year, when he transferred to Columbia, that he vowed to stop getting high and to commit himself to his studies and his future.

Phil Boerner, who was not only Obama's freshman-year hallmate but also his roommate when, two years later, they both transferred to Columbia, kept a diary as a young man, and in an entry from 1983 he recalled a typical late-night scene in the dorm featuring his friend:

Moment: Freshman year at Oxy. The stereo in Barry's room is on—a Hendrix or Stones record is being played—and the record is skipping. I'm in the hall—"The Annex" outside. I hear the record skipping, and conclude that something is amiss. I peek into the room—their door was always unlocked, and it wasn't even closed all the way this time—and see Barry crashed out on his bed. I tiptoe in to turn off the record. Just as I'm creeping up to the stereo, which is right beside his bed, he opens one eye and looks at me. He doesn't say anything, but I feel an explanation is necessary as to why I'm sneaking into his room. Certainly not to steal something, as he might have thought, if he'd been a suspicious person, which he wasn't, and isn't. Well, I said to him, "The record is skipping," and proceeded to turn off the stereo. He mumbled something—"Thanks," perhaps, and rolled over and returned to snoring softly. I crept out of the room, closing the door behind me.

Obama's circle was multiracial. Among his closest friends were three older students from South Asia: two Pakistanis, Mohammed Hasan Chandoo and Wahid Hamid, and an Indian, Vinai Thummalapally. "I think that one of the reasons he felt comfortable with us was because we were accepted by virtually all people," Hamid said. "We didn't come with a lot of predispositions about race. We weren't carrying that American baggage. We were brown, I suppose you could say, and we got along with people who were white and black. I think we had an immediate connection with him because we allowed him to be who he was, someone able to straddle things. And I think that is how Barack sees himself, as someone able to understand, for obvious reasons of his background, where both whites and blacks come from. As a politician, he is not your typical black candidate or white candidate—that's part of his strength—but it was harder when he was young. But by virtue of his strengths and his skills and talents, he was an endearing individual. People liked him rather immediately. He managed to get along. He was gifted that way—and those gifts allowed the world to be less problematic for him than it could have been for someone without those skills."

There were very few black students at Occidental in Obama's time there—around seventy-five out of sixteen hundred. "And you could count the black faculty members on two fingers," one of Obama's classmates said. African-American students really did negotiate Occidental in different ways. Some kept more or less to themselves, sitting at the "black tables" at lunch, constructing an enclosed social world out of a sense both of preserving black culture and of a lack of welcome from the white students. The college's weekly newspaper, *The Occidental*, quoted one black student, Earl Chew, as saying, "Coming here was hard for me. A lot of things that I knew as a black student—that I knew as a black, period—weren't accepted on this campus."

Obama moved fairly easily among groups, just as he had at Punahou. Louis Hook, who was a leader of the Black Students Association, recalled that Obama wasn't an especially active member of the group; rather, he "came in and out of it." He said most black students on campus were trying to sustain the "feel of the civil-rights movement" and some of Obama's friends and acquaintances wondered why he hung out with white and South Asian kids as often as he did. Obama, Hook concluded, "was a crossover guy," who "blended across the different communities. That was unusual. Some appreciated it, and some didn't look that highly on it. There was a split among black kids among people who really needed the reinforcement of their own culture and some who could deal inside it and outside it. Obama was in the category that didn't grow up in the African-American tradition. So for him, he could deal with it but was comfortable without it, too."

Obama discovered that, for the most part, the complaints of the black students at Occidental were the same as everyone else's: "Surviving classes. Finding a well-paying gig after graduation. Trying to get laid." In fact, Obama writes, "I had stumbled upon one of the well-kept secrets about black people: that most of us weren't interested in revolt; that most of us were tired of thinking about race all the time; that if we preferred to keep to ourselves it was mainly because that was the easiest way to stop thinking about it, easier than spending all your time mad or trying to guess whatever it was that white folks were thinking about you."

Like so many students, he was trying to figure out who he was. "He hadn't yet defined himself," Margot Mifflin, who was dating Obama's close friend Hasan Chandoo, said. "I didn't realize at the time how much work he had to do to define himself. One friend of his, and of mine, said to me not long ago, 'Since when is Barry black? He's as white as he is black.' She was saying that he was of mixed race. He'd grown up with white grandparents and a white mother. She didn't think there was anything cynical in the way that Barry identified himself, but we knew him as both black and white. I don't ever remember talking to him about his race. And we all called him Barry."

One of Obama's black friends at Occidental was an older student named Eric Moore, who, as the son of an Air Force officer, had grown up in Colorado, Ohio, and Japan. For three months, as part of the Operation Crossroads program, Moore worked at a rural medical clinic in the Siaya district of Kenya, near Lake Victoria and not far from where Barack, Sr., was born. The Luo tribe dominates the region, and Obama was eager to hear more about Moore's adventures in the villages there. "That was a source of connectivity between us," Moore recalled. "Coincidentally, in some ways I knew more about him than he knew about himself at that point."

One day, not long after returning from Kenya, Moore asked Obama, "What kind of name is 'Barry' for a brother?"

It was a natural question to ask, Moore said: "He wasn't embracing the Kenyan side, at least outwardly. He was proud, but he hadn't been there. So he told me his real name was Barack Obama. And I told him, 'That's a very strong name. I would embrace that.' I said, 'I would rock Barack.'"

There was no single moment when Obama declared an end to Barry—some friends never made the transition—but, by the time he left Occidental, after two years, he no longer introduced himself in the old way. He was coming to see himself as—to insist upon—"Barack Obama."

"It makes sense," his sister Maya said. "He was growing up. 'Barry' is a kid's name. In Indonesia he was 'Beri' and our Kansan grandparents struggled a little with 'Barack,' because of the rolling of the r's back then. His father, Barack, Sr., made some of the same adjustments. He called himself *Bar*-ack."

In his sophomore year, Obama shared an apartment in Pasadena with Hasan Chandoo. Handsome, smart, charming, rich, profane, and a political radical, Chandoo came from a Shia Muslim family that had lived all over the world and made a fortune in shipping. Chandoo had spent most of his life in Karachi; he went to an American-run high school there where he seemed to major in poker and golf. At Occidental, he became a somewhat more serious student, but he was well known for having leftist politics and late-night parties. He was more committed to the parties than to the politics. He was a flamboyant figure, who drove a flashy Fiat around campus.

Their apartment was plain and lightly tended. "It was a two-bedroom apartment that was distinctly underdecorated," Margot Mifflin recalled. "It looked like they never settled in. They were always throwing parties and Hasan would cook really hot food and tell us to cool it down with yogurt. And then there was a lot of dancing: the Talking Heads album 'Remain in Light' was out and Bob Marley was huge—and Barry had a taste for that not-so-great soft Grover Washington stuff."

Obama's South Asian friends "were very progressive, intelligent, worldly," Eric Moore said. "Hasan Chandoo was like Omar Sharif, the smoothest international playboy. They were Pakistanis, but bankers, business people, secular guys, American citizens. They were very cool and sophisticated."

Chandoo and Hamid, among others, helped "ignite" Obama politically. "In college, Hasan was a socialist, a Marxist, which is funny since he is from a wealthy family," Mifflin said. "But he was socialist in the way we were back then—an idealist who believed in economic equality, that's all. I am not sure how he defined it then, but he really studied it. Barack learned a lot from him, especially the notions of fairness and equality that you see in him today." Chandoo, for his part, readily admits to his youthful radicalism, but says that Obama was never the least bit doctrinaire: "The only thing doctrinaire about him was his austerity!"

To slap an ideological tag on Chandoo and Hamid, let alone Obama, is not only unfair; it also credits them with thinking far more programmatically than they did. "I would say we were *idealistic* and well-read in terms of understanding all the ideologies," Hamid said. "I remember going home to Pakistan and sitting across from my mother in the summer waxing eloquent about the benefits of socialism. She said, 'Wahid, this is all well and good, but I think you will grow up.' I guess that's what happened. We weren't Marxists. We were *idealistic* and believed in the betterment of the lot of the masses and not just the few. If you describe that as socialist, then maybe we did have some socialist thoughts at the time. Barack was pretty similar. I don't remember there being a dissonance between us. There was consistency in our thinking. We were all trying to improve."

"Barry and Hasan spent a lot of their time soap-boxing about politics," Mifflin said. "One of our friends remembers a group study session at which Obama got up to orate about one political subject or another and at the end someone said, 'You should be the first black President.' But, on the other hand, no one seriously thought of him as 'the one'—the one super-talented person who would become something huge. He was just one of our crowd."

For many years, Obama stayed in touch with his South Asian friends, particularly Hamid, who was for a long time an executive at PepsiCo, and Chandoo, who became a consultant and investor. During the campaign and even afterward, Hamid and Chandoo were wary of talking to the press, lest they say something that could be used against themselves or, worse, against Obama. They were well aware of the fact that some of Obama's most virulent opponents during the 2008 campaign were prepared to manipulate the Obama-as-Muslim myth at a moment's notice. "It got to the point where reporters were banging on our apartment door in the middle of the night," Hamid said.

The political conversation at Occidental when Obama arrived centered on the Soviet invasion of Afghanistan and Jimmy Carter's reaction to it. There were also candlelight walks against the proliferation of nuclear arms, a rally against Carter's reinstitution of registration for the draft, and, in 1980, denunciations of the election of Ronald Reagan. *The Occidental* published an endorsement of Jimmy Carter that was less notable for its rejection of Reagan than for its nose-holding support of the doomed incumbent. The headline was "Lukewarm."

Race, as both an on-campus political issue and a focus of national and international politics, was also at the center of discussion. Before Obama matriculated at Occidental, there had been an incident in which a popular professor of art history, an African-American named Mary Jane Hewitt, was denied a promotion. Two reporters from *The Occidental* heard that there were possible irregularities in the promotion process and, with the help of a cooperative campus security guard, broke into the administration building and got access to the tenure file. The editors of *The Occidental* did not publish the file but used it to guide their reporting. "We were very paranoid," one editor said. "We sat out on the fifty-yard line of the football field discussing what to do. Smoking pot all the time. It was L.A." Eventually, news of the break-in leaked and the two reporters were brought to an honor court proceeding; two of the more left-wing professors on campus, Norman Cohen and David Axeen, acted as faculty lawyers for the student-reporters. The students were not punished.

As with most college students, Obama had little notion of how to act on his political impulses. "I want to get into public service," Obama told Thummalapally. "I want to write and help people who are disadvantaged." What exactly he might do remained vague. In the eyes of some of his freshman-year friends, Obama became less happy-go-lucky as a sophomore. "I did see a change in him," said Kent Goss, a classmate who played a lot of basketball with Obama. "He was much more serious, more focused, more cerebral. . . . I saw him hanging out with a different crowd, which was a more serious crowd, a more intellectual crowd."

Obama took creative-writing courses, along with his more academic courses, and sometimes thought he might pursue a career as a writer. He published poems in *Feast*, the campus literary magazine, and also in a xeroxed magazine put out by one of his friends, Mark Dery, called *Plastic Laughter.* Dery was known as the "punk poet" on campus. The better, and longer, of Obama's two poems in *Feast* exhibited the influence of the free-verse poets of the time; "Pop" clearly reflects Obama's relationship with his grandfather Stanley Dunham. Obama showed it to his friends without telling them that it was about the man who had played such a big part in rearing him in Honolulu and his struggle, at once, to love and escape him as he made his way as an adult.

> Sitting in his seat, a seat broad and broken
> In, sprinkled with ashes,
> Pop switches channels, takes another
> Shot of Seagrams, neat, and asks
> What to do with me, a green young man
> Who fails to consider the
> Flim and flam of the world, since
> Things have been easy for me;
> I stare hard at his face, a stare
> That deflects off his brow;
> I'm sure he's unaware of his
> Dark, watery eyes, that
> Glance in different directions,
> And his slow, unwelcome twitches,
> Fail to pass. . . .

Not everyone in the Occidental literary crowd liked Obama. One classmate described him as "too *GQ*" and, according to Mifflin, "the artsier crowd said he was too sophisticated, too smooth somehow."

Obama was hardly a joyless *artiste*. By all accounts he was interested in women and dated fairly frequently, but he had no steady girlfriend in his two years at Occidental. "Some of us were all hooked up, but not Barry," Margot Mifflin said. "I never saw him date one person there for an extended time. . . . It wasn't as if Barry was just hanging out with the pretty ladies on campus. He was about ideas and engagement. He wanted to be with people who were thinking about things."

"Everybody liked him," Lisa Jack, a friend who took a series of photographs of Obama in 1980, said. "He was a hot, nice, everything-going-for-him dude. If he saw you sitting alone in The Cooler, he would come sit down with you. I don't know about deep relationships, but he had no problems getting women attracted to him. He wasn't lecherous or disrespectful. He managed to do it in a way that was cool. You couldn't help but like him."

Lawrence Goldyn, one of Obama's political-science professors at Occidental, was one of the very few openly gay teachers on campus. A Stanford-trained political scientist, Goldyn came to Occidental in the late-seventies. Obama took Goldyn's class on European politics. Goldyn was miserable at Occidental, where he felt the disdain of the administration. "I was sort of radioactive," he said. "I eventually had to go to medical school to make a living. It was a tough time. They told me I was too stuck on sexual politics . . . They looked at me and all they could see was homosexual, homosexual, homosexual." Goldyn became the adviser to the gay student union. "I got the left-outs, the black women, the gays gravitating to me," he said. "I don't think kids of color and gay people felt very welcome there. They felt like outsiders." Goldyn was grateful for students like Obama, who held him in high regard and sought him out after class. "There were a few like that—not a lot, a handful," he recalled. "There were some older political kids who gravitated to me because they liked my point of view. That a freshman or sophomore would do that showed intellectual courage."

During the Presidential campaign, Obama told a gay magazine, the *Advocate*, that Goldyn "was a wonderful guy. He was the first openly gay professor that I had ever come into contact with, or openly gay person of authority that I had come in contact with. He wasn't proselytizing all the time, but just his comfort in his own skin and the friendship we developed helped to educate me on a number of these issues."

There were many professors on campus who had been active in the sixties and who regaled their students with tales of civil-rights and antiwar demonstrations. That generation of professors was gradually replacing the men and women of the Second World War generation. "The transformation was happening right when Obama was here," Roger Boesche, who had been politically active as an undergraduate at Stanford in the sixties, said. Hearing about the exploits of those young professors was both fascinating and deflating. Among Obama's friends—among so many young people going to college in the seventies and eighties—there was a feeling of belatedness, a sense that political activism had lost most of its energy. They had come along too late for the March on Washington, Black Power, the Stonewall riots, the antiwar and women's-liberation demonstrations. Rightly or not, many of them felt they had the desire but not a cause.

Among campus political groups, the Democratic Socialist Alliance was one of the few with any energy and capacity for organization. A student named Gary Chapman, who now teaches technology policy at the University of Texas, formed the Alliance not long before Obama came to Occidental, and its supporters strung up a huge banner over the central quad bearing a portrait of Karl Marx. In 1978–79, the year before Obama matriculated, some students sympathetic to the Alliance had tried to push a political agenda—against apartheid; for increased diversity on campus—by running a slate of left-leaning candidates for student government. Caroline Boss, a friend of Obama's and one of the main leftist political leaders at Occidental, said that the college soon became the scene of intense discussion about American foreign policy, women's studies, gay rights, Latino studies, urban studies—and, especially, the apartheid regime in South Africa.

"A lot of work had been going on for the previous three years getting the campus more aware of practices at the college, looking at what was happening in South Africa," Caroline Boss said. "Already, before Barry, we'd had these rather sad, but nonetheless real, marches to Bank of America, to withdraw my twenty dollars."

Boss and many others began a campaign to get the board of trustees at Occidental to sell off stock invested in multinational corporations doing business in apartheid South Africa. The divestment movement had come to some notice in 1962, when the United Nations General Assembly passed a non-binding resolution calling for economic sanctions against South Africa. In 1977, a Baptist preacher and civil-rights activist, the Reverend Leon Sullivan, thrust the issue into the press. Sullivan, a board member of General Motors, the biggest American employer of blacks in South Africa, led a campaign of corporate responsibility directed against G.M. and other U.S.-based companies with an interest in South Africa. His draft of a code of corporate conduct, the Sullivan Principles, mandated that these multinationals provide equal rights for their black workers. On campuses across the country, students asked boards of trustees to divest from businesses that continued to work with the apartheid regime, and at some schools—Hampshire College, Michigan State, Ohio University, Columbia University, and the University of Wisconsin—the protests made a significant impact. There were pickets, sit-ins, teach-ins, the building of shantytowns, and other gestures modestly reminiscent of the civil-rights and antiwar movements. Nelson Mandela later said that the divestment movement helped hasten the collapse of the apartheid regime, by isolating it and causing billions of dollars in capital flight. The critics of divestment either accused its advocates of hypocrisy—why did they not ask the same of investors in Communist countries?—or, like Ronald Reagan and Margaret Thatcher, argued for a policy of "constructive engagement."

At Occidental, a small core of students put together a report for the trustees saying that divestment was the right thing to do, and that it would not demonstrably hurt the school's endowment. They were backed by the Democratic Socialist Alliance; an African-American student group called Ujima; Hispanic and gay groups; and a coordinating alliance called the Third World Coalition. But there was also a great deal of apathy on campus, especially among the pre-professional and fraternity crowds.

Obama went to meetings of these various groups, but not very often. "Obama was a person who was mainly an observer," Boss said. "He came into it gradually, but increasingly, in the political sense. He had strong intellectual curiosity. He was frustrated at the idea of living life passively. During his sophomore year he definitely had a distinctive kind of self-awareness that he grew into, a sense of purpose. That was really striking about him—for instance, when he announced himself as 'Barack' and not 'Barry' anymore. It came to him. And we talked about it, and he talked with others, too. He just announced it and said, 'Listen, I am using my full given name.' He associated it with connecting to his father. He was proud of his father and his heritage, even though he hadn't researched it yet. But he had this sense of his father as a man of destiny, as someone who could start as a goat herder and become a government figure. It was a legacy and something to take forward.

"He stepped from an international world and a Hawaiian world replete with ethnicities, very much the cosmopolitan," Boss continued, "and then he comes here and steps onto the continent, and gets with a crowd of African-Americans who have a keener sense of what that means and a deeper understanding of a slave history and the American experience. And so he was interested in what that meant for him personally. This discovery process, it's a bildungsroman, a person who is the quintessential cosmopolitan in this process of self-discovery, grappling with this question of 'Who am I?' "

Chandoo, Obama, Caroline Boss, and several other students, some from the Democratic Socialist Alliance, some from various ethnic associations on campus, planned a divestment rally for February 18, 1981. This was Obama's first foray as a public political actor.

It was, as Margot Mifflin recalled, a "sun-bleached winter day," with about three hundred students—activists, black and international students, blond surfers—milling outside Coons Hall, the main administration building, which was nicknamed "the Chrysler showroom" for its charmless, glass-paneled architecture. The board of trustees was scheduled to meet inside. The organizers of the rally came up with a list of speakers that included an American history professor, Norman Cohen; a visitor from South Africa named Tim Ngubeni; and a range of students: Caroline Boss, Earl Chew, Chandoo, and Obama. Students held signs reading "Apartheid Kills" and "No Profit from Apartheid."

Obama was to open the rally. In his memoir, he writes that, as he prepared his brief speech, he remembered his father's visit to his fifth-grade classroom and how he had won over everyone with his words. "If I could just find the right words," he thought. If he could do that, he could have an impact. He took the microphone in a "trancelike" state. The sun was shining in his eyes, but he could see in the distance, over the heads of the demonstrators, someone playing Frisbee in the distance.

"There's a struggle going on," Obama began. He could sense that only a few people had heard him. He raised his voice. "I say, there's a struggle going on! It's happening an ocean away. But it's a struggle that touches each and every one of us. Whether we know it or not. Whether we want it or not. A struggle that demands we choose sides. Not between black and white. Not between rich and poor. No—it's a harder choice than that. It's a choice between dignity and servitude. Between fairness and injustice. Between commitment and indifference. A choice between right and wrong . . ."

Obama was neither the best nor the most dramatic speaker at the rally. The school paper made no mention of him. What most people remember about his presentation is that, before he could get very far, two white students, acting the role of South African police goons, dragged him from the podium in a gesture of prearranged guerrilla theater. His moment was over.

The impact of the other speakers was greater. Ngubeni, who, as a student in South Africa, had been a member of the grassroots Black Consciousness Movement and an associate of Steve Biko, the martyred anti-apartheid leader, declared that the movement had to begin in the United States because "all the bosses are over here."

By the time the demonstration was over, Obama's euphoria had evaporated. He saw some white trustees watching them from inside the building, laughing. He worried that the protest and his own speech had been a childish farce. "After the rally, a pair of folk singers harmonized as we wandered off to class, feeling groovy," Mifflin wrote years later.

But Obama had made a slight impression, at least on some. "He spoke much the same way he does now—reasoned, with passion, but not some hothead spouting off," Rebecca Rivera, a fellow protester, said. "Then, before he could finish, the stupid skit they had planned took him offstage.

He was just getting going. I just remember thinking, Who is this guy? And why haven't we heard from him before? As people were dispersing, I remember saying to Barry, 'That was a great speech, I wish you would get more involved.' And, of course, that was the spring and soon he was gone. He was off to bigger and better things."

Obama's involvement in student politics had been earnest, but infrequent, cool, and removed. ("I was on the outside again, watching, judging, skeptical.") Rivera, and many others, remembered Obama as only fitfully engaged. "The impression he gave me was 'I get involved when it is important enough,' " she said. "The stuff we minority students were arguing about seemed important, but it was pretty small potatoes."

The faculty at Occidental had been opposed to apartheid, voting unanimously to divest, but the trustees stubbornly resisted; as late as 1990, with the white South African government in retreat, the trustees fended off a motion to divest. "And then it was clear," Boesche said, "that Nelson Mandela would have to take care of all this for us."

Despite all his political frustration, Obama enjoyed Occidental, but he wanted a bigger, more urban environment. He wanted to get away from the hothouse feeling of a small college. "I was concerned with urban issues," he said years later, "and I wanted to be around more black folks in big cities." He wanted to go East, preferably to New York. He looked into the possibility of transferring to Columbia University.

"We felt like we were in a groove and we wanted life to be more difficult," Phil Boerner, who also applied to Columbia that spring, said. "It was a country-club atmosphere. We wanted to make things harder for ourselves. Obama used to tell his friends that he wanted to go somewhere where the weather was cold and miserable so that he would be forced to spend his days indoors, reading."

Caroline Boss recalls Obama at college with admiring affection. "It's a story of self-discovery, isn't it?" she said. "He wants to get his feet wet, learn about the U.S. and being black as part of an American history and condition, and he gets that in California. And then California feels too pat, he is too dissipated, he is getting away with too much, hanging out too much, so he says to himself, Go put yourself in a very cold place. He picks Harlem."

Except for those he knew best, Obama seemed to slip out of sight with barely a word. Ken Sulzer, one of Obama's earliest friends on campus, recalled, "I remember in senior year, someone said, 'Hey, where's Obama?' We didn't realize he'd gone. But I thought, Good for him. A decade later, when I read about him becoming the first African-American president of the *Harvard Law Review,* I said to myself, What the hell? Barry Obama. He's Barack now? Who knew?"

In the summer of 1981, before arriving in New York, Obama traveled to Asia for three weeks, first to Pakistan to visit Chandoo and Hamid, and then to Indonesia to see his mother and Maya. "They took a trip in Pakistan together that Fox News tried to twist into something awful," Margot Mifflin said. In fact, the trip reacquainted Obama with some of the realities of the developing world. "When Obama came back," Mifflin said, "he said he'd been shocked by many things, but especially the poverty. When they rode through the countryside, he was amazed at how the peasants bowed to the landowners in respect as they passed. It blew his mind."

"It's true," Hamid said. "The trip gave him a grounding of sorts. To be exposed to a place like Pakistan as an adult, he saw how differently people live. He stayed with me and Hasan in Karachi, but he also wanted to get out in the countryside, and we went to rural Sindh, to the lands of a feudal landlord who was in school with me in high school and before. We went to this person's lands, where the feudal system is still strong. Barack could see how the owner lives and how the serfs and workers are so subservient. . . . Barack also met an individual there of African descent. Africans were brought to Pakistan years ago by the Arabs—part of the slave trade, though in another direction. And to see people like that was very striking for Barack. He sat across from him and, even though they didn't share a common language, they tried to communicate. It was a moment that stayed in his mind."

Obama spent much of his time in Pakistan with his friends' families— Chandoo's family is fairly wealthy, Hamid is upper-middle-class by Pakistani standards—but he also played basketball with kids in the street and explored the neighborhoods of Karachi during Ramadan. By talking with his friends, he got a deeper sense of the political and religious divisions of an infinitely complex political culture. "I am from the Sunni sect and Hasan from the Shia, so he learned a lot about the dialogue between the two," Hamid said.

As a transfer student, Obama wasn't able to get Columbia housing, and so for the next couple of years he lived in a series of cheap off-campus apartments. The first year he had made arrangements to share a third-floor walkup with his Occidental friend Phil Boerner, at 142 West 109th Street, off Amsterdam Avenue. They split the monthly rent of three hundred and sixty dollars. The apartment's charms included spotty heat, irregular hot water, and a railroad-flat layout. They adjusted, using the showers at the Columbia gym and camping out for long hours at Butler Library.

Obama's academic emphasis was on political science—particularly foreign policy, social issues, political theory, and American history—but he also took a course in modern fiction with Edward Said. Best known for his advocacy of the Palestinian cause and for his academic excoriation of the Eurocentric "Orientalism" practiced by Western authors and scholars, Said had done important work in literary criticism and theory. And yet Said's theoretical approach in the course left Obama cold. "My whole thing, and Barack had a similar view, was that we would rather read Shakespeare's plays than the criticism," Boerner said. "Said was more interested in the literary theory, which didn't appeal to Barack or me." Obama referred to Said as a "flake."

In his spare time, Obama wandered around the city, taking in Sunday services at the Abyssinian Baptist Church, a socialist conference at Cooper Union, African cultural fairs in Brooklyn and Harlem, jazz at the West End. He took long walks and runs in Riverside Park and Central Park. He shopped at the Strand downtown and Papyrus and the other bookstores around the Columbia campus. When Hasan Chandoo visited, they went to hear Jesse Jackson speak in Harlem. There was far less partying now. This was the beginning of what Obama has wryly referred to as his "ascetic period."

"When I transferred, I decided to buckle down and get serious," Obama told the Columbia alumni magazine two decades later. "I spent a lot of time in the library. I didn't socialize that much. I was like a monk." Obama often fasted on Sundays, vowed to give up drugs and drinking (he was less successful with cigarettes), and started keeping a journal, including, by his own admission, "daily reflections and very bad poetry." He wrote in the journal about his childhood and adolescence, and these entries helped feed the memoir that he wrote years later. He took a vow of self-improvement. He was a member of the generation primed to join and enjoy the first big Wall Street boom of the early eighties, but he was determined to resist the era's financial temptations. A certain self-righteousness and self-denial crept into his being: "Fearful of falling into old habits, I took on the temperament if not the convictions of a street-corner preacher, prepared to see temptation everywhere, ready to overrun a fragile will."

"You know, I'm amused now when I read quotes from high-school teachers and grammar school teachers, who say, 'You know, he always was a great leader,' " Obama told me. "That kind of hindsight is pretty shaky. And I think it's just as shaky for me to engage in that kind of speculation as it is for anybody. I will tell you that I think I had a hunger to shape the world in some way, to make the world a better place, that was triggered around the time that I transferred from Occidental to Columbia. So there's a phase, which I wrote about in my first book, where, for whatever reason, a whole bunch of stuff that had been inside me—questions of identity, questions of purpose, questions of, not just race, but also the international nature of my upbringing—all those things started converging in some way. And so there's this period of time when I move to New York and go to Columbia, where I pull in and wrestle with that stuff, and do a lot of writing and a lot of reading and a lot of thinking and a lot of walking through Central Park. And somehow I emerge on the other side of that ready and eager to take a chance in what is a pretty unlikely venture: moving to Chicago and becoming an organizer. So I would say that's a moment in which I gain a seriousness of purpose that I had lacked before. Now, whether it was just a matter of, you know, me hitting a certain age where people start getting a little more serious—whether it was a combination of factors—my father dying, me realizing I had never known him, me moving from Hawaii to a place like New York that stimulates a lot of new ideas—you know, it's hard to say what exactly prompted that."

Obama and Boerner lived cheaply. They ate bagel lunches in the neighborhood around Broadway. At night, they cooked beans and rice or ate the cheapest dishes at Empire Szechuan on Ninety-seventh and Broadway. Obama wore military-surplus khakis or jeans and a leather jacket.

One of Obama's first and closest friends in those early months in New York was Sohale Siddiqi. Born and brought up in Pakistan, Siddiqi had overstayed his tourist visa and was living, illegally, on the Upper East Side, working as a waiter and as a salesman in a clothing store; he was drinking, taking drugs, and getting by. Obama and Boerner had grown disgusted with their apartment and had decided to look for other accommodations. Obama, after living alone in a studio apartment for his second semester, agreed to room the following year with Siddiqi, in a sixth-floor walkup at 339 East Ninety-fourth Street.

"We didn't have a chance in hell of getting this apartment unless we fabricated the lease application," Siddiqi said. Siddiqi fibbed about his job, saying that he had a high-paying employment at a catering company; Obama declined to lie, but they managed to get the apartment anyway. Small wonder. The place was a dump in a drug-ridden neighborhood.

The roommates were friendly but lived entirely different lives. Siddiqi was a libertine, but Obama's days of dissolution, mild as they had been, were over. "I think self-deprivation was his shtick—denying himself pleasure, good food, and all of that," Siddiqi said. "At that age, I thought he was a saint and a square, and he took himself too seriously. I would ask him why he was so serious. He was genuinely concerned with the plight of the poor. He'd give me lectures, which I found very boring. He must have found me very irritating. . . . We were both very lost. We were both alienated, although he might not put it that way."

Despite his exasperation with Obama, Siddiqi learned to admire his forgiving temperament. Obama, he noticed, never said anything when Siddiqi's mother, who had never spent time around a black man, was rude to him. Long after Obama moved out, because of Siddiqi's constant partying, Obama proved a constant friend when Siddiqi developed a serious cocaine problem. Many years later, as a way of warding off the press, Siddiqi recorded a telling message for his answering machine: "My name is Hal Siddiqi and I approve of this message. Vote for peace, vote for hope, vote for change, and vote for Obama."

On the night of November 24, 1982, during Obama's first semester of his senior year at Columbia, his father got behind the wheel of his car after a night of drinking at an old colonial bar in Nairobi, ran off the road, and crashed into the stump of a gum tree. He died instantly.

Obama, Sr., had spent the day working on a new infrastructure plan for the Kenyan capital. Although he'd become, by all accounts, a bitter man, one in perpetual danger of losing any opportunity to work, he had had a decent day. He had heard rumors that he might be promoted to a relatively good government job, maybe in the Ministry of Finance, and he bought rounds of drinks for his friends that night. A man of promise, Obama had failed not only his ambitions, but also the dozens of family members who depended on him for financial help and prestige. "He couldn't cope," said Obama's sister Auma. "He was one person trying to look after hundreds."

An aunt called Barack, Jr., on a scratchy line from Nairobi to tell him the news. Hundreds of people in Kenya gathered to mourn Barack, Sr., but the government-controlled press paid him no great tribute. "At the time of his death," Obama wrote, "my father remained a myth to me, both more and less than a man."

At Columbia, Obama kept showing up at talks and lectures, including one by the former SNCC leader and Black Power proponent Kwame Ture—Stokely Carmichael—but he was not walking any picket lines or immersing himself in any movements. "I don't remember him going to rallies or signing petitions," Phil Boerner said.

At Columbia, Obama was a serious, if unspectacular, student. He majored in political science with a concentration in international relations and became interested in the nuclear standoff between the United States and the Soviet Union. In his senior year, in Michael Baron's course in American foreign policy and international politics, he wrote a seminar paper on prospects for bilateral disarmament. The class analyzed decision-making and the perils of "groupthink," the ways that disastrous policies, like the escalation of the Vietnam War, develop.

In March, 1983, Obama wrote an article for *Sundial*, a student weekly, titled "Breaking the War Mentality." Nominally a report on two campus groups—Arms Race Alternatives and Students Against Militarism—the article makes plain Obama's revulsion at what he saw as Cold War militarism and his positive feelings about the nuclear-freeze movement, which was very much in the air in the early years of the Reagan Administration, before the emergence in Moscow of Mikhail Gorbachev. He wrote:

> Generally, the narrow focus of the Freeze movement as well as academic discussions of first versus second strike capabilities, suit the military-industrial interests, as they continue adding to their billion dollar erector sets. When Peter Tosh sings that "everybody's asking for peace, but nobody's asking for justice," one is forced to wonder whether disarmament or arms control issues, severed from economic and political issues, might be another instance of focusing on the symptoms of a problem instead of the disease itself.
>
> Indeed, the most pervasive malady of the collegiate system specifically, and the American experience generally, is that elaborate patterns of knowledge and theory have been disembodied from individual choices and government policy. What the members of ARA and SAM try to do is infuse what they have learned about the current situation, bring the words of that formidable roster on the face of Butler Library, names like Thoreau, Jefferson, and Whitman, to bear on the twisted logic of which we are today a part.

Both in the seminar and in his muddled article for *Sundial*, Obama expressed sympathy for the urge to reduce, even eliminate, nuclear arsenals. In a letter to Boerner, he joked that he wrote the piece for *Sundial* "purely for calculated reasons of beefing up" his résumé. "No keeping your hands clean, eh?" At around the same time, he started sending out letters to various social organizations, looking for work.

Two months before graduation, Obama told Boerner he was bored. "School is just making the same motions, long stretches of numbness punctuated with the occasional insight," he wrote in a letter to Boerner. "Nothing significant, Philip. Life rolls on, and I feel a growing competence and maturity. Take care of yourself and Karen, and write a decent note, you madman, with a pen so the words aren't smudged by the postman's fingers. Will get back to you when I know my location for next year. OBAMA."

With everyone around him applying to law school, graduate school, and investment-bank training programs, Obama got it into his head to become a community organizer. He was a young man who lacked membership in a community and a purpose, and to work as an organizer would move him toward community, maybe even toward "the beloved community" that King had spoken of a generation before. In his early twenties, Obama admits, he was "operating mainly on impulse," full of a yearning both to surpass his parents' frustrations and to connect to a romantic past. He recalls staying up late at night thinking about the civil-rights movement and its heroes and martyrs: students at lunch counters defiantly placing their orders, SNCC workers registering voters in Mississippi, preachers and churchwomen in jail singing freedom songs. Obama wanted to be part of the legacy of the movement. But, since the movement was long gone, he applied for membership in that which persisted.

"That was my idea of organizing," he writes. "It was a promise of redemption." Obama, his friend Wahid Hamid said, "had already developed a sense that he wanted to get involved in community work and not go down the regular path. He was trying to figure out how to have the biggest impact and not succumb to a traditional path like being a research associate at an investment bank or a corporate lawyer."

In the summer of 1983, after graduation, Obama visited his family in Indonesia. He wrote a postcard to Boerner, saying, "I'm sitting on the porch in my sarong, sipping strong coffee and drawing on a clove cigarette, watching the heavy dusk close over the paddy terraces of Java. Very kick back, so far away from the madness. I'm halfway through vacation, but still feel the tug of that tense existence, though. Right now, my plans are uncertain; most probably I will go back after a month or two in Hawaii."

When Obama got back to New York, he found that the many letters he had written to organizing groups and other progressive outfits had gone unanswered. Frustrated and broke, he interviewed for a job, in late summer of 1983, with Business International Corporation, a publishing and consulting group that collected data on international business and finance and issued various newsletters and reports for its corporate clients and organized government roundtables on trade.

"I remember distinctly meeting him," Cathy Lazere, a supervisor at Business International, said. "He was lanky, comfortable with himself, smart. He was so young that his résumé still had his high-school stuff on it. He had taken some international economics in college. And, as you might expect, he talked about his name, a little about his mother in Indonesia, the Kenyan father. I hired him, and let's just say the salary was nowhere near enough to pay off his college debts." Founded by Eldridge Haynes, of McGraw-Hill, in 1953, Business International, or B.I., as it is known, was among the first research firms designed to provide information services for multinational firms.

Obama worked in the financial-services division, interviewing business experts, researching trends in foreign exchange, following market developments. He also edited a reference guide on overseas markets, called Financing Foreign Operations, and wrote for a newsletter called Business International Money Report. He wrote about currency swaps and leverage leases. (The currency swaps and derivatives that Obama covered for Business International Money Report were components of the financial engineering that led to the crash of 2008.) Obama also helped write financial reports on Mexico and Brazil.

In his memoir, Obama paints a picture of the office that is rather more corporate and formal than it was. He had no secretary, and he wore jeans more often than a suit. "We had Wang word processors that the young people shared," Lazere said, "and I remember Barack working hard and puffing away on Marlboros. You could still smoke in those days. He was very even-tempered, even-keeled. He definitely had a certain emotional intelligence, the ability to figure out what people wanted."

Obama was not uninterested in economics—he had taken a senior seminar at Columbia on foreign aid and capital flows between the developed and developing worlds—but he found himself doing research on companies, investments, and levels of risk, and, at times, found it stultifying, even morally discomfiting. He had a young idealist's disdain for even the most tentative step into the world of commerce: "Sometimes, coming out of an interview with Japanese financiers or German bond traders, I would catch my reflection in the elevator doors—see myself in a suit and tie, a briefcase in my hand—and for a split second I would imagine myself as a captain of industry, barking out orders, closing the deal, before I remembered who it was that I had told myself I wanted to be and felt pangs of guilt for my lack of resolve." He made his boredom plain to his mother in Indonesia. In a letter to Alice Dewey, Ann Dunham reported on her son:

> Barry is working in New York this year, saving his pennies so he can travel next year. My understanding from a rather mumbled telephone conversation is that he works for a consulting organization that writes reports on request about social, political, and economic conditions in Third World countries. He calls it "working for the enemy" because some of the reports are written for commercial firms that want to invest in those countries. He seems to be learning a lot about the realities of international finance and politics, however, and I think that information will stand him in good stead in the future.

Once in a while, Obama brought his ideals into the office. William Millar, a colleague on the money report, recalled that Obama told him they should boycott any firms doing business in South Africa. "I said he needed to realize that it's the non–South African companies who were hiring blacks and giving them positions of authority with decent pay," Millar recalled. "That's what accelerates change—not isolation."

Obama's supervisors liked him. They found him intelligent but removed, possessing a "certain hauteur, a cultivated air of mystery." They called him, affectionately, "Mr. Cool." One afternoon, Obama was having lunch at a Korean restaurant with a colleague when the subject of exercise came up. Obama mentioned that he worked out in Riverside Park after work and on weekends.

"I jog there, too," the colleague said.

"I don't jog," Obama replied. "I run."

People in the office had the distinct impression that Obama was a friendly guy looking to mark time, make some money, and move on. "When I gave him something to do, he would smile and say 'Gotcha,' " Lazere said. "The truth is, I thought he would end up as a novelist or something, taking the world in. He was a real observer, a little off to the side, watching, not totally engaged." Obama kept his work life and his social life separate, preferring to see his Columbia friends rather than socialize with his colleagues. "He always seemed a little aloof," said Lou Celi, who managed the global-finance division. "At the time, I just figured he was doing his own thing and wasn't as sociable as some of the others in the office. Some people, you know all about their lives outside work. Not Barack."

"There were several African-American women who worked in the library as our internal clipping service," said Cathy Lazere. They cut out relevant articles on business, finance, and trade, and often doubled as receptionists. "They would have been about ten years older than Barack—around my age or older," she recalled. "He created quite a frisson when he arrived on the scene, but to my knowledge he had very little interaction with them. Most people assumed from his bearing that he was a wealthy preppy kid. Some of the preppies I had met at Yale were like the Lost Boys of Peter Pan. I thought Barack might have been like that. Beneath his cool-cat façade, I sensed a little loneliness, since he was never fully engaged in what was going on around him."

Obama sometimes took part in an evening discussion group with Phil Boerner and his wife-to-be, Karen; Paul Herrmannsfeldt, who went on to work at McGraw-Hill; George Nashak, who works with the homeless; and Bruce Basara, who pursued a doctorate in philosophy. They read Nietzsche, Sartre, Rilke's *The Notebooks of Malte Laurids Brigge*, Samuel Beckett's *Murphy*. Boerner admitted that the group often either failed to do the reading or relied on what they remembered from their undergraduate courses, but it was a way to keep thinking and talking "about serious stuff after graduation."

Obama left B.I. after little more than a year, telling his colleagues that he was going to become a community organizer. A big mistake, Celi told him in his exit interview. "Now he seems so in charge, but back then Barack seemed like a lot of kids who graduate from college and don't know what they want to do with their lives," Celi said. "I thought he had the writing talent so that he could move up in publishing. Turned out he had other fish to fry."

"Despite all the self-assurance, Barack was trying to think through his life," Lazere said. "He was the only black professional in the office then, and I think New York was making him think about his identity and what to do with himself."

. . .

In early 1985, Obama took a job at the New York Public Interest Research Group, a nonprofit organization, begun in the seventies, with help from Ralph Nader, that promotes consumer, environmental, and government reform. He spent the next four months working mainly out of a trailer office at 140th Street and Convent Avenue, helping to mobilize students at the City College of New York. He got students to write letters and speak up on a variety of issues: a Straphangers Campaign to rebuild public transportation in the city; an effort to fend off construction of a municipal trash incinerator in Brooklyn; a voter-registration drive; and a campaign to increase recycling. Obama's first taste of organizing didn't last long and did little to shake the foundations of the city, but he did impress his supervisor, Eileen Hershenov, with his ambitions for the future.

"Barack and I had some really engaged conversations about models of organizing," she said. They talked about their admiration for Bob Moses's voter-registration drives with SNCC, the radically different organizing means of Saul Alinksy in Chicago and the Students for a Democratic Society during the Vietnam War. "And we talked about models of charismatic leadership, the pros and cons of that, what it can achieve, and the dangers of not leaving behind a real organization," Hershenov said. "Remember, this was the Reagan era. People were not exactly taking to the streets for a social movement. We weren't red-diaper babies, either. But we were thinking about how you engage the world: what works coming out of the sixties, what structures and models worked and what didn't."

Obama was working at City College with students who tended to be older, lower-income, some of them with families of their own already. "They were pressed for time," Hershenov said. "So how do you get them to organize, especially when what you were pushing was not something tied to identity politics or some sort of 'cool' Marxist, Gramsci, theory-oriented thing? NYPIRG was a Naderite group, and seen as kind of wishy-washy and bourgeois. But Barack was getting students involved in bread-and-butter community issues and he was very good at it. And, while Barack himself was not a radical, he had read, he could speak that language if need be. He had the gift of being able to talk with everyone: students on the left, in the center, faculty, everyone."

Obama drove to Washington with some student leaders to get members of the New York congressional delegation to oppose cuts in public funding for student aid. After delivering stacks of petitions to members with offices in the Rayburn Building, he and a few friends walked around the city and ended up on Pennsylvania Avenue, peering through the iron gates at the White House. Obama had never seen the building before. Inside, the high command of the Reagan Administration—an Administration that Obama and his friends saw as the ideological enemy—was at work. Obama was struck, above all, by the proximity of the White House to the street. "It embodied the notion that our leaders were not so different from us," he wrote later. "They remained subject to laws and our collective consent."

At the end of the academic year, Obama knew that he had had enough of New York. Hershenov tried to get him to stay another year. It was rare to get such a thoughtful organizer. "I asked him if it would help if I got on my knees and begged—and so I did," she said. "But it didn't help. It was time for him to go."

Part Two

In my body were many bloods, some dark blood, all blended in the fire of six or more generations. I was, then, either a new type of man or the very oldest. In any case I was inescapably myself.

—Jean Toomer, *Cane*

Chapter Four

Black Metropolis

In 1968, Saul Alinsky, the inventor of community organizing and one of the most original radical democrats America has ever produced, met an earnest young woman from Wellesley College named Hillary Rodham. Like many college students of the time, Rodham was in the midst of a political transformation—in her case, from Goldwater Republican to Rockefeller Republican and then to Eugene McCarthy supporter all in the space of a few years. It was the summer before her senior year and she was spending it as a kind of political tourist. In June and July, she worked in the Washington office of Melvin Laird, a Republican congressman from Wisconsin who became Richard Nixon's Secretary of Defense. Then, as a pro-Rockefeller volunteer, she went to the Republican National Convention in Miami, where she stayed at the Fontainebleau Hotel, shook hands with Frank Sinatra, and saw Nixon win the nomination. Finally, she spent a few weeks with her parents, in the Chicago suburb of Park Ridge; at night, with her friend Betsy Ebeling, she went downtown to the edges of Grant Park and, from a distance, witnessed Mayor Richard J. Daley's police beating up antiwar demonstrators. In Chicago, Rodham heard more and more about Saul Alinsky, who was always on the lookout for new recruits.

Alinsky had made his mark three decades earlier, in Chicago's Back of the Yards, a poor neighborhood of meatpackers and stockyards that formed the landscape of *The Jungle*, Upton Sinclair's documentary novel. A native Chicagoan and already a veteran of union organizing, the young Alinsky set out to organize in the Yards. "People were crushed and demoralized, either jobless or getting starvation wages, diseased, living in filthy, rotting unheated shanties, with barely enough food and clothing to keep alive," Alinsky recalled. "It was a cesspool of hate; the Poles, Slovaks, Germans, Negroes, Mexicans and Lithuanians all hated each other and all of them hated the Irish, who returned the sentiment in spades."

Alinsky had his own enemies in the Yards, including not just the ward heelers of City Hall, who resisted outside interference, but also the purveyors of racial hatred: Father Coughlin's National Union for Social Justice and William Dudley Pelley's Silver Shirts, who railed about the influence of international bankers and rapacious Jews. His main ally was the Catholic Church; at the time, Chicago had one of the most liberal archdioceses in the country. Alinsky thought of himself as a man of action, committed but unsentimental, a keen student of what made the world go around: power. He loathed do-gooders and moral abstractions; he valued concrete victories over dogma and talk. To combat the defeatism and apathy of the meatpackers, he appealed to their self-interest. He came to understand their most concrete grievances and went about organizing them to fight for themselves.

Alinsky staged rent strikes against slumlords and picketed exploitative shop owners. He arranged sit-ins in front of the offices of Mayor Edward Joseph Kelly, whose political machine was so ruthless and encompassing that, in Alinsky's words, it made Daley's version "look like the League of Women Voters." Alinsky was not only a democratic revolutionary but a consummate tactician. He was more than willing to exploit Kelly's vanity and innermost anxieties, as long as it brought results. Although Kelly was associated with the Memorial Day massacre of 1937, in which Chicago police opened fire on unarmed striking steelworkers, he still craved acceptance by the liberal, and pro-labor, President, Franklin Roosevelt. There was nothing Kelly would not do, according to Alinsky, to get an invitation to the White House. Alinsky, who had been an acolyte and biographer of John L. Lewis, the powerful head of the Congress of Industrial Organizations, told Kelly that if he would close a reasonable deal with the meatpackers' union, he would deliver the C.I.O.'s endorsement. Such an endorsement, he assured Kelly, would magically transform him into a "true friend of the workingman" and thus make him acceptable to F.D.R. Alinsky had found the avenue to Kelly's self-interest. A deal was struck.

As a pragmatist, the aging but still vigorous Alinsky disdained the leaders of the youth movement who were streaming into Chicago in August of 1968 for the Democratic Convention. He had little patience for these kids. What did they understand about power, about what real Americans wanted and needed? They were, in his view, dilettantes—spoiled Yippies who smoked pot, dropped acid, and had never met a working person in their lives. "Shit," Alinsky said, "Abbie Hoffman and Jerry Rubin couldn't organize a successful luncheon, much less a revolution."

Hillary Rodham was hardly a revolutionary. When she arrived at

Wellesley in 1965, her ambition was to become head of the campus Young Republicans. She fulfilled it. But, in time, as she gave increasing attention to the civil-rights movement and the war in Vietnam, her views began to shift. Not that she ever joined the radicals of S.D.S. She was elected head of the student government, and in that role she tolerated, even enjoyed, interminable committee meetings; she was a practical-minded liberal, concerned with easing dress codes, ending parietals, and reforming out-dated academic curricula. She certainly thought about national issues—particularly Vietnam, race, and the growing women's movement—but, unlike some of her classmates, she focused mainly on problems that she could actually solve. And so there was something about Alinsky that appealed to her.

After his success in the Back of the Yards, Alinsky organized other communities on the South Side of Chicago, in the barrios of Southern California, in the slums of Kansas City, Detroit, and Rochester, New York. He carried out his work with an absurdist flair. In 1964, he threat-ened Mayor Daley, who seemed to be backing out of a series of agreed-upon concessions to poor blacks on the South Side, with a prolonged "shit-in" at O'Hare Airport. The airport had been a cherished project of the Daley machine—its glass-and-concrete embodiment—and Alinsky threatened to bring its operations to a standstill by calling on a few thou-sand volunteers to occupy all the urinals and toilets at his signal. Daley made the concessions. And when Alinsky was working in Rochester's black community in the mid-sixties, he threatened to organize a "fart-in" at the Rochester Philharmonic in order to get Kodak to hire more blacks and engage with black community leaders. After a pre-concert dinner featur-ing "huge portions of baked beans," a hundred of Alinsky's people would take their seats among Rochester's élite. "Can you imagine the inevitable consequences?" he said, envisioning the ensuing "flatulent blitzkrieg."

Alinsky may not have been a theoretician, but his view of what was ail-ing post-war America influenced generations of community organizers. When an interviewer asked him if he agreed with Nixon that there was a conservative "silent majority" that disdained everything about the sixties, he dismissed the idea, but said that the country was in a state of terrible disruption and likely to move either toward "a native American fascism" or toward radical social change.

Right now they're frozen, festering in apathy, leading what Thoreau called "lives of quiet desperation." They're oppressed by taxation and inflation, poisoned by pollution, terrorized by urban crime, frightened by the new youth culture, baffled by the computerized world around them. They've worked all their lives to get their own little house in the suburbs, their color TV, their two cars, and now the good life seems to have turned to ashes in their mouths. Their personal lives are generally unfulfilling, their jobs unsatisfying, they've succumbed to tranquilizers and pep pills, they drown their anxieties in alcohol, they feel trapped in long-term endurance marriages or escape into guilt-ridden divorces. They're losing their kids and they're losing their dreams. They're alienated, depersonalized, without any feeling of participation in the political process, and they feel rejected and hopeless. . . . All their old values seem to have deserted them, leaving them rudderless in a sea of social chaos. Believe me, this is good organizational material.

Alinsky declared that his job was to seize on the despair, to "go in and rub raw the sores of discontent," to galvanize people for radical social change: "We'll give them a way to participate in the democratic process, a way to exercise their rights as citizens and strike back at the establishment that oppresses them, instead of giving in to apathy." That was as good a definition of community organizing as any.

Alinsky came to his conclusions about the state of American society via first-hand experience. His parents were Orthodox Jews who emigrated from Russia at the turn of the century to the slums of the South Side. His father started out as a tailor, ended up running a sweatshop, and then left the family. At sixteen, Alinsky himself was "shackin' up with some old broad of twenty-two." When his father died in 1950 or 1951, he left an estate of a hundred and forty thousand dollars—fifty dollars of it for Saul.

As a graduate student in criminology at the University of Chicago in the early nineteen-thirties, Alinsky decided to do research on the Outfit, Al Capone's gang, which dominated the city and City Hall. He used to hang out at the Lexington Hotel where Capone's men spent their evenings. Because Alinsky presented no threat to these invulnerable gangsters—he was a source of amusement to them—he was able to spend hours listening to Big Ed Stash, one of Capone's executioners, and Frank (The Enforcer) Nitti, a leading deputy, tell stories about bootlegging, women, gambling, and killing. "I was their one-man student body and they were anxious to teach me," Alinsky recalled. "It probably appealed to their egos." Alinsky never wrote his dissertation. Instead, he gathered up his understanding of the way power worked in Chicago and launched into progressive politics, raising money for the International Brigade in the Spanish Civil War, the Newspaper Guild, Southern sharecroppers, and various labor constituencies.

In the late nineteen-fifties, Alinsky was approached by some black leaders in Chicago about Woodlawn—a neighborhood on the South Side of Chicago, he said, that "made Harlem look like Grosse Pointe." In 1960, working with a young white organizer named Nicholas von Hoffman, who later became a prominent journalist, a black organizer named Robert Squires, and clergymen like Arthur Brazier, a Pentecostal minister who turned a storefront church into one of the largest congregations on the South Side, Alinsky formed what became known as the Woodlawn Organization, or TWO, whose goal was to head off the kind of deterioration and discrimination that had already laid waste to neighborhoods like Lawndale, on the West Side. "Those were the days of what was called urban renewal, which we saw as Negro removal," said Brazier.

Nick von Hoffman said, "There were no idealists around then. It was a wasteland, particularly because we were tiptoeing on the question of race relations. Any white person fooling around with that stuff was tagged as a Red. Two or three years earlier, we had made our first attempt to organize on the question of race on the southwest side of Chicago. We had money from the Roman Catholic Church. It was a boundary area between the white and black worlds that was in flames. The situation was, if a black family moved into the white area and their house were to catch fire, the fire engines would not come. The local banks formed a union with the local real-estate people to buy up empty houses that might be bought by black people."

Alinsky and von Hoffman, working with neighborhood activists and clergy, scored a series of improbable successes, going after the Board of Education for maintaining de-facto segregation, department stores for refusing to hire blacks, merchants for selling their wares at inflated prices, and the University of Chicago for trying to push out poor local residents to make room for new buildings. Von Hoffman haunted the Walnut Room of the Bismarck Hotel, where he met the heads of the Cook County Board of Supervisors and the Chicago Board of Realtors. Over lunch— "an ice cream soda and three Martinis"—he tried to cut deals with them. The Woodlawn Organization became a legendary paradigm of community organizing. Besides fighting the University of Chicago, it ran voter-registration drives, won better policing, and forced improvements in housing, sanitation facilities, and school conditions.

Hillary Rodham became so interested in what she was hearing about Saul Alinsky that when she returned to Wellesley for her senior year, she decided, together with her faculty adviser, Alan Schecter, to write her thesis on Alinsky and American poverty programs. Relying on both wide reading and her own interviews with Alinsky, Rodham produced a paper that probes beneath Alinsky's legend to consider his successes and his limitations as an organizer. She wrote of Alinsky as existing in a "peculiarly American" group of radical democrats who set aside high-flown rhetoric: "Much of what Alinsky professes does not sound 'radical.' His are the words used in our schools and churches, by our parents and their friends, by our peers. The difference is that Alinsky really believes in them and recognizes the necessity of changing the present structures of our lives in order to realize them."

Rodham's thesis is sometimes knotty with undergraduate display, but it is also a judicious analysis. She was prescient about the all-too-essential role that Alinsky played in his own movement. Without him, the movement would flounder, she warned. Alinsky's personality was large, distinct, and, likely, irreplaceable. Community organizing after his death—and it came soon, in 1972—would suffer the same internal debates and drift as psychoanalysis after Freud. While Rodham praised Alinsky for his cool-eyed methodology, she expressed concern about his reluctance to enter mainstream politics to effect change on a far broader scale.

"In spite of his being featured in the Sunday New York *Times*, and living a comfortable, expenses-paid life, he considers himself a revolutionary," she wrote in conclusion. "In a very important way he is. If the ideals Alinsky espouses were actualized, the result would be a social revolution." She placed Alinsky in the lineage of Eugene Debs, Walt Whitman, and Martin Luther King, all of whom, she wrote, were "feared, because each embraced the most radical of political faiths—democracy."

Alinsky wrote to Rodham offering her a place at his Industrial Areas Foundation Institute, where she would learn to be a community organizer. "Keeping in mind that three-fourths of America is middle class, a new and long overdue emphasis of the Institute will be placed on the development of organizers for middle class society," Alinsky wrote. Rodham, an honors student and a speaker at the Wellesley commencement, had a sparkling range of options for life after graduation: law school acceptances from both Harvard and Yale and Alinsky's invitation to train and work as a community organizer. She decided on law school, and Yale seemed more intellectually flexible than Harvard. In the endnotes to her senior thesis, she wrote that Alinsky's offer had been "tempting, but after spending a year trying to make sense out of his inconsistency, I need three years of legal rigor."

Sixteen years later, Barack Obama was in the Main Reading Room of the New York Public Library on Forty-second Street, leafing through newspapers, searching for the work he wanted most. He picked up a copy of *Community Jobs*, a small paper that carried ads for public-service work. In Chicago, an organizer named Jerry Kellman, a follower (more or less) of the Alinsky tradition, was looking for someone to work with him on the far South Side where the steel mills were closing and thousands of people were facing unemployment and a blistered landscape of deteriorating housing, toxic-waste dumps, bad schools, gangs, drugs, and violent crime. Kellman, who led the Calumet Community Religious Conference, a coalition of churches designed to help the people in the area, was especially desperate for an African-American organizer. The neighborhoods on the far South Side were nearly all black and he, as a wiry-haired white Jewish guy from New York, needed help.

For white organizers in those neighborhoods, "getting any traction was like selling burgers in India," Gregory Galluzzo, one of Kellman's colleagues, said. "Jerry *had* to hire a black organizer." Yvonne Lloyd, a South Side resident who worked closely with Kellman, said that African-Americans in the area were unreceptive to white organizers. "Black people are very leery when you come into their community and they don't know you," she said. Lloyd and another black activist who worked with Kellman, Loretta Augustine-Herron, pressed him hard to hire an African-American.

The ad in *Community Jobs* was long and descriptive. "I figured if I could paint a picture of the devastation and show it as a multiracial but mainly black area, it would interest someone," Kellman said. The address at the bottom of the ad was 351 East 113th Street, Father Bill Stenzel's rectory at Holy Rosary, a Catholic church on the far South Side. Kellman was using a couple of rooms there as his base of operations.

Obama sent Kellman his résumé.

"When I got it with the cover letter signed 'Barack Obama,' I thought, What the hell is this? And Honolulu? I thought, well, he's Japanese," Kellman said. "My wife was Japanese-American and so I asked her about it. She figured there was a good chance he was Japanese, too."

Like many young people of promise and ambition, especially ones with absent parents, Barack Obama had a hunger for mentors. He had the gift of winning over his elders and getting them to teach him about worlds that were alien to him. More than many of his peers, he sensed that there was much to learn from older people who had special knowledge of the way things worked, and his eagerness to learn brought out their eagerness to teach. In years to come, Obama befriended and absorbed all he could from elders like Laurence Tribe, at Harvard Law School; Jeremiah Wright, at Trinity United Church of Christ; Emil Jones, in the Illinois State Senate; Valerie Jarrett, Judson Miner, Abner Mikva, Newton Minow, David Axelrod, Penny Pritzker, Bettylu Saltzman, and many others in the worlds of politics and business in Chicago; Pete Rouse, Richard Lugar, and Richard Durbin in the U.S. Senate.

Jerry Kellman was the first of these mentors. And in the formation of Obama's ideas about community, effective political change, storytelling, and forming relationships, Kellman may well have played the most influential role in Obama's life outside of his family. Kellman was born in 1950 in New Rochelle, New York, a large and diverse suburb in Westchester County. When he was in seventh grade, the Supreme Court ordered the integration of New Rochelle's school system, the first such case in the North. When he was in junior high and high school, his political passions were Israel—he was so active in Jewish youth groups that he was selected to introduce David Ben-Gurion at an Israel Bonds dinner—and the civil-rights movement. In high school he helped run a black candidate's campaign for student-council president and then organized a series of discussion groups among white and black students. Kellman and his friends mourned the death of Martin Luther King, Jr.; the day after King's death, they launched a campaign to get the school board to stop using *Little Black Sambo* readers in the schools attended by kids in local projects. At graduation, he helped lead a walk-out to protest the war in Vietnam.

In August, 1968, Kellman enrolled at the University of Wisconsin in Madison, and it was clear from the start that he would be majoring in student protest. A regular at antiwar meetings and demonstrations, he helped organize a march of a thousand students to ban mandatory R.O.T.C. a week before he even began classes. The demonstration was a success and the policy was changed. In his freshman year, the Milwaukee *Journal* ran an article on the new breed of radical; Kellman was featured. But, despite a growing reputation on campus for political commitment, he thought that S.D.S., the dominant radical group on campus, was "nuts," its rhetoric of revolution comically impractical and dangerously violent. The next year, 1970, Kellman transferred to Reed College, in Oregon; not long afterward, a group of antiwar extremists bombed the math building at Wisconsin, killing a physicist named Robert Fassnacht and injuring several others. At Reed, a group of professors, tired of the traditional academic structure, set out to start a "commune-college." With a grant from the Carnegie Endowment, they started a "learning community" in a series of farmhouses and the inner city. Kellman spent most of his time there counseling people on the draft.

In the summer of 1971, Kellman went to Chicago, long acknowledged as the national center of community organizing. ("It was either that or going to live on a kibbutz.") He slept on people's floors and took jobs in restaurants; for a while, he chopped onions and grilled hot dogs at Tasty Pup. But mostly he learned organizing and the realities of Chicago: the isolation and dismal conditions in the poor black communities of the South and West Sides; the machine structure of political power; the discriminatory tactics of local mortgage bankers and real-estate developers. In such a grim and ironclad political culture, Kellman discovered, ordinary people go about their lives with little sense of community, cohesion, or possibility. They do not express their self-interest because they automatically relinquish any hope of fulfilling it. "What was drummed into us was self-interest," Kellman said. "That's Alinsky. It's all self-interest. Very hard-nosed. What is their self-interest and how to use it to organize."

In Austin, a neighborhood on the far West Side, he spent nights drinking with church and neighborhood leaders, learning people's life stories and the details of their disenfranchisement. He was no longer trying to end a war. He was trying to stop a bank from leaving the neighborhood, trying to get a pothole filled, a local drug dealer arrested, a stop sign replaced. He arranged meetings with priests to gain their support, with ordinary people to build up an energized community, with politicians to get them to do the right thing.

Like so many young organizers, Kellman became obsessive about his work. He did not stay long in any one place. He bounced from Austin to suburban DuPage County, from Lincoln, Nebraska, to Philadelphia. To slow down, and to please his wife, and maybe earn a decent living, he studied for a while at the University of Chicago, but it wasn't for him.

In 1982, Kellman trained organizers for the church-based group the United Neighborhood Organization, converted to Catholicism a couple of years later, and then joined the Calumet Community Religious Conference, which worked with black churches, and started organizing in the most poverty-stricken areas of the South Side. He and colleagues like Greg Galluzzo, an Alinsky apostle who had extensive organizing experience, and Mike Kruglik, a barrel-chested Chicagoan, took stock of the devastation in the wake of all the mill closings in the Calumet region, which ranged from the far South Side into Indiana. With thirty thousand workers in a single industry, Calumet was a kind of local Detroit; it had once produced more steel than Pittsburgh. But now, because of foreign competition and the cost of retooling plants, the men were out of work, the plants were rusting shells.

Kellman's early attempt to organize church leaders in the area got a boost when Cardinal Joseph Bernardin signaled that if local priests didn't join the effort they should rush to confession. Father Stenzel at Holy Rosary helped Kellman pull together ten parishes, which kicked in a thousand dollars apiece and promised to help organize willing parishioners. Kellman knew that he couldn't sustain an organization that tried to yoke together the white neighborhoods of Indiana and the black areas of the South Side; to deal with the South Side and gain access to greater funding, he conceived the Developing Communities Project for Chicago. He told his board of local activists, all of whom were black, that he would find an African-American organizer. What he could offer was a miserable salary, a resistant public, and only a slender hope of success.

"It was easier to promise than it was to deliver," Kellman said. "The logic is that you need someone very smart, but if you are smart enough to be an organizer you should be smart enough not to do it. And if you are black and the pride of the family, why become downwardly mobile? It doesn't make a lot of sense. It was hard. I got no one I liked. The heat was beginning to build. I procrastinated. I scrambled. Meantime, I kept taking out ads and looking at résumés. The *Tribune*. The *Times*. The Detroit *Free Press*. But also that one in *Community Jobs*."

Kellman read Obama's résumé and called him in New York. They spoke for two hours. ("Over the phone I figured out he wasn't Japanese.") A couple of weeks later, Kellman, in New York to visit his parents, met Obama at a coffee shop on Lexington Avenue. He looked very young to him. Obama was twenty-four. What concerned Kellman about very bright, very young candidates was the possibility of early burnout. Community organizing is isolating, tedious, and deeply frustrating work. More often than not, battles drag on, and then fizzle out without a satisfying result. A young person with some options is likely to leave at the first hint of boredom or defeat. Kellman had already known a young organizer who was so psychologically distressed by the work that he'd had to let the person go and find psychiatric help.

The terms for a training organizer like Obama were less than modest— a ten-thousand-dollar salary and a couple of thousand more for a car. "But preposterous propositions are what being an organizer is like," Kellman said. "So we went over Barack's story, and it was clear to me that he was never very long anywhere and he was different wherever he goes." Even in that early conversation, Kellman saw Obama as someone looking for himself and for a place to call home.

"He kept asking, 'What will you teach me, and how will you teach me?'" Kellman recalled. "I thought of him as an outsider, and he wanted to work with the poor, with people who have faced racial discrimination. His heroes were in the civil-rights movement, but that was over. This was as close as he could get. And he needed to live in a black community."

Kellman quizzed Obama about his background and, like most people, found the flood of details hard to absorb on first hearing. Kellman tried to push him: Why didn't he go to graduate school? Didn't he want to make money? Obama had said that he was excited by the election, in 1983, of a black mayor in Chicago, Harold Washington. So why not go work for him? Kellman asked. Why organize? But Obama kept repeating how inspired he was by the civil-rights movement and his desire to work on a grassroots level.

Obama admitted to Kellman that he had another motivation for wanting to be an organizer on the South Side. He was thinking about being a novelist. "He told me that he had trouble writing, he had to force himself to write," Kellman said. He was looking not only for experience, an identity, and a community; he was also in search of material.

Before Kellman could hire him officially, Obama had to be confirmed by a small board of directors, which met at St. Helena of the Cross, a Catholic church on the South Side. Many of the community activists on the South Side were middle-aged black women, and they were more eager than ever for Kellman to settle on an African-American organizer. "We interviewed three other people before Barack. Nobody really fit the bill of what we needed," one board member, Loretta Augustine-Herron, said. "We did want someone to look like us, but that wasn't the only thing. If Barack hadn't had the ability to understand our needs, it wouldn't have worked. He had the sensitivity. He was honest to a fault. He told us what he knew and what he didn't. When we described our plight, he understood. He didn't have a cockamamie idea to resolve some problem we didn't have." Augustine-Herron and the others had only one concern: "He was so young. Was he going to be up for this?"

Obama decided to move to Hyde Park, an integrated neighborhood and home of the University of Chicago. Obama found himself a cheap first-floor apartment on East Fifty-fourth Street and Harper Avenue. As he had in New York, he outfitted the apartment for monkish living: a bed, a bridge table, a couple of chairs, and some books. Eventually he went out and got a gray cat which he named Max. Hyde Park was the logical neighborhood for Obama from the start. The area was mainly black, but integrated, and, because of the presence of the University of Chicago, salted with intellectuals. From Hyde Park it was a short trip to the neighborhoods where he would be working, including Roseland and West Pullman on the far South Side.

During his first weeks in Chicago, Obama spent many hours with Kellman, touring the South Side and talking. "He was very idealistic—naïve only in his lack of experience," Kellman recalled. "He had no experience of Chicago ward committeemen and graft and the rest. We talked a lot about race, how to deal with it. We were trying to organize blacks with white priests. Barack has always had to deal with the way people react to him, which has nothing to do with him, but, rather, with the fact that he is black or looks black. A lot of the struggle for him was to figure out who he was independent of how people reacted to him. He was working on it. He had been in school all his life, which is not a very real environment in terms of race. This was the first time when he would be in one neighborhood and identified in one way. He had never encountered a place where race was so determinative."

Kellman drove Obama around to see the abandoned mills, the rusted ships in the abandoned port, and to meet with community leaders. "It was like going to an exotic country for him," Kellman said. "He had so much learning to do about how people live their lives, but he learned almost effortlessly. He had gifts. He was comfortable with people and talked easily with people."

The standard books for beginning organizers are Alinsky's two theoretical tracts: *Reveille for Radicals* and *Rules for Radicals*. Kellman thought those were trivial and glib and recommended Alinsky's biography of John L. Lewis and Robert Caro's *The Power Broker*, a titanic biography of the unelected master builder of New York, Robert Moses. The books were intended to give him a short course in the way cities and power really work. "Decisions in Chicago are not made where they are supposed to be," Kellman said. "Aldermen and state representatives make no decisions; ward committeemen do, and they are making a lot of those decisions because of their second professions as funeral-parlor directors, insurance salesmen, attorneys."

Obama spent most of his time methodically compiling lists of priests, ministers, and community leaders and arranging to interview them. The idea is that the organizer does not barrel into a neighborhood like some sort of Moses in a black leather jacket, ready to lead; first he *listens* and only then tries to engage enough people to form an effective leadership group. He helps them learn to analyze power and even speak in public. That group then goes on to confront elected officials and city bureaucrats and take power into its own hands.

At night, Obama wrote long meticulous reports about what he had learned in his interviews. He often drew sketches of his subjects in the margins to help him remember names and faces.

"He was very disciplined in the way he lived," Kellman said. "In the first few months when he was an organizer, he had no social life and I was worried that I was going to lose him. He wasn't dating. He was doing his interviews, doing his reports, reading—and on the weekends he was visiting black churches and writing short stories. He was very focused and disciplined, monkish not in the sense of being a celibate but of holing up and reading." To relax, Obama played basketball or took long runs by the lakefront, stopping only to reward himself with a cigarette—his most glaring vice. He ate sparingly. If his friend and fellow organizer John Owens ordered dessert, Obama would say, like a particularly ironic cleric, "Did you deserve that?"

"I don't think he had much of a life outside of work," Loretta Augustine-Herron said. "I used to worry about that! He worked seven days a week most weeks. Early-morning meetings and then meetings till ten that night. He went to places that I told him not to let the sun go down on you there, but he went anyway."

The more Obama got to know the South Side and the people who lived there, the more his writing became about what he was seeing and hearing. Occasionally, he sent drafts of his stories to old friends like Phil Boerner or gave them to Kellman and Kruglik.

"He gave me two or three of his short stories," Kruglik recalled. "They were about the streets of the South Side of Chicago, what they looked and felt like to him, the dreariness of the landscape in winter. One was about a pastor who is overwhelmed by his problems but he still wants to build a strong congregation and take care of himself, too. Something shines through the pastor's spirit that allows him to do that. The stories were very descriptive. At first, I wondered, how does he have the energy to do all this? I figured he must have copied it somehow from someone. But they were about people I knew." Obama was meeting, and becoming friends with, black church people on the South Side like Dan Lee, a deacon at St. Catherine's Church in West Pullman, and the Reverend Alvin

Love, the young minister at Lilydale First Baptist Church. Obama's fellow organizers had no problem identifying them in his fiction.

Kellman remembers reading a story about a small church: "Barack had the experience of being in a foreign land for the first time. The storefront church was as foreign as could be. At that point in his life, Indonesia was more familiar to him. But he was writing about what he was seeing." (Kellman says he probably should have kept copies of Obama's stories. "I would have made a killing on eBay.") Another story, "A Man of Small Graces," describes a character on the South Side who seemed to be based on Obama's stepfather, Lolo Soetoro.

When Obama did have free time he usually liked to spend it alone. Sometimes Kruglik would drag him out to a blues or jazz club—Obama was a fan of the Jazz Showcase downtown—or have him come over to watch a ballgame: the Bears, the Bulls, the White Sox. ("It was amazing how fast he became a Chicago partisan," Kruglik said. "I mean who else was he supposed to root for? Honolulu? Jakarta? It was all part of integrating himself into Chicago and making it home.") On summer afternoons, Kellman was occasionally able to lure Obama out for a walk at Montrose Harbor or to his house in Beverly, an Irish and black neighborhood on the South Side, for a backyard barbecue. "One thing I understood personally is that he wanted to be around us simply because we had a family," Kellman said.

One of Obama's organizing colleagues, Sister Mary Bernstein—"my father was Jewish and my mother won"—often teased him about his social life. "One morning," Sister Mary said, "I came in the office and he was sitting at his desk and stirring his tea and he said, 'How's it going, Sis-tuh?' He always called me 'Sis-tuh' and I called him 'O-bama.' And he said, 'Sis-tuh, how am I going to find a date?' And I said, 'Barack, everyone I know is too old for you, and they're all nuns. I'm the last person you should ask.' "

Kellman and many other of Obama's friends agree that, as engaging as Obama was, he was, at least for a long time, wary about revealing information about himself—his past and his emotions. But as he and Kellman spent more and more time together, it became clear that Obama was still thinking through questions about his family and his identity, about politics and his own future. One thing that struck Obama's friends and colleagues in Chicago was how much he admired his mother for her independence and her social idealism. His father was quite another story. "He didn't want to repeat his father's life," Kellman said. Observing Obama's seriousness, his cool, and his modest way of living, Kellman couldn't help but think that the younger man had cast himself in stark contrast to the bitter, brilliant, volatile, and wholly unreliable man who was his father.

Obama and Kellman took their walks in the park, ate lunch at a McDonald's near the old steel mills, and sometimes the talk drifted away from work. "Dating was a challenge," Kellman said. "How do you live in two worlds? Could he marry a white woman? Where would he live? Was it even right to ask? Is love all that matters? He thought a lot about marriage, his long-range plans, and how to handle the questions that arose out of it. Then there was money: How can you do what you believe in and still live decently? What degree of sacrifice? Or should I just be smart and make a lot of money? We would talk about all of this. Or politicians. How much should we work with them and how much in opposition? Were they enemies or were they allies? Should you work within the system or stand outside of it, advocating? Can you join the system and not lose your sense of what is just?"

Obama dated various women—in that department, Kellman said, "He was more than capable of taking care of himself." Toward the end of his time as an organizer, Obama had a steady girlfriend, a white University of Chicago student who was studying anthropology. Even though he knew that the relationship would come to an end, Kellman said, "They were both committed to paths that would lead to some dedication. They parted for geographic reasons. They both had commitments that would take them out of Chicago. Long term, in general, Barack wanted kids and he wanted a house. He wanted a family—even young and single and not having met Michelle and being in a relationship that he felt wasn't going to last."

By the time Obama came to Chicago, he had become comfortable not only with his given name but with his racial identity in particular. What his work on the South Side was bringing him was something larger—a deepening connection to an African-American community. He was no longer a student trying to make friends in the Black Students Association. This was life, daily and natural contact, whether at home in Hyde Park— a more middle-class, integrated, university-town environment—or farther south, among the poor and the dispossessed.

"Barack simply believed that he'd been black all of his life," Mike Kruglik said. "Part of it was, as he told me, that while all these people were thinking about his being biracial or asking was he black enough—all that stuff—when he walked down the streets of the South Side no one asked that question. No one asked that question when he tried to hail a taxi in

New York. Now he was a black community organizer in a black community with the purpose of creating an organization to give black people a voice. There was a synthesis of how he identified himself culturally and being a community organizer. Being a community organizer helped him create a black community. Before that, he'd had a romantic idea of a black community and found that there really was no community as he'd imagined it: the community was fragmented and largely destroyed. He had to re-create that community. I heard a lot of those things coming out of his mouth. There was this organic feeling about him, of being a serious young man helping people fight for their community. And he *willed* himself to be part of the community and then defend it."

One of his black colleagues in organizing, John Owens, had grown up in Chatham on the South Side, and he was fascinated by how "open-minded" Obama was about questions of race. "He was concerned about being fair about whites as well as about blacks, whereas the average African-American who grows up in the community, the concern with being fair is usually with your own. He always wanted to be even-handed in his analysis of things. In that regard, he was able to have stronger relationships with whites more than the average African-American."

Obama's early impressions of Chicago were best expressed in a long, handwritten letter to his old friend Phil Boerner:

Phil—

My humblest apologies for the lack of communications these past months. Work has taken up much of my time and the free margins I devoted mostly to catching my breath. Things have begun to settle into coherence of late, however, so hopefully you'll be hearing more from me in the future.

Now, what's your excuse?

Chicago—a handsome town, wide streets, lush parks, broad, lovingly crafted buildings, Lake Michigan forming its whole East side, as big and mutable as an ocean. Though it's a big city with big city problems, the scale and impact of the place is nothing like NY, mainly because of its dispersion, lack of congestion. Imagine Manhattan shrunk by half, then merged with the boroughs into a single stretch of land, and you've got some idea of what it's like. Five minutes drive out of the Loop (the downtown area) and you're in the middle of single story frame houses with backyards and tall elms.

The layout influences the people here. They're not as uptight, neurotic, as Manhattanites, but they're also not as quick on the pick-up. You still see country in a lot of folks' ways—the secretary in a skyscraper still has the expression of a farm girl; the sound of crickets on a hot Southern night lies just below the surface of the young black girl's words at a check-out counter. Chicago's also a town of neighborhoods, and to a much greater degree than NY, the various tribes remain discrete, within their own turf, carving out the various neighborhoods and replicating the feel of their native lands. You can go to the Polish section of town and not hear a word of English spoken, walk along the Indian section of town, colorful as a bazaar, and you'd swear you might be in a section of New Delhi.

Of course, the most pertinent division here is that between the black tribe and the white tribe. The friction doesn't appear to be any greater than in NY, but it's more manifest since there's a black mayor in power and a white City Council. And the races are spatially very separate; where I work, in the South Side, you go ten miles in any direction and will not see a single white face. There are exceptions—I live in Hyde Park, near the Univ. of Chicago, which maintains a nice mix thanks to the heavy-handed influence of the University. But generally the dictum holds fast—separate and unequal.

I work in five different neighborhoods of differing economic conditions. In one neighborhood, I'll be meeting with a group of irate homeowners, working-class folks, bus drivers and nurses and clerical administrators, whose section of town has been ignored by the Dept. of Streets and Sanitation since the whites moved out twenty years ago. In another, I'll be trying to bring together a group of welfare mothers, mothers at 15, grandmothers at 30, great-grandmothers at 45, trying to help them win better job-training and day care facilities from the State. In either situation, I walk into a room and make promises I hope that they can help me keep. They generally trust me, despite the fact that they've seen earnest young men pass through here before, expecting to change the world and eventually succumbing to the lure of a corporate office. And in a short time I've learned to care for them very much and want to do everything I can for them. It's tough though. Lots of driving, lots of hours on the phone trying to break through lethargy, lots of dull meetings. Lots of frustration when you see a 43% drop-out rate in the public schools and don't know where to begin denting that figure. But about 5% of the time, you see something happen—a shy housewife standing up to a bumbling official, or the sudden sound of hope in the voice of a grizzled old man—that gives a hint of the possibilities, of people taking hold of their lives, working together to bring about a small justice. And it's that possibility that keeps you going through all the trenchwork.

Two other guys on our staff, both white, in their late thirties, do the same thing in the white suburbs. What draws the two areas together is a devastated economy—the area used to be the biggest steel producer in the U.S., and now closed down mills lie blanched and still as dinosaur fossils. We've been talking to some key unions about the possibility of working with them to keep the last major mill open; but it's owned by LTV, a Dallas-based conglomerate that wants to close as soon as possible to garner the tax loss.

Aside from that, not much news to report. My apartment is a comfortable studio near the Lake (rents are about half those in Manhattan). Since I often work at night, I usually reserve the mornings to myself for running, reading and writing. I've enclosed a first-draft of a short story I just finished; if you have the patience, jot some criticism on it, let George mark it up, and send it back to me as soon as possible, along with some of the things you guys may have written.

It's getting cooler, and I live in mortal fear of Chicago winters. How's the weather over there? I miss NY and the people in it—the subways, the feel of Manhattan streets, the view downtown from the Brooklyn Bridge. I hope everything goes well with you, give my love to Karen, George, Paul, and anyone else I know.

Love—
Barack

Obama had arrived in Chicago in June of 1985, two years after Harold Washington won election as the city's first black mayor. To the African-Americans of the city, this was an epochal breakthrough, a seeming end to traditional white machine rule and what was commonly called the city's "plantation politics," and they were always ready to talk about it. Obama could walk into his barbershop or the Valois cafeteria and get a quick seminar on Washington's victory. He saw the campaign posters everywhere, tattered and yellowing but still displayed in shop windows. He saw the portraits in the South Side barbershops next to King and Malcolm and Muhammad Ali. Obama joined Washington's admirers and followed the daily drama of the Mayor's battles with a City Council that was still packed with old machine-style aldermen, the most famous of whom was "Fast Eddie" Vrdolyak.

There is no telling how Obama might have developed had he answered an ad to work in some other city, but it is clear that the history of African-Americans in Chicago—and the unique political history of Chicago, culminating in Washington's attempt to form a multiracial coalition—provided Obama with a rich legacy to learn from and be part of. "The first African-American president could *only* have come from Chicago," Timuel Black, one of the elders of the South Side and a historian of the black migration from the South, says. Tim Black came to Chicago from Alabama with his family as an infant, grew up on the South Side, and went on to write and assemble *Bridges of Memory*, a two-volume oral history of the black migration and African-American life in the city. For decades, Black has been a college teacher, political activist, and resident sage of the South Side, and he is one of the elders Obama sought out when he was an organizer. They met for the first time at a student hangout near the university, Medici on 57th, where Obama quizzed him for hours about the history of the migration and the political and social development of the South Side. Obama was not only fascinated by the history of black Chicago; he also chose to enter that history, to join it. Chicago was where he found a community, a church, a wife, a purpose, a political life—and he was absorbed in its past. "He soaked it up," Black said. "He made it his own."

African-Americans have lived in the lakeside portage that became Chicago for more than two centuries. According to legend, the Potawatomi Indians, who first lived there, had a saying: "The first white man to settle at 'Chickagou' was a Negro." A French-speaking black man, Jean Baptiste Point du Sable, was the first permanent settler, arriving in "Chickagou" at the end of the eighteenth century. Until the Civil War, blacks were officially banned from settling in Illinois, yet in the eighteen-forties and fifties pro-slavery polemicists called it "the sinkhole of abolition" because so many escaped slaves kept arriving via the Underground Railroad.

The Great Migration of African-Americans to Chicago began around 1910; the migration was a process that came in bursts, peaking in the nineteen-forties and fifties, but did not entirely end until the nineteen-seventies. In all, it raised Chicago's black population from a marginal two per cent to thirty-three per cent, transforming the politics and culture of the city. In the South, boll weevil infestations put cotton farmers out of work and, later, mechanization transformed cotton cultivation forever; at the same time, in the industrial North there were thousands of jobs available in the slaughterhouses and the mills and the factories, not least because the Great War and then the Immigration Act of 1924 shut off the borders to Europeans while so many whites were being shipped off to war. The Great Mississippi Flood of 1927 also sent hundreds of thousands of black sharecroppers looking for work and a place to live. Throughout the migration, the most important of the black newspapers, the Chicago *Defender,* a weekly edited by Robert S. Abbott, a Georgia native, published milk-and-honey appeals to Southern blacks asking them to question their conditions in the South and come North for a life of freedom and plenty:

> Turn a deaf ear to everybody. . . . You see they are not lifting their laws to help you. Are they? Have they stopped their Jim Crow cars? Can you buy a Pullman sleeper where you wish? Will they give you a square deal in court yet? Once upon a time we permitted other people to think for us—today we are thinking and acting for ourselves with the result that our "friends" are getting alarmed at our progress. We'd like to oblige these unselfish souls and remain slaves in the South, but to their section of the country we have said, as the song goes, "I hear you calling me," and have boarded the train singing, "Good-bye, Dixie Land."

Trainloads of black families arrived every day at Illinois Central Station. Between 1916 and 1919, half a million blacks arrived in Chicago from the South. A Black Belt began to take shape on the South Side, a triangle running between Twenty-sixth Street on the north and Fifty-fifth Street on the south, from State Street to Lake Michigan. It was a huge, dense neighborhood that came to be known as Bronzeville. To some extent, the *Defender*'s boosterish appeals were genuine. Blacks really did find greater opportunity in Chicago and, in a world of de-facto segregation, Bronzeville became a lodestar of black life in America, a "parallel universe," as Timuel Black calls it, of "parallel institutions": black churches, theaters, nightclubs, and gambling parlors known as "policy wheels." John (Mushmouth) Johnson became Chicago's first black gambling czar and he, in turn, helped Irishmen like "Hinky Dink" Kenna and "Bathhouse John" Coughlin develop their careers as the political bosses of the First Ward.

Still, many whites in Chicago resisted the influx, the expansion of Bronzeville, by every means possible. Between July, 1917, and March, 1921, a bomb went off in a black-occupied house roughly every three weeks. The community association in Kenwood and Hyde Park determined that blacks could not move east of State Street and "contaminate property values." Real-estate tycoons ran scams that played on white fears. One of the major white real-estate barons, Frederick H. Bartlett, handed out leaflets to whites in Douglas, Oakwood, and Kenwood reading, "Negroes are coming. Negroes are coming. If you don't sell to us now, you might not get anything." And so whites suffering from "nigger mania" sold cheap and the realty companies, accepting tiny down payments, sold the same houses for double and triple the price to newly arrived blacks. Realtors would sell to whites promising that there was a restrictive covenant and they could be assured of having no black neighbors. At the same time, black resentment of white racism was growing; black soldiers who had fought in Europe and returned home only to be treated once more as inferior beings helped stoke a growing sense of militancy.

The event that ignited the long saga of racial conflict in Chicago came on the afternoon of July 27, 1919. A black teenager named Eugene Williams went swimming in Lake Michigan and floated across an imaginary line marking Twenty-ninth Street, and into a "white area." A group of white youths stoned him to death. As a group of blacks tried to get care for Williams, they grabbed George Stauber, one of the white youths, and tried to get a white policeman to arrest him. The officer refused and a fight broke out, setting off four days of violence, spreading into the taverns and the pool rooms, from one neighborhood to the next. Members of Irish "athletic clubs," armed with clubs and other weapons, went out looking for "jigs" and "smokes"; to their surprise, the blacks fought back, even torching houses near the stockyards and the railroad. The August 2nd issue of the *Defender* described "a blaze of red hate flaming as fiercely as the heat of day"; the paper wrote about streets and alleys filled with abandoned corpses, mobs controlling whole areas of Chicago, city police unable, or unwilling, to regain the upper hand, a metropolis consumed with fear, violence, and rage: "Women and children have not been spared. Traffic has been stopped. Phone wires have been cut." Spearheading the riot was a white gang in the Irish neighborhood of Bridgeport known as the Hamburg Athletic Club. One of its members—and one of its eventual leaders—was a teenager named Richard J. Daley. When the battles were finally over, thirty-eight men and boys had been killed—twenty-three of them black.

That summer, the Jamaican-born poet Claude McKay, who was living in Harlem, published a sonnet called "If We Must Die" about the lynchings and race riots raging throughout the country. The opening lines reflected the sense of outrage and determination among black men and women in places like Harlem and the South Side:

If we must die, let it not be like hogs
Hunted and penned in an inglorious spot,
While round us bark the mad and hungry dogs,
Making their mock at our accursed lot.

Throughout Chicago, the borderlines between white neighborhoods and black remained tense for years after the 1919 riot. *The Property Owner's Journal*, the Kenwood and Hyde Park Association's official publication, issued a warning that reflected the depth of hatred and foreboding:

Every colored man who moves into Hyde Park knows that he is damaging his white neighbor's property. Therefore, he is making war on the white man. Consequently, he is not entitled to any consideration and forfeits his right to be employed by the white man. If employers should adopt a rule of refusing to employ Negroes who persist in residing in Hyde Park to the damage of the white man's property, it would soon show good results.

Chicago's blacks sought refuge in the Republican Party. Partly out of loyalty to the party of Lincoln, they voted for William Hale Thompson for mayor. During his three terms—from 1915 to 1923 and then from 1927 until 1931—Mayor Thompson, dubbed Big Bill and Bill the Builder, welcomed blacks into his coalition. He gave so many city jobs to blacks that his opponents took to calling City Hall Uncle Tom's Cabin. During his political races, Democratic Party campaign workers were sent out on the streets with calliopes to play "Bye, Bye, Blackbird" and to distribute leaflets showing Thompson piloting trainloads of blacks from Georgia with a caption reading, "This train will start for Chicago, April 6, if Thompson is elected."

The pioneer black politician of the South Side was a well-to-do businessman—a contractor, decorator, and real-estate broker—named Oscar Stanton De Priest. Born to former slaves in Florence, Alabama, De Priest won election as an alderman in 1915 but stepped down two years later when he was indicted on a Mob-connected corruption charge; with Clarence Darrow as his attorney, De Priest was acquitted. In 1928, running in Chicago's first congressional district as a Republican, De Priest became the first black member of the House of Representatives since Reconstruction.

With the rise of Franklin Roosevelt, blacks in Chicago began to shift their loyalty to the Democratic Party and to a new mayor, Anton Cermak, who built the foundations of a political machine that ruled the city for half a century. Cermak was mayor only between 1931 and 1933, but he helped bring Poles, Ukrainians, Jews, Czechs, Italians, and blacks into city government. He even helped bring in the lower-class Irish from Bridgeport and Back of the Yards. On February 15, 1933, at a public ceremony, in Bayfront Park, in Miami, Cermak was shot in the chest while shaking hands with President-elect Roosevelt. The bullet was most likely intended for Roosevelt. Cermak's supposed last words to F.D.R.—"I'm glad it was me instead of you"—are inscribed on a plaque in his honor at Bayfront Park.

White ethnic politicians dominated the Chicago machine, but someone needed to control the black South Side. A get-along pol named William Levi Dawson, who had switched from the Republicans to the Democrats, soon became the boss of what was called the "sub-machine"— a black extension of City Hall. Dawson was born in Albany, Georgia. His grandfather had been a slave, his father a barber. When his father's sister was raped by a white man, and he retaliated, he was forced to head North. Young Dawson graduated from Fisk in 1909 and worked as a porter and a bellhop. Fighting in France in the First World War, he was gassed. Along the way, he lost one of his legs in an accident.

A mild but clever man with a neat pencil moustache, Dawson returned to Chicago and went to work in a ward political office on the South Side. As a local politician and then as a congressman, his priority was to bring relative economic and political well-being to the black neighborhoods of the South and West Sides. Any talk of ideology and reform, of civil rights and empowerment, seemed to him an indulgence, the self-defeating radicalism of young hotheads. In Congress, he stood in direct contrast to Adam Clayton Powell, Jr., of Harlem, who was a militant and flamboyant spokesman for civil rights. Dawson was tied to the leading ministers, the *Defender*, the ward leaders—Chicago's parallel universe of black institutions. He was a master at defusing any rebellion in the ranks. When the local branch of the N.A.A.C.P. denounced Dawson for failing to speak out about the murder of Emmett Till in 1955, he fought back. He had had his loyal precinct captains run for delegate positions to the local N.A.A.C.P. convention; they won, and he took control of the organization. In 1956, he opposed a federal bill to end segregation in the schools because he feared a loss of federal funding. And, in 1960, he advised the Kennedy campaign, "Let's not use words that offend our good Southern friends, like 'civil rights.' "

Dawson believed that he was acting in the tradition of Booker T.

Washington, waging winnable battles and leaving the rest for another day. The advice he gave to Kennedy was, in his mind, hardheaded politics, a way to win votes among Southern congressmen for concrete aid to the poor. The social realities of black Chicago in the post-war era, however, were extremely complex, and not something that Dawson's old-fashioned attitude to power was capable of dealing with. Accommodation was winning very few battles.

Even so, the South Side was one of the most culturally vibrant black communities in the country. With the ferment of the Harlem Renaissance a memory, the South Side was arguably the capital of black America. Joe Louis lived there. The *Defender*, which, in 1956, began to publish a daily edition, was there. Joseph H. Jackson, the pastor of the Olivet Baptist Church and the head of the conservative National Baptist Convention, was there. All the best blues performers, gospel singers, jazz musicians, and actors came to the Savoy Ballroom and the Regal Theater. Chicago was home to establishment figures like Dawson and Jackson, but also to a range of political radicals, religious leaders, and cultists, including Elijah Poole, who, as Elijah Muhammad, moved the headquarters of the Black Muslims from Detroit to the South Side. Richard Wright, who had come North from Mississippi to Chicago as a young man, insisted that life was so hard on the South Side that no one should be surprised at what political ferment might one day arise there. "Chicago is the city from which the most incisive and radical Negro thought has come," he wrote in his introduction to *Black Metropolis*, St. Clair Drake and Horace Cayton's classic 1945 study of the South Side. "There is an open and raw beauty about that city that seems either to kill or endow one with the spirit of life. I felt those extremes of possibility, death and hope, while I lived half hungry and afraid in a city to which I had fled with the dumb yearning to write, to tell my story. But I did not know what my story was."

By the nineteen-forties, the rise of a distinct, heterodox, and growing black population on the South Side inspired the white press to publish countless scare headlines. The white neighborhoods on the South Side built "improvement associations" designed to prevent the influx of blacks. White taverns installed locks and buzzers to keep out blacks. A black Chicagoan had to be careful not to wander into the wrong neighborhood lest he ignite a riot like the one near the lake in 1919.

Even after the 1948 Supreme Court ruling in the case of Shelley v. Kraemer barred state enforcement of restrictive covenants and promised an end to housing segregation, Chicago remained one of the most racially segmented cities in the country. (It remains so, today.) When, in 1951, a black family moved into an apartment in the white working-class town of Cicero, thousands attacked the building for several nights in a row until the National Guard was ordered to end the violence. Mayor Martin Kennelly, a son of Bridgeport and a product of the machine, sent police to the South Side to raid the policy wheels, and Bill Dawson decided to assert his will. The Cook County Democratic Central Committee had to decide whether to re-anoint Kennelly as its mayoral candidate in the 1951 election. Furious with City Hall's assault on the policy wheels, Dawson sent word from Washington that he opposed Kennelly's nomination. Dawson told Kennelly, "Who do you think you are? I bring in the votes. I elect you. You are not needed, but the votes are needed." The Central Committee decided on a compromise: it would allow Kennelly one more term and then, in 1955, turned to another son of Bridgeport, Richard J. Daley.

At first, Mayor Daley built on Cermak's principle of machine politics that an effective organization would come not merely from the Irish base but from a coalition of all ethnic groups and the effective use of patronage systems. For Daley, blacks were a dependable source of support. They were crucial to his first election. And yet Daley could not tolerate a wholly independent sub-machine. Almost immediately after taking office, he undermined Dawson, taking away his right to appoint the committeemen in his wards.

Daley's ruthless efficiency could not be doubted. Through a web of loyal aldermen, committeemen, and precinct workers, he dispensed thousands of jobs—forty-five thousand at the machine's peak. He was so intimately involved in the city's workforce, it was said, that he could greet many of the forty thousand employees by name. Daley was shrewd enough to bridge a political culture that ranged from buffoonish ward hacks to independent liberals like Governor Adlai Stevenson and Senator Paul Douglas. While more than a few members of the machine over the years took bribes or committed other crimes, Daley lived modestly, went to Mass every day, and showed at least a grudging respect for some of his political foes. Still, as the radio broadcaster and oral historian Studs Terkel once said of Daley, "He's marvelous when it comes to building things like highways, parking lots, and industrial complexes. But when it comes to healing the aches and hurts of human beings, he comes up short." This was especially so in the case of race.

Daley had inherited ugly, racist sentiments about black men and women. When he became mayor, his antipathy to blacks showed itself gradually at first, and then, for many, wholly eclipsed his better qualities. However delusionally, he thought of himself as fair-minded and believed that blacks would assimilate and advance in much the same way that other ethnic groups had. His condescension was brutally offhand. When a young man from South Carolina named Jesse Jackson moved to Chicago after making a name in the Southern civil-rights campaigns, Daley offered him a job—as a toll-taker on the highway.

Daley enforced policies of de-facto segregation, not so much because of closely held theories of black inferiority as because of his view of political power and how to retain it. In the late fifties and sixties, he built a series of vast housing projects—Henry Horner Homes on the near West Side; Stateway Gardens on the South Side; Cabrini-Green on the near North Side; and the twenty-eight sixteen-story towers of the Robert Taylor Homes. To isolate Robert Taylor and Stateway from any white neighborhoods, he routed the Dan Ryan Expressway so that it locked in the separation of the races.

Beginning in 1959, when the League of Negro Voters ran an independent candidate for city clerk, there were signs of some resistance to Daley in the black community. At a national convention of the N.A.A.C.P. in 1963, in Chicago, Daley was booed off the stage, mainly because he had so consistently opposed the integration of the public-school system. The half dozen blacks who won seats on the City Council by the nineteen-sixties, however, were so compliant that they were known as "the Silent Six." The most outspoken alderman on questions of race was Leon Despres, who was white; Despres was a leading example of the post-war liberal Democrats who kept their distance from the machine and called themselves independents. Some admiring blacks called Despres "the lone Negro on the City Council."

"Whenever I would raise a point about discrimination, segregation, oppression, civil rights, or an ordinance on those matters, which I increasingly did, Daley would always sic one of the 'Silent Six' to answer me," Despres said. One of the six, Claude W. B. Holman of the Fourth Ward, practiced a form of loyalty and devotion to Daley that seemed almost North Korean in its blind passion. Despres recalls Holman once telling Daley, with the cameras on, "You are the greatest mayor in history—greatest mayor in the world and in outer space, too."

Even as the civil-rights movement came to the forefront of American political life, doing battle and making advances in the South, black activists in Chicago like Willoughby Abner, Timuel Black, Albert Raby, and Dick Gregory could make little headway against Daley's implacable machine. "A good legitimate Negro wanting to go into politics in Chicago," Gregory said in the mid-nineteen-sixties, "not only has to run against a handkerchief-head Negro but also against a machine getting kickbacks from dope and prostitution. . . . You have to respect Daley. He has a big job being mayor, governor, prosecutor, and president of the Chicago Branch of the N.A.A.C.P."

The most dramatic challenge to Daley's hegemony came in the mid-sixties, from Martin Luther King, Jr. After winning victories on the streets of Selma, Montgomery, and Birmingham, after successfully pushing Lyndon Johnson on voting rights, King and his lieutenants started debating where and how to bring the campaign North. Adam Clayton Powell, among others, was unenthusiastic about having the movement come to New York, and so King started thinking that Chicago, with eight hundred thousand blacks, might be the right choice. At a downtown rally in 1965, King said:

> Chicago is the North's most segregated city. Negroes have continued to flee from behind the cotton curtain, but now they find that after years of indifference and exploitation, Chicago has not turned out to be the new Jerusalem. We are now protesting the educational and cultural shackles that are as binding as those of a Georgia chain gang.

Despite the warnings and the opposition of some members of his inner circle, King planted himself in Chicago and launched a bold, if vaguely conceived, anti-poverty and anti-discrimination plan. He rented an apartment in a grim building in Lawndale, on the West Side. "King decided to come to Chicago because Chicago was unique in that there was one man, one source of power," Arthur Brazier, the Pentecostal minister who worked with Saul Alinsky in Woodlawn, and then with King, said. "This wasn't the case in New York or any other city. He thought that if Daley could be persuaded of the rightness of open housing and integrated schools that things could be done."

Daley proved an elusive and stubborn foe. In the South, King had been helped by the grotesque dimensions and reliable brutality of his adversaries. Bull Connor, Jim Clark, and George Wallace were ideal foils for a movement steeped in the language of the Gospels and the tactics of Mahatma Gandhi. The moral contrast was, to millions of Americans, increasingly self-evident. In Daley, King faced a far craftier opponent, one gifted in the art of political manipulation, public compromise, and private deceits. And he was on his home turf.

At first, King's associate Andrew Young said, "We didn't see Mayor Daley as an enemy. In 1963, he had held one of the biggest, most successful benefits that S.C.L.C. had ever had at the time of Birmingham. Mayor Daley and Mahalia Jackson put it together." Daley's fear now was primal: if the civil-rights movement succeeded in registering more voters, it might threaten his coalition and the very existence of the machine. "The machine had served the black community well, but its days were over and we were there to announce that," Andrew Young said. "But Daley wasn't ready to turn loose."

Daley could rely on more than just the compliance of a cadre of black politicians. Many black clergymen, for instance, realized that if they sided overtly with King against City Hall they might suddenly lose their patronage. Who would give jobs to their parishioners? Who would pick up the garbage, repair the roads, maintain electricity and sewage, and prevent crime in the neighborhood? King could not provide these things, but Daley could take them away. He had the capacity to make life miserable. Dorothy Tillman, who came to town with King and the Southern Christian Leadership Conference, and who later became an alderman, said, "Chicago was the first city that we ever went to as members of the S.C.L.C. staff where the black ministers and black politicians told us to go back where we came from."

The Nation of Islam, under Elijah Muhammad, was a growing presence on the South Side, especially for disaffected young black men and women who had grown tired of the more obedient Christian ministers. But King could not expect any help from the Nation, which denounced integration. "If anything they were more zealous in support of segregation than Mayor Daley, since the mayor paid lip service to racial tolerance and the Muslims were black supremacists," Ralph Abernathy, King's closest adviser, wrote. "They would probably have joined us if we had proposed killing all the white people, but they certainly didn't want to listen to anyone preach the gospel of brotherly love."

The prospects for victory in Chicago were so grim that there was real division in King's own ranks. "I have never seen such hopelessness," Hosea Williams, a King adviser, said. "The Negroes of Chicago have a greater feeling of powerlessness than I've ever seen. They don't participate in the governmental process because they are beaten down psychologically. We are used to working with people who want to be free."

Nevertheless, King organized a huge rally for July 10, 1966, at the city's main football stadium, Soldier Field. On a ninety-eight-degree day, with thirty-eight thousand people in the seats, King was driven to the speaker's platform in the backseat of a white Cadillac convertible. Members of the Blackstone Rangers gang hoisted a Black Power flag. Mahalia Jackson, Stevie Wonder, and Peter Yarrow performed. And King, introduced by a leader of the Chicago archdiocese, gave a speech that announced the movement's weariness with the status quo in Chicago and the other industrial cities of the North:

> Yes, we are tired of being lynched physically in Mississippi, and we are tired of being lynched spiritually and economically in the North. We have also come here today to remind Chicago of the fierce urgency of now. This is no time to engage in the luxury of cooling off or to take the tranquilizing drug of gradualism. We have also come here today to affirm that we will no longer sit idly by in agonizing deprivation and wait on others to provide our freedom. . . . Freedom is never voluntarily granted by the oppressor. It must be demanded by the oppressed. . . .
>
> This day, henceforth and forever more, we must make it clear that we will purge Chicago of every politician, whether he be Negro or white, who feels that he owns the Negro vote rather than earns the Negro vote.

King not only employed one of his favorite phrases—"the fierce urgency of now," a phrase that he had employed at the March on Washington three years earlier to signal an unwillingness to delay—but also recognized the growing appeal of a more radical Black Power movement and tried to suggest the moral interdependence of the races: "The Negro needs the white man to free him from his fears. The white man needs the Negro to free him from his guilt. Any approach that overlooks this need for a coalition of conscience is unwise and misguided. A doctrine of black supremacy is as evil as a doctrine of white supremacy."

Then, after leading demonstrators on a long march downtown to City Hall, King, in an echo of Martin Luther nailing his ninety-five theses to the Castle Church door in Wittenberg, attached a list of demands for equality in housing, employment, and education to the Mayor's door.

Daley did not deny King an audience. Rather, he invited him into his office and then, with a combination of courtesy and stubborn guile, he paid lip service to greater equality if King would, in exchange, end his demonstrations and leave town. Occasionally, Arthur Brazier recalled, Daley poked King by noting that he was the head of the Southern Christian Leadership Conference, and saying, "So why are you here in Chicago? Why don't you go back South?"

King kept up the pressure, staging marches on the West Side, in black neighborhoods, where he was received warmly, and in white neighborhoods like Marquette Park, where he was greeted with shouts of "Go back to Africa!" and a rock that was hurled at his head, hitting him. "I've never seen anything like it in my life," King said. "I think the people from Mississippi ought to come to Chicago to learn how to hate."

"I'd never seen whites like these in the South," Dorothy Tillman said. "These whites was up in trees like monkeys throwing bricks and bottles and stuff. I mean, racism, you could almost cut it, a whole 'nother level of racism from hatred. And the sad thing about it was that most of those neighborhoods we went to were like first- or second-generation Americans. . . . Most of them were fleeing oppression."

Roger Wilkins, a young African-American lawyer working in Johnson's Justice Department, was dispatched to Chicago to talk to both sides and report back to Washington. Wilkins discovered that the tactics that had worked for the S.C.L.C. in the South had been rendered toothless in Chicago. Wilkins visited King at his apartment in Lawndale—"It was ugly and the stairwells stank of urine"—and found him negotiating with leaders of two gangs, the Blackstone Rangers and the Devil's Disciples, to march nonviolently against Daley and participate in various community programs. "The Illinois National Guard was out there in armored personnel carriers and these kids wanted to throw Molotov cocktails and Martin was saving their lives," Wilkins recalled. "He wouldn't let them go. He was conducting a nonviolence seminar." After the gang leaders left, King told Wilkins what he was learning in Chicago was that, in Wilkins's words, "you can have all the rights in the world, but if you were impoverished, those rights meant nothing; and if you went to a terrible school, you were nowhere. Martin now understood that the whole system was out of balance and, the way it was tilted, poor black people fell off. What he wanted to do now was not just about race. It was deeply about poverty." Wilkins was among those who thought that if King hadn't been killed, less than two years later, he would have started an anti-poverty movement no less profound than the civil-rights movement he had led in the South.

Daley made promises that he broke and offered compromises that he had no intention of adhering to. Tired and temporarily defeated, King left Chicago. "Like Herod, Richard Daley was a fox, too smart for us, too smart for the press . . . too smart for his own good, and for the good of Chicago," Ralph Abernathy wrote.

King's trials in Chicago, however, along with the war in Vietnam, helped to radicalize him. He began to realize that the problem of racism was even more deeply rooted than he had imagined. Chicago, David Halberstam wrote in a profile of King in *Harper's*, left him "closer to Malcolm than anyone would have predicted five years ago—and much farther from traditional allies like Whitney Young and Roy Wilkins." It was a defeat that led to his proposal, in 1967, for a Poor People's Campaign and a multibillion-dollar Marshall Plan for the inner cities.

When King was assassinated in Memphis on April 4, 1968, there was rioting in Chicago. Whole blocks on the West Side, the more recent of Chicago's black enclaves, were leveled. At a press conference, Daley betrayed how deep his antipathy toward the city's blacks now ran. He thought that the police had behaved with excessive restraint. Policemen should have had instructions, Daley said, "to shoot, to maim or cripple any arsonists and looters—arsonists to kill and looters to maim and detain."

It appeared that Daley, using both political guile and sheer brutality, had crushed the forces of reform that had "invaded" his city: the Woodlawn Organization, the S.C.L.C., the hippies, the Yippies, and S.D.S. Daley's victories, however, were far from permanent. Gradually, even some of the older, obedient politicians of the black sub-machine changed their minds.

Ralph Metcalfe, a silver medalist in the hundred-meter dash at the 1936 Olympics in Berlin and a boss of the Third Ward, was a prime example. Metcalfe was Dawson's protégé and his successor in Congress—a loyal member of the machine. When King came to Chicago, Metcalfe was among those black leaders who said that he wasn't wanted: "We have adequate leadership here." In 1972, police pulled over a black dentist, a friend of Metcalfe's, and handcuffed and bullied him for no reason. Not long afterward, another black dentist who was driving had a stroke and hit a parked car; the police held him in jail for five hours and he went into a coma. Metcalfe asked Daley to come to his office, but Daley refused; after these outrages, Metcalfe broke with Daley and the machine, saying, "The Mayor doesn't understand what happens to black men on the streets of Chicago and probably never will."

Richard J. Daley died, in 1976, after twenty-one years in office. Even his most loyal aides could not say that he had succeeded in holding off racial change in Chicago. "What Daley did was smother King," his press secretary, Earl Bush, told the Chicago *Sun-Times* in 1986. "What Daley couldn't smother was the civil-rights movement."

Daley was succeeded by Michael Bilandic, another machine politician from Bridgeport, who served ineptly until 1979, and then by Jane Byrne, who ran as a reformer in the city's first post-Daley election but, once elected, ignored her minority allies from the campaign and governed with an assemblage of machine hacks. When it was time for her re-election campaign in 1983, she faced two opponents, the scion, Richard M. Daley, and Harold Washington, a congressman from the South Side.

Harold Washington started out as a cog in the machine—his father was a precinct captain in Bronzeville; his mentor was Ralph Metcalfe—but both as a state senator in Springfield and as a member of Congress, he became a favorite of liberal whites along the Lakefront and South Side blacks looking for an effective new generation of leadership. Despite the shadow cast by Daley, there was a progressive tradition in Chicago politics: Ida Wells, Jane Addams, Saul Alinsky, Adlai Stevenson, Paul Douglas, the Independent Voters of Illinois, the various streams of black integrationists and more radical activists on the South Side. Washington, who was far more intellectual than he usually let on, was a student of his city's progressives, and he set out to win the mayoralty by drawing on those traditions and on his own deep experience in the maelstrom of Chicago politics.

In the Democratic primary, Washington's supporters hoped that Byrne and Daley would split the white ethnic vote and that Washington could succeed with a combination of blacks and just enough white liberals to win. In majority-black cities like Gary, Cleveland, and Detroit, a new generation of black mayors had already come to office. In Chicago, where African-Americans made up just forty per cent of the population, the demographics were less stark. Washington, using rhetoric that was echoed (if less bluntly) by Barack Obama a generation later, refused to assume the mantle of a racial candidate.

"I'm sick and tired of being called 'the black candidate,' " he said at the opening of a campaign office. "They don't talk about Jane Byrne as the white candidate. I don't even want to be called 'intelligent.' That's a put-down. It's manifestly obvious I am intelligent. Nor is it necessary to constantly refer to me as 'articulate.' Why don't they just come out and say I know what I'm talking about? Richard M. Daley believes he should be mayor simply because his father was. We don't have the divine right of kings in this country, I don't think."

Washington did not start out with a great deal of national help. Former Vice-President Walter Mondale, who was hoping to upset President Reagan the following year, supported Daley; Edward Kennedy, an important figure for Illinois Democrats, supported Byrne. The only newspaper to endorse Washington was the *Defender*. His fund-raising was limited and much of his grassroots support came from local churches.

Among the ministers who worked hard for Washington was the charismatic leader of the Trinity United Church of Christ on Ninety-fifth Street, the Reverend Jeremiah Wright. Wright and some of his colleagues collected names for a pro-Washington advertisement in the *Defender*. The ad said that the black church "which stands firmly in the tradition of Dr. Martin Luther King, Jr.," and "stands on the shoulders of those African slaves who sang 'Before I'd be a slave, I'd be buried in my grave,' " could only support Harold Washington. To describe their point of view, the writers of the advertisement called themselves "unashamedly black and unapologetically Christian"—a phrase that Wright eventually adopted as the motto of his church.

Washington crushed Daley and Byrne in the debates, and his strategy paid off with a narrow win in the primary. "You don't have to be blessed with a great imagination to see the parallels between Harold Washington in 1983 and Barack Obama in 2008," Clarence Page, a Pulitzer Prize–winning Chicago *Tribune* columnist who covered both races, said. "In 1983, you had the strong female incumbent, Byrne; the populist of the bungalow belt, Richie Daley; and the black spoiler. The breakthrough quality for Harold Washington was his oratory. The morning after that first debate, after Harold won so decisively, you saw Washington buttons all around town. And then, of course, the moment he won the Democratic primary a miracle occurred—half of Chicago went Republican overnight. And you had the black base asking if Harold was 'black enough' and whites thinking he was 'too black.' Sounds a little familiar, doesn't it?"

Chicago had long been a bastion of Democratic Party rule, but now, whites all over the city were newborn Republicans, and it barely mattered who the Republican nominee was. Racial animosities were so intense that nearly any sentient white Republican stood at least some chance of beating an African-American Democrat. The Republicans also had a point of attack: they were able to bring up, repeatedly, the fact that Washington had failed to file his income-tax forms for many years (although he paid the actual tax revenue); in 1972, a federal judge handed down a two-year sentence, then suspended all but five weeks of it.

Washington's Republican opponent, Bernard Epton, was from Hyde Park and had a reputation as a principled man. He was an early opponent of McCarthyism. He had marched with the sanitation workers in Memphis after Martin Luther King was there. As a state representative, he'd fought against racist real-estate practices. Epton ran for the Republican nomination with the expectation that (a) he would be running against Daley or Byrne and (b) that he would probably lose.

When Washington won the nomination, Epton said the right thing: "I don't want to be elected because I am white." But he rapidly betrayed himself. As his ambition intensified, he began to give himself over to Washington, D.C.-based Republican consultants who came up with a campaign slogan that appealed to racist instincts: "Epton for Mayor. Before It's Too Late." Some of Epton's supporters distributed leaflets saying they refused to vote for a "baboon"; others wore buttons that were just white. On the streets of white ethnic neighborhoods there were leaflets describing Washington's "campaign promises": "Raise Whitey's Taxes!" was one. "Replace CTA buses with Eldorados!" was another. The leaflets had Washington moving City Hall to Martin Luther King Drive and relocating a city bureaucracy to Leon's Rib Basket. Another flyer implied that Washington was guilty of child molestation.

Leanita McClain, a black member of the *Tribune*'s editorial board, described in a column the vicious racial atmosphere during the campaign:

> The Chicago *Tribune* endorsed Harold Washington in a long and eloquent Sunday editorial. It was intended to persuade the bigots. It would have caused any sensible person at least to think. It failed. The mail and calls besieged the staff. The middle range of letters had the words "LIES" and "NIGGER LOVERS" scratched across the editorial.
>
> Hoping to shame these people, make them look at themselves, the newspaper printed a full page of these rantings. But when the mirror was presented to them, the bigots reveled before it. The page only gave them aid and comfort in knowing their numbers. That is what is wrong with this town; being a racist is as respectable and expected as going to church.
>
> Filthy literature littered the city streets like the propaganda air blitzes of World War II. The subway would be renamed "Soul Train." . . . In the police stations, reports were whispered about fights between longtime black and white squad-car partners. Flyers proclaiming the new city of "Chicongo," with crossed drumsticks as the city seal, were tacked to police station bulletin boards. The schools actually formulated plans to deal with racial violence, just in case.

Haskel Levy, an aide to Bernard Epton, told him that he was becoming the unwitting tool of a racist campaign. But, instead of repudiating racism, Epton repudiated Haskel Levy. He threw Levy's coat into the hall and told him, "Get the fuck out!"

The erstwhile man of principle doubled down as he smelled victory. "I am not ashamed of being white!" Epton now declared. He told a crowd of Republicans in the Forty-seventh Ward, "Some of my great liberal friends feel they have to prove they are liberal by voting for a black who was sentenced to jail and who's supposed to run a city budget of two billion dollars plus. They call that liberalism. I call it sheer idiocy." Epton now seemed to relish his ability to rev up white crowds and their resentments. A young reporter for the *Tribune*, David Axelrod, described Epton as "volatile and capricious, prone to inexplicable outbursts and fits."

Naturally, Harold Washington was furious. He accused Epton, who had once been a friendly colleague in Springfield, of unleashing "the dogs of racism."

There was no doubt that Epton had done the unleashing, but Washington used wit rather than anger to deflect the worst of it. When asked on a radio call-in show if, as mayor, he would replace all the city's elevators with jungle vines, Washington cracked, "I don't think we have three million Tarzans in this city."

The racist fury was never more in evidence than on March 27, 1983, Palm Sunday. Accompanied by Vice-President Mondale, Washington went to St. Pascal's, a Catholic church in the northwest of the city. He was greeted by a racist mob shouting, "Nigger die" and "Carpetbagger!" and "Epton!" Someone had scrawled the graffito "Nigger die!" on the church. During the service, the demonstrators outside were so disruptive that Mondale and Washington had to leave. Soon afterward, the campaign became a national story with *Newsweek* publishing a cover feature on "Chicago's Ugly Election." David Axelrod covered the event for the *Tribune*. "It was one of the worst things I have ever seen," he recalled. "The racism was unguarded, full-throated. I thought people were going to get hurt, or worse."

In Chicago, Democrats routinely beat Republicans for mayor and just about every other local office, by landslides. But, despite that history, and the huge difference in party registration, Washington beat Epton by just over three per cent of the vote. Washington's campaign had united integrationists, black nationalists, Lakefront liberals, business people, community activists, church people, college students, and sixties-era leftists. That was just enough. An alarming number of whites, traditional Democrats, loyal to the old and hobbled machine, crossed over and voted for Epton—or, rather, against Washington. In the end, Washington's victory was due mainly to a record turnout among African-Americans.

When Washington's team organized a "unity breakfast" after the election and invited Epton to come, Epton refused, preferring to escape to

Florida instead. But nothing could deflate the elation of the winner's supporters. "For blacks, Washington's victory was like the coming of the messiah," Don Rose, one of his campaign aides, said. "The feeling was: the veil of oppression was lifted by one of us, and we did it. It was the original 'Yes We Can.' "

As a young organizer, Obama absorbed these momentous events. He read up on them, asked about them, sought out conversations with people who remembered not just Daley and King but Dawson and De Priest. In *Dreams from My Father*, he captures the adulation of Harold Washington in his Hyde Park barbershop, describes the sense of hope the new city administration brought to the slums of the West Side and the housing projects of the South Side. It was part of the talk Obama, as a young community organizer, was hearing every day.

In office, Washington set out to be the mayor of all the city's neighborhoods and people. He also wanted to create a governing coalition capable of resisting the anti–New Deal ideology, racial indifference, and draconian cutbacks of Ronald Reagan, who had come to power two years before.

Harold Washington had worked as a teenager for the Civilian Conservation Corps, served in an engineering battalion in the Pacific theater during the Second World War, and worked his way up through the political ranks in Chicago's Third Ward. His sympathies were with the thousands of steelworkers who had been laid off and then denied benefits when the mills closed. In Washington's eyes, his victory was not solely an African-American victory, but a victory—no matter what the polls suggested—for a "multiethnic, multiracial, multilanguage city," as he said in his first inaugural address. At his victory celebration the band played "Take the 'A' Train" but also "Hava Nagila," "Bésame Mucho," "When Irish Eyes Are Smiling," "Auf Wiedersehen," "O Sole Mio," and "Fanfare for the Common Man." Washington's desire to extend a hand even to his enemies, rather than concentrate his efforts on the people who had elected him, alienated some of the nationalist activists in his electoral coalition—important voices like the journalist Lutrelle Palmer. "He never became what I would consider the black Mayor," Palmer once said. "Black people wanted something that was so simple: fairness. . . . Harold was *too* fair."

Obama was too young to have memories of the Kennedys and King. Harold Washington was the first elected politician in his lifetime who inspired him. For Obama, Washington's career suggested the value of a life on the inside, in politics. Mike Kruglik believed almost from the start that Obama was considering running for office one day—for mayor, perhaps. "Barack admired Harold Washington, he was inspired by him," Kruglik said, "and when he thought about the path to power himself he thought of becoming a lawyer, then a state legislator, then a congressman, then mayor—like Harold. Even before Harvard Law School, he thought about that. He would say, 'If you really want to get something done, maybe being mayor will help.' It was a matter of power integrated with purpose."

Obama's admiration was not absolute. Washington ran a disorganized office and was faced with constant opposition from the old machine aldermen on the City Council. "We were cynical about Harold, even though you couldn't help but like him," Jerry Kellman said. "Harold was interested in Harold. Barack was frustrated sometimes with the lack of responsiveness of Washington to the community and saw him as complex and flawed." The problem, Kellman said, "was that if Barack was going to get to a position of political power in Illinois his only option was Washington's path—from the state legislature, to Congress, to mayor. Racial politics precluded anything else. This was true as far as any of us could see at the time. But Barack did not see himself as another Harold Washington. He saw himself as having skills and a perspective from organizing that Harold did not have, and Barack hoped to find a way to put them to use."

For the time being, though, Obama could not afford to linger over the ramifications of political forces beyond his control. His daily work was in church basements, high-school gymnasiums, the waiting rooms of broken bureaucracies. These were the scenes of his political education. He was interviewing people: priests, ministers, activists, local officials, police officers, teachers, principals, workers, hustlers, shopkeepers. An organizer interviews people incessantly, asking them about their lives, their tragedies and frustrations, their desires and aspirations. Obama and his colleagues counted themselves failures if they were seen as visitors. The more they made themselves fixtures in the community, the better their chances of success.

"Narrative is the most powerful thing we have," Kellman said. "From a spiritual point of view, much of what is important about us can't be seen. If we don't know people's stories we don't know who they are. If you want to understand them or try to help them, you have to find out their story."

While Obama formed friendships in Hyde Park, the greater South Side was his community, the focus of his work and life. The closer he became to people on the South Side, the more he was able to get them to trust in the possibility of change. "Barack enjoys people and forms strong attachments," Kellman said. "He had the opportunity to do that here, unlike in New York City. There was an opportunity for intimacy. He wanted to get to know the black community and he felt very much at home. He wanted to be effective. And people would ask him questions: 'What church do you belong to?' 'Are you just here for a few months or are you really going to stay in Chicago?' 'Who are your mom and dad?' These questions, which seemed pretty innocent for most people, were very complicated for Barack. But he gradually became a Chicagoan and really fell in love with the city. He was in his element on the South Side. He comes to a community that is thought to be homogeneous but it really is diverse in income and many other ways. Give Barack diversity and he is king of the room. The diversity of the black community was a real plus. He could move in different worlds here, more so than anywhere else. There are so many communities in Chicago. Al Sharpton could never have risen to the kind of prominence he has in New York in Chicago. With time, even Jesse Jackson began to seem not sophisticated enough for this community."

Community organizing has a miserable success rate. For every triumph like Alinsky's in Woodlawn, there are dozens of failures, projects begun with high hopes that fizzle out in a splutter of indifference and frustration. To the local residents, young organizers can seem a vaguely comical, if well-meaning, nuisance. "We were always asking each other, 'Why do this work that busts your balls so bad all the time?' " Mike Kruglik recalled.

One winter morning, soon after he started working as an organizer, Obama was waiting outside a school to deliver some leaflets. An administrative aide from the school who had got to know him said, "Listen, Obama. You're a bright young man, Obama. You went to college, didn't you?"

Obama nodded.

"I just cannot understand why a bright young man like you would go to college, get that degree, and become a community organizer."

"Why's that?" Obama said.

" 'Cause the pay is low, the hours is long, and don't nobody appreciate you."

In South Side neighborhoods like Roseland, West Pullman, and Altgeld Gardens, a grimly isolated project on the far South Side, Obama tried to make inroads. Relying largely on the support of ten Catholic parishes (and their white priests), Obama hoped to organize black neighborhoods whose residents were, for the most part, Baptist or Pentecostal. He moved from church to church, trying to enlist ministers in his effort. One day he rang the doorbell at the Lilydale First Baptist Church on 113th Street. A young minister named Alvin Love answered and wondered, Who *is* this skinny kid?

"I didn't know what an organizer was," Love said. "I was young and had about two hundred members. And we started talking. He gave me his spiel about his name and his background. He said his accent was Kansan and explained why." Obama asked what issues were on Love's mind, and Love talked about crime, graffiti, break-ins, gangs, the explosion of crack cocaine. "We were both young, and I was trying to figure out how to get my church involved in the community," Love said. "I saw him as a gift from Heaven." Obama explained that, until then, the organizers had been white and Catholic; he was trying to broaden things to reach all the "stakeholders" in the area.

"So I threw in with him," Love recalled. In the months to come, Obama kept trying to widen his circle of activists in Love's parish and elsewhere, training them at weekly sessions in church basements and community rooms.

Most of Obama's days were pure frustration. It was the norm to work for years on a project—a battle against the expansion of dangerous toxic-waste dumps, for example—and head toward a seeming victory, only to have it all be forgotten on some bureaucrat's desk downtown. But Obama was getting an education: political, racial, and sentimental. He met all kinds of people he had never encountered in Hawaii or in college: young black nationalists, full of pride, but also too willing to listen to conspiracy theories about Koreans funding the Klan and Jewish doctors injecting black babies with AIDS. He met teachers full of idealism and compassion, but also exhausted by the chaos in their classrooms. He met government officials, preachers, single mothers and their children, school principals, small-business people, all of them telling Obama their fears and frustrations. He had learned a lot from books, but there was something far more immediate, visceral, and lasting about the education he was getting now. It was the nature of his work to ask questions, to listen. He called the narratives he was collecting "sacred stories."

Obama had read Saul Alinsky, but he did not adopt his confrontational style. He was methodical about his interviews and compiling his reports; polite, even charming, with his contacts; but reluctant to mix it up. Kellman's steely approach to organizing was not Obama's. Kellman worried that his protégé was too analytical and mild. He also worried that he had asked too much of Obama, that it was easy for him to get lost on the vast South Side. There were some small victories: the creation of a drug-prevention program in the schools called Project Impact; an initiative to get the city to release promised funding for a majority-black school, the Chicago High School for Agricultural Sciences on 111th Street. But Kellman feared that a tide of frustration would sweep Obama away. He asked Obama to come work with him in Gary, but Obama refused. He had made a life on the South Side.

"What I saw in Barack was caution, lots of caution," Kellman said. "I have the opposite tendency, which is impulsivity. Barack thinks. He agonizes before doing anything risky. And when you are an organizer you have to do things that are designed to get a reaction. Every time he had to gather people and bring them to someone's office, he worried: Am I being too confrontational? He didn't want to betray a relationship. That's why he wasn't Alinsky-like. There is a machismo which makes organizers afraid to admit that they are moved by ideals rather than self-interest. But most of what we do in life is, of course, a combination of both. Barack understood this, and so did I, and so the Alinsky teaching on self-interest was balanced with Dr. King's appeals to our mutuality. What he did embrace completely was the need for power to get anything done and the operating definition of power in a democracy as organized people and organized money. He thought he could fold organizing into politics and saw himself as an organizer-politician. He still does, as far as I can tell."

In his first year in Chicago, Obama worked part of the time in Altgeld Gardens, a vast project on the far South Side. Altgeld Gardens—or "the Gardens," as residents call it—unlike towering projects such as the Robert Taylor Homes (now torn down), is a sprawl of two-story bungalows with around fifteen hundred apartments. Opened in 1945 to house returning African-American war veterans, Altgeld is the most isolated project in the city, distant from any shopping or public services, though it is not the poorest. The apartments are modest but usually well kept. By the time Obama arrived, most of the residents were single mothers living, and struggling, on public assistance. The menace of the place came from the gangs, which made it dangerous at night; from a sewage treatment plant to the north that emitted what Obama called a "heavy putrid odor"; from the grim, sour-smelling Calumet River to the west, with its rusted tankers; and from the foul, unregulated landfills all around.

Obama spent his first months at Altgeld just talking with people in the schools and churches. He clearly did not have access to funds to improve the most obvious problems. So he asked people at school parents' meetings to fill out complaint forms.

At around the same time, in the spring of 1986, Linda Randle, an organizer at the immense Ida B. Wells public housing project on Martin

Luther King Drive, arrived at Building 534 and noticed an enormous yellow tarp and, behind it, a loud machine. As she came closer, flecks of an unknown substance hit her in the face. She asked what was going on.

"Two guys came out in space suits," Randle recalled. "I knocked on their masks and said, 'What are you all doing?'"

"We're removing asbestos," one of them said. Once used as insulation, asbestos, as it crumbles, can lead to lung cancer and other diseases if inhaled.

"From the whole building?" Randle asked.

"No, just on the first floor."

The building was huge, and Randle wondered why the workers were limiting themselves to the administrative offices. More than ten thousand people lived at Ida B. Wells and the workers weren't touching the apartments where the residents lived. Randle stripped some insulation—asbestos—off a pipe and put it in a bag. She talked to the director of tenant services and asked what was going on: "He told me, 'Linda, there is no money to be made in this. Leave it alone.' I told him, 'O.K.,' and went out the door to another neighbor's house. I called the E.P.A. and asked them to come out and analyze it. I also pulled up loose floor tiles. And so he came out and he took the stuff to be analyzed."

While waiting for the test results, Randle called Martha Allen, a writer for *The Chicago Reporter*, an investigative monthly. Some of the residents told Randle and Allen that children had been eating fallen bits of asbestos. Allen interviewed residents, doctors, officials from the E.P.A., and the city, and compiled a brilliant investigative article for *The Reporter*'s June, 1986, issue. It concluded that thousands of people living at the Ida B. Wells Homes were living at risk. The photograph on the front page showed a seven-year-old girl named Sarah Jefferson, holding her niece, Mahaid, on her lap; next to them is a heating pipe covered with tattered asbestos insulation.

Randle went to an organizing group called the Community Renewal Society. There she met Obama for the first time. ("He looked so young!") Obama told her that he had had a similar experience at Altgeld Gardens. Since 1979, people in the project had been trying to do something about asbestos, and recently a woman at the Gardens had pointed out a classified ad in a local paper: the Chicago Housing Authority was soliciting bids to remove asbestos—not from all the apartments but from the management office. Obama organized a delegation of Altgeld women to go to the manager and confront him. The manager lied, saying that there was no asbestos in the residential units.

Obama and Randle soon learned that sixteen of the nineteen public housing projects in Chicago had asbestos: Wells was the largest of them, and Altgeld the second largest. "We talked about the injustice of it," Randle said. "We knew we had to do something about this."

In Chicago and in most cities, Kellman said, "environmental issues didn't usually lead to action in those days—people were most concerned about drugs and gangs and crime—but you could work with a sense of outrage about privilege."

At Altgeld, Obama worked with his colleagues Yvonne Lloyd and Loretta Augustine-Herron. In 1966, Augustine-Herron, her husband, who was employed at the post office, and their children had been forced to move out of the project because they no longer met the low-income requirement. In 1967, her oldest daughter was stricken with leukemia and, two years later, died. "Altgeld is built on polluted ground and I'd read and heard rumors about pollution causing cancer," she said. "As I became more interested in this, I realized that more and more of my neighbors were getting sick with cancer and respiratory diseases. The problem was who to turn to and what to do to make things better." She found solace in talking to Obama. "Barack had the sensitivity," Augustine-Herron said. Even before the asbestos issue arose, Obama spent many hours talking with her at her kitchen table about her family, and the problems of the South Side. "Barack is six months older than my eldest child," she said. "I think I got to know him really well. And I talked a lot to him about my daughter."

At first, Obama and the others thought that they could solve the problem by arranging a meeting with the executive director of the Chicago Housing Authority, Zirl Smith. When Obama, Randle, and about ten others arrived downtown in a rented schoolbus for an 11 A.M. meeting with Smith, he kept them waiting. Randle, however, had called reporters and told them to show up at noon. When the reporters arrived, they started asking questions about the asbestos problem at Altgeld Gardens and Ida B. Wells. A local television station filmed one of the women describing the problem and put her on the air later that day. Once Smith's secretary noticed the reporters, though, she quickly ushered the group into an empty office.

"They offered us coffee and doughnuts and said, 'The director will be with you soon,'" Randle recalled. "Now the media couldn't see us." They waited for two more hours. Finally, Randle told Obama they should leave, and they did. While they were waiting for the bus, Randle told Obama, "Barack, this is the beginning of a long struggle for us. We can't do C.H.A. first; we have to go to H.U.D. first"—the federal Department of Housing and Urban Development. "You go first to the top of the mountain." When they got back home, Obama and Randle started giving out the number of Zirl Smith to residents of the projects. "Light up the phones," they told them.

What thrilled Obama was not so much the subsequent news coverage as the fact that the women he had helped organize and brought downtown on the bus were able to speak so clearly, if nervously, in front of the cameras. His delegation was smaller than he had hoped, but its members had banded together, wryly calling themselves Obama's Army. They had a nickname for Obama—Baby Face.

Obama wrote that the trip to the C.H.A. with his little army changed him "in a fundamental way." It wasn't the smattering of publicity that they received, and it certainly wasn't any concrete success—the asbestos remained for years. Rather, for a young man not long out of college, it was an indication of what might be possible. But he soon saw the limits of that promise.

When Obama and the others finally met with officials from H.U.D. and the C.H.A., they were told that they could not get both asbestos removal *and* basic repairs. ("I had a *big* hole in my bathtub!" Randle said.) The agencies tried to undermine the organizers by going to key residents and fixing their plumbing. After yet more meetings, Zirl Smith agreed to try to do better. "He didn't know where he was going to get the money for asbestos but he would try," Randle said. "I called Barack and said, I don't know if he is playing games, but we have to continue working on this."

Martha Allen's article in *The Chicago Reporter* created interest in the larger, mainstream media in town. Walter Jacobson did a report on WBBM and both the *Tribune* and the *Sun-Times* began to write about the problem.

At that point, Obama organized a mass meeting at Our Lady of the Gardens with Zirl Smith. More than seven hundred people showed up in the church's stiflingly hot gym—most of them single women, but also older people, children, and even reporters.

Ordinarily, Obama had a penchant for organization—scripting meetings, preparing speakers and backup speakers, jotting notes on a clipboard, and then holding follow-up sessions to evaluate how they had done. But he could not lead this meeting the way he had hoped. The crowd, which was already angry, was incensed when Smith was more than an hour late. The public-address system was scratchy and weak. Kellman tried to take the lead, orchestrating a chant, but Obama quickly pulled him aside, telling him that perhaps it was not the best idea to have a white organizer leading a pep rally at Altgeld Gardens.

"He asked me to be a little less visible," Kellman recalled. "He was very stressed. It was still his first year."

Obama kept handing the microphone over to his activists, hoping that they could educate the crowd on the asbestos problem and kill time until Zirl Smith arrived. There was shouting and booing. At last, Smith showed up; Obama told one female activist that they should not give up the microphone lest Smith monopolize the entire discussion. Randle began by asking Smith whether he was going to address the problem—yes or no. As Smith prepared to respond, she did not hand him the microphone but, rather, pointed it toward his mouth. He began by promising to work on the problem—"We're trying to determine the severity of the asbestos. . . ."—but made it plain that if she didn't give him the mike he was going to leave. After nearly two hours of waiting, the crowd was in a state of sweaty irritation. Someone in the crowd fell ill. Smith said that he would call an ambulance from his car. Still, no one would give him the mike. And so after ten minutes, he left the church gymnasium in a huff.

"Chaos! Our wonderful meeting had turned to chaos!" Randle said.

"No more rent!" some of the Altgeld tenants cried as Smith headed for his car.

Obama was humiliated. The possibility that he had felt at the C.H.A. office in the Loop had now evaporated. Several women approached him and yelled at him for embarrassing them, for making them look like fools in front of city officials and the TV cameras.

That night, Obama called his colleague John Owens, an African-American organizer who had gone with him that summer to a training retreat at a monastery near Malibu, California. Obama was stricken. At the retreat they had worked hard on all the fundamentals of organizing—preparation, interviews, power analysis, tactics—but now his plans had ended in a shambles. "Barack was really embarrassed," Owens said. "He thought he hadn't prepped everyone the way he should have."

This was 1986. Most of the asbestos was not removed until 1990 and some was not removed for years after that. But the city did begin to act. The C.H.A. started more testing, established an "asbestos hotline" to answer questions about health hazards, and appealed to the federal government to pay for asbestos removal in the projects. It would take time, but by organizing standards that was a good outcome.

Yet most of what was miserable about Altgeld Gardens in 1986 is still miserable. And over the next two years, working on issues of school reform, job banks, and public safety at the Gardens and in other neighborhoods on the South Side, Obama made far less progress.

"It was hard for all of us," Linda Randle said. "In your struggles as an organizer, you have more losses than you have wins. It goes with the territory. You are out there all day and you talk with people and you think they are getting it but they haven't really. So you have to step back and maybe go at it from a different angle and figure out where they want to go. Over and over again."

"Organizing is a Sisyphean endeavor," Kruglik said, recalling that night in Altgeld. "The power structure in a place like Chicago is not much different than it was thirty or forty years ago. Barack was angry about how people suffered, the injustice of that kind of poverty. He knew that people suffered like that because of the decisions that people in power made."

In those years, Obama spent a lot of time thinking about faith and religion. At every church and community center he visited, sooner or later someone asked him what church he belonged to. Obama danced around the question, changed the subject.

"He was constantly being pressured about joining a church," Alvin Love, of Lilydale First Baptist Church, said. "I didn't push the way other ministers in D.C.P. [Developing Communities Project] did, so he was comfortable talking about it with me. He knew it was inconsistent to be a church-based organizer without being a member of any church, and he was feeling that pressure. He said, 'I believe, but I don't want to join a church for convenience' sake. I want to be serious and be comfortable wherever I join.' He would *visit* churches. You never knew when he was visiting whether he was doing that as an organizer or coming to worship. Over the years, I had the feeling it was to worship as much as it was for work."

Love recommended that Obama seek the advice of an older pastor, L. K. Curry, at Emmanuel Baptist Church on Eighty-third Street. After hearing Obama talk about both his spiritual search and his interest in issues of social justice, Curry recommended that Obama pay a call on one of the best-known ministers on the South Side, Jeremiah Wright, the pastor of Trinity United Church of Christ on Ninety-fifth Street. No organizing effort would fail to gain from Wright's support—and, besides, Curry told Obama, he might like what he found inside the chapel.

The son and grandson of pastors, Jeremiah Wright grew up in the racially mixed neighborhood of Germantown, in Philadelphia. He attended Virginia Union University from 1959 to 1961, a historically black college in Richmond, and then spent six years in the military—he was in the Marines from 1961 to 1963 and then trained as a cardiopulmonary technician at the National Naval Medical Center in Bethesda,

Maryland. In 1966, the year before he left the military, he was part of a team that cared for Lyndon Johnson after he underwent heart surgery. Wright finished his bachelor's degree and got a master's in English at Howard University, and then received another master's, in the history of religions, at the University of Chicago.

Compared with most African-Americans, in the South and in the Northern cities, Wright had a middle-class upbringing, but not a sheltered one. In a sermon that deeply affected Obama, "The Audacity to Hope," Wright confided that when he was fifteen he was arrested for auto theft and that when he went away to college he briefly left the church and, under the influence of Malcolm X, flirted with Islam: "I tried one brief time being a Muslim: '*As salaam alaikum.*' " He had experienced racism—in Virginia, in the military, even in enlightened Germantown—and understood the complexes that came with it. "When I was growing up," he said in a sermon called "Unhitch the Trailer," "folks used to buy a bleaching cream called Nadinola to try to change what God had done."

In the nineteen-sixties, the United Church of Christ, a mainly white denomination, established a small parish on the South Side, at Ninety-fifth Street, hoping to draw on the privately owned homes in the area. In the early nineteen-seventies, the parishioners at the new church, Trinity, wanted to play gospel music rather than the traditional Anglo-European hymns; they wanted the church to be more involved in the civil-rights movement, in social activism, in African culture. Most of the ministers on the South Side at the time were cultural conservatives: wary of the black liberation movement; wary of reform in their services; reluctant to adopt political positions that would put them in opposition to their patrons in City Hall. As a result, young people, searching for greater black identity as well as a spiritual home, were leaving the church for the Nation of Islam, black nationalism, or small sects like the Black Hebrew Israelites. Trinity promised a Christian home for young people who were politically and socially aware, and wanted that awareness to be part of their church.

Jeremiah Wright, who arrived in Chicago in 1969 and became Trinity's pastor in March, 1972, was among the young clergymen who reacted to the changing political atmosphere and rose to the challenge from rival confessions and sects. He had grown up in an educated household filled with both memories of segregation in Virginia and intense discussion about the heroes of black culture and education. At Virginia Union, he had become increasingly politicized, and at Howard he had heard Stokely Carmichael preach the ideas of Black Power, read the books of Afrocentric scholars such as Cheikh Anta Diop, and studied with some of the faculty's most charismatic black scholars, including Sterling Brown. That was the moment, he said, "when the kids turned black." Wright, like many other young, educated preachers, felt that the time had come for a black church that was a center of racial solidarity and social justice, just as it had been in the years leading toward the Civil War. It was, Wright felt, as if he had been preparing to take over at a church like Trinity all his life.

"The members of this church said, 'No, no, no—we're not going to become Islamic or Hebrew, we're Christian,' " Wright told me. "We're going to be a black church in the black community. As a matter of fact, we're doing nothing in this community. We need to change." In Chicago, Wright had seen churches that either had "throw-down good music" or "a strong social justice component," but rarely both. Wright wanted both. He presented himself to Trinity as a devout intellectual, seminary-trained, and also as a modern race man determined to build a church community committed not only to civil rights but to the day-to-day problems that afflicted so many on the South Side: crime, gangs, drugs, pregnant teenagers, discrimination, poverty, poor education.

Wright began at Trinity with fewer than a hundred worshippers. At first, he told Roger Wilkins for the 1987 PBS documentary "Keeping the Faith," Trinity was a "white church in blackface." Eventually, he expanded the church to more than six thousand parishioners. He created dozens of educational programs and became one of the leading exemplars of black-liberation theology in the country. Wright's politics embraced not only the liberal and radical leaders of civil rights and Black Power—in 1977, he hung up a banner on the church reading, "Free South Africa"—but also an unusually progressive set of social views. He approved of female pastors, preached tolerance of homosexuals, and provided counseling for victims of H.I.V./AIDS. Above all, Wright was considered a brilliant preacher. In 1993, *Ebony* published a poll of the top fifteen black preachers in the country; Wright was second only to Gardner Taylor, and was one of the youngest in an august group including Samuel D. Proctor, Charles Adams, and Otis Moss, Jr.

An important contemporary intellectual influence on Wright and his church was James Cone, a brilliant young professor of divinity from Fordyce, Arkansas. After enduring the humiliations of the Jim Crow South in his youth, Cone reacted to the ferment of the 1967 riots in Detroit by writing *Black Theology and Black Power,* an impassioned manifesto for a black church determined to "emancipate the gospel from its 'whiteness' so that blacks may be capable of making an honest self-affirmation through Jesus Christ." The book was published in 1969, when Cone was thirty-one.

A student of the modern European theologians—Paul Tillich and Karl

Barth, in particular—Cone recognized that, while his church preached justice and mercy, it had little or nothing to say about the suffering in his community. In an America that continued to oppress blacks, the church that preached a gospel of Christ must demand radical change: "Unless theology can become 'ghetto theology,' a theology which speaks to black people, the gospel message has no promise of life for the black man—it is a lifeless message." Cone had thought about leaving the church but decided instead to transform it. Blackness, for Cone, became a central metaphor for Christian suffering and Christianity itself a "religion of protest against the suffering and affliction of man." The text of *Black Theology and Black Power* cites the European theologians that Cone had been studying as a divinity student and as a young pastor, but it also leans on the ideas and language of Frederick Douglass, Frantz Fanon, the Declaration of Independence, Martin Luther King, Malcolm X, and James Baldwin. Its tone is unapologetically ferocious. By way of explanation (and certainly not apology), Cone quotes Baldwin: "To be a Negro in this country and to be relatively conscious is to be in rage almost all of the time." Cone's book conceives a radical synthesis of Christian faith and Black Power, King's message of love and Malcolm's of insistence. For Cone, Christianity must focus on the oppressed, and for that role God has obviously chosen black men and women. (At times, Cone cautions that his concept of "blackness" is not restricted to African-Americans but, rather, is a metaphor for the dispossessed; he is not a separatist or a supremacist.)

Cone reminds the reader that the American black church, born in slavery, was a singular institution, posed against a white society that had robbed black men and women of their liberty, families, languages, and social cohesion. The spirituals, Cone writes, were not merely protest songs but a "psychological adjustment to the existence of serfdom."

The black-liberation theology that Cone conceived and that Wright brought to his church is rooted in nineteenth-century ideas: in David Walker's abolitionist *Appeal*, published in 1829, which refers to the "God of the Ethiopians"; in Frederick Douglass's slave narrative that distinguishes between the Christianity of Jesus Christ ("good, pure, and holy") and Christianity in America ("bad, corrupt, and wicked"); in Bishop Henry McNeal Turner's newspaper, *Voice of Missions*, where he wrote, "We have as much right biblically and otherwise to believe that God is a Negro, as you buckra or white people have to believe that God is a fine looking, symmetrical and ornamented white man." In *The Negro Church in America*, E. Franklin Frazier writes, "The 'color' of God could only assume importance in a society in which color played a major part in the determination of human capacity, human privilege, and human value. It was not and is not a question of whether God is physically black, but it is a question of whether a man who is black can identify with a white God and can depend on His love and protection." Cone and Wright were part of a deep tradition when they married notions of rebellion and faith. Black-liberation theologians reminded their readers that Nat Turner, Gabriel Prosser, and Denmark Vesey were not just rebel slaves; they were preachers. The A.M.E. Zion Church was known as the "freedom church," because it was a spiritual home for abolitionists like Frederick Douglass, Harriet Tubman, Sojourner Truth, and Eliza Ann Gardner.

Wright was not a pure follower of Cone. Relying on his own reading in Afrocentric history and theology, Wright rejected Cone's notion that the white slave masters had stripped the black man of his spiritual and cultural links to Africa. Unlike Cone, Wright insisted on the African origins of spirituals and the blues; he was more deeply influenced by Afrocentric thinking, in general. In church, Wright often wore African-patterned robes. He also came to believe in some of the more dubious theories linked to Afrocentrism. For instance, to explain the so-called differences in European and African "learning styles," Wright endorsed the idea that Africans and African-Americans were "right-brain" people, who are not "object-oriented" but, rather, "subject-oriented": "They learn from a person" rather than a book.

Initially, Obama approached Wright as an organizer. He wanted Trinity, with its thousands of parishioners, to consider joining a coalition of other churches on the South Side.

Wright welcomed the young man but laughed at his idea. "That isn't going to happen in this city," he said. "I ain't seen it. I've been in this city since 1969. We don't agree with each other on whether you baptize in the name of Jesus or baptize in the name of the Father, Son, and the Holy Ghost." The churches in Chicago, he insisted, were just too various, too at odds. Some believe in speaking in tongues, some are sedate and traditional. Some support homosexuals and female ministers; others, most decidedly, did not. The divisions ran deeper than the divisions between Orthodox and Conservative Jews, between Hasidim and Reform, Wright said. The idea of organizing all the churches in and around Roseland, as Obama proposed, was impossible. Wright teased Obama for his dewy idealism, saying, "You know what Joseph's brothers said when they saw him coming across the field: 'Behold, the dreamer!' "

Wright's reaction was typical among the pastors of some of the largest black churches on the South Side. Ministers like James Meeks, at Salem

Baptist, told organizers that it was easier for them, politically, if they just picked up the telephone and called the Mayor. Meeks worked with the Developing Communities Project for a short while, Alvin Love recalled, "but Barack couldn't keep him in. One of the biggest problems for a community organizer is managing egos when you deal with the pastors." Wright, Love said, "figured he was already way ahead of any organizer on social-justice issues. Why deal with an organizer?"

Nevertheless, Obama was fascinated by Jeremiah Wright and began to discuss more intimate things with him. Ann Dunham had always described herself as "spiritual" and did not hesitate to have her children read sections of the Old and New Testaments, the Koran, the Bhagavad Gita, and other religious texts, but she was never a churchgoer, never a believer in the standard sense. Not having been brought up in the church, Obama was full of questions, academic and theological. Wright said, "His search was: 'I need a faith that doesn't put other people's faiths down, and all I'm hearing about is you're going to hell if you don't believe what I believe.' He didn't hear that from me."

Obama's colleagues were not surprised that he had found his way to the black church—particularly to Jeremiah Wright and Trinity. "Barack had no problem moving into the black church because it is rooted in social justice," Kellman said. "Some ministers can be awful and 'Where is mine,' but historically, this church saw these folks through from slavery. It was almost all they had to work with and it still is around these communities. He was vaguely aware of this but until he came to Chicago he didn't experience it. He had heard tapes of King, the music of it. He knew the church was central to the civil-rights movement. He wanted to be part of a community of people who make values part of the center of their lives. In Judaism, there is no individual salvation. It's community. Barack moves into that sense of the church. It took him years to figure out how to use some of that in his own rhetoric."

If it was merely a large and influential church he sought, Obama could have chosen the Reverend Arthur Brazier's enormous Pentecostal church on the South Side. Brazier had worked with Alinsky in the Woodlawn Organization and had been one of the black ministers who stood by King in Chicago. But Wright was even more politically involved and more progressive. "Reverend Wright and I are on different levels of Christian perspective," Brazier said. "Reverend Wright is more into black liberation, he is more of a humanitarian type who sought to free African-Americans from plantation politics. My view was more on the spiritual side. I was more concerned, as I am today, with people accepting Jesus Christ. Winning souls for Christ. The civil-rights movement was an adjunct; as a Christian, you couldn't close your eyes to the injustice. But in my opinion the church was not established to do that. It was to win souls for Christ."

The more Obama attended services at Trinity, the more Wright's rhetoric infused his thinking and language. Obama admired the way Wright responded to the needs of his community—he helped parishioners with AIDS, created support groups for addicts and alcoholics, developed an "African-centered" grade school, the Kwame Nkrumah Academy, and, every summer, took church members to Africa.

The political pronouncements by Wright that, two decades later, plagued Obama's Presidential run were not yet in evidence. "The only troublesome issue was how to relate to Louis Farrakhan," Kellman recalled. "And in the black community people were willing to cross the line and not care about anti-Semitism as long as he was helping people. And I don't think Barack was engaging Wright on that issue."

Obama's black and white friends say that his motives for joining Trinity were complicated, yet Trinity was undeniably a "power church" in town. Obama "saw it as a power base," Mike Kruglik said. "You can't interpret what Obama does without thinking of the power factor. Even then. For a long time, I wouldn't talk about this, but he told me way back then that he was intrigued by the possibility of becoming mayor of Chicago. His analysis was that the mayor in this town is extremely powerful and all the problems he was dealing with then could be solved if the mayor was focused on them."

In fact, Obama, who was working with the poor and the working class, was initially concerned about Trinity from a class point of view. There were black churches—and white churches, too—that put affluence next to godliness and he wanted to make sure that he was in the right place. "Some people say that Trinity is too upwardly mobile," he remarked to Wright.

In 1981, a committee at Trinity, chaired by a parishioner named Vallmer Jordan, had adopted a twelve-point document of "self-determination" called "The Black Value System." The document, which was written under the influence of the Black Power movement and came under scrutiny during Obama's Presidential campaign, calls for commitment to God, the black community, and family, dedication to education ("We must forswear anti-intellectualism"), a strong work ethic and self-discipline, charity for black institutions, and support for worthy black politicians. Article 8, on the "disavowal of the pursuit of 'middleclassness,'" warns that the black community is weakened by the division between its most fortunate and talented members and those whose lives are consumed by misfortune, crime, and incarceration ("placing them in concentration camps, and/or structuring an economic environment that induces captive youth to fill the jails and prisons"). And while it is permissible to pursue middle-class prosperity "with all our might," members of the community must be wary of being seduced "into a socioeconomic class system which, while training them to earn more dollars, hypnotizes them into believing they are better than others and teaches them to think in terms of 'we' and 'they' instead of 'us.' "

Vallmer Jordan admitted that there had been a "hunk of resistance" to the article on "middleclassness" among church members, until it was made very clear to congregants, not least to the substantial number of well-to-do members who no longer lived in the neighborhood, and who drove to church each Sunday, that they were being warned against their own potential alienation, a drift away from the community.

"We refuse to be silk-stocking," Wright says. The standing joke is that Trinity has B.A.s, B.D.s, M.D.s, J.D.s, Ph.D.s, and A.D.C.s, too—Aid to Dependent Children. "We've got welfare, those letters don't matter here," Wright said. "What matters is that you're made in the image of God. That kind of message, and trying to push that kind of message, is what makes us different."

When conservative critics suggested during the campaign that Trinity's Black Value System was a kind of black-nationalist manifesto, Obama replied, "Those are values that the conservative movement in particular has suggested are necessary for black advancement. So I would be puzzled that they would object or quibble with the bulk of a document that basically espouses profoundly conservative values of self-reliance and self-help."

After a couple of years, Obama had built the Developing Communities Project into a good, small program, but he could readily see its limits. His relationship with Kellman had grown frayed at times, but they still were able to meet, take walks, talk about their work and politics. Obama found himself thinking about a larger arena, about ways to make a greater impact. Obama knew that he could not live the conventional life of a corporate lawyer or executive. Once, Kellman sent him out to Northbrook on a project, and Obama found himself dressing in a suit and commuting on the train. "I never want to do this on a regular basis," Obama told him. "I can't live like this. It's my idea of a nightmare."

In late October, 1987, his third year as an organizer, Obama went with Kellman to a conference on the black church and social justice at the Harvard Divinity School. One night, as they took a walk in Cambridge, Obama told Kellman that he was thinking seriously about leaving Chicago. Obama talked with him about his father, about how he was learning from encounters with various half siblings how Barack, Sr., had lived the last years of his life—impotent with rage, unable to fulfill any of the personal and political dreams he had had when he was a promising student at the University of Hawaii. Obama was determined to do better; he was determined to acquire the proper tools to make his mark on a far broader canvas than he ever could as a community organizer.

It was time, Obama told Kellman, for him to get a legal education. He wanted to go to Harvard.

"Harvard Law School was also a personal security decision," Kellman said. "He wanted to make a living, a decent living. He wasn't a materialist at all. He wanted security to support a family." Money certainly was a part of his decision. By then, Obama's salary had gone up to thirty-five thousand dollars. He was not uninterested in making more than that. He wanted a family, and a reliable income. But above all he wanted to move on, acquire the tools he needed for politics. More often than not, Obama said, organizing ended up in failure; the gains were too small, too rare. Kellman, who soon left organizing himself for a while, did not argue the point. If anything, his level of frustration ran deeper. The conversations at the divinity school intensified Kellman's conviction that one day Obama would return to Chicago and run for public office.

On November 25, 1987, Harold Washington, who had been re-elected the year before, died at his desk at City Hall—a death, Obama wrote, that was "sudden, simple, final, almost ridiculous in its ordinariness." Like most of the city, Obama spent much of that Thanksgiving weekend watching on television as the lines of mourners at City Hall stood in the cold rain; he listened to WVON, the main black talk-radio station in town, take calls from African-Americans who regarded Washington as a fallen king. In many ways, Obama revered Washington, but he also despaired that Washington had not left behind a strong political organization: "Black politics had centered on one man who radiated like a sun." After eight days of negotiations, the City Council installed Eugene Sawyer, a black member of the old machine, as mayor. Sawyer had shown support for Washington but now had to rely on the white conservative aldermen like the "Eddies," Edward Vrdolyak and Ed Burke, Washington's archenemies in what was known as the "Council Wars." (Vrdolyak, the epitome of a corrupt machine alderman, finally ended his long career in 2008 with a string of federal indictments and a conviction for mail and wire fraud.)

Obama went to City Hall to witness what he called "the second death": Sawyer's official elevation. Outside, Obama watched as the crowd, mainly older black men and women, denounced the African-American aldermen who were doing business with Vrdolyak and waved dollar bills at Sawyer, calling him an Uncle Tom. In the weeks after Washington's death and the sorry spectacle of Sawyer's installation, some of Obama's friends, including Mike Kruglik, became even more convinced that he would one day return to Chicago and run for office.

Toward the end of his time as an organizer, Obama met with Bruce Orenstein, an organizer for the United Neighborhood Organization, who had worked with him in an attempt to devise a way to profit off of the local landfills to fund community improvements on the far South Side. A proposal they had put together had won support from Harold Washington, but it collapsed after he died. Sawyer was not Harold Washington. Both Obama and Orenstein were frustrated and ready to move on—Obama to law school, Orenstein into video projects. When Orenstein asked him over a beer where he planned to be in ten years, Obama replied, "I'm going to write a book and I want to be mayor of Chicago."

Obama asked John McKnight, a co-founder, with Greg Galluzzo, of the Gamaliel Foundation and a professor of communications at Northwestern, and Michael Baron, his politics professor at Columbia, to write letters of recommendation for him to Harvard Law. (He also applied to Yale and Stanford.) McKnight had met Obama when he arrived in Chicago as a trainee. Obama told him that now that he had seen what could be done on a "neighborhood level," he wanted to explore what could be done in public life. McKnight, who has been involved with organizing for decades, and who shared the organizer's traditional wariness of politicians, cautioned him: an organizer was an advocate for people and their interests; a politician, he said, is "the reverse," someone who synthesizes and compromises interests. Would he be satisfied with that? "That's why I want to go into public life," Obama replied. McKnight agreed to write the letter. He had the idea that Obama had not received exceptional grades as an undergraduate—"I don't think he did too well in college"— but he had been deeply impressed by his intelligence and his commitment as an organizer.

Just after he left his job as an organizer, Obama published a short article in a local monthly, *Illinois Issues*, entitled "Why Organize? Problems and Promise in the Inner City." In the article, Obama makes clear that he came away from the experience in Chicago believing that neither electoral politics nor government development programs would help the inner cities unless they were "undergirded by a systemic approach to community organization." Despite the hope created by the election of black mayors like Washington, in Chicago, and in Gary, Indiana, the high-school dropout rates were still at nearly fifty per cent; the old forms of discrimination had been replaced by institutional racism; the flight of the middle class and a Reagan-era decline in public support had left inner cities in despair.

Obama was not entirely frustrated with his experience in Chicago. He credited the Developing Communities Project and programs like it with gains in job training, school accountability, and better crime and drug programs. He and his colleagues had been able to set up a jobs-training center on Michigan Avenue in Roseland, on the site of a shut-down department store. (Harold Washington himself came to the ribbon-cutting.) And yet, like so many projects that Obama and his fellow organizers worked on, the jobs initiative floundered because there was so little work around. The center closed after three years. "I do know that we got some training done," Alvin Love said. "But I don't know how many people really got new jobs."

By 1988, Obama's ideas about organizing no longer focused much on Saul Alinsky. For Obama, organizing was a way of thinking about fixing specific problems and also building a culture. "We tend to think of organizing as a mechanical, instrumental thing," Obama said in 1989 at a roundtable discussion organized by the Woods Charitable Fund, in Chicago. "I think Alinsky to some extent may not have emphasized this, but I think the unions that Alinsky saw—I think John L. Lewis understood that he was building a culture. When you look at what's happened to union organizing, one of the losses has been that sense of building a culture, of building up stories and getting people to reflect on what their lives mean and how people in the neighborhood can be heroes, and how they are part of a larger force. That got shoved to the side."

Obama now saw Alinsky's theories and opinions as deeply flawed. Alinsky's critique of Martin Luther King, for example, showed a dismissal not only of charismatic leadership but also of long-term vision. Obama particularly disputed Alinsky's emphasis on confrontation. He thought the time had come to find new ways to reach young African-Americans. "They are not necessarily going to town hall meetings, and they are not going to pick up *Reveille for Radicals*," Obama said. "They are going to see the Spike Lee film, or they are going to listen to the rap group."

Obama was clearly thinking about broader politics now and about how he, or anyone, could bring the experience of organizing to elected office. "How do you link up some of the most important lessons about organizing—accounting, training, leadership, and that stuff—with some powerful messages that came out of the civil-rights movement or what Jesse Jackson has done or what's been done by other charismatic leaders?" he asked the panel. "A whole sense of hope is generated out of what they do. Jesse Jackson can go into these communities and get these people excited and inspired. The organizational framework to consolidate that is missing. The best organizers in the black community right now are the crack dealers. They are fantastic. There's tremendous entrepreneurship and skill. So when I talk about vision or culture it has to do with how organizing in those communities can't just be instrumental. It can't just be civic. It can't just be, 'Let's get power, call in the alderman,' etc. It has to be recreating and recasting how these communities think about themselves."

Obama could not have foreseen the full scope of his political future, but it's evident that he was thinking about the effect that someone like him could have both in imbuing a community with a sense of hope and in providing the organized framework for making that hope an asset for reform. He rejected organizing's "suspicion of politics." To disdain politics, he told the panel, was to disdain "a major arena of power. That's where your major dialogue, discussion, is taking place. To marginalize yourself from that process is a damaging thing, and one that needs to be rethought."

Obama, who had been attracted to community organizing by the example and the romance of the civil-rights movement, was, by the time his experience with it was over, thinking about how to combine elements of charismatic leadership, the principles of organizing, and a set of liberal political and policy principles. He was no longer interested in being an outsider; his thoughts were turning to elective politics. Going to law school—and, not incidentally, going to an institution like Harvard—was part of learning the fundamentals of a system he had seen mainly from the street.

Obama never completely left the world of community organizing. On vacations from law school, he visited a new girlfriend in Chicago named Michelle Robinson, and also Kellman and Kruglik. He later served on the boards of the Woods Fund and the Lugenia Burns Hope Center, which helped fund organizing efforts in the city. He spoke at numerous retreats and training sessions. And while he learned a tremendous amount from his experience, he had also come to embrace the possibilities of charismatic leaders—whether an outsider like King or an insider like Washington—and what can be reaped in a political process of battle and compromise.

In May, 1988, Obama made a clean break with the first chapter of his life in Chicago. He had split up with his old girlfriend. ("I ran into her a couple of weeks after he left and she seemed upset, brokenhearted," John Owens recalled. "Barack tends to make a strong impression on women.")

As Obama handed over the leadership of the Developing Communities Project to Owens, he was determined to work on a broader level. "Barack's biggest success in Chicago had not been in bricks and mortar," his friend and comrade Reverend Alvin Love said. "He'd found out things about himself and his community. That was important. But what he really did was give people like me and Loretta, John Owens, and Yvonne Lloyd, and dozens and dozens of others, the tools to keep the work going, whether he was around or not."

Before leaving, Obama gave his cat, Max, to Jerry Kellman. Then he said good-bye to his friends and drove out of town.

Chapter Five

Ambition

In the early fall of 1988, Obama arrived in Cambridge sure that he would learn what he later called "a way of thinking." He was taking on thousands of dollars in debt for the privilege. Unlike many students who end up in law school without quite knowing why, apart from its value as another blue-chip credential, Obama approached Harvard purposefully, as a serious place that offered dimensions of knowledge that he could never acquire as an organizer on the South Side of Chicago. At Harvard, he would join the world of the super-meritocrats of his generation, shifting from outsider to insider. "I would learn about interest rates, corporate mergers, the legislative process, about the way businesses and banks were put together; how real-estate ventures succeeded or failed," he wrote. "I would learn power's currency in all its intricacy and detail, knowledge that would have compromised me before coming to Chicago but that I could now bring back to where it was needed, back to Roseland, back to Altgeld; bring it back like Promethean fire." Harvard also had a personal dimension: Barack, Sr., had left his wife and his two-year-old son to go there. If Obama had inherited anything from his father it was the notion that Harvard was the sine qua non, the place you went to go the farthest, achieve the most. At Harvard he would match his father, then surpass him; at Harvard he would acquire his serene self-confidence and a sense of his own destiny.

A modern would-be politician, particularly a Democrat like Barack Obama, arrives at Harvard Law School keenly aware that the law school—its students and faculty—provided much of the brainpower for the New Deal, the New Frontier, and the Great Society. Before Obama, Rutherford B. Hayes was the only President to graduate from the law school, but Harvard alumni have always been well represented in Congress and, especially, on the Supreme Court. On the current Supreme Court, John

Roberts, Antonin Scalia, Anthony Kennedy, and Stephen Breyer all graduated from the law school. (Ruth Bader Ginsburg attended for a year and
made the *Law Review*, then moved with her husband to New York, and finished at Columbia.)

The law school, which is just a short walk north of Harvard Yard, is a
jumble of architectural styles, ranging from Austin Hall, the Romanesque
creation, in 1883, of H. H. Richardson, to the Harkness Commons, a
fairly brutal concoction from the Bauhaus catalogue of Walter Gropius.
The land was the bequest of the Royall family, Southern plantation owners who brought their slaves North, to an estate in Medford, Massachusetts. In 1781, Isaac Royall, Jr., left Harvard an endowment that served to
establish the college's first chair of law. The proceeds from the sale of the
Medford estate, in 1806, became the seed money of the law school as a
whole. The school, which was established in 1817, was small at first and
fairly insignificant, until, in 1870, Christopher Columbus Langdell came
to Harvard and instigated a new curriculum, based on the study of individual legal cases and a style of Socratic inquisition.

By the time Obama arrived at Harvard, the law-school curriculum had
grown much more flexible than in Langdell's day and the student body
more diverse, but the school was still a fractious place, riven by political
conflict and intramural resentments. As if to flaunt its own unhappiness,
the law-school community commonly referred to itself as a bastion of
Levantine infighting—alternately "Beirut on the Charles" and "the Beirut
of legal education."

Obama said that Harvard Law School was the "perfect place to examine how the power structure works." Indeed, the "power structure"—a
phrase common in organizing circles—and how it is, or is not, examined
by the likes of Harvard Law School was the focus of a battle that had
already raged for a decade when Obama enrolled. In 1977, a group of legal
academics—radicals, as most would readily have identified themselves—
met at a conference in Madison, Wisconsin, to discuss a barely formed
school of thought that was soon to be called Critical Legal Studies. Influenced by post-structuralism, the Frankfurt School of critical theory, and
the Legal Realism of the nineteen-twenties, the scholars interested in
Critical Legal Studies sought to demystify the law and the language of law
and legal studies, to challenge its self-regard as a disinterested system of
precedent. Critical Legal Studies posited that law is politics by other
means, that the practice and discourse of law—and legal education—is
merely another lever of entrenched power, a way of enforcing the primacy
and perquisites of the wealthy, the powerful, the male, and the white.

According to the adherents of Critical Legal Studies, many of the conditions of the legal status quo—the high incarceration rates among people of color, the higher penalties for drugs used mainly among the poor—are inscribed in a legal system that only pretends to be consistent and nonideological.

Many students at Harvard in the late seventies, the eighties, and the early nineties, who were not necessarily left-wing, were excited by this analysis. The leading Crits at Harvard were three vastly different scholars: Morton Horwitz, Duncan Kennedy, and Roberto Mangabeira Unger.

"Barack didn't study directly with Horwitz or Kennedy, but they were very much in the air, and he absorbed what was going on," Obama's classmate Kenneth Mack, who is now himself a professor of law at Harvard, said. "The Crit who was most important to his studies—not that he was an acolyte—was Roberto Unger."

Unger, a social theorist, born in Brazil, was one of those academics who combine a personal charisma and a mode of study that attract young students. The American legal system, Unger contends, *pretends* to neutrality and a reliance on precedent, but what it actually does is enforce the permanence and the property rights of élites; the law guards against radical challenges to the élites and engages only in narrow issues. Unger is less a legal scholar than a political philosopher, and the more conventional students at Harvard avoided his courses. "His course descriptions in the catalogue were impenetrable and you knew he was worse in class," a near-contemporary of Obama's said.

Obama took two of his courses. The first was Jurisprudence. As Unger taught the course, Jurisprudence was a radical critique of contemporary Western political thought and legal theory and Obama's most prolonged academic exposure to the rudiments of Critical Legal Studies. A classmate who took the course with Obama described Jurisprudence as a "multi-step argument" that inspected, and then undermined, the presumptions of American legal thought. In his third year, Obama enrolled in Reinventing Democracy, a course in which Unger combined a critique of Western democracies—or neo-liberalism, as he referred to it—and the potential forms democracy could, or should, take. Unger argued against the "mandarins" who presided over contemporary democratic society and tried, in often highly experimental terms, to urge a rethinking of Western institutions. He urged the adoption of a "universal social inheritance" going well beyond the terms of the New Deal.

"The Reinventing Democracy course was relatively small and very intense," Unger said. In class, Unger contrasted the "bold but shapeless" course of F.D.R.'s initiatives in the early days of the New Deal, his "institutional experimentalism," with the more "restrictive focus" of his later years in office. He also expounded on what he saw as the Democratic Party's failure in the second half of the twentieth century to follow up on the efforts of the early New Deal. The reforms of the Johnson Administration, for example, were deemed modest. The class debated the Republican ascendancy in post-war America—its concessions to moneyed interests and its cultural rhetoric, directed toward the white middle-class majority.

"Everyone recognized that this late-twentieth-century exercise in conservative statecraft would not have enjoyed such success had the Democratic Party, and the progressives in general, not abdicated so completely their responsibility to build and to defend a national alternative," Unger said. "Many worried, however, that it would be hard to undo this defeat and supply the alternative without the *deus ex machina* of a crisis of dimensions resembling that of the Depression of the nineteen-thirties."

Unger, who later served in the Brazilian government of Luiz Inácio Lula da Silva, disputed the idea, proposed by some classmates, that Obama was put off by the abstruse theoretical nature of the course. "Obama shared in the more philosophical part of the discussion as vigorously as he did in the more context-oriented part," he said by e-mail from São Paulo. "The impression you report, of impatience with speculative exploration, is false. It does justice neither to him nor to me to represent these conversations under the lens of the trope of philistine activist against starry-eyed theoretician. He was always interested in ideas, big and small."

Unger continued to communicate sporadically with Obama by "e-mail and BlackBerry correspondence" over the years, keeping in touch through the Presidential campaign, but he added, "At no time can I say I became his friend." He avoided inquiries from the press for "a simple reason":

I am a leftist, and, by conviction as well as by temperament, a revolutionary. . . . Any association of mine with Barack Obama in the course of the campaign could do only harm.

Unger said that, as a student and afterward, Obama shared with other gifted Americans "a very strong sense of the limits that American politics and political culture impose on what can be said and done, and ultimately on what can be felt and thought." That sense of caution crimps political debate and diminishes the capacity for political boldness: "Obama is probably smarter than Franklin Roosevelt was but lacks the full thrust of Roosevelt's providential self-confidence." Unger also offered an analysis of Obama's personality and "subjectivity":

> Obama's manner in dealing with other people and acting in the world fully exemplifies the cheerful impersonal friendliness—the middle distance—that marks American sociability. (Now allow me to speak as a critic. Remember Madame de Staël's meetings that deprive us of solitude without affording us company? Or Schopenhauer's porcupines, who shift restlessly from getting cold at a distance to prickling one another at close quarters, until they settle into some acceptable compromise position?) The cheerful impersonal friendliness serves to mask recesses of loneliness and secretiveness in the American character, and no less with Obama than with anyone else. He is enigmatic—and seemed so as much then as now—in a characteristically American way.
>
> Moreover, he excelled at the style of sociability that is most prized in the American professional and business class and serves as the supreme object of education in the top prep schools: how to cooperate with your peers by casting on them a spell of charismatic seduction, which you nevertheless disguise under a veneer of self-depreciation and informality. Obama did not master this style in prep school, but he became a virtuoso at it nevertheless, as the condition of preferment in American society that it is. As often happens, the outsider turned out to be better at it than the vast majority of the insiders.
>
> Together with the meritocratic educational achievements, the mastery of the preferred social style turns Obama into what is, in a real sense, the first American élite President—that is the first who talks and acts as a member of the American élite—since John Kennedy. . . .
>
> Obama's mixed race, his apparent and assumed blackness, his non-élite class origins and lack of inherited money, his Third-World childhood experiences—all this creates the distance of the outsider, while the achieved élite character makes the distance seem less threatening.

By the time Obama appeared on campus, there had also appeared an increasing number of conservative and libertarian scholars centered on the Federalist Society, a many-branched group that had begun in 1982 at Harvard, Yale, and the University of Chicago. The main tenet of the Federalists was, in their terms, judicial restraint; critics argued that the Federalist vision of restraint was a form of conservative activism. The founders included such conservative jurists as Robert Bork. (On the current Supreme Court, Antonin Scalia and Samuel Alito are Federalists.) Some Federalists believe in the Law-and-Economics approach, a theoretical marriage of Milton Friedman's free-market economics and judicial minimalism, and they look to the pioneering work not only of Smith and Pareto but of the economist Ronald Coase, and such jurists as Frank Easterbrook and Richard Posner. At Harvard Law School, where an A.C.L.U. liberal is considered a centrist, the advent of the Federalists—a vocal minority—heightened the political tension on campus.

"Posner wasn't at Harvard, of course, but Barack was extremely interested in what he was saying and writing, too," Mack said. "Some students on the left just wouldn't read about the 'law and economics' school on general principle. That wasn't Barack."

The combination of C.L.S. radicals, A.C.L.U. liberals, and Federalist conservatives made for constant fights at the law school, particularly over tenure decisions. In the fall of 1987, one of the younger Critical Legal Studies adherents, Clare Dalton, a specialist in family law and the wife of the economist Robert Reich, was denied tenure, despite overwhelming support from the outside review committee. When Derrick Bell, the first black professor to gain a place on the Harvard Law School faculty, staged a sit-in supporting Dalton, Robert Clark, a leading professor at the law school, cracked, "This is a university, not a lunch counter in the Deep South." He eventually apologized for the remark, but the tone of the conflict was set.

"By the time Barack got to campus, in 1988, all the talk and the debates were shifting to race," said Elena Kagan, who became dean of the law school and then, in 2009, was named Obama's Solicitor General. In part as a result of affirmative action, ten to twelve per cent of the student body at the law school was African-American, and the racial atmosphere, as at so many other institutions, was marked by a general undertone of resentment and disquiet. At meals, blacks sat mainly with blacks, whites with whites. Some of Obama's classmates told me that, as students in their early and mid-twenties, they were beginning to imagine their professional lives in the "white world"—in law firms, corporations, public service—and the process of finding a sense of confidence and identity and balance was not easy at Harvard Law.

"You had the sense that there were a lot of white students thinking to themselves about us, Do you, the black students, really belong here?" Earl Martin Phalen, a friend of Obama's, said. "So many of us carried a chip around, angrily insisting, 'We're as smart as you. There are a lot more people that got in as legacies than from affirmative action.' "

The law-school class, with more than five hundred students, is divided into four sections; Obama took all his first-year classes in Section Three. His professors included a pro-life feminist and eventual Bush Administration ambassador to the Holy See, Mary Ann Glendon, for property; a human-rights specialist, Henry Steiner, for torts; Richard Parker, a constitutional scholar, for criminal law; a civil-rights specialist, David Shapiro, for civil procedure; and a visiting scholar from Northwestern, Ian Macneil, for contracts. "We felt as if we had the hardest, worst, most inflexible section," one of Obama's section mates, David Dante Troutt, complained. "We felt like a control group in the presence of folks receiving the revolutionary new drug."

To Mack, Obama seemed far more mature and centered than his classmates; he seemed "wise in the ways of the world," not merely because he was older by a few years but also because of his serene manner, his intellectual engagement, and his evident desire to enter public service rather than serve a corporate firm. Mack, and other first-year friends, like Cassandra Butts, knew little about Obama's complicated background at first. From his appearance, they could hardly guess at his complicated background. Obama looked African-American and identified himself as such.

"We were friends fairly immediately and then over the next two years, we saw each other all the time," Mack said. "He wasn't interested in a lot of the things young people are interested in. He was much more serious from the beginning. He didn't go to many big parties. We'd go over to his house for drinks and dinner. That was more his idea of a good, social night than going to the sort of big party that twenty-somethings go to. I went to a lot of parties and I don't think I ever saw Barack at one of them. But he could talk about sports, about politics, public policy, foreign relations. He wanted to talk about everything. And he was very much interested in Martin Luther King and the civil-rights movement. He was versed in King's ideas and rhetoric. He had really thought a lot about it on a level most students had not. Even then there was that quote of King's that he always loved and recited: 'The arc of the moral universe is long but it bends toward justice.' That appealed to Barack in the sense that things were going to take a long time to accomplish and that you need to have faith, long-term faith."

Obama lived much as he had in New York and Chicago. He rented a seven-hundred-dollar-a-month basement apartment in Somerville, a working-class town near Cambridge, and he outfitted it with secondhand furniture. He played basketball with friends at the gym, ate his meals at a sandwich shop in Harvard Square, and, like most of his classmates, spent nearly all of his time studying. The novelist Scott Turow, who became a friend and an early political supporter in Chicago, came to the law school in 1975; the first-year grind he describes in his memoir *One L*—nerve-racked, sleep-deprived, tobacco-driven—rang true when Obama read it. Obama, who carved out a regular space at the law library and put in long study days, told Turow that they had shared much the same experience of Harvard. Beyond the "boot camp" details of the book, Turow writes of the way the school encourages a steely ambition in its students, the "almost inescapable temptation to scramble, despite obstacles and ugliness and bruises, for what sometimes looks to all of us to be the very top of the tallest heap."

Almost from the start, Obama attracted attention at Harvard for the confidence of his bearing and his way of absorbing and synthesizing the arguments of others in a way that made even the most strident opponent feel understood. Once, at a debate over affirmative action with the staff of the *Harvard Law Review*, Obama spoke as if he were threading together the various arguments in the room, weighing their relative strengths, never judging or dismissing a point of view. "If anybody had walked by, they would have assumed he was a professor," Thomas J. Perrelli, a friend of Obama's who went on to work in his Justice Department, said. "He was leading the discussion, but he wasn't trying to impose his own perspective on it. He was much more mediating."

Obama's earnest, consensus-seeking style became a source of joking among his friends. A group would go together to the movies and tease Obama by imitating his solicitude: "Do you want salt on your popcorn? Do you even *want* popcorn?"

In a political atmosphere where bitter arguments were commonplace, Obama's open-mindedness seemed strange even to his friends. "In law school, we had a seminar together and Charles Fried, who is very conservative, was one of our speakers," Cassandra Butts, who first met Obama at the financial-aid office, recalled. The issue of the Second Amendment came up, and Fried was expressing the view of a Second Amendment absolutist. "One of our classmates was in favor of gun control—he'd come from an urban environment where guns were a big issue," Butts continued. "And, while Barack agreed with our classmate, he was much more willing to hear Fried out. He was very moved by the fact that Fried grew up in the Soviet bloc"—in Czechoslovakia—"where they didn't have those freedoms. After the class, our classmate was still challenging Fried and Barack was just not as passionate and I didn't understand that."

Obama also impressed his teachers with his capacity to be heard without showing off. Ian Macneil, the visiting contracts professor from Northwestern, said that even in his large class Obama stood out. "I was always a little too impatient in class, so if students went off the track I would interrupt before I should. When I did that with Barack, he said, 'Let me finish.' He wasn't rude, just firm."

Although Obama was popular, he was not voracious in his social networking. Obama always needed time to himself. "Barack never absorbed energy from being with a crowd of random people," David Goldberg, a classmate who is now a civil-rights lawyer in New York, said. "Barack needs some kind of context. He doesn't have the ability to walk into any situation and be attracted to people. He needs a little momentum, some kind of challenge."

As Obama's friends learned more about his background, they began to draw conclusions about his distinctive bearing and his way of dealing with other people, intellectually and personally. "Barack is the interpreter," Cassandra Butts said. "To be a good interpreter means you need fluency in two languages, as well as cultural fluency on both sides. When you go to a foreign country and you don't know the language, your interpreter is someone you rely on, because he is your compass. Barack has been that for me from the time I met him. He has been the ultimate interpreter in his political life. As a biracial person, he has had to come to an understanding of the two worlds he's lived in: his identification as an African-American man and the white world of his mother and his grandparents. Living in those worlds, he functions as an interpreter to others. He has seen people in both worlds at their most intimate moments, when their humanity and imperfections shone through. His role is as an interpreter, in explaining one side to the other."

As much as anyone can, Obama had chosen his racial identity, pursued it. By the time he got to Harvard, the issue was long settled. Without hesitation, he became active in the Black Law Students Association. "He's operating outside the precincts of black America," Randall Kennedy, an African-American professor at the law school, said. "He is growing up in Hawaii, for godssakes. And then when he comes to the mainland and tries to find his way, he has to work at it. He does have to go find it. He is not socialized like other people. I can't help thinking that he might have thought it a burden at the time, but maybe some of the things he missed out on were a benefit to miss out on. For one thing, the learned responses, the learned mantras and slogans, the learned resentments of that time that one got in college—he talks in his book how useful it was to get along easily with white people. You remember that at the time for some black people getting along with white people was seen not as a virtue but as a vice."

Both Obama and Butts signed up for Kennedy's course, an elective called "Race, Racism and American Law." Kennedy had caused some controversy, writing critically in *The New Republic* and elsewhere about some aspects of affirmative action. At the first class, Obama and Butts watched as a predictable debate unfolded between black students who objected to Kennedy's critique and students on the right, almost all white, who embraced it. Obama feared a semester-long shout-fest. He dropped the course.

For many black students, the most welcoming faculty member was Charles Ogletree, a civil-rights lawyer and scholar who was born into a family of farmers in California's Central Valley. Ogletree, known to his friends and students as Tree, joined the Harvard faculty in 1985 and was counsel to Anita Hill during Clarence Thomas's Senate confirmation hearings for the Supreme Court. At Harvard, he led "the Saturday School," a freewheeling seminar at which he presented outside speakers, staged debates, coached first-year students in their coursework and the art of taking law exams, and, in general, led discussions on subjects ranging from the political controversy of the day to the past achievements and future goals of the civil-rights movement to special topics in legal history. Ogletree brought in a survivor of the Japanese internment camps during the Second World War; Jesse Jackson to talk about the political scene; and the boxing impresario Don King, who, in his youth in Ohio, had been involved as an unnamed numbers runner in Mapp v. Ohio, an important search-and-seizure case in the early sixties. The students at the Saturday School were generally African-American, but everyone was welcome. Sometimes, Ogletree had upperclassmen in the law school act out the arguments of a controversial case. "Barack came to a lot of those sessions," Ogletree recalled. "It gave everyone an extra opportunity to learn about the law, listen to faculty work out their ideas and also prepare for classes, get ready to take an exam. Barack was interested in the vitality of the debate about power and the law and the underrepresentation of certain groups.

"Black identity was not given to him—he sought it," Ogletree went on. "It was clear at the Harvard Law School that most of his closest buddies were African-American males, and he shared with them a whole range of experiences, from talking trash on the basketball court to talking about the issues of law and politics. He was well read. He had taken the time in college to read the books of the black-studies movement. He had certainly read Richard Wright and James Baldwin, but he also knew all about the generation of Thurgood Marshall and all those trained at historically black colleges. He came well-steeped in the history of the civil-rights movement and wanted to know even more."

.   .   .

The professor who became Obama's intellectual mentor at Harvard was a mainstream liberal—the constitutional scholar Laurence Tribe. A civil libertarian, Tribe is, by almost any standard, among the most brilliant scholars of constitutional law of his, or any other, generation, a dazzling mind engaged in issues of political significance.

The year before Obama began law school, Tribe, at the invitation of the Senate Judiciary Committee and its chairman, Joseph Biden, of Delaware, testified against Ronald Reagan's nomination of Robert Bork to the Supreme Court. So fluid and commanding was Tribe in oral argument that Biden decided to make him his cornerstone witness. In three hours of testimony, Tribe attacked Bork's judicial writings, insisting that he was "out of the mainstream" on issues of privacy, reproductive rights, school selection, and many other issues. As a liberal, Tribe believes that the Constitution is a living document that requires constant interpretation in light of an expanding vision of human dignity; he argues that "original intent," the mantra of conservatives like Bork, is a cover for resisting evolutionary social change. Tribe was, in many ways, the intellectual backbone of the effort to spurn Bork. No one questioned his credentials; he had won nine of twelve cases that he argued before the Supreme Court. The Senate voted, 58–42, to reject Bork, and Reagan ended up nominating Anthony Kennedy instead. (Although Kennedy hardly proved a liberal, he has been far less conservative in his votes and written opinions than Bork would have been.)

Tribe's testimony and his many television appearances were so effective, however, that they made up a kind of kamikaze mission where his future was concerned. Tribe craved a seat on the Supreme Court and he hoped that a Democratic President would nominate him, but, after the Bork hearings, Republican elephants, blessed with long memories, vowed that they would never forgive him.

Tribe was born in Shanghai in 1941, to Jewish parents who had fled the tsarist pogroms. His father was held in a Japanese-run internment camp near Shanghai, and, when the war was over and he was released, he brought the family to San Francisco. Tribe was a versatile prodigy. He won a full scholarship to Harvard and wound up studying math and graduating summa cum laude having done all the coursework for a doctorate. He did not pursue a career in mathematics because he saw that he could not match his contemporary at Harvard Saul Kripke, an eccentric logician and philosopher, who had been writing about modal logic since he was seventeen.

Looking for a field with "real-life ramifications," Tribe went to Harvard Law School and, after graduation, began teaching. Tenured at Harvard at twenty-nine, he published, in 1978, a seventeen-hundred-page treatise entitled *American Constitutional Law*, the most authoritative volume on modern constitutional doctrine. As a litigator at the Supreme Court, Tribe has presented cases on free speech, homosexual rights, and women's rights. In 1986, he took on Bowers v. Hardwick, a case in which he argued for the rights of gay men and women to practice consensual sex without fear of state prosecution. The Court ruled against Tribe's client, Michael Hardwick, and for the State of Georgia, five to four. Not long after Lewis Powell retired from the Court, he publicly admitted that he regretted voting with the majority, and, in 2003, in a case called Lawrence v. Texas, Bowers was overturned. Anthony Kennedy, who, in great measure, owed his job to Tribe, wrote the opinion for the majority.

Tribe also distinguished himself among academics by becoming a wealthy man litigating corporate cases. For helping to win a ten-billion-dollar judgment for Pennzoil against Texaco, his fee was reportedly three million dollars. Not a few of his colleagues were shocked by a 1994 article in *The American Lawyer* called "Midas Touch in the Ivory Tower: The Croesus of Cambridge" that reported that Tribe was earning between one and three million dollars a year.

By the time the Class of 1991 arrived on campus, Tribe had taught thousands of students. One afternoon—on March 29, 1989–he jotted a note to himself on his desk calendar. It read, "Barack Obama, One L.!" He wanted to remind himself of an encounter that day with an impressive student who had come by his office to talk. "Barack wanted to get to know me because he was interested in my work," Tribe recalled. "I soon saw that he was very purposive about being at the law school. It wasn't a school of maintaining options as it is for many students. Barack had a clear sense that he wanted to know about the legal infrastructure of things: corporate law, constitutional law as the framework. I was impressed by his maturity and his sense of purpose, his fluency."

Tribe signed up Obama as his primary research assistant, and they worked on three projects together: Tribe's book *Abortion: The Clash of Absolutes;* a highly theoretical article called "The Curvature of Constitutional Space," in which Tribe called on metaphors derived from quantum physics and Einsteinian relativity to describe matters of societal obligations and the law; and an article called "On Reading the Constitution." Obama caught up quickly in subjects, like physics, in which he had no background. For their work on "The Curvature of Constitutional Space," Tribe and Obama spent hours discussing the case of DeShaney v. Winnebago County, a children's-rights issue that reached the U.S. Supreme Court in 1989. The case centered on a boy named Joshua DeShaney. When his parents divorced in 1980 in Wyoming, his father was given custody, and the boy then moved with him to Wisconsin. Soon, social-services workers received reports of the father hurting the child. After an abuse report and hospitalization in January, 1983, the Winnebago County Department of Social Services got a court order to keep the boy away from his father and in the hospital, but a "child-protection team," consisting of a psychologist, a detective, several social-services caseworkers, a pediatrician, and a county lawyer, recommended that the juvenile court return the boy to his father. The beatings—and the complaints—resumed. In 1984, the father beat his son so severely that Joshua was in a coma and had to undergo brain surgery. As a result of repeated traumatic beatings, the boy became severely retarded and paralyzed. Nevertheless, the Supreme Court absolved Winnebago County of any constitutional responsibility for the child.

Chief Justice Rehnquist wrote for the majority, "A state's failure to protect an individual against private violence" was not a denial of the victim's rights. "While the state may have been aware of the dangers that Joshua faced in the free world, it played no part in their creation, nor did it do anything to render him any more vulnerable to them." This decision provoked an unusually passionate response from Harry Blackmun in dissent: "Poor Joshua! Victim of repeated attacks by an irresponsible, bullying, cowardly and intemperate father, and abandoned by [county officials] who placed him in a dangerous predicament. . . . It is a sad commentary upon American life and constitutional principles."

In his discussions with Obama, Tribe called the majority's decision a form of "Newtonian blindness." In other words, he said, "the law recognized only forces at a distance and not the arrangement of the way the space around the kid was warped. Barack and I talked about this metaphor from physics, the way state power curves and bends social action.

"In going over the literature on Einstein," Tribe continued, Obama pointed out that "if one deemed the state responsible, then there would be no social space for private choice. The theme of arranging the world so that people become more accountable to themselves as agents. I remember him talking about how the case related to black fathers needing to be responsible. The theme that so often emerged was the theme of mutual responsibility, that legal institutions had to encourage people to take care of each other, and any institutional arrangement that left people completely to their own devices was fundamentally flawed."

The article was Tribe's, not Obama's, but they spent many hours together in Tribe's office or taking walks along the Charles River talking about such cases. Obama didn't talk with Tribe about running for office, but he made it plain that he had come to the law school to find better ways of "helping people whose lives had been ripped apart," as Tribe put it. When an unsigned legal note by Obama on abortion surfaced years later during the Presidential campaign, Tribe said: "It was consonant with the ways he thought with me about the puzzles of abortion, the incommensurability of the arguments: bodily integrity on one hand and the value of unfinished life on the other. He kept both values in mind in a way that would be meaningful to both sides."

What Tribe and Obama mainly discussed was the law itself. They rarely waded into ideological abstraction. "To make a beeline to Larry Tribe is to say that you want to be a lawyer," Martha Minow, a liberal who taught a course in law and society, said. "It was the kids who self-consciously identify themselves as radical or quite left-wing who head for elsewhere. That wasn't Barack."

Minow, who became dean of the law school in 2009, was another of Obama's mentors at Harvard, and they formed a friendship that had great implications for Obama's professional and personal life. Minow grew up in Chicago; the daughter of Newton Minow, who was chairman of the Federal Communications Commission in the Kennedy Administration and a partner at the corporate law firm of Sidley Austin. Obama met his future wife, Michelle Robinson, at the firm as a summer intern. The more Minow learned from Obama and about his past, the more she came to understand his capacity to discuss the most explosive political or racial issue with an uncanny balance of commitment and dispassion. "Obama is black, but without the torment," she says. "He clearly identifies himself as African-American, he clearly identifies with African-American history and the civil-rights movement, but his life came largely—not completely, but largely—without the terrible oppression.

"Barack is a universalist who doesn't deny his particularity," Minow continued. "He is very specifically African African-American, but he is also someone with a white mother and white grandparents. He could and would identify with different people. In America, you are 'raced' whether you have chosen it or not. He struggled with that as a college student and as a law student. But he came to accept and embrace what and who he is, and, at the same time, he has this very special sense of universalism that would become such an important part of his political message later on."

At Harvard and, later, in a seminar led by the political scientist Robert

Putnam, Minow noticed Obama's ability to shift his tone and language just enough to put anyone—the white Harvard professor, a black friend from the inner city, a bank president, clergymen, conservatives, liberals, radicals—at ease. Later, when he entered politics, reporters who followed him noticed the same thing. "He can turn on and off the signals that work best," she said. "That's not a bad thing at all—just the opposite. I think that's the promise of a multicultural society.

"It's partly because he is biracial, partly because of his father and being abandoned, and Indonesia," Minow went on. "All of this leads to a search for self-definition and gives him a non-knee-jerk way of thinking about race."

Over the years, Obama stayed in touch with Tribe and Minow. They discussed electronic eavesdropping, Guantánamo, the politicization of the Justice Department under the Bush Administration, future Supreme Court justices. And they have occasionally disagreed—about same-sex marriages, for instance, which Tribe supported and Obama opposed.

"Overall, Obama has, and had then, a problem-solving orientation," Tribe said. "He seems not to be powerfully driven by an a-priori framework, so what emerges is quite pragmatic and even tentative. It's hard to describe what his presuppositions are, other than that the country stands for ideals of fairness, decency, mutual concern, and the frame of reference that is established by our founding and the critical turning points of the Civil War and the New Deal, as a frame to identify who we are. When Earl Warren was Chief Justice, he would ask, after an oral argument, 'But is it fair?' For Barack, the characteristic question is, 'Is that what we aspire to be as a country? Is that who we are?'"

In the speech he made in March, 2007, at Brown Chapel, in Selma, commemorating Bloody Sunday, Obama observed that, as a member of the Joshua generation, he stood "on the shoulders of giants." At Harvard, the giant was Charles Hamilton Houston. Very few students arrived at the law school knowing the name. And yet Houston was, in his way, as crucial to the civil-rights movement as the marchers in Selma. He was their precursor. At Harvard, he was Obama's precursor, too.

In May, 1915, *The Crisis*, the official publication of the N.A.A.C.P., published a one-sentence item: "Charles H. Houston, a colored senior of Amherst College, has been elected to the Phi Beta Kappa." This is the first public recognition of the man who became, in the nineteen-thirties and forties, the chief architect of the legal war against school segregation.

Houston's civil-rights movement, however, was not one of culture or protest. It was a movement of lawyers, who argued a stream of cases that sought equal rights of citizenship for people of color. Following the end of the Civil War and, between 1865 and 1870, the passage of the Thirteenth, Fourteenth, and Fifteenth Amendments, the hopes of Reconstruction faded and were overrun by nearly a century of lynchings, segregated public schools and facilities, and all the other elements of institutionalized racism in America. "Charles Houston became the critical figure who linked the passion of Frederick Douglass demanding black freedom and of William DuBois demanding black equality to the undelivered promises of the Constitution of the United States," Richard Kluger wrote in *Simple Justice*, his history of the fight for desegregation and Brown v. Board of Education.

Born in 1895, Charles Hamilton Houston was raised in Jim Crow Washington. His father was a well-to-do lawyer, a member of the capital's tight-knit black bourgeoisie. A member of Harvard Law School's class of 1922, Houston was the first black ever to win a spot on the *Law Review*.

After Harvard, Houston taught at Howard University. Founded in 1867, Howard was an outgrowth of the Freedman's Bureau; the original property was a beer hall. Many of the doctors, dentists, lawyers, nurses, engineers who emerged from that era and created a black middle class and a black intelligentsia attended Howard. The great power behind the school's expansion was its first black president, the economist and minister Mordecai Johnson. On the advice of Louis Brandeis, Johnson reorganized the law school and hired Charles Houston to assemble a faculty—and it was to be a faculty with a distinct political purpose. Houston's most important student was Thurgood Marshall, who became his protégé at the N.A.A.C.P. Legal Defense Fund.

Attacking the "separate but equal" principle of the Supreme Court's 1896 decision Plessy v. Ferguson, Houston piled up numerous victories for racial justice. In the 1936 case of Murray v. Pearson, for example, Houston established that the University of Maryland could not exclude African-American students—as it had Thurgood Marshall. Missouri ex rel. Gaines v. Canada required equal educational opportunities for young people of all races, a principle that was extended to the entire country by the Supreme Court. Houston was committed to purpose; as he put it, "a lawyer's either a social engineer or he's a parasite on society."

The battles that Houston and protégés like Marshall, Spottswood Robinson, A. Leon Higginbotham, and William Hastie waged at the time had little support in the white world. As Houston's biographer Genna

Rae McNeil points out, Houston came along before the rise of King and the civil-rights movement, at a time when other courses of action were limited to "advocacy of black separatism, accommodation to the system, collaboration with the predominantly white working-class" left, or "affiliation with groups promoting justice for all through the overthrow of the government."

Houston died in 1950, four years before Marshall argued Brown v. Board of Education, the case that ended the legal structure of school segregation. Houston was just fifty-four. After the great victory in Brown, Marshall paid tribute to Houston, saying, "We were just carrying his bags, that's all."

For African-American students at Harvard, Houston was an important symbol. "Houston was a big figure in the background of our minds," Ken Mack said. "And when Barack and I arrived it happened to be a moment when Houston was being recovered in historical memory. He was an especially big figure for all the black students on the *Law Review*. That book"—Genna Rae McNeil's 1983 biography of Houston, *Groundwork*— "had come out. You'd walk through the building and there are all these pictures of the editors since 1900, all these white faces, dozens each year, until you hit 1922—and then you see that one black face. Houston. It was a powerful thing to think that you were in some way the heir of one of the most powerful civil-rights figures in American history." (In 1991, Obama filmed, for TBS, a "Black History Minute" on Houston's life.)

For decades, the *Law Review* retained all the characteristics of an élite American institution, including racial prejudice. In its first eighty-five years, there were precisely three black members: Houston; William Henry Hastie, who later worked with Houston at the N.A.A.C.P. and became a federal appeals-court judge; and William Coleman, who was appointed Secretary of Transportation in the Ford Administration. (The first female president of the *Review* was Susan Estrich, who was elected in 1976 and went on, in 1988, to run Michael Dukakis's ill-fated Presidential campaign.)

The *Harvard Law Review* is a precipitate of the school's best and most ambitious students: only about three or four dozen are selected out of a class of more than five hundred students. Felix Frankfurter once said that life at the *Review* creates the "atmosphere and habits of objectivity and disinterestedness, respect for professional excellence, and a zest for being very good at this business which is the law." There are other publications on campus—the *Harvard Civil Rights–Civil Liberties Law Review* (where

Obama had some experience), the *Harvard Journal on Legislation*, the *Harvard International Law Journal*, the conservative *Harvard Journal of Law and Public Policy*—but the *Law Review* has always been the focus of greatest attention, whether from corporate law firms, investment banks, or judges looking for clerks. The sense of election and entitlement could not be greater among the editors. It is an old tradition. Oliver Wendell Holmes and Louis Brandeis began automatically selecting, each year, two high-ranking *Law Review* editors as their clerks. The *Review*'s alumni include Felix Frankfurter ('06); Antonin Scalia ('60); Richard Posner ('62); Nuremberg trial counsel Telford Taylor ('32); former Secretary of State Dean Acheson ('18); former Attorney General Elliot Richardson ('47); Senators Thomas Eagleton ('53) and Robert Taft ('13); former Yale president Kingman Brewster ('48); Washington *Post* publisher Philip Graham ('39); the poet Archibald MacLeish ('19); and Alger Hiss ('29).

Obama nearly botched his bid to get on the *Law Review*—and join this inner sanctum of the establishment—when, on the way to the post office to mail his application form, his balky Toyota Tercel broke down. After a flurry of frantic phone calls, he got a ride from his classmate Rob Fisher. Obama's grades were good—he graduated magna cum laude—and he got in.

The *Law Review* is situated in Gannett House, a white three-story Greek-Revival house. It is named for Caleb Gannett, a minister who lived nearby in the eighteenth century. *Law Review* editors routinely spend forty, fifty, sixty hours a week there, with first-year editors proofreading and copyediting articles and checking footnotes and citations, all according to the strictures of *A Uniform System of Citations*. (The style guide, better known as *The Bluebook*, is sold by the *Review* and is the publication's biggest money-maker.)

The masthead positions on the *Law Review* are filled by second-year students, who compete for them. The top position is president; there are also Supreme Court co-chairs, a treasurer, a managing editor, a few executive editors, two notes editors, and three supervising editors. Any one of those positions is an enormous boost in the race for jobs at the best law firms, judges' chambers, and corporate offices.

Obama's first year on the *Law Review* was typical: excruciating detail work and meetings, relieved only by the necessity of going to classes and keeping up with coursework. What spare time he had he spent playing basketball or hanging around the editors' lounge at Gannett House. The lounge, Mack recalled, is "the place where impressions and assessments quickly took root among a group of very ambitious people."

The political debates at Gannett House were even more furious than elsewhere on campus. Radicals argued with liberals, liberals argued with the conservative Federalists; as one editor put it, "Everyone was screaming at everyone else." Brad Berenson, a classmate of Obama's and a member of the Federalist Society who went on to work for the Bush Administration, said, "I've worked in Washington for twenty years—in the White House, in the Supreme Court—and the most bitter political atmosphere I've ever experienced was at the *Harvard Law Review*."

Both as undergraduates and as law students, the African-Americans on the *Law Review* were negotiating an élite white world, but here the arguments and status anxieties were particularly vivid. "Being on the *Law Review* was the most race-conscious experience of my life, and race-based attitudes and prejudices crossed political and ideological lines among the ambitious law students on its staff," Mack said. "Many of the white editors were, consciously or unconsciously, distrustful of the intellectual capacities of African-American editors or authors. Simply being taken seriously as an intellectual was often an uphill battle."

"Honestly, we were just very polarized on the *Law Review*," Christine Spurell, an African-American who was a friend and classmate of Obama's, said. "It's like you got to campus, and the black students were all sitting together. It was the same thing with the *Law Review*. The black students were all sitting together. Barack was the one who was truly able to move between different groups and have credibility with all of them. . . . I don't know why at the time he was able to communicate so well with them, even spend social time with them, which was not something I would ever have done . . . I don't think he was agenda-driven. I think he genuinely thought, Some of these guys are nice, all of them are smart, some of them are funny, all of them have something to say."

In the summer of 1989, Obama's professor and friend Martha Minow recommended to her father, Newton Minow, that he hire Obama as a summer associate. She called him "the best student I've ever had." As it turned out, the firm's recruiter had already seen to it. At Sidley, in Chicago, Obama met an associate and Harvard Law graduate named Michelle Robinson. She was slated to be his "adviser" for his three-month stint there. Robinson, like everyone at the firm, had heard about Obama— this "hotshot," as she called him—and it was her job to take him to lunch and watch out for him. She had heard that Obama was biracial and had grown up in Hawaii. For Robinson, who was born and reared on the

South Side, Hawaii was not where anyone was from; it was where rich people went on vacation. Obama's background and his intellectual reputation were all daunting.

"He sounded too good to be true," she said to David Mendell of the Chicago *Tribune*. "I had dated a lot of brothers who had this kind of reputation coming in, so I figured he was one of these smooth brothers who could talk straight and impress people. So we had lunch, and he had this bad sport jacket and a cigarette dangling from his mouth and I thought, 'Oh, here you go. Here's this good-looking, smooth-talking guy. I've been down this road before.' "

To her surprise, Robinson found Obama funny, self-deprecating, "intriguing"—"We clicked right away"—but she was intent on keeping their relationship professional. She fended off Obama's requests for a date. At the beginning of the summer, Michelle had made a "proclamation" to her mother: "I'm not worrying about dating . . . I'm going to focus on me." Besides, she and Obama were two of the very few African-Americans at the firm; the idea of dating Obama struck Michelle as "tacky." Instead, she introduced him to a friend. This did not put Obama off. "Man, she is hot!" Obama told a friend. "So I am going to work my magic on her."

Finally, Robinson agreed to go out with Obama—"but we won't call it a date." Robinson was living with her parents in South Shore, not far from Obama's apartment, in Hyde Park. They spent a long summer day together. They went first to the Art Institute and then had lunch in the museum's courtyard café. A jazz band played as they ate. Then they walked up Michigan Avenue and went to Spike Lee's latest film, "Do the Right Thing." Michelle thought to herself that Obama was pretty good: he knew something about art and now he was showing off his "street cred." She was both amused and smitten. Not long after, they wound up back in Hyde Park, at a Baskin-Robbins, the ice-cream chain where Obama had worked as a teenager in Honolulu. They also had their first kiss and, as Obama recalled years later, "It tasted like chocolate."

"Probably by the end of that date," Michelle said, "I was sold."

Robinson had dated, but she had never had a serious boyfriend before; none had ever made the grade. Barack, for his part, had dated quite a lot but bothered to bring a girl home to meet his family in Hawaii only once before. After a few dates, Michelle invited Barack to dinner at her parents' house, a modest brick bungalow on Euclid Avenue, in South Shore. He won over her parents, who had been concerned about Obama's being biracial. Like their daughter, they had never met anyone like him. The Robinsons had not had to fashion an African-American identity for themselves in the prolonged and complicated way that Obama had. The richness and history of black American life was evident in their family history: Michelle's great-great grandfather Jim Robinson worked as a slave harvesting rice on Friendfield Plantation, near Georgetown, South Carolina. But the genealogical complexity that is so common among African-Americans was a fact of life among the Robinsons, too. The genealogist Megan Smolenyak eventually discovered that Michelle Obama's great-great-great-great-grandparents included a slave named Melvinia who gave birth in 1859 to a biracial son, the result of a union with a white man. Although most sexual unions between blacks and whites then were coercive, nothing is known of the father of Melvinia's first-born son except for his race. Michelle Obama's family background also includes a Native American strand.

The Robinson family had come North with the Great Migration. The students at Michelle's high school, a magnet school for gifted kids, were mainly African-American; the school was named after civil-rights leader Whitney Young. One of Michelle's closest friends there was Santita Jackson, Jesse Jackson's daughter. Michelle's father, Fraser Robinson III, worked for the city for thirty years, doing maintenance on boilers and pumps at a water-filtration plant. He was eventually promoted to foreman. He was also volunteer precinct captain for the Democratic Party. He suffered from multiple sclerosis and walked with two canes; when he could no longer walk he used a motorized wheelchair. (Fraser Robinson died of complications from kidney surgery, in 1991.) Michelle's mother, Marian, stayed at home with the children until they were in high school and then worked as a secretary for the Spiegel's catalogue store.

The Robinsons were hard-working, close, and ambitious for their children. "When you grow up as a black kid in a white world, so many times people are telling you—sometimes not maliciously, sometimes maliciously—you're not good enough," Craig Robinson, Michelle's brother, said. "To have a family, which we did, who constantly reminded you how smart you were, how good you were, how pleasant it was to be around you, how successful you could be, it's hard to combat. Our parents gave us a little head start by making us feel confident."

In 1981, Michelle followed Craig, a basketball star, to Princeton. In a class of fourteen hundred, she was one of ninety-four African-Americans. Among African-Americans at Ivy League schools, the feeling was that Princeton was an especially unwelcoming place. Even as late as the nineteen-eighties there were pockets of the university—some of the eating clubs, in particular—that supported its lingering reputation as "the northernmost college of the old Confederacy." There were only five tenured African-Americans on the faculty and just a handful of courses in African-American studies. One of Michelle's freshman-year roommates at Pyne Hall, a girl named Catherine Donnelly, from New Orleans, moved out midway through the year. Donnelly's mother was so upset at the notion of her daughter rooming with a black girl that she telephoned influential alumni and hectored the university administration to get Catherine another room. "It was my secret shame," Donnelly recalled.

In her sophomore year, Robinson roomed with three other women of color and joined various black organizations, including the Organization of Black Unity. Much of her social life revolved around the Third World Center. Robinson majored in sociology, with a concentration in African-American studies, and wrote a senior thesis entitled "Princeton-Educated Blacks and the Black Community." "My experiences at Princeton have made me far more aware of my 'Blackness' than ever before," she wrote. "I have found that at Princeton no matter how liberal and open-minded some of my White professors and classmates try to be toward me, I some-times feel like a visitor on campus; as if I really don't belong. Regardless of the circumstances under which I interact with Whites at Princeton, it often seems as if, to them, I will always be Black first and a student sec-ond." Michelle sent out hundreds of questionnaires for her thesis to black alumni asking about their lives, their attitudes, and whether they favored an "integrationist and/or assimilationist" ideology or a "separationist/and or pluralist" view. The thesis conveys a deep disappointment that, in her view, so many black alumni assimilate so quickly and completely into mainstream white society. The thesis shows a young woman struggling not only with Princeton but also with the larger questions faced by some-one who grew up on the South Side, acquired an Ivy-League credential, and then has to decide how to live her life.

Marvin Bressler, a sociology professor at Princeton who knew Craig and Michelle Robinson well as undergraduates, said that the two grew up in an African-American version of a "Norman Rockwell family": a tight-knit family that emphasized loyalty, hard work, church, respect for their elders. Their world was the South Side and almost entirely African-American. To come to Princeton, Bressler said, was for kids like Craig and Michelle profoundly disorienting: "You show up as a freshman. There already exist, with respect to race, competing organizations that want you. And they are asking, 'Is your fundamental identity as a woman? Or is it as an African-American?' Hovering over this is an intense discomfort that you think of initially as prejudice. There is no discrimination in the old sense, but you come from Chicago and now there are these Gothic towers and all those smooth Groton types looking so confident and secure."

Michelle continued to worry that the longer she stayed inside white-dominated institutions the more tenuous her connection to black life might become. Robin Givhan, an African-American woman from Detroit, was a year behind Michelle at Princeton and now covers her for the Washington *Post*. "When you're in college, everything revolves around you and your drama—my paranoia, neuroses, insecurities," Givhan recalled. She described the radically different ways that her black friends at Princeton worked out their various dramas. There was Crystal, from New Jersey, "who left for a trip to Africa with her hair in a bun and came back with cornrows and deeply conscious of her race—that became the defining aspect of her personality." There was Beverly, from Michigan, who was friendly with Brooke Shields, avoided the Third World Center, and "took on this 'I'm-not-really-that-black' temper." The way Michelle Robinson approached Princeton, Givhan said, reflected a genuine, and understandable, urge to hold on to a sense of community, and an anxiety about being assimilated too completely into "the white mainstream." White kids, taken up with their own dramas, had a way of looking straight past students like Michelle.

Years later, Givhan, reading white columnists' praise of Michelle Obama's self-possession, found the descriptions ignorant and patronizing: "There was a part of me that thought, How low were your expectations? She went to Princeton and Harvard. She was an executive. Why the sense of awe? There was a part of me that found it irritating. I could line up a dozen of my friends who are Michelles and then some. What she did was just normal. In many ways, she is exceptional and it was disheartening that she had to ratchet her exceptionalism down to normal."

By the time Michelle Robinson got to Harvard Law School, she was far less anxious about the complications of negotiating such an institution. Charles Ogletree, who was her faculty mentor at Harvard, recalled, "The question for her was whether I retain my identity given to me by my African-American parents, or whether the education from an élite university has transformed me into something different than what they made me. By the time she got to Harvard, she had answered the question. She could be both brilliant and black."

Michelle Robinson took a different path at the law school than Obama did. She was far closer to Ogletree than to any white professor. She was more active in the black student association, joined one of the African-American-oriented publications, and worked for the Legal Aid organization, helping indigent clients in landlord and tenant cases. She thought hard about working for Legal Aid after law school, but Ogletree assured her that she could "do good and do well" if she practiced at a firm like Sidley Austin, where she had been a summer intern, as long as she obtained a promise that she could spend part of her time on pro-bono cases.

Despite their differences of background and emphasis, it was clear that Michelle and Barack were not going to spend their careers at a place like Sidley Austin. When they were first getting to know each other, Obama told Craig Robinson, "I think I'd like to teach at some point in time, and maybe even run for public office." Robinson asked if that meant running for alderman. "He said no, at some point he'd like to run for the U.S. Senate," Robinson said. "And then he said, 'Possibly even run for President at some point.' And I was, like, 'O.K., but don't say that to my aunt Gracie.'" Obama, for his part, doesn't remember the remark, but added, "If the conversation did come up, and I said I was interested in electoral politics . . . my aspirations would have been higher than being alderman."

The ultimate prize at the *Law Review* is its presidency. A comical proportion of each year's law-review cadre (as many as half) ordinarily run for the presidency. At first, Obama was reluctant to run. The competition would take place in February of his second year. He was gaining a reputation among his African-American peers and among many faculty members. Christopher Edley, Jr., whose father had been a protégé of Thurgood Marshall's, had been elected to the *Review* in 1975, the first black editor in many years. As a professor, he saw great promise in Obama.

"There are a couple of things about legal education that can be enormously valuable," Edley said. "One, of course, is studying how institutions of governance and property operate: how courts, legislatures, regulatory agencies operate. Second, it instills habits of mind that I think are enormously powerful even when you are not dealing with something that one would narrowly consider to be 'law.' For law students it's very important to understand the other side of the argument. If you are a litigator, a critical skill is trying to anticipate and dissect the best argument your opponent is going to make, so you drill down and understand his argument as well as your own. That gives you a certain humility, because it forces you to face the weaknesses in your own position and to appreciate that any difficult problem has, by definition, good arguments on both sides. That's where Barack was so strong. Now, why did he seem to hate debates in the Presidential race, and wasn't particularly good at them at first? Because the difference between someone who is a great lawyer and merely a great debater is that the lawyer appreciates nuance and only subsequently focuses on how to communicate. His talent, that habit of mind, was also evident in his openness in engaging people with whom he disagrees. It's antithetical for a good lawyer to have a self-righteous conviction that he has a monopoly on truth. You are trained to have an appreciation for complexity. It's not relativistic, but principled and humble at the same time. You come to the problem with your own compass, your opinions and principles, but you have to be open. That was Barack."

After talking with close friends like Cassandra Butts, Obama decided to run for president of the *Law Review.* "Most of my peers at the *Law Review* were a couple of years younger than I was," Obama said. "I thought I could apply some common sense and management skills to the job. I was already investing a lot of time in the *Law Review,* and my attitude was Why not try to run the *Law Review?*"

Maturity, not ideology, seemed to be Obama's appeal. "One thing that is hard to remember, but was true, was that there was at times some eye-rolling at the *Law Review* about Barack because it was almost as if he was part of the faculty, bigger than a law student," David Goldberg, who was a liberal rival for the presidency, said. "A lot of professors were usually indifferent to students. But they were almost sycophantic to him. It was clearly both because he was brilliant and because he was African-American. He was also incredibly mature and thoughtful and still had his heart in the right place."

In Obama's year, nineteen of the thirty-five second-year members of the *Law Review* editorial board decided to run for president. The outgoing students joined the second-year students who were not in the hunt in a large meeting room in Pound Hall, where they would caucus and vote. The presidential prospects were left to sit and wait in an adjacent kitchen; they were supposed to cook meals for the selectors during deliberations. The selectors studied thick "pool files" on the candidates, containing their writing samples and work for the *Law Review.* The process—detailed, argumentative, self-important—went on all day and late into the night.

"At various points," Goldberg recalled, "someone would poke his head into the kitchen and say X, Y, and Z come back into the room. These were the people who were now out of the running and they joined the selectors. And in the kitchen there would be a sigh of relief."

The only conservative who stayed in the race past the early elimination rounds was Amy Kett, a skilled but relative long-shot candidate. Her hardy but outnumbered faction of conservatives knew that she had no chance, but, together, they figured they might have some influence on the outcome. Brad Berenson and the other conservatives were looking for someone who dealt with them open-mindedly "and didn't personalize political differences."

"At places like Harvard and Yale, young people often demonize folks who have differing political views," Berenson said, "and there were plenty of those at Harvard in 1990, when things were so political. Barack wasn't one of them. He earned the affection and trust of almost everyone. The only criticism from conservatives was that he was somewhat two-faced and made everyone think he was all things to all people, that he was concealing his true feelings. But I never subscribed to that criticism."

When members of the *Law Review* recall the election process today almost all think of it in terms of reality television, a prolonged and brainy episode of "Survivor." A representative for the electors came into the kitchen and made the announcement. Amy Kett was out—off the island. (Not that her career suffered; Kett went on to clerk at the Supreme Court for Sandra Day O'Connor.)

"At that point, the choice was among the liberals, and I recall that *en masse* the conservative vote swung over to Barack," Berenson said. "There was a general sense that he didn't think we were evil people, only misguided people, and he would credit us for good faith and intelligence."

By twelve-thirty, the only candidates left were David Goldberg, a white liberal who was headed toward a career in civil-liberties law, and Barack Obama.

Finally, someone came to get the two of them and give them the news. Obama was president. "Before I could say a word, another black student"—Ken Mack—"just came up and grabbed me and hugged me real hard," Obama recalled. "It was then that I knew it was more than just about me. It was about us. And I am walking through a lot of doors that had already been opened by others."

The news of Obama's historic election—he was the first African-American president of the *Law Review*—was picked up by news media all over the world. Interviewed for the New York *Times* by Fox Butterfield, Obama reacted with unerring diplomacy, acknowledging both the expectations that his fellow African-American students had for him and his broader responsibilities. "The fact that I've been elected shows a lot of progress," he said. "It's encouraging. But it's important that stories like mine aren't used to say that everything is O.K. for blacks. You have to remember, that for every one of me, there are hundreds or thousands of black students with at least equal talent who don't get a chance. . . . I personally am interested in pushing a strong minority perspective. I'm fairly opinionated about this. But, as president of the *Law Review*, I have a limited role as only first among equals."

Obama's friend Earl Martin Phalen was one of the many African-American students on campus who were overcome by the election. They had formed bonds in class listening to the outrages that had been committed against their forebears—crimes of slavery, lynching, Jim Crow, myriad forms of discrimination and humiliation—and so, for this generation, this victory, Obama was their Charles Hamilton Houston. "It was an affirmation of intellectual prowess and belonging for people of color," Phalen, who is now an education activist, said. "Barack was also very proud of the fact and aware of the historical significance, but it wasn't like reparations for him." Phalen is black; he was adopted by and reared in a large white family outside of Boston. "You appreciate race," Phalen said, "and you understand its significance, but at the end of the day we were similarly brought up and we knew the main thing was that it's about content of character. Barack knew that."

Obama gave many interviews after his election and only slipped once when he airily informed a reporter for the Associated Press, "The suburbs bore me." Nearly all the articles contained what the writer Ryan Lizza has called the "essential elements of Obama-mania": "the fascination with his early life, the adulatory quotes from friends who thought that he would be President one day, and Obama's frank, though sometimes ostentatious, capacity for self-reflection." Obama told the Boston *Globe* something that he has repeated throughout his political career: "To some extent, I'm a symbolic stand-in for a lot of the changes that have been made."

The next step for the new president of the *Law Review* was to assemble an editorial team, a process made complicated by ego, politics, and race. Obama could have loaded the masthead with liberals and African-Americans. Instead, he followed the traditional system of selection and the result was that three of the four executive editors were conservatives: Amy Kett, Adam Charnes, who later worked in the Bush Justice Department, and Jim Chen, who became an academic after clerking for Clarence Thomas. Brad Berenson, Kenneth Mack, Julius Genachowski, and Tom Perrelli also got masthead jobs—a mixed ideological cast.

It was almost inevitable, considering the atmosphere of resentments and the long decades of racial denial at the *Law Review*, that Obama would fail to satisfy everyone, including other African-Americans. His friend

Christine Spurell had never really understood Obama's penchant for listening so intently to the conservatives and synthesizing their views; in those days, she was much more impatient than her friend. But she had worked upwards of sixty hours a week during her first year on the *Review* and worked well together with Obama editing an article about Martin Luther King. "My heart was bursting with pride," she said, when Obama became president. She also counted on his awarding her a masthead position. When he did not, she felt betrayed.

"A few weeks later he called me into his office and he said, 'We have to fix this problem between us,' " she recalled. "I was so angry with him. He said something to the effect of, 'I don't know what our problem is. Maybe it's that we're both half-white? I don't know.' I think he was saying that maybe that makes us so familiar to each other that we irritate each other or are suspicious of each other. I remember I was crying during that conversation, mostly out of anger and frustration, which shows how significantly I felt let down. I remember saying something to the effect of 'I don't care what our problem is, we're not likely to resolve it, nor am I interested in resolving it.' "

After their talk, the two came to a "détente," Spurell said, and nearly two decades later, she said that she came to see that Obama sidelined her because she was too confrontational, too abrasive—qualities that he could not bear. "I had no patience for the idiots on the other side and Barack did, which annoyed me, even angered me sometimes, but it made him the better person, certainly a better one to be the president of the *Law Review*," she said.

The highlight of Obama's year-long stint as president may well have occurred at the annual banquet, at the Harvard Club, in Boston, which celebrates the journal's changing of the guard. A formal occasion, the banquet brings together the staff of the *Review*, along with alumni and their spouses. Nearly all the banquet guests were white; the waiters, dressed in starched white uniforms, were largely African-American. Obama spoke about how a skinny black kid with "a funny name" being elected to the presidency of the *Law Review* was important not for him, mainly, but as a breakthrough for everyone. As he expressed his gratitude to the people who had "paved the way," some of Obama's classmates noticed the black waiters standing at the back of the room listening intently. At the end of the speech, as everyone stood and applauded, one of the older waiters hurried up the aisle to shake Obama's hand.

.   .   .

The *Harvard Law Review* publishes monthly during the academic year—more than two thousand pages in all—and Obama spent forty to sixty hours a week at Gannett House reading, meeting with editors, and editing articles. He did not, however, take the journal too seriously. He was well aware of the absurdity of law students' selecting and editing the work of experienced jurists and scholars, and he had no illusions of the *Law Review*'s effect in the larger world of academia and jurisprudence. The *Review* has a circulation of four thousand and is the most frequently cited journal of its kind, but, very often, when arguments got out of hand, Obama would say, "Remember, folks, nobody reads it." David Ellen, who succeeded Obama as president of the *Law Review*, said, "We spent the most time together talking when we were making the transition from him to me, and his whole message was about keeping the *Review* in perspective. He knew that this was not a very big deal out in the real world, and he knew because he had already been out there."

"Barack could motivate people to do things that were against their self-interest, and he got people without much in common to stay responsible to the greater project—and he had a very light touch," David Goldberg said. "Politically, I thought he was, clearly, on the issues, a liberal. I never thought of him as a transformative thinker but as a thoughtful person."

Obama was editor of Volume 104 of the *Law Review*. There is no discernible ideological accent in his issues except for a desire to mix things up. In that period, the *Review* published articles that ranged over a spectrum—one article was a foursquare assault on affirmative-action policy—but were, in the main, liberal. There were articles calling for the elderly, women, and African-Americans to have a greater capacity to file discrimination suits. And yet, if Obama was a liberal, he was not always predictable. He worked closely with Robin West, a professor at the University of Maryland at the time and an expert on feminist legal theory, on an article that was critical of conservative judges and even of liberals who make a priority of rights before liberation. Quoting Václav Havel, West wrote that a citizen's sense of responsibility was no less important than his or her rights. She argued that goals of tolerance and diversity might be "weakened, not strengthened, by taking rights so 'super seriously' that we come to stop examining our responsibility." Obama, West said, clearly agreed with her, "and so it wasn't at all surprising to hear him, so many years later, making similar arguments about race, racism, and responsibility and not allowing that discourse to fall into the hands of social conservatives and libertarians."

Obama's issues featured an unsigned note on feminist theory and the state's legal position toward pregnant women and drug abuse. There were multiple responses to a controversial article by Randall Kennedy in an earlier volume, "Racial Critiques of Legal Academia," that accused white academia of too readily accepting mediocre work by black academics. Obama also oversaw the publication of an article by Charles Fried, a conservative professor at Harvard Law School and the Solicitor General during the Reagan Administration, attacking affirmative action as "racial balkanization."

In its own small universe, the *Harvard Law Review* is often judged on its efficiency—Does it come out on time? Is it well edited and proofread? Every year until his death in 1994, Erwin Griswold, the former dean of the Law School and former U.S. Solicitor General, sent frequent letters to the president—"Grizzer-grams," they were called—lauding a good article or, far more often, pointing out flaws of prose, reasoning, editing, or timeliness. Obama's "Grizzer-grams" were mainly complimentary.

In January, 1960, ten years after Charles Houston's death and six years after Brown, Derrick Bell, a young lawyer in the Justice Department, left the government and joined Thurgood Marshall full-time at the N.A.A.C.P. Legal Defense Fund. This was not a difficult decision for Bell. The Justice Department had angered him by demanding that he give up his membership in the N.A.A.C.P. lest it compromise his legal objectivity.

"That was kind of *nervy*, don't you think!" Bell recalled.

He spent the next eight years in the civil-rights movement and then entered the academy, where he has remained a self-described "ardent protester" on behalf of African-Americans.

Derrick Bell was, in Barack Obama's time, the most vivid symbol of racial politics at Harvard Law School. His maternal grandfather was a cook on the Pennsylvania Railroad. His father's side of the family was from rural Alabama, the Black Belt, and joined the migration North, to Pittsburgh. His father had less than a junior-high-school education and worked as a steelworker and as a janitor in a Pittsburgh department store. In 1962, Bell helped James Meredith win admittance to the University of Mississippi. In the town of Harmony, Mississippi, in 1964, he worked alongside a tough-minded local organizer named Biona MacDonald. Many of the local whites resisted every move toward change, staging intimidating shows of force, firing shots through black people's windows. Local banks foreclosed on the mortgages of people sympathetic to the movement. Bell was astonished by the fearlessness of Biona MacDonald, and how she continued to lead protests against segregation, despite threats and beatings, and so he asked her how she managed to endure. "I can't speak for everyone," she told Bell, "but as for me, I am an old woman. I *lives* to harass white folks."

Bell tried to make the transition from civil-rights lawyer to legal academic, but he was turned down for jobs at Michigan, George Washington, and a half dozen other schools. He was good enough, it seemed, to lecture at Harvard or to get offers for low-paying visiting-professor jobs, but not for the tenure track. It was only after the assassination of Martin Luther King, Jr., in 1968, that law schools on the level of Harvard felt compelled to break the color barrier. Administrators finally realized that the legal victories of Brown v. Board of Education and the 1964 Civil Rights Act barring discrimination in employment had not done much to integrate university faculties. The riots that followed the assassination focused their attention.

Derek Bok, the dean of Harvard Law School, flew to Los Angeles to offer Bell a job, and assured him, "You'll be the first, but not the last." That was fine, Bell replied, "because I don't want to be the token."

After two years on the faculty, Bell threatened to resign. For the next two decades he repeatedly threatened to resign in order to get Harvard to hire more African-American men and, eventually, women. "My life," Bell said, "is a living manifestation of taking no shit."

At Harvard, Bell also disturbed the peace with his iconoclastic writing. In "Serving Two Masters," a 1976 essay published in the *Yale Law Journal*, and in the 1987 book *And We Are Not Saved*, he reassessed his role in the movement to integrate American institutions and found himself, and the civil-rights movement, to have been sadly deluded. He was losing faith in the American capacity to make progress. Bell wrote, in "Serving Two Masters," "The time has come for civil rights lawyers to end their single-minded commitment to racial balance." He insisted on a new sense of "racial realism"—a realism that some would interpret as despair. "Black people will never gain full equality in this country," he wrote in the book *Faces at the Bottom of the Well*. "Even those herculean efforts we hail as successful will produce no more than temporary 'peaks of progress,' short-lived victories that slide into irrelevance as racial patterns adapt in ways that maintain white dominance. This is a hard-to-accept fact that all history verifies. We must acknowledge it, not as a sign of submission, but as an act of ultimate defiance." Bell argued that in some ways Brown v. Board of Education, despite its good intentions, led to a *failed* integration. As whites left the cities for the suburbs, the tax base contracted and blacks were left behind in miserable, underfunded schools. The situation might have been better, Bell argued, had the "equal" part of the "separate but equal" ideal of the 1896 case of Plessy v. Ferguson been enforced.

In Obama's second year in law school, after Harvard declined to give a tenure-track offer to a visiting professor from the University of Pennsylvania, a black woman named Regina Austin, Bell threatened to take an indefinite, unpaid leave from the university. Bell championed Austin's writing on racial and gender barriers, but Austin had no federal clerkships or law-review appointments in her background; her credentials, in the conventional sense, were deemed unexceptional. "Still, I thought Regina was perfect," Bell said. "She was saying what needed to be said. And she was a lot more militant than I ever was. But they"—the appointments committee at the law school—"were always saying no. They always wanted to see the next one and the next one." By 1990, there were five black men on the faculty, but no black women. According to Martha Minow, Erwin Griswold, who was dean from 1946 to 1967, used to invite what few women students there were on the law-school campus to tea and say, "Now, why are you here, taking up the place of a man?"

On April 9, 1990, without consulting Regina Austin, Bell wrote to the dean, Robert Clark. The letter, Bell told Clark, was an "inadequate but quite firm notice of my intention to request a leave without pay" that would, he said, continue indefinitely "until a woman of color is offered and accepts a tenured position on this faculty." "This was all going on while my wife, Jewel, was very sick with cancer," Bell said. "When I told her what I planned to do, she said, 'Derrick, why does it always have to be you?' " Much of Bell's letter to Clark was apologetic—apologetic for failing to realize sooner the importance of having black women on the faculty.

Bell released the letter to his colleagues and staged a hunger strike. Some students discussed another plan of action to support diversity: they declared, not without an element of grandeur, that they would take their final exams but, rather than turning them in, place the papers in escrow until the university hired more minorities.

To his classmates, how Obama would react to Derrick Bell's protest was a matter of some interest. Obama supported greater diversity on campus, but he had never been a leading activist in the Bell controversy or on any other political issue. Obama's popularity and stature as a Harvard "first" was such that Cassandra Butts asked him to speak at a campus rally.

"Barack's being president of the *Law Review*—being the first African-American president—that was a very big deal, so I was glad he came out,"

Derrick Bell said. "That was not exactly a bastion of affirmative action over there at the *Law Review*. Around that time, there had been a huge battle just to add a writing competition as an additional criterion to get on the *Review*."

Dressed in khakis and a light-blue dress shirt, Obama stepped to the microphone outside the Harkness Commons, surrounded by students, Bell, and placards reading "Diversity Now" and "Reflect Reality." Obama spoke in support of Bell's struggle to win a tenured position for a woman of color. He called Bell the "Rosa Parks of legal education": "I remember him sauntering up to the front," Obama said, "and not giving us a lecture but engaging us in a conversation." He commended Bell for "speaking the truth," and then, his speech concluded, he hugged him in front of a cheering crowd. Charles Ogletree recalled that Obama's speech stood out for its eloquence and emotional force, "even though he wasn't the most vocal and central advocate in that debate."

Everyone remembers Obama in much the same way: that he held generally progressive views on the political and racial controversies on campus, but never took the lead. He always used language of reconciliation rather than of insistence.

"Barack was someone who was politically engaged, but it was not a central part of his institutional personality," Christopher Edley, Jr., said. "As a community organizer, he had been doing the real thing in Chicago before coming to Harvard. The institutional politics at Harvard Law School can be quite consuming if you don't have the perspective provided by familiarity with politics of a more consequential sort. My sense was that, while he was sympathetic to those local struggles, he was really about something beyond all of that. And, frankly, that was what was so appealing. I felt something of a connection to him because of my own experience in national politics. For him it was difficult to get too excited about Zip Code 02138."

Bell soon left Harvard and never returned. (He teaches at New York University.)

In discussions at the *Law Review*, Obama held fast to a consistent theme: that students at Harvard and other privileged institutions needed to work for the public good. "One of the luxuries of going to Harvard Law School is it means you can take risks in your life," Obama said in one of his interviews at the time. "You can try to do things to improve society and still land on your feet. That's what a Harvard education should buy—enough confidence and security to pursue your dreams and give something back."

One debate that Obama engaged in with some passion at the *Review* was over affirmative action. He supported it, and when his friend Cassandra Butts decided to review Shelby Steele's influential book *The Content of Our Character*—a conservative analysis of race relations that saw affirmative action as a policy that reinforced a victim psychology among blacks and flattered the virtue of whites—Obama spoke with her about her critique. The "simplistic rhetoric" that, in 1989, Butts criticized in her article for the *Harvard Civil Rights–Civil Liberties Law Review* is very similar to Steele's rhetoric nearly two decades later in his book *A Bound Man: Why We Are Excited About Obama and Why He Can't Win*. Steele asserted that Obama was caught in a racial dynamic in which black candidates are either "challengers," who accuse white Americans of ongoing racism and demand outdated policies like affirmative action, or "bargainers," who agree to minimize the history of American racism in exchange for white political support.

At Harvard, in the midst of a debate over the low number of women on the *Law Review* and whether to employ some form of affirmative action to increase it, Jim Chen, one of the most vocal conservatives at the journal, wrote a tough-minded letter to the *Harvard Law Record*. He decried affirmative action for the tarnish that it leaves on its beneficiaries.

Obama wrote to the *Record*, defending affirmative action and closing with a more introspective argument:

> I'd also like to add one personal note, in response to the letter from Mr. Jim Chen which was published in the October 26 issue of the *Record*, and which articulated broad objections to the *Review*'s general affirmative action policy. I respect Mr. Chen's personal concern over the possible stigmatizing effects of affirmative action, and do not question the depth or sincerity of his feelings. I must say, however, that as someone who has undoubtedly benefited from affirmative action programs during my academic career, and as someone who may have benefited from the *Law Review*'s affirmative action policy when I was selected to join the *Review* last year, I have not personally felt stigmatized either within the broader law school community or as a staff member of the *Review*. Indeed, my election last year as President of the *Review* would seem to indicate that at least among *Review* staff, and hopefully for the majority of professors at Harvard, affirmative action in no way tarnishes the accomplishments of those who are members of historically underrepresented groups.
>
> I would therefore agree with the suggestion that in the future, our concern in this area is most appropriately directed at any

employer who would even insinuate that someone with Mr. Chen's extraordinary record of academic success might be somehow unqualified for work in a corporate firm, or that such success might be somehow undeserved. Such attributes speak less to the merits or problems of affirmative action policies, and more to the tragically deep-rooted ignorance and bias that exists in the legal community and our society at large.

Barack Obama
President, *Harvard Law Review*

Note the deft and confident wave of the lance: the way Obama points out that affirmative action might also help an Asian-American, one like Jim Chen. (Though he forgets that affirmative action is hardly uncontroversial among Asian-Americans.) As a mature politician, Obama came to reject the need for affirmative action for African-Americans who, like his own children, were already cosseted by American advantage. Some of his Harvard friends say that Obama believed that affirmative action had likely helped him get into Columbia and Harvard. "I have no way of knowing whether I was a beneficiary of affirmative action either in my admission to Harvard or my initial election to the *Review*," Obama told the *Journal of Blacks in Higher Education*. "If I was, then I certainly am not ashamed of the fact, for I would argue that affirmative action is important precisely because those who benefit typically rise to the challenge when given an opportunity. Persons outside Harvard may have perceived my election to the presidency of the *Review* as a consequence of affirmative action, since they did not know me personally. At least one white friend of mine mentioned that a federal appellate court judge asked him during his clerkship whether I had been elected on the merits. And this issue did come up among those who were making the hiring decisions at the [University of Chicago] law school—something that might not have even been raised with respect to a white former president of the *Review*."

Nearly all of Obama's colleagues on the *Review* came to appreciate his talent for mediation. They even came to know enough about his past to make fun of him. In the annual parody issue of the *Law Review*, "the Revue," they "quoted" Obama on his complicated background: "I was born in Oslo, Norway, the son of a Volvo factory worker and part-time ice fisherman. My mother was a backup singer for ABBA. They were good folks." In Chicago, "I discovered I was black, and I have remained so ever since." After being elected, he united people into "a happy, cohesive folk" while "empowering all the folks out there in America who didn't know about me by giving a series of articulate and startlingly mature interviews to all the folks in the media."

In Obama's last year of law school, he was starting to think hard about his future—and his teachers were thinking about it, too. Christopher Edley, Jr., was one of many faculty members who sensed that future was bound to be large and ambitious: "He was noticeable to a certain degree in class, but not one of the more vocal students. It was outside of class when he would come by my office to chat that I really got a sense of him. I claim to have been the first to use the phrase 'preternatural calmness' to describe him. That's what was so striking about him. Even as we would talk about career paths, he seemed so centered that, in combination with his evident intelligence, I just wanted to buy stock in him. I knew that the capital gains would be enormous."

David Wilkins, a young African-American professor at the law school, said, "After Barack was elected president of the *Law Review*, I talked with him—to congratulate him and also to talk with him about what he was going to do with it going forward. And so I said, 'Well, of *course* you're going to clerk for someone on the Supreme Court, and you'll probably even have your choice of which justice to clerk for. And then maybe you'll become a law professor'—as if that were the highest thing to attain to. And then he gave me that calm look that we've grown so used to seeing, kind of both bemused and respectful. There was a long pause. And then he said, 'Well, I am sure that would be a great *honor* and all, but that's not really what I had in mind for myself.' That's the guy: totally grounded. And he knew, more or less, *exactly* what he wanted to do."

Abner Mikva, a former congressman from Chicago who sat on the U.S. Court of Appeals for the District of Columbia Circuit, offered Obama a clerkship, but the young man turned him down. Mikva was shocked. His was the second-most-important court in the land, a sure stepping-stone to a Supreme Court clerkship. Was Obama angling for the Supreme Court right away? Was he trying to figure out exactly *which* justice to clerk for? *That* was a little cheeky. No, that wasn't it, either.

At Harvard, Obama secretly found the study of law, he wrote, "disappointing at times, a matter of applying narrow rules and arcane procedure to an uncooperative reality; a sort of glorified accounting that serves to regulate the affairs of those who have power." The language was not far from the left-leaning instruction on campus. But Obama also saw the law as a form of memory, "a long-running conversation, a nation arguing with itself." In the language of the founding documents of the nation, he could hear, he wrote, the language of Frederick Douglass and Martin Delany, the struggles of the civil-rights movement, Japanese-Americans in intern-ment camps, Russian Jews in sweatshops, immigrants at the Rio Grande, the tenants of Altgeld Gardens—all of them "clamoring for recognition" and asking the same question that Obama directed at the ghost of his father: "What is our community, and how might that community be rec-onciled with our freedom? How far do our obligations reach? How do we transform mere power into justice?" The idealist had now formulated his questions, gathered his tools.

Michael McConnell, a conservative constitutional scholar who was later appointed to the federal-appeals bench by George W. Bush, was so impressed with the meticulous and fair-minded editing that Obama dis-played on a piece he wrote for the *Law Review*, "The Origins and Histori-cal Understanding of Free Exercise of Religion," that he told the chairman of the appointments committee of the University of Chicago Law School, Douglas Baird, and told him to keep Obama in mind for a teaching job. McConnell was impressed that Obama had edited the piece so that it was a better version of itself rather than so transformed it that the author no longer recognized it. Baird felt that McConnell was a superb judge of talent, and so he called Obama and asked if he was interested.

"Well, no, actually," Obama said. "What I want to do is write this book."

Chapter Six

A Narrative of Ascent

When Obama left Cambridge to start his public life, he could not have anticipated some of the breaks that would accelerate his career: the political elders who stepped aside and provided him with crucial openings; a devastating electoral loss that turned out to be a kind of gift; political rivals who imploded as the news of their unfortunate personal lives became public; invitations to speak at an antiwar rally in 2002 and, two years later, at a national convention. In retrospect, the greatest break of all may have been that Jerry Kellman called him not from an immensity like New York (where he might have got lost or waited far longer to emerge), or from a city like Detroit or Washington, D.C. (where he might have run for mayor, but without hope of a larger career). Chicago itself was, for Obama, a stroke of fortune: a big-time metropolis and a political center with a large African-American base, but situated in a state whose demographics reflected the country as a whole. After the fall of the old Daley machine, Chicago was opening up to younger politicians, to blacks and Latinos. Chicago was home for Obama, it was a community; it was also an ideal place to begin a life in politics. Obama did not stay long enough to become a fixture of Chicago—his roots were not deep—but the city provided a series of profound lessons and opportunities.

When Obama returned to Chicago after graduation, he certainly could have taken a job with the corporate law firm or investment bank of his choosing. Instead, he accepted a place at the best-known civil-rights firm in town, Davis, Miner, Barnhill & Galland. The firm, with around a dozen lawyers, had its offices in a brick town house on West Erie Street, north of the Loop; the concentration was on voting rights, tenant rights, employment rights, anti-trust, whistleblower cases—a classic liberal "good guy" firm. Judson Miner, a liberal advocate who had been Harold Washington's corporation counsel, brought Obama to the firm and convinced him over a series of long lunches that he could work on cases that would "let him sleep soundly at night." The work, Miner promised, would feel like an extension of his work as an organizer on the South Side.

Obama also had Doug Baird's offer to teach law part-time at the University of Chicago. He was given the rank of a lecturer—a non-tenured, adjunct position—and provided with a stipend, benefits, and a small office on the sixth floor of the D'Angelo Law Library. At first, Baird did not require Obama to teach at all; both he and the dean, Geoffrey Stone, understood that Obama would spend most of his time writing a book about race and voting rights. When he decided to turn the book into a more personal rumination on family and race, they were unfazed.

All of Obama's employers in Chicago—Allison Davis and Judson Miner at the law firm, the deans at the university—proved indulgent of Obama's divided attentions; sooner or later, they figured, he would increase his commitments or go into politics. His intelligence, charm, and serene ambition were plain to see. The first time he met Geoffrey Stone, Obama was not yet thirty, and yet Stone's assistant, Charlotte Maffia, joined the legion predicting something large for him: she said that he would soon be governor of Illinois. Only occasionally were there rumbles of resentment about the young lawyer taking time to indulge his literary ambition. "He spent a lot of time working on his book," Allison Davis admitted to a reporter for *Chicago* magazine. "Some of my partners weren't happy with that, Barack sitting there with his keyboard on his lap and his feet up on the desk writing the book."

Obama was starting his new life in Chicago in a far different spirit than he had the first time. Gone was the self-conscious asceticism, the intermittent periods of loneliness. When he started his life as a lawyer and teacher in 1992, he had a community and a partner. The writing was going slowly, but his relationship with Michelle Robinson had survived the separations during law school. They were living together now in Hyde Park and were engaged to be married.

In the spring of 1992, before he could get much work done as a lawyer or complete his book, Obama made a commitment to lead a voter registration drive in the African-American and Hispanic communities called Project Vote. The drive was aimed at combating the Reagan Administration's rollback of social programs by registering as many as a hundred and fifty thousand of the four hundred thousand unregistered African-Americans in Illinois. The work had to be accomplished by October 5th.

Project Vote, which was founded by the civil-rights activist Sandy Newman in 1982, just before Harold Washington's first successful race for City Hall, could not rely on the old Democratic Party machine's method of padding the rolls by handing out cash payments known as "bounties." The program needed a director who was familiar with the city and who had organizing skills, someone who could reach people in the churches, the schools, the community centers, and on the street. "I kept hearing about Obama in community-organizing circles," Newman, who was Project Vote's national director, said. A well-known activist in town, Jacky Grimshaw, pressed Newman to interview Obama, saying that he had the right managerial and diplomatic skills to recruit volunteers and persuade community groups to join in the effort. After talking through the job with Obama, Newman called John Schmidt, a partner at the law firm of Skadden Arps, who had agreed to co-chair the Chicago branch of Project Vote, and asked him to meet with Obama.

Schmidt called Obama, who was doing some training work with organizers on the West Side, and invited him to the office. As they talked, Schmidt realized that in his long career in law and as a close aide to Richard M. Daley at City Hall, he had never before met someone who had deliberately spurned a sure clerkship at the Supreme Court. The work they discussed was tedious, and Schmidt worried that Obama would walk away from it after a few days or weeks. Traditionally, the Chicago machine did not want anyone registering to vote if that person was not going to vote with the machine. As a result, election law in the city required that registrars come for training sessions at the Board of Elections, downtown, teach people to fill out the forms precisely, collect the forms, and get them on the rolls. It meant getting people, mainly churchwomen, to stand outside of Sunday services all over the city and persuade people to sign up.

Obama said he didn't mind the prospect of such work. His one reservation about taking the job was that he would miss the deadline, June 15th, for handing in his book manuscript. He wondered if he could work on Project Vote part-time—a suggestion that Newman dismissed. "I told him, 'Do you want to write this memoir at such a young age or rescue democracy?' " Newman recalled. The stakes were high: the Reagan-Bush era was in its eleventh year, and the Democrats in Illinois had a chance not only to elect Bill Clinton to the White House, but also to elect an African-American, Carol Moseley Braun, to the Senate. Obama accepted Newman's offer to run Project Vote in Illinois—which would be centered mainly in Cook County. The salary was around twenty-five thousand dollars. To a great degree, it was an extension of his work as a community organizer, but it was also a bridge to electoral politics. Through Project Vote, he had to call on committeemen, aldermen, state legislators, lawyers, activists, clergy—the intricate web of associations that formed the political culture of Chicago and the state of Illinois. If he could register a significant number of new Democratic voters, he would bank the sort of capital that counts most: political I.O.U.s.

Obama heard that Sam Burrell, an alderman on the far West Side, in the Twenty-ninth Ward, had done successful work registering voters and so he arranged to meet with one of Burrell's aides, a young woman named Carol Anne Harwell, and tried to enlist her to help with Project Vote. "I don't think Barack had ever been that far west," Harwell recalled. "He came to the office in his raggedy black car and he was wearing a leather bomber jacket and carried a briefcase and a satchel." Obama struck Harwell as intelligent and eager, but despite his years as an organizer, lacking in street savvy. "He didn't know all the slang," she said. "If you had said, 'Oh, that's dope,' he wouldn't have known that. Hip-hop wasn't his thing." After Harwell agreed to work as Obama's assistant, she discovered what Obama was carrying around in his satchel—a laptop and his book manuscript.

Obama had some money to work with. Ed Gardner, whose family owned the SoftSheen hair-products company, agreed to help underwrite the campaign. The co-chairs of the finance committee were Schmidt and John Rogers, the founder of Ariel Investments, one of the biggest black-owned businesses in town, and a teammate of Craig Robinson's at Princeton. Schmidt and Rogers called on wealthy Chicagoans like the developer and ex-alderman Bill Singer and the developer and arts patron Lewis Manilow.

Obama was more concerned with the apathy and the political disconnection of unregistered voters than with resources. "Today, we see hundreds of young blacks talking 'black power' and wearing Malcolm X T-shirts," he told the *Sun-Times* columnist Vernon Jarrett early in the campaign, "but they don't bother to register and vote. We remind them that Malcolm once made a speech titled 'The Ballot or the Bullet,' and that today we've got enough bullets in the streets but not enough ballots." Obama had visited the one-party state of Kenya, and he told Jarrett that his African relatives and friends looked at their American brothers and sisters with envy: "They can't understand why we don't relish the opportunity to vote for whomever we please."

Obama set up an office on South Michigan Avenue and went looking for registrars who could be both persuasive and reliable. He himself

trained seven hundred registrars—there were eleven thousand overall—
and helped devise a public-relations campaign with a black-owned firm
called Brainstorm Communications. Obama and his team thought that
posters and registers using a straightforward slogan like "Register to Vote"
would do nothing to appeal to young people. That year, Spike Lee had
come out with his popular biopic of Malcolm X, and Obama and his colleagues thought for a while about using Malcolm's slogan, "By Any Means
Necessary." They settled on "It's a Power Thing."

"We took the 'X' from Malcolm, put it on some kente paper, and made
posters and T-shirts with the slogan 'It's a Power Thing' that were so popular that we ended up trademarking them," Carol Anne Harwell said. "Of
course, people in the African-American community knew that the 'X'
referred to Malcolm, but we also had white girls going around wearing
them, and one told us, 'Look at this! I'm Number Ten!' "

Project Vote volunteers put up the posters all over African-American
neighborhoods and in Hispanic areas like Pilsen. The two major black-
owned radio stations in town, WVON and WGCI, ran ads that told people where they could sign up; black-owned fast-food restaurants allowed
registrars to approach potential voters over their burgers and fries.

Obama faced generational resistance from some longtime activists and
black nationalists. Lutrelle (Lu) Palmer, the head of the Black Independent Political Organization and a popular journalist-activist known as "the
Panther with a pen," was one of a small contingent that saw Obama as too
young, too haughty, and too inexperienced to be taken seriously. Palmer
helped register thousands of voters for Harold Washington's 1983 campaign; he had no patience for Obama's desire to continue along the same
lines. In an interview with the Chicago *Reader*, Palmer said that Obama
"came to our office and tried to get us involved [in Project Vote], and we
were turned off then. We sent him running. We didn't like his arrogance,
his air."

But, relying on his connections with black church leaders and community activists from his organizing days, Obama more than overcame the
resistance. Project Vote met its extraordinary goal of registering nearly a
hundred and fifty thousand new voters. For the first time in the history of
Chicago, registration in the majority-black wards was greater than that in
the majority-white wards. Project Vote played a pivotal role in the election of Carol Moseley Braun, the first African-American woman ever
elected to the Senate and only the second African-American to be elected
to the chamber since Reconstruction. Bill Clinton, in a three-way race
with George H. W. Bush and Ross Perot, became the first Democratic

candidate to win Illinois since Lyndon Johnson overwhelmed Barry Gold-water, in 1964.

Obama, who was now thirty-one, was so successful in his leadership of Project Vote that Democratic Party political operatives in Chicago took notice. At the press conference announcing the results of Project Vote, Obama stood quietly to the side and let Jesse Jackson, Bobby Rush, and other senior Democratic Party politicians get the attention. "It wasn't modesty. Barack is not modest," Schmidt said. "But rather than grab the spotlight, it was more important to him to have these people as potential allies down the road. That was way more important than to be a star at a two-bit press conference in 1992. That is very rare. He has always had a level of assurance and foresight that was very unusual."

Obama's effort also attracted the attention of the business community. *Crain's Chicago Business* reported that Obama had "galvanized Chicago's political community, as no seasoned politico had before."

One of the more important connections Obama formed during Project Vote was with Bettylu Saltzman, the daughter of Philip Klutznick, a rich developer who had been Secretary of Commerce in the Carter Administration. Saltzman was a well-known member of the Lakefront Liberals, left-leaning Chicagoans, predominantly Jewish, who lived in the high-rises along Lake Michigan and were vital fund-raising sources over the years for Illinois Democrats like Paul Douglas, Adlai Stevenson, Paul Simon, and Harold Washington. Saltzman was a regular at a group called the Ladies Who Lunch—a group of influential women in Chicago who included Christie Hefner, the chairman of Playboy Enterprises; the philanthropist Marjorie Benton; Isabel Stewart, who ran the Chicago Foundation for Women; Amina Dickerson, of Kraft Foods; the columnist Laura Washington; and Julia Stasch, of the MacArthur Foundation. Saltzman was also friendly with the wealthiest Jewish business families in town: the Crowns and the Pritzkers. When Obama paid a visit to Saltzman to ask for help on Project Vote, she joined the growing contingent of people who came home to tell a spouse that she had just met the man who could be the first black President. "I told everyone I knew about this guy," she said. "Everyone," in Saltzman's case, turned out to be a core of wealthy Chicagoans who one day would help form the financial base of Obama's political campaigns.

The meeting with Saltzman, and others like it during Project Vote, was Obama's introduction to the northern reaches of Chicago. He already had an education in the diversity of the South Side—the churches, the African-American neighborhoods, the liberal politics of Hyde Park and the university. Now he was reaching to the Gold Coast, the near North Side, the northern suburbs—liberal enclaves, too, but with a great deal more money.

Don Rose, a political consultant who worked with Martin Luther King, Jr., during his Chicago years and with a raft of Democratic politicians, said, "Obama is possibly the best networker I've ever seen. Bill Clinton might be his rival, but Barack is amazing. First, he comes to Chicago with a reference from Newton Minow's daughter, Martha. Then Newt introduces him to a circle of high-class liberal lawyers. He gets this job with the churches as an organizer, and he finds himself a network of pastors and people working in related non-profits and foundations. He also finds himself at the University of Chicago, and that has a network at the law school, the business school—and they are all bowled over to discover this brilliant black guy. There is also a Harvard network. There are also liberal, élite funders and agency heads: Bettylu Saltzman was also part of the Minow grouping and *she* has lots of friends. It's circle after circle that sometimes touch—or they can be bridged. An ambitious young man can get to know a whole lot of people. If you've impressed one or two people in three or four of these groupings, and you make it your business to do this for business or politics or social prestige, you can really go far."

Saltzman also had friends in the political world. She made sure to contact David Axelrod, a former Chicago *Tribune* reporter who had become a campaign consultant for Democratic candidates. Axelrod, a strategist who concealed his cunning behind a laconic charm, had worked for Simon, Stevenson, and Harold Washington, and, in 1991, was running the doomed Senate campaign of a personal-injury lawyer named Al Hofeld. He was especially involved with Richard M. Daley. "Bettylu called me up and said, 'I want you to meet this young guy who's running Project Vote,'" Axelrod recalled. "She said, 'I know this is an odd thing, but I think he could be the first black President.' She really did say it. And I thought, Well that's a little grandiose, but I'd like to meet him." Saltzman also knew people in the foundation world, the business world, and the political world. "Barack quickly became part of that circle, and they all took an interest in him, because he was an impressive young guy," Axelrod said.

When a reporter who was writing a profile of Obama for *Chicago* magazine after the success of Project Vote asked him about running for office, Obama answered coyly. This was clearly not the first time someone had raised the question. "Who knows?" he said. "But probably not immediately. Was that a sufficiently politic 'maybe'? My sincere answer is, I'll run if I feel I can accomplish more that way than agitating from the outside. I don't know if that's true right now. Let's wait and see what happens in 1993. If the politicians in place now at city and state levels respond to African-American voters' needs, we'll gladly work with and support them. If they don't, we'll work to replace them."

Obama married Michelle Robinson, on October 3, 1992, just as Project Vote was winding down before the election. Surrounded by guests from Kenya, Hawaii, and Chicago, Jeremiah Wright presided over the ceremony at Trinity. Wright talked about the importance of marriage and responsibility, especially for black men. Because Michelle's father, Fraser, had died the previous year, her brother Craig walked her down the aisle. At the reception, held at the South Shore Cultural Center, the music was "old-school stuff, music you could move to," Carol Anne Harwell recalled. Santita Jackson, Michelle's high-school classmate and Jesse Jackson's daughter, sang.

Obama's relationship with Michelle was not without its complications. Barack's ambitions and considerable ego often clashed with Michelle's desire for stability and a sense of partnership. But the relationship was his emotional anchor. A few years after the wedding, but before Obama declared his intention to run for his first political office, a photographer named Mariana Cook visited Barack and Michelle at their apartment in Hyde Park and photographed them sitting together on a couch under a couple of Indonesian prints. Cook also interviewed them for a book she was assembling about marriage.

Obama, for his part, clearly believed that he had found something profound in his wife. "All my life, I have been stitching together a family, through stories or memories or friends or ideas," he told Cook. "Michelle has had a very different background—very stable, two-parent family, mother at home, brother and dog, living in the same house all their lives. We represent two strands of family life in this country—the strand that is very stable and solid, and then the strand that is breaking out of the constraints of traditional families, traveling, separated, mobile. I think there was that strand in me of imagining what it would be like to have a stable, solid, secure family life."

Michelle's remarks were no less loving, but it was clear that she felt that her husband was headed into potentially dangerous waters. "There is a strong possibility that Barack will pursue a political career, although it's unclear," she said. "There is a little tension with that. I'm very wary of politics. I think he's too much of a good guy for the kind of brutality, the skepticism. When you are involved in politics, your life is an open book, and people can come in who don't necessarily have good intent. I'm pretty private, and like to surround myself with people that I trust and love. In politics you've got to open yourself to a lot of different people."

With Project Vote and the election over, Obama again turned to his book. He had been committed to writing a book about race since his days at Harvard. Just after he was elected president of the *Harvard Law Review*, in February, 1990, Jane Dystel, a literary agent in New York, noticed the article in the New York *Times* about Obama's winning the post. Dystel called Obama in Cambridge and suggested that he write a book. She urged him to put together a proposal that she could submit to publishers. Dystel, whose father had been head of Bantam Books, clearly saw something in Obama, who came to visit her in New York. Her associate Jay Acton, who represented James Baldwin, said maybe they could get Obama to write a book like *The Fire Next Time*.

Later, when Obama recounted his discussions with publishers to his friend and law colleague Judd Miner, he was amused by the assumptions they made about him. He recalled that one publisher "asked me to write about being poor and rising from the ghetto of Chicago. I told them, 'I never did take that trip but I would like to write about the trip I have taken.'"

After conducting an auction with a few other publishers, Dystel sold Obama's book to Poseidon Press, a small imprint of Simon & Schuster run by an editor named Ann Patty. The advance was reportedly over a hundred thousand dollars. Obama received half that amount on signing the contract.

While Obama was still at Harvard, he made notes for a book. Fairly soon, he realized that he had no interest in writing a straight book about issues—about civil-rights law, affirmative action, or organizing. Instead, he wanted to write about himself, about his struggle with identity and the elusive ghost of his father. Relying on the journals that he had been keeping since his days as an undergraduate, he started working in earnest. After his wedding and honeymoon, he spent a month alone, writing, in a rented hut on Sanur Beach, in Bali.

Obama took a long time to finish. "He had to come to terms with some events in his life that some people pay years of therapy to get comfortable revealing," his friend Valerie Jarrett said. The writing went slowly, she said, "because everything was so raw."

Along the way, Obama experienced some minor dramas of the publishing trade. In the summer of 1993, Simon & Schuster closed Poseidon. When publishers close an imprint, they usually transfer books for which they have high hopes to another imprint inside the house and try to get rid of projects without much promise. Obama had missed deadlines and handed in bloated, yet incomplete, drafts. "We took fliers on things," Ann Patty said, "but, when Poseidon went down, Simon & Schuster kept the gold and got rid of the fliers."

Dystel took the book, now entitled *Dreams from My Father*, to Times Books, an imprint at Random House run by the former Washington *Post* reporter and editor Peter Osnos. Times Books paid Simon & Schuster forty thousand dollars for the book—a very good deal, it turned out, for Random House. Simon & Schuster ended up losing the rest of the advance it had paid.

Henry Ferris, the editor at Times Books who worked directly with Obama, communicated with him almost entirely by telephone and express mail. Obama proved receptive to editing. Ferris asked him to reduce one thirty-page episode to fifteen pages; Obama did it without complaint or hesitation. "He was a quick study," Ferris said. (In a preface to the 2004 paperback edition, Obama writes that he now winces when he reads the book and still has the "urge to cut the book by fifty pages or so" and get rid of "mangled" sentences and expressions of emotion that seem "indulgent or overly practiced.")

Ferris was impressed by his young author's sturdy ego and sense of his own potential. "He thought enough of himself and his story that he thought to write his autobiography at the age of thirty," Ferris said. "He knew his story was special, his parentage was interesting. He had that much of a sense of story. I saw him as a person who at that time was in a position to talk about race relations in this country in a way that certainly I can't and few can. He understood the white world and the black world and he was tossed back and forth between them. That was something that I remember him talking about, being in a position to speak about things in a way that others couldn't."

With *Dreams from My Father*, Obama was working in the oldest, and arguably the richest, genre of African-American writing: the memoir. The memoir tradition begins with the first slave narratives: *A Narrative of the Uncommon Sufferings and Surprizing Deliverance of Briton Hammon, a Negro Man*, a pamphlet published in Boston in 1760; *A Narrative of the Most Remarkable Particulars in the Life of James Albert Ukawsaw Gronniosaw, an African Prince, as Related by Himself*, in 1770; and then, in 1789, an international best-seller, *The Interesting Narrative of the Life of Olaudah Equiano, or Gustavus Vassa, the African, Written by Himself.* Equiano recounted the story of his capture as a boy of eleven, his purchase by a sea captain, and then, after he buys his own freedom, his life in England as an abolitionist. There are more than six thousand slave narratives known to scholars, and, as the literary scholar Henry Louis Gates, Jr., writes, these texts arose out of the writers' need to assert their own identity, and that of their people, as thinking human beings and not, as they were viewed by American law, as the animal possessions of white men: "Deprived of access to literacy, the tools of citizenship, denied the rights of selfhood by law, philosophy, and pseudo-science, and denied as well the possibility, even, of possessing a collective history as a people, black Americans—commencing with the slave narratives in 1760—published their *individual* histories in astonishing numbers, in a larger attempt to narrate the collective history of 'the race.' "

Any canon or college syllabus of African-American autobiography tends to begin with certain cornerstone texts: the three slave narratives of Frederick Douglass; *Up from Slavery*, by Booker T. Washington; Harriet Jacobs's *Incidents in the Life of a Slave Girl: Written by Herself; The Souls of Black Folk* and *Dusk of Dawn*, by W. E. B. DuBois; *The Big Sea*, by Langston Hughes; *Black Boy*, by Richard Wright; *Dust Tracks on a Road*, by Zora Neale Hurston; *Notes of a Native Son* and *Nobody Knows My Name*, by James Baldwin; *The Autobiography of Malcolm X; I Know Why the Caged Bird Sings*, by Maya Angelou. (James Weldon Johnson's *The Autobiography of an Ex-Colored Man* and Ralph Ellison's *Invisible Man* are novels, and yet they are so clearly based on the events of the authors' lives that they are often discussed alongside these memoirs.) Depending on which critic is doing the accounting, the canon of memoirists also includes Ida B. Wells, William Pickens, Anne Moody, Claude Brown, Eldridge Cleaver, Ralph Abernathy, Roger Wilkins, George Jackson, Angela Davis, Alice Walker, Amiri Baraka, John Edgar Wideman, Audre Lorde, John Hope Franklin, bell hooks, Brent Staples, and Itabari Njeri. Some co-authored memoirs by entertainers such as Billie Holiday (*Lady Sings the Blues*), Dick Gregory (*Nigger*), Sammy Davis, Jr., (*Yes I Can*), and Count Basie (*Good Morning Blues*) can also claim a place on the extended list. One way that Obama joins this tradition is that usually, in European literature, a writer writes his or her novels, plays, and poems, and then, toward the end, writes a memoir; it is more common among African-American writers than Europeans to *begin* their writing lives by asserting themselves with an autobiography.

As a young man, Obama searched for clues to his own identity by very purposefully reading his way through DuBois, Hughes, Wright, Baldwin, Ellison, and Malcolm X. He has also mentioned texts by Douglass, Marcus Garvey, Martin Delany, and a range of novelists—in particular, Toni Morrison. In fact, reading as a way of becoming is a feature of African-American autobiography, as it is of so many outsider-memoirists of any ethnicity. In memoirs of all kinds, a young person in search of a way to rise above his circumstances or out of his confusion invariably goes to the bookshelf. Malcolm X, for one, provides an extended account of his self-education. He reads histories by Will Durant and H. G. Wells, which gave him a glimpse into "black people's history before they came to this country"; he reads Carter G. Woodson's *The Negro in Our History*, which "opened my eyes about black empires before the black slave was brought to the United States, and the early Negro struggles for freedom." In *Soul on Ice*, Eldridge Cleaver recounts his reading of Rousseau, Paine, Voltaire, Lenin, Bakunin, and Nechayev's *Catechism of the Revolutionist* as a means of detailing his own radical catechism. Young autobiographers also read other memoirs to learn the form. Claude Brown told an audience in New York in 1990 that he carefully studied the structures of Douglass's slave narratives and Richard Wright's *Black Boy* before writing *Manchild in the Promised Land*, his memoir of growing up in Harlem in the nineteen-forties and fifties. Even Sammy Davis, Jr., in his Harlem-to-Hollywood autobiography, *Yes I Can*, is eager to tell the reader that, while he was on "latrine duty" in the Army, he became an obsessive reader of Wilde, Rostand, Poe, Dickens, and Twain; and that helped him endure the racism of his fellow soldiers.

While it is safe to assume that by the time Obama published he was thinking about public office, even he, for all his ambition and his self-assurance, could not have envisioned that *Dreams from My Father*, just thirteen years later, would provide a trove of material for voters, journalists, speechwriters, and media consultants during a Presidential campaign. After Obama's emergence as a national politician, it was difficult to read it solely in the spirit in which it was written; the book became a sourcebook of stories endlessly called upon for use in politics. *Dreams from My Father* is important precisely because it was written when Obama was young and unguarded. "Barack is who he says he is," Michelle Obama said. "There is no mystery there. His life is an open book. He wrote it and you can read it. And unlike any candidate he has really exposed himself, pre-political ambition, so it's a book that is kind of free from intent. It is the story of who he is."

Many journalists eager to write or film profiles of Obama when he became a candidate read *Dreams from My Father* and expressed dismay that he had not written his book according to the precise standards of scholarly or journalistic veracity. In fact, Obama, unlike most other memoir writers, alerts his reader to the flexible terms of his book. He signals his awareness of "the temptation to color events in ways favorable to the writer" and "selective lapses of memory." He does not pretend to a purely factual rendition. He appropriates some of the tools of fiction. While the book is based on his journals and conversations with family members, "the dialogue is necessarily an approximation of what was actually said or relayed to me." Moreover, some of the characters are composites; the names (with the exception of family members or well-known people) are altered; and chronology, he admits, has been changed to help move the story along. What's exceptional about this is not that Obama allows himself these freedoms, but, rather, that he cops to them right away.

W. E. B. DuBois set a standard for forthrightness about the genre of memoir, writing, "Autobiographies do not form indisputable authorities. They are always incomplete, and often unreliable. Eager as I am to put down the truth, there are difficulties; memory fails especially in small details, so that it becomes finally but a theory of my life, with much forgotten and misconceived, with valuable testimony but often less than absolutely true, despite my intention to be frank and fair." His book *The Autobiography of W. E. B. Du Bois*, he admits, is merely "the Soliloquy of an old man on what he dreams his life has been as he sees it slowly drifting away; and what he would like others to believe."

Obama's memoir is a mixture of verifiable fact, recollection, re-creation, invention, and artful shaping. The reader is hardly to be blamed for asking the difference, quite often, between a memoir and a novel that is obviously based on facts. A modern writer like Philip Roth constantly invokes this crossfire of genre distinctions and deliberately arouses in the reader an urge to ask what is true and what is not, all the while reminding the reader that life, as it is lived, is an unstructured mess, whereas the fiction writer constructs the impression of reality by shaping it, using it as the verbal clay he needs to tell his story and thereby reveal emotional or philosophical truths.

African-American autobiographies often follow a structure that the literary scholar Robert Stepto calls a "narrative of ascent." The narrator begins in a state of incarceration or severe deprivation. He breaks those bonds so that he may go out, discover himself, and make his imprint on the world. (When the young Frederick Douglass finally fights back against the evil overseer and "slave-breaker" Edward Covey, he writes, "You have seen how a man was made a slave; you shall see how a slave was made a man.") Sometimes the narrator will not know one or more of his parents; he may not know his date of birth. ("Of my ancestry," Booker T. Washington writes in *Up from Slavery*, "I know almost nothing.") He assesses and describes his deprivations, the oppression that keeps him down. He goes through trials. He takes a journey: he travels the Middle Passage; he escapes his slave-master; or, like Wright, he leaves the Jim Crow South for the Northern city, or, like Washington, heads *back* into the Deep South, or, like Malcolm X, goes from place to place, courting trouble, winding up in prison. He reads. He studies. He has experiences. He struggles with the absence of a father or struggles with the father who is there but cannot be relied upon. He *learns*. And, as he accumulates experience and endures his trials, he begins to discover his identity, often taking a new name as he does so.

In the case of many authors, including Douglass, Hughes, and Malcolm X, part of that struggle for identity includes wrestling with the fact of a white parent or grandparent. The narrator begins to find his place in a community of African-Americans. He discovers his mission and sets out to fulfill it. Douglass becomes a leading abolitionist, meets with Lincoln in the White House, and presses him to integrate the Union forces. DuBois helps found the N.A.A.C.P., becomes a giant of American scholarship, and ends his long life in Ghana.

Obama's reading of black memoirists when he was still living in Hawaii was the "homework" of a young man trying "to reconcile the world as I'd found it with the terms of my birth." And yet, in all the books he reads, he keeps finding authors filled with a depressing self-contempt; they flee or withdraw to varying corners of the world, and to Obama they are "all of them exhausted, bitter men, the devil at their heels."

For Obama, the great exception is Malcolm X. Despite their obvious differences of era, religion, temperament, and politics, it is not impossible to figure out why Obama is so taken with Malcolm. Malcolm's is a narrative of mixed raced, a missing father, and self-invention. He starts life as Malcolm Little, becomes "Detroit Red" on the street, "Satan" in prison, Minister Malcolm X, and then El-Hajj Malik El-Shabazz. "His repeated acts of self-creation spoke to me," Obama writes. "The blunt poetry of his words, his unadorned insistence on respect, promised a new and uncompromising order, martial in its discipline, forged through sheer force of will."

Obama was disturbed by one line of Malcolm's: "He spoke of a wish he'd once had, the wish that the white blood that ran through him, there by an act of violence, might somehow be expunged." The reference is to a moment in *The Autobiography of Malcolm X* when, as a minister of the Nation of Islam, Malcolm gives a speech in Detroit and talks about the rape of his grandmother:

> We're all black to the white man, but we're a thousand and one different colors. Turn around, *look* at each other! What shade of black African polluted by the devil white man are you? You see me—well, in the streets they used to call me Detroit Red. Yes! Yes, that raping, red-headed devil was my *grandfather*! That close, yes! My mother's father! . . . If I could drain away his blood that pollutes *my* body, and pollutes *my* complexion, I'd do it! Because I hate every drop of the rapist's blood that's in me! And it's not just me, it's *all* of us! During slavery, *think* of it, it was a *rare* one of our black grandmothers, our great-grandmothers and our great-great-grandmothers who escaped the white rapist slavemaster. . . . Turn around and look at each other, brothers and sisters, and *think* of this! You and me, polluted all these colors—and this devil has the arrogance and the gall to think we, his victims, should *love* him!

Obama, who has been raised by a loving white mother and white grandparents, writes that even as a teenager, he knew that the presence of white family, white blood, could never become an abstraction: "If Malcolm's discovery toward the end of his life, that some whites might live beside him as brothers in Islam, seemed to offer some hope of eventual reconciliation, that hope appeared in a distant future, in a far-off land. In the meantime, I looked to see where the people would come from who were willing to work toward this future and populate this new world."

Obama's Malcolm is not the Malcolm of mid-career. He admires "The Ballot or the Bullet" but not the strains of militancy and separatism, the faith in the cosmology of Elijah Muhammad. He admires Malcolm's masculine pride, his eloquence, his determined self-evolution, and the revelation at the end of his life that religious faith and separatism are incompatible. At law school, Obama's habit of mind was always conciliatory. That is the Malcolm he desires as well—the self-confident, charismatic, eloquent leader who comes to see his faith in a broader, more humanist light, the militant who begins to see the value of a broader embrace.

After he became President, Obama told me, "I think that I find the sort of policy prescriptions, the analysis, the theology of Malcolm full of holes, although I did even when I was young. I was never taken with some of his theorizing. I think that what Malcolm X did, though, was to tap into a long-running tradition within the African-American community, which is that at certain moments it's important for African-Americans to assert their manhood, their worth. At times, they can overcompensate, and popular culture can take it into caricature—blaxploitation films being the classic example of it. But if you think about it, of a time in the early nineteen-sixties, when a black Ph.D. might be a Pullman porter and have to spend much of his day obsequious and kow-towing to people, that affirmation that I am a man, I am worth something, I think was important. And I think Malcolm X probably captured that better than anybody."

In the original Simon & Schuster contract, dated November 28, 1990, *Dreams from My Father* had been tentatively titled "Journeys in Black and White." As Obama writes, the book is a "boy's search for his father, and through that search a workable meaning for his life as a black American." Obama told me that he was quite "conscious" of the great tradition of African-American memoir and knew that he had a more modest story to tell. "I mean, at that point I'm thirty-three and what have I done?" he said. "The only justification for anybody wanting to read it was to be able to use my experiences as a lens to examine what's happened to issues of race in America, what's happened to issues of class in America, but also to give people a sense of how it's possible for a young person to pull strands of himself together into a coherent whole." The most limited way to read the book is to comb it for its direct referents to reality, to discover "who is who." One can discover that "Marty" is (for the most part) Jerry Kellman. Or that the saturnine nationalist known as "Rafiq" is based on a community activist in Chicago named Salim al Nurridin. Or that the militant-sounding "Ray" at Punahou is an ex-con named Keith Kakugawa. And so on. Some of these real people made news during the campaign when they protested some aspect of their portrayals. (Kakugawa said he wasn't as obsessed with race; al Nurridin disputed the rendition of his ideology.) Ann Dunham, who was dying, in Hawaii, of uterine and ovarian cancer, read drafts of her son's book, and although she admired it, even she had quibbles. She told her friend Alice Dewey that she was really not quite so naïve about race as her son made her out to be.

Dreams from My Father is the extended and relatively guileless self-expression of Obama *before* he became a public man, a politician. We read him, as a young man reflecting on a still younger man, dealing with countless questions: What is race? What does it mean to be African-American?

What does it mean to be raised by whites and identify oneself as black? What is the right way to live a life? And how is race relevant to such moral considerations?

Obama's story contains many of the familiar features of African-American autobiography: a search for a missing parent; a search for a racial identity; a search for a community and a mission; a physical journey that echoes all his other searches. Obama, however, is in many ways more privileged than his literary predecessors. He is middle-class. He has bene-fited from the passage of time and from many laws. He enters institutions of privilege often denied his precursors. And, both as a person and as a storyteller, this poses a problem for him. The lawns and quadrangles of Punahou, Occidental, Columbia, and Harvard Law School are not ordi-narily the landscapes of epic struggle.

Moreover, Obama has grown up, sometimes to his frustration, *after* the civil-rights movement. His is hardly a world free of racism, but it is a world in which the popular culture around him is rich with African-American stars, from the musicians he watched on television as a child in Hawaii to the enormously influential figures of his adulthood. What's more, his white friends have listened to those records, watched those shows, idolized those same stars. Knowingly or not, they have come to accept Ralph Ellison's idea that what we understand to be American is, in countless visible and invisible ways, impossible without African-Americans. One of his earliest recognitions of racism comes when, watch-ing television in Indonesia, thousands of miles away from black America, he notices that the Bill Cosby character in "I Spy" never gets any women, while his white partner, Robert Culp, makes out on a regular basis. Back in Hawaii, a classmate asks to touch his hair the way she might tentatively touch the coat of a farm animal. Painful, but, again, they are hardly moments worthy of *Manchild in the Promised Land.*

Narratives of ascent, by their nature, must begin with deprivation, oppression, and existential dread. Obama seems to sense this problem and, at the very start of his book, darkens his canvas as well as he can. He is twenty-one and living in New York, on East Ninety-fourth Street, between First and Second Avenues. This has always been a world away from East Ninety-fourth Street and Park or Madison or Fifth Avenues, and the block was markedly worse then than it is now. Veteran residents of the building told a reporter for the New York *Times* that there had been assaults in the hallways and that drug use was common. And yet it was not Bushwick, either. Elaine's and the Ninety-second Street Y are nearby. Obama places himself in that "part of that unnamed, shifting border between East Harlem and the rest of Manhattan," knowing that the mere mention of Harlem, to some white non–New Yorkers, will resonate in a minor key. The block is "uninviting," "treeless," shadowy; the buzzer is broken; the heat is spotty; the sounds of gunfire echo in the night, and a "black Doberman the size of a wolf" prowls nearby, an empty beer bottle clamped in its jaws. And, to flavor the menacing picture with a dash of class resentment, Obama reports that "white people from the better neighborhoods" walk their dogs on his street "to let the animals shit on our curbs."

Obama heightens the facts of his spare and lonely life. His "kindred spirit" is a silent and solitary neighbor who lives alone, and eventually dies alone, a crumpled heap on the third-floor landing. "I wished that I had learned the old man's name," the narrator reports gravely. "I felt as if an understanding had been broken between us—as if, in that barren room, the old man was whispering an untold history." A paragraph later we realize the literary effect for which Obama is striving: the death of the old man with his "untold history" foreshadows by a month the death of the Old Man, Obama's father, who, of course, is himself the great untold story that Obama will set out to explore and tell. As he is cooking his eggs "on a cold, dreary November morning," Obama gets the news on a scratchy line from Nairobi.

Obama's book is a multicultural picaresque, a search both worldly and internal that will take him to Honolulu, Jakarta, Los Angeles, New York, Chicago, Nairobi, and his ancestral village of Kogelo. Along the way he accumulates knowledge, he peels back layer after layer of secrets, until he becomes his mature, reconciled self. When Obama writes a new preface for the 2004 edition, he is the Democratic Party nominee for U.S. senator from Illinois, and he insists that "what was a more interior, intimate" quest has now "converged with a broader public debate, a debate in which I am professionally engaged, one that will shape our lives and the lives of our children for many years to come." His quest is not just his own; it becomes emblematic of a national political quest. Writers rarely insist so boldly on the importance of their own books.

At the end of each of the memoir's three long sections ("Origins," "Chicago," and "Kenya"), the narrator is in tears and experiences an epiphany: first, he weeps when he sees his father in a dream and resolves to search for him; then he cries in Jeremiah Wright's church when he realizes that he has found both a community and a faith; and, finally, he collapses in tears at his father's grave, when he realizes that after discovering so much about his father—his intelligence, his failures, his tragic end—he is reconciled to his family and his past.

It is not difficult to understand why politically sympathetic readers were prepared to make extravagant, extra-literary claims for Obama's book during his Presidential campaign. They were reading him not as the civil-rights lawyer and law professor he was when the book was first published, but as a candidate who hoped to succeed George W. Bush, a President who was insistently anti-intellectual, an executive who resisted introspection as a suspect indulgence.

Race is at the core of Obama's story and, like any good storyteller, he heightens whatever opportunity arises to get at his main theme. When he is writing about the more distant past of his mother's side of the family, he tries to plumb the racial memories of his grandparents, people who "like most white Americans at the time" had "never really given black people much thought." Jim Crow around Wichita, Kansas, where they grew up, was in its "more informal, genteel form": "Blacks are there but not there, like Sam the piano player or Beulah the maid or Amos and Andy on the radio—shadowy, silent presences that elicit neither passion nor fear." But when the Dunhams lived briefly after the war in north Texas, they begin to feel the presence of race. At the bank, Toot, Obama's grandmother, is told that a "nigger" like the janitor, Mr. Reed, should never be called "Mister." His mother, Ann, who was eleven or twelve, is harassed as a "nigger lover" and a "dirty Yankee" for having a black girl as a friend. Here Obama is careful to signal his own doubt; memory, and its deceptive nature, is also his theme. "It's hard to know how much weight to give to these episodes," he writes. Obama is skeptical when his grandfather says that he and Toot left Texas for Seattle to escape Southern racism; Toot suggests that a better job opportunity was more likely the case. Obama's predilection, as the book will show, is to reconcile possibilities. He comes to suspect that, in his grandfather's mind, the wounds of blacks "merged with his own: the absent father and the hint of scandal, a mother who had gone away," the sense that as a young man he had been shunned as not quite respectable— a "wop," his in-laws called him. "Racism was part of that past, his instincts told him, part of convention and respectability and status, the smirks and whispers and gossip that had kept him on the outside looking in."

Obama is also wise to Hawaii, to the "ugly conquest" of the islands through "aborted treaties and crippling disease," the exploitation by missionaries and the cane and pineapple barons. "And yet, by the time my family arrived"—in 1959, the same year as statehood—"it had somehow vanished from collective memory," he writes, "like morning mist that the sun burned away." There is something deeply attractive about Obama in this mode, when he is unsentimentally trying to grasp the complexity of things.

Obama's novelistic contrivances can sometimes feel strained. In Chapter 2, he recalls a day when he is nine years old and living with his family in Indonesia. He is sitting in the library of the American Embassy, in Jakarta, where his mother teaches English. The scene is painted in palpable detail: the traffic-choked road to the embassy, with its rickshaws and over-crowded jitneys; the "wizened brown women in faded brown sarongs" with their baskets of fruit; the "smartly dressed" Marines at the embassy; his mother's boss, who "smelled of after-shave and his starched collar cut hard into his neck." Obama recalls ignoring the World Bank reports and geological surveys and finding a collection of *Life* magazines. He thumbs through the ads: "Goodyear Tires and Dodge Fever, Zenith TV ('Why not the best?') and Campbell's Soup ('Mm-mm good!')." Then he comes on a photograph of a Japanese woman "cradling a young, naked girl in a shallow tub": the girl is gnarled and crippled. Then he comes across a photograph of a black man who has used a chemical treatment to whiten his complexion. "There were thousands of people like him," he learns, "black men and women back in America who'd undergone the same treatment in response to advertisements that promised happiness as a white person." Reading this, Obama recalls, "I felt my face and neck get hot." The article is like an "ambush" on his sensibilities and innocence. "I imagine other black children, then and now, undergoing similar moments of revelation," Obama writes.

During the Presidential campaign, a journalist from the Chicago *Tribune* searched for the article. No such article ran. Obama responded feebly, "It might have been an *Ebony* or it might have been . . . who knows what it was?" Archivists at *Ebony* could not find anything, either. It might have been that Obama was thinking of John Howard Griffin's book *Black Like Me*. Griffin, a journalist and a burly white Texan who was wounded in the Second World War, decided, in 1959, to explore the lives of African-Americans in the South. On assignment for *Sepia*, a black-oriented magazine, Griffin shaved off his hair, exposed himself to long sessions of ultraviolet rays, and took huge doses of medication prescribed by a dermatologist to darken his skin; he then traveled around Louisiana, Georgia, Alabama, and Mississippi where he discovered the indignities suffered by men and women of color. His book, which was published in 1961, was a best-seller and remained popular for decades in American schools; however, in the Texas town where Griffin lived with his family, he was hanged in effigy.

Obviously, Obama was after an emotional truth here, and there certainly were articles published over time about black men and women who used whitening creams. The scene cannot help but echo that famous moment in Malcolm X's autobiography when he gets his first "self-defacing" conk, allowing a barber to take the kink out of his hair with a stinging lye-and-potato mixture called congolene.

Obama is not always easy on Ann Dunham. That is part of the drama of his book: his obvious love for a woman who is intelligent, idealistic, brave, and engaged with the world but also, at times, maddeningly naïve and frequently thousands of miles away. Obama's father, who is almost completely absent from Obama's life as anything more than a ghost, is angry and self-indulgent, brittle with his son on his one trip to Hawaii, and yet he is the singular object of the narrator's imaginings, at the center of a young man's quest to claim a race and a history.

Obama is proud of his mother's broadmindedness, her insistence that her family avoid behaving abroad like "ugly Americans." She demands that the family resist the temptation to treat anyone as an "other," as a "foreigner" or a benighted "local." More than her Indonesian husband, she does not automatically assume that an American habit of mind or culture is superior to the Indonesian. She aspires to be cosmopolitan. This clearly had an enormous influence on Obama, as a person and as a politician. And yet, early in the book, Obama is reflexively suspicious of his mother. He is the adolescent whose vanity resides in the way in which he "sees through" his parent. "My mother's confidence in needlepoint virtues," he writes, "depended on a faith I didn't possess, a faith that she would refuse to describe as religious; that, in fact, her experience told her was sacrilegious: a faith that rational, thoughtful people could shape their own destiny." He could hardly bear her self-conscious admiration for black culture. When she brings him Mahalia Jackson records and recordings of the speeches of Martin Luther King, Jr., he rolls his eyes. "Every black man was Thurgood Marshall or Sidney Poitier; every black woman Fannie Lou Hamer or Lena Horne," he writes, echoing the sarcastic tone of his teenaged self. "To be black was to be the beneficiary of a great inheritance, a special destiny, glorious burdens that only we were strong enough to bear."

Obama realizes that he has to learn how to be an African-American almost entirely on his own. It is not something that his mother and grandparents, however well intentioned they may be, can provide.

Obama sometimes felt himself a fake when he tried to imitate the language and resentments of his few black friends. When they would talk about "how white folks will do you," the phrase felt "uncomfortable in my mouth." "I felt like a non-native speaker tripping over a difficult phrase." Poignantly, Obama "ceased to advertise" his mother's race "when I began to suspect that by doing so I was ingratiating myself to whites." But, at the same time, he is well aware that he is no Richard Wright, who made the classic migration from Mississippi to the South Side; nor is he Malcolm Little, whose father, a Baptist minister and Garveyite organizer, was killed in Lansing.

"We were in goddamned Hawaii," Obama writes. "We said what we pleased, ate where we pleased; we sat at the front of the proverbial bus. None of our white friends, guys like Jeff or Scott from the basketball team, treated us any differently than they treated each other. They loved us, and we loved them back. Shit, seemed like half of 'em wanted to be black themselves—or at least Doctor J."

Nevertheless, Obama is lost, almost completely without African-American adults around to help him figure himself out. For an adolescent black kid in an almost wholly white world, Hawaii was a vexed and confusing paradise. "As it was, I learned to slip back and forth between my black and white worlds, understanding that each possessed its own language and customs and structures of meaning, convinced that with a bit of translation on my part the two worlds would eventually cohere."

Obama is hardly humorless in private. Occasionally a wry, mocking wit comes through in his public appearances. As a writer, though, he is usually earnest in the extreme. Chapter 5, which covers his years at Occidental, opens with him stretched out on his couch at three in the morning, listening to Billie Holiday singing "I'm a Fool to Want You" after a party at his apartment. Hasan has gone off to his girlfriend's house. He has a drink, a cigarette; we are led to believe that he has been partying pretty hard. He thinks about his father, about the drugs he has taken, about his youthful disaffection, his tussles with his mother. Then the record ends. "I suddenly felt very sober," and he pours himself another drink: "I could hear someone flushing a toilet, walking across a room. Another insomniac, probably, listening to his life tick away. That was the problem with booze and drugs, wasn't it? At some point they couldn't stop that ticking sound, the sound of certain emptiness." It is a 3 A.M. scene in which Sinatra meets Sartre.

Obama emphasizes two aspects of his life at Occidental, nearly to the exclusion of everything else: he rehearses different kinds of African-

American voices and describes his increasing politicization. The audio-book version of *Dreams from My Father* is arguably of greater interest than the text, and one of the reasons is that Obama, who admits that he has become a master of shifting his own voice and syntax to fit the situation, expertly mimics his black Occidental friends: Marcus, "the most conscious of brothers" with a sister in the Black Panthers; Joyce, who insists on her multiracial identity; Tim, with his argyle sweaters and peculiar taste for country music. As the book progresses, he is equally adept at imitating "Rafiq," the black nationalist, "Marty," the organizer, and his Kenyan relatives. He does not mock them; but there is a comic affection in those voices, a rich texture to the performance. He is also telling us something about the diversity of the black community, its range of qualities, anxieties, talents, and backgrounds.

The specifics of Obama's background are sui generis, but at Occidental he begins to identify with a nagging, and fairly common, problem: an anxiety about authenticity. He is reminded again of his bland good fortune at this pleasant college campus near Pasadena: "I was more like the black students who had grown up in the suburbs, kids whose parents had already paid the price of escape. You could spot them right away by the way they talked, the people they sat with in the cafeteria. When pressed, they would sputter and explain that they refused to be categorized. They weren't defined by the color of their skin, they would tell you. They were individuals." But Obama sees the lie in that, too. Race is a "fact." The kids who insist completely on their own individuality, the ones who want to trip the lock of color, of tribe, are also deluded. "They talked about the richness of their multicultural heritage and it sounded real good, until you noticed that they avoided black people."

The role model who shocks Obama into a sense of the life he ought to pursue is the straight-talking Chicago girl he calls Regina. She pointedly asks to call him Barack. She is delightful. She lives with her mother (the father is absent) on the South Side of Chicago. She talks about taverns and pool halls and close-knit neighbors, "about evenings in the kitchen with uncles and cousins and grandparents, the stew of voices bubbling up in laughter." Hers is a vision of black life that fills Obama with longing—"a longing for place, and a fixed and definite history." Not only does he get involved in the anti-apartheid movement; he also resolves to live, as an adult, in a large African-American community. The appearance of Regina, we come to feel, is a harbinger of Michelle Robinson.

Obama is on the move in his book, but he moves not to escape the onerous bonds known to the early memoirists—the bonds of slavery, Jim

Crow, prison, or an oppressive home. He is on the move in order to satisfy an inner search, to answer the questions of his divided self.

As a well-read student who is coming of age in the era of multiculturalism and critical theory, Obama is keenly aware of the academic notions that identity is, in some measure, a social construction. Race is a fact, a matter of genetics and physical attributes, but it is also a matter of social and self-conception. A commanding theme of the book is a young man's realization that he has a say in all of this; that he is not merely a "product" of family history; he has to make sense of his circumstances and his inheritances, and then decide what he wants to make of it all and who he wants to be. Identity and race are matters over which he has some influence.

In Chicago, Obama enters a realm of political work where an essential part of his job coincides with his internal search: he essentially canvasses the South Side. And, as he asks about the problems of one pastor, priest, and community activist after another, he adds to his store of knowledge about the way people live. Every possible form of black politics and political thinking—liberal integrationism, black nationalism, Afrocentrism, apathy, activism, even the tendency to conspiracy thinking—is heard and, in the memoir, given voice. At a meeting with a colleague called Deacon Will, a roomful of people are inspired by Will's moving description of his own life. "Then, as if the sight of this big man weeping had watered the dry surface of their hearts, the others in the room began speaking about their own memories in solemn, urgent tones," Obama writes. "They talked about life in small Southern towns: the corner stores where men had gathered to learn the news of the day or lend a hand to women with their groceries, the way adults looked after each other's children ('Couldn't get away with nothing, 'cause your momma had eyes and ears up and down the whole block'), the sense of public decorum that such familiarity had helped sustain. In their voices was no little bit of nostalgia, elements of selective memory; but the whole of what they recalled rang vivid and true, the sound of shared loss." The scene is sentimental, but the reader cannot help thinking that it, and a hundred instances like it, shaped Obama's thinking and political style: the belief in "sacred stories" as a form of political communication, understanding, and cohesion.

Obama is less sentimental about politics. In fact, as he recalls his daily encounters with the despair of the de-industrialized South Side, his instinct to personalize his vision is combined with a capacity to see problems with a certain dispassion, a clear-eyed sense of how markets and shifting economic fortunes create or destroy places like the South Side with a historical ruthlessness:

I tried to imagine the Indonesian workers who were now making their way to the sort of factories that had once sat along the banks of the Calumet River, joining the ranks of wage labor to assemble the radios and sneakers that sold on Michigan Avenue. I imagined those same Indonesian workers ten, twenty years from now, when their factories would have closed down, a consequence of new technology or lower wages in some other part of the globe. And then the bitter discovery that their markets have vanished; that they no longer remember how to weave their own baskets or carve their own furniture or grow their own food; that even if they remember such craft, the forests that gave them wood are now owned by timber interests, the baskets they once wove have been replaced by more durable plastics.

It is a passage that sounds strikingly similar to his mother's descriptions in her dissertation of how modern economic change threatened the culture of the Javanese villages where she was finishing her doctoral fieldwork. In Chicago, Obama is doing his own sort of fieldwork.

On the South Side, Obama could take in the full range of black political opinion. His neighborhood, Hyde Park–Kenwood, was also home to Louis Farrakhan, to Jesse Jackson's headquarters, and to intellectuals of varying ideologies and tempers. Obama's exposure to the sort of political viewpoints that are aired regularly on the street and black radio, but never on "Meet the Press" or "Washington Week," is something that he takes seriously. Obama allows Rafiq many paragraphs to dilate on a black-nationalist vision, one that interests, but, finally, frustrates the narrator. He reads issues of *The Final Call*, the newspaper of the Nation of Islam, and he listens to the nationalists on the radio, but he worries that what had been a generation ago, in Malcolm X's voice, a wake-up call and a summons to pride, has now become fantastical delusion, "one more excuse for inaction." Obama determines that the sort of black nationalism he is hearing from Rafiq and others has "twin strands": one that is an affirming message "of solidarity and self-reliance, discipline and communal responsibility" and another that depends on hatred of whites. Obama concludes that Rafiq is right to think that "deep down, all blacks were potential nationalists. The anger was there, bottled up and often turned inward." But a nationalism that depends on racial animosity, that is subject to conspiracy theory, contradicts the morality that his mother taught him, a morality of "subtle distinctions" between "individuals of goodwill and those who wished me ill, between active malice and ignorance or indifference." Obama concludes that nationalism, like Reagan's own sunny right-wing vision, depends on "magical thinking." African-Americans, he says, are those "who could least afford such make-believe." If community organizing insists on anything, it is pragmatism. And, since nationalism lacks "a workable plan," Obama looks elsewhere.

Chicago was also a place where Obama was trying to divine how race figured into his life as a man. How does tribe, especially when tribe is so complicated and mixed, figure into the question of whom to love, whom to marry? Obama dates both black and white women, and he is not reluctant to make that experience, too, a part of his narrative. In New York, he tells us, he loved a white woman: "She had dark hair, and specks of green in her eyes. Her voice sounded like a wind chime." They dated for a year. At one point, the woman invites him to her family's country house. It is autumn. They go canoeing across an icy lake. The family knows the land, "the names of the earliest white settlers—their ancestors—and before that, the names of the Indians who'd once hunted the land." The house is a family inheritance, and so, it seems, is the country itself. The library is filled with the pictures of dignitaries whom the grandfather had known. And Obama, who needs not remind us that his own inheritance is a more elusive thing, sees the gulf between him and this woman. "I realized that our two worlds, my friend's and mine, were as distant from each other as Kenya is from Germany," he writes. "And I knew that if we stayed together I'd eventually live in hers. After all, I'd been doing it most of my life. Between the two of us, I was the one who knew how to live as an outsider." He is like the "ethnic" in a hundred novels, the outsider who, with a mixture of wonder and apprehension, enters the world of the established order through romance.

The connection is fraught. After leaving a theater where they have seen a bitterly funny play about race, Obama's girlfriend is confused. She asks why black people are so "angry all the time." They argue. It is a familiar moment of romantic culture-clash; Obama is like one of Jhumpa Lahiri's young Bengali-Americans in the town house of his wealthy Wasp girlfriend. But Obama, as ever, refuses to describe their breakup as evidence of a hopeless gap. "Maybe even if she'd been black it still wouldn't have worked out," he writes. "I mean, there are several black ladies out there who've broken my heart just as good."

Obama ends the Chicago section by discovering Jeremiah Wright's Trinity United Church of Christ. The scene doesn't merely flirt with melodrama; as the portrayal of revelation, it insists on our good faith. As he sits in the pews early one Sunday morning, he hears in the music and in the minister's voice the convergence of "all the notes" of the many life stories he has been listening to for the past three years. Then, as in so many (far greater) memoirs, from Augustine to Malcolm X, Obama dramatizes his spiritual shift, his own leap of faith. Until now, he has resisted or deferred that leap, despite the blandishments of so many well-meaning ministers and activists, but now the stories of suffering and redemption suddenly link with *the* story of suffering and redemption. "In that single note—hope!—I heard something else; at the foot of that cross, inside the thousands of churches across the city, I imagined the stories of ordinary black people merging with the stories of David and Goliath, Moses and Pharaoh, the Christians in the lion's den, Ezekiel's field of dry bones. Those stories—of survival, and freedom, and hope—became our story, my story; the blood that had spilled was our blood, the tears our tears; until this black church, on this bright day, seemed once more a vessel carrying the story of a people into future generations and into a larger world. Our trials and triumphs became at once unique and universal, black and more than black." Obama's tears this time are not tears of despair, as they were at the end of "Origins." They are tears of release, the joy of having gained something profound: the comfort of community, the immensity of faith.

Obama begins the section on his journey to Kenya, which he made in the summer of 1988, with a series of portentous gestures. He spends three weeks in Europe before going to Africa and he reports gloomy disappointment with Paris, London, and Madrid (a plaza has "De Chirico shadows"). He is a "Westerner not entirely at home in the West, an African on his way to a land full of strangers." On the road between Madrid and Barcelona, he encounters a Spanish-speaking African, a *doppelganger* from Senegal. ("What was his name? I couldn't remember now; just another hungry man far away from home, one of the many children of former colonies— Algerians, West Indians, Pakistanis—now breaching the barricades of their former masters, mounting their own ragged, haphazard invasion. And yet, as we walked toward the Ramblas, I had felt as if I knew him as well as any man; that, coming from opposite ends of the earth, we were somehow making the same journey.") It is not an especially convincing sequence; even the highly sympathetic reader senses a young man wanting to dramatize his loneliness with maximal symbolic freight and artificial political meaning.

The symbol-laden atmosphere carries over to his five-week tour of Kenya. At the Nairobi airport, he encounters the beautiful Miss Omoro who helps him with his lost baggage and dazzles him by recognizing his name. Throughout the book (and, as we know, throughout his political career), Obama's name has been a symbol of his identity, both of his wrestling match with identity and of the way others see him. "For the first time in my life," Obama writes, "I felt the comfort, the firmness of identity that a name might provide, how it could carry an entire history in other people's memories." And he hasn't even left the airport.

On his first day, he experiences the shock of recognition: everyone looks like him! "All of this while a steady procession of black faces passed before your eyes, the round faces of babies and the chipped, worn faces of the old; beautiful faces that made me understand the transformation that [Obama's friends] claimed to have undergone after their first visit to Africa. For a span of weeks or months, you could experience the freedom that comes from not feeling watched, the freedom of believing that your hair grows as it's supposed to grow and that your rump sways the way a rump is supposed to sway. . . . Here the world was black, and so you were just you."

But Obama's naïveté and his eagerness to be transformed recedes as he starts listening to his storytelling relatives, men and women who deepen his knowledge about his father and all that his father has come to stand for in his mind. Obama's sister Auma, who studied in Germany, had spent time with Obama in the States. During that first encounter, she not only relayed the basic facts of their father's life in Nairobi—his work for an American oil company and various ministries; the political intrigues in Nairobi; his sad deterioration—but was prepared to separate myth from reality. She is, unlike so many others, properly skeptical, as well as highly intelligent. When she tells a story about how Jomo Kenyatta summoned the Old Man (as she calls Barack, Sr.) and warned him to "keep his mouth shut," she adds, "I don't know how much of these details are true." What is certain is that Barack, Sr., was a man made miserable by his political disappointment, and also by his "survivor's guilt," as one who was lucky enough to be airlifted to another world and return with an education. Auma is sympathetic, but she is also far more clear-eyed than Obama's mother was. The Old Man, she reports, was a miserable husband and a worse father. Drunk and raging, he would stagger into Auma's room late at night, wake her, and rail at her about how he had been betrayed. Obama realizes rather quickly that when he was ten and his father came to visit him, Barack, Sr., was already in the midst of his decline. The revelations are utterly at odds with Obama's long-held myth of his father's grandeur, a myth propagated by his loving and well-meaning mother. It is a myth, he comes to understand, that he can no longer rely on. "I felt as if my world had been turned on its head," Obama writes of his discoveries about his father, "as if I had woken up to find a blue sun in the yellow sky, or heard animals speaking like men." He realizes that he had been "wrestling with nothing more than a ghost." And in that discovery there is a dawning sense of wisdom and, even, liberation: "The fantasy of my father had at least kept me from despair. Now he was dead, truly. He could no longer tell me how to live."

As Obama spends more time in Kenya with Auma and his aunts, cousins, nephews, nieces, and step-siblings, his own vanities begin to peel away. Sitting with his relatives in the shabby apartment belonging to one of them, with its "well-worn" furniture and "two-year-old calendar," he recognizes the same attempt to ward off poverty, the same chatter, the same "absence of men" that he knew on the South Side. The apartment is "just like the apartments in Altgeld." In Africa, he sees that his self-willed collegiate asceticism is "hopelessly abstract, even self-indulgent." And as he walks in the vast Nairobi slum called Mathare, with its tin shacks and open sewage, he, too, comes to see what survivor's guilt is all about.

One day, he and a reluctant Auma go on a safari. Here, again, Obama cannot resist the symbolic weight of what he is seeing. In the Great Rift Valley, where remains of the early hominids, including "Lucy," were found, the same place that Obama's father described to the eager school-children in Hawaii, Obama sits at twilight watching hyenas feed on the carcass of a wildebeest and vultures loom on the perimeter of the kill. "It was a savage scene, and we stayed there for a long time, watching life feed on itself, the silence interrupted only by the crack of bone or the rush of wind, or the hard thump of a vulture's wings as it strained to lift itself into the current," Obama writes. "And I thought to myself: This is what Creation looked like. The same stillness, the same crunching of bone. There in the dusk, over the hill, I imagined the first man stepping forward, naked and rough-skinned, grasping a chunk of flint in his clumsy hand, no words yet for the fear."

Finally, Obama visits the scene of his own origins. With his sister Auma, his stepmother Kezia, his aunt Zeituni, and his brothers Roy and Bernard, he boards a train for Kisumu, the town closest to his ancestral village of Kogelo. He is riding on tracks that the British began laying in 1895, the year that Hussein Onyango Obama was born. While he rides the night train, Obama experiences one of his not infrequent reveries. Colonialism and its legacy are a persistent theme in Obama's book, and once more he crosses the wires of the personal and the political and imagines the result. Would a British officer on the train's maiden voyage "have felt a sense of triumph, a confidence that the guiding light of Western civilization had finally penetrated the African darkness? Or did he feel a sense of foreboding, a sudden realization that the entire enterprise was an act of folly, that this land and its people would outlast imperial dreams?"

In Kogelo, Obama meets "Granny" (this is Mama Sarah, as she is known locally, Barack, Sr.,'s stepmother) and learns from her his family's history as if from a Homeric singer of myth and epic. In interviews with visiting journalists, Sarah is plainspoken. When Obama gets her to recount family history, she is a vatic presence. Sitting outside her simple house, she speaks at great length, beginning:

> First there was Miwiru. It's not known who came before. Miwiru sired Sigoma, Sigoma sired Owiny, Owiny sired Kisodhi, Kisodhi sired Ogelo, Ogelo sired Otondi, Otondi sired Obongo, Obongo sired Okoth, and Okoth sired Opiyo. The women who bore them, their names are forgotten, for that was the way of our people.

She tells the whole story: The family's migration from Uganda to Kogelo. Battles with the Bantu. The saga of Onyango. It is a story of Genesis, of Exodus, of generations—all recalled and told in the Luo language, with the sagacity of a village ancient. The opening soliloquy lasts for more than ten pages and, after some narrative business, resumes for eighteen more. It's probably safe to say that these extended quotations are constructed out of Obama's effortful attempts to derive as much information from her as he could, and that he re-created her words in the most poetic way possible, but it is not a wholesale invention. Such recitation is a rich Luo tradition; often, even illiterate elders can recite their family histories for many generations.

The story of father and son, Onyango and Barack, Sr., and their attempts to move out into the greater world and then return, their attempts to be cosmopolitans—one at the high noon of colonialism, the next as colonialism dwindles and disappears—is a remarkable and tragic story. Onyango is, in many ways, an unsympathetic figure: brusque, cruel. But his curiosity and his ambition fascinate his grandson. Onyango, Sarah tells him, "became curious and decided that he must see these white men for himself." He sets out on foot for Nairobi, and returns "many months later" wearing the white man's clothing: trousers, a shirt, and "shoes that covered his feet," a sight that frightened the village children. They think that he has been circumcised or is somehow unclean and, therefore, hiding under these strange garments. He is an exile from Eden, and is now estranged from his village world. Soon, the white man's presence extends to every corner of Kenya and, as Sarah says, infects black Africa and economic norms and cultural values: "With tea, we found that we needed sugar, and teakettles, and cups. All these things we bought with skins and meat and vegetables." Then the Luo start working for wages, for "the white man's coin." Guns, war, a wholesale fall from grace soon follow. "Respect for tradition weakened, for young people saw that the elders had no real power. Beer, which once had been made of honey and which men drank only sparingly, now came in bottles, and many men became drunks. Many of us began to taste the white man's life, and we decided that compared to him, our lives were poor."

At the end of the long day with her grandson, Mama Sarah rummages around in a trunk that contains a few invaluable scraps of the past and gives them to Obama "like messages in bottles": the frayed document that Onyango carried as a servant among British officers, one of Barack, Sr.,'s letters of application to an American university. ("This was it, I thought to myself," Obama writes ruefully. "My inheritance.") Finally, he leaves his grandmother's hut and goes out into the yard to contemplate two concrete slabs covered in tile, the graves of his grandfather and father:

> Standing before the two graves, I felt everything around me—the cornfields, the mango tree, the sky—closing in, until I was left with only a series of mental images, Granny's stories come to life. . . .
>
> For a long time I sat between the two graves and wept. When my tears were finally spent, I felt a calmness wash over me. I felt the circle finally close. I realized that who I was, what I cared about, was no longer just a matter of intellect or obligation, no longer a construct of words. I saw that my life in America—the black life, the white life, the sense of abandonment I'd felt as a boy, the frustration and hope I'd witnessed in Chicago—all of it was connected with this small plot of earth an ocean away, connected by more than the accident of a name or the color of my skin. The pain I felt was my father's pain. My questions were my brothers' questions. Their struggle, my birthright.

The epilogue of *Dreams from My Father* ties things together neatly. The dreamy spell of recovering the past is broken before Obama leaves for home. A history teacher named Rukia Odero, a friend of his father's, warns against coming to Africa in a false quest for the "authentic." Obama must realize, she tells him, that every question has not been resolved.

Then the narrator brings us up to date. He admits that Harvard Law School was not always fun ("three years in poorly lit libraries"), but his idealism and heightened rhetoric are undiminished. In the words of the

Declaration of Independence, he says, he also hears the spirit of Frederick Douglass and Martin Delany, of Martin and Malcolm, of Japanese families in internment camps and Jewish piece-workers in sweatshops, of dust-bowl farmers and the people of Altgeld.

The story ends as traditional comedies do—with a wedding. When Michelle Robinson appears in the story, everything falls into place. Surrounded by his American and African family, by friends from organizing and from law school, from Punahou, Occidental, and Columbia, Obama and Michelle are married by Reverend Wright. "To a happy ending," Obama says as a toast and, in the African tradition, dribbles a little of his drink on the floor for the elders buried in the earth. Everything is reconciled. As befits the form of so many narratives of ascent, Obama has found himself and he has found a wife, a family, a community, a city, a faith, and a cause. At the same time, he has avoided his father's mistakes and grown out of his own. He is at ease. His wedding unites black and white, America and Kenya. And, since nearly all of the millions of people who have read the book read it in the light of an even greater quest, the hero and his story are elevated to mythic levels.

Peter Osnos and his colleagues at Times Books did not have outsized commercial ambitions for *Dreams from My Father*. "We had mid-list hopes for Obama," Osnos said. "Most galleys were done plain then, but we did a nice advance reader's edition, which indicates a certain interest. We were going for the multicultural thing." The book was reviewed positively in the New York *Times*, the Washington *Post*, and the Boston *Globe*, but it received scant publicity. Obama was interviewed in Los Angeles for the cable-television show "Connie Martinson Talks Books"; at the end of the show, Martinson turned to the author and said, "You know, I've never said this to anyone, but you would have a terrific career in politics." As part of a modest book tour, Obama gave readings for small crowds at bookstores including his local, Fifty-seventh Street Books, in Hyde Park. At Eso Won Books, an African-American bookstore in Los Angeles, just nine people came to see him, and Obama simply sat everyone in a circle and, after reading for a few minutes, shared details of his life and, ever the community organizer, asked people, "Tell me your name and what you do."

Times Books shipped about twelve thousand copies of *Dreams from My Father* and sold nine thousand. For less than ten thousand dollars, Times Books licensed the paperback to Kodansha, a Japanese-owned house, which was specializing in multicultural books for an American audience.

Dreams first appeared in the summer of 1995. The nineteen-nineties were rich with books by authors eager to write about themselves, their families, their deprivations, addictions, incarcerations, hallucinations, love affairs, illnesses, losses, and redemptions. Some of these books—like William Styron's *Darkness Visible*, Frank McCourt's *Angela's Ashes*, Mary Karr's *The Liar's Club*, Susanna Kaysen's *Girl, Interrupted*, Paul Monette's *Becoming a Man: Half a Life Story*, and James McBride's *The Color of Water*, all published by 1996—fulfilled Obama's literary ambitions: honesty, literary achievement, and astonishing sales. Obama waited more than a decade before his book became a best-seller.

Obama is hardly the only President to exhibit a literary bent before running for office. The most prolific of the literary Presidents was Theodore Roosevelt, who began his first book, a naval history of the War of 1812, while still an undergraduate at Harvard. As a reader, Roosevelt was heroic, capable of consuming two or three books in a night. His biographer Edmund Morris writes that in 1906 (as President!) Roosevelt read five hundred books or more, including *all* of Trollope's novels, the complete works of Thomas De Quincey, the complete prose of Milton, the poetry of Scott, Poe, and Longfellow, and William Dudley Foulke's *Life of Oliver P. Morton*. In all, Roosevelt wrote thirty-eight books, including, prior to his political career, biographies of Thomas Hart Benton, the Missouri senator and advocate of westward expansion, and Gouverneur Morris, the author of the preamble of the Constitution; a four-volume history, *The Winning of the West*; accounts of his many hunting trips; and scores of literary reviews and scientific articles. Woodrow Wilson, who had a doctorate in history and political science from Johns Hopkins, wrote *Congressional Government* and other academic studies well before his election as governor of New Jersey and then as President. Herbert Hoover was not unliterary. With his wife, Lou, he translated from Latin the Renaissance treatise on mining by Agricola, *De re metallica*. John Kennedy's literary efforts carried with them the aura of gilded sponsorship and professional assistance: his father promoted for publication his Harvard thesis "Why England Slept" and his aide Theodore Sorensen and others were more than helpful in the industrial production of *Profiles in Courage*.

Dreams from My Father ought not to be overvalued as a purely literary text; other writer-politicians such as Václav Havel and André Malraux wrote immensely greater and more mature work before holding office. But few American politicians of consequence before Obama have ventured to describe themselves *personally* with anything like the force and

emotional openness of *Dreams from My Father*. It is enough to say that *Dreams from My Father* is a good book that became, through political circumstance, an important one.

Early in the history of the Republic, it was impossible to imagine political self-projections at all. The Founding Fathers were philosopher-statesmen who saw the executive branch as a check on the unruly and corruptible legislature. Campaigning itself was a degradation of the office. "Motives of delicacy," Washington said, "have prevented me hitherto from conversing or writing on this subject, whenever I could avoid it with decency." Washington established the American Presidency as an office neither to be sought nor to be declined. Even in a democracy, it was somehow bestowed, not battled for. The historian M. J. Heale has called the early Presidential posture "the mute tribune."

Self-presentation in the American political culture begins in earnest with Andrew Jackson. After retiring from the military, in 1815, and setting up house on a thousand-acre plantation near Nashville, Jackson hired John Eaton, a young lawyer and one of his former soldiers in the War of 1812, to write his biography. Several years later, Jackson used Eaton's hagiographic *Life of Andrew Jackson* for his 1824 presidential race. The book, considered the first campaign biography ever published in the United States, presented Jackson as something utterly new in American politics: "the self-made man." When Jackson ultimately won the Presidency in 1828, his choice for Secretary of War was his biographer, John Eaton.

Jackson's brand of self-description has never faded from American politics. In 1852, just after completing *The Blithedale Romance*, Nathaniel Hawthorne wrote a slapdash biography of his Bowdoin College friend Franklin Pierce. It took around a month to complete. Hawthorne's reward was a consulship in Liverpool; the country's reward was a miserable President. William Dean Howells wrote a biography of Lincoln in the course of a few weeks and without ever meeting the man. The portrait, which was published in 1860, is the foundation of a million others: the "rude cabin of the settler," the earnest, rail-splitting autodidact, the "young backwoodsman" reading Blackstone's *Commentaries on the Laws of England* "under a wide-spreading oak" in the woods near New Salem. "People went by, and he took no account of them," Howells wrote of Lincoln's studies in the forest, "the salutations of acquaintances were returned with silence, or a vacant stare."

The stories have their variations: the modest warrior-statesmen dominate, though there occasionally appears an intellectual woodsman, like

Lincoln. But the template remains basically the same: the rise from modest circumstances to an adulthood of selfless service to flag and country. The biographers recount Jackson's mother telling her boys about the poverty of Ireland; Henry Clay's loss of his father in childhood; William Henry Harrison's log cabin; and Teddy Roosevelt at San Juan Hill. F.D.R.'s early biographers describe the classrooms of Groton as if they were carved from pinewood. "American campaign biographies still follow a script written nearly two centuries ago," the historian Jill Lepore writes. "East of piffle and west of hokum, the Boy from Hope always grows up to be the Man of the People. Will we ever stop electing Andrew Jackson?"

Obama's *Dreams from My Father* was not intended as a campaign biography, but it ended up acting as one. For a politician who was making the personal political and placing his own story and background at the center of his candidacy, writing *Dreams from My Father* was the ultimate act of self-creation. Its stories are at the center of Obama's thinking, his self-regard, his public rhetoric.

In the closing weeks of the 2008 Presidential campaign, as it seemed more and more evident that only a miracle worthy of Dorian Gray could rescue John McCain from defeat, a little-known conservative writer, magazine editor, and former talk-radio-show host named Jack Cashill advanced a theory popular on various right-wing Web sites, including American Thinker and World Net Daily, that Barack Obama was not the author of *Dreams from My Father*. This was a charge that, if ever proved true, or *believed* to be true among enough voters, could have been the end of the candidacy. Obama himself admitted that many people had got involved in his campaign "because they feel they know me through my books." This accusation of fraud possessed a diabolical potency for those who wished him ill. It suggested that the man poised to become the first African-American President, one celebrated for his language and his eloquence, could not possibly be such a good writer.

The true author of Obama's book, Jack Cashill suggested, was likely Bill Ayers, best known as the co-founder of the Weather Underground and the "terrorist" referred to in speeches by Sarah Palin. Cashill wrote that he had carefully studied books by Ayers, who had written a memoir and books about education, and through a process that he called "deconstruction," this latter-day Derrida charged that these volumes contained too much in common to skirt suspicion. For instance, Cashill wrote, they both misspelled Frantz Fanon as "Franz." They were both obsessed with eyes: "Ayers is fixated with faces, especially eyes. He writes of 'sparkling' eyes, 'shining' eyes, 'laughing' eyes, 'twinkling' eyes, eyes 'like ice.' . . . Obama is also fixated with faces, especially eyes. He also writes of 'sparkling' eyes, 'shining' eyes, 'laughing' eyes, 'twinkling' eyes. . . . Obama also used the highly distinctive phrase 'like ice.' "

And so on.

Cashill's assertions might well have remained a mere twinkling in the Web's farthest lunatic orbit had it not been for the fact that more powerful voices hoped to give his theory wider currency. A writer for the *National Review*'s popular blog The Corner declared Cashill's scholarly readings "thorough, thoughtful, and alarming." And Rush Limbaugh, during his nationwide radio broadcast on October 10, 2008, digressed from a mocking segment about *Dreams from My Father* to take up the Ayers-as-author theory:

> You know, there are stories out there, he may not have written this book. . . . There's no evidence that Obama has ever written anything prior to this except a poem, and the poem was as dumb as "A River, Rock, and Tree" that Maya Angelou did at the Slickster's inauguration back in 1993. There's no evidence that he has any kind of writing talent. We haven't seen anything he wrote at Harvard Law, or when he was at Columbia, or any tests that he's written. But if you read his books, if you listen to his audio reading of the book here, you don't hear this when Obama goes out and speaks. I would like for him to be given a test on his own book. You know how Charles Barkley once said he was misquoted in his own book? (laughs) I would like for Obama to actually be given a test on his own book.

This may not have been Limbaugh's most racist insinuation of the campaign. His delighted airing of the song "Barack, the Magic Negro," sung to the tune of "Puff, the Magic Dragon," probably reached a wider audience, and his description of Obama as a "Halfrican American" was, perhaps, more immediately pernicious, as it played on the rumors that the candidate lacked a proper American birth certificate, attended a madrassa as a boy in Indonesia, and was, in fact, either a Kenyan or an Indonesian citizen.

Still, Cashill's and Limbaugh's libel about Obama's memoir—the denial of literacy, the denial of authorship—had a particularly ugly pedigree. Writing elevated a slave from non-being, from commodity, to human status, as Henry Louis Gates, Jr., has written: a slave wrote, above all, to "demonstrate her or his own membership in the human community." In Frederick Douglass's narrative, his master, Mr. Auld, says, "Learning would spoil the best nigger in the world. . . . If you teach that nigger (speaking of myself) how to read, there would be no keeping him."

And yet writers like Douglass had to call on white men to authenticate their texts, the better to disprove the antebellum Jack Cashills and Rush Limbaughs ready to declare fraud. For the wary white readership, the abolitionists William Lloyd Garrison and Wendell Phillips provided prefaces for Douglass's book that represented seals of white endorsement. Garrison had first heard Douglass describe his life story at a speech at the Atheneum on Nantucket, in 1841, and now he was prepared to vouch for his text. "Mr. Douglass has very properly chosen to write his own Narrative, in his own style," Garrison wrote, "and according to the best of his ability, rather than to employ some one else. It is, therefore, entirely his own production." Garrison vouched for Douglass's literacy. The title, too, indicates a need to deny a sham. It is called the *Narrative of the Life of Frederick Douglass, an American Slave, Written by Himself.*

A century and a half later, thinking a degree of racial progress had been achieved, Barack Obama and his publisher had not thought to collect such endorsements.

Part Three

So he tested these truths of his against the blight of Chicago.
—Saul Bellow, *The Dean's December*

Chapter Seven

Somebody Nobody Sent

In the summer of 1991, Barack Obama moved back to Chicago and waited for his public life to begin. Abner Mikva, a fixture of liberal independent politics in Chicago and a judge on the D.C. Circuit Court of Appeals, had offered him a clerkship, and although Obama turned him down, the two men became friends, having breakfast or lunch downtown or at the Quadrangle Club in Hyde Park to talk politics. Obama confided that at some point—soon, he hoped—he wanted to run for office. Mikva was coming to see that, while Obama was more serene than Bill Clinton, far less grasping and needy, he was immodest in his ambition. "I thought, this guy has more chutzpah than Dick Tracy," Mikva said. "You don't just show up in Chicago and plant your flag."

By way of avuncular counsel, Mikva told Obama one of the most famous stories in the history of Chicago politics. Mikva grew up in Milwaukee, where the political culture was so open that, legend had it, someone who volunteered at party headquarters in the morning could wind up county chairman by nightfall. In 1948, Mikva, a student at the University of Chicago Law School, wanted to work for the Democratic Party, which was running two liberals: Paul Douglas for the Senate and Adlai Stevenson for governor. On the way home from class one night, Mikva stopped by the ward headquarters. "Timothy O'Sullivan, Ward Committeeman" was painted on the window. Mikva went in and asked if he could work for Stevenson and Douglas. The ward committeeman took the cigar out of his mouth and asked, "Who sent you?"

"Nobody sent me," Mikva replied. "I just want to help."

The committeeman jammed the cheroot back in his mouth and frowned.

"We don't want nobody that nobody sent," he said and dismissed the young law student.

Recalling the story and Obama's resigned reaction, Mikva said, "That's Chicago. It's a place where people put their relatives in jobs, where the machine ruled and, to an extent, still does. You just don't show up and come barging in."

Obama did his best to steer clear of the machine. He spent a dozen years as a lawyer and as a teacher. His part-time work in both professions also helped shape his political sensibility, deepen his thinking (especially about the law and race), and widen his web of associations. Judson Miner, who was Obama's mentor at Davis Miner, was a model of anti-establishment, anti-machine politics. In 1969, two years after graduating from law school and a year after the riots at the Democratic Convention, he founded the Chicago Council of Lawyers, an organization of progressive attorneys intent on creating an alternative bar association to challenge the failings of the legal system and improve services for the poor. The council issued reports analyzing candidates for the bench, campaigned for judicial reforms, and placed articles in the local press. Miner did not cultivate the radical reputation of a William Kunstler, but, when he was still in his thirties, he gained a singular reputation in civil rights. In Chicago, he was *the* civil-rights lawyer, known for representing plaintiffs in sex- and race-discrimination suits, voting-rights suits, tenants'-rights and corporate-whistleblower cases. Among African-Americans, especially, Miner was celebrated for having been Harold Washington's corporation counsel—the top legal job in City Hall—in his final two years in office.

Davis Miner was a boutique firm with around a dozen lawyers. As with all small civil-rights firms, one of its biggest problems was that, when it sued the city or a large corporation, it was almost always in opposition to a huge LaSalle Street firm that was able to throw armies of associates into the fray, filing one defense motion after another, swamping the plaintiff under an avalanche of work and accumulating fees.

From 1992 to 1995, Obama was an ordinary associate at Davis Miner, even though he spent a great deal of time writing and some time teaching. From 1997 until 2004, when he ran for the U.S. Senate, he was "of counsel," a part-time position paid by the hour. Obama rarely went to court and his overall legal record was modest. He appeared in court as counsel in five district-court cases and five cases heard by the Seventh Circuit Court of Appeals. All told, Miner said, Obama "contributed" to thirty cases, often in a secondary or tertiary role. Mainly, he drafted memoranda and motions, and prepared depositions. "I was one of the better writers," Obama recalled. "I ended up doing the more cerebral writing, less trial work. That's actually something I regret, not doing more trial work."

Obama may not have compiled a voluminous case record, but the cases he worked on reflected the sense of virtue he sought when he turned down corporate jobs and judicial clerkships. Unlike so many of his Harvard classmates, who were making six-figure salaries at corporate firms and expecting more, Obama, at a salary of around fifty thousand dollars a year, was battling corporations in court rather than defending them. In 1994, he worked on a suit against Citibank and its mortgage practices regarding minorities. The same year, he was on a team of lawyers that, in the Seventh Circuit, defended a securities trader named Ahmad Baravati, who had been blackballed by his employer, Josephthal, Lyon & Ross, after reporting fraudulent practices at the firm. Arguing that an arbitrator had the right to award Baravati a hundred and twenty thousand dollars in punitive damages, Obama parried with Judge Richard Posner, one of the leading conservative jurists in the country. In the end, Posner sided with Obama's client. ("I wrote the opinion on the case, but I don't remember any of the lawyers," Posner said. "It wasn't a memorable case.")

In 1995, the governor of Illinois, Jim Edgar, refused to implement legislation that allowed citizens to register to vote when they applied for a driver's license. Edgar, a Republican, was wary of the legislation, for it was sure to lead to the registration of many more Democrats than Republicans. A number of progressive groups, including the League of Women Voters and the Association of Community Organizations for Reform Now (ACORN), represented by Obama, joined the Justice Department in a lawsuit. Obama, whose keenest legal interest at Harvard and Chicago was voting rights, did not speak during the courtroom proceedings but his side won its case.

As a lecturer at the University of Chicago, Obama entered a world quite apart from community organizing on the South Side, civil-rights law downtown, and even Harvard Law School. Obama had known plenty of conservatives at Harvard; he won the presidency of the *Law Review* in part because the conservative minority thought that he was a liberal who would listen to them. The law-school faculty at Chicago was ideologically diverse—and prided itself, above all, on an atmosphere of fierce and open argument—but the conservative strain ran deep.

There were plenty of liberals on the faculty; Geoffrey Stone, Abner Mikva, Lawrence Lessig, Elena Kagan, David Strauss, Diane Wood, Martha Nussbaum, and Cass Sunstein were among Obama's acquaintances and friends. But, like the department of economics, the law school had a strong contingent of "law and economics" libertarians, like Richard Epstein, Alan Sykes, and Reagan-appointed jurists like Richard Posner and Frank Easterbrook. Just as the economics school attracted students wanting to get a full dose of the monetarist theory developed there by Milton Friedman and George Stigler, many Chicago students set aside acceptances at Harvard, Yale, or Columbia in order to study with the contingent of right-leaning rationalists in Hyde Park. Their views were no less varied than the liberals', but they were, as a whole, far less interested in terms like "justice" and "fairness" ("terms which have no content," according to Posner) than in the economic liberty and interests of the individual. Since the late nineteen-seventies, generally speaking, the conservatives at Chicago had disdained what they saw as a vapid consensus among liberal legal academics. They opposed government regulation, judicial activism, and legislation that aimed at redistributing income. They spoke as much about markets as they did about legal precedent. They argued in favor of a less restricted Presidency and against social policy imposed by judicial decree.

Chicago's law school is a third the size of Harvard's, but, proportionally, the number of conservatives on the faculty and of students active in the Federalist Society was far greater. One consequence of the Reagan revolution, however, was that the Chicago faculty had lost members to the federal bench, the Justice Department, and the regulatory agencies. As a result, some of the conservatives who remained when Obama arrived thought that the school's uniqueness had eroded several years earlier. "The height of the conservatism was in the late nineteen-seventies, which was a bad period, a lot of disorder, with a sense of the country declining and a lot of over-regulation," Posner said. "There was a fair amount of resistance to affirmative action and to the relaxing of academic standards, and the conservatives, even into the eighties, were outspoken and distinctive. But even as elements of conservatism persisted at Chicago, it's important not to exaggerate it, that it is a relative matter. In every election, a majority of the Chicago faculty votes for the Democrat, whereas at Harvard or Yale law school it's probably closer to ninety percent." In 2008, Posner, perhaps the most distinguished conservative on the federal bench, came to admire Obama—"especially," he said, "after one of my clerks, who had worked with him at the *Harvard Law Review*, told me that he wasn't even all that liberal. I was reassured."

At Chicago, the constitutional-law curriculum is divided into separate courses on structural questions and individual rights. Obama taught the latter, focusing on such issues as equal protection, voting rights, and privacy, rather than on such questions as the separation of powers.

Obama also taught a seminar course called Current Issues in Racism and the Law. He had small groups of students prepare presentations on one of a range of complicated questions: interracial adoptions; all-black, all-male schools; the gerrymandering of voting districts according to race; discriminatory sentencing; hate crimes; welfare policy; the reproductive freedom of women who have taken drugs during pregnancy or neglected their children; reparations for the descendants of slaves; hate speech; school financing. Rather than assign whole books, Obama, like many other professors, assembled a thick packet of readings. To establish a historical and theoretical understanding of race, he assigned excerpts from George Fredrickson's *The Arrogance of Race* and Kwame Anthony Appiah's *The Uncompleted Argument: DuBois and the Illusion of Race*. Both readings deal with historical arguments over whether race is a matter of biology or of social construction. In order to confront Andrew Jackson's Indian Removal policy, of shifting Native American populations west of the Mississippi River, he assigned not only court cases and Jackson's proclamation but also excerpts from *The Law of Nations*, by Emeric de Vattel, a Swiss legal philosopher of natural law, who exerted a strong influence on the American Founders. He assigned the essential court cases on slavery, a speech by the nationalist Martin Delany, and two texts by Frederick Douglass: "Is It Right and Wise to Kill a Kidnapper?" and "The Right to Criticize the American Institutions." Similarly, he covered Reconstruction, retrenchment, and the rise of Jim Crow by assigning the essential legislation and court cases—the Emancipation Proclamation, the South Carolina Black Codes, the Thirteenth, Fourteenth, and Fifteenth Amendments, Plessy v. Ferguson—and a series of documentations of lynchings, and excerpts from *Up from Slavery, The Souls of Black Folk*, and speeches by Marcus Garvey, the leading figure of early black nationalism. In covering the civil-rights era, Obama assigned King's "Letter from Birmingham Jail" and speeches by Malcolm X but also conservative critiques like Robert Bork's "Civil Rights—A Challenge." He included an ideologically pitched exchange on affirmative action and civil-rights law among Randall Kennedy, the liberal African-American law professor at Harvard; Charles Cooper, a conservative litigator who worked in the Reagan Justice Department; and Lino Graglia, a law professor at the University of Texas who refers to affirmative action as a "fraud." The three essays that Obama assigned were first presented by the Federalist Society at Stanford in 1990, at a symposium on the future of civil-rights law, and published the following year in a special issue of the right-leaning *Harvard Journal of Law and Public Policy*.

In the final part of the course, Obama's students read another series of ideologically opposed texts: Shelby Steele's conservative essay "I'm Black, You're White, Who's Innocent?"; Derrick Bell's radical critique in *Faces at the Bottom of the Well*; Bart Landry's analysis of the scale and nature of the new black middle class; John Bunzel's study of racial tension at Stanford University; and an excerpt from William Julius Wilson's *The Truly Disadvantaged*, a sociological examination of the social isolation of the African-American poor.

When, during the Presidential campaign, the New York *Times* published Obama's syllabus online, the reporter Jodi Kantor solicited opinions of the course from four prominent law professors across the ideological spectrum. Akhil Reed Amar, a constitutional scholar at Yale, praised the "moral seriousness" of Obama's syllabus for the race seminar and went so far as to compare Obama to Lincoln as a legal and moral thinker, a politician who, Amar said, understood the Constitution better than the Supreme Court justices of his era. "Some of the great mysteries and tragedies of human life and American society—involving marriage, divorce, childbearing, cloning, the right to die with dignity, infertility, sexual orientation, and yes, of course, race—are probed in these materials in ways that encourage students to think not just about the law, but about justice, and truth, and morality," Amar wrote. The results were effusive on the right as well. John C. Eastman, a law professor at Chapman University and a former clerk to Clarence Thomas, said that Obama was "leading his students in an honest assessment of competing views," and a libertarian, Randy Barnett, a professor of law at Georgetown and a senior fellow at the Cato Institute, remarked that Obama's summaries of key legal questions of race and the law were "remarkably free of the sort of cant and polemics that all too often afflicts academic discussions of race." Overall, Pamela S. Karlan, a voting-issues specialist at Stanford Law School, inferred from reading Obama's syllabus and his examination questions for the constitutional-law class that he "could have been a first-rate academic had his interests gone in that direction."

The extravagance of these professional opinions was undoubtedly influenced by the emotions of the 2008 election campaign, but they accord with what Obama's students say about their experiences in his classes over the years. Liberal students considered Obama a "godsend," one former student said, for his open-mindedness and his personality. His teaching ratings were among the highest at the law school and invariably gave him credit for a capacity to get students to see the complexities of a given question, and for a cool yet welcoming demeanor. One student,

Byron Rodriguez, who took courses with Obama in both racism and the law and voting rights, said that he was especially sympathetic to students from disadvantaged backgrounds and was clearly liberal, but his style was always to try to present all views and challenge the students to argue with them without being dismissive. "I remember reading Bork's opposition to the Civil Rights Act and Obama even putting that into the best light," Rodriguez said.

"He was different from other professors at Chicago," Daniel Sokol, a student in Obama's class on Race and the Law, who teaches law at the University of Florida, said. "A lot of the faculty was heavily Socratic in method, even in upper-level courses. Obama was demanding with questions, but he wouldn't just stick on one student. It was a small seminar. It felt more pleasant when he asked tough questions. It wasn't the inquisition model of teaching, which was so popular at U. of C."

One senior faculty member, Richard Epstein, a libertarian known for his corrosive wit and his fire-hose Socratic style, laughed as he acknowledged stylistic differences with Obama, saying that some professors— "guys like me"—listen to a student make a wrong-headed analysis and pounce on it, goading the student into studying, and thinking, harder. Obama, Epstein said, was more the kind of teacher who listened to a wrong-headed analysis and then, by way of reframing it, corrected and deepened it, always careful to make the student feel listened to.

In a fairly traditional way, Obama insisted that students learn to understand and argue all sides of a question. "But there was a moment when he let his guard down," one former student recalled. "He told us what he thought about reparations. He agreed entirely with the *theory* of reparations. But in practice he didn't think it was really workable. You could tell that he thought he had let the cat out of the bag and felt uncomfortable. To agree with reparations in theory means we go past apology and say we can actually change the dynamics of the country based on other situations where you saw reparations. For example, the class talked about reparations in other settings: Germany and the State of Israel. American Indians. We talked about apology and the South African Truth Commission. After fifteen minutes of this, as the complexities emerged—who is black, how far back do you go, what about recent immigrants still feeling racism, do they have a claim—finally, he said, 'That is why it's unworkable.' "

As he was as an organizer and as a law student, Obama was known for his impulse to reconcile opposing points of view, to see where the convergences were, and, by doing so, to form alliances. Cass Sunstein, a prolific legal scholar who taught at Chicago and later also at Harvard, was one of

Obama's closest friends at the law school. Sunstein regards himself as both a liberal and a judicial minimalist, and shares Obama's intellectual temperament—a reluctance to be too far ahead of the electorate on a prevailing legal and moral question. During the Presidential campaign, when Sunstein was asked about Obama's view of legal ideology, it seemed that there was not a great deal of difference between the attitudes he expressed in the classroom at Chicago and those he expressed as a politician. "If there's a deep moral conviction that gay marriage is wrong, if a majority of Americans believe on principle that marriage is an institution for men and women, I'm not at all sure [Obama] shares that view, but he's not an in-your-face type," Sunstein told the writer Larissa MacFarquhar. "To go in the face of people with religious convictions—that's something he'd be very reluctant to do," he added. "[John] Rawls talks about civic toleration as a modus vivendi, a way that we can live together, and some liberals think that way. . . . But I think with Obama it's more like Learned Hand when he said, 'The spirit of liberty is the spirit which is not too sure that it is right.' Obama takes that really seriously. I think the reason that conservatives are O.K. with him is both that he might agree with them on some issues and that even if he comes down on a different side he knows he might be wrong. I can't think of an American politician who has thought in that way, ever."

Obama was not much involved in the workshops, seminars, and lunches at which faculty members regularly exchanged ideas and discussed their works-in-progress. He was somewhat removed: first because he was working on Project Vote, his book, and his own law cases, and later because of his life as a politician. "My sense is that he was really close only to Cass Sunstein and a couple of other liberals," Richard Posner said. Nevertheless, he was well known and well liked. "He always had that aura: He said 'good morning' and you thought it was an event," Epstein said. "He has that kind of charisma—just like Bill Clinton, but without the seediness of Clinton. He makes you feel embraced and listened to. Clinton was always seducing you. This is a more wholesome version of the experience."

Obama was a consistent presence in Hyde Park for a dozen years; when he won a seat in the state legislature and had to be in Springfield for much of the week, he moved his class schedule to Monday mornings and Friday afternoons. Although he was a devoted teacher, he showed little interest in becoming a legal academic. He never published a single academic article. Nevertheless, the deans at Chicago regarded him so highly, and were so eager to increase the diversity of their faculty, that they eventually gave him the rank of "senior lecturer," a title that had been given to three judges on the Seventh Circuit, two conservatives (Richard Posner and Frank Easterbrook) and a liberal (Diane Wood). Even though he had no publications to his name, they hinted at the possibility of tenure. Obama politely demurred. "Barack did not focus on academic publication, because he knew where he was going, and that was to public service," the philosopher Martha Nussbaum, who teaches at the law school, said. "That's what made him happy. That's what made his eyes light up."

Before embarking on the story of the political rise of Barack Obama, it may be useful to take time out for a mental exercise. Here it is:

Name your state senator.

No, not the two legislative titans who represent your state in Washington, D.C. The question is, who represents your district in your state capital?

Fine. Now that you have Googled the name and are trying to wrap your mind around the pronunciation and other such details, imagine that this undoubtedly decent, if generally anonymous, man or woman emerges in a very few years from Trenton or Harrisburg, Tallahassee or Lansing to become, as if in a reality television show, President of the United States. Add into the equation that he or she is African-American, while every previous resident of the White House, for more than two centuries, has been a white male Protestant, except for the thousand-day interregnum when the President was a white male Roman Catholic.

Who could have predicted it? As it happens, one of Barack Obama's friends from Hawaii. In his memoir, *Livin' the Blues*, the poet and radical sage of the Waikiki Jungle, Frank Marshall Davis, wrote, "Until the election of Franklin D. Roosevelt, we could aim our hope no higher than selection for what was termed the president's 'Kitchen Cabinet.' Since then we have been inching our way slowly toward the oval room." Still, it's hard to imagine that Davis had in mind the skinny, disaffected kid who used to come around for advice in Waikiki about how to live his life as a black man in America.

As late as 1994, Barack Obama's ambitions for public life existed mainly in the realm of fantasy; the avenues of approach, the paths to office, seemed blocked. All the interesting political positions, and even most of the dull ones, were taken.

Starting a political career requires a great deal more than the desire to do so. It requires an opportunity, and a network to seize it. When Obama returned to Chicago in 1991, it was not at all clear where the opportunity would be. City Hall, where his closest organizing friends thought that he would wind up, was out of the question, perhaps for many years to come. Richard M. Daley, who had vastly improved his skills since losing to Harold Washington and had adapted to the racial diversity of the city in a way that his father never could, seemed a permanent fixture. City Hall had become no less dynastic than the House of Habsburg. The congressman in Obama's district, the former Black Panther Bobby Rush, routinely won re-election with minimal campaigning. The alderman in the Fourth Ward—Obama's ward, in Hyde Park—was a former high-school history teacher, an African-American woman named Toni Preckwinkle. It had taken a couple of tries before she won the post, in 1991, but Preckwinkle was popular, her seat secure. The fact that she was light-skinned and married to a white man, a teacher named Zeus Preckwinkle, was sometimes a source of nasty talk in some parts of the ward, but it wasn't much of a problem; she was seen as honest, independent, liberal, with deep roots in the community. Finally, the state senator in Obama's area, another former educator, Alice Palmer, was no less beloved than Rush and Preckwinkle. She was known for supporting progressive legislation in Springfield and helping to lead anti-apartheid rallies in Chicago. A veteran of the Harold Washington campaigns, Palmer had especially solid support among civil-rights-era leaders in town, including an influential contingent of black nationalists. Palmer's husband was also a source of her popularity. Edward (Buzz) Palmer had been a leader of the Afro-American Patrolmen's League, a progressive organization in a police department with a reputation for racism and unwarranted violence.

And so Obama had to practice patience.

In the meantime, he went about meeting people. Obama, it turned out, was a world-class networker. Just as he had gone from church to church as an organizer, now he and Michelle accepted countless invitations to lunches, dinners, cocktail parties, barbecues, and receptions for right-minded charities. They also joined the East Bank Club, downtown, a vast gym and social center on the Chicago River, where so many Chicagoans of a certain class gathered to exercise, eat lunch, get their nails done or their hair cut, and, as if by total accident, run into one another. The East Bank Club was, as one member described it, the "world's first urban country club," a place where you would see Oprah Winfrey in her sweats, members of the Joffrey Ballet stretching out; you saw local politicians, business people, Jews, African-Americans—a place, according to one prominent member, that "reinforces a center to this provincial town and provides a nexus of relationships for people obsessed with being buff." The member-ship price, by the standards of New York or Los Angeles, was modest, and so, too, was the level of snobbery.

The Obamas' social world began to expand exponentially. They were intelligent, attractive, eager, and ambitious, and they entered many worlds at once: the liberal, integrated world of Hyde Park; the intellectual world of the University of Chicago; the boards of charitable foundations; the growing post-civil-rights world of African-Americans who went to prestigious universities and were making their fortunes and ready to exert political influence. The Obamas were young and idealistic, and older people wanted to befriend and guide them. Despite Obama's rejection of a job offer at Sidley Austin and Michelle's decision to quit the firm, Newton Minow took them to the Chicago Symphony at the Ravinia Festival, where they ran into prominent friends. Bettylu Saltzman, the heiress and political activist who befriended Obama during Project Vote, helped guide Barack and Michelle to some of the wealthiest people in town. And, through his teaching colleagues, Obama became increasingly familiar with the professors, attorneys, physicians, and executives at the central intellectual institution in town.

An example: one of the partners at Obama's law firm, Allison Davis, was a member of a small, élite coterie in Hyde Park—African-American families who had compiled records of achievement over two or three generations. Davis's great-grandfather was an abolitionist lawyer; his grandfather chaired the anti-lynching commission of the N.A.A.C.P.; his father was valedictorian at Williams (though, as a black man, he was not allowed to live in the dorms) and an anthropologist who was the first African-American scholar to be awarded a full, tenured position at the University of Chicago or any major American research university. In 1947, Davis's father brought the family to Hawaii, so that he could study the uniquely integrated school system there. Davis is light-skinned, so much so that he became a kind of anthropologist himself, tuning in to what whites say about blacks when there are, seemingly, no blacks around to overhear them.

Allison Davis was an elder in a new breed. There had long been a moneyed black élite in the city, like the real-estate man Dempsey Travis, who was active in old-line Democratic politics and wrote histories of black politics and jazz in the city. On the South Side, there had been well-to-do black doctors, lawyers, car dealers, and merchants. Now there was a critical mass of African-Americans who, having gone to the country's best universities, were intent on creating a new élite. Davis hosted many dinner parties and, around the Christmas–New Year holiday, he threw a huge bash; he invited the younger people from the university, from City Hall, from among Cook County pols, from the foundations and the arts. "The Old Guard wasn't there—this was the next generation," Marilyn Katz, a former S.D.S. radical who was running a public-relations business, with clients from City Hall, said. "You would see a range of people from black professionals, the white progressive intelligentsia, the North Side–development scene people like Buzzy Ruttenberg, people from the University of Chicago, the parents at private schools like Parker, St. Ignatius, and the Lab School, in Hyde Park. Eventually, years later, there would be a big overlap of these schools and the finance committee of the Obama campaign in Illinois. Early on, Barack was there, but he wasn't a star yet."

Davis knew everyone, it seemed, and everyone came to his parties: John Rogers, who had grown up in Hyde Park—a street there is named for his mother, Jewel Lafontant, a lawyer and a prominent figure in Republican politics—and founded the investment firm Ariel Capital Management. Jim Reynolds, Jr., of Loop Capital Markets. Robert Blackwell, Jr., of the tech-consultancy firm Electronic Knowledge Interchange. The publisher Hermene Hartman. All of them became Obama's friends. "I tried to include Barack and Michelle in everything," Davis said.

Obama also met some Chicago operators of dubious value and intent. When he was still in law school, he got a job offer from the Rezmar Corporation, a developer of low-income housing run by a Syrian immigrant named Antoin (Tony) Rezko. Rezko came to Chicago when he was nineteen, intending to study civil engineering. He made a fortune setting up fast-food franchises—Panda Express Chinese restaurants and Papa John's pizzerias—and even did some business with Muhammad Ali. Rezko could see that one of the swiftest ways to riches in Chicago was through political connections, and he soon began to climb. At Ali's request, he held a fund-raiser in 1983 for Harold Washington. In 1989, Rezko and his associate Daniel Mahru set up Rezmar and, partnering with various community groups, got government loans to develop apartments on the South Side. In 1990, one of Rezko's vice-presidents, David Brint, called Obama at Harvard, after reading about him in the newspaper, and offered him a job—one of many that he turned down. As it happened, Allison Davis was appointed by the mayor to the Chicago Plan Commission and Davis Miner did the legal work for a joint venture between the Woodlawn Preservation and Investment Corporation and Rezmar. Obama did not do much real-estate work at Davis Miner; in all he spent just five hours on work for Rezmar. But the contact was made and a friendship was formed. When the time came for Obama to enter politics, Tony Rezko was ready.

If Obama was on the make politically, his new friends and acquaintances thought, he carried it off with a certain élan. "Barack made lots and lots of alliances," Davis said, "but he was so affable and gregarious that I never had the sense that he was mining the invitees for future campaign contributions." Davis felt that, given the proper opening, Obama could make a political career in Chicago. "All the deals have been made in New York, everything has been divided up and dealt out," he said. "If you look at the social page of the New York *Times* on Sundays, it's stagnant, more European in terms of traditions and entry into positions of influence. Here in Chicago, you don't confront the same barriers."

By far the most important new friend in Barack and Michelle Obama's lives was Valerie Jarrett. A graduate of Stanford and Michigan Law School, Jarrett began her professional life working for a corporate law firm. The work was so dull, so detached from her desire to make a social and political impact, that she often just closed the door and stared out the window of her office on the seventy-ninth floor of the Sears Tower, crying, wondering what she was doing with her life.

Jarrett came from perhaps the most talented and prestigious African-American family in the city. Her great-grandfather was Robert Taylor, one of the first accredited African-American architects. One of her grandfathers was Robert Rochon Taylor, the head of the Chicago Housing Authority; ironically, one of Daley's most hideous public housing projects was named for him. Jarrett was born in Shiraz, in Iran, where her father, James Bowman, a prominent pathologist and geneticist, was running a hospital. Valerie's mother, Barbara, was a specialist in early-childhood education. When the Bowmans returned home to Chicago, Valerie was fluent in Farsi and French, as well as in English.

On Election Day in 1983, she had campaigned door-to-door for Harold Washington at a housing project near Cicero. When she wore her "Washington" button to work she took note of the suspicious glances of many of the white lawyers in the firm. After his victory at the polls, Washington persuaded many of the black professionals in town to come to work at City Hall. In 1987, Jarrett went to work for Judson Miner in the corporation counsel's office on various redevelopment projects near O'Hare Airport. After Washington's death, many of the committed black professionals at City Hall, disenchanted with his successor, Eugene Sawyer, who was so much weaker, so much more pliant to the will of the machine, left, and, if they didn't leave then they left when Daley was elected, in 1989. Jarrett, who came to believe that the younger Daley was not a racist like his father, stayed on, eventually becoming a deputy chief of staff in Daley's office and the Commissioner of the Department of Planning and Development. Working for Daley, in the view of some of Jarrett's friends, was a form of selling out, of racial betrayal, but she was soon one of the best-connected people in Chicago.

The Harvard law professor David Wilkins, a native of Hyde Park, spent between 1995 and 1999 working on a research project about blacks in the legal profession. Most of the lawyers in town, he discovered, knew Jarrett. "No one in my generation of black people in Chicago is more respected than Valerie," Wilkins said. "Valerie was the liaison between the white North Shore élites and the black South Side élites. Daley was smart enough to realize that he needed black people supporting him in order to rule. He knew that there had to be another Harold Washington out there, and he had to position himself against that threat. In the meantime, Valerie saw the real way that power is wielded. She knew everyone. And after a while she ran the housing authority, the transit authority, and the Chicago stock exchange—all quasi-independent regulatory bodies with a lot of power."

In July, 1991, a colleague of Jarrett's at City Hall, a lawyer named Susan Sher, handed her the résumé of an impressive young woman at Sidley Austin: Michelle Robinson. Someone had written across the résumé that Robinson wanted to leave the firm; she was bored and wanted to "give back."

"They said she was a terrific young woman, disenchanted with the practice of law," Jarrett recalled. "And I thought, I know that type, because that's exactly what I was. I thought that sounds like somebody I would get along with."

"She is made for you," Sher told Jarrett.

Jarrett met with Robinson and, almost immediately, offered her a place in her office. But, before Robinson accepted, she asked Jarrett if she would have dinner with her and her fiancé, Barack Obama.

Although Jarrett was older and infinitely more experienced in the public life of Chicago, she was nervous about meeting Obama. She had already heard a lot about him. As the first black president of the *Harvard Law Review*, she said, "he was a really big deal within the African-American legal community."

They met at a restaurant called Café Le Loup and immediately fell into a long discussion of their childhood travels. "Barack felt extraordinarily familiar," Jarrett said. "He and I shared a view of where the United States fit in the world, which is often different from the view people have who have not traveled outside the United States as young children." Through her travels, Jarrett felt that she had come to see the United States with a greater objectivity as one country among many, rather than as the center of all wisdom and experience. "We were also both, in a sense, only children," she went on, "because his sister is so much younger than he is, and I am an only child. We were forced to be with adults at a very young age, and, therefore, if not to participate, be in the room where there were adult conversations going on about world politics. We were both inundated with a lot of diverse information, which gives you a lot of appreciation for diversity of thought and how that shapes you. And I think that's why we clicked."

Jarrett also observed Barack and Michelle together. They were not yet married, but it seemed to her that they were already "kindred spirits."

"I was struck then by how you could have people that were raised in such different worlds, yet have the same values," she said. "Michelle had a lot of what Barack missed in childhood: two parents, everyone home for dinner, a brother, family unity, a place to call their own. It was a nuclear family grounded in one neighborhood, but with the same values of work, personal responsibility, treating each other the way you want to be treated, and compassion, and just core decency. That's how they both were raised in the end. Barack's father abandoned him, and that left, I think, a hole in his heart. By finding Michelle and her dad and seeing their really close relationship, he thought, This is what I want in my life. Often times, you re-create your childhood. Often people say that children who had alcoholics as parents become alcoholics. And I think sometimes you decide that I'm going to do the opposite. In this case Barack said, I want to be the opposite kind of husband and father that my father was."

Michelle Robinson took the job with Jarrett, and Jarrett soon began inviting her and Obama to numerous social occasions. She wanted to open up to them the various worlds of Chicago that she knew so well through her parents and through her own work. Eventually, Jarrett became their emissary to everyone from the leaders of the growing black business community to media titans like Linda Johnson Rice, the publisher of *Ebony* and *Jet*, and to various city and state politicians.

"I wasn't shy about calling people and saying, You've *got* to meet this guy: coffee, or lunch, or whatever," Jarrett recalled. "Sometimes I'd go along, sometimes I wouldn't. My parents have a big backyard, and we're always inviting people over, and Michelle and Barack were there all the time, and so they met a lot of people. I always felt that I was doing someone a favor by introducing that person to him. It wasn't like I was doing this just to help his political career.

"I think Barack knew that he had God-given talents that were extraordinary. He knows exactly how smart he is. . . . He knows how perceptive he is. He knows what a good reader of people he is. And he knows that he has the ability—the extraordinary, uncanny ability—to take a thousand different perspectives, digest them, and make sense out of them, and I think that he has never really been challenged intellectually. I mean, he's the kind of guy you'd hate in law school, who would pick up his book the night before the final, read it, and ace the test. So what I sensed in him was not just a restless spirit but somebody with such extraordinary talents that they had to be really taxed in order for him to be happy." Jarrett was quite sure that one of the few things that truly engaged him fully before going to the White House was writing *Dreams from My Father.* "He's been bored to death his whole life," she said. "He's just too talented to do what ordinary people do. He would never be satisfied with what ordinary people do."

Mike Strautmanis, a young lawyer who had met Michelle when he worked as a paralegal at Sidley Austin, became friends with the Obamas—and eventually a trusted aide to both Obama and Jarrett. A native Chicagoan, Strautmanis could see how Jarrett was linking her new protégés to one social and political circle after another. "Valerie is the one," he recalled. "She was the one who could lead him to the black aristocracy. The lawyers. The business people. The politicians, even. And not only the black aristocracy but all the movers and shakers in Chicago. She invited them to Martha's Vineyard for vacation. She had dinner parties where she had all kinds of important people for Barack and Michelle to meet. She invited them to charity events, to sit on the boards of foundations. Without Valerie, it would have taken Barack a lot longer."

Judd Miner's networks were less business-oriented. He introduced Obama to people who worked for various liberal foundations and to progressives like Salim Muwakkil, an African-American journalist who had written for the Chicago *Tribune,* and, at various points, for the newspaper of the Nation of Islam and the democratic socialist paper *In These Times.* Miner, Muwakkil recalled, "wanted to hook [Obama] into progressive networks."

Before Obama ran for any office, he had a long conversation with Muwakkil at the Davis Miner offices. "We talked a lot about the esoterica of the black movement," Muwakkil said. They discussed the long-running debates between Martin Delany and Frederick Douglass, between Washington and DuBois and their points of convergence. Obama talked about the Black Arts Movement of the nineteen-sixties and seventies and how, in his view, racial dogma had suffocated its vitality. Obama said that he identified with Douglass and saw the limits of a nationalist politics.

"I sensed that he was vaguely on the left," Muwakkil said. "His ambitions were well disguised. His cool manner was always there, and it underplayed his ambition. One reason that he was so knowledgeable about the arcana of black politics is that he studied it and he crafted himself. He doesn't share the traditional ancestral narrative. That's not part of his being. One of the reasons he is so attractive to a lot of people is that he doesn't have this sense of cultural grievance. He never had that sense of a family being socialized to subservience. He has an ease of interaction with whites that a lot of African-Americans don't have. He had to learn that cultural repertoire of African-Americans. The notion that you are socialized in an environment that insisted that you were inferior, that you spend much of your energy proving that you aren't inferior, that kind of double consciousness—he didn't have to deal with that. He has Malcolm's capacity for self-creation. That's what Barack did. He made himself, like a kind of an existential hero. He picked this out and that out, and he created himself."

A crime opened the political door for Barack Obama.

On August 21, 1994, Mel Reynolds, representing the Second Congressional District of Illinois, was indicted by a Cook County grand jury for witness tampering and for an array of sexual crimes, including having sex with a sixteen-year-old campaign worker named Beverly Heard and asking her to take lewd photographs of an even younger girl. Reynolds, born in Mound Bayou, Mississippi, the son of a preacher, seemed a young man of great promise: he graduated from a public university in Illinois, won a Rhodes scholarship to study at Oxford, and earned a master's in public administration at Harvard. For five years, he fought to unseat Gus Savage, a nationalist whose penchant for anti-Semitic pronouncements proved so outrageous to the Jewish community that Reynolds had been able to win support not only from the Pritzkers and the Crowns, in Chicago, but from contributors across the country. Savage had also referred to Ron Brown, the first black head of the Democratic National Committee, as "Ron Beige" and to his critics as "faggots"; mocked "the suburban Zionist lobby"; and embraced Louis Farrakhan's depiction of Adolf Hitler as a "great man." Reynolds, who had worked on the Presidential campaigns of Edward Kennedy and Jesse Jackson, failed to unseat Savage in 1988 and 1990; in 1989 he was accused of sexually assaulting a twenty-year-old college student, but was acquitted. He won election to the House in 1992. Now, as he watched his brief career in Congress implode, he referred to Beverly Heard as an "emotionally disturbed nut case." During the trial in the summer of 1995, the judge ruled as admissible a series of tapes of Reynolds talking to Heard in the most obscene terms. The transcripts ran in the *Tribune*. Admitting that he made "mistakes" but denying to the end that he had had sex with an under-age girl, Reynolds went on "Larry King Live," on September 1, 1995, to announce his resignation from Congress. "You can't discuss race in Chicago," Reynolds said, casting about for excuses. "If you do, you will be relegated to the fringe." Beverly Heard, he added manfully, "set me up."

In November, 1994, three months after the Reynolds indictment, Alice Palmer, the respected state senator in Obama's district—the thirteenth—formed a fund-raising committee to "explore" her prospects for succeeding Reynolds in Congress. On June 27, 1995, she formally announced her candidacy. In September, when the governor, Jim Edgar, announced a special election, for November 28th, to fill Reynolds's seat, Palmer hoped that she would run unopposed. She miscalculated. The opposition was plentiful and tough. Emil Jones, the most powerful Democrat in the State Senate and a savvy machine politician from Morgan Park, on the far South Side, declared, and so, too, did a teacher named Monique Davis, and, most significant, Jesse Jackson, Jr. After his two Presidential races, Jesse Jackson, Sr., had hoped that his son would succeed him as the preeminent black politician in the city, and that he would pursue a national career. Jesse, Jr., who was just thirty and not anything like the academic star Obama had been, did not heed his father's advice to start modestly, with a run for alderman or the State Senate.

Obama was watching these events closely, and, with Palmer's seat in the thirteenth district now open, he sounded out local politicians, like his alderman, Toni Preckwinkle, and state representative, Barbara Flynn Currie, about running. He needed to get the support of the politicians and committeemen who had the capacity to raise money and marshal the door-to-door volunteers who were crucial in a local race. Obama approached Ivory Mitchell, a political veteran on the South Side, who was chairman of the Fourth Ward's Democratic organization. On the third

Saturday of each month, Mitchell held an open bacon and egg breakfast to discuss the ward's problems and to hear from local officials. In election years, Mitchell mobilized those people to work on behalf of the candidates the local party organization had endorsed. "In other words, I come with a ready-made army," Mitchell said.

Obama told Mitchell that he wanted to run for office, probably the seat that Alice Palmer was leaving behind.

"O.K.," Mitchell said. "How much money do you have?"

"I don't have *any* money," Obama replied.

"Well, if you don't have any money, we're going to have to finance the campaign for you," Mitchell said.

Mitchell had a good feeling about Obama—"He was intelligent and he was *hungry*"—so he sent him to see Preckwinkle. She remembered Obama from Project Vote and told him that she, and others in the area, would support him as long as he got Alice Palmer's blessing. Obama was confident that, with a little time and persuasion, he could do just that.

Obama invited Carol Anne Harwell, his old friend and aide at Project Vote, to his apartment to talk. Harwell had run successful campaigns for two judges and for Sam Burrell, an alderman on the West Side, in the Twenty-ninth Ward. She had also kept on file much of the voter information she and Obama and their colleagues had accumulated during Project Vote—information that could prove valuable in a political race. By the end of their conversation, Harwell agreed to manage Obama's campaign.

Obama had a more difficult time trying to persuade his wife of the wisdom of a race for State Senate. He had just finished writing his memoir, a project that had kept him locked up alone in small rooms for endless hours. Michelle wanted a family and a career, and now her husband proposed to spend much of his time in Springfield? "I married you because you're cute and you're smart," she recalled telling him, "but this is the dumbest thing you could have ever asked me to do." What was more, she was dubious about the entire enterprise of electoral politics. "I wasn't a proponent of politics as a way you could make change," she said. "I also thought, Was politics really a place for good, decent people?"

Harwell recalled, "Michelle felt that Barack wasn't going to make any money. He'd be away from home all the time. She felt that he could accomplish more by teaching and by working at the law firm. She was not a happy camper." But, finally, Obama prevailed. And once the decision was made, Michelle worked hard on the campaign, not least because the neighborhood that her husband was hoping to represent was her own. "She knew those people," Harwell said. "They were *her* people."

Alice Palmer, like Michelle Obama's family, lived in one of the modest bungalows of South Shore. In the eyes of her constituency—the African-American neighborhoods of Englewood, South Shore, Woodlawn, and Hyde Park—she was from unassailably heroic stock. One of her grandfathers, Joseph Henry Ward, was a slave. In the late nineteenth century, he left North Carolina for Indianapolis where he cleaned stables for doctors. When Ward was twenty, one of the doctors took a liking to him and helped him learn to read. Ward went to medical school and later, in segregated Indianapolis, opened a hospital for African-Americans. One of Palmer's grandmothers, Zella Louise Locklear Ward, was a free black who arrived in Indianapolis in the late nineteenth century, helped found the Colored Women's Improvement Club, and ran a tent city for black tuberculosis patients.

Alice Palmer reached the State Senate by appointment, replacing Richard Newhouse, the first African-American ever to run for mayor of Chicago, who had to step down because of illness. Palmer, the local Democratic committeewoman, was a welcome choice among local activists. Her background as an activist and in local politics was unimpeachable. She had a doctorate in education from Northwestern and went to Springfield determined to win greater funding for Chicago schools. She became popular among her constituents—popular enough, she believed, to win a seat in Congress.

In the late spring of 1995, after a series of conversations, Obama won Alice Palmer's support. Alan Dobry, a former Democratic ward committeeman and a fixture in Hyde Park politics, had been concerned about the open State Senate position until, at a meeting to kick off her campaign for Congress, Palmer told him, "I found this wonderful person, this fine young man, so we needn't worry that we'd have a good state senator."

Before announcing his intention to run, Obama wanted to be absolutely sure that Palmer was committed to the congressional race and that she would not get back in the State Senate race, even if she lost in the Democratic primary to Emil Jones or Jesse Jackson, Jr.

"I hadn't publicly announced," Obama recalled. "But what I said was that once I announce, and I have started to raise money, and gather supporters, hire staff and opened up an office, signed a lease, then it's going to be very difficult for me to step down. And she gave me repeated assurance that she was in [the congressional race] to stay."

Palmer doesn't dispute that. He "did say that to me," she said. "I certainly did say that I wasn't going to run [for State Senate]. There's no question about that."

Obama also understood that he had her endorsement. ("I'm absolutely certain she . . . publicly spoke and sort of designated me.") On that point, Palmer disagrees: "I don't know that I like the word 'endorsement.' An endorsement, to me, having been in legislative politics . . . that's a very formal kind of thing. I don't think that describes this. An 'informal nod' is how to characterize it."

Palmer announced her candidacy for Congress on June 27th, and, the following week, the local papers announced Obama would run to succeed her. Her intentions, as she stated them at the time, could not have been clearer. "Pray for Mel Reynolds and vote for me," she told reporters. In the last paragraph of a story in the Hyde Park *Herald*, the reporter, Kevin Knapp, took up the subject of a successor, mentioning Obama, "an attorney with a background in community organization and voter registration efforts," as the likeliest possibility. Later that month, Obama filed the necessary papers to create a fund-raising committee. He received his first campaign contributions on July 31, 1995: three hundred dollars from a downtown lawyer, a five-thousand-dollar loan from a car dealer, and two thousand dollars from two fast-food companies owned by an old friend, Tony Rezko.

In many ways, it was a trying time to want to be a Democratic legislator. Bill Clinton was in the White House, but the Party had suffered major losses in the 1994 midterm elections. Newt Gingrich had declared a conservative counterattack and Clinton had begun to rely more heavily on illiberal advisers like Mark Penn and Dick Morris, who were disdained by the more progressive aides and constituencies that had supported him in 1992. In Illinois, the governor was a Republican and both houses of the legislature had Republican majorities. Legislators in the minority in Springfield had very little to do: the governor set the agenda and his party fell into line.

But for all the limitations of the office, Obama had to start somewhere. He had to get in the game and learn its skills and hidden rules. As he began to think about fund-raising and organization, he called on dozens of local politicians at the ward, city, and county levels, as well as on neighborhood activists who might support him. With Palmer committed to the congressional race, Obama had every reason to believe that he would face little opposition in the March Democratic primary; and, in his district, the chance of a Republican winning was about as likely as an African-American winning the White House.

Bill Ayers and Bernardine Dohrn were among the many neighbors and acquaintances in Hyde Park who were interested in Obama. Ayers and Dohrn were former leaders of S.D.S. and the Weather Underground, and were unapologetic about their support for violent resistance to the Vietnam War. They were now known as community activists, mainly in the field of education. Collectively, they were also the Elsa Maxwell of Hyde Park, frequently inviting guests to their house for readings, discussions, and dinners, and many people in the neighborhood, whether they approved of their behavior in the sixties or not, came.

"Some of us draw a line between what Bill and Bernardine did when they were young and now, when they are doing unimpeachable work in the community," the novelist Rosellen Brown said. "Hyde Park is a pretty small, insular community, and everyone, from Studs Terkel to schoolteachers working on juvenile-justice issues, came to their house to meet interesting people."

The son of a wealthy Chicago business executive, Ayers was a professor at the Chicago campus of the University of Illinois and was one of the founders of the Chicago Annenberg Challenge, a foundation that distributes grants to educational programs. Ayers helped bring Obama onto the Annenberg board. One guest at a dinner at Ayers's house remembers sitting next to Michelle, who had taken a community-relations job at the university. The discussion was about race, class, and family, and Michelle talked about her grandmother's final days. Her grandmother was immensely proud of the fact that Michelle and Craig had graduated from Princeton, and, in Michelle's case, Harvard Law School. They were thriving. They had broken through. On her deathbed, the old woman told Michelle, "Don't you start the revolution with my great-grandchildren. I want them to go to Princeton, too!"

"She knew that her Princeton education was valuable, and no one, having had advantages, wants to give them up," the guest said, recalling the conversation. "She knew that having stepped up to the class defined by a privileged education, she obviously did not have everything in common with the people she grew up with."

Before Obama formally announced his candidacy, Ayers and Dohrn were asked to throw a small informal reception for him. According to Ayers, Alice Palmer made the request. And although Ayers and Dohrn were not particularly interested in electoral politics—they believed that real change came from popular movements and viewed Obama as someone far more to the center than they were—they agreed. "It was Alice's initiative to have the event in order to hand over the baton," Ayers recalled. "She was running for Congress and she wanted to introduce him to the political community. It was good for her and it was good for him. . . . The thing about Obama was, he struck me from the first moment as the smartest sort of guy. He was compassionate and clear and a moderate, middle-of-the-road Democrat. How into him was I? Not very. I liked him as a person. I did it because I was asked. We had lots of things: readings, book signings, dinners, talks. For us, it's part of being a citizen."

The guests at the reception included Quentin Young, a doctor who had long campaigned for a single-payer health-care system, the Palestinian-American professor Rashid Khalidi, the novelist Rosellen Brown, and Kenneth Warren, who teaches literature at the university, and his wife, Maria Warren, who writes a blog called Musings & Migraines. Young remembered that Palmer introduced Obama as her successor. When Obama was introduced to Rosellen Brown, he told her that he had read *Civil Wars*, her novel about a couple of refugees from the civil-rights movement and their lives a decade later. ("After that, like any novelist, I probably would have voted for him for anything," Brown said.) Most of the guests either liked Obama's short talk or had no real objections, but a few, like Maria Warren, were frustrated.

"I remember him saying very generic things and one of the people there said, 'Can't you say something of more substance?'" Warren recalled. "He didn't generate that much excitement, and a few people were saying, 'It's too bad Alice isn't going to run for her seat again.' I remember Barack getting kind of defensive and shaking his head." In 2005, long before Obama was a Presidential candidate, Warren wrote on her blog, "His 'bright eyes and easy smile' struck me as contrived and calculated—maybe because I was supporting another candidate. Since then, I've never heard him say anything new or earthshaking, or support anything that would require the courage of his convictions."

Thirteen years later, during the Presidential campaign, this brief, otherwise forgettable gathering would be introduced into evidence by the Republican Party that Obama had a dangerously radical background, that leaders of the Weather Underground had "launched" his political career. Which was ridiculous. It is true that Obama saw Ayers in the years to come at quarterly board meetings and other occasions. Obama praised Ayers's book *A Kind and Just Parent: The Children of Juvenile Court* in the *Tribune*, though his own views on education were much less left-wing. They once spoke on the same panel about juvenile justice—an event put together by Michelle Obama in 1997, when she was associate dean of student services at the University of Chicago. But no matter what one thought of Ayers's past—and Obama said that Ayers had been guilty of "despicable" acts during the antiwar movement—the notion that the two men were close friends or ideological soul mates was false.

As Obama continued to call on various politicians and activists in the district, he sometimes got perplexing advice. One African-American politician suggested that he change his name; another suggested he make sure to put his picture on all his campaign materials, "so people don't see your name and think you're some big dark guy." Another adviser told him sternly to make sure that he was never photographed holding a glass— even if it was filled with water or juice—lest the electorate take him for a drinker.

"Now all of this may be good political advice," Obama told Hank De Zutter, a writer for the Chicago *Reader*, "but it's all so superficial. I am surprised at how many elected officials—even the good ones—spend so much time talking about the mechanics of politics and not matters of substance. They have this poker-chip mentality, this overriding interest in retaining their seats or in moving their careers forward, and the business and game of politics, the political horse race, is all they talk about."

On September 19, 1995, at the Ramada Lakeshore, in Hyde Park, Obama formally announced his candidacy. Cliff Kelley, a former alderman and the host of the most popular call-in show on WVON, was master-of-ceremonies. "Politicians are not held to highest esteem these days," Obama told the packed room. "They fall somewhere lower than lawyers. . . . I want to inspire a renewal of morality in politics. I will work as hard as I can, as long as I can, on your behalf."

Palmer may not have used the word "endorsement" to describe her enthusiasm for Obama, but, at the Ramada that day, there was no mistaking her enthusiasm for the thirty-four-year-old organizer and lawyer. "In this room, Harold Washington announced for mayor," she said. "It looks different, but the spirit is still in the room. Barack Obama carries on the tradition of independence in this district, a tradition that continued with me and most recently with State Senator Newhouse. His candidacy is a passing of the torch, because he's the person that people have embraced and have lifted up as the person they want to represent this district."

Carol Anne Harwell looked for a campaign office. She thought she had found something affordable and adequate on Seventy-first Street. "It was clean and had a bathroom, and the important thing was that it had phone jacks," Harwell recalled. "Michelle walked in there and she just went, 'No, no, no. Uh-uh.' We ended up farther west in a nicer place. Michelle was determined to run a top-notch campaign, no cheesiness. She brought elegance and class to the campaign. She was the taskmaster and she was very organized, even if she didn't know a lot about politics then. When we started collecting petitions, we would set a goal for, say, two hundred signatures that day. There would be a blizzard and we would come back with only a hundred and fifty. Michelle would be furious and we'd have to go out and get the rest."

On Saturday mornings, Michelle Obama and her friend and the campaign's issues coordinator, Yvonne Davila, went out knocking on doors to collect signatures to get on the ballot. They were much more efficient than Obama, who went out in the evenings with Harwell. "It was so slow," Harwell said. "The old ladies loved him. He would introduce himself and ask them what they needed. They wanted to mother him. They would go on forever about their grandchildren. Barack was not Chicago-smart yet. He didn't know how to keep moving. He even went out campaigning in a leather jacket, no gloves, no hat. I think I had to introduce him to the concept of long underwear."

By the modest standards of a campaign for State Senate, Obama's started unevenly. He was not much of a speaker at first. He was stentorian, professorial, self-serious—a cake with no leavening. In the most critical speaking realm of all, the black churches of the South Side, he came off as flat and diffident; it would take hundreds of speeches in pulpits around the city before he acquired the sense of cadence, Biblical reference, and emotional connection that marked his performances later on.

But he was lining up the support he needed. Sam and Martha Ackerman, an influential family of Hyde Park independent Democrats, held a coffee for Obama. Ministers in the area were welcoming. Palmer, his alderman, Toni Preckwinkle, and the local ward chairman, Ivory Mitchell, were all on his side, along with a group of longtime liberal Hyde Park activists. Since the end of the Second World War, the neighborhood had been the center of political defiance of the machine. The Independent Voters of Illinois was the most important political organization in Hyde Park, and anti-Daley politicians, like the legendary alderman Leon Despres, carried its banner. Veterans of numerous I.V.I. campaigns, like Alan Dobry and his wife, Lois Friedberg-Dobry, canvassed door-to-door. A chemist with a Ph.D. from the University of Chicago, Alan Dobry was a typical old-line Hyde Park independent, working for Despres when he ran for reelection as alderman in 1959, in the Fifth Ward, which includes Hyde Park, as well as in black neighborhoods in Woodlawn.

"Everything seemed to be falling into place that autumn," Dobry recalled. "Obama had friends who would put up the money for him: people from Judd Miner's law firm, Harvard people, colleagues at the University of Chicago. He knew people in the habit of funding independent political campaigns." Harwell was from the West Side but she was managing this South Side campaign with evident skill. She brought in Ronald Davis, a math professor at Kennedy-King College who had also been a Project Vote coordinator, to be the field coordinator. Young volunteers, like Will Burns, who soon became a political-science graduate student at the University of Chicago, handed out flyers and, with Obama, campaigned door-to-door. Burns later wrote a master's thesis on how Harold Washington, a machine politician, turned himself into a spokesman for black empowerment and how he built coalitions. After Washington's death, there had been a vacuum in black politics in Chicago; Burns thought that he saw in Obama a kind of successor, free of the old language and cronyism.

In mid-October, Obama took a break from campaigning and went to Washington for the Million Man March, a mass demonstration on the Mall organized principally by Louis Farrakhan, the head of the Nation of Islam. Many of the issues that the march was intended to highlight were on Obama's mind: the soaring incarceration rates among young black men; disproportionate levels of poverty, unemployment, and high-school dropouts; the distorted portrayal of African-Americans in the media. But because of the central role played by Farrakhan, who had made hateful statements about Jews and white America, it was a complicated event for Obama, a liberal African-American running for office in a district that was mainly black but also heavily Jewish, especially near the university. The speakers in Washington included Gus Savage, Malcolm X's widow, Betty Shabazz, Jesse Jackson, Rosa Parks, Maya Angelou, and, of course, Farrakhan.

When he returned, Obama spoke gingerly of the events he had witnessed in Washington. Rather than give the reporter Hank De Zutter a pithy quote for his story in the *Reader*, he delivered a measured, nuanced view of race in America that sounds very much like what he said thirteen years later, at a crisis point in his run for the Presidency:

What I saw was a powerful demonstration of an impulse and need for African-American men to come together to recognize each other and affirm our rightful place in the society. . . . There was a profound sense that African-American men were ready to make a commitment to bring about change in our communities and lives.

But what was lacking among march organizers was a positive agenda, a coherent agenda for change. Without this agenda a lot of this energy is going to dissipate. Just as holding hands and singing "We shall overcome" is not going to do it, exhorting youth to have pride in their race, give up drugs and crime, is not going to do it if we can't find jobs and futures for the 50 percent of black youth who are unemployed, underemployed, and full of bitterness and rage. Exhortations are not enough, nor are the notions that we can create a black economy within America that is hermetically sealed from the rest of the economy and seriously tackle the major issues confronting us. . . .

Any solution to our unemployment catastrophe must arise from us working creatively within a multicultural, interdependent, and international economy. Any African-Americans who are only talking about racism as a barrier to our success are seriously misled if they don't also come to grips with the larger economic forces that are creating economic insecurity for all workers—whites, Latinos, and Asians. We must deal with the forces that are depressing wages, lopping off people's benefits right and left, and creating an earnings gap between C.E.O.s and the lowest-paid worker that has risen in the last 20 years from a ratio of 10 to 1 to one of better than 100 to 1.

This doesn't suggest that the need to look inward emphasized by the march isn't important, and that these African-American tribal affinities aren't legitimate. These are mean, cruel times, exemplified by a "lock 'em up, take no prisoners" mentality that dominates the Republican-led Congress. Historically, African-Americans have turned inward and towards black nationalism whenever they have a sense, as we do now, that the mainstream has rebuffed us, and that white Americans couldn't care less about the profound problems African-Americans are facing.

But cursing out white folks is not going to get the job done. Anti-Semitic and anti-Asian statements are not going to lift us up. We've got some hard nuts-and-bolts organizing and planning to do. We've got communities to build.

Obama's analytical, unemotional, intricate, Farrakhan-free, yet sincere response echoed his reaction to Rafiq, the nationalist in his memoir, his comments a few years earlier about the death of Harold Washington, and his discussions of the pressures of a global economy on local destiny. Obama was increasingly directing his attention to the problems of class, systemic change, and elective politics. As a younger man, he was paying his respect to the elders of the movement, but he clearly felt that the days of nationalism and charismatic racial leadership were outdated and played out.

At around the same time, Obama got the news that he would not be alone on the ballot. The Hyde Park *Herald* reported that there would be at least two other candidates: Marc Ewell, a thirty-year-old real-estate inspector and the son of a former state legislator, Raymond Ewell, and Gha-is Askia, a community-affairs liaison in the Illinois attorney general's office. Askia was the more interesting of the two. Born a Baptist, Askia was the sixteenth of eighteen children and a Muslim convert. His name means "One who relieves those in distress." Askia won the endorsement of several local politicians; his friend Muhammad Ali promised to have a fundraiser for him.

As the campaign began to develop, Obama learned that his mother was gravely ill. In 1992, living in Indonesia, Ann Dunham had finished her thousand-page doctoral dissertation on the craftsmen of Java, dedicating it to her mother, to her mentor Alice Dewey, and "to Barack and Maya, who seldom complained when their mother was in the field." In 1992 and 1993, she lived in New York City and was a policy coordinator for Women's World Banking, where she worked on issues of microfinancing for women in the developing world. (One of her jobs was to help generate policy materials for the 1995 United Nations International Women's Conference in Beijing; Dunham and her colleagues believed that the best advocate for microfinancing at the Beijing meeting would be Hillary Clinton.) In the fall of 1994, while visiting some friends in Jakarta, Dunham felt intense abdominal pains. Her Indonesian doctors diagnosed a digestive malady. At first, she barely spoke of her illness to Barack, in Chicago, or to Maya, who was studying secondary education at New York University. Finally, at the urging of her family and friends, she went to see doctors at Kaiser Permanente in Honolulu, who determined that she had advanced uterine cancer. At Memorial Sloan-Kettering Cancer Center in New York, specialists told her that the cancer was too advanced for effective treatment.

Dunham returned to Hawaii. One of her colleagues in Indonesian studies, Bronwen Solyom, recalled, "She was tough, she was very brave. She went on staying interested in what we always talked about and not about being sick. But by the time she came home from Indonesia it was probably too late."

In early November, she was admitted to the Straub Clinic in Honolulu. "I was working on my master's degree in New York at the time when the doctors in Hawaii said there was no hope," Maya Soetoro-Ng said. "My goal was to finish my degree and go live with her in Hawaii for her last days. But because she was so young, I thought we had more time. I was in a state of denial and thought she might last for years. But when I returned one day from class she called and made it clear she didn't have much time. I told her that I was scared and she said, 'Me, too.' I got on a flight that day."

Maya arrived in Honolulu on the afternoon of November 7th. "When I got to my mother's hospital room, she was surrounded by my grandmother and some friends," Soetoro-Ng said. "My grandmother was so tired, so I sent her home. It was clear that things were ending. I read to my mother from a book of Creole stories that I had been reading with my students. I read her a story about taking flight, because it was clear that she wasn't coming back. I told her that it was time to go." That night, at around eleven, Ann Dunham died. She was fifty-two.

To his great distress, Obama did not arrive in Honolulu until the next day. He had been in constant contact with his mother, with visits, telephone calls, and letters. Dunham wrote her son many letters encouraging him in his pursuits. More and more, he had come to admire his mother not only for the moral example she had set but also for the room she had given him to explore his own identity. Only as he grew older could he appreciate how young she was when she gave birth to him and how resilient she had been when Barack, Sr., left. She was just a teenager, a smart, sweet-tempered nineteen-year-old pushing a stroller and her African-American toddler along the sidewalks of Honolulu and Seattle in 1963. She never thought twice about it. Dipping in and out of one culture after another, Ann was an idealist about race, not least when it came to her own family. Finishing her dissertation and nearing fifty, she half-seriously told Alice Dewey that she was thinking of adopting a third child—the more ethnically complicated the better.

"She thought having an African-American kid was wonderful," Dewey recalled. "When she was in Hawaii, Americans were starting to adopt Asian kids. It had started in Korea, children of American soldiers. They were awfully cute. She saw one on TV and she said, 'Oh, I want one!' That really would have completed the set! And I wouldn't have been surprised."

"She was a superb mother in a number of ways," Maya said. "In spite of not being able to provide us with a stable two-parent household or a big house or any of those things, she gave us a sense of wonder and curiosity, empathy, a sense of responsibility and service, a love of literature. She was incredibly kind, so we had a steady, loving voice around us at all times, which helped us to be brave, and helped my brother to be brave when he had enormous decisions to make. Those things were present in her work.

You see it in the empathy for the people whom she writes about. It's a grounded voice that balances idealism and pragmatism."

A few days later, Obama and Maya attended a memorial service for their mother held in a Japanese garden at the University of Hawaii's East-West Center conference building, on campus. Maya and Barack gave short speeches recalling Ann's nature, her travels, and her scholarly passions. Afterward, they drove to a cove near Lanai Lookout, on the south shore of Oahu, where the cliff is steep and the waves crash into the rock and swirl in pools of foam. They climbed down the rocks and stood near the waves. Barack and Maya cast the ashes of Stanley Ann Dunham into the waters of the Pacific.

On November 28th, Jesse Jackson, Jr., walloped the Democratic competition in the special primary for the Second Congressional District. His father's celebrity, his network of connections in the black community, ranging from Operation PUSH to the churches, and his capacity to raise money far outstripped that of Emil Jones, who finished second, and Alice Palmer, who, coming in third, received barely five thousand votes, around ten per cent. Disappointed as she was, Palmer told her supporters that she had no intention of changing her mind and running to reclaim her State Senate seat. At fifty-six years old, Palmer seemed more likely to return full-time to education.

"Barack called her, they spoke several times, and Alice said, 'I gave my word and I am not going to [get back in the race],' " Carol Anne Harwell recalled.

Besides, rejoining the race would be complicated. To get on the ballot, candidates had to get the signatures of seven hundred and fifty-seven registered voters in the district. On December 11th, the first filing day for nominating petitions, Obama handed in more than three thousand signatures collected by his campaign. By now, however, a small but influential circle of community activists and friends of Alice Palmer—the journalist Lu Palmer; the political scientist Adolph Reed, Jr.; the historian Timuel Black and his wife, Zenobia; the academic and journalist Robert Starks; the state legislators Lovana Jones and Donne Trotter; the alderman Barbara Holt—had started to form a Draft Alice Palmer Committee intended to persuade Obama to withdraw in favor of Palmer. These were mainly veterans of the civil-rights movement and the Harold Washington campaigns. Alice Palmer was one of them. Obama, in their view, was a callow newcomer from Hawaii and Harvard, too smooth, too willing to dismiss what he called "the politics of grievance." They did not trust him to be nearly as progressive as Palmer had been. He could wait his turn. Even Jesse Jackson, Jr., appeared to support Alice Palmer and sent his field organizer to her meetings.

The Chicago *Defender* and the black-oriented tabloid *N'Digo* began to run articles sympathetic to Palmer. The *Defender* reported that some of her supporters were now calling on Obama to "step aside like other African Americans have done in other races for the sake of unity and to release Palmer from her commitment." The *Defender* had a long history with Palmer and an even longer one with Buzz Palmer, who had been the strongest voice for reform inside the Police Department for many years. Local politicians began to choose sides: Toni Preckwinkle stayed with Obama, citing Palmer's promises; Emil Jones went with Palmer. Writing in the *Defender*, Robert Starks, who taught political science at Northeastern Illinois University and was well known on the South Side, raised the unlikely prospect that the seat would be lost to a machine politician: "If [Palmer] doesn't run, that seat will go to a Daley supporter. We have asked her to reconsider not running because we don't think Obama can win. He hasn't been in town long enough. . . . Nobody knows who he is."

In early December, the informal pro-Palmer committee invited Obama to a meeting at Lovana Jones's house. Obama went to the meeting with his field coordinator Ron Davis. They knew what was coming. Appealing to Obama's sense of propriety, the members of the committee asked him to get out of the race.

"He said he had enough petitions and would not pull away," Timuel Black recalled. "I was kind of angry. When we asked Barack to withdraw, for reasons of seniority, membership on important committees, and so on, we didn't know him the way we knew her. Our confidence in her was deeper. We promised if he ran for anything else, he would get our support. But he said he was already organized and had money."

Some of Obama's supporters saw a motive other than loyalty behind the Draft Alice Palmer Committee: funding. Linda Randle, the veteran South Side activist who had worked with Obama on the anti-asbestos campaign at Altgeld Gardens, said that Palmer had helped her supporters get money for their community projects. "They could see with Barack that wasn't getting ready to happen," she said. "They worried about losing their funding, because Barack was less sympathetic to them—much less. Barack is cheap. If he puts money out there, he wants to see how you use it. Alice less so, because those were her friends."

"In Chicago you wait your turn, like in the Chinese Communist Party, when you take into account who was with Mao on the Long March—and Barack wasn't even from Chicago," Will Burns said. "But he was a very different kind of cat. He wouldn't walk away."

"They wanted to bully Barack but he wasn't going to be punked like that," Carol Anne Harwell said.

Palmer decided to run to retain her seat, saying that if Michael Jordan could make a comeback, so could she. She and her supporters believed that no matter what was said about a deal, the seat was rightly hers. "Not to belittle it or anything, but Obama did not have the representative experience of a black man on the South Side," Buzz Palmer said. "We were the activists of the South Side and we had never *heard* of Barack Obama. He said he was an organizer, but I would have heard about it if he was something important. Obama came to politics completely out of the blue. We felt he could wait it out. And if they ran against each other, there wasn't any way Alice could lose to Barack Obama."

Palmer's supporters scrambled to get the signatures required to get on the ballot, and by December 18th, the deadline, they filed 1,580 signatures, twice what she needed. Palmer held a press conference at a banquet hall in Woodlawn saying that the "draft" effort was too compelling to resist.

That day, Obama told the *Tribune* that Alice Palmer had pressured him to drop out but that he had refused. "I am disappointed that she's decided to go back on her word to me," he said.

During the holidays, Obama and his team decided to take part in a long Chicago political tradition—they would challenge the signatures on his opponents' petitions. This is a routine, and often effective, tactic: in 2007, sixty-seven out of a total of two hundred and forty-five candidates for alderman were eliminated because of insufficient or bad signatures on their petitions. It is less common, however, in the case of an incumbent.

Palmer's volunteers had had only a few days to collect signatures, increasing the likelihood that they had accumulated "bad names": signatures that were either fakes, had addresses outside the district, or were not from registered voters. Some were printed rather than written in cursive script, as required. In campaigns where signatures were a problem, it was common Chicago practice to "roundtable the sheets"—meaning that volunteers would get together in a closed room, sit around a table with a telephone directory, scour the book for potential names and addresses, and forge the signatures they needed. On the day after Christmas, the Obama campaign filed challenges against all of his opponents: Palmer, Askia, Ewell, and Ulmer D. Lynch, Jr., a retired laborer and precinct captain who had been trying, without success, to win a spot on the City Council for decades. Ron Davis went by train to Springfield, where all petitions had to be filed. He brought back copies of Palmer's petition lists and everyone could see that they were especially slipshod, containing names like Superman, Batman, Squirt, Katmandu, Pookie, and Slim.

On January 2nd, Harwell and other volunteers went to the Chicago Board of Election Commissioners—an office on the third floor of City Hall—and asked to see the petition sheets for Obama's opponents. They spent the next week carefully combing through the lists. The Obama campaign was hardly alone: the Commission office was filled with campaign officials and volunteers checking signatures against registration rolls. "It's like old home week," said Alan Dobry, who, along with his wife, Lois, joined the petition review effort.

Obama, who was relatively new to Chicago politics, was ambivalent about the process. "He really wanted to win a race," Harwell said. "He didn't understand that people challenge petitions all the time. People have a right to battle. We told him that they couldn't hand in garbage petitions. Once we showed him the Superman and Pookie sheets, he came around."

Obama and his supporters knew that he could easily lose to Palmer in a head-to-head primary. If he agonized over the decision to challenge the petitions, he did not agonize for long. "To my mind, we were just abiding by the rules that had been set up," Obama recalled. "I gave some thought to . . . should people be on the ballot even if they didn't meet the requirements. . . . My conclusion was that if you couldn't run a successful petition drive, then that raised questions in terms of how effective a representative you were going to be." In private, Obama absorbed a less righteous sense of tactics: "If you can get 'em, get 'em," Davis told Obama. "Why give 'em a break?" To help with the petition survey, Davis brought in Thomas Johnson, a Harvard-educated lawyer who had been involved in the Harold Washington campaigns and had helped Obama on Project Vote.

As Obama's campaign workers reviewed the petitions, it soon became clear that all of Obama's opponents had done, at best, a sloppy job of gathering signatures. There were addresses in the wrong district, bogus names, printed names.

"My wife and I worked on the petitions and we remember how the machine used to do this to our independents and knock us off the ballot, so we had to learn in order to protect ourselves," Alan Dobry recalled. "When I ran for ward committeeman in 1986, against Mike Igoe, the son of a federal judge, one of his precinct captains put in a clumsy forgery for the dean of students at the University of Chicago—which was a problem because they misspelled his name *and* he was on sabbatical in France at the time they collected it.

"Alice did not believe she would lose," Dobry continued. "She is a nice person and a real expert on educational issues, but she was not a good politician. She is not good at organizing campaigns."

Marc Ewell filed 1,286 names and Obama's challenge found him eighty-six short. Askia filed 1,899 names and was sixty-nine names short. Askia admitted that he had paid Democratic Party precinct workers five dollars a sheet for some of the petitions and that they had likely used "roundtabling" to fill out the effort. "That's a standard thing in Chicago—you pay people to circulate petitions," Askia said. "Even the mayor does it." He said that the Obama campaign was wrong to use "loopholes" if Obama was going to claim to be a new kind of politician.

Palmer had filed about twice the number of names required, but Obama's people asserted that two-thirds of them were invalid, leaving her two hundred shy of the required seven hundred and fifty-seven. According to Robert Starks, one of her main supporters, "We were in too much of a rush and that leads to bad signatures."

Even some of Palmer's friends in the State Senate could see she was in trouble. Rickey Hendon, a self-described "street guy" whose district was on the West Side near the United Center, said that he had no objection to Obama's tactics: "Hell, I do it and people have tried to do it to me. It's the Chicago way. People can make stuff up in this town. You can't let it slide. That's bullshit. Alice should have taken care of business." Hendon, who was one of Obama's antagonists in Springfield, also had no doubts about the repercussions of the incident. Obama, he said, "wouldn't be President if Alice had stayed on the ballot. I don't know anyone who thinks Alice wouldn't have won at that time and in that era. She was the queen. She was loved."

The Obama volunteers filled out long forms describing each challenge, and, in the end, the government upheld their case. When the result arrived, eliminating Palmer from the ballot, Obama told his volunteers not to betray any glee. "It was very awkward," Obama recalled. "That part of it I wish had played out entirely differently."

"This was not the optimal outcome," Will Burns said. "He didn't want us backslapping like we had done something great." (Nonetheless, Alice Palmer always resented Barack Obama, and privately she said that he ended up disappointing her, that he was not the progressive she thought he was when she first endorsed him. In 2008, Palmer supported Hillary Clinton for President.)

With the petition drama over, the Independent Voters of Illinois-Independent Precinct Organization (IVI-IPO), the most important anti-machine group to emerge in Chicago after the Second World War, endorsed Obama. There was now no way that he could lose the primary save for some unforeseen disaster. From his law partners and friends like Valerie Jarrett, who was now chairman of the board of the Chicago Transit Authority, he had raised more than sixty thousand dollars. His two opponents in November were insignificant: a sixty-seven-year-old Republican teacher named Rosette Caldwell Peyton; and David Whitehead, for the Harold Washington Party, who had run unsuccessfully for a slew of offices, including, four times, for alderman. The Chicago *Tribune* and the Chicago *Sun-Times* both endorsed Obama.

In the end Obama won, with eighty-two per cent of the vote.

What kind of politician did Obama intend to be? The most comprehensive portrait of him that appeared during the campaign was Hank De Zutter's long article in the Chicago *Reader*. An almost completely sympathetic piece, it portrayed Obama as a young man who admired Harold Washington but was critical of him as a leader whose dream of a principled coalition politics fell apart the day he died, in 1987. "He was a classic charismatic leader," Obama said, "and when he died all of that dissipated."

At one point, De Zutter watched Obama teaching a workshop for "future leaders" in the Grand Boulevard community, on the South Side, organized by ACORN and the Centers for New Horizons. Dressed "casually prep" and looking like an "Ivy League graduate student," Obama met with eight black women to discuss the way power was organized in the city. For a while, the women talk about "they" and "them," and how these unnamed people have come to control the lives and wealth of Chicago. Obama cuts it off.

"Slow down now. You're going too fast now," he says. "I want to break this down. We talk 'they, they, they' but don't take the time to break it down. We don't analyze. Our thinking is sloppy. And, to the degree that it is, we're not going to be able to have the impact we could have. We can't afford to go out there blind, hollering and acting the fool, and get to the table and don't know who it is we're talking to—or what we're going to ask them—whether it's someone with real power or just a third-string flak catcher."

At that point, Obama saw himself trying to bridge his activity during his first sojourn in Chicago to the world of practical politics, a bridge between the church-basement meetings of the South Side and the confer-ence rooms of the Loop. He offered De Zutter a kind of credo for his career:

> What if a politician were to see his job as that of an organizer, as part teacher and part advocate, one who does not sell voters short but who educates them about the real choices before them? . . . The right wing, the Christian right, has done a good job of building these organi-zations of accountability, much better than the left or progressive forces have. But it's always easier to organize around intolerance, narrow-mindedness, and false nostalgia. And they also have hijacked the higher moral ground with this language of family values and moral responsibility.
>
> Now we have to take this same language—these same values that are encouraged within our families—of looking out for one another, of sharing, of sacrificing for each other—and apply them to a larger soci-ety. Let's talk about creating a society, not just individual families, based on these values. Right now we have a society that talks about the irresponsibility of teens getting pregnant, not the irresponsibility of a society that fails to educate them to aspire for more.

Obama's idealism was part of what attracted young people like Will Burns, who eventually ran for office himself on the South Side, to the campaign. Obama seemed to promise a new kind of politics or, at least, a marriage of conventional liberal-policy positions to a temperament that relied on reconciliation rather than on grievance. The problem was that Obama was also given to a certain naïveté. In a tone of rueful apology, he admitted that he would have to raise money from people of means in order to win the election, but, "once elected, once I'm known, I won't need that kind of money, just as Harold Washington, once he was elected and known, did not need to raise and spend money to get the black vote." As a Presidential candidate, Obama not only raised an unprecedented amount of cash, from both the wealthy and ordinary supporters, but also dropped a promise to abide by spending limits, and then outspent his Republican opponent by a gigantic margin.

Obama had won his first elected office, but he alienated some on the left, both whites and blacks. They were suspicious not only of his shallow roots in the community but also of his post-civil-rights liberalism. He lacked a certain authenticity, some of them felt; he was too privileged, too willing to compromise on the "black agenda." "Chicago politics, whether it was the old Daley or Harold Washington, is a gutsy, boots-on-the-ground game and it's got to reflect the community," Robert Starks said. "It could be Daley from Bridgeport or Washington from the South Side. Now here comes Obama and he turns that idea upside down—he escapes the whole Chicago tradition of coming from the bowels of the community."

Adolph Reed, Jr., a professor of political science who was then teaching at Northwestern, and who had also been involved in the attempt to draft Palmer, published an article in the *Village Voice* that was the clearest expression of the deep and early suspicion of Obama, his origins, and his ideological makeup:

In Chicago, for instance, we've gotten a foretaste of the new breed of foundation-hatched black communitarian voices: one of them, a smooth Harvard lawyer with impeccable do-good credentials and vacuous to repressive neoliberal politics, has won a state senate seat on a base mainly in the liberal foundation and development worlds. His fundamentally bootstrap line was softened by a patina of the rhetoric of authentic community, talk about meeting in kitchens, small-scale solutions to social problems, and the predictable elevation of process over program—the point where identity politics converges with old-fashioned middle-class reform in favoring form over substance. I suspect that his ilk is the wave of the future in U.S. black politics here, as in Haiti and wherever the International Monetary Fund has sway. So far the black activist response hasn't been up to the challenge.

Obama's unseating of Palmer had planted some bitter seeds. He discovered that when, in Springfield, he joined the Black Caucus and again, to greater distress, in 2000, when he challenged the former Black Panther Bobby Rush for his seat in Congress. The Palmer affair, Will Burns said, had a dual effect on the South Side. On the one hand, Burns said, "people learned that he was going to play hardball. They learned that just because you write an editorial and tell him to do something, doesn't mean he is going to do it. It put people on notice." On the other hand, the resentment against him lingered, especially in the communities where the percentage of African-Americans was highest and the income level lowest. "The seeds of the 'not-black-enough' stuff started as a consequence of that first election," Burns said.

·   ·   ·

Despite the wide margin of his victory, Obama knew that he needed to expand his base of recognition. He understood that Hyde Park was a special sort of enclave—it was not considered the real South Side. So he established his district office in South Shore, the working- and middle-class black neighborhood where his wife had grown up.

Obama was sworn in on January 8, 1997. In the light of his future, it is all too easy to look at this first office with a portentous sense of gravity. After all, just seven years later, while he held the same office, people would hear him give a speech in Boston and start to wonder if he, "a black man with a funny name," just might be the future of Presidential politics in the Democratic Party. A state senator! But in 1997 being a Democratic state senator in Illinois was to hold an office without status. (Even in the best of times, Democratic state senators in Chicago with ambitions dreamed of becoming aldermen and congressmen or holding state office.) The Republican leader, or president, James (Pate) Philip, was an aging hack given to racist innuendo, and any Democrat rash enough to initiate a piece of progressive legislation found that initiative buried forever in the rules committee. Philip was the sort of racist who would first announce his lack of political correctness and then blunder on about the deficiencies of blacks: "It's probably a terrible thing to say, but I'll say it: some of them do not have the work ethics we have. . . . I don't know what you do about that, but it's kind of a way of life."

Pate Philip, Obama once told me, "was not a neoconservative but the original paleo-conservative. He was a big, hulking guy. He looked like John Murtha, but had very different politics, and would chomp on cigars and make politically incorrect statements, and he had adopted Newt Gingrich's—not just the Contract with America—he had adopted Newt Gingrich's rules for running the House. As a consequence, you couldn't even amend a bill without his approval."

The two legislative chambers in Springfield were almost entirely controlled by "the Four Tops": the Senate president, the House speaker, and the two minority leaders. They controlled committee assignments, legislative agendas, staff, and even campaign money. Run-of-the-mill Democratic legislators were known as "mushrooms" because they were kept in the dark and made to eat shit. Obama was a newly sprouted mushroom.

Ideology was a simple matter for the Republicans. Pate Philip, who was a Marine veteran and a sales manager for Pepperidge Farm, worked mainly to keep taxes low and to make any plans for reform "dead on arrival." The minute he took over the leadership seat, in 1992, he called for the abolition of bilingual education ("Let 'em learn English").

Obama commuted to Springfield. Most weeks when the Senate was in session, he made the three-plus-hours' drive to Springfield, along Interstate 55, late Monday and returned Thursday night. He usually stayed in the President Abraham Lincoln Hotel, on East Adams Street, a short walk from the Old State Capitol. Within a couple of days of arriving in Springfield for the first time, he called Judd Miner and asked him to take him off salary; he would be paid by the hour for any work he did for the firm.

Even in Springfield, where many of his colleagues were suburban and downstate senators who could not have cared less about the internecine battles of the South Side, there was still a price to be paid for knocking Alice Palmer off the ballot and out of the Senate. Two African-American senators in particular, Rickey Hendon, from the West Side, and Donne Trotter, who represented a district that extended from the South Side into the south suburbs, were not keen to give Obama a warm welcome. They viewed him as too lawyerly, too Harvard, too much in a hurry, insufficiently Chicago, and insufficiently black. Theirs was a less ideologically sophisticated version of the view taken by Adolph Reed, Jr.: that Obama was "vacuous" and inauthentic. Obama's book had been reviewed and even excerpted in the Hyde Park *Herald*, and so some of his colleagues already knew about his background. They teased him about smoking dope as a kid and about being reared by his white mother and grandparents. They asked him if he had figured out what race he belonged to. Hendon teased Obama that he was from Hawaii and lived in Hyde Park: "What do you know about the street?"

Hazing is a first-year ritual in Springfield. Obama's turn took place on the Senate floor in mid-March. To help the unemployed, Obama had introduced a bill to create a guide to community-college graduates for potential local employers—a bill of relatively small significance. Rickey Hendon jumped on it.

HENDON: Senator, could you correctly pronounce your name for me? I'm having a little trouble with it.
OBAMA: Obama.
HENDON: Is that Irish?
OBAMA: It will be when I run countywide.
HENDON: That was a good joke, but this bill's still going to die. This directory, would that have those 1–800 sex line numbers in this directory?
PRESIDING OFFICER: Senator Obama.
OBAMA: I apologize. I wasn't paying Senator Hendon any attention.

HENDON: Well, clearly, as poorly as this legislation is drafted, you
    didn't pay it much attention, either. My question was: Are the
    1–800 sex line numbers going to be in this directory?
OBAMA: Basically this idea came out of the South Side community
    colleges. I don't know what you're doing in the West Side com-
    munity colleges. But we probably won't be including that in our
    directory for the students.
HENDON: I wish—I wish Senator Collins was here to make that—hear
    that comment. Let me just say this, and to the bill: I seem to
    remember a very lovely Senator by the name of Palmer—much
    easier to pronounce than Obama—and she always had cookies and
    nice things to say, and you don't have anything to give us around
    your desk. How do you expect to get votes? And—and you don't
    even wear nice perfume like Senator Palmer did. . . . I'm missing
    Senator Palmer because of these weak replacements with these
    tired bills that make absolutely no sense. I—I definitely urge a No
    vote. Whatever your name is.

Hendon said later that part of his motive was just a ritual of sarcastic
welcome—"He wasn't going to be above freshman hazing, as far as I was
concerned. It's been a tradition forever"—but Obama definitely irritated
him. Hendon, Trotter, and others quickly determined that Obama had his
eyes fixed on higher office: alderman, congressman, mayor, governor.
Hendon joked that Obama would likely run for "president of the world."
Hendon had marched in support of the Black Panther Party in 1971, after
the murder of Fred Hampton. He remembered the first Mayor Daley, Dr.
King, the riots on the West Side—he was a *real* Chicagoan, he insisted,
and not from Hyde Park. Hendon didn't take Obama's main claim to
authenticity—his three years as a community organizer—seriously. Street
cred, he said, "is something you really earn and it takes some time. He
didn't have the time in as a community organizer. I was *in* the streets. I
stood up. Look, I have friends like Barack. I understood him. He was not
any kind of mystery to me: I have friends from Africa, biracial friends,
college-educated lawyer friends, and sometimes we have battles and differences. My friends with all those degrees like to compromise and live in
nice rich neighborhoods. They don't see things as they really are. You're
not as willing to compromise if you see the poverty all the time. When we
were talking about racial profiling, he told us he'd never been pulled over.
I've been pulled over a *lot*."
    Donne Trotter, a more polished legislator and given to natty bow ties,

was no less contemptuous of his new colleague in the Black Caucus. "Barack didn't have a clue," Trotter said. "He was a new kid on the block, an unknown entity, a blank sheet of paper. I'm not into conspiracy theories but no one knew who was backing him. It sure wasn't the community he was trying to represent. Who was this guy?"

Like Hendon, Trotter had no compunction about getting in Obama's face. "As Harold Washington said, 'Politics ain't beanbag,' it's a contact sport, so it's not as if what I was talking about was so out of line," he said. ("Beanbag" was actually a coinage of Mark Twain's Chicago friend the journalist Finley Peter Dunne.) "It wasn't a question of black enough. What we did know, by his own admission in his book, was that he grew up in Hawaii. It wasn't the issue of a white mother, that's not so unusual, but he didn't have our black experience. On the South Side, it's twenty below zero. In Hawaii, it's eighty degrees—and he's supposedly roughing it."

Obama brushed off the insults from Trotter and Hendon, and he focused instead on forming useful alliances where, and with whom, he could. One of the first things he did in Springfield was to call on the Democratic leader, Emil Jones, whom he had first met as an organizer while staging a street demonstration near Jones's house. Emil Jones was far more important than Hendon and Trotter. A legislator since 1973, he was one of eight children. His father had been a truck driver, a bailiff in the Cook County Circuit Court, and a Democratic precinct captain in the Thirty-fourth Ward organization on the far South Side. Gruff, earthy, and a chain-smoker, Jones made it his business in the Senate not only to pass progressive legislation but to bring home the pork to the African-American community. He helped to build institutions like Kennedy-King College, in Englewood, the DuSable Museum of African American History, the Bronzeville Children's Museum, and the Beverly Arts Center. Jones was an old-style apparatchik, and Obama had a lot to learn from him. Jones, in turn, realized that in Barack Obama he had a unique, if raw, talent that he could mold. It was not every day, he told an aide, that a black Harvard Law School graduate—earnest, sincere, ready to work—showed up on his doorstep.

"Barack was very idealistic when we first met," Jones said. "He wanted to get things done but didn't know how to solve the problem. He thought you could press a button and it would be done." Jones easily sensed the animosity of senators who had been friends with Alice Palmer and felt that Obama had somehow betrayed her. "I knew the feeling was there, but they didn't know that I'd known Barack for a long time," he said. Pedigree was also a problem—"Harvard and all the rest"—but Jones did not feel threatened. Instead, when Obama came asking for hard assignments, Jones gave them to him. Democrats could not easily initiate legislation, but they could get involved in the negotiations, and Jones made Obama his lead negotiator on a welfare-to-work package being pushed by the Republicans. This annoyed Hendon and Trotter, but Obama knew that Jones's favor was invaluable in Springfield.

Obama also formed friendships among white legislators from the suburbs and downstate. During his freshman orientation session, he met a Democrat named Terry Link, who had just pulled off an upset in a district north of Chicago. Link was white, ran a forklift business, and "barely got out of high school," but, he said, "We hit it off right away."

"One thing Barack has is the ability to adapt, and in the State Senate he discovered that things weren't clear-cut," Link recalled. "We were sitting on the floor at eleven-forty-five on the last night of our first session and we were handed the budget, a foot thick, at that time. We broke it up into five bills and had to vote on it. We were in the minority and we had just minutes before we had to vote. Barack had such a stern face, and he said, 'Do you really think our forefathers designed our Constitution to do the state's business like this?' That's when I think it hit him that things weren't being done the way he might have hoped."

Denny Jacobs, a Democrat from a downstate district, East Moline, recalled that Obama was long-winded in his early appearances on the floor, and his performances were sometimes greeted with eye-rolling, coughing, and annoyed muttering. "The state legislature is not a place for eloquence," Jacobs said. "You don't win with persuasive arguments. It's down-and-dirty politics, and he learned how to play that. You better be prepared to trade part of a bill if you are going to survive. If you want to get a little piece of a health-care bill, say, as Barack did, you had to give things up, because most people, including myself, were opposed to his all-out comprehensive bill. He had to withdraw his own beliefs." Early on, Jacobs said, Obama irritated him with constant requests for clarification and tutorials. In the midst of a revenue-committee hearing, Jacobs recalled, Obama was "asking all these damn questions. Finally, I leaned over and said, 'Do me a favor. Get your information on your own time.' Didn't fluster him at all. He just said, 'O.K., Jacobs, I will.' "

To make any progress, the Democrats had to form relationships with centrist Republicans. "We weren't treated as a hot commodity," Link said. "Without good relationships, you were never consulted or invited to meetings." And so Obama, Link, and others made a serious effort to learn more about the Republicans and then compare notes.

The social lives of Illinois lawmakers in Springfield were not, traditionally, an edifying spectacle. Some legislators treated the capital as a
marital hideaway, carrying on affairs and staying out late with friends.
Obama led a blameless and relatively spartan after-work existence. Most
nights, when he was in Springfield, he would make a quick stop at one or
two of the many receptions being held around town—lobbyists, interest
groups, visiting groups from Chicago—and then get back to his hotel
room where he would read, mark exams, watch a few cycles of SportsCen-
ter on ESPN, spend up to an hour talking on the telephone with Michelle,
and then, finally, fall off to sleep. Sometimes he went out to dinner with
lobbyists or fellow legislators; he was never much of a drinker. Early
mornings, he played basketball with a lobbyist from Ameritech at a local
Y.M.C.A. or went running.

Link organized Wednesday night sessions of the Subcommittee Meeting: a dollar-ante poker game held first at Link's house in Springfield and,
later, at the offices of a lobbying group, the Illinois Manufacturers Association. Link invited Obama, other legislators such as Denny Jacobs and
Larry Walsh, a senator-farmer from Elmwood, and a few lobbyists. Everybody involved in the game says that Obama was a cautious player, folding
hand after hand, waiting for his moment to bluff or go big on a good hand.
The game was never high-stakes—to win or lose a hundred dollars was
a dramatic night. Obama's caution, hidden behind a cloud of cigarette
smoke, could be maddening. One Republican, Bill Brady, of Bloomington,
told Obama, "You're a socialist with everybody's money but your own."

Obama enjoyed the poker games but he was also aware that for him,
"Mr. Harvard," taking part in the game was a good thing to do. It made
him seem more like a regular guy. He said, "When it turned out that I
could sit down at [a bar] and have a beer and watch a game or go out for a
round of golf or get a poker game going, I probably confounded some of
their expectations."

Friends in Chicago had also told Obama that in Springfield a lot got
done on the golf course, and so he often went with Link and others at the
end of the day to play nine holes before dusk. But on Thursday afternoons, as soon as the bell rang for the end of the session, Obama climbed
into his Jeep Cherokee, Illinois license-plate No. 13, and sped off to I-55
and Chicago. "He was on the road immediately—he didn't hang around,"
Link said.

Obama tried to form alliances with younger black senators who were
not turned off by his education, his manner, or his ambition. In 1998, his
second year in the Senate, a twenty-nine-year-old black woman named

Kimberly Lightford won a seat in Oak Park and other suburbs west of Chicago. Lightford called on Emil Jones, who told her that she should go see Obama. "He's the future of the Senate," he told her.

Lightford visited Obama at his law office. "I saw this articulate handsome young man," she recalled. "All these other guys were older white males. He was very polite. He told me all about Michelle. They had their daughter Malia," who had been born in 1998. "I was engaged to be married, too. He told me all about my campaign, and I said, 'You were paying attention?' He asked me about resources: I'd won with twelve thousand five hundred dollars, going door-to-door in a seven-person race. He pulled out a checkbook and wrote me a check for five hundred dollars. I thought, This is my new big brother. When we arrived in Springfield that November, they were having elections, and he nominated me as chairman of the Senate Black Caucus."

Rickey Hendon, who had been chairman, went along with Lightford's nomination. But in sessions of the caucus he and Trotter continued to razz Obama. "If Barack got tired of them in the meeting, he would laugh them off, or he would just leave the meeting," Lightford said. "He avoided any blowouts. I'd never seen anyone keep his cool like that."

Lightford was especially impressed by Obama's manners. "I was the first in the Senate to have a baby," she said. "Barack nurtured me through my whole pregnancy in Springfield. I always got the shoulder massage, or 'Do you need a footrest, you need a blanket?' He had a wife at home pregnant, so he knew. We were two weeks apart."

Lightford, Jacobs, and Link all assumed that their friend would not make a career of Springfield. "The day I met Barack," Link recalled, "I knew I would be in the Illinois Senate a lot longer than him, and he would go on to something bigger and better: mayor or president of the Cook County Board or whatever. He wanted to go on to something else. He could see that what was going on in Springfield, especially being in the minority, he couldn't accomplish much." Lightford added, "It was too easy for him in Springfield. He had figured it all out. He was a step ahead."

In his first year, Obama took on a particularly thorny assignment from Jones. Paul Simon, the retired U.S. senator from Illinois, was running a public-policy institute at Southern Illinois University and trying to draft new state ethics guidelines. Illinois politics had long been an ethical bog. Under state law, legislators could spend their leftover campaign funds without much restriction; some bought cars, paid school fees for their children, added rooms to their houses, set up a retirement fund. Members were also free to accept gifts from lobbyists and constituents—golf trips, memberships in clubs and golf courses, lavish dinners. Abner Mikva suggested that Simon and Jones call on Obama; the Republicans called on Kirk Dillard, a moderate from DuPage County. Obama was not quite as lonely a warrior on the issue as he portrayed himself in 2008, but along with Dillard and two members of the lower house, he was a lead sponsor of the new ethics bill, making speeches on the floor and negotiating with recalcitrant legislators. Dillard recalled that Obama was mocked in his own party caucus when he tried to push a comprehensive bill limiting contributions from unions and corporations and the traditional ability of the Four Tops to distribute campaign funds to other members; Trotter called Obama "the knight on the white horse." Finally, in 1998, the legislature passed a bill that, while it grandfathered in funds that had already been collected, prohibited lawmakers in the future from mixing campaign and personal accounts and taking substantial gifts; the bill also called for far greater disclosure than had ever existed in Illinois. The legislation helped put Obama on the map as a reformer.

Obama had at least one consistent, if modest, outlet for his ideas: an occasional column in the Hyde Park *Herald* entitled "Springfield Report." Between 1996 and 2004, he published more than forty columns in the *Herald*. When he first announced for the Senate seat, he filled out a "general candidate questionnaire" issued by the I.V.I.-I.P.O. asking for his endorsements (Sierra Club, A.F.L.-C.I.O., the firefighters), a biographical sketch, and a series of "yes/no" questions on various issues. In that questionnaire, Obama reflected a fairly standard liberal Democratic profile: support for public-campaign financing, domestic-partnership legislation, a single-payer health plan for Illinois, Medicaid funding for abortion; opposition to electronic eavesdropping and legalized gambling for Cook County. In his columns, however, he was able to give these positions more texture.

In the spring of 1997, when a thousand young African-American men assembled at the Dirksen Federal Building, in Chicago, to protest the drug and conspiracy trial of Larry Hoover, a convicted felon and the head of a street gang known as the Gangster Disciples, Obama wrote, "Something is terribly wrong: at the very least, it should give us some indication of the degree to which an ever-growing percentage of our inner-city youth are alienated from mainstream values and institutions, and regard gangs as the sole source of income, protection, and communal feeling. The reason for such alienation isn't hard to figure out. Close to half—that's right, half—of all children in Chicago are currently growing up in poverty."

In other columns, he wrote about exorbitant utility rates, onerous welfare reform, drunk-driving legislation, the need to keep genetic-test results confidential, the forty million dollars in no-bid contracts extended to a Springfield contractor who——"it may not surprise you to hear"——was a major campaign contributor to various Republican politicians, including Governor Jim Edgar.

Obama shed his rookie idealism and now spoke readily of his willingness to compromise. During a debate, in Springfield, he said, "I probably would not have supported the federal legislation [on welfare reform], because I think it had some problems. But I'm a strong believer in making lemonade out of lemons." Once, as Obama and Jacobs were walking in the halls of the Old Capitol building they noticed a civics-lesson poster that listed the steps needed to pass a piece of legislation. Both men laughed and agreed that the poster might be more useful as toilet paper. "He realized that sometimes you can't get the whole hog, so you take the ham sandwich," Jacobs said. "Barack wised up pretty quickly." This willingness to take the ham sandwich when the whole hog was unavailable would characterize Obama's pragmatic view of politics straight into the Oval Office.

The more Obama learned to deal with Republicans, suburban and downstate senators, lobbyists, and other seeming antagonists, the less he cared about the approval of Trotter and Hendon. His capacity to listen, learn the rules, compromise, avoid taking offense, and move forward was winning the parental approval of Emil Jones. His performance on the ethics bill gave him a reputation as a conciliator, a negotiator.

Even as he was gaining a good reputation as a legislator, Obama could not conceal his feelings about the day-to-day work of a state senator. He didn't mind the modest salary—forty-nine thousand dollars a year—and the long drives between Chicago and the state capital gave him time to think, make phone calls, and listen to music and books on tape. And his seat was his as long as he wanted it. In 1998, Obama had to run again. His luck was such that he ran against, as Will Burns put it, "the one person with a name funnier than Barack's": Yesse Yehudah. A Republican, Yehudah managed to get just eleven per cent of the vote; Obama was now safely in office until 2002.

But to be in the minority in the State Senate, to glimpse the infantile resentments, the mulish infighting, and the sausage-factory atmosphere was hardly what Obama had hoped for. Sometimes he told Michelle stories about the playground atmosphere in Springfield, the carousing and late-night drinking, and she could hardly believe it. He was also bored—bored with the details of so much work that seemed without impact on the lives of people in his district.

"Springfield may be the most boring place on earth," Obama's friend the novelist Scott Turow said. "For someone who had been living in Hyde Park, it was an intellectual desert. He expressed that. He felt that he couldn't engage anyone down there in a policy discussion. I think he was unprepared for how basic the terms of debate were: this one wants this, the other wants that, and the leadership wants this. . . . In Springfield, his initial response was 'I think I wanna get out of here and be a writer.' "

One of Obama's colleagues at the law school, Dennis Hutchinson, recalled, "Obama was unhappy in the State Senate. He saw Springfield as something he had to go through in order to establish a public record. He knew that the real deal was in Washington. He chafed, too, at the control that Mayor Daley and the Democratic establishment exerted. I asked him once why there was no successor to Harold Washington. He said, 'That's easy,' as if I knew nothing and he was going to gently explain. 'Every time there is a vacancy or a death or a conviction, the Mayor handpicks a successor and creates his own power base in the black community.' He seemed deeply schooled in Chicago politics and history going back to the first Daley and Martin Luther King in the sixties and the co-opting of the black ministers. That was all in his intellectual inventory."

Back in Chicago, Obama took part in various panels and discussions. Between 1997 and 2000, he also took part in the Saguaro Seminars, on civic engagement, held every few months and led by Robert Putnam, a professor at the Kennedy School, at Harvard. Putnam, who was best known for a book on the decline of community called *Bowling Alone*, assembled a diverse group of scholars (William Julius Wilson, Martha Minow, Glenn Loury, and Amy Gutmann), evangelicals (Ralph Reed and Kirbyjon Caldwell), journalists (E. J. Dionne, George Stephanopoulos), artists (Liz Lerman), and conservative politicians (Vin Weber) to discuss everything from the lessons of the Progressive Era to religion and ways of increasing civic engagement in modern life. "We had a giant jigsaw puzzle in putting together the group—left, right, white, brown—and Obama fell in the category of young, urban, black, community organizer," Putnam said. "My son was on the *Law Review* and played basketball with him. He came home to say he had met the most impressive person he had ever met in his life."

Obama was among the least well-known people in the seminar but he immediately attracted attention. "Obama is the same person all the time. When we see him in public, it is not a face he is putting on—it's him," Putnam said. "There is no mask, or at least the mask is so well integrated in his life that it's disappeared. He was thoughtful, but not self-revealing.

People who think they know him well are never unaware that he is restrained in self-revelation. The striking feature was his style in the discussion of hot topics with a lot of big egos. His style was to step back and listen. There were some important people who looked pretty bored; he was not, he was following. He carefully listened. Bill Clinton is also a power listener, but Obama, who has this capacity, is less forward than Clinton in letting you know what he thinks. But then he would say, 'I hear Joe Smith saying X, and Nancy saying Y, but I think Joe and Nancy actually agree on Z.' And it wouldn't be pabulum. It is not a trivial thing to listen for a whole day and see common themes in the midst of an arguing bunch. It's a personal skill or a personality trait. I don't think I have ever seen that same ability in anyone else." Putnam said that Obama seemed to the group "endearingly ambitious" as a politician, and they were soon referring to him as "the governor" and asking him what he was going to run for next.

By 1999, Obama was looking hard at his options on the South Side. The congressman in his district, Bobby Rush, had decided to challenge Mayor Daley for the Democratic nomination. Rush thought of himself as the second coming of Harold Washington, an authentic man of the streets poised to break a leader of the old machine; he was convinced that he could repeat the triumphs of 1983 and 1987 by drawing a record black vote, along with the Lakefront liberals. He barely got the black vote. Daley won by more than forty per cent. Suddenly, Bobby Rush seemed vulnerable and his congressional seat was up in 2000. Perhaps, Obama thought, the door to Washington was opening.

Chapter Eight

Black Enough

By 1966, the nonviolent tactics and the churchly aura of the Southern Christian Leadership Conference no longer had a singular hold on the movement for black liberation. Stokely Carmichael, speaking the language of Black Power, had radicalized SNCC, and more militant organizations grabbed the attention of young black men and women. Martin Luther King, Jr., himself had ignored the advice of many of his closest advisers and deepened his critique of American society, denouncing the war in Vietnam; in the last year of his life he spoke out for a redistribution of American wealth that he referred to as democratic socialism.

In October, 1966, Huey P. Newton and Bobby Seale, who met as students at Merritt College in Oakland, California, formed the Black Panther Party. Newton was born in Monroe, Louisiana; his father was a sharecropper and a minister. In college, Newton read Marx, Lenin, and, especially, Malcolm X, studied the slave revolts of Nat Turner and Gabriel Prosser, and helped campaign for a black-history course—a rarity in those days. Seale, who was born in Dallas, served four years in the Air Force and worked in a sheet-metal plant. Both young men were enraged by frequent cases of police abuse in Oakland and conceived the Panthers, initially, as an armed self-defense patrol to protect black neighborhoods in the city. They had been inspired by Carmichael—not only by the brazen style of his rhetoric but by his leadership of the Lowndes County Freedom Organization, which was registering voters in Alabama. The L.C.F.O.'s symbol was the black panther, and Newton and Seale adopted it.

Seale was the chairman of the Party, Newton was minister of defense; together they drafted a ten-point political manifesto calling for self-determination of black communities, full employment, restitution for slavery, and the release of black prisoners. Their brand of black nationalism, Newton said, "was structured after the Black Muslim program—

minus the religion." The Panthers adopted the uniform of black leather jackets, starched blue shirts, and black berets—berets, Newton explained, "because they were used by just about every struggler in the Third World. They're sort of an international hat for the revolutionary."

As part of an ongoing counter-intelligence program known as COIN-TELPRO, the F.B.I. under J. Edgar Hoover had been investigating the civil-rights movement and seeking to discredit Martin Luther King. The program was a well-funded symptom of government paranoia. In August, 1967, Hoover initiated a more comprehensive effort. "The purpose of this counterintelligence endeavor," Hoover wrote in a confidential memorandum, "is to expose, disrupt, misdirect, discredit, or otherwise neutralize the activities of Black Nationalist, hate-type organizations. . . ." Hoover was out to "prevent the rise of a 'messiah' who would unify, and electrify, the militant black nationalist movement. Malcolm X might have been such a 'messiah'; he is the martyr of the movement today. Martin Luther King, Stokely Carmichael, and Elijah Muhammad all aspire to this position." Hoover added the Panthers to his list. In September, 1968, five months after King's assassination in Memphis, Hoover called the Black Panther Party "the greatest threat to the internal security of the country."

The Panthers were not to be mistaken for the S.C.L.C. By the 1968 Presidential election, Newton was in jail—charged with the voluntary manslaughter of an Oakland police officer. He was also on the ballot for a California congressional seat. Kathleen Cleaver and Seale ran for seats in the California legislature. Eldridge Cleaver ran for President on the Peace and Freedom Party line and received thirty thousand votes. Symbolic runs all, but they infuriated the F.B.I. "This was all at a time when the F.B.I. was committed to wiping us out," Seale said. "Hoover knew we didn't care if they kept dragging us into court—we *loved* going to court, we had lots of bail funds—so they were committed to undermining us and killing us if necessary."

After the 1968 election, a charismatic young man named Fred Hampton helped open the Illinois chapter of the Panthers on the West Side of Chicago. As a teenager, Hampton had been president of the N.A.A.C.P. Youth Council in Maywood, an integrated suburb west of the city. He won a measure of local fame when he campaigned for the town to build a new swimming pool, since blacks were denied access to pools in white communities.

Hampton's closest allies in the Illinois chapter of the Black Panther Party were Bob Brown, a former SNCC organizer, and a young man named Bobby Rush. Born in Albany, Georgia, Rush moved with his family to Chicago, in 1953, when he was seven years old. His mother, a part-time teacher, opened a beauty salon on the South Side, and moved into an apartment near the Cabrini-Green public-housing complex. A Boy Scout as a child, Bobby dropped out of high school when he was seventeen and enlisted in the Army. He married two years later and moved with his wife to the Hilliard Homes, on the South Side. In 1968, deeply affected by the King assassination and disgusted with his superior officers, Rush joined SNCC and, when Stokely Carmichael encouraged him and others to organize a branch of the Black Panthers in Chicago, he responded immediately.

Under Fred Hampton's leadership, the Panthers in Chicago forged links with both street gangs and a range of multi-ethnic groups on the left: the Young Lords, the Young Patriots, S.D.S., and the Red Guard Party. In Chicago, the Panthers staged weekly demonstrations. They tried to win credibility among the working-class communities on the South and West Sides, setting up free breakfast programs, medical clinics, and political-education seminars. Armed and always ready to advertise their capacity for violence, the Panthers were not mistaken for a social welfare program, but they were, for the most part, welcomed in those neighborhoods.

"Being a Panther was a search for self-expression, an identity in a big world, a search for a relevant life—that's why I went to certain extremes," Rush recalled. "I read all these philosophical works by Nietzsche, Erik Erikson—who else did Huey have us read?—Hegel, Marx. Huey had us reading all this stuff and it satisfied my search for knowledge."

Everyone in the Illinois branch of the Black Panthers was in Hampton's thrall. He was handsome, brash, and physically brave. His speeches were not nearly as sophisticated as King's or Malcolm's—they were filled with invective against the "motherfuckers" and the "pigs" and laced with half-digested clumps of Third-World revolutionary clichés—but he had a visceral presence that appealed to many young black men and women who, after witnessing so many incidents of brutality on their streets, after living through so many assassinations of their leaders and heroes, were receptive to a message of self-assertion, dignity, and armed defense. "Fred Hampton was, for me, the most dynamic person I'd ever known," Rush said. "He personified strength, maleness, life, and love."

As Black Panther organizations across the country marched in demonstrations, got into battles with the police, and served up militant rhetoric on the evening news, Hoover commanded the F.B.I. to step up its efforts to infiltrate the local chapters. On November 25, 1968, he ordered his men "to exploit all avenues of creating further dissension in the ranks of the B.P.P."

The F.B.I. tapped Hampton's mother's phone and put him high up on the agency's "agitator index." But what the bureau really needed was a spy, a snitch. In Chicago, police identified an African-American teenager named William O'Neal who had stolen a car and gone on an extended joyride. Roy Mitchell, an agent working in the Racial Matters division of the Chicago field office, recruited O'Neal as an informer. In exchange for dropping the felony charge and paying him a small monthly salary, Mitchell persuaded O'Neal to infiltrate the Panthers office and report to the bureau.

O'Neal became Hampton's bodyguard and he described for the F.B.I. details about the membership, their conversations and plans, their evening political-education sessions on Marx, Mao, Fanon, Malcolm X. "We'd go through political orientation, and we would read certain paragraphs, and then Fred Hampton and Bobby Rush would explain to us, the new membership, basically what it meant and what was happening," O'Neal said. "And they'd draw parallels to what was going on in the past revolutions in the various countries, for instance China or Russia."

In May, 1969, Hampton was convicted of stealing seventy-one dollars' worth of ice-cream bars from a Good Humor truck in Maywood. The judge denied him an appeal bond because he was deemed a supporter of "armed revolution." And, in November, two Chicago police officers were killed; the suspect was a Black Panther named Jake Winters. At this point, O'Neal said, law-enforcement officials were determined to crush the Panthers. At the same time, other dramas were playing out in Chicago: the trial of the Chicago 8 defendants—including Jerry Rubin, Abbie Hoffman, and Bobby Seale—who had been charged with trying to incite riots during the 1968 Democratic National Convention, and the Days of Rage, an attempt by the Weather Underground to "bring the war home" and accelerate the uprising against the American presence in Vietnam.

On December 3, 1969, the Panthers held a political-education meeting at a church on the West Side that went late into the night. Afterward, Hampton; his pregnant girlfriend, Deborah Johnson; Mark Clark, the twenty-two-year-old head of the Panthers branch in Peoria; and a small group of friends and comrades went to Hampton's apartment on West Monroe Street. Weeks earlier, O'Neal had provided the F.B.I. with a detailed layout of the apartment.

Sometime after 4 A.M. on December 4th, a fifteen-man contingent of the Chicago police encircled Hampton's house. The pretext for the raid, organized by the Cook County state's attorney, Edward Hanrahan, an ally of Mayor Daley's who had been groomed as a potential successor or as a potential governor, was to serve a search warrant for illegal weapons. At around 4:45 A.M., the officers stormed the apartment from the front door and the back, spraying automatic weapon fire. Mark Clark, who had been sitting with a shotgun in the front room, got off one errant shot; he was killed instantly. The officers headed to Hampton's bedroom. Deborah Johnson tried to shake Hampton awake.

"Chairman, chairman, wake up!" someone shouted out. "The pigs are vamping! The pigs are vamping!"

The officers shot their way into the bedroom and wounded Hampton. Later, a Panther named Harold Bell testified that after the officers came through the door they found Hampton in his bed, bleeding from the shoulder. He said the following exchange between officers took place:

"That's Fred Hampton."

"Is he dead? Bring him out."

"He's barely alive. He'll make it."

Then, Bell said, two shots went off.

"He's good and dead now," one of them said.

The police held a press conference later that day and spoke of the arsenal in the apartment and, with self-admiration, their restraint in not killing all the Panthers present. At the Maxwell Street District lockup, some of the surviving Panthers told their lawyer Flint Taylor that they overheard police officers saying, "Rush is next."

Police officers raided Rush's apartment, in the Hilliard Homes complex, only to find it abandoned. Rush had been hiding in a Catholic church. He then went to the regular Saturday meeting of Jesse Jackson's group, Operation Breadbasket, the forerunner of Operation PUSH. In front of five thousand people and protected by members of the Afro-American Patrolmen's League, Rush turned himself in.

"You see this man?" Jackson told the crowd as he stood next to Bobby Rush. "We're turning him over with no scars, no marks, and we expect to get him back that way." Two black police officers quietly took Rush to the local precinct house.

After he was released, Rush led reporters on a tour of Hampton's house, which the police had failed to seal. Rush claimed that "a look at the holes in the walls would show anyone that all the shots were made by persons who entered the apartment and then went from room to room firing in an attempt to kill everyone there." Only the most loyal defenders of the police believed that the Panthers had engaged them in a firefight. The columnist Mike Royko wrote, "The Panthers' bullets must have dissolved in the air before they hit anybody or anything. Either that or the Panthers were shooting in the wrong direction—namely, at themselves."

In the eyes of the African-American community, Fred Hampton became a martyr and Bobby Rush a living symbol of black resistance. Thousands filed past Hampton's coffin at the Rayner Funeral Home on the South Side. Among the mourners at his funeral in the First Baptist Church of Melrose Park were Ralph Abernathy, Jesse Jackson, Benjamin Spock, and leaders of various left-wing groups in the city including the Black Disciples, the Latin American Defense Organization, and the Young Lords. The church was crowded with people and overflowing with anger and grief—people shouted out slogans against the government, some fainted. Bobby Rush said, "Hampton had the power to make people see that the power structure has genocide in their minds." The service ended with the singing of "We Shall Overcome" while members of the Panthers chanted, "All power to the people."

A few weeks later, the F.B.I. gave William O'Neal a bonus for "uniquely valuable services, which he rendered over the past several months." It was a check for three hundred dollars.

The killing of Fred Hampton initiated the decline of the Black Panthers but became an emblematic moment in the history of race relations in Chicago. The murder thrust Bobby Rush, a far more awkward speaker than Hampton, into the leadership role of the Chicago Black Panthers. "Bobby is a good leader, but a quiet one," Seale said. Rush, who had worked hard to overcome a childhood stammer, did manage to express his insistence on bearing arms. At a speech to Chicago college students, he said, "I don't go around saying 'We shall overcome' unless I have a gun in my hand." In 1971, he served a six-month prison term for weapons possession.

The last real triumph of the Panthers before they left the political stage was the political defeat, in 1972, of Ed Hanrahan, who was running for re-election as state's attorney. The Panthers joined the conventional political campaign to throw him out of office. Hanrahan's defeat was hardly the only consequence of the police violence.

Hampton's murder was such a galvanizing event, Rush said, that it "laid the foundation" for Harold Washington's election as mayor. By 1974, though, the Panthers had played themselves out as a political force. "We'd gone from five thousand members to a few hundred at most," Seale said. In Chicago, at least, martyrdom was their most effective legacy. Rush quit the Black Panther Party to enroll at Roosevelt University, where he studied political science. He failed in an attempt to win a seat on the City

Council and for a while he sold insurance to make a living. In 1983, the year of Washington's transformative victory, Rush, riding his coattails, was elected alderman from the Second Ward. On the City Council, Rush was a loyal Washington supporter in the endless "Council Wars," in which resentful white aldermen like "Fast Eddie" Vrdolyak blocked Washington's initiatives at nearly every turn.

In 1992, Rush decided to run for Congress, in Illinois's First Congressional District, challenging Charles Hayes, who had succeeded Washington after he was elected mayor. Hayes had been a founding member of Operation PUSH with Jesse Jackson and a supporter of King. The First District has long been a seat of great importance in black politics, and, in addition to Washington, Oscar De Priest, William Dawson, and Ralph Metcalfe were among those who had held it. More than seventy per cent of the district's residents are black, and it has been represented by an African-American politician longer than any other district in the country. It includes portions of Englewood, Woodlawn, Douglas, Oakland, Avalon Park, Chatham, Beverly, South Shore, and Hyde Park, along with suburban Oak Forest, Evergreen Park, and Blue Island. Rush was able to beat Hayes by reminding voters of his role in the Black Panthers and of a banking scandal involving Hayes, who had been discovered to have more than seven hundred overdrafts on his House checking account. It was a contest of racial bona fides and authenticity, and it got national attention. Soon after entering Congress, Rush said of his colleagues, "Some were amazed I didn't have bandoliers or a gun." Once he took office, it seemed that he would win re-election, term after term, without serious challenge. "Bobby Rush went from being the vice-chairman of the Illinois Black Panther party to the vice-chairman of the Illinois Democratic Party," Clarence Page, the veteran *Tribune* columnist, said. "Only in America."

As Obama's boredom in Springfield deepened, he thought about his options. Was Bobby Rush, who was his congressman, vulnerable to a challenge? Could Obama convince the voters of his own rationale—that Rush was a relic of the old racial politics of Chicago, an out-of-touch legislator of little consequence in Washington? Hardly anyone Obama talked to thought that he could reasonably challenge Rush. Newton Minow, Valerie Jarrett, his close friends Marty Nesbitt and John Rogers, various local political allies on the South Side, his colleagues at the law firm and the university—almost no one, it seemed, thought it was even remotely a good idea.

Arthur Brazier, one of the most prominent black ministers in Chicago and a friend of Obama's, told him that there was no way he could support him. "I didn't want to cross Bobby Rush," Brazier said, "and I didn't think Barack could win." Obama's three years of making friends with clergymen on the South Side was not enough. (In fact, early in the campaign, Rush held an event at Fellowship Missionary Baptist Church at which a hundred ministers, including Brazier, stood in front of a banner reading, "We Are Sticking With Bobby!")

"I thought it was a terrible idea," John Schmidt, Obama's old friend from Project Vote, said. "The State Senate was not a disgraceful place to be. But it goes to Barack's lack of modesty. The State Senate wasn't a big enough stage."

Michelle Obama was also wary of the idea of her husband running for Congress. She was working hard at the University of Chicago on community-relations projects. When Barack was in Springfield, she was home alone with Malia. What if he won? Would they need two homes? They could barely afford the co-op they had, to say nothing of the college and law-school loans that they were still paying off. She admired her husband's passion to do good, but what law firm in town would not pay him the better part of a fortune to take on a mixture of corporate and pro-bono cases? Michelle Obama did not hide from her friends the fact that the pressures of work, family, separation, and her husband's ambition had put an enormous strain on the marriage. She did not hide her resentment. When the congressional campaign asked her to go to fundraisers, she usually refused.

"Michelle wasn't around much during the campaign," Chris Sautter, Obama's media and direct-mail consultant, said. "She was there for the announcement and on Election Night, but I don't really remember her much other than that. There were times when Barack couldn't get back from Springfield for events and she was asked to stand in for him, but she mostly wouldn't do it. She didn't become really committed to his career until he was going to win the nomination for Senate four years later."

Obama, who desperately wanted to graduate from Springfield, kept looking for a credible plan in order to run against Rush. The rule in American politics is that to unseat an incumbent member of the House the challenger has, in essence, to convince voters that the incumbent should be fired for cause. The incumbent needs to be vulnerable, embroiled in scandal or weakened politically. Black incumbents in black districts were especially hard to dislodge. Rush was hardly Daniel Webster—his speeches were clumsy, his legislative record was undistinguished—but his popularity in the district was close to unassailable. And yet Obama reasoned that he could form a base in places where Rush was weak, neighborhoods like Beverly and Mount Greenwood, in the Nineteenth Ward. This was an area with a lot of whites and city workers, and in the mayoral race Rush had run poorly there. Obama also had the support of four South Side aldermen: Toni Preckwinkle, Leslie Hairston, Terry Peterson, and Theodore Thomas.

"The First Congressional District seat is a bellwether of black leadership in Chicago," Ted Kleine wrote in the Chicago *Reader.* "When Rush took it from 74-year-old Charles Hayes in 1992, his victory was seen as a sign that the militants who'd come of age in the late 1960s were taking over from the preachers and funeral directors who led the integration marches in the days of Dr. Martin Luther King." Could Obama, who was younger and more educated, now persuade enough voters that the days of the aging militant were over? Will Burns, who signed on to help Obama once more, said, "This was the first time he ran on a message of change, a different kind of leadership."

When Obama called on his local Democratic organization chairman, Ivory Mitchell, for support, Mitchell said, "O.K., get your petitions drawn up and have a lawyer look at them." When Obama returned a few days later, he confessed that his wife didn't want him to run. So when another South Side state senator, Donne Trotter, decided to run against Rush and approached Mitchell, Mitchell gave him his support.

"Then, when Michelle changed her mind and Barack decided to run, I told him that I had promised Donne I'd support him, and, besides, if Obama got in he would end up splitting the anti-Bobby vote and it would be a disaster," Mitchell recalled. "Barack said, 'No, I can beat them both.' He had his mind made up."

When Rush heard that Obama might challenge him, he was unworried, despite his poor showing against Daley. "I first met Obama in 1992, late spring or summer," Rush recalled, in his Washington office, in the Rayburn Building, near the Capitol. "I was Clinton's national director of voter registration. It was my responsibility to monitor the voter-registration efforts and to see that the allocations of resources for friends of Clinton were going smoothly. Obama at that time was working for Project Vote in Illinois. I remember we met in an office in a town house on the near North Side. He was a very *persuasive* young man, and even then he had a certain charisma about him. He had a sunny disposition, too. I knew all about his community-organizing background, and so I felt he was an ally. I felt a kinship to him.

"But when he decided to run against Alice Palmer," Rush continued, "I was well aware of the process that had gone on. Alice had a commitment from him, and he reneged on his promise. A lot of my comrades and colleagues were just outraged. I wasn't shocked, though. It takes a lot to surprise me. I felt that Barack had betrayed Alice and Alice's allies. He betrayed her faction of the progressives, and we were coming from a hotbed of liberal politics. She represented a challenge to the white liberal élites." Rush disliked the old Democratic independents like Leon Despres, Abner Mikva, and Newton Minow and saw Obama as their African-American plaything.

"Barack was an instrument for their efforts to unseat Alice. His ambition became the force that they used to challenge Alice, to deny her the opportunity to run for her Senate seat," Rush said. "Barack was just no threat. The forces that created him were the same forces that were always coming after me. I could never reconcile why they came after me. Ideologically, we were on the same side. But Barack was backed by that same liberal élite cadre or cabal that came out of Hyde Park. These folks, they didn't like me. I wasn't upper crust. I came from the streets of Chicago. I'm not Harvard or Ivy League, although I've got two master's degrees. I'll never be accepted as a member of the élite. I'm a former Black Panther! I was a high-school dropout! And Barack was the antithesis of a street person. I saw this as racist. They wanted someone with a better pedigree. . . . Barack wasn't the first to come at me in that way. There were others of the same ilk. And I cleaned their clocks, too!"

To Rush it was almost as if Obama's pedigree and his supporters' admiration were a personal rebuke. "It was evident then that there was this strain of élitism that existed—it wasn't *necessarily* racial, but that was an element," Rush continued. "These people were allies and friends, ideologically. Barack was so desirable to them, he was so in demand for these élitists, these white liberal élites. His ambitions and their desires coalesced. I didn't express anger at the time. I made a decision not to get involved. But people like Lu Palmer and Tim Black were really angry. See, you've got to have a history in Chicago politics, and if you want to challenge someone who has a history you better come strong, you better be bringing something of your own."

Rush disdained not only Obama's association with the white Lakefront liberals but also his sense of racial identification. "It's amazing how he formed a black identity," Rush said, rising from his desk and starting, theatrically, to sashay across his office, mimicking Obama's sinuous walk. "Barack's walk is an adaptation of a strut that comes from the street.

There's a certain break at the knees as you walk and you get a certain *roll* going. Watch. You see?" Rush laughed at his own imitation. "And he's the first President of the United States to walk like that, I can guarantee you that! But, lemme tell you, I never noticed that he walked like that *back then!*"

Rush sat down, smiling with satisfaction.

"But this isn't new," he said. "I really admire the way he learned. I don't denigrate it. He's been adapting all his life. He had the discipline to accomplish it and the foresight to see what his vision of himself required, you know? Barack's calculating in almost every decision in terms of how he wanted to project himself. Life is not a bunch of accidents, especially for someone with a huge vision for himself. He planned it out. If you desire to be great, the projectile of your life has to be there, you have to map it out. And that's what he did in every sense. To his credit, Barack didn't deny his African-American identity. He desired it so much. He adapted, he took on a lot of the culture. His desire to be a community organizer was also a product of being too young to have been an activist in the civil-rights movement."

Rush grinned and leaned back in his enormous chair. "If he'd been old enough, I could even see Barack being a Black Panther—especially the group that was really into the theoretical part," he said. "That would have fed his intellect. He might even have carried a gun, I wouldn't deny that!" (Rush seemed to delight in causing his old rival trouble.)

Rush was not impressed with Obama's three years as a community organizer, dismissing it as the trivial pursuit of feckless youth, as if, in comparison to his own experiences with Fred Hampton and the Black Panthers, it had been a junior year abroad. "I mean, you can't portray yourself as an activist if you are only a pale reflection of the real thing," Rush said. "You have to admit the truth—especially when you are running against the real thing."

Obama decided to get into the race in July of 1999 and spent the summer trying to assemble a campaign team and appeal to potential donors. (The primary was the following March.) His campaign manager was Dan Shomon, a former reporter for U.P.I. and the Corpus Christi *Caller-Times.* Shomon, a street-smart, chunky, high-strung political operative, had quit journalism while working for the wires in Springfield and taken a job as a legislative aide to Emil Jones, the Democratic leader. In 1997, Jones, through his chief of staff Mike Hoffmann, had assigned Shomon to be

Obama's legislative aide. At first, Shomon balked. He had spent some time shooting the breeze with Obama in the hallways of the Capitol, and he could readily tell that Obama was a hyper-ambitious freshman, someone with "wide eyes," as he put it, who wanted to pass landmark legislation covering health care, economic justice for the poor, job training, and many other issues. Shomon thought that Obama would be better off if he "stayed in the weeds," as the saying went in Springfield, "because if you stick out too much, too soon, you get whacked." Shomon didn't need the headache of dealing with an aggressive, starry-eyed freshman.

"I don't want to deal with Obama," he told Hoffmann. "He's trying to change the world in fifty seconds and he's got a safe seat. I have five senators I need to take care of. I don't have time to deal with this guy."

Hoffmann and Emil Jones persuaded Shomon to think otherwise, and Shomon went out to dinner with Obama. Like everyone else in the chamber, Shomon knew that Obama was a graduate of Harvard Law School, erudite and idealistic, but also that he was not very familiar with the counties of rural and suburban Illinois. Shomon knew, too, that Obama had been "spanked" by the black caucus and many of his fellow Democrats.

"Have you ever been south of Springfield?" Shomon asked him.

Obama admitted that he had never been south of the Mason-Dixon line.

Shomon said, "Obama, I'm going to take you to southern Illinois and we're going to play some golf and we're going to meet some people."

It was the early summer of 1998. Michelle was pregnant with Malia and Obama figured that this was his only chance before the baby arrived. Shomon crafted a trip around a week-long golf outing at a resort on Rend Lake, in Franklin County. In fact, they played every day, even though the temperature hovered around a hundred degrees all week. They went to barbecues and drank beer, though "Barack was never a big drinker," Shomon said. "One or two and that was it."

Southern Illinois is closer to Arkansas and Tennessee than it is to Chicago, and the general political outlook on social issues like gun control is much more conservative. Both men saw the short journey as a meandering fact-finding mission. Shomon gave his charge a few tips: "Don't order anything crazy, like Dijon mustard." Don't wear fancy clothing. Driving downstate in Obama's green Jeep Cherokee, Shomon and Obama touched base with a political favorite in the area, State Senator Jim Rea, and went to a golf outing and fundraiser for him. They met one of the state's U.S. senators, Richard Durbin, at a barbecue in Du Quoin. They stopped to talk with small-town mayors. The state's attorney in Du Quoin told them about an all-white branch of the Gangster Disciples, which was selling drugs. They stopped in at Southern Illinois University, in Carbondale, and played golf with the athletic director, Jim Hart, a former quarterback for the St. Louis Cardinals. They visited one of the best-known farming families in southern Illinois, Steve and Kappy Scates, who were impressed with how outgoing and engaged Obama was. The Scates family grew beans and corn and their farm stretched across two counties at the southern end of the state. Obama, Kappy Scates joked, "learned that Illinois is a lot longer than he thought it was."

"When he got back he realized these folks could vote for me—I mean, these folks could help me, they could support me," Shomon said. "I think it was really a revelation to him that he had a lot of appeal as a politician." Shomon thought that the diversity of Illinois—its differences of ethnicity, class, geography, and economy—would be a plus for Obama. If he had been from Wisconsin or Vermont, or even a black congressman absorbed in a traditional African-American district, he would not have encountered the same degree of differences. "What those trips proved is that he appealed to rural white people," Shomon said. "They would vote for him, they liked him. That was essential for a statewide race."

But now Obama was asking Shomon, a white guy who got a master's in public administration at the University of Illinois in Springfield, to help him win a congressional district that was seventy per cent black.

Shomon accepted, though an internal poll he took gave Obama only a limited chance to succeed. The campaign's biggest difficulty, it seemed at first, was to get Obama better known in the district. He was not, after all, running for the presidency of the University of Chicago. Except to the political aficionados of Hyde Park, he was a well-kept secret with a foreign-sounding name. The early poll showed Rush with ninety-per-cent name recognition, Obama with nine per cent. Another early poll showed that while Obama's Ivy League résumé validated him with white voters, made him seem comfortably moderate, someone they could vote for, it had little effect on the African-American majority, which greatly esteemed Bobby Rush. That summer, Steve Neal, the dean of Chicago political columnists and an early fan of Obama's, wrote a piece in the *Sun-Times* praising him and the *Tribune* speculated that Obama would run for Congress.

In mid-August, Obama took part in the annual Bud Billiken Parade and Picnic, a tradition started on the South Side in 1929 by Robert S. Abbott, the founder of the Chicago *Defender*, to celebrate and organize the kids who delivered his paper. With hundreds of floats and tens of thousands of participants, the parade was a big event for politicians on the South Side, with loads of celebrities and wide television coverage. Obama gamely marched along in the vast crowd, attracting very little attention. Al Kindle, a gruff and wily African-American political operative who had been working on the South Side for various candidates for many years, was now doing field operations for Obama—a fancy way of saying that he was working the bars, the churches, even the gangs, to get the word out on the candidate. When he saw Obama at the parade, he said, "No one knew who he was. He seemed a little embarrassed." Obama spent much of the summer trying to increase his name recognition, attending coffees in private homes and dinners at small, neighborhood places all over the district.

On September 26, 1999, Obama made his formal declaration in front of a few hundred people at a reception at the Palmer House, a famous old pile of a hotel in the Loop. "I'm not part of some longstanding political organization," Obama said at the kickoff rally. "I have no fancy sponsors. I'm not even from Chicago. My name is Obama. Despite that fact, nobody sent me," he said, echoing Mikva's story about the cigar-chomping committeeman. "The men on the corner in Woodlawn drowning their sorrows in alcohol . . . the women working two jobs . . . they're all telling me we can't wait."

Before the campaign began, a tragedy took place that altered the emotional texture of the race and paralyzed Obama for months. On October 18th, Rush's twenty-nine-year-old son, Huey, was shot by two robbers outside his home, on the South Side. Named for Huey Newton, the young man died four days later. Bobby Rush was devastated by his son's death. ("I always thought it was me who wouldn't get to thirty.") As a Panther leader, Rush had been part of an ostentatiously armed revolutionary group; as a mainstream politician, he supported strict gun-control laws. "Our responsibility—*my* responsibility—is to eliminate violence from our neighborhoods and from our nation," he said. This had always been, for Bobby Rush, a message that resonated with the voters in his district, but now it was all the more powerful after the death of his son. Rush formally announced his candidacy for re-election three days after Huey's funeral.

Not long afterward, Rush's elderly father died in Georgia. "I know my faith is being tested," Rush said after learning the news. "However, it is only that faith and the loving support of my wife, family, and friends that supplies me with the strength to keep going."

From then on, Rush ran a minimalist, Rose Garden campaign, avoiding most invitations to appear alongside his opponents, Obama and Donne Trotter, Obama's nemesis in the State Senate. Trotter did not have the money or the support to win the race, but he had deep roots in the South Side. His great-grandfather had arrived in Chicago from Mississippi in 1900 and his grandfather, Walter Trotter, had been a prominent minister in Hyde Park. A resident of South Shore, Trotter had even worked with the Black Panthers. And since he loathed Obama, he seemed almost as intent on damaging Obama as he did on beating Bobby Rush.

Rush mainly stayed in Washington and relied on his precinct workers and sympathetic interviews with the local press. When he did appear on the South Side, it was most often to campaign for gun control, tying his personal tragedy to gun deaths across the country. He had already co-sponsored dozens of gun-control bills in Congress, but now the press, including the national press, could not resist the story of a former Black Panther, who used to advocate armed resistance, mourning the loss of his son to gun violence and campaigning for greater restrictions. "I believe that this glorification of a gun is something that has to be dealt with," he said. "Many males don't feel as if they're empowered unless they're packing."

Obama knew that he could not go on the full offensive against Rush. For several weeks, he effectively suspended his campaign. Then, around the year-end holidays, he was severely mocked for missing a crucial vote in Springfield on a crime bill called the Safe Neighborhoods Act, which included gun-control provisions. The bill had the support of both the Democratic mayor, Richard M. Daley, and the Republican governor, George Ryan. As he did every year at Christmas, Obama took his family to Hawaii to visit his grandmother, who was approaching eighty. The Obamas left on December 23rd and planned to return five days later in time for the resumption of the legislative session. On the day of the flight back to Chicago, Malia Obama woke with a high fever. She had the flu. Barack and Michelle decided to wait another day and then either they would fly back together or Barack would return while Michelle and Malia stayed behind a little longer.

The gun-control measure might have lost anyway, but Obama was slammed for missing the vote. The *Tribune* ran an editorial criticizing him and other legislators who failed to vote. "What a bunch of gutless sheep" it began. In one of his columns in the Hyde Park *Herald*, Obama tried to appeal to his constituents' sympathies, pointing out that if he hadn't gone to Hawaii, his ailing grandmother would have had to spend Christmas alone. "We hear a lot of talk from politicians about the importance of family values," he wrote. "Hopefully, you will understand when your state senator tries to live up to those values as best he can."

It did no good. The sympathy was all for Bobby Rush.

"The black community doesn't turn its back on you when you are down," Will Burns, who was now a deputy campaign manager, said. "The campaign was suspended effectively almost to January. We had to be respectful. You couldn't attack a man who was grieving, who was mourning. Then there was the vote in Hawaii. We had asked him not to go. We were worried that something would happen. Between all those things, we had trouble. And we had come in so late."

Obama soldiered on, campaigning door to door and on freezing subway platforms, wearing no hat, no gloves. "We called him 'the Kenyan Kennedy,' " Will Burns said. But the complications continued. Jesse Jackson, Sr., still an influential figure on the South Side, was among the many black leaders who endorsed Rush. Jackson and the others saw no reason to throw their old comrade out in favor of someone whose most memorable act had been to maneuver one of their own, Alice Palmer, into retirement. What was more, Jackson was not eager to see Obama elevated and become a rival to his son. "Bobby had deeper roots," Jackson said. "We knew Bobby in ways that we did not know Barack."

One of the saving graces of Obama's campaign was that while he was constantly running into older African-Americans who found him diffident or lacking deep roots in the community or possessing insufficient commitment to a traditional "black agenda," he attracted a core of younger people, including well-educated black men and women, who saw that he represented something different from Rush's generation of leaders. Even as they trailed behind Rush and, in their most clear-headed moments, anticipated a loss, Obama and his team acquired a certain spirit. They were a "random-ass mix," Burns said, of "guys with no teeth waiting to get their next Old Grand-Dad and then these Shiraz-drinking, *Nation*-reading, *T.N.R.*-quoting young black folk."

One of those devoted young volunteers, a black lawyer named Mike Strautmanis, who had met Obama through Michelle, later became an intimate friend of the family and, in the White House, Valerie Jarrett's chief of staff. "I came back after my senior year of college to Sidley to work as a paralegal," he said. "There were probably five black lawyers there and I went knocking on doors trying to meet all of them. One day, I knocked on Michelle's door to introduce myself. At that time, she was doing intellectual-property law. She was looking over the storyboard for Keystone Beer—the ad about 'Bitter Beer Face.' Sometimes we talked about

Barack. I'd heard about him. *Everyone* had heard of him after he became president of the *Harvard Law Review*.

"So we developed a friendship. What we talked about most was fundamental questions about what we were doing, how we wanted to make a larger difference in the world. I was trying to figure out how to use my law degree to do something useful for other people."

Strautmanis's parents were from the South Side. His father left the family before he was born but his mother was a commanding presence in his life. "She made me think that I could be in a room and someone's entire impression of African-Americans might depend on me, how I behaved," he said. "I was always trying hard to be polite, to be intelligent, to work hard, to be *perfect*. I used that to motivate myself. My friends and family were mostly on the South Side because I *chose* to identify as an African-American, to culturally identify. My white liberal teachers put pressure on me to do really well. I was important to them, and it made them feel good."

Strautmanis grew up with the model of a black mayor battling a stubbornly conservative, and often racist, City Council. "Harold Washington was like the Lone Ranger to me," he said. "There were the bad guys and the good guys and every day you tuned in to see who won on the next episode. I still have my Harold Washington button—it was blue with white rays, like the rays of the sun."

As a volunteer canvassing door-to-door for Obama, Strautmanis was among a small group of young, educated African-Americans who saw their candidate as the incarnation of generational change. "I thought it was just so obvious: Barack was brilliant. Barack felt that Bobby Rush was politically weakened by his unsuccessful mayoral race and he hadn't done shit in Congress. He thought, What is Bobby Rush doing there? What had he put his stamp on? What was his crusade? I mean, why was he there at all?"

As a campaigner, Obama was an awkward, if earnest, novice. He was pedantic, distant, a little condescending at times, a better fit for the University of Chicago seminar room than for the stump or the pulpit of a black church in Englewood. In debates, he was in the habit of crossing his legs and holding his chin up at an imperious angle while an opponent spoke, as if his mind were elsewhere or the proceedings were beneath consideration. Too often, Obama reminded reporters and voters of the great sacrifice he had made by forgoing a Supreme Court clerkship or a mega-salary downtown to engage in public service. This was not a choice that a civil servant was likely to view with sympathy.

"He went to an élite institution like Harvard and spoke with twenty-five-cent words, and so he had that tendency to talk over, or down to, people," said Al Kindle, who, among Obama's campaign operatives, had the keenest ear for the street.

Ron Davis, who had worked with Obama in 1996 and was working for him again, would tell Obama, "Motherfucker, you got to talk better, you got to *talk* to the people!" Davis, Kindle said, "would talk nasty to get Obama mad."

Newton Minow, who held a fundraiser for Obama, remembers, "Barack wasn't that good. Someone would ask a question and he would give a professorial answer. His answers were just too long and boring. I never thought he could defeat Rush. I've represented a number of black businesses in Chicago, and when I called fifteen or twenty of them, including the publisher of *Ebony*, none of them would contribute. They all said the same thing: 'Let him wait his turn.'"

Dan Shomon, Ron Davis, Al Kindle, Toni Preckwinkle, and Will Burns all urged Obama to keep things simple, to avoid lecturing, to loosen up and show some emotion, to be a little more aggressive. "Originally he was short with us about that," Kindle said. "He didn't like the fact that people were telling him he was arrogant. And there was all this talk that he was 'sent by the white man,' that he really is white in black clothing, that his job was to break up and rape the black community."

Kindle, who was in and out of barbershops, beauty parlors, and coffee shops, who talked with ministers and gang leaders, knew that precinct workers for both Bobby Rush and Donne Trotter were putting the word out that Obama was an effete outsider, a product of a rich Jewish "cabal" from the Lakefront and the near North Side, that he had been brought up in Hawaii and Indonesia by his white mother and grandparents, that he "wasn't black enough."

"Barack wasn't raised in the black community, his mother was white, and the question was whether he was another Clarence Thomas," Kindle said. "You couldn't come out and say it on TV, but it was in the streets. That's why he needed me to get out in the neighborhood and try to validate him in the neighborhoods. We could say, yes he knows about poor people, yes he is black enough.

"There is a lot of mistrust in the community and so for someone from Hyde Park it's easy to generate it," Kindle went on. "The University of Chicago had a history of financing operations that were land grabs and he worked there. And there was that money coming in that was Jewish money, so it was an issue of class struggle."

Carol Anne Harwell, who had been with Obama from the beginning, recalled that the campaign was deflating for him. "Barack took a lot of stuff," she said. "They talked about his mama; they talked about his speech; they said he wasn't a brother—it was really hard. They saw him as a carpetbagger from Hyde Park in a district that had the 'hood in it."

Those sentiments would often emerge on WVON, a local black radio station whose call letters once stood for "the Voice of the Negro" but were later changed to "the Voice of the Nation." "The WVON audience is not huge but it has people who are hubs of information within discrete communities," Will Burns said. Callers on Cliff Kelley's popular show on WVON slammed Obama, drawing a humiliating comparison between the heroic elder, Bobby Rush, and the entitled young man who wanted to unseat him. "There were no flyers or stuff stuck in doors, but there was a steady drumbeat," Burns said. "Part of this was Barack's comeuppance for what the nationalists felt he had done to Alice Palmer."

Rush's and Trotter's grassroots campaign workers kept up an effective whispering campaign. They pointed to campaign contributions from prominent white supporters like Minow, Mikva, Schmidt, and the novelists Scott Turow and Sara Paretsky, saying that it reeked of an "Obama Project," a shadowy plan by moneyed whites to propel their favored, and obedient, black man up the political ladder. It hardly mattered that Obama's finance committee was made up of younger black businessmen or that he had the support of some important black aldermen—Toni Preckwinkle, Ted Thomas, and Terry Peterson. Rush's and Trotter's supporters dismissed such people as "buppies."

Mike Strautmanis recalled, "I went to my grandmother and I told her I was working for Barack and we were going to take Bobby Rush's congressional seat. Barack was on the cover of the *Sun-Times* and I showed it to my grandmother. She looked up at me with this *look* and she said, 'Why is he gonna take Bobby's job?' For a while, I was lost for anything to say. I thought, Oh, shit. If I can't convince my grandmother to vote for Barack, we're in trouble."

By the New Year, Obama had a bad feeling about the campaign. He had raised almost as much money as Rush—including a ninety-five-hundred-dollar loan to himself—but there seemed no way he could win. The campaign could do little about Rush's strategy of exalting his own racial authenticity and, through surrogates, questioning Obama's. "Less than halfway into the campaign, I knew in my bones that I was going to lose," Obama recalled. "Each morning from that point forward I awoke with a vague sense of dread, realizing that I would have to spend the day smiling and shaking hands and pretending that everything was going according to plan."

With coverage of the race dominated by the murder of Huey Rush, Obama often seemed to lose focus and motivation. "Barack in that first race didn't show the commitment you need to win," Obama's media consultant, Chris Sautter, said. "He had never had to run in a competitive race before. He hadn't appreciated the grueling hours you have to put in. He didn't appreciate the scale of time needed for raising money or going door-to-door. And after Huey Rush's murder, he was just not enthusiastic about anything."

Obama didn't run negative ads or mail pieces. He mainly just kept talking about his experience as an organizer, his work as a lawyer on voting-rights cases, his experience in Springfield on welfare reform, gun control, ethics, racial profiling, and aid to poor children. Inevitably, he began his speeches with well-practiced self-deprecation: "The first thing people ask me is, 'How did you get that name, Obama?' although they don't always pronounce it right. They say 'Alabama,' or 'Yo Mama.' " Then he would recount his multi-ethnic journey and detail his liberal credentials. He never lost his cool, and he radiated a feeling that, even if he lost, he was a new kind of African-American politician.

"He never gave you the sense he felt he was going to go down in flames," Burns said. "Maybe he felt we needed that or we might want to pack it up. He's funny. He's got a dry wit, a wicked sense of humor. There had been a shooting in one of the wards we were trying to win. I was in charge of a rally for gun control at a church. We had walked the flyer, we'd made phone calls, we really put a lot of time and energy into it. We had the meeting. And the cameras are there—and there were like ten people. The buses never showed up. It was a disaster. The one thing you don't want with Barack is to fail on a mission. Some politicians start screaming and throwing shit. He tapped me on the shoulder after he spun it out as a press conference. He said to me, 'You know, Will, when I call a rally, normally you have people there. *That's* a rally.' "

In private, as the campaign floundered, Obama even talked with Ron Davis and Al Kindle about his ultimate ambition. "He has always wanted to be President—it's like a waking dream," Kindle said. "The first time it came up was the summer he was running for Congress. Ron would say,

Martin Luther King, Jr., in 1965, leading protesters in Selma across the Edmund Pettus Bridge

Obama and John Lewis at Brown Chapel AME Church in Selma, on March 4, 2007, commemorating "Bloody Sunday"

Tom Mboya *(rear, left)* with scholarship students leaving on the "airlift" for Kenyan students to the United States

Barack Hussein Obama, Sr., as an exchange student in Honolulu, in 1962

Obama, age two, at home in Honolulu, in 1963, with his mother, Stanley Ann Dunham

Ann Dunham with her second husband, Lolo Soetoro; their infant daughter, Maya Soetoro; and Obama, in Jakarta, Indonesia, 1968

After transferring to Columbia, Obama with his grandparents, Stanley Armour Dunham and Madelyn Lee Payne Dunham

Obama at Occidental College, in 1980, clowning and smoking a cigarette

During his first trip to Kenya, in 1987, Obama posed with members of his Kenyan family, including his half-sister Auma, lower left; Auma's mother, Kezia; and his grandmother Sarah

Obama's grandmother Sarah, at home in the village of Kogelo in northwestern Kenya

Obama at Harvard Law School, in 1990, just after being elected president of the *Harvard Law Review*

Obama's leadership of the Project Vote registration drive in Illinois during the 1992 elections gave him a political boost, especially on Chicago's South Side.

Barack and Michelle Obama at their home in Hyde Park in 1996, photographed by Mariana Cook, who interviewed them for her book on couples

Chicago mayor Harold Washington was a political role model for Obama.

Campaigning for the Illinois State Senate in 1996 on the South Side

Bobby Rush and Fred Hampton as
Black Panthers

As an incumbent congressman, Rush easily
defeated Obama in 2000—a race that Obama
considered his political education.

Obama speaking at a 2002 anti–Iraq War rally, in Chicago—an event that was a boost to his Presidential hopes six years later

Obama campaigning in 2004 for the U.S. Senate

The Obamas soak in the applause after his keynote address to the Democratic National Convention, in Boston, on July 27, 2004.

Another moment of triumph as Obama easily wins a seat in the U.S. Senate, defeating Alan Keyes.

Getting a haircut at his barbershop in Hyde Park

OPPOSITE: Rushing up the Capitol steps to a vote in November, 2005

Obama and John McCain, at a Senate hearing room in February, 2006, pose like fighters after a heated exchange of letters during a dispute about ethics reform.

A frosty moment with Hillary Clinton before a primary debate at the Kodak Theatre, in Los Angeles

Obama with his friend and pastor, the Reverend Jeremiah Wright, in March, 2005

The Reverend Joseph Lowery was one of the civil-rights-era leaders who was with Obama from the start of the 2008 Presidential campaign

John Lewis, one of Obama's heroes, started out loyal to Hillary Clinton and then switched sides after sensing he was "on the wrong side of history."

The Election Night celebration in Grant Park, in Chicago

One of more than a million people who gathered in Washington for the inauguration of Barack Obama on January 20, 2009

'Don't tell anyone, but this boy wants to be President.' We laughed and Ron would say, 'He's loony!' "

Obama did get one break. On March 6th, the *Tribune* endorsed him:

Eight years ago, the Tribune endorsed Rush with these words criticizing Hayes: "He's a politician who can't shake the old ideas of government interventionism even though it is so clear in his district that the old ideas have failed." The same now seems true of Rush. He touts experience and seniority, but his approach to problems has not produced many results. And maybe that would be good enough, if he did not have an outstanding opponent.

Obama is smart and energetic. He was the first black president of the *Harvard Law Review*, and he is committed to his community. He has fresh ideas on governing and he understands that, as congressman for the 1st District, he would become a spokesman for African-American concerns nationally and an important voice in shaping urban politics in Chicago and the nation.

On Sunday, March 12th, Obama got a friendly reception in Beverly when he marched, along with three hundred thousand others, in the annual South Side Irish Parade. Over the years, the parade had become known as a drunken bacchanal and Obama was anxious about participating. Shomon convinced him to do it. "It's great," Shomon said. "You have corned beef and cabbage with your family and then you march around the block and have a beer with your cousin Jimmy." Obama began the day at a Catholic Mass and a soda-bread-and-casserole brunch at the home of Jack and Maureen Kelly, and with neighborhood volunteers like John and Michelle Presta, who ran a bookstore in the area. Obama marched on Western Avenue alongside the beer-drinking bagpipers and the teenaged kids with Mardi Gras beads and their green-dyed hair. A couple of nights later, he gamely fought to another draw with Rush and Trotter at a dull candidates' forum hosted by "Chicago Tonight," a program on WTTW.

The *Tribune* endorsement and the parade were boosts to the spirit, but Obama was not deluded. At the time, working-class blacks, the heart of the Democratic electorate in the district, tended to read the *Sun-Times*. On March 16th, the paper's editorial declared that Obama and Trotter had "failed to make their case" and endorsed Rush. Obama could not even win over the liberal alternative press. Ted Kleine's article in the Chicago *Reader*, entitled "Is Bobby Rush in Trouble?," appeared just before the primary on March 21st; it was balanced but contained some lethal moments.

Rush was quoted as saying that Obama "went to Harvard and became an educated fool. . . . We're not impressed with these folks with these eastern elite degrees."

The piece described how Rush had been able to turn the generational tables on Obama. At a debate on WVON, moderated by Cliff Kelley, Rush talked about leading a protest march in 1995 after an off-duty police officer killed a homeless man. Obama jumped in, saying, "It's not enough for us just to protest police misconduct without thinking systematically about how we're going to change practice." Rush found his opening, saying, "We have never been able to progress as a people based on relying solely on the legislative process, and I think that we would be in real critical shape when we start in any way diminishing the role of protest. Protest has got us where we are today."

"A week later," Kleine reported, "Rush was still rankled by Obama's suggestion that the black community's protest days are past. 'Barack is a person who read about the civil rights protests and thinks he knows all about it,' he said. 'I helped make that history, by blood, sweat, and tears.' " The exchange made Obama look callow and ungrateful.

Kleine interviewed the candidates at length and concluded that Obama spoke in "a stentorian baritone that sounds like a TV newscaster's." He also allowed Trotter to hold forth with a series of remarks that deepened the impression that Obama was insufficiently black. "Barack is viewed in part to be the white man in blackface in our community," Trotter told Kleine. "You just have to look at his supporters. Who pushed him to get where he is so fast? It's these individuals in Hyde Park, who don't always have the best interests of the community in mind."

The article depicted Obama as being on the defensive during the campaign, fending off attacks that, to Obama, were not only offensive but reflected a tragic suspicion of higher education among some voters. Obama told the *Reader* that when his opponents ripped him for going to Harvard Law School or teaching law at the University of Chicago, they were sending a signal to black children that "if you're well educated, somehow you're not keeping it real." He insisted that his kind of background allowed him to live in more than one world—an essential quality for a modern politician.

"My experience being able to walk into a public-housing development and turn around and walk into a corporate boardroom and communicate effectively in either venue means that I'm more likely to be able to build the kinds of coalitions and craft the sort of message that appeals to a broad range of people, and that's how you get things accomplished in Congress," he said. "We have more in common with the Latino community, the white community, than we have differences, and you have to work with them, just from a practical political perspective. . . . It may give us a psychic satisfaction to curse out people outside our community and blame them for our plight. But the truth is, if you want to be able to get things accomplished politically, you've got to work with them."

Obama's campaign raised over six hundred thousand dollars and spent some of it on a series of three radio spots that cast Obama as the new wave, an earnest idealist tough enough to work effectively in Congress. One of the spots, written by Chris Sautter and his brother, Craig, was called "Blackout":

MAN'S VOICE: Oh, man, there go the lights again.
WOMAN'S VOICE: Another blackout!
MAN'S VOICE: I'm tired of this. When's somebody going to do something?
WOMAN'S VOICE: Obama.
MAN'S VOICE: Say what?
WOMAN'S VOICE: State Senator Barack Obama. He's fighting for reforms that would force Con Ed to refund customers who lose power.
VOICEOVER: Barack Obama, Democratic candidate for Congress. As a community organizer, Obama fought to make sure that residents in Roseland and Altgeld Gardens received their fair share of services. Barack Obama. As a lawyer, Obama fought for civil rights and headed up Project Vote, registering over a hundred thousand minority voters. Barack Obama. Elected to the Illinois Senate, Barack Obama pushed to make health insurance available to everyone, regardless of income, and brought millions of dollars into our community for juvenile crime prevention.
MAN'S VOICE: Here come the lights. Con Ed must have heard from that Senator Bama.
WOMAN'S VOICE: That's *Obama*, Barack Obama. And they'll be hearing a lot more from him.
VOICEOVER: Barack Obama, Democrat for Congress. New leadership that works for us.

The play on Obama's name and the down-home "Say what?" had little effect. Neither did his rare appearances alongside his opponents. In debates sponsored by the Urban League and the League of Women Voters, Obama failed to draw a real distinction between himself and Bobby Rush. Obama's volunteers were encouraged by his ability to fence with Rush, but even to some allies, he seemed aloof to the point of arrogance. Obama "was kind of snotty," Toni Preckwinkle said. "His head was up in the air, he acted like he was too good to be there."

If there were any doubts where this primary was headed, they were shelved when Bill Clinton came to town just before the balloting to campaign for Bobby Rush.

Clinton's popularity on the South Side had only intensified during his impeachment saga. Rush had stood close to Clinton on the White House lawn after the House vote on impeachment. Clinton had not forgotten. He taped a thirty-second radio commercial for Rush that played constantly on WVON and other important stations. "Illinois and America need Bobby Rush in Congress," Clinton said, and even referred to the killing of Huey Rush to make the ad more emotionally resonant. "Bobby Rush has been an active leader in the effort to keep guns away from kids and criminals long before his own family was the victim of senseless gun violence."

The commercial ran on March 13th and Clinton campaigned for Rush in Chicago that day, dominating local television news. "Until then, for us to win, you had to find Bobby with a live boy or a dead girl," Will Burns said. "When Clinton came into the picture, it was game over."

On March 21st, Bobby Rush won sixty-one per cent of the vote. Obama got thirty percent, Trotter seven per cent, and a retired police officer from Calumet Heights, George Roby, won one per cent. The only area that Obama won was the Nineteenth Ward, with its Irish-Catholic teachers, firefighters, and police officers. He also scored well in the small part of the district that extended into southern suburbs like Evergreen Park and Alsip.

The next morning, Obama went around to the houses in the district that displayed blue "Obama for Congress" signs and knocked on doors, thanking his supporters.

In November, Rush beat the Republicans' sacrificial candidate, Raymond Wardingley, by seventy points. The last Republican to win the congressional seat in the First District had been a son of slaves, Oscar De Priest.

Nine years after beating Obama, Rush recalled the experience with an almost unseemly relish. "Barack was not a good debater," he recalled. "He was too academic. He'd lose the crowd. And I knew something about political theater, after all. The message was simple: Where did this guy come from? Who is he? What's he ever done? . . . My whole effort was to make sure that people knew that Barack Obama was being used as a tool of the white liberals. Now, these people later on also helped launch him as a candidate to the U.S. Senate and as President. You cannot deny Obama's brilliance, his disciplined approach. He is a very political guy, very calculating."

The night of his defeat, Obama, speaking to his supporters at the Ramada in Hyde Park, said, "I confess to you, winning is better than losing."

It was not clear that Obama would ever run for office again. Steve Neal, in a column in the *Sun-Times*, said that Obama would surely be heard from again—maybe he would run for Illinois Attorney General or State Treasurer—but for Obama himself even the prospect of getting Michelle's support for another campaign was forbidding. "I've got to make assessments about where we go from here," he told his supporters. "We need a new style of politics to deal with the issues that are important to the people. What's not clear to me is whether I should do that as an elected official or by influencing government in ways that actually improve people's lives."

Long after the loss, Obama recalled the sting of it: "It's impossible not to feel at some level as if you have been personally repudiated by the entire community, that you don't quite have what it takes, and that everywhere you go the word 'loser' is flashing through people's minds."

Obama is not given to rages or to depression, but the loss to Bobby Rush was decisive in every way. Years later, Obama told me, "I was completely mortified and humiliated, and felt terrible. The biggest problem in politics is the fear of loss. It's a very public thing, which most people don't have to go through. Obviously, the flip side of publicity and hype is that when you fall, folks are right there, snapping away." Not only had he lost by a margin of more than two-to-one, he had been repeatedly insulted as "not black enough," as dull, professorial, effete. Was he stuck in Springfield? If Bobby Rush couldn't come close to beating Richard Daley, how could he? In addition to the professional anxieties, there were financial ones: thanks to the campaign, Obama was sixty thousand dollars in debt.

"He was very dejected that it might all be over," Abner Mikva said, "and he was thinking how else could he use his talents." Obama began to wonder if he, and his family, wouldn't be better off if he didn't have to deal with the "meaner" aspects of political life: "the begging for money, the

long drives home after the banquet had run two hours longer than scheduled, the bad food and stale air and clipped phone conversations with a
wife who had stuck by me so far but was pretty fed up with raising our
children alone and was beginning to question my priorities."

Michelle Obama also had things to say post–Bobby Rush. She had
been against the run in the first place and now she was wondering when
her husband would settle down and figure out a practical way of reconciling his family's financial needs and the urge to contribute to the community. She did not see it in electoral politics. The family was hardly
poor—their annual income was now more than two hundred thousand
dollars—but the fact that they could be living immeasurably better was
not lost on either of them. As graduates of Harvard Law School, both
Obamas had serious earning potential, and Michelle had talked about
spending all her time with the family if her husband would only tend to
business. "My hope was that, O.K., enough of this," she said, "now let's
explore these other avenues for having impact and making a little money
so that we could start saving for our future and building up the college
fund for our girls."

Michelle Obama had long been displeased with the life of a political
wife. "She didn't understand Springfield," Dan Shomon said. "She worried that he was wasting his time. He could have been making so much
money and here he was mired in mediocrity." Barack was always on the
move, campaigning, traveling, working in Springfield, teaching, or practicing law, but Michelle did not hesitate to make it clear that she expected
her husband to do his share at home when he was there. "I found myself
subjected to endless negotiations about every detail of managing the
house, long lists of things that I needed to do or had forgotten to do, and
a generally sour attitude," Obama wrote later in his second book, *The
Audacity of Hope*. Dan Shomon told a reporter for *Chicago* magazine that
Michelle said to her husband, " 'O.K., Barack, you're going to do grocery
shopping two times a week. You're to pick up Malia. You're going to do
blah, blah, blah, and you're responsible for blah, blah, blah.' So he had his
assignments, and he never questioned her, never bitched about it. He said
that Michelle knows what she's doing—I trust her child rearing and the
family rearing." (Sasha, the Obamas' second child, was born in 2001.)

Obama certainly could have gone back to the University of Chicago or
his law firm. Another option that he considered was leaving the State Senate and becoming the head of the Joyce Foundation, which was built on a
great timber fortune and doled out around fifty million dollars a year to
community projects in the city.

"It was a sweet job—around a million a year, two country-club memberships, and I thought, Here it is, finally the day that all our hard work would pay off," said Dan Shomon, who imagined working as Obama's chief aide at the foundation. "Barack could have given out money to all kinds of good, progressive groups. He went into the interview, though, and his hands were shaking for fear that he would get the job. He knew that if he got it, that was it—he would be out of the game, out of politics."

Obama sparkled in the interview, but, ultimately, both he and the board of directors knew that his heart wasn't in it. "For God's sake, Barack," one of the board members, Richard Donahue, said, "this is a great job. But you don't want it." Relieved, Obama promptly walked away from the foundation world.

"That was the one thing Michelle didn't quite understand yet," Shomon said. "As much as he complained about Springfield, Barack had the addiction. And the narcotic was politics. He wanted to be an elected official. No matter what, politics completed him as a person, and he wasn't finished with it. Even when Barack was morose, when he was down and out after the race with Bobby, I never thought he would chuck politics. He had to pick up the pieces. But, ultimately, if it hadn't been for that race, there would be no Barack Obama. That was boot camp. That's what got him ready to do what he had to do."

Chapter Nine

The Wilderness Campaign

A month after losing to Bobby Rush, Obama bought a cheap plane ticket and flew to Los Angeles for the Democratic National Convention, where the Party would put forward the ticket of Al Gore and Joe Lieberman. Obama was not a delegate. He had not gained much favor in the Illinois Democratic Party by trying to unseat Rush. He didn't even have a floor credential, but his friends urged him to go and make some contacts. Later, Obama realized that they were trying to get him back on the horse and have some fun.

When Obama arrived at the airport in Los Angeles, he went to the Hertz counter to rent a car only to have his American Express card declined. He finally managed to convince a supervisor that he was good for the money. That may have been his most successful act of persuasion in months. For a couple of days, he watched speeches gazing up at a JumboTron at the Staples Center while thousands of Democrats, many of them in funny hats and all in sure possession of floor passes, streamed by him. He made his way into the skyboxes, but he could not get to the floor. He didn't stay long in Los Angeles.

Back in Springfield, Obama endured a round of "we-told-you-so"s at his Wednesday poker game. He became even closer to Emil Jones, who told him what had been so clear from the start of the campaign. The First Congressional District was not the right political arena for him. "It was a predominantly African-American district where you had to campaign solely on those issues," Jones said, recalling his conversations with Obama. "And Barack did not campaign that way, so as a result he lost. Which was good."

With time Obama and his small circle of political advisers and operatives began to see the value in having lost to Rush. Obama came to understand his defeat as a political education. He could not match the local appeal of Rush, who, while hardly the noblest exemplar of the civil-rights generation, boasted a historical credibility that Obama, as a man in his late thirties, could not. Rather, Obama, as a member of what he later called the Joshua generation, had a broader, more modern kind of appeal; and, because he had greater access to the élite institutions of American life, to Columbia and Harvard, to the liberals and the downtown business establishment, he had a familiar kind of education, an acceptable set of positions, a capacity to attract constituencies that Rush never would.

"Bobby did us a favor by running the campaign the way he did—it helped define Obama," Al Kindle said. "If Obama had tried to be 'more black' or be more like Rush to beat him, and if he'd been successful, he would have been forever pigeonholed. We already knew that he wasn't a traditional black politician. The race gave him exposure. He was not Harold Washington. He wasn't Bobby Rush. He was a different leader that the community had to grow toward, white and black. There was no model for it yet. The model was the flip side of what Harold couldn't be because the city back then was too divided racially. At this point in history, the city was less overtly racist and we didn't have the same lightning-rod politicians like Eddie Vrdolyak who organized on the basis of race. Obama became the next generation."

It was hard to imagine, in 2000 and 2001, when and how Obama's political second chance would emerge—if ever. Many in the African-American community were searching for the next generation of progressive leaders; the men and women of Rush's generation did not have the capacity to challenge Richard Daley. The situation in the Senate was not especially promising: Richard Durbin was the popular Democratic successor to Paul Simon, and Peter Fitzgerald, a wealthy young Republican, had toppled Carol Moseley Braun after a single term that had been plagued by accusations of ethical misdemeanors. When Fitzgerald's term was up in 2004, Braun could easily run again. Despite bungling her campaign finances and gaining a reputation in some quarters for low-grade corruption, she had far greater name recognition than Obama.

After the loss to Rush, Obama and Dan Shomon started traveling around the state again in earnest. According to Shomon, between 1997 and 2004, they put in nearly forty thousand miles stopping in at dinners, country fairs, Elks-club meetings, political rallies—any conceivable event that could get him better known in the state.

"In the car, it was just the two of us and we talked about everything, from his marriage to golf to life to women to politics," Shomon said. "A lot of it was me listening to his ideas about politics and strategy, and then I thought about how those ideas would fit into reality and how to advance him politically."

Obama quizzed Shomon about every political player in the state. He no longer thought about running for mayor: attorney general, governor, U.S. senator—those were the offices on the horizon of his ambition now. In the meantime, he was teaching and legislating, and he even brought in some legal work to his old firm. Obama's friend the African-American entrepreneur Robert Blackwell, Jr., thought there was money to be made in Ping-Pong, what he called "the No. 1 participation sport in the world." For fourteen months, Blackwell paid Obama's firm a monthly fee of eight thousand dollars to work on contracts. (The deal became a matter of controversy when Obama, in his capacity as Blackwell's state senator, wrote a letter recommending that Blackwell's Ping-Pong firm, Killerspin, receive a tourism grant to help sponsor international tournaments in Chicago.)

It was not clear, at first, where all this traveling and exposure would lead, but one thing was clear—that Michelle Obama was concerned about what it meant for their future. When Barack called in from the road to report how well a speech had gone, she would, Shomon recalled, reply something on the order of, "Malia is sick, so that's what I'm concerned about."

Obama was not deterred. Michelle's practiced dyspepsia was also part of the style of their relationship. She understood his ego and his self-involvement; this was her way of keeping it in check. Although politics was a strain on their relationship, it was never fatal. It is a mistake to make of her in those days, as some accounts have, a cartoonish nag; Michelle Obama was also proud of her husband and shared his desire to do good.

"I don't think Barack ever worried that their marriage was going to end," Shomon said. "He was worried about his future, if he was electable, if he was going to be stuck in the minority, if Michelle was going to be mad at him for this or that. But I never sensed his marriage was *really* in trouble."

"Without Michelle, there is no Barack," Al Kindle said. "He needed her as an image, and, of course, he really loved her. If she hadn't agreed to a political life, he wouldn't have run. A divorce would have killed him. After the congressional race, she wanted to know, 'Where are we going?' She needed him to make a decision. He decided, 'I am going to run one more time.' He was ready to leave the state legislature and he was looking for the next thing. He was evaluating his options. Some of what she was doing was forcing him to figure out what he wanted."

. . .

On September 19, 2001, the Hyde Park *Herald* published a gallery of reactions to the catastrophic terrorist attacks the week before at the World Trade Center in New York, and at the Pentagon. The two Illinois senators, Peter Fitzgerald and Richard Durbin; the House member for Hyde Park, Bobby Rush; the aldermen Toni Preckwinkle and Leslie Hairston; and the state representative Barbara Flynn Currie all provided fairly predictable messages of sympathy and vigilance. In 2001, Obama was still too insignificant a politician to be called on for comment in the national media, but in the *Herald* he provided a reaction to the events that is worth quoting in full for its attempt to explore the political meanings of the attacks:

Even as I hope for some measure of peace and comfort to the bereaved families, I must also hope that we as a nation draw some measure of wisdom from this tragedy. Certain immediate lessons are clear, and we must act upon those lessons decisively. We need to step up security at our airports. We must reexamine the effectiveness of our intelligence networks. And we must be resolute in identifying the perpetrators of these heinous acts and dismantling their organizations of destruction.

We must also engage, however, in the more difficult task of understanding the sources of such madness. The essence of this tragedy, it seems to me, derives from a fundamental absence of empathy on the part of the attackers: an inability to imagine, or connect with, the humanity and suffering of others. Such a failure of empathy, such numbness to the pain of a child or the desperation of a parent, is not innate; nor, history tells us, is it unique to a particular culture, religion, or ethnicity. It may find expression in a particular brand of violence, and may be channeled by particular demagogues or fanatics. Most often, though, it grows out of a climate of poverty and ignorance, helplessness and despair.

We will have to make sure, despite our rage, that any U.S. military action takes into account the lives of innocent civilians abroad. We will have to be unwavering in opposing bigotry or discrimination directed against neighbors and friends of Middle Eastern descent. Finally, we will have to devote far more attention to the monumental task of raising the hopes and prospects of embittered children across the globe—children not just in the Middle East, but also in Africa, Asia, Latin America, Eastern Europe, and within our own shores.

Years later, in the wake of the invasion of Iraq, of many more incidents of terrorism, of warrantless wiretaps and prisoner abuse, of profiling and intensified security, Obama's comments might seem commonplace. But in the days and weeks after 9/11, any attempt to understand "the sources of such madness," to understand how a young man comes to be a terrorist—how he might be shaped by economic and political despair and the demagoguery of fanatical leaders—was viewed by many with tremendous suspicion, as if an attempt at understanding constituted a lack of outrage at the terrorists or grief for the thousands of victims. And, in a reaction of just three paragraphs, to raise the question of civilian deaths in any U.S. military action was not at all a common sentiment at the time.

After the Al Qaeda attacks, Obama discovered that his name, never a great advantage in his political races, was, post 9/11, a kind of gruesome punchline. He had scheduled a meeting that month with Eric Adelstein, a media consultant for Democratic political candidates, to talk discreetly about the possibility of running for statewide office—possibly Illinois attorney general or U.S. senator. He had just been crushed by Bobby Rush and was deep in debt. Now his name rhymed with that of the most notorious terrorist alive. "Suddenly Adelstein's interest in the meeting had diminished!" Obama told the *Tribune* reporter David Mendell. "We talked about it and he said that the name thing was really going to be a problem for me now."

As he waited for his next political opportunity, Obama was determined to be a more engaged legislator in Springfield. He had come a long way. When he first arrived in the State Senate, he struck his colleagues as stiff, academic, arrogant. Over time, he became friendlier, more collegial. He did not radiate, as he once had, a sense of superiority. Obama had studied Bill Clinton on television. He had even watched Rod Blagojevich, a mediocre intellect, but a gifted one-on-one campaigner. "Barack wasn't Mr. Personality when he first got to the State Senate," Dan Shomon said. "He learned the Mr. Personality aspect of politics, the charm, only later. He even learned to get around the camera at public events, that you weren't there if you weren't in the picture. He learned ways to bring people toward him."

At the same time, Obama became a more effective advocate for serious issues. He was hardly on the left wing of his party, but he spoke out consistently for a moratorium on executions and against racial profiling. Like most Democrats in the legislature, he was especially wary of the

conservative-era impulse to slash both social spending and income taxes—
a far more concrete specter in the states, where budgets must be balanced.
George Ryan, a moderate Republican who was elected governor in 1999,
came to office with a glimmer of hope for the Democrats, and Obama
was pleased that, in 2000, Ryan put a moratorium on capital punishment.
He hoped that this signaled a more progressive trend in Illinois state politics, but in February, 2002, the state faced a budget crisis—a shortfall of
more than seven hundred million dollars—and Ryan prepared to cut back
on crucial state welfare programs. Writing in the *Herald*, Obama said that
the state now faced one of the "paradoxes" of a recession. "The worst
thing state government can do during a recession is cut spending," he
wrote.

And yet one incident during the Democratic attempt to hang on to as
many social-service programs as possible showed that Obama's problems
with some of his African-American colleagues were not over. On June
11th, Rickey Hendon made a heartfelt speech on the Senate floor urging
that funding for a child-welfare facility in his West Side district be pre-
served. Hendon had been especially angered by two terrible incidents over
the years—the cases of the Keystone 19 and the Huron 12—when children on the West Side were found living in the most desperate conditions.
There was no way that Hendon could succeed in his appeal—the Republican majority voted against him—but what surprised him was that Obama
voted against him, too. Incensed, Hendon, who sat up front with the
minority leadership, headed back to what was known as Liberal Row,
where Obama sat with three other Democrats: Terry Link, Lisa Madigan,
the daughter of the speaker of the Illinois House, and Carol Ronen, who
was particularly active on gay issues.

"Rickey was very upset—screaming and hollering," Terry Link
recalled.

Obama tried to calm Hendon down, saying something about keeping
spending under control.

"He explained to me that we had to show fiscal responsibility during
tough budget times," Hendon recalled. "Before I could ask him about the
poor children, I found myself walking back to my seat in a daze. I sat
down, like in a daydream, or nightmare, kind of blur, and continued to
vote no on cut after cut along with all the Democrats, including Liberal
Row. Finally I heard the bill number called for a cut on the South Side in
Senator Obama's district. Barack rose to give an emotional speech condemning this particular cut. He asked for compassion and understanding.
Now, this facility they wanted to close was very similar to the one he just

voted to close on the West Side. His fiscally prudent vote took place only about ten minutes earlier and now he wants compassion!"

Hendon got up to speak and called out Obama on the floor of the Senate:

> HENDON: I just want to say to the last speaker, you got a lot of nerve to talk about being responsible and then you voted for closing the [Department of Children and Family Services] office on the West Side, when you wouldn't have voted to close it on the South Side. So I apologize to my Republican friends about my—bipartisanship comments, 'cause clearly there's some Democrats on this side of the aisle that don't care about the West Side either, especially the last speaker.
>
> PRESIDING OFFICER (SENATOR WATSON): Senator Obama, do you wish to speak? Senator Obama.
>
> OBAMA: Thank you, Mr. President. I understand Senator Hendon's anger at—actually—the—I was not aware that I had voted No on that last piece of legislation. I would have the record record that I intended to vote Yes. On the other hand, I would appreciate that next time my dear colleague, Senator Hendon, ask me about a vote before he names me on the floor.

After Obama attempted, in vain, to have his vote changed, he angrily walked toward Hendon's seat on Leaders Row. As Hendon recalls it, Obama "stuck his jagged, strained face into my space" and told him, "You embarrassed me on the Senate floor and if you ever do it again I will kick your ass!"

"What?"

"You heard me," Obama said, "and if you come back here by the telephones, where the press can't see it, I will kick your ass right now!"

The two men walked off the floor of the Senate to a small antechamber in the back. In Hendon's self-dramatizing version of the incident, the confrontation got physical and came just short of a real fight with Emil Jones dispatching Donne Trotter to break things up before they descended to the level of the World Wide Wrestling Federation. Terry Link and Denny Jacobs say that Hendon has hyped the incident—that Obama never cursed at Hendon and that no blows were exchanged—but no one denies it was an emotional schoolyard confrontation that could have gotten out of hand.

In *Black Enough/White Enough: The Obama Dilemma*, an often bitter book, Hendon writes that the incident proved that Obama was "bipartisan enough and white enough to be President of the United States." It also proved, in his dubious analysis, that Obama was sufficiently tough to occupy the Oval Office. "If we were attacked by terrorists, would he pull the trigger?" he wrote. "There's no doubt that he would." When asked what would have happened if Trotter and others hadn't separated the two men, he said, "I don't think anybody walking the face of the earth can whup me! It probably would have been the end of my career if I'd lost because of the neighborhood I represent. That's the kind of fight it would have been. Thank God cooler heads prevailed. I couldn't go back to the West Side getting beat up by a guy from Harvard. Or from the South Side. I would have been through." Such, on occasion, was the level of debate in Springfield, Illinois. And Barack Obama was eager to leave it behind.

That same month, in June, 2002, Obama was campaigning for Milorad (Rod) Blagojevich, then a two-term congressman, who was the Democratic candidate for governor. The son of a Serbian-born steelworker from the Northwest Side, Blagojevich had been an indifferent law student at Pepperdine ("I barely knew where the law library was") and got his political start through his father-in-law, an alderman named Richard Mell. In 2002, Blagojevich was one of eighty-one Democrats in the House of Representatives who voted to authorize the use of force in Iraq. In the gubernatorial primary, Blagojevich had defeated the former state attorney general, Roland Burris, and the Chicago schools head, Paul Vallas. Obama had supported Burris in the primary but turned his support to Blagojevich in the general election. Rahm Emanuel, who was then a member of the House, told Ryan Lizza of *The New Yorker* that he and Obama "participated in a small group that met weekly when Rod was running for governor. . . . We basically laid out the general election, Barack and I and these two." (Blagojevich's campaign adviser, David Wilhelm, refined Emanuel's remarks later, telling Jake Tapper of ABC that Obama was a member of an advisory council, not one of the principal strategists.) Years later, when Blagojevich was facing federal corruption charges, Obama was circumspect about his relations with him, but during the campaign he proved a loyal party man. Appearing in June, 2002, on Jeff Berkowitz's local cable show ("Berkowitz is my name, politics is our game"), Obama said, "Right now, my main focus is to make sure that we elect Rod Blagojevich as Governor."

BERKOWITZ: You working hard for Rod?

OBAMA: You betcha.

BERKOWITZ: Hot Rod?

OBAMA: That's exactly right. You know, I think having a Democratic
governor will make a big difference. I think that I am working
hard to get a Democratic senate and Emil Jones president, replacing Pate Philip, and once all that clears out in November, then I
think we'll be able to make some good decisions about the [U.S.]
Senate race.

In effect, Obama was closing his eyes and thinking of the Democratic
Party. "He and Blagojevich had no relationship at all," Pete Giangreco, a
direct-mail consultant who was working then for Blagojevich, said. "They
came from two different planets politically. Barack was Hyde Park and the
University of Chicago. Rod was an admitted C-student who had a not
even thinly veiled contempt for intellectuals. He hated anyone from the
North Shore or Hyde Park and he wore his contempt as a badge of honor.
And there was some racial politics mixed up in there, too. They were not
allies."

In 2001, Richard Durbin, the state's senior senator, hosted a group of
Democratic Party activists and politicians. For the occasion, Dan Shomon
printed up buttons reading "Obama: Statewide in 2002." But what
statewide office did he and Obama have in mind? Lisa Madigan, Obama's
friend on Liberal Row, was a likely candidate for attorney general. Peter
Fitzgerald's seat in the U.S. Senate was the only attractive possibility.
Fitzgerald had got into battles with his own party in both Washington and
Springfield, but so far he showed no sign of stepping aside and the fact of
the family's enormous banking fortune meant that he was perfectly capable of financing another race.

With the 2002 elections just over a month away, Obama confided to
Abner Mikva that he was thinking about taking a run at Fitzgerald's U.S.
Senate seat in 2004. Mikva told him, "You have to talk to the Jackson boys
first." Jesse, Jr., who had won a seat in the House, in 1995, was also thinking about the Senate, Mikva said. Obama said he knew: "I'm working on
that." At a lunch at 312, an Italian restaurant on LaSalle, Obama told Jackson that if Jackson was running he would not. Not to worry, Jackson
replied; he was staying in the House.

By the late summer of 2002, the Bush Administration was intensifying its public rhetoric about an invasion of Iraq. On September 12th, Bush went to the General Assembly of the United Nations and declared, "If Iraq's regime defies us again, the world must move deliberately, decisively to hold Iraq to account. We will work with the U.N. Security Council for the necessary resolutions. But the purposes of the United States should not be doubted." Within a month, he would have the support of Congress to use force in Iraq.

On September 21st, Bettylu Saltzman, Obama's wealthy friend and patron on the near North Side, was having dinner with her husband and two other couples at a Vietnamese restaurant downtown called Pasteur. Saltzman, by then, had eight grandchildren and had not been to an anti-war rally of any kind since Vietnam, but as the group discussed their despair at the Administration's obvious desire to send troops to Iraq, Saltzman said, "We've got to do something!" Early the next morning, she called an old friend who might know how to put together a rally: Marilyn Katz, a raspy-voiced, chain-smoking raconteur, who had been a leader of S.D.S. in her youth and now ran a communications firm that regularly won contracts with Mayor Daley. Part of Richard Daley's Machiavellian skill had been to modernize the Chicago political structure, removing its mailed fist but retaining its toleration of corruption in the name of making things work. Daley's loss to Harold Washington in 1983 had taught him that he could not govern in opposition to the African-American community; he had to bring African-Americans into the process. By making City Hall more inclusive, by doing business with people his father could not tolerate—African-Americans, Hispanics, Lakefront liberals, old leftists like Marilyn Katz and Bill Ayers, and independent Democrats—he built a far broader coalition. In 1989, just weeks after winning his first of six mayoral elections, Daley became the first Chicago mayor to march in the city's annual Gay Pride parade. In Richard M. Daley's Chicago, a city of strange bedfellows, it was only natural that a wealthy liberal like Bettylu Saltzman would find an ally in an ex-radical like Marilyn Katz.

"Marilyn is a very good organizer, I am not," Saltzman said. "So I woke her up."

"Thank God you called," Katz said, and the two talked about how to proceed.

Two days later, the two women convened a meeting of about a dozen people at Saltzman's penthouse apartment, including a number of veteran left-wing activists, Michael Klonsky and Carl Davidson, and Rhona Hoffman, who ran a well-known art gallery. "We all took assignments," Saltzman said. Robert Howard, a local attorney, got permission to use Federal Plaza on South Dearborn at midday on October 2nd. Marilyn Katz and Davidson, another S.D.S. veteran, knew that with a well-aimed e-mail spray they could get a core of left-wing groups to come to Federal Plaza. Then they tried to assemble a list of speakers, which included Jesse Jackson, Sr., and various clergy and local politicians. Saltzman called John Mearsheimer, a political scientist at the University of Chicago, but he already had a speaking engagement in Wisconsin. Later in the week, she called Barack Obama at home. Michelle answered and said she would give him the message.

"I finally spoke to him on Monday for a Tuesday rally," she recalled. "Few knew who he was. The only people who really knew him were in Hyde Park, people who were his friends and associates."

Saltzman called on Obama simply because she had a sense that he had a future. "I didn't know him as well as Valerie Jarrett and Marty Nesbitt did. I am a North Sider. I'm white. It's a different group of people. I don't really know what he had in place. I just had this instinct about him."

Before agreeing to speak at the rally, Obama called a few trusted friends to discuss the political ramifications. He had already commissioned a benchmark poll to explore a Senate run and was fairly sure he was going to do it. For a Hyde Park politician, the risk of speaking was mild— at the university both the left and many on the right opposed an invasion of Iraq—but the issue got more complicated the farther away you went from Chicago. "Nationally, the conventional wisdom was to support the war," Will Burns said. "The war hadn't started yet, there was lots of triumphalism, lots of talk about mushroom clouds. If you are running for Senate, there's the chance of looking 'soft on terror.' This was just a year after 9/11."

Pete Giangreco, who had agreed to advise Obama and do his direct-mail campaign for a potential Senate campaign, got a call from Obama to discuss the invitation to speak. "The war was pretty popular then," Giangreco said. "Opposing it wouldn't be a problem in the primary, but it could be a really big problem in a general election. All kinds of people might have a problem with being 'soft': Reagan Democrats, downscale ethnic folks in Chicago, and people downstate who didn't live in college towns. Talking from a targeting standpoint, I said we already had a challenge with these folks. His name, Barack Obama, was *different* and not very helpful, and, while Roland Burris and Carol Moseley Braun had won statewide races, it's always a challenge for an African-American. So I said, 'You might be able to capture the folks on the left who are against this war, and against *any* war, frankly, but there were all the others to take into account.' He just took it all in. He finally said, 'Well, my instinct is to do this.' And my reaction was 'If this is what you really believe, you'll score huge points for courage and saying what you think.' "

"Politically, the reason why Barack's political advisers were saying it was a good idea for him to speak was because the coalition he needed to get elected was blacks and liberals, and he wasn't going to get liberals if he was supporting Bush in the war," Chris Sautter, Obama's media consultant in the 2000 congressional race, said. As Obama talked it through further with Giangreco, Shomon, and David Axelrod, he concluded that he could devise a rhetorical construction that would express his opposition to an invasion of Iraq without making him seem disqualifyingly weak on terror.

In defiance of the weather report, on October 2nd, the sun was shining. People milled around the speaker's platform holding up antiwar signs. Estimates of the crowd ranged from the *Tribune's* "about 1,000" to the Chicago *Defender's* "nearly 3,000." The organizers thought it was somewhere in the middle. Some of the trappings of the demonstration were comically reminiscent of earlier times. While the old John Lennon tune "Give Peace a Chance" played on the public-address system, Obama leaned over to Saltzman and said, "Can't they play something else?"

The *Tribune* reporter at the rally, Bill Glauber, described the crowd as a combination of college students, veterans of the anti–Vietnam War movement, and "a few second-generation activists following in the wake of parents radicalized by Vietnam." Bill Ayers was there; so were most of the board members from the Woods Foundation and students from Northwestern and other colleges in the area. Remarking on the calm atmosphere at the rally, Glauber said that it "wasn't a replay of the Days of Rage—it was more like a gentle call to arms for a nascent peace movement desperate to head off a new Gulf War."

The demonstration lasted less than an hour. Marilyn Katz read a statement from Senator Durbin, who had come out in opposition to the war: "When the Senate votes this week on President Bush's resolution to wage war against Iraq with preemptive force, I will vote no. I do not believe the Bush Administration has answered one simple question: Why now?"

By 2002 in Chicago, Jesse Jackson, Sr., was viewed, even by longtime allies, black and white, with mixed feelings. People paid tribute to his work in the civil-rights movement and to his historic Presidential campaigns in 1984 and 1988, but they were also weary of his penchant for self-centeredness. Obama's relationship with Jackson was never entirely warm, despite the fact that Michelle Obama had grown up as a close friend of the family. The point of conflict, even early on, was simple: Jackson tended to treat young black politicians in Chicago with wariness, at best, and Obama, while he respected Jackson, also saw him as vain and out of date. Nevertheless, Jackson remained a reliable speaker against the Bush Administration, and he performed well that day.

"This is a rally to stop a war from occurring," Jackson said, and then he asked the crowd to look at the sky and count to ten. Looking down again, Jackson said, "I just diverted your attention away from the rally. That's what George Bush is doing. The sky is not falling and we're not threatened by Saddam Hussein." Jackson accused the Administration of trying to divert public attention, above all, from its economic failures.

In addition to Jackson and Obama, the speakers included the Reverend Paul Rutgers, the executive director of the Council of Religious Leaders of Metropolitan Chicago, and a former state senator, Jesus Garcia.

Obama's speech, which ran just a few minutes, was an exquisitely calibrated rhetorical performance, signaling both his opposition to war with Iraq and a willingness to use force when necessary. It was a speech intended as much to assure people that he was not a wide-eyed pacifist as it was to show his antiwar solidarity.

> Let me begin by saying that although this has been billed as an anti-war rally, I stand before you as someone who is not opposed to war in all circumstances. The Civil War was one of the bloodiest in history, and yet it was only through the crucible of the sword, the sacrifice of multitudes, that we could begin to perfect this union, and drive the scourge of slavery from our soil. I don't oppose all wars.
>
> My grandfather signed up for a war the day after Pearl Harbor was bombed, fought in Patton's army. He saw the dead and dying across the fields of Europe; he heard the stories of fellow troops who first entered Auschwitz and Treblinka. He fought in the name of a larger freedom, part of that arsenal of democracy that triumphed over evil, and he did not fight in vain. I don't oppose all wars.
>
> After September 11th, after witnessing the carnage and destruction, the dust and the tears, I supported this Administration's pledge to hunt down and root out those who would slaughter innocents in the name of intolerance, and I would willingly take up arms myself to prevent such tragedy from happening again. I don't oppose all wars. And I know that in this crowd today, there is no shortage of patriots, or of patriotism.
>
> What I am opposed to is a dumb war. What I am opposed to is a

rash war. What I am opposed to is the cynical attempt by Richard Perle and Paul Wolfowitz and other armchair, weekend warriors in this Administration to shove their own ideological agendas down our throats, irrespective of the costs in lives lost and in hardships borne.

What I am opposed to is the attempt by political hacks like Karl Rove to distract us from a rise in the uninsured, a rise in the poverty rate, a drop in the median income, to distract us from corporate scandals and a stock market that has just gone through the worst month since the Great Depression. That's what I'm opposed to. A dumb war. A rash war. A war based not on reason but on passion, not on principle but on politics. Now let me be clear—I suffer no illusions about Saddam Hussein. He is a brutal man. A ruthless man. A man who butchers his own people to secure his own power. He has repeatedly defied U.N. resolutions, thwarted U.N. inspection teams, developed chemical and biological weapons, and coveted nuclear capacity. He's a bad guy. The world, and the Iraqi people, would be better off without him.

But I also know that Saddam poses no imminent and direct threat to the United States, or to his neighbors, that the Iraqi economy is in shambles, that the Iraqi military is at a fraction of its former strength, and that in concert with the international community he can be contained until, in the way of all petty dictators, he falls away into the dustbin of history. I know that even a successful war against Iraq will require a U.S. occupation of undetermined length, at undetermined cost, with undetermined consequences. I know that an invasion of Iraq without a clear rationale and without strong international support will only fan the flames of the Middle East, and encourage the worst, rather than best, impulses of the Arab world, and strengthen the recruitment arm of Al Qaeda. I am not opposed to all wars. I'm opposed to dumb wars.

Carl Davidson, one of the rally's organizers, was listening to the speech when a friend sitting next to him nudged him and said, "Who does he think this speech is for? It's not for this crowd." Davidson said he thought, This guy's got bigger fish to fry.

"It was a great rally and it wasn't an easy thing to do," Bill Ayers said. "There was a howling storm of patriotic nationalism going on. I remember Obama's speech vividly because it was all done in the cadence of the black church. 'I'm not against all war, just a foolish war . . .' That's so Obama: smart, unifying, and very moderate."

Obama received polite applause and his admiring sponsor, Bettylu

Saltzman, thought he had performed effectively. But another civic leader at the rally, Juan Andrade, Jr., the president of the United States Hispanic Leadership Institute, said that while he has since seen Obama give magnificent speeches, "there was nothing magic" about his performance that day. "There was nothing about that speech that would have given anybody any sense that he was going places. We were just glad that he was one of those who was willing to step up at a time when very few people seemed to be willing to do that." One of the organizers, Michael Klonsky, an S.D.S. leader who became a professor of education, remembers thinking at the time how qualified Obama's opposition to the war was. "He knew the war was a dead end but he was kind of clever," Klonsky said. "At the time, I didn't see much point in giving a treatise on just and unjust wars. Looking back, this was a guy with political ambitions who didn't want to box himself in."

The 2002 antiwar speech was a precursor to Obama's speech on December 10, 2009, in Oslo, when he accepted the Nobel Prize for Peace. There, too, Obama spoke, to some extent, at cross-purposes with the audience in front of him. In Oslo, he made plain that the choices facing a head of state, a commander-in-chief, are not the same as those of the head of a movement, like King or Gandhi. In front of a Norwegian audience that could not have been entirely pleased with his decision just a week earlier to send an additional thirty thousand troops to Afghanistan, Obama refused the purity of pacifism and insisted on the complexity of the real world ("I face the world as it is . . .") and the need, unfortunately, to rely on force when diplomacy has failed and the moral and political circumstances demand it. In Oslo, Obama implicitly rebuked the Bush Administration's use of torture and its invasion of Iraq, but it was this insistence on complexity, the refusal to adopt a purely pacific rhetoric, that was reminiscent of the speech on Federal Plaza.

While some of Obama's advisers worried that phrases like "a dumb war" might come back to haunt Obama, it would turn out that the war was far worse than dumb. It was a catastrophe that went on longer than the Second World War. But when Obama's team would eventually make use of the speech to advertise their candidate's strategic and moral judgment, they discovered there was no videotape. "There wasn't any, just some crappy snippet," Giangreco said. Had Obama been a certain, well-organized candidate for the Senate, he might have made sure there was someone there with a camera. "I would kill for that," David Axelrod said years later. "No one realized at the time that it would be a historic thing."

Toward the end of the rally, Obama told Bettylu Saltzman that he couldn't stick around long. He was headed downstate to Decatur, the county seat of Macon County.

"There really was no doubt he was running," she recalled. "Why else do you go to Decatur, Illinois?"

The 2002 elections were hugely successful for the Illinois Democrats—a statewide rebuke to the Bush Administration. Promising "to end business as usual," Rod Blagojevich was elected governor over the Republican, George Ryan, and both houses of the state legislature now had Democratic majorities—for the first time in twenty-six years. In the State Senate, Emil Jones got the post of president, displacing Pate Philip.

In the early spring of 2002, Obama went to see Emil Jones. Since 1997, Jones had been his mentor in the persistent realities of Illinois politics. He had helped soothe the friction between Obama and antagonists like Hendon and Trotter. Jones, a former sewer inspector and an old-school Party regular, could see that Obama was a new breed:

> He said to me, he said, "You're the Senate president now, and with that, you have a lot of *pow-er.* " . . . And I told Barack, "You think I got a lot of *pow-er* now?" And he said, "Yeah, you got a lot of *pow-er.*" And I said, "What kind of *pow-er* do I have?" He said, "You have the *pow-er* to make a United States *sen-a-tor!*"
>
> I said to Barack, "That sounds good!" I said, "I haven't even thought of that." I said, "Do you have someone in mind you think I could make?," and he said, "Yeah. Me." The *most* interesting conversation. And so I said to him, "Let me think about this." We met a little later that day, and I said, "That sounds good. Let's go for it."

Before he became president of the Senate, Emil Jones had not yet gained great respect in the legislature. People looked on Michael Madigan, the Democratic speaker of the House and Lisa's father, as the Party's pillar. "The truth is, Emil was always underestimated," Will Burns, who worked for Jones before joining Obama's congressional campaign, said. "It was thought he didn't have the same political acumen as Madigan or Richie Daley. But he was underestimated, really, because he was black. No one would say it, but as an African-American I can't easily dismiss the effect of race on people's perceptions. There was the sense that he was just an old pol and that's it. So, for Emil, the challenge of helping Barack, using his position and leverage, to elect him to the Senate, was good for Barack and it was also good for him."

The most important thing that Jones could do now for Obama was to provide him with an increasingly substantive legislative docket—something that no Democrat could boast while languishing in the minority. Obama, like many others in the Senate, had been in the habit of dodging controversial votes (including on abortion measures) by voting "present" rather than "yea" or "nay." This was a well-known tactic that could be adopted to avoid being drawn into a vote whose only purpose was to expose the opposition in one way or another, but, still, Obama's frequent use of it—a hundred and twenty-nine times—allowed opponents to criticize him for lacking the courage of his convictions. A "present" vote has variously been described as "a soft 'no' " and " 'no' with an explanation." But Emil Jones, of all people, was not interested in idealistic flameouts. Such creatures were alien to him. After their meeting, Jones started to funnel bills to Obama, some of which had lain dormant in committee for years. Jones knew that Obama had developed a penchant for compromise. He could work with Republicans and downstate Democrats with far greater finesse than most of his colleagues. When the bills passed, they would have Obama's name on them, as sponsor, and potentially help him in a run for higher office.

"We attained the majority in the seventh year and I passed twenty-six bills in a row," Obama told me. "In one year, we reformed the death penalty in Illinois, expanded health care for kids, set up a state earned-income tax credit. It wasn't that I was smarter in year seven than I was in year six, or more experienced; it was that we had power. . . . You can have the best agenda in the world, but if you don't control the gavel you cannot move an agenda forward."

Eventually, Jones was known around the Senate chamber as Obama's "godfather." (And when Obama became a national political phenomenon, Jones set the ring tone on his cell phone to play the opening bars of Nino Rota's theme for the "Godfather" films.) Donne Trotter said that there were days when nearly every bill had Obama's name on it. Jones, for example, let Obama be the main sponsor of a bill insisting that police videotape interrogations as a check on brutality cases and false confessions. Obama was able to bring on board not only Republicans but also police associations that had initially balked at such legislation. Even Blagojevich had initially opposed the measure, which was the first of its kind in the country. In May, 2003, it passed the Senate unanimously and Blagojevich withdrew his objections. "I had reservations about supporting it without the participation of law enforcement," the Governor said. "But Senator Obama ironed out some of the practical challenges that concerned me."

Obama also co-sponsored legislation banning ephedra, a diet supplement that had led to the death of a Northwestern University football player. He won a ban on the use of pyrotechnics in nightclubs after scores of people were killed in two tragic incidents. Forging a compromise between police associations and civil-liberties organizations, he crafted a series of racial-profiling measures that demanded that police record the race of every motorist they pulled over and send the records for analysis to the Department of Transportation. ("Driving while black, driving while Hispanic, and driving while Middle Eastern are not crimes.") He sponsored a bill that allowed twenty thousand children to be included in Kid Care, a program for kids without health insurance. And he passed legislation that provided added tax relief for low-income families with the Earned Income Tax Credit.

Working with health-care providers, insurance lobbyists, and other interest groups, Obama led a commission that studied expanding care to more citizens of the state. He had repeatedly expressed support for single-payer health care, but the commission was limited to modest reform. Obama, who had played poker with lobbyists and taken legal campaign contributions from insurance lobbyists, said in a debate during the U.S. Senate campaign that he had "worked diligently with the insurance industry" and with Republicans after concerns were raised about across-the-board state health coverage. "The original presentation of the bill was the House version, that we radically changed—we radically changed—and we changed in response to concerns that were raised by the insurance industry," he said.

Jones also extracted promises from black politicians like Hendon and Trotter, who had not shown Obama much love, to endorse Obama. They agreed only after many loud discussions. "I made them an offer," Jones recalled telling Obama. "And you don't want to know."

As he grew more experienced, Obama was also recognizing that, in order to rise in Illinois politics, in order to transcend the hermetic, somewhat independent base of Hyde Park, he needed to play ball with people higher up than Jones: in particular, with Richard M. Daley. To remain pristine in Chicago politics—to follow the path of someone like the independent alderman Leon Despres—was to put a cap on ambition. To advance, to have the means to win a statewide election, meant navigating the murky politics of Chicago. The city under the Daleys had avoided the fate of other industrial Midwestern cities like Detroit. Just as his father had built highways, O'Hare Airport, the convention center, parks, and countless office buildings, Richard M. Daley had transformed the Loop, building projects like Millennium Park, complete with its magnificent Frank Gehry–designed bandshell. Daley the Younger had been a far better mayor than his father when it came to schools, allowing more experimentation and building magnet schools and charter schools; he also leveled many of the city's horrendous high-rise projects, which housed tens of thousands of people and had become centers of gang violence. Daley showed no predilection for amassing a personal fortune. But Daley, also like his father, failed to transform the political culture of legalized bribery, the routine funneling of huge city contracts to friends of City Hall—the reality known as "pay to play." Millennium Park may be a source of civic pride and a great tourist attraction, but it was also millions over-budget. Chicago is no less a one-party political city than Beijing; only one of the fifty aldermen is a Republican. And so the impulse to reform these practices is minimal. Stories of corruption, enormous and banal, regularly appear in the *Tribune* and *Sun-Times*, but the citizenry kept increasing Daley's margins of victory.

Sooner or later, any ambitious Chicago politician had to do business with the Mayor and had to think many times before criticizing him. In 2005, in the midst of a series of corruption investigations, which had been described at length in the *Sun-Times*, Obama told the paper that the articles gave him "huge pause." An hour later, though, he called the paper back and told the reporter that he wanted to clarify his remarks. Daley, he now said, was "obviously going through a rough patch" but the city "never looked better." To talk about endorsing Daley, or not, was "way premature." In January, 2007, Obama endorsed Daley, praising him as "innovative" and "willing to make hard decisions."

When Obama was not in Springfield or teaching or spending time with his family, he was back to networking. Sometimes that meant making more trips downstate. Sometimes it meant attending the myriad events going on in Chicago: lunches at the business clubs, cultural events, fundraisers on the Lakefront and in the suburbs. After losing so badly to Rush, he started mending fences with black community leaders, clergy, Democratic committeemen, aldermen, and city officials. He attended a regular discussion group at Miller Shakman & Beem, a law firm where Arthur Goldberg and Abner Mikva had practiced. There Obama would talk politics with Abner Mikva, David Axelrod, Newton Minow, Don Rose, Bettylu Saltzman, and various other Democratic activists. Obama wanted to re-establish himself as a Democrat independent of the Daley circle and organization, but also as someone who would not wage an overtly anti-Daley race. He was willing to make common cause with the activists on the South Side as well as with Party regulars like Emil Jones. "This was a guy who was a quick learner," Don Rose said of that period between the congressional and Senate races. "When Obama makes a mistake, he only makes it once."

The return of the Democrats to power in 2002 also helped Obama in a more subtle way. Like that of many other state senators, his district—the Thirteenth—was reconfigured. In the spring of 2001, anticipating a Democratic sweep, Obama had gone to see a Democratic Party consultant named John Corrigan in a room at the Stratton Office Building, in Springfield, known as the "inner sanctum." The room is locked down; to get in it was necessary to use a fingerprint scanner and tap a code into a keypad. Inside was an array of computer monitors. The Senate Democratic caucus in the legislature had hired Corrigan to look into the details of re-aligning districts in the state to the Party's advantage. This was perfectly legal. The majority party has the right, within legal guidelines, to rearrange legislative borders. The Republicans, of course, preferred to maximize the percentage of African-Americans in a particular district. Because blacks voted almost solely for Democrats, it was better to have one district be close to a hundred-per-cent black and a neighboring district have a minimum number of blacks. The Democrats preferred to spread out their black voters. As Corrigan showed Obama on a computer screen, the best thing that could happen to his district would be to retain the Hyde Park base, along with Englewood and other black neighborhoods, but to push the district north toward the Loop rather than west into poorer black neighborhoods. The district would remain reliably majority African-American and Democratic, but it would also provide more black voters for another district. For Obama, there was an added bonus as he looked forward to a race for the U.S. Senate: his constituency would now include many more wealthy, liberal whites—many of them Jewish—along Lake Michigan. As far as Corrigan could tell, his friend was no longer depressed about the loss to Bobby Rush. He was preparing for the next act.

"I have seen people who have run for lesser office than Congress and just disappear after losing," Corrigan said. "Barack has always been calm, cool, and collected. Nothing seems to faze him. He doesn't get mad. He is always creative when someone presents a barrier to get through. He can always think or talk his way through things."

In October, 2002, Obama was touring downstate with Dan Shomon again. One evening, they were standing beside Route 4 in Carlinville, a town of about seven thousand in Macoupin County. The town was known for houses ordered from the Sears catalogue. The two men, who were heading to a political dinner, were discussing what effect a Senate race would have on Obama's family. Shomon knew that Obama was the kind of person who tends to feel guilty, and he thought the race would end up making him feel guilty for the pressures it would put on Michelle. He was already feeling bad that he was missing so much of his little girls' child- hood. When they pulled over to the side of the road, Shomon said, "I don't think you should run."

"I'm running anyway," Obama replied.

Chapter Ten

Reconstruction

In the generation after the Civil War, men of color—some born free, some born into slavery—began to fight their way into statehouses and the halls of Congress. These were, in the main, men of intelligence and bravery: There was Robert Smalls, who stole a Confederate ship in Charleston Harbor and handed it over to Union forces; in Philadelphia, after the war, he caused a sensation when he was thrown off an all-white streetcar and then led a black boycott of the city's transit system. In 1875, Smalls was elected a member of the South Carolina delegation to the House of Representatives. There was Hiram Revels, of Mississippi, a brilliant seminarian and itinerant minister, who had been imprisoned in 1854 in Missouri for preaching to blacks; in 1870, the Mississippi State Senate voted to send him to Washington to serve out the term for a U.S. Senate seat left vacant during the war. Revels, the first African-American in the Senate, served just one year. And there was Blanche Kelso Bruce, a wealthy landowner in Mississippi, who was born to a slave in Virginia. In 1875, he was elected to the U.S. Senate, where he fought for open immigration and the rights of Native Americans; at the 1880 Republican National Convention, Bruce received eight votes for Vice-President.

For black men and women, however, Reconstruction was a short-lived interregnum between slavery and Jim Crow, between iron subjugation and the rise of insidious voting restrictions and the lynching parties of the Ku Klux Klan. The ability of blacks to run for, and hold, higher office faltered miserably after neo-Confederate insurrection and terror in the mid-eighteen-seventies finally forced Washington to withdraw federal protection of blacks from white violence; by 1900, Southern states began to deny blacks, *de facto* and *de jure*, their right to vote. As Eric Foner, the leading historian of Reconstruction, points out, the resistance to black political empowerment was well and cruelly embodied by one of the country's greatest filmmakers and a best-selling historian: D. W. Griffith's "Birth of a Nation" (1915) and Claude Bowers's best-seller *The Tragic Era* (1929) depicted black office-holders as flamboyantly corrupt mountebanks and helped justify disenfranchisement of black citizens and the brutality of the Klan.

On January 29, 1901, a black representative from North Carolina, George H. White, stepped forward to give his last speech in the Capitol—and what proved to be the last speech of any black lawmaker in Washington for a generation. White had initiated anti-lynching legislation, but his efforts had come to nothing. The racism that he now faced at home was unbridled. The Raleigh *News and Observer* expressed parochial shame that "North Carolina should have the only nigger Congressman." The paper's anxieties were soon relieved.

"This, Mr. Chairman, is perhaps the Negroes' temporary farewell to the American Congress," White told his congressional colleagues, "but let me say, Phoenix-like he will rise up some day and come again. These parting words are in behalf of an outraged, heart-broken, bruised and bleeding, but God-fearing people, faithful, industrious, loyal people, rising people, full of potential force. . . . The only apology I have for the earnestness with which I have spoken is that I am pleading for the life, the liberty, the future happiness, and manhood suffrage for one-eighth of the entire population of the United States."

The next time an African-American was elected to Congress was in 1929—this was Oscar De Priest of Chicago. There were no black Southerners in the House until 1973, with the arrival of Barbara Jordan, of Texas, and Andrew Young, of Georgia. The first African-American senators elected in the modern era were Edward Brooke, a Republican from Massachusetts, in 1966, and Carol Moseley Braun, a Democrat from Illinois, in 1992. It was Carol Moseley Braun who was very much on Barack Obama's mind in the fall of 2002.

Moseley Braun had served only one six-year term in the Senate—a term troubled by allegations of financial impropriety and by an unsanctioned meeting with the Nigerian dictator Sani Abacha. Moseley Braun lost her bid for re-election in 1998 to the wealthy conservative Republican Peter Fitzgerald, who spent fourteen million dollars of his own money on his campaign. When that race was over, she accepted an offer from Bill Clinton to serve as an ambassador—to New Zealand. Fitzgerald's career, it appeared, would be just as brief as Moseley Braun's. After battling for six years with his own state party organization and the Bush White House, Fitzgerald was rumored to be going back to private life and his career as a banker. After losing in 1998, Moseley Braun had said that she would never return to elective politics—"Read my lips. Not. Never. Nein. Nyet."— but she was anything but predictable. Now, in late 2002, Obama was waiting to see if she would attempt to return to the Senate. Operatives in the Democratic Party organization tried to find her a lucrative job offer, but that went nowhere. And Moseley Braun, for her part, cared no more for Obama than, in the end, Alice Palmer did.

Obama's dilemma was plain: in the 1992 Democratic primary, Moseley Braun won a narrow victory against two white candidates—the incumbent Alan Dixon and a personal-injury lawyer, Albert Hofeld. The way for Obama to win a primary in a crowded field would be to dominate the black and progressive votes in Chicago and the suburbs and to get at least some votes among the more conservative electorate downstate. Moseley Braun's presence in the race would be problematic and probably prohibitive. "Our bases overlapped so much—not just that she was African-American, but that she came out of the progressive wing of the party . . . and our donor bases would have been fairly similar," Obama said. "So it would have been difficult, I think, to mobilize the entire coalition that was required for me to run." If Moseley Braun decided to run, he said, "I would probably have stepped out of politics for a while."

Obama had been traveling the state, alone and with Dan Shomon, from Rockford to Cairo, from East St. Louis to Paris, for many months as an undeclared candidate, but he had not yet sold his closest circle of friends and advisers—much less his wife—on the wisdom of running. Both Valerie Jarrett, who had become a close and trusted friend of the Obamas, and David Axelrod, who was now advising Obama informally, told him that after his loss to Bobby Rush, to lose in a Senate race would finish him in politics. Jarrett and Axelrod felt that Obama would be better off waiting for Richard M. Daley, who had been mayor for more than twelve years, to retire and then run to replace him. He could transform Chicago in a way that Harold Washington hadn't. After all, Obama had been thinking about City Hall since his days as a community organizer.

Jarrett conspired with Michelle Obama to organize a breakfast at her house and, together with two other friends, the investor John Rogers and the parking-lot magnate Martin Nesbitt, they planned an intervention. Jarrett said that she carefully "stacked the deck" to tell Obama the disappointing news: "We were all against him. We all thought it was a big mistake for his career and that he shouldn't do it.

"But unlike what he normally does, which is to go around the room and say, 'Tell me what you think,' Barack started out by saying, 'I want to run, and let me explain to you why,' " Jarrett recalled. "We were all kind of taken a little bit aback, because we thought the purpose was to talk about it, not that he'd made a decision. He went through all of his logic. He said, 'I didn't have a big political supporter when I ran for Congress. Now I have Emil Jones. I've already lined him up. I think I can get the necessary aldermanic support. I think it's going to be a crowded field, and that will work to my advantage.' "

Obama said that he had learned from the mistakes he'd made against Bobby Rush. In that race, he had challenged a powerful black politician with deep roots in a heavily black district—an act of impiety without sufficient justification. Congressional campaigns are waged door-to-door; they are neighborhood battles that often hinge on longstanding name recognition, ethnic solidarity, and personal connections. In a Senate race, Obama's particular talents—his ability to reach out to white suburbanites as well as to blacks and Hispanics; his increasingly evident talent to project on television—would be crucial, especially if he could raise enough money. Obama believed that if Moseley Braun stayed out of the race, he had a chance. According to Jarrett, Obama said, "I told Michelle if I lose, I'm out of politics. That would make her happy." He added, "If what you're worried about is fear, if I'm not afraid to fail, then you shouldn't be afraid to fail. And I need you in order to be successful. So why don't you step up and decide you're going to help me raise some money, because that's the one piece that I don't have worked out."

By the end of the breakfast, Jarrett had agreed to chair Obama's finance committee. Rogers and Nesbitt agreed to donate both time and money. Nesbitt, in addition to running a parking-lot management company, was a vice-president of the Pritzker Realty Group, a division of the Pritzker empire, one of the biggest fortunes in Chicago. Not long after the breakfast, in the summer of 2002, Nesbitt got the Obama family invited to Penny Pritzker's country house, on Lake Michigan. After talking with the Obamas, Pritzker and her husband, Bryan Traubert, went for a run near their house and, along the way, decided to play a key role in financing Obama's race. They were soon joined in the campaign by other wealthy Chicagoans: John Bryan, the head of the Sara Lee Corporation, James Crown, and old friends of Obama's like Newton Minow and Abner Mikva.

Michelle also agreed to go forward, though her anxieties were hardly allayed. "The big issue around the Senate for me was, how on earth can we afford it?" she said. "I don't like to talk about it, because people forget his credit card was maxed out. How are we going to get by? O.K., now we're going to have two households to fund, one here and one in Washington. We have law-school debt, tuition to pay for the children. And we're trying to save for college for the girls. . . . My thing is, is this just another gamble? It's just killing us. My thing was, this is ridiculous, even if you do win, how are you going to afford this wonderful next step in your life? And he said, 'Well, then, I'm going to write a book, a good book.' And I'm thinking, 'Snake eyes there, buddy. Just write a book, yeah, that's right. Yep, yep, yep. And you'll climb the beanstalk and come back down with the golden egg, Jack.' "

John Rogers, who had helped Moseley Braun re-establish herself in Chicago after she returned from Auckland, thought that he could sound her out about her plans. "My role was to talk to Carol and determine whether she was going to run and to even nudge her away from it," he said. But Moseley Braun was infuriatingly inscrutable. All Obama could do was continue to make contingency plans, travel around the state speaking at one event after another, and wait.

Finally, on February 18, 2003, Moseley Braun ended her indecision and announced that, in fact, she was running for office. The office was President of the United States.

Eric Zorn, an influential liberal columnist for the *Tribune*, was among the dumbstruck, writing that Moseley Braun was "ethically challenged" and was now "making reservations for fantasy land." In any event, the Senate race, for both parties, was absolutely open with no incumbent and not a single dominant candidate on the horizon. Obama called David Axelrod for advice and planned a press conference. He was in.

Obama's intentions did not yet impress everyone as entirely serious. Some of his colleagues at the University of Chicago still thought that he could be persuaded to give up politics for good and accept a tenured teaching position. At a fundraiser for Bill Clinton's charitable foundation, Obama's law-school colleague Geoffrey Stone watched his friend work the room. Stone felt pity for Obama. "After the defeat by Bobby Rush, people here thought Barack's political career was over," Stone recalled. "At the reception, I saw Barack in the crowd, and he was doing the politician thing, shaking hands, looking people in the eye, and I was thinking, What a waste! What is he doing this for? Twenty minutes later, we were at the shrimp bowl. I said to him, 'As your friend, I tell you, I was watching you work the room and I can't believe you're doing this. Why not settle down and be a law professor?' He says, 'Geoff, I appreciate that, but I really have to do this. I think I can make a difference. I've got to try.' As he disappeared into the crowd, I thought, What a putz. What a waste."

Luck is not the least of the many factors that figured into the rise of Barack Obama. First came the unseemly fall, in 1995, of Mel Reynolds, which led to Alice Palmer's decision to run for Congress and Obama's subsequent decision to succeed her in the Illinois State Senate. As a candidate for the statehouse, Obama enjoyed an easy path to office: he faced nominal competition in his first two campaigns and none at all in his third. Following the decisive loss to Bobby Rush—a campaign in which everything that could go wrong did—Obama was, in his run for the U.S. Senate, the beneficiary of one fantastic stroke of fortune after another. The first was Moseley Braun's unforeseen decision to run for President.

At the press conference opening his campaign, Obama declared that Peter Fitzgerald had done "zilch" for the general welfare. "Four years ago, Peter Fitzgerald bought himself a Senate seat, and he's betrayed Illinois ever since," he said. "But we are here to take it back on behalf of the people of Illinois." But before he had to answer any return volleys Fitzgerald retired from the Senate. He had recommended Patrick Fitzgerald, a crusading prosecutor from New York, as U.S. Attorney—whose appointment led to the indictments of corrupt officials in both parties. Peter Fitzgerald's biggest opponents to that appointment had been the Republican Speaker of the House, Dennis Hastert, and George W. Bush. He had battled his own party on everything from environmentalism (he was for it) to the funding of the Lincoln Library. After six years, he had tired of bankrolling a life in politics.

In the nearly three years since losing to Bobby Rush, Obama had, like an athlete in training or a musician woodshedding, worked hard at his craft. Not only had he become a far more engaged legislator (especially after the Democrats came into the majority); he had also lost his diffident bearing when it came to retail politics. After countless speeches, cocktail parties, panel discussions, fund-raising dinners, business lunches, and state fairs, after speaking in the pulpits of black churches in Chicago and in V.F.W. halls downstate, he had become a better orator, a smoother campaigner, a more disciplined fundraiser. Obama was beginning to develop his signature appeal, the use of the details of his own life as a reflection of a kind of multicultural ideal, a conceit both sentimental and effective. He was no longer straining to be someone he was not. Instead, he was among those politicians who were forging a new identity for the next generation of black leaders, men and women with no direct connection to the civil-rights movement except in the ways the movement had helped them to gain greater access to the best colleges and law schools and other realms of American opportunity. Unlike the elder generation of black politicians, many Southern-born and educated at historically black colleges and seminaries, Obama navigated Harvard and Roseland, the Loop and Altgeld Gardens. He was adept at pitching his cadences one way in black churches, another way at a P.T.A. meeting downstate, and yet another at a living-room gathering in Hyde Park or the near North Side. Some of his critics took notice of these differences in intonation and body language and counted Obama as a phony, but there was no doubt that for the vast majority of his audiences he was developing into a fresh, compelling candidate. What was more, he was utterly aware of his shape-shifting capacities.

"The fact that I conjugate my verbs and speak in a typical Midwestern newscaster voice—there's no doubt that this helps ease communication between myself and white audiences," Obama said. "And there's no doubt that when I'm with a black audience I slip into a slightly different dialect. But the point is, I don't feel the need to talk in a certain way before a white audience. And I don't feel the need to speak a certain way in front of a black audience. There's a level of self-consciousness about these issues the previous generation had to negotiate that I don't feel I have to."

Salim Muwakkil, the left-wing columnist who had come to know Obama in the early nineties, noticed that Obama had also become much more comfortable campaigning in the kinds of lower-income black communities where he had lost so badly in his 2000 congressional race. "One day, Barack was at Wallace's Catfish Corner on the West Side, an outpost where black politicians met, run by a former alderman, Wallace Davis," Muwakkil recalled. "His talk was interrupted by a radical group composed of ex-inmates who said, 'We're tired of you uppity Negroes treating us like trash. No one cares about ex-inmates. We're growing in strength and we want to be dealt with.' Barack acknowledged their plight. He gave a calm, well-grounded response, in words they could understand, how they were barking up the wrong tree if they thought this was aiding their cause. They didn't buy it all, but it was hard-won respect."

Obama was also proving to be an African-American politician who made white voters—white voters who could never have imagined themselves voting for a black man for senator—come around to him. Eric Zorn, of the *Tribune*, followed Obama into various receptions and marveled at his ease with everyone in the room. "Obama was somehow all about validating *you*," Zorn said. "He was radiating the sense that 'You're the kind of guy who can accept a black guy as a senator.' He made people feel better about themselves for liking *him*." Obama's manner, his accent, his pedigree, his broad approach to the issues, told white voters, among other things: *I am not Jesse Jackson.* Jackson was a man of his time and place and history: he was born in the segregationist South, steeped in the civil-rights movement. Jackson certainly learned to navigate the broader world, but the difference in generation, psychology, speech, politics, and history was unmistakable. Jackson demanded painful change; the largest part of his history was one of heated rebuke, the rightful demand for redress. It was an illusion to think that all the victories were won, but Obama, so much younger, fluent in so many languages, possessed a manner of cool, yet winning embrace.

Obama seemed capable of making whites forget even the most alien detail about him—his name. Early on, Dan Shomon had polled Obama's name, asking voters if they would not prefer "Barack (Barry) Obama." They did, by a small percentage. "From the start of Obama's career, a lot of people mistakenly thought he was a Muslim from his name, especially a lot of blacks," Shomon recalled. "But Barack refused to change it. He was who he was and that was it."

Emil Jones, a creature of the South Side and the statehouse, accompanied Obama on one of his trips to southern Illinois and was amazed at the younger man's talent. "A little old lady said to me, 'I'm eighty-six years of age. I hope I live long enough because this young man's going to be President and I want to be able to vote for him,' " Jones recalled. "It was a little old white lady! It was astounding. There were three thousand people there. There were three blacks: him, me, and my driver."

Obama was at ease even doing what he liked least—raising money. "I remember one of Barack's first fund-raisers," his direct-mail consultant Pete Giangreco recalled. "It was in Evanston in the backyard of Paul Gaynor, a left-leaning lawyer. He's from an old lefty family: his father was a big lawyer, Mickey Gaynor, and his mother, Judy, a great fund-raiser. Their block seceded from the United States of America during the Vietnam War; it was that kind of block in the People's Republic of Evanston. Anyway, the fund-raiser was packed with the old-time progressive establishment people—but regular people, not stars. It was a warm, late-summer night. And Obama gave that riff about how if there was a senior downstate who can't get her prescription drugs, it matters to me even if it's not my grandmother; if a kid on the South Side can't read it matters to me even if it's not my kid; if a Muslim is hassled unjustly at the airport it affects my freedoms, too. It was one of those rare moments: goosebumps. And to a person they all walked out of there saying, 'Sign me up.' It was not a high-dollar thing but the buzz was there. These were people who had memories of Paul Simon, Harold Washington, Bobby Kennedy, and they were waiting and wanting to believe again. The word went out: this was the guy."

David Wilkins, the Harvard Law School professor who grew up in Hyde Park, threw one of the earliest out-of-state fund-raising events for Obama at his house in Cambridge. "I had to *beg* people to come and pay a hundred dollars," Wilkins recalled. "We got about twenty-five people to come and I remember feeling so bad. Collectively, we probably got about ten thousand dollars. And Barack sat right over there, right against that window, and he talked with us for three hours. He was *dazzling*. This was before he was a *thing*. It was like seeing Hendrix in a club before he was Hendrix."

To win, Obama needed top-level professional help. At first, his campaign manager was Dan Shomon, who had a keen understanding of the state and long experience with the candidate. Al Kindle took a leave of absence from Toni Preckwinkle's staff to make sure that Obama had an effective ground operation in Chicago's black neighborhoods. Kindle, who had worked for Harold Washington and Carol Moseley Braun, was especially adept at get-out-the-vote operations on Election Day. But, much more important, Obama now had the guidance of David Axelrod, who had established himself as the leading Democratic political and communications strategist in the state. A shambling, easygoing personality, Axelrod was a great believer in the use of narrative and biography to put across a candidate to the public; he was also not at all reluctant to use negative ads if the situation required it. Axelrod had first met Obama through Bettylu Saltzman during Project Vote in 1992, and had spent plenty of time learning the details of Obama's story and his personality in preparation for a campaign.

Obama and Axelrod remained friends and talked frequently about politics, but when it came time to hire a staff, Obama did not immediately leap into Axelrod's embrace. Axelrod was unblemished, but he was also a close associate of the Daley family, a certified member of the city's political establishment. Just as Obama wanted to meet Valerie Jarrett before Michelle accepted her offer of a job at City Hall, he also wanted to think through signing on with David Axelrod. In the end, though, it was not an agonizing decision: Obama wanted to win. He liked and trusted Axelrod.

Going with Axelrod made him less of an outsider, perhaps, but it also helped make him a serious candidate for the United States Senate.

Born in 1955, Axelrod grew up in Stuyvesant Town, a post-war middle-class apartment development in Manhattan, just north of the East Village. His parents were liberal Jewish intellectuals and the household was full of talk about politics. Axelrod's mother was a reporter for the left-leaning newspaper *P.M.* and his father was a psychologist. In 1960, when he was five, his parents separated; he remembered seeing John Kennedy make a campaign speech near his building to a crowd of five thousand people that same year. When he was thirteen, he and a friend sold campaign materials at the Bronx Zoo supporting Robert Kennedy's Presidential campaign. R.F.K.'s assassination in 1968 was, outside of his parents' separation and divorce, the most devastating memory of his childhood.

As an undergraduate at the University of Chicago, Axelrod became obsessed with the city's politics and managed to get a job writing a column called "Politicking" for the Hyde Park *Herald*. In one fantastical column published in 1974, he described having a dream about Chicago and then waking to see a headline in the newspaper: "Daley in 20th year as Mayor." In fact, Richard J. Daley died two years later; Axelrod eventually worked not only for political independents but for the resumption of the Daley dynasty.

The year Axelrod started working for the *Herald*, his father committed suicide. Soon afterward, Axelrod decided to make his life in Chicago. On the recommendation of the political strategist Don Rose, who lived in Hyde Park and read the *Herald*, the *Tribune* gave Axelrod an internship right after his graduation, in 1976. After covering crime and other city stories for three years, Axelrod started working as a political reporter and soon became the paper's lead political writer.

At the *Tribune*, Axelrod's favorite editors included an ex-Marine who had penetrated a crime syndicate for a story. "It was a real 'Front Page' cast of characters," he said, "and they could get you excited about your work. They made you feel that journalism was really a calling."

Axelrod was an aggressive reporter with a future at the *Tribune*, but, after a while, he started to lose his taste for the paper. "The news side became much more permeated by the business side," he said. "In other words you could see the warning signs of where the news business was going." Axelrod and his wife, Susan, have a daughter, Lauren, who suffered irreparable brain damage from years of seizures caused by epilepsy.

"The H.M.O.s wouldn't cover a lot. We were paying eight, ten thousand dollars out of pocket, and I was making forty-two thousand a year. It was a lot. The only reason I could even think about leaving is because my wife is a saint. She basically said, 'You've got to be happy or otherwise what's the point?' . . . Besides, I always thought that the only two jobs worth having at the paper were writer and editor. The rest was middle management."

Axelrod left the *Tribune* in 1984 and helped manage Paul Simon's successful Senate campaign against the incumbent, Charles Percy. The Simon campaign attracted a group of young people who soon became fixtures in Illinois politics, including Rahm Emanuel. After the election, Axelrod turned down a chance to work for Simon in Washington and set up his own political consulting business and worked for Democrats, both independents like Harold Washington and "organization" candidates, most notably Richard M. Daley. Axelrod turned down roles in both Bill Clinton's and Al Gore's Presidential campaigns—his daughter's seizures were still too severe for him to travel as often as would have been necessary—but his reputation grew as he helped with successful campaigns for African-American mayoral candidates in Detroit, Washington, D.C., Cleveland, Houston, and Philadelphia.

Among the recent campaigns that Axelrod had worked on before joining Obama was that of Rahm Emanuel, in 2002, when he ran for Congress from the Fifth District, on the North Side—the seat abandoned by Rod Blagojevich when he was elected governor. Although Emanuel was born and reared in Chicago, he spent many years working in Washington, as an aide to Bill Clinton, and then making a fast fortune as an investment banker. When he ran for Congress, he faced accusations of being a "millionaire carpetbagger." Axelrod helped silence those charges when he did a television ad for Emanuel featuring a Chicago police sergeant named Les Smulevitz. The setting was a Chicago diner. "I've been a Chicago police officer for a long time, and I've seen it all—the guns, the gangs, the drugs," the officer said. Then he praised Emanuel's crime-fighting bona fides as an aide to Clinton. "That's why the Fraternal Order of Police and Chicago firefighters backs Rahm Emanuel for Congress. And I'd tell you that even if I weren't his uncle."

Axelrod was a magnet for first-rate help. With Shomon, he brought in Peter Giangreco, the direct-mail expert, who had just advised Rod Blagojevich's successful run for governor; Paul Harstad, a polling expert who had helped Tom Vilsack, of Iowa, in his gubernatorial race; and, as deputy campaign manager, Nate Tamarin, who worked for Giangreco. Axelrod was Obama's chief strategist and media guru, but he could not manage the campaign. In the spring of 2003, he invited Jim Cauley, a tough, plain-spoken political operative from the Appalachian territory in Kentucky, to talk with him and Obama about replacing Dan Shomon as campaign manager. The relationship between Shomon and Obama had grown more distant, and it was time, some in the campaign believed, to bring in someone with wider experience.

Cauley had impressed Axelrod when, in 2001, he helped Glenn Cunningham, an African-American and a former police officer and U.S. marshal, become mayor of Jersey City. The challenge of electing an African-American where blacks were not in the majority was something that Cauley had spent years thinking about and he had succeeded brilliantly with Cunningham.

When Cauley first met Obama at his modest campaign offices, he told him, "If you want to run an old-school African-American race, it's not my thing. I don't know how to do it."

But after listening to Obama talk for a while, Cauley could see that he was far less attuned to the generation of Jesse Jackson, Sr., and Bobby Rush. His natural cohort included younger African-American office-holders like Harold Ford, Jr., of Tennessee; Deval Patrick, of Massachusetts; Artur Davis, of Alabama; and, eventually, Adrian Fenty, the mayor of Washington, D.C., and Cory Booker, the mayor of Newark. These were young men who had little, if any, direct memory of the civil-rights movement, but who possessed a distinct sense of debt to that past. Their experiences were hardly uniform: Ford, for instance, grew up in a prominent Memphis family and, as the son of a congressman, attended the St. Albans School for Boys and the University of Pennsylvania. Patrick was born in the Robert Taylor Homes projects on the South Side of Chicago and his father, a musician in the Sun Ra Arkestra, left the family. Patrick got a boost from A.B.C.—a nonprofit organization called A Better Chance, which helped send him to Milton Academy—and that led to Harvard College and then Harvard Law School. Cauley and Axelrod were eager to work with Obama. They agreed that he was not only individually gifted and politically progressive, but also that he was an exemplar of this new generation of black politicians who could potentially win elections—governorships, Senate seats—that had always been considered out of reach.

Even with Moseley Braun out of the Illinois Senate race, Obama faced a dizzying array of opponents in the Democratic primary. In more or less ascending order of importance:

Vic Roberts, a retired coal miner from southern Illinois.

Joyce Washington, an African-American health-care consultant from Chicago, who had once run for lieutenant governor.

Nancy Skinner, a liberal radio-talk-show host on WLS-AM, who had a degree in business from the University of Michigan but no experience at all in politics.

Gery Chico, a Hispanic former school-board president and top aide to Richard M. Daley.

Maria Pappas, the Cook County treasurer, whom the *Tribune* described as "known for such public eccentricities as twirling a baton and carrying a poodle in her purse."

Dan Hynes, the thirty-five-year-old Illinois comptroller, was a serious candidate and had the greatest name recognition in the field. Hynes had traditional union support and the endorsement of establishment politicians loyal to his father, Tom Hynes, the former Cook County assessor and president of the State Senate, who was also the Democratic Party boss on the Southwest Side. With his father's connections, Dan Hynes had lined up the support of Democratic stalwarts including the Democratic Party chairman, Michael Madigan; the Cook County Commissioner (and the Mayor's brother), John Daley; and John Stroger, the Cook County Board president. (Richard Daley did not make endorsements.) Hynes was earnest and decent, but he was also self-defeatingly cautious, a reluctant self-promoter, a poor campaigner, and irredeemably dull. In the Obama campaign's earliest poll, Hynes led the field by a wide margin, but that seemed mainly an indicator of name recognition.

Finally, there was Blair Hull. Of all Obama's opponents, he was the one whom Obama's team took most seriously. Hull was proof that, just when you believed that the politics of Illinois could get no stranger, there was always tomorrow. Hull grew up in Los Gatos, California. His father was a judge. After studying mathematics, computer science, and business, he taught high-school science and math for a year and then worked as a securities analyst. In the early nineteen-seventies, Hull took an interest in the blackjack theories of Ed Thorp, the author of *Beat the Dealer*, a cult classic for card-counters. Visiting Las Vegas several days a month, Hull refined his technique. Using a method called the "Revere Advanced Point Count," an even more sophisticated system than Thorp's, Hull and some teammates started to make thousands of dollars each. The run came to an end in 1977, when one of Hull's teammates, Ken Uston, published a memoir called *The Big Player*.

Hull used his winnings to start a computerized options firm. This proved more lucrative than blackjack. In 1999, he sold the firm to Goldman Sachs, for three hundred and forty million dollars. Living in Illinois, where there was no legal limit on the amount of money a candidate could spend on his own campaign, Hull figured that he could go far in politics—even though he never expressed any compelling reason for wanting to be elected. "He was rich and bored," one of his consultants said. "He thought being a senator might be cool. That was the whole thing."

Hull had thought first about running for the House of Representatives against Rahm Emanuel and Nancy Kaszak, in the Fifth District. According to Hull, Emanuel had made a fund-raising call to him and was so abrasive—"He was just being Rahm, which is why he is loved by so many people!"—that he decided to run himself. Hull paid to have some polling done, however, and he realized that he couldn't win. "So I went to see Richie Daley in City Hall and Daley wanted to be with Rahm," Hull said. "He says, 'You don't want to be in the House. It takes forever to get seniority and get anything done. You should be in the Senate. You don't have to work as hard.' . . . I would never have thought about the Senate. It was way above my league."

But the Democratic side of the race was so wide open and Hull's pockets were so deep that he decided to run. Like Michael Bloomberg in New York, or Jon Corzine in New Jersey, he would run as an "anti-politician," someone who lacked a political past but was so wealthy and accomplished in business that the voters might see him as incorruptible and somehow "above" ordinary politics. This was the traditional conceit of such candidates; to be "above" things. The problem was that Hull often came off as yet another in a long line of eccentric technocrat-businessmen who thought that all problems of policy and politics could be solved using the same equations with which they had made financial fortunes. When Joshua Green, a writer for *The Atlantic Monthly*, asked Hull if he could devise an algorithm for political success, Hull said, "Sure! You'd create a persuasion model based on canvassing that says 'The probability for voting for Hull is . . . plus some variable on ethnicity . . . with a positive coefficient on age, a negative coefficient on wealth, and that gives us an equation . . .'" Hull then wrote down an equation in Green's notebook that he thought was a kind of mathematical map to victory:

Probability = $1/(1 + \exp(-1 \times (-3.9659056 + (\text{General Election Weight} \times 1.92380219) + (\text{Re-Expressed Population Density} \times .00007547) + (\text{Re-Expressed Age} \times .01947370) + (\text{Total Primaries Voted} \times -.60288595) + (\% \text{ Neighborhood Ethnicity} \times -.00717530))))$

Then he said to Green, "That's the kind of innovation I will bring to problems in the United States Senate." Years later, when asked if he had been joking by providing a regression analysis for winning a seat in the Senate, Hull was quiet for a while, then said, "Well, no. That wasn't light-hearted."

If Hull had been a man of ordinary means, his bizarre reliance on probability theory and his utter lack of knowledge about policy would have been disqualifying. But in Illinois, there was fresh experience of a candidate purchasing his seat as if it were on a sale rack at Marshall Field's. In 1998, Peter Fitzgerald had spent fourteen million dollars of his family's banking fortune to defeat Carol Moseley Braun. Hull declared that he was ready to spend triple that amount.

Hull hired veritable armies of consultants: issues experts; direct-mail, media, and Internet gurus; a communications director in Chicago; a communications director downstate; two separate teams of pollsters—all for top-dollar fees. Few of them came to work for Hull because they believed in him. There was nothing to believe in. In the summer of 2002, Hull's advisers taped a mock interview with Hull and played portions of it for a focus group of potential voters. Hull struck everyone in the room as almost comically banal and unpolished. "One woman thought she was being punked for an episode of 'Candid Camera,' " Mark Blumenthal, one of Hull's pollsters, said.

Hull needed help. He had approached David Axelrod before deciding whether to run against Emanuel for a House seat or against Obama, Hynes, and the others for Senate. Axelrod, who had not yet signed on with Obama, was not immune to the charms of a rich, self-financing client; in 1992, he had helped run the woeful campaign of Al Hofeld, a wealthy attorney, who had spent a great deal of money trying to win the Democratic nomination for the U.S. Senate against the incumbent, Alan Dixon. Axelrod met with Hull several times. Like many others, Axelrod had heard rumors about Hull: that he had been treated for substance abuse, that he had been through an ugly divorce, in 1998, from a successful real-estate broker named Brenda Sexton (whom he had married twice). There were even rumors that Hull had hit Sexton. In long, frank discussions, Hull confirmed the rumors about his troubled divorce and admitted that he had also had a problem with alcohol and cocaine.

In the end, however, Hull decided to run for the Senate and Axelrod went to work for his friend Obama. Axelrod was already convinced that he had signed on with a "once in a lifetime" politician, though Obama had a less than even chance of getting the Democratic nomination.

"Into the teeth of those two winds, Hynes and Hull, stepped Barack Obama, whose only real electoral history was getting the shit kicked out of him by Bobby Rush," Pete Giangreco said. "People who knew him loved him. The question was: Could we get his story out? Would we have the money? Could we get people to know him the way we knew him?"

Since many voters were unfamiliar with the candidates, the early focus in the 2004 primary race was on endorsements, particularly among labor unions and the traditional political organizations. More than a hundred elected officials in Chicago and downstate came out for Dan Hynes, and, thanks to his family name, so did the most traditionally minded unions, including the A.F.L.-C.I.O. But Obama surprised the Hynes campaign by picking up the support of three activist unions, the Service Employees International Union (S.E.I.U.), the Illinois Federation of Teachers, and the American Federation of State, County, and Municipal Employees (A.F.S.C.M.E.). Obama's reputation as a left-of-center politician skilled in the arts of compromise—especially his work on health care, child-care benefits, and judicial and ethics reform—appealed to the labor leaders, and he had courted them for years in Springfield and Chicago.

Obama had also, of course, established himself as an early opponent to the Iraq war. By the beginning of 2004, the war had lasted far longer than the Bush Administration had predicted and there was no sign at all of the chemical, biological, or nuclear weapons that had been the main premise for invasion. The contrast between Hynes's support for the war and Obama's early opposition to a "dumb war" at the rally in October, 2002, on Federal Plaza, served Obama well as he picked up strength in liberal suburbs like Evanston.

Obama also impressed reporters and his small audiences with his performance on the stump. He began his speeches with some form of the now familiar riff on his "funny" name: "People call me 'Alabama.' They call me 'Yo Mama.' And that's my supporters! I won't say what my opponents call me." And then he would weave his own story into the larger story of community and the American future. His were not especially original liberal sentiments and positions, but when they came from the mouth of a young biracial man named Barack Obama audiences absorbed them at a different emotional level.

"The thing about Barack was that there were some aspects of campaigning that he enjoyed, like test-driving new devices in speeches," Giangreco said. "But he would complain sometimes about the campaigning.

He wasn't like Bill Clinton, who loved the retail stuff and the strategizing. He just didn't have that relish for the game. He wasn't the happy warrior. But he was still damned good at it."

One of Obama's commercials ended with a peroration of hope and possibility: "Now they say we can't change Washington? I'm Barack Obama and I am running for the United States Senate and I approve this message to say, 'Yes, we can." *Yes, we can.* It was a phrase that resonated with Obama's career in community organizing. In 1972, the United Farm Workers, led by Cesar Chavez and Dolores Huerta, had used the slogan "*Sí, se puede*": "Yes, we can," or "Yes, it can be done." A few years later, the second baseman for the Philadelphia Phillies, Dave Cash, started the rallying cry "Yes, we can" after the team swept the Montreal Expos in a double-header. At first, Obama was dismissive of the phrase, thinking it exceedingly banal, a mode of cynical packaging. "He thought it was a little schlocky at first," Giangreco recalled. But both Axelrod and Michelle Obama convinced him that it would help rouse the spirits of African-Americans and other voters who had grown so accustomed to hard times and their own sense of resignation. Obama's first direct-mail piece was also meant to summon a certain emotional sense of resurgence in African-Americans and progressives. "Finally, a Chance to Believe Again" was the rubric; it was a phrase that later became "Change We Can Believe In."

Howard Dean's 2004 Presidential campaign had enlightened the world of political operatives about the benefits of the Internet, but Obama's Senate campaign didn't have the money for a major effort on the Web—and certainly not for the kind of daily tracking polls that would allow them to calibrate their progress. Obama was frustrated by the campaign's initial approach to the Internet. "We are technologically illiterate," Obama told some volunteers at a parade in Evergreen Park, in July, 2003. Later in the campaign volunteers organized Dean-style "meetups" and an Obama for Senate Yahoo Group, but the efforts were modest.

Hull's pollster, Mark Blumenthal, and his media consultant, Anita Dunn, thought that, even though Obama began the race far behind, his appeal to African-Americans and Lakefront liberals, a significant sector of the Illinois Democratic electorate, would eventually make him the man to beat. "I remember being on the conference call when the opposition researcher talked about Obama," Blumenthal said. "There was nothing. Nice family, no trouble with the law, Columbia, Harvard. There was the mention of drugs in his book, but there was no way Blair Hull, with problems in the past with cocaine and alcohol, could do anything about that. Then the oppo guy finally said, 'Well, Obama is *really* liberal. His record in Springfield was really liberal.' And we said, 'So? We're not Republicans. That doesn't help.' "

Not long afterward, the Hull campaign organized a focus group to analyze Obama's potential appeal. It showed people a clip of his announcement speech, then footage of a black clergyman and Jesse Jackson, Jr., praising Obama at the event. Obama's kickoff event had been aimed, at least in part, at the African-American base. After the loss to Bobby Rush—who had, vindictively, come out for Hull—Obama could not just assume black support. At the focus group, Hull's team noticed that the whites in the room reacted poorly to the film. They didn't mention race, but they said they wanted "something new" or "That's Chicago politics." Hull's advisers suspected that they were reacting to Jackson, whose family was unpopular with many moderate and conservative whites. When they showed those same white voters footage of Obama alone and emphasized his biography—especially the lines about being the first black president of the *Harvard Law Review* and teaching at the University of Chicago—his numbers increased dramatically, particularly among liberal, well-educated voters.

Over the fall and winter of 2003, Hull had spent heavily on media all over the state to get from zero to the mid-teens in the polls—a strategy his campaign called the "steady burn"—but then he stalled. The Hull team also carried around the secret about their candidate's divorce. In the summer of 2003, he had told his lawyers, pollsters, and consultants even more details than he had revealed to David Axelrod. The question was, should they tell the story early and let any controversy die down long before the primary or should they try to keep it all quiet? If they released the facts, would the news immediately and conclusively damage Hull's candidacy? At a marathon meeting with Hull, his advisers and lawyers said that the divorce records could not be unsealed without legal permission—and such permission was unlikely. Hull also assured his team that Brenda Sexton would be on his side should there be a leak. He made no mention of a damning deposition that she had given at the time of the divorce. Hull asked his aides about running a poll in Ohio, in which they would test public opinion in the event that the news got out, but they quickly assured him that he could save his money. A poll would surely tell him that news of spousal abuse would be fatal.

Hull decided to stay in the race and keep the records sealed as long as he could. There had been disagreement among the consultants, but they all stayed with him—and kept receiving their monthly checks. "We should have been screaming at him louder than we were," Blumenthal said. "The amount of money people were making was a factor."

The primary date was March 16th. All winter, Hull spent heavily on television, radio, and print advertising. The ads portrayed him as a loyal union member, a veteran (the only one in the race), a smart businessman, a protector of women and the elderly, an anti-politician fit to lead. It was the best campaign that money could buy. Hull traveled the state in a luxurious private jet and in a chartered red-white-and-blue R.V. nicknamed Hull on Wheels. He handed out "Give 'Em Hull" baseball caps by the thousands. He employed more than a hundred people, and a squad of workers, who pounded in yard signs for seventy-five dollars a day. Even some people who came to cheer for him at campaign stops got money from the Hull organization.

The *Tribune*'s lead writer covering the campaign, David Mendell, was so deeply struck by the expensive emptiness of the Hull campaign that he described it in the paper as " 'The Truman Show' meets 'The Candidate.' "

Mendell enjoyed covering Obama. In the world of Chicago politics, Obama seemed unsullied, intelligent, committed; even his sometimes thin-skinned self-regard, which Mendell found to be outsized at times, was interesting. "The only thing he had a hard time laughing at was himself," Mendell recalled. "During the campaign, some of his opponents were criticizing him for casting all of those 'present' votes in Springfield. Once we were in an elevator and Obama pressed the button and it didn't light up. He did it again and it still didn't light up. Finally, I said, 'It's like all those present votes you cast! It won't commit.' Obama just stared at me. He wouldn't crack a smile."

But the truth was that Obama, at first, was not the center of the story. Hull was. Hynes, Pappas, and Chico, in particular, were all but ignored by the press in favor of Hull. For months, Hull appeared confident in his capacity to purchase victory and he seemed on his way. His efforts downstate undermined Dan Hynes. Unlike many of his consultants, Hull did not consider Obama to be a strong competitor. "Barack, at the end of the campaign, was a strong candidate, but at the beginning he wasn't," Hull recalled. Money, the Hull campaign believed, would keep the candidate safely ahead of Hynes and Obama.

Obama tried to overcome Hull's financial advantage with wry dismissals. "I don't begrudge extraordinarily wealthy people spending their money," he said. "But what I do know is that although you can buy television time, you can't buy a track record and you can't buy the experience that's necessary to hit the ground running when you get to the United States Senate." Laura Washington, a columnist at the *Sun-Times* and an ardent Obama supporter, wrote on February 15th, "There's some good and bad news there for Obama. My aunt Muriel, a Jewish grandmother in

Highland Park, has been in Obama's corner for months. But these days she's feeling the heat from friends who have been wooed by Hull's commercials. She says Obama needs to get on TV—right now. 'You sense his honesty, you sense his commitment, you sense his brilliance. If he were on television, you'd fall in love with him,' she said." Laura Washington's aunt Muriel proved herself one of the keenest analysts of the race.

Dan Hynes, mystified that his campaign was stuck despite his many endorsements, watched the Hull ascension with despair. Hynes's campaign spokesman, at lunch with David Mendell, handed over a folder of opposition research. The folder contained papers indicating that the records of Hull's divorce from Brenda Sexton were sealed, but that she had filed a restraining order against him. "The Hynes people were doing the dirty work," Mendell said.

Soon after the meeting with the Hynes aide, Mendell interviewed Hull for a profile for the *Tribune* and he asked him about the divorce, the restraining orders, and much else. Hull refused to talk about any personal matters. "He was squirming in his chair but he just wouldn't address it," Mendell said. Mendell referred to the restraining order deep in his story. David Axelrod mentioned it to the *Tribune*'s liberal columnist, Eric Zorn, who had already seen it, and who then wrote about it. At the same time, Mike Flannery, an aggressive reporter for WBBM, the CBS affiliate, started pressing Hull on the same documents.

For months Axelrod had been absorbed in figuring out how to present Obama in a media campaign that he was conceiving for late in the race. He and Cauley were mapping out the electoral math and the timing of the campaign. Their strategy was based on a set of simple premises: around two-thirds of the Illinois electorate lived within range of the Chicago media market. Obama's success would rest on capturing nearly the entire African-American vote and attracting progressive whites in the city, Cook County, and perhaps in the "collar counties" surrounding Chicago: DuPage, Kane, Lake, Will, and McHenry Counties. In Illinois, the black vote was ordinarily twenty-two or twenty-three per cent of the primary vote; by making sure that more African-Americans registered and got to the polls, Obama stood to gain tens of thousands of votes. The campaign also thought that Obama should focus as well on white liberal women, who vote in high numbers. Obama's team figured that in a seven-person primary race he shouldn't need much more than thirty-five per cent overall to win.

"We had done a focus group in Evanston with thirty-five-year-old-and-up white women," Jim Cauley said. "We showed them footage of

Blair Hull, Dan Hynes, and Obama. When we showed them Hynes, one lady said, 'Dan Quayle.' When we showed them Hull we heard 'Mr. Potato Head' and 'embalmed.' Then we showed them Obama and we heard 'Denzel.' Another woman said, 'No, Sidney Poitier.' That was my eureka moment when I thought, Shit, we're gonna win this thing. This was five weeks out."

The race was shifting. At a radio debate in Springfield in late February, Hull's Democratic opponents started to call on Hull to release his divorce records and to attack him personally. One of the candidates, Maria Pappas, told Hull that he and his ex-wife "need to get inside of a room" and hash out their problems. Obama preferred to jab at Hull on the issue of the Iraq war. "The fact of the matter is, Blair, that you were silent when these decisions were being made," Obama said, rebutting Hull's contention that he had been an opponent of the war. "You were AWOL on this issue."

In mid-February, Hull's tracking polls had showed him slightly ahead. But on February 25, a CBS 2/Newsradio 780 poll showed that Obama had started to edge in front of Hull, twenty-seven per cent to twenty-five—not a decisive statistic but the beginning of a trend. Not long afterward, Obama gleefully announced that he had received a ten-thousand-dollar check from Michael Jordan, easily the biggest celebrity in Chicago. ("We debated whether to frame it in the office but—pragmatists that we were—we decided to go ahead and cash it.")

Early in the campaign, Hull had gambled that his divorce records would remain a secret. Now he tried to let the steam out of the story with a foolish maneuver. His spokesman, Jason Erkes, called in David Mendell to look at the divorce documents—but off the record. Mendell refused to cooperate under those terms. The *Tribune* and WLS-TV prepared to sue to get the papers unsealed by a judge. "What we discovered now was that everyone had the divorce deposition—everyone except for us in the campaign," Anita Dunn said. "And we knew now that we weren't going to win a case in court to keep it sealed."

On February 27th, Hull and his ex-wife, Brenda Sexton, decided to unseal the divorce papers themselves. Five years later, Hull said that he was woefully late in making the move. "I knew there was a chance this would come out," he said. Holding on to the files, he added, "was a risk that I thought was worth taking." Once he released them, it was easy to see why his consultants had hoped they would remain a secret. The documents revealed that on March 12, 1998, Sexton had asked a Cook County Circuit Court judge for protection because her husband had threatened to kill her. "I am in great fear that if this court does not enter a protective order in my favor and against Blair, as well as exclude him from my residence in which I am residing with my child . . . Blair will continue to inflict mental, emotional and physical abuse upon me as he has done in the past," it said. "At this point, I fear for my emotional and physical well-being, as well as that of my daughter." The papers described multiple allegations of verbal and physical abuse, including one, from December 2, 1997, in which Sexton said, "Blair and I were calmly talking about trust issues, and I remarked everyone has a trust issue with him. Blair suddenly responded by saying, 'You evil bitch. You are a f—— c——,' repeatedly. He then hung on the canopy bar of my bed, leered at me and stated, 'Do you want to die? I am going to kill you, you f—— bitch.'" Reporting an incident from February 9, 1998, Sexton said, "He then held one of my legs and punched me extremely hard in the left shin. After that, he swung at my face with his fists a couple of times in a menacing manner just missing me."

Sexton had asked for a ten-million-dollars settlement, and eventually agreed to three million dollars plus half the value of their house, on the North Side. Hull informed the *Tribune* that he and Sexton "remain friends." At the same time, people inside Hull's campaign were telling reporters that Hull and Sexton could not bear to be in each other's company.

Hull insisted that the documents should not disqualify him from the Senate. "It is my total reputation in my life, my sixty-one years, that you should look at," he told reporters gamely.

But he knew. Hull called one of his advisers and kept saying, "We're done, right?" He was devastated. Blumenthal recalls that the morning after the story broke in the *Tribune*, Hull went to the same coffee shop he had been going to for a decade for a cup of coffee and a muffin. The people there had always greeted him with a friendly word. Now they looked away. "He felt like a pariah," Blumenthal said.

Hull now claims that Sexton's allegations in the files were false or exaggerated, merely part of a complex struggle for a financial resolution to an unhappy union. "Divorces are about two things: money and children," he said. "And there were no children." Hull insisted that any of the abuses recounted in the file were fiction.

Publicly, Obama kept his distance from Hull's personal travails. (Privately, he told Dan Shomon, "If you want to be in politics, do not beat your wife.") But one *Tribune* account suggested that the Obama campaign was not wholly innocent in the affair, and that its operatives had encouraged the press to look more deeply into the matter before Hull and Sexton finally decided to make a full disclosure. When I asked about that, Hull said only, "I'll let you come to your conclusions." He then hastened to describe his financial and political support of Obama's Presidential campaign. In 2004, the Obama Senate campaign paid for "books"—full-scale studies and opposition research—on its leading opponents, Hull and Hynes, but that was routine. (Each book cost around ten thousand dollars.) Obama's aides deny taking any strong or sneaky action to press the story about Hull's divorce records. Two key members of Obama's team insisted that the rumors about Hull were so current around Chicago, especially in political circles, that "everyone" knew about them.

"Ax didn't leak the story, but he might have fanned the flames to help our candidacy," Dan Shomon said. "Barack actually thought that if Blair Hull dropped out it would be a negative for us. We wanted Hynes and Hull to split the more conservative white vote."

Obama's advisers, like everyone else in Chicago politics, could readily see that, with just a few weeks left before the primary, the damage to Hull was probably fatal. "Women were not thrilled to read in the *Sun-Times* that [Hull] had called his wife the c-word," Jim Cauley recalled. "They peeled away from him in no time and went to where they were comfortable. Barack was a non-threatening, charismatic, intelligent guy with a beautiful wife and kids."

The revelation about Hull's ugly divorce came just after the start of the Obama media blitz that Axelrod had been planning for months. Axelrod's strategy from the start had been to hold off until the closing weeks of the campaign, and then, when voters were paying attention, spend on a round of ads for Obama. The strategy, whether or not it was informed by Axelrod's knowledge of Hull's past and the suspicion that it might eventually go public, worked in swift and remarkable fashion.

First came an introductory ad with Obama talking about his success at Harvard Law School and his progressive votes in Springfield. Obama's presence on the screen is soothing, competent, and dynamic. Compared with Hull or Hynes, he was Jack Kennedy. And Axelrod got the ending he wanted from his reluctant candidate: "I'm Barack Obama, I'm running for the United States Senate, and I approved this message to say, 'Yes, we can.' "

The Hull campaign showed the first Obama ad to a focus group to assess its potential effect. They were astonished. "It was a fabulous spot, Obama just exploded off the screen," Blumenthal said. "The people were saying, 'Wow, I want to know more about him. Anita Dunn says that's where it all changed. At that moment, he stopped being a typical South Side politician for people. Now they were seeing someone who transcended race and the old racial politics. After that, Obama just shot up and out of sight."

Axelrod thought that he could deepen Obama's image as the inheritor of a progressive legacy in the state by enlisting Paul Simon, who was widely admired even in conservative downstate counties for his integrity and his lack of pretension. Simon agreed to come out for Obama, but just before the endorsement was announced, he suffered complications during surgery to repair a heart valve and died—a terrible blow to old friends and colleagues like Axelrod, whose first campaign had been Simon's Senate race twenty years earlier. After the funeral, Axelrod came up with an idea to "replace the irreplaceable," Pete Giangreco said. Simon's daughter Sheila appeared in a thirty-second spot, saying that Obama and her father were "cut from the same cloth."

"That ad was so effective," Dan Shomon said. "Barack had always had Paul Simon's endorsement if he wanted it, but he got something better: he got him speaking from the grave."

A final commercial featured archival footage of both Simon and Harold Washington, evoking the proudest moment in the history of progressive politics in Chicago. "There have been moments in our history when hope defeated cynicism, when the power of people triumphed over money and machines," the narrator said while images of Simon and Washington appeared and dissolved on the screen.

The campaign had originally planned to use these commercials during a two-week television blitz in the Chicago market at a cost of around eight hundred thousand dollars. But the combination of Blair Hull's nose-dive and Obama's increasingly impressive fund-raising machinery changed everything. As if overnight, the campaign raised enough money to intensify the media effort in the vote-rich Chicago media market and also run ads downstate. They were able to run ads on stations in Carbondale and even Paducah, Kentucky, which broadcasts into southern Illinois. "The money was pouring in," Cauley said. "We just kept adding markets." The ad campaign, one of Hull's advisers admitted to Giangreco, put the Obama campaign "on a rocket sled."

The money hadn't just fallen out of the sky. One of the things that Obama had learned since the congressional campaign was to sit down and make a long string of fund-raising calls. And when he went on fund-raising missions to the living rooms of wealthy supporters, he refused to stop at giving his usual stump speech and taking questions. Many candidates let their hosts or surrogates make the appeal for funds, but Obama would often say, "I like to do my own dirty work" and put the arm on his supporters himself. To donors who told Obama that they could "do five"—meaning donate five thousand dollars—Obama would say, "I need your help. Can you do ten?" "Go the extra mile!" "I need you to feel some pain!" He was not shy. Steven Rogers, a businessman who taught at Northwestern, told the New York *Times* that he was once paired with Obama in a golf game and, by the sixth hole, Obama had told him that he wanted to run for Senate—"and by the ninth hole, he said he needed help to clear up some debts."

Hull's presence had complicated the financial picture of the race. According to the so-called millionaire amendment in federal election laws, if a wealthy self-financing candidate is in the race, his opponents can accept contributions many times the usual limit. Among those who donated the maximum, or close to it, to Obama's campaign were members of the Pritzker and Crown families, the developer Antoin Rezko, and members of the George Soros family, as well as friends such as John Rogers, Valerie Jarrett, and Marty Nesbitt; classmates from Harvard; and colleagues at the University of Chicago. Because of the millionaire's amendment, nearly half of Obama's total funds came from fewer than three hundred donors. At the start of the campaign, Obama had told Nesbitt, "If you raise four million, I have a forty-per-cent chance of winning. If you raise six million, I have a sixty-per-cent chance of winning. You raise ten million, I guarantee you I can win." In the end, Obama and his team raised more than five million for the primary alone. Sometimes, during the final media blitz, the campaign would run out of cash and they would have to hold their commercials for a day or two; but, in general, the funds were there to run strong to the end.

Obama had started out the campaign riding around the state in his Jeep Cherokee, often alone, barely able to draw crowds downstate of fifty or a hundred. He'd ride around from one event to the next, smoking cigarettes, talking on his cell phone, listening to books on tape. But as the money came in and as his chances increased, Cauley and the others persuaded Obama to stop driving himself—"The guy was wasting time looking for parking spaces!"—and sell the Jeep. By Thanksgiving of 2003, he was being driven around in an S.U.V.

By early March, it was all but over for Blair Hull—and he knew it. He skipped one of his own press conferences, leaving his spokesman to explain that the candidate had been spending time taking senior citizens to Canada to buy cheaper prescription drugs. The disasters kept coming for Hull: a little more than a week before the Democratic primary, he admitted that he had smoked marijuana and used cocaine "occasionally" in the nineteen-eighties and had been treated for alcohol abuse.

As if Hull's downfall had not been lurid enough, a story in the *Tribune* revealed that Jack Ryan, the Republican frontrunner, had sealed his 1999 divorce records and that the paper was trying to gain access to them. Ryan had been married to a Hollywood actress named Jeri Ryan, the star of two major television series: "Boston Public," an earnest high-school drama series in which she played a teacher named Ronnie Cooke, and "Star Trek: Voyager," in which she played an equally earnest former Borg drone named Seven of Nine from the home planet of Tendara Colony, where everyone apparently wears form-fitting one-piece Lycra suits. Jeri Ryan met her husband in 1990, when she was dealing blackjack at a charity event.

For Obama, victory in the primary was assured. Hull was spiraling downward, Hynes was stuck, and the rest of the candidates never got much traction. Obama had all but escaped criticism in the press. Not only did he impress voters and the media with his intelligence and seriousness, he had also avoided being the focus of attention until late in the race. He was never the subject of a negative ad. "When you are at sixteen percent, no one is kicking your ass because no one thinks you are for real," Jim Cauley said. One of the few criticisms of Obama that Cauley could recall from late in the race came when a conservative Jewish group complained that, in filling out a questionnaire, Obama had referred to Israel's security "wall" rather than calling it a "fence."

Just before the primary vote, Obama collected glowing endorsements from the *Tribune*, the *Sun-Times*, the Chicago *Defender*, and many outlets in the suburbs and downstate. With Hull's candidacy in ruins, downstate voters were migrating not to Hynes, as everyone expected, but to Obama. "The conventional wisdom even as late as 2004 was that there were hardly any African-Americans downstate and people there would never dream of voting for a black man named Barack Obama," Anita Dunn said. "This was a part of the country where the Klan had been active in the nineteen-twenties. But it turned out that when people were suffering economically, they were ready for a change. You saw the phenomenon of people feeling better about themselves for supporting an African-American. It was a real harbinger of the future." Dunn went on to become a close aide to Obama during his Presidential run four years later and his first White House communications director.

On the Sunday night before the primary, Obama was at his campaign headquarters with Jim Cauley, discussing his prospects. "A survey we had said he was at forty-eight, and I thought, No way in hell," Cauley said. "I thought we had a ceiling—in a seven-way race you can't get over forty-five. Barack said, 'You think we're at forty-five?' But now we weren't this tiny campaign anymore. Now there were four hundred people on board. He had run around the state and no one in the press would talk to him, but once he was on TV in those ads his life changed. And I said, 'Yeah, dude, you're a different human now.' "

On Primary Day, March 16th, Obama's campaign focused on maximizing the African-American turnout. It sent fifteen-seat vans all over the South Side to get people to the polls. If someone wasn't home, volunteers put a sticker on the door. Later, if the sticker was gone, they'd know the resident was home. Then they would knock on the door again and try to persuade the person to vote—and then call the van.

Eric Zorn, the *Tribune* columnist, spent time with Obama on Primary Day and wrote that he "carried himself with the engaged serenity you often see at a wedding in the father of the groom: focused, but not preoccupied; happy, but not ecstatic." The Obama family camped out in a suite on the thirty-fourth floor of the Hyatt Regency Chicago, a hotel operated by the Pritzker family. When, just after 7 P.M., the call came that WBBM-TV had projected him the landslide winner, Michelle Obama gave her husband a high-five and took on the voice of Sally Field at the Academy Awards: "They like you! They really like you!"

In the last three weeks of the campaign, Obama had gone from sixteen per cent to fifty-three per cent. As the television news crews filed in to film the scene, Obama pointed to Malia and Sasha, who were wearing their Sunday best for the victory party. Obama said his biggest concern was if "these dresses will hold up until ten o'clock." At 8:13 P.M., Hull called Obama to concede. When Paul Simon's daughter, Sheila Simon, introduced Obama later that night to the cheering crowd, she held up one of her father's signature bow ties and said that the tie was the only real difference between the winner and her father.

"I think it's fair to say that the conventional wisdom was we could not win," Obama told his supporters. "We didn't have enough money. We didn't have enough organization. There was no way that a skinny guy from the South Side with a funny name like 'Barack Obama' could ever win a statewide race. Sixteen months later we are here, and Democrats all across Illinois—suburbs, city, downstate, upstate, black, white, Hispanic, Asian—have declared: Yes, we can!"

Joining Obama on the stage that night with his family was Jesse Jackson, Sr. The Obama-Jackson relationship was deeply complicated. Jackson, who had been an impetuous protégé of Martin Luther King both in the South and in Chicago, had made history in 1984 and 1988 with his Presidential campaigns. Now he was witnessing the rise of a generation that, he knew, viewed him with ambivalence. They were displacing him. Jackson had spurned Obama before, endorsing Alice Palmer for State Senate and then Rush for Congress, but this time he stood with Obama for the U.S. Senate. On primary night he told the crowd, "Surely Dr. King and the martyrs smiled upon us."

The next morning, Obama had breakfast with his opponents, and with the state's Democratic Party leadership. A triumphant Emil Jones was there, and so was a chastened Bobby Rush.

Later in the day, Obama flew around the state—to Springfield, to Quincy, to Marion—to thank the voters. And for perhaps the thousandth time, he told reporters that he would not be held back by race even as he prepared for a general election campaign to become the only African-American in the U.S. Senate. "I have an unusual name and an exotic background, but my values are essentially American values," he said (not for the first time, and not for the last). "I'm rooted in the African-American community, but not limited by it."

About a week after the primary, Obama witnessed the most dramatic evidence possible that his appeal was not limited by race. With Senator Durbin, he traveled to the southernmost tip of Illinois, to the small town of Cairo. In the nineteen-sixties and seventies, Cairo had been a center for the White Citizens Council. The schools were segregated. There were cross burnings and harassment of blacks and Jews. As Obama and Durbin were driving into town, Durbin said, "Let me tell you about the first time I went to Cairo. It was about thirty years ago. I was twenty-three years old and Paul Simon, who was lieutenant governor at the time, sent me down there to investigate what could be done to improve the racial climate in Cairo." When Durbin arrived in town, a resident picked him up and brought him to a motel.

As Durbin was getting out of the car, the man said, "Excuse me, let me just give you a piece of advice. Don't use the phone in your motel room because the switchboard operator is a member of the White Citizens Council, and they'll report on anything you do." Durbin checked into the room and unpacked. A few minutes later there was a knock on his door and there was a man at the door who said, "What the hell are you doing here?" Then he just walked away.

"Well, now Dick is really feeling concerned and so am I because, as he's telling me this story, we're pulling into Cairo," Obama recalled the following year, at an N.A.A.C.P. dinner in Detroit. "So I'm wondering what kind of reception we're going to get. And we wind our way through the town and we go past the old courthouse, take a turn and suddenly we're in a big parking lot and about three hundred people are standing there. About a fourth of them are black and three-fourths are white and they all are about the age where they would have been active participants in the epic struggle that had taken place thirty years earlier. And as we pull closer I see something. All of these people are wearing these little buttons that say 'Obama for U.S. Senate.' And they start smiling. And they start waving. And Dick and I looked at each other and didn't have to say a thing. Because if you told Dick thirty years ago that he, the son of Lithuanian immigrants born into very modest means in East St. Louis, would be returning to Cairo as a sitting United States senator, and that he would have in tow a black guy born in Hawaii with a father from Kenya and a mother from Kansas named 'Barack Obama,' no one would have believed it. But it happened."

Chapter Eleven

A Righteous Wind

The Illinois Senate race of 2004 did not take place in a political vacuum, of course; that same year, George W. Bush was running for re-election. Bush had come to office in 2000 only after a five-to-four vote of the U.S. Supreme Court effectively ended the Florida recount with Bush in the lead. The vote denied the Presidency to Al Gore, who had, by nearly any rational count, won the popular vote both nationally and in Florida. In the race for the 2004 Democratic nomination, John Kerry, the junior senator from Massachusetts, fended off the early challenge of Vermont's governor, Howard Dean, and, after a string of primary victories, was able to start planning for the race against Bush.

One of the best and earliest opportunities that a challenger has to frame his candidacy—to project his political ideas, and his character, to millions of people all at once—is at the nominating convention. Television audiences for the Conventions have diminished over time, but the candidates for President and Vice-President can still make an important initial impression not only with their acceptance speeches but also with speeches and theatrics on the first nights of the Convention.

The Kerry campaign chose Jack Corrigan, a Boston lawyer who was a Party veteran, to help run the Convention, which was to take place in late July at Boston's FleetCenter. Corrigan was in his late forties. As a student, he had taken off so much time to work for various Democratic candidates that his friends joked that he would be on Social Security before he got his law degree. He had been an aide to Edward Kennedy, Geraldine Ferraro, Michael Dukakis, and Walter Mondale, and he had been one of Al Gore's point men in Palm Beach County during the 2000 recount fight. Kerry's campaign manager, Mary Beth Cahill, asked Corrigan to play a larger role in the campaign, but he preferred to stay home and take the job of running the Convention: by early spring, he had started working on stagecraft, media arrangements, union contracts, and the list of potential speakers.

"One of the things you have to figure out is a keynote speaker, which is just one domino in a complicated mosaic," Corrigan said. He had done his first serious political work when he was an undergraduate at Harvard and volunteered for Abner Mikva in his 1976 and 1978 congressional races. During those campaigns, Corrigan became friendly with Henry Bayer, a former teacher and union organizer. Whenever Corrigan and Bayer got together they would have five-hour dinners and talk politics. By 2003, Bayer was running the Illinois chapter of A.F.S.C.M.E., the biggest union in the country for public employees and health-care workers. Bayer called his friend and said, "You really have to raise money for this guy, Barack Obama. He's running for Senate in Illinois and he's the real deal."

"Why would I want to get involved in that?" Corrigan asked.

"Because," Bayer answered, "Ab Mikva says he is the most talented politician in fifty years."

Mikva not only came from the state of Douglas, Stevenson, and Simon; he had also worked as White House counsel to Bill Clinton. The best politician in fifty years? This moment of hyperbolic praise caught Corrigan's attention. Corrigan called Elena Kagan, a classmate at Harvard Law School and one of Mikva's former law clerks. He had learned that Obama had been president of the *Law Review* and thought that Kagan might have known him there. As it turned out, Kagan knew him not from Harvard but because they were both teaching at the University of Chicago. She praised Obama to Corrigan in terms nearly as extravagant as the ones Mikva had used.

So now, Corrigan recalled, "I'm thinking: this is *really* interesting." He resolved to do something for Obama's Senate campaign, maybe assemble some phone banks and put together a fundraiser at the home of Larry Tribe, Obama's mentor at Harvard. But he was distracted by his law practice and the Presidential race and, by early February, other friends were telling him that Blair Hull was a decent candidate and, using his vast pile of cash, had built a lead over Dan Hynes and Obama.

"I visited Mary Beth Cahill in Washington," Corrigan recalled, "and I said, 'Listen, there is this kid in Chicago who is great and he is about to lose his primary. We should hire him.' Mary Beth nodded and we moved on. This was just one of about ten things I had to tell her." Cahill had also heard encouraging things about Obama.

Corrigan went back to Boston and, after a few weeks, Obama pulled ahead to win the primary. "And so by then," Corrigan went on, "I've got a lot of problems with the Convention. Construction is running behind. The schedule is tight, a lot of headaches. So I thought, Well, Obama could give a speech, but maybe not the keynote. I threw him on a list. When you think about the speakers at a Convention, you have to take a lot of things into consideration: demographics, states that are in play, local races. He was worth thinking about.

"And then," Corrigan continued, "I got a call from an old friend in the Dukakis campaign, Lisa Hay, who'd become a public defender in Portland, Oregon. She was attending a conference in Boston and we had a cup of coffee and she was really on me about how Kerry wasn't strong enough against the war in Iraq. And so I said, 'Lisa, you've got to get with the program and help out.' Finally, she said, 'O.K., I'll help, but I'm saving my money to help my friend Barack Obama.' It turns out she ran against him for president of the *Law Review* and lost." Hay told Corrigan about the banquet celebrating the new officers of the *Law Review* at the Boston Harvard Club, and how, at the end of Obama's speech, the black waiters put down their trays and joined in the applause.

"If you really want someone who can speak, he's your guy," Hay told Corrigan.

"The whole story was moving and a little eerie," Corrigan said. "I had a vision in my mind. Lisa's story had reminded me of Mario Cuomo." In the long history of Convention speeches, from F.D.R.'s eloquent endorsements of Al Smith, in 1924 and 1928, to Barbara Jordan's performance in 1976 ("My presence here is one additional bit of evidence that the American dream need not forever be deferred"), perhaps none was as exquisitely crafted or as movingly delivered as Mario Cuomo's 1984 keynote, "A Tale of Two Cities." The speech debunked Ronald Reagan's "Shining City on a Hill" as a chimerical and exclusive land for the rich and the lucky. Cuomo talked about "another city"—a city of the poor and the middle class watching their dreams "evaporate." His use of direct address to the sitting President was a solemn yet effective technique: "There is despair, Mr. President, in the faces that you don't see, in the places that you don't visit, in your shining city." Corrigan and Cahill started thinking of Obama as someone capable of speaking in those emotionally memorable terms.

In late May, Corrigan, together with Mary Beth Cahill, put Obama on a list of possible keynote speakers that also included the Michigan governor, Jennifer Granholm, Janet Napolitano, of Arizona, and Mark Warner, of Virginia. "We were also thinking about having an Iraq veteran or a teacher," Cahill recalled. "It was a long process and we started looking at videos of all of them."

Cahill and others made calls to get full reports on the possible keynoters; in Obama's case, she spoke to Rahm Emanuel, Richard Durbin, and both Richard and William Daley in Chicago. "The reports on Obama," she said, "were glittering." Obama himself was hardly passive in the process. Axelrod and the campaign's chief of staff, Darrel Thompson, began to lobby for Obama with Kerry's people once they heard that his name was under consideration. Donna Brazile, Minyon Moore, and Alexis Herman—African-American women who had played significant roles in the Party during the Clinton and Gore campaigns—also lobbied for Obama to deliver the keynote.

Obama's drawbacks were obvious. Even though he was the Democratic nominee for the Senate in Illinois, he was still only a state legislator. There was also the matter of his outright condemnation of the war in Iraq, which conflicted with Kerry, who, like Hillary Clinton and many other Democrats, had voted, in 2002, to authorize military action. In Obama's favor was his youth, his race, and the Party's desire for a Democrat to win back the second Illinois Senate seat. In April, 2004, Kerry had spent a couple of days campaigning in Chicago with Obama, appearing with him at a vocational center, a bakery, a town-hall meeting, and a fundraiser at the Hyatt downtown. As Kerry watched Obama speak at the town hall and at the Hyatt, his national finance chairman, a Chicago-based investment banker named Louis Susman, whispered to him, "This guy is going to be on a national ticket someday." Kerry told Susman that he was considering him for a spot at the Convention. "He should be one of the faces of our party now," Kerry said, "not years from now."

In the Republican primary, Jack Ryan, a former partner at Goldman Sachs, had defeated a crowded field, but he began the general election lagging far behind Obama, who was starting to attract national attention. The prospect of a young politician of the post-civil-rights era becoming the sole black senator in the midst of a close battle between Bush and Kerry was an irresistible story. In a Profile published in *The New Yorker*, William Finnegan portrayed Obama as he went to visit A.F.L.-C.I.O. leaders in Springfield. In the primary campaign, the union had endorsed Dan Hynes.

"This is a kiss-and-make-up session," Obama told Finnegan as they entered a room of twenty-five white union leaders in windbreakers and golf shirts. He spoke about the jobs lost during the Bush Administration, federal highway funding, non-union companies homing in on big contracts. Finnegan, who was not alone in being struck by Obama's ease in front of all-white crowds, followed Obama to central Illinois and a community center near Decatur, where two major factories had closed. Obama began with his usual riff about his name and then gave a rousing speech about the Bush Administration's instinct to protect the interests of the powerful and abandon the powerless to feed on clichés about self-reliance. As they drove from the rally in the flatlands of central Illinois toward Chicago, Obama said, "I know those people. Those are my grandparents. The food they serve is the food my grandparents served when I was growing up. Their manners, their sensibility, their sense of right and wrong—it's all totally familiar to me."

Jan Schakowsky, a Democratic congresswoman from the northern suburbs of Chicago, told Finnegan that she had recently been to the White House for a meeting with President Bush. As she was leaving, she noticed that the President was looking at her Obama button. "He jumped back, almost literally," she said. "And I knew what he was thinking. So I reassured him it was 'Obama,' with a 'b.' And I explained who he was. The President said, 'Well, *I* don't know him.' So I just said, 'You will.'"

Bush was already aware of Jack Ryan, the attractive Republican candidate. Ryan was as handsome as a surgical resident on daytime television; he was intelligent and financially fixed—a Goldman Sachs partner who made his fortune and then went off to teach on the South Side of Chicago at Hales Franciscan, an all-male nonprofit high school that was almost entirely African-American. He grew up in the suburb of Wilmette and earned graduate degrees in both law and business from Harvard. He was a pro-life, pro-gun, free-market conservative. Ryan said the school where he taught was an example of economic freedom in action—an independent school helping people. And since he was giving his time, not just his money, Ryan radiated credibility; in the era of "compassionate conservatism," he could argue that his was more than a slogan. Although he, too, had helped finance his own race, Ryan was more appealing, and less technocratic, than Blair Hull.

Ryan's fortunes collapsed, however, in late June, when Robert Schneider, a Los Angeles Superior Court judge, ruled in favor of the *Tribune* and WLS-Channel 7 in their lawsuit to unseal Jack and Jeri Ryan's divorce records. Ryan had long maintained that the papers should remain closed to public inspection in order to protect their nine-year-old son. Although the Ryans' divorce lacked the suggestion of violence featured in Blair Hull's documents, it was instant fodder for cable news and the Internet, which unfailingly provided photographs of Jeri Ryan in various states of immodest dress. Smoking Gun and other sites quickly posted Jeri Ryan's testimony:

> I made clear to Respondent that our marriage was over for me in the spring of 1998. On three trips, one to New Orleans, one to New York, and one to Paris, Respondent insisted that I go to sex clubs with him. These were surprise trips that Respondent arranged. They were long weekends, supposed "romantic" getaways.
>
> The clubs in New York and Paris were explicit sex clubs. Respondent had done research. Respondent took me to two clubs in New York during the day. One club I refused to go in. It had mattresses in cubicles. The other club he insisted I go to. . . . It was a bizarre club with cages, whips and other apparatus hanging from the ceiling. Respondent wanted me to have sex with him there, with another couple watching. I refused. Respondent asked me to perform a sexual activity upon him, and he specifically asked other people to watch. I was very upset. We left the club, and Respondent apologized, said that I was right and he would never insist I go to a club again. He promised it was out of his system.
>
> Then during a trip to Paris, he took me to a sex club in Paris, without telling me where we were going. I told him I thought it was out of his system. I told him he had promised me we would never go. People were having sex everywhere. I cried, I was physically ill. Respondent became very upset with me, and said it was not a "turn on" for me to cry. I could not get over the incident, and my loss of any attraction to him as a result. Respondent knew this was a serious problem. I told him I did not know if we could work it out.

The documents also quoted Jeri Ryan's mother, Sharon Zimmerman, saying, "Jeri Lynn told me that she was tired of being told what to eat, how to sit, what to wear, tired of being criticized about her physical appearance and told to exercise."

Ryan said in the filing that he had been "faithful and loyal" to his wife during their marriage. "I did arrange romantic getaways for us, but that did not include the type of activities she describes," he said. "We did go to one avant-garde nightclub in Paris which was more than either one of us felt comfortable with. We left and vowed never to return." Ryan made it sound as if they had walked out on an underground production of *Ubu Roi*.

Obama was at a fund-raising dinner in distant Carbondale when the news broke. How to react to a story as strange as a *second* sex scandal? In

April, after his primary victory, Obama had hired a new communications director, Robert Gibbs, a shrewd operative from Alabama, who had worked for Ernest Hollings, of South Carolina, in the Senate and on the campaign trail with John Kerry. In 2002, Gibbs had worked for another Joshua generation politician, former Dallas mayor Ron Kirk, who had tried, and failed, to beat John Cornyn for a Senate seat in Texas. Like Cauley, Gibbs was a white Southerner with sharp instincts about the politics of race. The issue now, however, was sex. Obama and Gibbs worked quickly to come up with a suitably dignified, and anodyne, response. "I've tried to make it clear throughout the campaign," Obama told reporters, "that my focus is on what I can do to help the families of Illinois and I'm not considering this something appropriate for me to comment on." (The invoking of "families" was an inspired touch.) Later, Obama would lower his head in embarrassed silence as reporters shouted questions at him like "Do you think a sexual fetish defines a person's character?"

While the Obama campaign stepped back in studied (and stunned) silence as yet another opponent endured a humiliating implosion, Jay Leno weighed in:

> In the Senate race in Illinois, the Republican candidate Jack Ryan just went through an ugly divorce and in court papers, his wife accused him of taking her to sex clubs where he tried to make her have sex with him in front of strangers. Aren't Republicans the family-values people? That's the difference between Republicans and Democrats on family values. Democrat politicians cheat on their wives. Republicans cheat, too—but they bring the wife along. Make it a family event! They include the whole family!

For a few days, Ryan seemed to think he could get past the crisis by emphasizing the potential damage done to his son and his outrage at the judge who had released the papers. "A lot of people were saying to me the last three months it's politically damaging to keep these files sealed, just release the files," Ryan told reporters. "But what dad wouldn't do the same thing I did? What dad wouldn't try to keep information about your child, that might be detrimental to the world knowing, private? Even the things moms and dads say to each other, about each other, should be kept away from children." Ryan insisted that he had done nothing illegal. Jeri Ryan followed with a statement that, while not denying the accuracy of her testimony in the divorce papers, underscored that her ex-husband had never been unfaithful or abusive.

"Jack is a good man, a loving father and he shares a strong bond with our son," she said. "I have no doubt that he will make an excellent senator."

Ryan also found support from the man he hoped to succeed, Peter Fitzgerald (who had voted to find President Clinton guilty during his impeachment trial) and from the Fox News host Bill O'Reilly, who said, "Just think about it, any politician or somebody thinking about running for office, if they have an ex-wife who is mad at them or an ex-girlfriend, they are dead, they are toast, because you can make any accusation in the world."

But political endorsements from Jeri Ryan and Bill O'Reilly were not going to sway the state Republican Party organization. At the start of the campaign, Judy Baar Topinka, the Republican chairwoman in Illinois, had asked Ryan if there was anything damaging or embarrassing in the files. He had assured her that there was not. "I consider him an honest man and I take him at his word," she said just before the primary vote. The state Republican leadership now made it plain, on and off the record in the press, that Jack Ryan was no longer a viable candidate. Raymond LaHood, a Republican moderate from central Illinois, was among those who called on Ryan to leave the race. (Obama appointed LaHood to his Cabinet, as Secretary of Transportation, in 2009.)

On June 25th, Ryan complied with his Party's wish, but not without complaining that the *Tribune* had held him to a "higher standard than anyone else in the history of the United States." One politician who showed some pity for Ryan was Blair Hull. "He is the closest thing to a saint that you can find," he said years later. "He's a kind and generous person. It was sad. It's funny where these turns in life take you. He could be where Obama is right now. He looked like John Kennedy."

Obama continued to keep his rhetoric, and his public face, as impassive as possible. "What happened to him over the last three days was unfortunate," he said of Ryan. "It's not something I certainly would wish on anybody. And having said that, from this point forward, I think we will be continuing to talk about the issues."

At around the time Ryan was enduring his public humiliation, the Obama campaign was hearing rumors that the Kerry team was going to ask him to give the keynote address at the Convention. Both parties often used the keynote address as a way to focus on the next generation of leadership. In 1988, the Democrats called on the Texas state treasurer, Ann

Richards, to give the keynote at the Convention nominating Michael Dukakis, and Richards delivered an attack on George H. W. Bush that had more one-liners than a midnight monologue. ("Poor George. He can't help it. He was born with a silver foot in his mouth.") The speech propelled Richards to victory in the Texas gubernatorial campaign.

To Mary Beth Cahill, the short list for keynoter seemed dull—except for Obama. Everything she had seen of Obama on the video reel that his campaign had sent convinced her that he was a gamble worth taking. Just before the July Fourth weekend, she recommended Obama to Kerry, and Kerry, who was not deeply involved in the details of the Convention, waved it forward. Obama was riding from Springfield to Chicago when he got the call telling him the news. After hanging up, he turned to his driver and said, "I guess this is pretty big."

Obama was able to spend far more time on the speech than if he had had an actual opponent to campaign against. The press was filled with reports that the Republicans were grasping at ideas to replace Jack Ryan: there was Mike Ditka, the celebrated former tight end and coach for the Chicago Bears, and there was Orion (The Big O) Samuelson, a radio broadcaster known for his popular daily spot, "National Farm Report," and his recording of Yogi Yorgesson's "I Yust Go Nuts at Christmas." Andrea Barthwell, the deputy drug czar in the Bush Administration, was the favorite of the moderate wing of the nineteen-person Illinois Republican Central Committee, but the conservatives blocked the idea and continued searching for someone who leaned harder to the right. None of the candidates who finished behind Ryan seemed either sufficiently appealing or willing to enter a race that they were likely to lose.

While the Republicans continued their search, Obama worked in Springfield on a first draft of his speech, making notes and sketching passages on yellow legal pads at his desk in the Senate chamber. Sometimes, in order to get away from his colleagues and the budget debates on the floor, he worked in the men's room, near the sinks. In the course of the campaign, Obama had developed a keen sense of what lines and ideas from his speeches played well with audiences, and much of the writing process was a matter of cobbling together a new text out of his stump speeches.

Obama faxed his first draft to Axelrod, who was on vacation in Italy, and to the Kerry campaign. The point person among Kerry's aides for Obama's speech was Vicky Rideout, who had been a campaign aide to Dukakis and the lead speechwriter for Geraldine Ferraro, when she ran with Walter Mondale, in 1984. The Kerry campaign had determined from polling numbers that the public did not want to witness a fusillade of negativity about the Bush Administration at the Convention—especially when the country was at war. Rideout was keeping a careful watch for anti-Bush rhetoric in all the speeches to be delivered in Boston. Some people in the campaign thought this reluctance to attack Bush was foolhardy, that voters routinely told pollsters that they disliked negative campaigning even though it plainly worked, but Robert Shrum, who spoke for the Kerry campaign, prevailed, and so Obama delivered a draft that focused on hope—which was his disposition anyway.

"My distinct impression was that Obama was writing this himself," Rideout recalled. "He e-mailed the draft to me a little late. I was getting nervous because he was a high-risk speaker, no one really knew him, and this was the most important speech outside of the nominees. When I read it I breathed a sigh of relief. I had no idea what to expect from a guy who had been a state senator for a few terms. We didn't want an Ann Richards, vituperative, lashing kind of speech. This was uplifting. The only problem was that it was twice as long as it should have been."

One touch that Obama did not use often on the campaign trail but added to the speech draft was a phrase that was a turn on the title of one of Jeremiah Wright's sermons—"the audacity to hope." This phrase was to be the refrain of the speech's climax, the clarion call to optimism, to vote for Kerry, and to a renewed national spirit.

Working with Rideout and his own aides, Obama went about the work of cutting the speech, which was scheduled for July 27, 2004, the second night of the four-day-long Convention. There is nothing like excessive length to kill the rhythm and effectiveness of a political speech. None of the Kerry people had forgotten Bill Clinton's windy address at the 1988 Convention, which drew its loudest applause when he arrived at the phrase, "In conclusion . . ." Obama had a hard time reconciling himself to the cuts at first and despaired of the initial instruction that the draft, which ran twenty-five minutes, be reduced by half. Rideout told Obama that he needed to cut back on the more provincial material about Illinois and "turn up the volume a bit" on the words in praise of John Kerry and his running mate, John Edwards, and place them earlier in the speech.

Three days before the speech, Obama, Axelrod, and Gibbs boarded a chartered Hawker jet late at night in Springfield. By now, Obama had trimmed the text to twenty-three hundred words and had it more or less memorized. He had practiced in Axelrod's office on a rented teleprompter; he'd never used the machine before. Since the start of his political career, he had worked either from notes, from a full text, or purely from memory.

With the teleprompter, he had to work on not squinting or taking on a mesmeric, metronomic rhythm as he shifted reading from the two screens flanking the lectern. He also had to realize that he was speaking both to a packed arena and, more important, to millions of people watching on television. If he shouted, he would come off on television as abrasive, unhinged. In Chicago, he practiced the speech fifteen times or more on the teleprompter. As they flew to Boston, Obama told the story of his miserable, brief stay at the Los Angeles Convention four years before.

"Let's hope this Convention goes a whole lot better," he said.

They arrived at Logan Airport after midnight and went straight to the Hilton Boston Back Bay to get some sleep. But Obama couldn't sleep and, for a while, he just wandered around the hotel lobby. "He'd been at it for weeks," Jim Cauley recalled. "He told me, 'No mistakes. We have got to nail this one.' "

Over the next two days, Obama split his time between rehearsing his speech in one of the windowless locker rooms of the FleetCenter and doing interviews. At rehearsals, he worked with Michael Sheehan, a long-time speech coach for Democratic politicians, who started out as a producer of Shakespeare at the Folger in Washington. Sheehan worked with Obama on various techniques unique to a venue like the FleetCenter. First, he and Obama toured the cavernous, empty hall, just to get a feel for the enormity of the place. Sheehan had been giving these tutorials to Democratic nominees since 1988 and he was accustomed to meeting egotistical politicians who insisted on moving with big entourages; he was struck by how Obama went around with, at most, two or three people: Axelrod, Robert Gibbs, and Jonathan Favreau, a speechwriter in his mid-twenties, whom Gibbs knew from the Kerry campaign. Then, once they went down to the basement rehearsal room, Sheehan encouraged Obama to "surf," to speak over applause rather than waiting for it to die down, thereby avoiding a start-stop, start-stop cadence that would have the rhythm of a car in heavy traffic and play poorly on television. They worked on emphases and accents, pauses before punch lines, pacing and timbre. Sheehan showed Obama videotapes of some "counter-examples," like Alfonse D'Amato, the New York Republican, who had botched their speeches with singsong deliveries and clumsy pacing. Above all, he counseled Obama not to bellow or shout, as if he were in a small auditorium or a state fair; he had to let the microphone do the work for him and vary his volume only moderately to indicate a heightening emotional pitch.

"To trust the microphone in a hall like that was a leap of faith," Sheehan said. "It's like that moment in one of the Indiana Jones movies where he comes to a chasm and there is an invisible bridge. You have to have that kind of confidence. . . . Barack was never nervous. He was all about 'Show me what I need to know.' And then he assimilated it. There is a massive misconception about him that he is totally a community organizer. I look at him and I see the law professor. He studies."

In his interviews with the national press, Obama was asked about everything from his views on Iraq to his own burgeoning celebrity status. If Obama was in the least bit nervous about this deluge of attention, he did not show it. Equanimity was part of his appeal. "I love to body surf," he said. "If you're on a wave, you ride it. You figure at some point you're going to get a mouthful of sand. It doesn't last forever." Obama even felt confident enough to be a little critical of John Kerry's limitations. When he was asked about the nominee's relationship with African-American voters, he said, "There's no doubt John Kerry has not captured the hearts of the black community the way Clinton did. His style is pretty buttoned down. He's not the guy who is going to play the saxophone on MTV."

Obama did so many interviews and rehearsed his speech so often that by Tuesday, the day of the speech, he was feeling a little hoarse. At noon, he was scheduled to speak at a rally assembled by the League of Conservation Voters. He cut his remarks short. Apologizing, he said, "I can't throw out my throat for tonight or I've had it."

Obama was on edge especially when the Kerry campaign, which reviewed all the speeches in order to check for thematic consistency and to avoid overlap, called to say that Obama's extended riff on there not being red states or blue states, only the *United* States, was a problem. Kerry, they said, wanted to say something very similar. They asked for cuts. "For Obama, this was the emotional peak of the speech, his signature lines—it's what he had been saying for months—and so I wanted to be absolutely sure the Kerry people thought it was a really big deal to do this at the last minute," Vicky Rideout recalled. "I discussed it with the campaign's speechwriters and I approached Obama and said, 'We have a little challenge here.' "

Rideout explained what she'd been told, half-expecting Obama to lose his temper. He was, after all, wound up about the speech and had been working on it for weeks. A last-minute excision of the heart of the text was sure to throw him.

"All he said was, 'Jeez, really?' He was upset but he didn't show that much anger," Rideout said. "It was that temperament—'no drama Obama' all the way. He didn't cheerfully slap me on the back the way Bill Richardson might have but there was no steam coming out of his ears, either."

Perhaps not, but when Obama got in the car afterward with Axelrod and another campaign aide, he was furious, according to an account in *Chicago* magazine. "That fucker is trying to steal a line from my speech," Obama said, according to the campaign worker. Axelrod, for his part, did not recall Obama's language but said that Obama, after being upset, eventually cooled off. In a subsequent conversation with Vicky Rideout, Obama asked whether the request to cut the passage was coming directly from Kerry or from a nervous staff member. Rideout checked and was told that Kerry had made the request himself. "In that case, it's John's convention," Obama said, and he pared back the passage somewhat but retained the crucial lines.

At around two that afternoon, Obama rehearsed in a room just under the stage. He was still adjusting to the teleprompter and it was very hard to tell, without crowd noise, without the dual audiences of the arena and the television camera, if he was going to be entirely at ease that night. Network television no longer carried the event live—that was left to the cable stations——but there was no doubt that he would get coverage if he scored or if he bombed. Some politicians, including Clinton, had survived a disastrous performance at a Convention, but not many. Despite all the pressure, the story most frequently repeated in Obama's circles about the day of the speech centers on a moment he had with his close friend Marty Nesbitt. As crowds milled around on the streets and in the hotel lobbies of Boston, asking him to sign autographs or pose for cell-phone pictures, Nesbitt said to him, "You know, this is pretty unbelievable. You're like a rock star."

"It might be a little worse tomorrow," Obama said.

"Really?" Nesbitt said. "Why do you say that?"

Obama smiled and said, "It's a pretty good speech."

Obama called his grandmother Toot in Hawaii and his daughters, Sasha and Malia, who were back in Chicago. Michelle Obama, who had watched one of her husband's rehearsals the day before, had one piece of advice: "Smile a lot." Before the speech, the Obamas waited with Richard and Loretta Durbin in a blue-carpeted holding room backstage. Obama wore a black suit, a white shirt, and a tie that he'd borrowed from Gibbs.

When Obama emerged from behind the curtain, he smiled at the applause and heard the pulsing beat of Curtis Mayfield & the Impressions singing their civil-rights-era hit, "Keep on Pushing." (He was relieved to see five thousand blue and white Obama signs in the hands of delegates. Jim Cauley had hired two college kids to drive a U-Haul filled with the signs from Chicago to Boston and they had broken down somewhere outside of Cleveland; with little time to spare, they got back on the road.) After a half-minute of applause, Obama stepped to the podium and began:

> On behalf of the great state of Illinois, crossroads of a nation, land of Lincoln, let me express my deepest gratitude for the privilege of addressing this convention. Tonight is a particular honor for me because, let's face it, my presence on this stage is pretty unlikely.
>
> My father was a foreign student, born and raised in a small village in Kenya. He grew up herding goats, went to school in a tin-roof shack. His father, my grandfather, was a cook, a domestic servant to the British. But my grandfather had larger dreams for his son. Through hard work and perseverance my father got a scholarship to study in a magical place, America, that has shone as a beacon of freedom and opportunity to so many who had come before him.
>
> While studying here my father met my mother. She was born in a town on the other side of the world, in Kansas. Her father worked on oil rigs and farms through most of the Depression. The day after Pearl Harbor, my grandfather signed up for duty, joined Patton's army, marched across Europe. Back home my grandmother raised a baby and went to work on a bomber assembly line. After the war, they studied on the G.I. Bill, bought a house through FHA and later moved west, all the way to Hawaii, in search of opportunity.
>
> And they too had big dreams for their daughter, a common dream born of two continents.

Obama began the speech, as he had begun hundreds of others, with a highly compressed summary of his origins. He didn't stumble, but he was, at the beginning, somewhat ordinary, a little stiff, finding his way. Vicky Rideout and Jack Corrigan stood in the wings and watched Obama. Rideout had spent weeks going through the text with him and his team and thought it was a good speech, a winner, but she could see that there was nothing electrifying about Obama in the opening minute or two. He possessed neither the measured gravity of Mario Cuomo nor the theatrical passion of Jesse Jackson, whose Convention speeches remained embedded in the Party's collective memory.

The speech was structured to go from a passage on autobiography to one connecting the speaker to the diversity and the history of the nation ("I stand here knowing that my story is part of the larger American story"), and then to the stories of specific, emblematic people. And by the time Obama began to talk about the suffering of the people he had met on the campaign trail—the union workers in Galesburg whose plant moved to Mexico; the bright young women in East St. Louis who can't afford college; the people in the collar counties around Chicago angry about waste in both the Pentagon and "a welfare agency"—somewhere in there, Obama began to find his rhythm. This speech was by no means the best he had written and far from the best he ever delivered. To some extent it was a condensed, if more polished, version of a stump speech that he had been honing for nearly two years. But almost no one in the hall or in the television audience had heard it before or had ever seen Obama and his skills, his melding of the professorial and the pastoral. Rideout said that she felt Obama "pull into another gear." His shoulders relaxed, his head was raised up a little higher, his voice took on a greater sense of abandon as he surfed the applause, just as he had rehearsed. From that point on the speech riveted both the hall and, even more, the television audience. "At that moment," Rideout said, "you could see that Obama felt he was *meant* to be there, delivering this speech—it was what he was *meant* to do." Watching Obama and the speech take off, as it did, reminded Michael Sheehan of the moment of brightness and fire just before a rocket gathers speed and truly launches.

In the closing flourish, which Obama had trimmed to please the Kerry campaign, he called on familiar themes of common purpose and national unity but put them in such a way that the speech would be talked about for many years to come:

> If there's a child on the South Side of Chicago who can't read, that matters to me, even if it's not my child.
>
> If there's a senior citizen somewhere who can't pay for their prescription drugs and has to choose between medicine and the rent, that makes my life poorer, even if it's not my grandparent.
>
> If there's an Arab-American family being rounded up without benefit of an attorney or due process, that threatens my civil liberties.
>
> It is that fundamental belief—I am my brother's keeper, I am my sister's keeper—that makes this country work. It's what allows us to pursue our individual dreams, yet still come together as one American family: *E pluribus unum*, out of many, one.
>
> Now even as we speak, there are those who are preparing to divide us, the spin masters and negative ad peddlers who embrace the politics of anything goes. Well, I say to them tonight, there is not a liberal America and a conservative America; there is the United States of

America. There is not a black America and white America and Latino America and Asian America; there is the United States of America.

The pundits, the pundits like to slice and dice our country into red states and blue states: red states for Republicans, blue states for Democrats. But I've got news for them, too. We worship an awesome God in the blue states, and we don't like federal agents poking around our libraries in the red states.

We coach Little League in the blue states and, yes, we've got some gay friends in the red states. There are patriots who opposed the war in Iraq, and there are patriots who supported the war in Iraq. We are one people, all of us pledging allegiance to the Stars and Stripes, all of us defending the United States of America.

In the end, that's what this election is about. Do we participate in a politics of cynicism, or do we participate in a politics of hope?

The applause in this section of the speech was loud and, if it is possible to interpret applause, seemed to reflect years of frustration with the Republican culture wars, partisan warfare, and a political strategy of divide and conquer. Like the 2002 antiwar speech, it served a progressive message in a way that sounded deeply patriotic even to people who might consider themselves Republicans or independents. The speech seemed to many a long-awaited rebuke to the sneering moralism on display at earlier Republican Conventions when figures like Pat Robertson and Pat Buchanan took the stage. Obama's speech depended on an audience ready to recognize the demographic and cultural shifts in the country. Nixon's strategy in 1968, with its implicit racial appeals, had been the fulfillment of L.B.J.'s prediction that his support of civil rights and voting rights for African-Americans would hand over the South to the Republicans for a generation. Whether it was a wish or a reality, Obama insisted, in the political and poetical terms of his speech, that the women's movement, gay liberation, immigration, affirmative action, and many other factors and patterns had helped to reverse that reality.

Finally, Obama used that phrase of Jeremiah Wright's—the audacity of hope—to distinguish between "blind optimism" and "something more substantial."

It's the hope of slaves sitting around a fire singing freedom songs; the hope of immigrants setting out for distant shores; the hope of a young naval lieutenant bravely patrolling the Mekong Delta; the hope of a mill-worker's son who dares to defy the odds; the hope of a skinny kid with a funny name who believes that America has a place for him, too.

Hope in the face of difficulty, hope in the face of uncertainty, the audacity of hope: in the end, that is God's greatest gift to us, the bedrock of this nation, a belief in things not seen, a belief that there are better days ahead.

I believe that we can give our middle class relief and provide working families with a road to opportunity.

I believe we can provide jobs for the jobless, homes to the homeless, and reclaim young people in cities across America from violence and despair.

I believe that we have a righteous wind at our backs, and that as we stand on the crossroads of history, we can make the right choices and meet the challenges that face us.

America, tonight, if you feel the same energy that I do, if you feel the same urgency that I do, if you feel the same passion that I do, if you feel the same hopefulness that I do, if we do what we must do, then I have no doubt that all across the country, from Florida to Oregon, from Washington to Maine, the people will rise up in November, and John Kerry will be sworn in as President. And John Edwards will be sworn in as Vice-President. And this country will reclaim its promise. And out of this long political darkness a brighter day will come.

As the camera panned the audience, there was not just the usual orchestrated applause and listless waving of signs. Some of the delegates were crying, some stomping their feet—for a state senator from Illinois. Professionals like Hillary Clinton, who stood applauding, fully recognized that they had been introduced to an extraordinarily talented young politician. "I thought that was one of the most electrifying moments that I can remember at any Convention," she said the next day. "I have campaigned and have done fund-raising for him, and a friend of mine asked who is this Barack Bama?" Clinton said she replied the name was Barack Obama. "It's Swahili for Bubba."

Vicky Rideout, who had been writing and editing speeches for a long time, stood in the arena, as the Curtis Mayfield song revved up again and Obama embraced his wife and waved and the applause kept coming in waves, and she thought she had never witnessed anything like it: "To see an absolute newbie set the place on fire like that? It was astonishing."

Chicagoans who had spent time with Obama might have been the slowest to see what had happened. Will Burns, who had been Obama's deputy campaign manager and field manager for the Rush campaign, was moved by the spectacle but also told friends, "That was a speech he used to give to crowds of ten people!" Eric Zorn, the *Tribune* columnist, had also seen Obama deliver similar speeches and watched this one from the arena. He thought Obama had done well enough, but he had no idea of the depth of the reaction until he went to the press center where journalists had watched it on television. "What was clear is that, good as he had been live, it was way better on the screen," Zorn said.

The cable anchors all praised Obama and the networks scurried to get video for their late broadcasts and morning shows. Almost instantly, Obama's team was getting invitations to appear on network television. Even the remote sultans of the Chicago and Illinois political organizations set aside their usual studied indifference to embrace Obama. Richard Daley, who had maintained a kingly aloofness during the primary campaign in Illinois, acknowledged that Obama had hit a "grand slam," and the governor, Rod Blagojevich, said of the Senate race, "If present trends continue, Barack Obama is on the verge of getting a hundred per cent of the vote." Even Bobby Rush, who wore his disdain of Obama like a gold watch, had to admit that his old rival was now a bona-fide star: "Do you know what 'Barack' means in Hebrew? It means 'one who God favors.' That's lightning. You don't fool with that." Then he smiled and said, "And besides, some people live a charmed life."

Clarence Page wrote in the *Tribune:*

A superstar is born. It is difficult for many of us to contain our enthusiasm for Barack Obama, yet we must try. We owe that to him. We should not reward his blockbuster performance last week at the Democratic National Convention by loading his shoulders with the fate of the nation. Not yet, anyway. That can wait, perhaps until, say, his 2012 Presidential campaign?

For the rest of the week in Boston, as Obama went from the Convention floor to various interview appointments, people circled around him asking for autographs, urging him to run for President.

At Logan Airport, where Obama was going to catch a flight back to Chicago with other members of the Illinois delegation, people asked for autographs. It seemed that the only people at Logan who didn't recognize him worked at security. As he went through the security checks, a guard pulled aside Obama, "a skinny black guy with a funny name," for extra screening. Jim Cauley, who was traveling with him, was shocked and wanted to protest as a security guard passed a wand over Obama's arms, legs, and body.

Obama smiled and told his campaign manager, "Dude, it's happened to me all my life. Don't worry about it."

Once they got past security and were walking to the gate, Cauley heard his cell phone ringing. He answered. It was an English-speaking aide to Mikhail Gorbachev in Moscow. Gorbachev, who had been running a foundation since stepping down as the Soviet leader, in 1991, had heard the speech and wanted to speak to Obama. The most important foreign leader of the post-war era was on the line: Obama took the call.

Still, people kept crowding around Obama, making it hard to move. Cauley cajoled someone in charge of Delta's first-class lounge to let them inside. Later, Cauley ran into the senior senator from Delaware, Joe Biden.

While Obama spoke on the phone, Biden told Cauley that he was impressed and expected to see Obama soon in Washington.

"He's a good man," Biden said, "but tell him he needs to go slow when he gets to the Senate."

Even before Obama got back to Chicago, his fund-raising accelerated on the strength of his speech; much more was on the way. But Obama's newfound fame also brought an accompanying pang of anxiety, especially among African-Americans old enough to remember what had happened to some of the country's greatest black political figures. As energized as many black men and women in Illinois and across the country were by Obama's rise, many were immediately concerned with his safety. Just a few weeks before, when Obama gave a graduation speech at the Lab School, the private school in Hyde Park that his daughters attended, one of his leading black financial supporters and fellow parents repeatedly heard that anxiety. "A lot of friends of mine were saying, 'You tell that brother to be careful,' " the supporter recalled. Now that anxiety, accompanied by enormous pride, only increased.

In the meantime, the Republicans had still not come up with a candidate to replace Jack Ryan. Rather than rest on his lead against a phantom opponent, Obama embarked on a long-planned statewide campaign binge, hitting thirty counties and thirty-nine cities and towns. The *Sun-Times* printed one of his daily schedules:

8:30 A.M.: Champaign County rally, Urbana
10:05 A.M.: Douglas County rally, Tuscola

11:45 A.M.: Coles County rally, Mattoon
12:45 P.M.: Cumberland County rally, Neoga
2:40 P.M.: Jefferson County rally, Mount Vernon
3:55 P.M.: Wayne County rally, Fairfield
5 P.M.: Wabash County rally, Mount Carmel
5:45 P.M.: Lawrence County rally, Lawrenceville
6:30 P.M.: Richland County rally, Olney
8 P.M.: Marion County rally, Salem

The problem was that when he came home from Boston, Obama was exhilarated and exhausted. He knew, vaguely, that he and his family were going on an R.V. trip throughout the state, but he thought that there would be plenty of time to spend together—a kind of vacation with a little campaigning thrown in. When he actually checked his schedule and saw that it was a five-day jamboree of non-stop rallies, he called Jeremiah Posedel, his downstate director.

"This was a Friday night and the tour began that Saturday," Posedel recalled. "Barack called me at my house in Rock Island and I could tell he was pissed off. He said, 'What the hell are you trying to do to me? This schedule is out of control. This is a *death march*.' "

When Obama made a campaign stop downstate in Rock Island County a year earlier, Posedel had made calls to twenty-five counties, frantically trying to gather people for a "rally." Obama drove three hours to the event. Thirty people showed up. "In those days, if you talked to people on the phone and tried to get them interested in Barack Obama, they would say, 'Who is he?' '*What* is he?' which was a way of asking about his race. The only reason a few might come is because I worked for Lane Evans, a downstate Democratic congressman who had endorsed Barack early. But even then, they were probably still voting for Hynes. Barack would make a great impression, but a lot of people still said, 'I don't think he can win.' They wouldn't mention race but they used every other excuse in the book."

Now, on his five-day triumphal "death march," in towns where Posedel expected, at most, forty or fifty people at each stop, Obama was drawing hundreds, even thousands. Suddenly, he was working rope lines, shaking countless hands, and speaking in packed auditoriums with parents holding their children up on their shoulders. At each event, he performed well, remembering names, shaking hands, speaking with clarity and enthusiasm, but, back in the car, he barely talked to Posedel. Even at a birthday party that Posedel threw for Obama at his house in Rock Island, Obama was cool to him. Finally, on the last stop of the tour, Obama pulled

Posedel into an alley and said, "You did a great job. This trip was unbelievable. It was great." Part of the strategy of the trip was to forever inoculate Obama against charges that he was unfamiliar with, and never visited, downstate Illinois—a charge that had plagued Moseley Braun. In every regard, Obama now had to admit, the journey had been a success. Then he tapped Posedel in the gut with mock menace. "But don't ever fucking do this to me again!"

Obama recognized that he was now a political phenomenon. The first edition of *Dreams from My Father* was now an expensive item on eBay. Rachel Klayman, an editor at Crown, the publishing house that had rights to the book, immediately started thinking about a new edition.

Obama did his best to project equanimity about his new life. "This is all so, well, interesting. But it's all so ephemeral," he told David Mendell of the *Tribune* as they were driving between campaign stops in DeKalb and Marengo. "I don't know how this plays out, but there is definitely a novelty aspect to it all. The novelty wears off, and it can't stay white hot like it is right now."

His campaign staff was also taking on a more big-time national cast. Dan Shomon, who had been by Obama's side since his earliest days as a state senator, was now barely a presence on the campaign. Shomon's mother had just died of cancer and, he said, "I needed a break." As an adviser, his influence was greatly reduced. Shomon had been helpful to Obama since his first years as a state senator, but his experience was limited to Illinois. Gibbs, Cauley, and Axelrod were advisers of much broader experience. As Obama became an increasingly national figure, a handful of Chicago politicians and organizers who were essential to his career in the early days—his alderman, Toni Preckwinkle, for instance—came to resent him and feel that he had grown egotistical, heedlessly casting aside old allies when they were no longer useful to him and cozying up to wealthy patrons farther north in Chicago. "I think he is an arrogant, self-absorbed, ungrateful jerk," one old South Side ally said. "He walked away from his friends." Dan Shomon, however, if his feelings were hurt, kept his counsel and eventually turned his attention to making money as a lobbyist.

Finally, in early August, the Republican Party's central committee settled on a candidate: Alan Keyes. African-American, Catholic, and an official in the State Department and the United Nations bureaucracy during the Reagan Administration, Keyes, on paper, might have seemed an interesting challenge for Obama. He earned a doctorate at Harvard, studying with the political scientist Harvey Mansfield and writing a dissertation on Alexander Hamilton and constitutional theory. He was, briefly, the president of Alabama A&M University. His mentor was Jeane Kirkpatrick. The Republican Party leadership thought that perhaps Keyes might cut into Obama's strength among blacks and win voters downstate.

In reality, Keyes was a stranger to the state and a hopeless choice for the Republicans, a Hail Mary pass for the religious right. Born on Long Island, he had lived in many places in the United States and abroad. Illinois was not one of them. Keyes was the most blatant sort of carpetbagger, a vagabond Quixote of the conservative movement. In 1988 and 1992, he ran for the Senate in Maryland against two popular Democratic incumbents, Paul Sarbanes and Barbara Mikulski, respectively, and he lost both races by spectacular margins. In each, he espoused the ideology of the religious right—abortion was his singular issue—and his attacks on his opponents resembled those of a tent-revival preacher reviling the heathen. In 1996, he ran for President, putting on an outlandish performance; he showed up at one debate to which he was not invited and had to be detained by the police. In 2000, he challenged George W. Bush for the Republican nomination; he received fourteen per cent of the vote in Iowa and, in order to keep hammering away at the abortion issue, stayed in the race long past the point of being a laughingstock. Now Keyes, who opposed the Seventeenth Amendment, a product of the Progressive Era that provides for the direct election of U.S. senators, was going to get on a plane to Chicago and rent an apartment in the south suburbs and run—for the U.S. Senate. Strident moralism was again to be his entire candidacy. Within a few weeks he was telling the people of Illinois, "Jesus Christ would not vote for Barack Obama."

When Obama learned that his opponent would be Alan Keyes, he could not help but betray incredulous delight.

"Can you believe this shit?" he said to Jim Cauley.

"No, dude," Cauley replied. "You are the luckiest bastard in the world."

On a hot evening in mid-August, a rented Budget truck pulled up in front of an apartment building in the suburb of Calumet City, south of Chicago near the Indiana border. Two young campaign workers unloaded a box spring and a mattress and carried everything up to a two-room apartment on the second floor—Alan Keyes's first apartment in the state of Illinois. Keyes had chosen Calumet City, a victim of deindustrialization, after asking his hastily assembled staff for an appropriately hardworking place he could call home. It was an odd choice for an evangelical candidate. Originally known as West Hammond, the town was once a headquarters for Al Capone, a center for gambling, prostitution, and bootlegging. It became known as Sin City.

Keyes never shed his carpetbagger image. In his announcement speech, he had tried to overcome it by declaring, "I have lived in the land of Lincoln all my life." The media, to say nothing of the voters, remained unmoved by such finesse. One *Tribune* editorial said, "Mr. Keyes may have noticed a large body of water as he flew into O'Hare. That is called Lake Michigan."

Obama treated the contest with Keyes the way a boxer treats the final round of a fight against a wounded opponent who has a reputation for last-ditch bursts of distemper. He cut back on the number of debates and tried to steer clear of Keyes, somberly acknowledging their differences and engaging him only when absolutely necessary. Neither white suburbanites nor African-Americans showed much interest in Keyes and his constant attacks on abortion laws, welfare, and gay marriage. What was more, Keyes had no money to run a proper campaign. His rhetoric was too excessive, his odds too long, for him to draw serious donors. When Keyes denounced the daughter of the Vice-President, Mary Cheney, for being a lesbian, even the chairman of the state Republican Party, which had put Keyes forward in the first place, denounced him as "idiotic."

By early October, Obama was leading in the polls by a margin of forty-five per cent. He had large reserves of cash to spend on media—sufficient to run against a far more formidable candidate. He spent time out of state, campaigning for fellow Democrats in closer races. Keyes ran a symbolic race in which he was prepared to say almost anything, to inflict whatever damage he felt necessary, to bring attention to his issues.

In a series of debates in October, Keyes was usually even-tempered when the discussion was about Iraq, national security, foreign policy, or local issues. But at times, he would call Obama's policy positions "wicked and evil," Marxist, and socialist. Usually, Obama's strategy was to absorb the blow impassively and, when it came time to speak, answer in a way that, at least subtly, made it clear that, at best, Keyes was to the right of the Illinois mainstream and, at worst, a demagogic fool. In the second debate, a televised session held during the deciding game of the National League Championship Series between the Houston Astros and the St. Louis Cardinals, Keyes reiterated his attack on Obama as a candidate whom Jesus would never support. As he spread his arms far apart, Keyes said, "Christ is over here, Senator Obama is over there—the two don't look the same."

Obama did not wholly conceal his disgust. "That's why I have a pastor," he replied, speaking past Keyes and to the viewer. "That's why I have a Bible. That's why I have my own prayer. And I don't think any of you are particularly interested in having Mr. Keyes lecture you about your faith. What you're interested in is solving problems like jobs and health care and education. I'm not running to be the minister of Illinois. I'm running to be its United States senator."

Keyes would not accept the distinction and said that Obama was putting himself forward as a man of faith only in order to win votes. "At the hard points when that faith must be followed and explained to folks and stood up for and witnessed to," Keyes said, "he then pleads separation of church and state, something found nowhere in the Constitution, and certainly found nowhere in the Scripture as such."

Onstage, Obama tried to mask his feelings about Keyes, but David Axelrod, among others, noticed that these attacks really bothered Obama and, at times, put him on his heels. Keyes was a religious absolutist and Obama, who described his own faith with a sense of ambiguity and doubt, was clearly undone at times by his opponent's attacks. On one occasion, Obama poked Keyes in the chest when they started an impromptu debate at an Indian Independence Day parade; a camera crew caught the encounter and repeatedly showed Obama's irritated gesture in slow motion. This worried Axelrod. He wondered if Obama would be able to absorb the more serious attacks that would inevitably occur in a tougher, closer race. Did he have the stomach for it, the taste for combat—and a capacity for moving on? Keyes was nothing, Axelrod knew. If Obama was going to go further in his career, he would have to learn to fend off far uglier, more effective attacks than Alan Keyes, a marginal candidate, could manage. He needed to be tougher.

In late October, the editorial page of the *Tribune*, which leaned to the center-right, endorsed Obama. The paper noted elsewhere the incredible dearth across the country of blacks elected to statewide office, pointing to Mississippi, which had an African-American population of thirty-six per cent—"the largest in the nation, yet it has not elected a single black person to any statewide office since Reconstruction."

A few days later, Obama won another endorsement—or at least an implicit one—from the most powerful political institution of all: Richard M. Daley. During the primary campaign, Daley, as usual, did not make an endorsement, but everyone, Obama included, assumed that Dan Hynes, with all his machine connections, had the Mayor's blessing. According to Bill Daley, Obama wrote the Mayor a letter during the Senate primary campaign, saying, "You're with Hynes, I understand that. I just hope that after the primary you can help me if I was to win this thing." Bill Daley, who recounted the letter for James L. Merriner of *Chicago* magazine, said that Obama's decision to send the note to the Mayor "was a very smart thing to do. I think he did that with a lot of people."

Throughout his political life in Chicago and the state of Illinois, Obama had gone to great lengths to reconcile his desire to be an independent Democrat with the need to maintain friendly relations with City Hall. Obama's détente with City Hall, his ability to maintain his Hyde Park credentials and still forge a useful bond with Emil Jones—"one of the hackiest of the hacks," according to the strategist Don Rose—was, in Chicago, a sign of both skill and ambition. Obama was not alone in this. Among others, Abner Mikva, Richard Newhouse, Harold Washington, Barbara Flynn Currie, Carol Moseley Braun, and Paul Simon were also independents who had made their arrangements with the Daleys in order to achieve their political goals. In later years, Obama said little about the patronage scandals that arose in Daley's administration and, in 2006, he declined to endorse a reformer (and David Axelrod's business partner), Forrest Claypool, over a proven hack, Todd Stroger, an African-American, who was loyal to Daley, for Cook County Board president. What Obama understood from the start of his political career was that a purist, an anti-machine politician like the Hyde Park alderman Leon Despres, might gain a stronger foothold on the path to Heaven but would never advance far on the path to power. Obama could borrow from the cadences of King, he could advertise his genuine admiration for the civil-rights movement, but he was a politician, not the leader of a movement. And to be a successful politician you had to make a few compromises along the way. Obama rarely failed to make them.

Daley's motives for coming around to Obama were relatively simple: Obama was a Democrat, first of all, and Daley was not about to waver from his party now that the primary was over. In addition, with Obama safely ensconced in Washington, Daley would not have to worry about a strong challenge from an African-American politician who once aspired to be mayor and now happened to be the hottest political celebrity in the country. "There were very few people on the Fifth Floor"—Daley's offices at City Hall—"who had given much thought to Barack until then," Pete Giangreco said. "But the modern Daley world revolved around racial divisions, which are as large and nasty in Chicago as anywhere in the country. It was always No. 1 on their agenda to make nice with black politicians in a way the Old Man"—Richard J. Daley—"never really did." As a Hyde Park independent, Obama had not been one of those state senators who consistently did Daley's bidding in Springfield, but now their interests converged. Obama going to the U.S. Senate was good for both of them.

With a full media contingent, Obama and Richard M. Daley met for lunch at Manny's, a deli on the near North Side. They ate matzo-ball soup and corned-beef sandwiches. They shook hands with everyone in the place and talked long after the television crews had packed up and gone off to the next story.

As the campaign headed into its final weeks, Obama grew accustomed both to the beat reporters who were following him around Illinois and on his travels out of the state, and to the growing blandishments and attentions of the national media. In many ways, the Illinois Senate race was a rehearsal for things to come and these reporters now focused less on the contest with Keyes than on Obama's biography, his rhetoric, his temperament, his staff, and his capacity for organization and fund-raising. The Illinois campaign also raised some of the same complicated discussions about Obama and race that came to the center of the American political debate a few years later. Of the many articles written in print or online, no piece rehearsed those themes more thoroughly during the Illinois campaign than a three-thousand-word article in the Chicago *Tribune*'s Sunday magazine called "The Skin Game: Do White Voters Like Barack Obama Because 'He's Not Really Black'?"

The author of the article was Don Terry, a forty-seven-year-old Chicagoan who had lived in Hyde Park nearly all his life. The parallels with Obama's background gave Terry's piece its resonance. Don Terry's father was black, his mother white; his parents had moved from Evanston to Hyde Park because it was integrated. Like Obama, Terry had a mother who taught him to value and explore his racial identity. She told him that Martin Luther King, Jr., was the "greatest man in the world" and that Paul Robeson "was an American hero with the singing voice of God."

Terry published his article on October 24th when Obama was sure of victory:

At the time, I was on assignment and speeding to a federal prison camp in a green Mercedes. The color of money. The white woman behind the wheel made sure I knew the car was 10 years old. She didn't have to be defensive with me. I know you can't judge a progressive by the car she drives. Besides, I never bite the hand that gives me a lift.

"I love Barack," said the woman, a middle-aged filmmaker, as we zipped past a campaign-style yard sign shoved into the dirt on the edge of a cornfield. The sign proclaimed, "Guns Save Lives."

"He's smart. He's handsome. He's charismatic," she continued. "He has the potential to be our first minority president."

"I hear what you're saying," I said. "But tell me. Why don't you say he has the potential to be our first black president?"

She seemed taken aback by my question and took a few moments to answer. "I guess it's because I don't think of him as black," she said.

Terry was disturbed by this notion—one that had been thoroughly rehearsed by Bobby Rush, Donne Trotter, and many others. He was equally disturbed by an article in *The New Republic* that said that Obama was "an African-American candidate who was not stereotypically African-American." Terry knew what these people were getting at, however awkwardly. Obama was the son of an African and a white secular Protestant; unlike Terry, he had not grown up around other black people. And yet what was implicit is that if the woman *had* thought of Obama as black, she would not have felt the same way.

Terry visited Obama at his campaign headquarters on South Michigan Avenue. The office was decorated with framed posters of Abraham Lincoln and of Muhammad Ali, in Lewiston, Maine, in 1965, standing over the prostrate body of Sonny Liston. On his desk was a copy of a book called *One Drop of Blood: The American Misadventure of Race*, by Scott L. Malcomson, a journalist who had caught Obama's eye with an op-ed in the New York *Times* entitled "An Appeal Beyond Race" about his speech at the Convention in Boston. Malcomson, like Terry, was among a growing number of journalists who were trying to make sense of this young politician and how he seemed the embodiment of a new generation.

Obama put his feet up on the desk. He said that as a young man he had written an autobiography of his struggle with the complexities of his racial identity, but now, as a politician, he protested that it was the pundits, and not voters, who were focusing on his identity as an explanation for his appeal. "After the primary, the pundits were trying to figure out my ability to win in black as well as white neighborhoods," he told Terry. "It was easy to attach to the fact that I'm of mixed race. To some degree, my candidacy has been a convenient focal point to try to sort out issues" of ethnicity, assimilation, and diversity. He said that his capacity to succeed in both black and white areas was "not a consequence of my DNA. . . . It's a consequence of my experience." Obama pointed out that Bill Clinton did well among black voters, and "as far as I know, he doesn't have any black blood in him."

Terry concluded his article by saying that he had recently turned on the television "hoping for a few minutes of distraction from the American Dilemma." He watched "Guess Who's Coming to Dinner," and it was clear to him that Sidney Poitier's character, Dr. John Wade Prentice, "a super-qualified, super-handsome, super-dashing doctor living in Hawaii," had a "lot in common" with Barack Obama. Like Dr. Prentice, who had to be extraordinary to win the hand of a "vacant" white woman, Terry wrote, Obama had to be no less extraordinary to confront the challenge of persistent racism and win higher office. "Race," Terry wrote, "still matters."

Terry's article did not engage all the questions that eventually surrounded Obama, but he succeeded in setting forth one of the most essential aspects of his unique appeal: that much of the excitement about him had to do with the beholder, with the anxieties, complexes, and hopes of the American voter. "He's a Rorschach test," Terry wrote of Obama. "What you see is what you want to see."

The urge to see something large in Obama was obvious: he had come along at just the point when American confidence was at a low ebb. The Iraqi insurgency was growing and casualties were rising. In May, 2004, CBS and *The New Yorker* revealed that Iraqi prisoners at Abu Ghraib prison had been tortured and sexually humiliated by American soldiers. The emblem of the scandal was a sickening photograph of one prisoner outfitted in a peaked hood and dark caftan and made to stand on a box with electric wires attached to his hands. For millions of people, George Bush was a national and personal embarrassment—an incurious, rash, flippant, pampered, dishonest leader. In Boston, Obama had seemed almost entirely the opposite: intelligent, idealistic, and engaged. Part of his glamour, at least for those inclined to read the Rorschach test this way, had to do with his race, his youth, his African name. As he presented his story—a narrative that said as much about his multicultural family as it did about Harvard or his apprenticeship in Chicago politics—he represented himself as the best of a post-civil-rights America, a fresh start. If his speeches were occasionally salted with platitudes, if his experience and his accomplishments were still slight, well, for so many Americans despairing of George Bush, that was O.K. They studied the Rorschach test that was Obama and they saw the outlines of promise. At the start of the campaign, Obama had won over crowds big enough to fit in Paul Gaynor's backyard in Evanston; now, even before he had faced the electorate of Illinois, he was reaching the country. The odd thing was that Barack Obama seemed to take it all in stride.

"When he won the Illinois primary for Senate, he demonstrated the breadth of his appeal—white folks, black folks everywhere," his law partner Judd Miner said. "He won every suburban district in the primary. He won overwhelmingly in those white districts. And then he carried that forward to the campaign itself for the seat itself. He just gained more and more confidence. People felt he was so different and intelligent. He never thought there was something he couldn't do."

On Halloween night, Alan Keyes held a last get-out-the-vote rally at the Spirit of God Fellowship Church in the Chicago suburb of South Holland, delivering a long disquisition on the need for religious virtue in politics. As he had throughout the race, Keyes denounced the media for trying "to portray me as some sort of inflammatory person." He spoke of going to Washington, but it was clear that he had come with the thought not of winning but of gaining a new pulpit.

On November 2, 2004, Obama voted just after seven in the morning at the Catholic Theological Union in Hyde Park. As the cameras followed him and his family, Michelle Obama said, "Don't you think he's been on TV enough?"

"I'm waiting for you to be at the top of the ticket!" one resident called out.

By early evening, the Chicago *Defender* started distributing a special edition with the headline, "Mr. Obama Goes to Washington." The Obamas went to a suite at the Hyatt Regency where they watched television and waited for the first vote tallies. A crowd of some two thousand gathered in the ballroom downstairs.

Not long afterward, it was clear that Obama had won the Illinois Senate race in a landslide, defeating Keyes by forty-three points, seventy per cent to twenty-seven. Obama was so far ahead in the closing weeks of the campaign that he'd started giving away money to other Democratic candidates and the Democratic Senatorial Campaign Committee. He sanctioned many of his volunteers to go and work on other races. Despite the fact that Keyes had said that it would be a "mortal sin" to vote for a candidate who supported abortion rights, Obama won three-quarters of the Catholic vote. He also won ninety-one per cent of the black vote.

Sometime after nine on Election Night, Obama went down to the hotel ballroom to greet his supporters, who were chanting the now familiar phrase: "Yes, we can! Yes, we can!"

"Thank you, Illinois! I don't know about you, but I'm still fired up!" he said. "Six hundred and fifty-six days ago, I announced in a room a little smaller than this . . . for the United States Senate. At the time, people were respectful but nevertheless skeptical. They knew the work that we had done . . . but they felt that in a nation as divided as ours there was no possibility that someone who looked like me could ever aspire to the United States Senate. They felt that in a fearful nation, someone named Barack Obama could never hope to win an election. And yet, here we stand!"

Part Four

If you don't have enough self-awareness to see the element of megalomania involved in thinking you should be President, then you probably shouldn't be President. There's a slight madness to thinking you should be the leader of the free world.

—Barack Obama, November 1, 2007, ABC News

Are you going to try to be President? Shouldn't you be Vice-President first?

—Malia Obama to her father at his swearing-in as U.S. Senator

Chapter Twelve

A Slight Madness

After accepting the last words of congratulations for his landslide election to the Senate, Barack Obama slept for two hours. Then he woke to answer questions about his prospects for running for President of the United States. This was now the velocity of his life.

Obama had agreed to a morning-after meeting with reporters at his campaign headquarters downtown—a tradition of winning politicians and fighters. The questions dwelled little on the campaign, for all its low comedy. Instead the reporters focused almost solely on one subject: Was he going to run for the White House in 2008? Obama had not spent five minutes in an office higher than that of an Illinois state legislator and he had never really been in a close competitive election, yet this was not an entirely disingenuous line of inquiry. At the Convention and afterward, Obama had hardly shunned media attention—his advisers scheduled as many national broadcast and print interviews as he could handle. In all those interviews, he was described as a new "hope" or "face" for the Democrats. When he was asked about running for President, Obama shyly dismissed it as absurd conjecture. But his novelty and glamour resided partly in the fact that he was asked the question in the first place.

Obama knew the rules. Even to hint at an interest in the White House would be unseemly. Election Night, 2004, had been misery for the Democrats. George W. Bush won back the White House. John Kerry's inability to rebuff the smears on his character and his record—particularly the attacks on his war record by the well-funded group called the Swift Boat Veterans for Truth—had cost him dearly. The Democrats also lost four seats in the Senate, including their leader, Tom Daschle, of South Dakota.

Obama had many qualities; he would have to work at modesty. Come January, 2005, when he was to be sworn in, he would be a junior senator in the minority party and, as he knew from his backbench years in Spring-field, there were strict limits to such a position. At least on this November morning, Obama needed to appear the awed and eager apprentice of the Senate. The hype about the Presidency needed to be "corrected," as he put it. Each time the question was asked, with slight variation, Obama's level of irritation rose:

"I am not running for President. I am not running for President in four years. I am not running for President in 2008."

"Come on, guys, the only reason I am being definitive is because until I am definitive, you will keep asking me this question. It's a silly question."

And then: "Guys, I am a state senator. I was elected *yesterday.* I have never set foot in the U.S. Senate. I have never worked in Washington. And the notion that somehow I am going to start running for higher office, it just doesn't make sense. My understanding is that I will be ranked ninety-ninth in seniority. I am going to be spending the first several months of my career in the U.S. Senate looking for the washroom and trying to figure out how the phones work."

Obama got especially irritated with Lynn Sweet, a persistent veteran reporter for the *Sun-Times.* "Lynn, you're dictating the answers as well as the questions," Obama said wearily. "Let me move on to the next ques-tion." Later, he guided her out to the hall to admonish her further.

Obama and his aides said that he was tired after campaigning. And, of course, it was true: he'd been at it, non-stop, for well over a year. In order to be a decent legislator, he would have to learn to parcel out his time and be discriminating with the national press and the constant invitations to give speeches around the country. Michelle, Malia, and Sasha were going to remain in Chicago; Obama rented a one-bedroom apartment near the Capitol in a high-rise near Georgetown Law School and shuttled back home for the weekends to see his family and meet with constituents. One of Moseley Braun's many mistakes as a senator was to spend too much time in Washington and grow remote from her constituents; Obama was determined not to do the same. In his first year, he held thirty-nine town meetings in Illinois.

At the Convention, Joe Biden had advised Obama to "go slow" in Washington. Obama knew that he had at least to *seem* unhurried. He would have to balance his tasks as the sole African-American senator and as a newborn political celebrity with his straightforward role as an institu-tional plebe. He had to avoid at least the appearance of placing national celebrity before sincere rookie effort.

"It's going to be important for me to say no, when it just comes to appearances, wanting to be the keynote speaker at every N.A.A.C.P. Freedom Fund dinner across the country," he told one reporter. "You know, those are the kinds of things where I'm just going to have to explain to people that there are limits to my time. I've got a family that I've got to look after. But when it comes to speaking out on issues that are of particular importance to the African-American community, I don't think that's a conflict with my role as an effective legislator for the people of Illinois."

After the press conference, Obama went to Union Station to be filmed thanking voters. But there, too, he spent time answering the same question again and again. David Axelrod put out the deflecting message, even if the reporters were not willing to accept it. "I don't think we're trying to dampen expectations, we're trying to douse them," he said. "We're trying to pour as much water as we can find on them. We don't want even a smoldering ember when it comes to this."

But, despite his modest words about wanting to be a good apprentice, to learn the craft of legislation and the customs of the institution, Obama was acutely aware that, as a rookie, his most powerful leverage in the Senate would be the force of his celebrity and his importance as the only African-American in the chamber. He did not have to wait to go slowly up the seniority ladder to gain a public platform. In the last week of November, Obama went to New York for a publicity tour to help plump sales for the paperback re-issue of *Dreams from My Father*—a publishing phenomenon, ignited by the Boston speech, that lasted for years; the book helped to spread word of his story and forever eased his family's financial concerns.

The tour, of course, was a strange way to correct the hype and put an end to outsized expectations. In a matter of hours, Obama was everywhere, and the questioning was not exactly rigorous. On ABC's daytime show "The View," Meredith Vieira predicted that Obama would be a "huge force in this country for the better"; not to be outdone, Barbara Walters put Obama in the same sentence with Nelson Mandela.

"I didn't spend twenty-seven years in prison," Obama solemnly reminded Walters.

Obama agreed to interviews with Charlie Rose, Wendy Williams, Leonard Lopate, Don Imus, and David Letterman. On Letterman's show, Obama seemed ready for admission to the Friar's Club:

LETTERMAN: The thing about your name, it's easy to pronounce and it's cool.
OBAMA: Well, that's what I think, that's what I think. You know, there were some advisers who told me to change my name.
LETTERMAN: Really?

OBAMA: Yeah, and somebody suggested "Cat Stevens," for example. . . .

LETTERMAN: Now, was there a guy running for Senate, maybe an incumbent, maybe not, I think a Republican, and he had a problem because he and his wife would go to strip clubs and have sex.

OBAMA: Well, that was—

LETTERMAN: Did I dream that? Does any of this ring a bell?

OBAMA: There were some issues, some allegations.

LETTERMAN: (laughs) Yeah.

OBAMA: But we didn't touch that stuff.

LETTERMAN: I see.

OBAMA: We took the high road, and—

LETTERMAN: Now is this who you were running against, or he dropped out, right?

OBAMA: Yeah, he dropped out—yeah, the Republicans, you know, they seem to have a lot of fun given all their moral values stuff. They enjoy themselves.

LETTERMAN: It sounded like fun to me. . . . Have you met the President? You must know the President?

OBAMA: Well, you know, he called me. He was very gracious. After the election, he gave me a call and we both agreed that we'd married up, and then he invited me over to the White House and we had breakfast with Dick Cheney and Karl Rove, and it was a real fun time.

LETTERMAN: Yeah, it sounds like Mardi Gras.

A couple of weeks later, Obama was in Washington. He had not yet been sworn in, but he was a headline speaker at the Gridiron Club. Adopting a tone of flagrant self-deprecation, he admitted that he was now so overexposed that he made "Paris Hilton look like a recluse."

"I figure there's nowhere to go from here but down," he said. "So, tonight, I'm announcing my retirement from the United States Senate."

There is no underestimating the importance of *Dreams from My Father* in the political rise of Barack Obama. After the 2004 Democratic Convention, his increased prominence had caught the attention of Rachel Klayman, an editor at Crown. She was inspired to re-issue the paperback version of *Dreams* after she read an article on Salon.com, by Obama's Chicago friend the novelist Scott Turow, touting him as "the new face of the Democratic Party." Obama was pleased by the sales of the re-issue, but he now realized that if his agent, Jane Dystel, had acted more quickly to regain the rights and spark an auction, he could have made even more money. He decided to end his business relationship with Dystel and to have Robert Barnett, an attorney at Williams & Connolly, in Washington, handle his literary affairs. Obama had met Barnett at the Democratic Convention and not long afterward Barnett prepared a debate-prep memorandum for Obama. Not only was Barnett far better connected than Dystel—he has negotiated book deals for everyone in the Washington establishment, from Bob Woodward and Alan Greenspan to the Clintons—he was also less expensive. As an attorney, Barnett charged up to a thousand dollars an hour—a hefty fee—but, in the end, far less than the normal fifteen-per-cent fee of an agent. Woodward once called him the "last bargain in Washington."

Two weeks before Obama was sworn in as a senator, Crown, a division of Random House, announced that he had signed a contract to write three books; the deal was for just under two million dollars. The press release was a model of diplomacy, saying that the agreement had been "initiated" by Dystel but "negotiated and concluded" by Barnett. Since that time, Dystel has avoided talking to reporters.

"Obama showed a kind of dry-eyed practicality by getting rid of Jane to get Barnett," Peter Osnos, the former head of Times Books, which had originally published *Dreams from My Father,* said. "I have to admit that even though it is common practice in Washington now, it startled me that practically the first thing that Obama did after being elected to the Senate was to sign a contract for two million dollars with Crown." Obama's contract called first for *The Audacity of Hope,* an account of his first year in the Senate and his thoughts on various issues, from religion and race to foreign policy. There was to be an illustrated children's book (with the proceeds going to charity), and the third book would be determined later. Unlike members of the House of Representatives, who are not permitted to accept book advances, only royalties, senators have no such restrictions, and, with the contract, Obama, like Hillary Clinton, who also signed a huge book deal before taking her Senate seat, transformed his financial life. It did not go unnoticed that *The Audacity of Hope* was to be published in the fall of 2006, a tight deadline, and just in time to ignite a round of publicity and further speculation about a run for the White House.

Although Peter Osnos counted himself an admirer of Obama, he later wrote an article for the Century Foundation in which he said of Obama's book deal, "I just wish that this virtuous symbol of America's aspirational class did not move quite so smoothly into a system of riches as a reward for service, especially before it has actually been rendered."

But even if Osnos was right and Obama's decision to sign a three-book deal was a hasty move to capitalize on his political celebrity and provide a tool for the next Presidential campaign, that celebrity was not something that he could control. Not long after the Convention speech, Eli Attie, one of the writers and producers for NBC's hit television series "The West Wing," was starting to flesh out a character to succeed President Josiah (Jed) Bartlet, the wry and avuncular head of state played by Martin Sheen. Although the series, the creation of Aaron Sorkin, first went on the air during the Clinton years, many Democrats watched it during the Bush Presidency as a kind of alternative-reality show. Bartlet, a Nobel Prize–winning economist and a devout Catholic with liberal values, was, for that audience, everything that Bush was not: mature, curious, assured, skeptical, and confident of his own intelligence.

Attie wanted the new character to be no less a liberal ideal, but this time he wanted someone of the "post-Oprah" generation, as he put it, someone black or Hispanic, but not an older figure closely tied to the rhetoric of the civil-rights movement and identity politics. Attie had serious political experience. He had written speeches for the former New York mayor David Dinkins, and had been an aide to Richard Gephardt in Congress, and to Bill Clinton in the White House; he was Al Gore's chief speechwriter through the 2000 Presidential campaign. When he watched Obama, he thought he saw the model for his character, Matt Santos: a young urban progressive with dignified bearing, a "bring-the-electorate-along-slowly candidate" who was neither white nor focused on race. "Faced with the task of fleshing out a fictional first-ever and actually viable Latino candidate for President, I had no precedent, no way to research a real-life version," he said.

Attie called David Axelrod, whom he had known from Democratic political campaigns, and asked him dozens of questions about Obama's history and psychology. Axelrod talked with Attie about the change in Obama's life after the Convention speech, the crowds that surrounded him everywhere he went, the incredible expectations people had for him even before he went to Washington. Santos, like Obama, wasn't an ortho-dox liberal, of the Edward Kennedy mold; instead, Attie came to see San-tos the way Axelrod saw Obama and the way Obama saw himself—as both a progressive and a cautious coalition-builder.

"Those early conversations with David turned out to play a huge role in my shaping of the character," Attie said. "One of the main things was Obama's attitude about race, his almost militant refusal to be defined by it, which became the basis for an episode I wrote called 'Opposition Research,' in which Santos said he didn't want to run as the 'brown candidate,' even though that's where all his support and fund-raising potential were. Also, there was Obama's rock-star charisma, the way people were drawn to him and were pulling the lever for him even though they didn't exactly think he'd win."

In the final two seasons of "The West Wing," which aired in 2005 and 2006, Matt Santos, played by Jimmy Smits, runs for President against a Republican from California named Arnold Vinick, played by Alan Alda. Press-friendly, winningly acerbic, and unusually independent, Vinick is suspicious of the religious right and positions himself to the left of his Party on a variety of issues. At least in his ideological flexibility and outspokenness, Vinick resembled John McCain—particularly the self-fashioned maverick who ran in 2000 against George W. Bush for the Republican nomination.

A couple of years later, those seasons of "The West Wing" proved so eerily prescient that David Axelrod sent Attie an e-mail from the campaign trail reading, "We're living your scripts!" And yet, while he was making those shows, Attie thought there was "no way" that the real character, Barack Obama, could go much farther than the Senate. "I just didn't think he could be the President of the United States in my lifetime, given the color of his skin," he said.

Just before Obama's Senate swearing-in ceremony, in January, 2005, *Newsweek* put him on the cover as the future of his Party and a unifying figure for the country. Printed across the photograph of Obama was the headline "Seeing Purple," a play on his rhetoric of red-blue convergence in Boston.

Obama was thrilled to learn that one of the previous occupants of his assigned desk on the Senate floor had been Robert Kennedy. As the junior senator from New York, Kennedy occupied the seat for just over three years, before entering the 1968 race for the Presidency.

Obama could not have been more junior in the Senate, and he understood that he needed a first-rate chief of staff who knew the people and ways of the Senate thoroughly. His old law school friend Cassandra Butts, who had worked as policy director for Gephardt's 2004 Presidential campaign, arranged a meeting for him with Pete Rouse, a thirty-year veteran of Capitol Hill. Rouse, a stout, phlegmatic workaholic in his late fifties, had been thinking about retiring on his government pension; he had lately been chief of staff for the Senate Majority Leader, Tom Daschle, who had lost his seat by a few thousand votes. Rouse had been so influential in the Senate that he was known around the Capitol as "the hundred-and-first senator." He met with Obama at the Mandarin Oriental Hotel, where Obama had been attending an orientation session for the freshmen of the 109th Congress, and, after the two had talked for an hour or so about the process of getting started in Washington, Obama asked him if he would be interested in being his chief of staff. Like anyone involved in politics, Rouse had heard a lot about Obama, but he hadn't focused on him—he hadn't even seen the Convention speech. But, after some long thought over the next couple of weeks, he agreed to Obama's offer. Rouse, in turn, helped staff Obama with refugees from Daschle's office.

"I know what I'm good at, I know what I'm not good at," Obama told Rouse at the beginning. "I know what I know and I know what I don't know. I can give a good speech."

"Oh yes, you can," Rouse said. "We all agree with that."

"I know policy," Obama continued. "I know retail politics in Illinois. I don't have any idea what it's like to come into the Senate and get established in the Senate. I want to get established and work with my colleagues and develop a reputation as a good senator, and we'll see what happens." This was precisely the approach that Hillary Clinton had taken when, in 2000, she won her seat in New York: undercut the image of a celebrity senator with hard work and deference to colleagues and the institution. The attention would come without asking for it.

Obama asked Rouse to help him assemble a staff that was made up of both Washington insiders and independent experts who could bring some intellectual heft to the office. Obama had also hired Robert Gibbs, who had long experience as a press aide on Capitol Hill and became Obama's protector during the campaign. He told his staff that he would rather have "some extraordinary people for a shorter time than ordinary people for a long time." In April, Obama met at a Capitol Hill steakhouse with Samantha Power, a journalist who, in 2002, published *A Problem from Hell*, a study of modern genocide and American foreign policy that had won the Pulitzer Prize. Obama did not strike Power as a liberal interventionist or a Kissingerian realist or any other kind of ideological "ist" except maybe a "consequentialist." In foreign policy, Obama said, he was for what worked. He hired Power as a foreign-policy fellow in his office.

Diversity was also a priority for Obama. More than half the staff of about sixty were people of color, including ten of the top fifteen salaried aides. Obama told Rouse that while he was perfectly aware that he was the only African-American in the Senate, a position that bore special responsibilities, "I don't want to be a black senator. I want to be a senator who happens to be black."

Rouse took on the assignment sensing that Obama could have a big future but certain that a national race was not imminent. He planned to help Obama set a direction for himself, and then, he recalled thinking, "We'll see what happens. I'll be in my rocking chair when he runs [for President] in 2016 or whatever." With Gibbs and Axelrod, Rouse drafted a document called "The Strategic Plan." The plan was about mastering the craft, procedures, and courtesies of the Senate; it was about building relationships with colleagues, including Republicans, and demonstrating an emphasis on Illinois.

In his first year, Obama carried out the plan with single-minded determination. He traveled extensively among his constituents in Illinois and even had his office keep in close contact with African-American leaders to his left. "He was worried that they would attack him on WVON," Dan Shomon, who stayed on Obama's payroll until 2006, said. "All that stopped when everyone fell into line when he ran for President."

In Washington, Obama worked on legislation that had particular impact on the state, including bills on highway construction, alternative energy, and ethanol. It was more important, his advisers felt, for him to work quietly to gain the confidence of his colleagues and desirable committee posts than to step forward and speak out on national issues like the war on Iraq.

As Rouse had predicted, the glitz took care of itself. Oprah Winfrey declared him "more than a politician. He's the real deal." *Vanity Fair* published a two-page spread on Obama, a rarity for any senator, much less a rookie. The magazine *Savoy* had a cover feature on Obama with the headline "Camelot Rising." At times, Obama's celebrity definitely had an erotic edge to it: the character Grace on the NBC sitcom "Will & Grace" dreamed that she was in the shower with the new senator from Illinois—and he was "Baracking my world!"

Obama did not ignore the attention, but he made a point of emphasizing his freshman learning and rituals. One of the first books that he read after his election was *Master of the Senate*, the third installment in Robert Caro's multivolume biography of Lyndon Johnson. (He didn't want to be seen reading the book during the campaign; now he made a point of mentioning it.) The book, in addition to covering Johnson's career in the Senate in bountiful, dramatic detail, opens with a long history of the institution and then an intricate set piece on Johnson's mentor, Richard Russell of Georgia. Russell served in the Senate from 1933 until 1971, when he died, and was the dominant figure in the conservative Southern faction that controlled the Senate until the rise of the civil-rights movement and the Kennedy assassination. Russell had supported Roosevelt's New Deal legislation but he was also an unapologetic proponent of Jim Crow. A virtuoso of Senate procedure and cloakroom persuasion, he blocked civil-rights legislation by whatever means available, including the repeated use of the filibuster. Nevertheless, Obama told Jeff Zeleny, the *Tribune* reporter who chronicled his career on the Hill most closely, that he was especially taken with Caro's passages about Russell's years in the Senate. Much of Obama's self-confidence resided in his belief that he could walk into any room, with any sort of people, and forge a relationship and even persuade those people of the rightness of his positions. Jim Cauley, Obama's Senate campaign manager, said he thought Obama believed that he could win over a room of skinheads. "All of us are a mixture of noble and ignoble impulses, and I guess that's part of what I mean when I say I don't go into meetings with people presuming bad faith," Obama has said. Now he seemed to think that he would have had a fighting chance with Russell: "Had I been around at all in the early sixties and had the opportunity to meet with Richard Russell, it would have been fascinating to talk to somebody like that. Even if you understood that this enormous talent would prevent me from ever being sworn in to the Senate."

When Obama paid a visit to the Senate elder Robert Byrd, of West Virginia, who as a young man had been a member of the Ku Klux Klan, he listened sympathetically as the old man described the sins of his youth as "the cross around my neck." It was the Rorschach effect all over again: Byrd saw in Obama a welcoming, forgiving face. And Obama, who was a gifted reader of other people, replied soothingly to Byrd, "If we were supposed to be perfect, we'd all be in trouble, so we rely on God's mercy and grace to get us through."

Obama knew that if he made enough of these respectful visits, if he made enough gestures of modesty and obeisance to the institution, he could go a long way toward forming alliances and ease any jealousies. Obama tried to make these conspicuous shows of humility and the transcendence of political history a hallmark of his way of doing business. He did not hesitate to advertise them.

Meanwhile, the true voice of sustained humility in Obama's life was his wife, who was back home in Chicago. Michelle Obama regarded the unending clamor and sycophancy that now attended her husband with a bracingly astringent bemusement. At the swearing-in ceremony, she observed all the commotion and said, "Maybe one day he will do something to warrant all this attention."

In his three years as an active senator, Obama proved a reliable Democrat, voting with his Party more than ninety-five per cent of the time; at one point, he even earned the rating of "most liberal" from relatively uncontentious arbiters like *The National Journal*. And yet he sought, above all, to emphasize his flexibility and pragmatism. "Over the next six years, there will be occasions where people will be surprised by my positions," he told Zeleny. "I won't be easy to categorize as many people expect."

Obama voted against Bush's nominee for Attorney General, Alberto Gonzales, but he supported Bush's second-term nomination for Secretary of State, Condoleezza Rice, offering the rationalization that despite her unquestioning involvement in the planning of the Iraq war, a war that he had judged "a dumb war," Rice was a committed and intelligent diplomat and the President was not likely to nominate someone less conservative if she was rejected. He did not vote to punish. He also voted against a defense appropriations bill that would have included a firm date for the withdrawal of troops from Iraq. Despite lobbying by John Kerry, Obama supported the White House on legislation capping payoffs in class-action lawsuits. He voted for bills strengthening environmental protection and free trade. He voted consistently for abortion rights.

Obama had wanted an appointment to the Commerce Committee, in order to be able to get some pork for his constituents in Illinois. He had hoped that his campaigning for Democratic candidates in the 2004 elections—which he had been able to do because his own race was not in doubt—would be enough to gain him the appointment. The Party leadership placed him instead on the committees for Environment and Public Works, Veterans Affairs, and Foreign Relations. At committee sessions, Obama, as the most junior senator, was eighteenth in line to ask questions; the committee room would often be all but empty when his turn at the microphone came. During Rice's confirmation hearings in the Foreign Relations Committee, Obama grew increasingly bored during one of Joe Biden's bloviations. Finally, Obama leaned back in his chair and handed one of his aides a note. The aide was excited to receive his first serious communication from the Senator. The note read, "Shoot. Me. Now."

Obama's closest friend in the Senate was his Illinois colleague, Richard Durbin. For Obama, Durbin was a link to the glory days of Illinois liberalism. When Durbin was an undergraduate at Georgetown, he'd served as an intern in the office of Paul Douglas; as a young lawyer, he was counsel to Paul Simon when he was lieutenant governor. Durbin was elected to the House in 1982 and to the Senate in 1996; for Obama, he was a teacher unthreatened by the younger man's glossy public image and boundless prospects.

Richard Lugar of Indiana, a Republican who was the longtime chairman of the Foreign Relations Committee and an advocate of tighter control of nuclear- and conventional-weapons stockpiles, also tutored Obama. Lugar had worked with Sam Nunn, of Georgia, on the Cooperative Threat Reduction Program to secure weapons stockpiles across the former Soviet Union. Obama had made a name for himself by opposing the invasion of Iraq, but there was not much he could do on the Foreign Relations Committee about Iraq. He thought he could make a concrete impact, with Lugar's help, by becoming an active voice on proliferation issues.

In August, 2005, as a member of a congressional delegation that also included Lugar, Obama went to Russia, Ukraine, and Azerbaijan to meet with officials and inspect various weapons-storage facilities. He had traveled fairly widely in Asia, Africa, and Europe, but this was his first trip to the former Soviet Union. The folkways of political missions to Moscow were alien to him. Faced with the prospect of mutual, and repeated, toasts, Obama asked to have his shot glass filled with water instead of vodka. Obama experienced what Lugar had many times before: rides in rickety buses to secret weapons sites; the dismantling of aging rockets; interminable briefings from officials telling partial truths. In Kiev, Obama went with Lugar to a dilapidated laboratory that had been used in the old Soviet biological weapons program. "So we enter into the building," Obama recalled for an audience at the Council on Foreign Relations in Washington a few weeks after the trip. "There are no discernible fences or security systems. And once we are inside, some sort of ramshackle building, there were open windows, maybe a few padlocks that many of us might use to secure our own luggage. Our guide, a young woman, takes us right up to what looked like a mini-refrigerator. And inside the refrigerator there were rows upon rows of test tubes. She picked them up, and she's clanking them around, and we listened to the translator explain what she was saying. Some of the tubes, he said, were filled with anthrax and others with plague. And you know, I'm pretty close and I start sort of backing off a little bit. And I turn around . . . and say, 'Hey, where's Lugar? Doesn't he want to see this?' And I turn around and he's way in the back of the room, about fifteen feet away. And he looked at me and said, 'Been there, done that.' "

Lugar had made countless such trips, but, for Obama, it was a revelation. He had studied arms-control issues at Columbia; now it stunned him to see the weaponry up close. "When you are there you get a sense of the totality of the nuclear program and the stockpiles of conventional arms," Mark Lippert, Obama's foreign-policy adviser, said. "It made an incredible impact on him to see the industrial complex behind it all. When we were in Ukraine, we went to a factory where they were disassembling conventional weapons. There were just piles and piles of shells. They told us that, working at the rate they were working, it would take eighty years to disassemble them all. At one chem-bio plant, we saw a freezer for the pathogens kept closed by just a string."

Three months after the trip, Lugar and Obama published an article on the Washington *Post*'s op-ed page called "Junkyard Dogs of War," warning against the spread of loose conventional weapons from the former Soviet Union and elsewhere, "particularly shoulder-fired antiaircraft missiles that can hit civilian airliners." Lugar and Obama introduced legislation to gain the cooperation of other nations and tighten control of arms caches in the former Soviet Union that were being routinely plundered, and whose contents were being used to make improvised roadside bombs in the Middle East and to fuel civil wars in Africa. The legislation helped strengthen systems to detect and intercept illegal shipments of materials used in chemical, biological, and nuclear weapons.

Obama's work with Lugar was not the only instance of his cooperating with Republicans and Democratic centrists. He worked with Mel Martinez, a Republican from Florida, on immigration reform, and with Tom Coburn, a right-wing Republican from Oklahoma, on legislation to bring greater transparency to government contracting. He was getting along with his own Party and with his colleagues in general.

"I am sure it was in the back of my mind that he would run for President someday," Lippert said, "but he felt we had to be serious and map out very particular policy issues where we could be heard. Obama's basic mantra is, You figure out the policy and I will figure out the politics."

During his term, Obama also called on journalists like Fareed Zakaria, of *Newsweek*, and Thomas Friedman and David Brooks, of the New York *Times*, to talk about policy. Obama was comfortable with them, eager to exchange ideas and, at the same time, playfully aware of the game of mutual seduction. When Brooks, a moderate conservative, wrote a column attacking the Republicans in Congress on fiscal issues and then added an additional attack on the Democrats, Obama sent him a friendly e-mail saying, "If you want to attack us fine, but you are only throwing in those sentences to make yourself feel better." Brooks felt caught out. "He was calling me to my better nature," Brooks said, wryly. As a conservative, Brooks was disappointed that Obama was such "an orthodox Democrat," but impressed with his intellect and the collective intelligence of the people whom he appointed.

Obama struck journalists as a voracious reader, deliberative, versed in policy and political philosophy. He could talk Reagan and Burke with Brooks and foreign policy with Zakaria and Friedman, all with the politician's gift of making his guest feel that he agrees with him. They were all struck by his charm and lack of neediness, his intelligence and what one called "his gargantuan self-confidence"—a freshman senator who was convinced he could get in a room with foreign-policy realists and idealists and somehow transcend the battle and reconcile the two sides. Their conversations started from the assumption that Obama had read their books and articles and he spent nearly all of the meetings listening.

As a law professor, Obama used to say that he had to know Antonin Scalia's side of arguments as well as Scalia did in order to win the debate. But for all his talk about seeing both sides of a question and occasionally siding with the opposition, Obama was, ideologically, squarely in the center of the post–Bill Clinton Democratic Party. His views, foreign and domestic, were generally progressive, but their expression was more analytic and deliberative than passionate. Passionate moralism would never be his dominant key. He could admire Edward Kennedy's ferocious advocacy of universal health care or the strong human-rights orientation of some of his other colleagues, but he was wary of what he saw as emotional absolutism. This was especially true for foreign policy.

"The sense I got from him then was that his fundamental view of the world was rooted as much in the struggle for development and economic growth as it was in missiles and the Cold War," Zakaria recalled. "I think this came first from his mother and Indonesia. His first memory of a foreign-policy event was not of Vietnam or of the Soviet Union but of life on the ground in Jakarta. The struggle for survival and development— that's the prism through which he sees the world. That is why the neocon agenda or even the recent formulation of the liberal internationalist agenda is not something he leaps toward immediately. It's not because of some coldness about democracy, but rather because he understands that, for the vast majority of the world, there is first a basic struggle for dignity and survival. I think that view comes from the Kennedy era, even though Kennedy was a cold warrior: the Alliance for Progress, the Peace Corps, the age of Pell Grants, aid to Africa, the Green Revolution in India. His mother was absorbed in that and so is he.

"Obama is a kind of practical idealist," Zakaria went on. "He told me that he admired George H. W. Bush's diplomacy, his careful management of the end the Cold War and his emphasis on productive relations with the world's other major powers. I can't think of many Democrats then who said that. He writes in his book about reading Fanon and other leftists when he was young, but it seemed to me that, in his view of the world, he moved beyond that. He is a sober type. And part of that seems to come from another influence: the University of Chicago. He was steeped in the atmosphere of law and economics. He may not have taken on their arguments, but something rubbed off in his view of the world—the realism and the logic."

In late August, 2005, Hurricane Katrina submerged much of the city of New Orleans, the Mississippi Gulf Coast, and, it seemed, the Bush Presidency. The storm overwhelmed the levees and emergency systems of New Orleans, and the public officials at the center of the tragedy—the mayor, Ray Nagin; the governor of Louisiana, Kathleen Blanco; the chief of the Federal Emergency Management Agency, Michael Brown; and most of all, President Bush—underperformed to such a degree that countless people caught up in the tragedy, along with millions who witnessed it on television, blamed those officials almost as if the hurricane had been an act of pure human agency rather than a force of nature. Bush's clueless fly-over detachment in the first days of the tragedy seemed to many a domestic version of his arrogance and deceit during the run-up to the war in Iraq, his hapless management of its prosecution, and his blithe indifference to the reports of torture. In Katrina's wake, the facts and images of incompetence, mismanagement, and callousness became as indelibly fixed as the images of the storm itself. The Bush Presidency was now, like the Lower Ninth Ward, underwater.

For eight months, Obama, even as he was ubiquitous on magazine covers and on television programs as a political celebrity of certain promise, had been a mild presence in the national debate. He had shied away from out-of-state speaking engagements and the Sunday talk shows. He avoided controversy. This studied reticence was part of the first stage of the plan that Rouse and his team had drafted for him. Obama had not wanted to get ahead of himself and seem like a preening show horse, the least desirable breed in the Senate stable. But as the sole African-American in the Senate, he could not avoid speaking out about Katrina.

Among Democrats, at least, there was not much debate about the performance of the President and the local government officials; the question for Obama was what tone to adopt. Jesse Jackson, and also black intellectuals like Cornel West, compared the images of crowds of African-Americans herded into the Superdome or left to broil on highway overpasses without food or water to Africans in previous centuries being herded onto slave ships. White Democratic Party leaders, including Howard Dean and Hillary Clinton, joined in the criticism, accusing the Administration of acting so slowly because of lingering racism.

When the hurricane made landfall, Obama had been in Russia, but the week after the storm he went to the Gulf Coast with former Presidents Bill Clinton and George H. W. Bush. Obama stood silently with Hillary Clinton as the two ex-Presidents spoke to reporters at various disaster sites. Then, appearing on ABC's Sunday morning talk show "This Week," with George Stephanopoulos, Obama criticized the government response, but painstakingly, without attacking anyone directly. His tone was many degrees less fierce than that of Jesse Jackson or Cornel West. "Whoever was in charge of planning was so detached from the realities of inner-city life in a place like New Orleans," Obama said, "they couldn't conceive of the notion that [people] couldn't load up their S.U.V.s, put a hundred dollars' worth of gas in there, put some sparkling water, and drive off to a hotel and check in with a credit card."

Obama's initial response was calibrated to express a sober awareness of reality—"It was apparent on the first day that blacks were disproportionately impacted"—not a sense of outrage or blame. In an interview with the *Tribune*, Obama was almost as hard on the Democrats as he was on Bush. "It is way too simplistic just to say this Administration doesn't care about black people," he said. "I think it is entirely accurate to say that this Administration's policies don't take into account the plight of poor people in poor communities and this is a tragic reflection of that indifference, but I also have to say that it's an indifference that is not entirely partisan. We as Democrats have not been very interested in poverty or issues relating to the inner city as much as we should have. Think about the last Presidential campaign: it's pretty hard to focus on a moment on which there was any attention given."

Even if Obama was privately outraged by the Bush Administration's early indifference to the suffering on the Gulf Coast—an outrage that he did express later—he clearly saw that his job as a senator was to forge a broader political consensus for reform rather than embody the popular anger. This rhetorical tact was partly a matter of temperament, and partly indicative of a generational shift. It was hard to imagine many older African-American legislators or mayors using the rhetoric of calm conciliation in Katrina's wake. Obama said that the "encouraging thing" about Katrina was that "everybody" was generous to the victims: "white suburban Republicans as well as black liberal Democrats."

"The burden is on us as Democrats, the burden is on me as a U.S. senator to help bridge that gap," he said.

Although his votes in the Senate were more predictably liberal than he advertised, Obama felt it was essential to show that he possessed a distinctive equanimity and cool. Conciliation was his default mode, the dominant strain of his political personality. After witnessing the partisan political wars that stretched from Watergate to the Clinton impeachment trial and the battles now being waged over the Bush Presidency on the Internet and cable television, Obama insisted on a rhetoric of common ground. He was instinctively wary of ideology, and sometimes this left even sympathetic colleagues and critics frustrated and wondering what he really believed in, what was essential to his view of the world. This had been his way since Harvard when he extended a hand to conservatives even at the cost of disappointing some fellow liberals.

In the fall of 2005, Obama and his Democratic colleagues were faced with the Bush Administration's nomination of John Roberts, a conservative federal judge, to succeed William Rehnquist as Chief Justice of the Supreme Court. Obama held long discussions with his staff over how to vote. As in the case of the nomination of Condoleezza Rice as Secretary of State, Obama knew that the Administration was not likely to put forward a less conservative nominee if somehow the Roberts nomination failed to gain approval from the Senate. Obama admitted that Roberts had a good legal mind and that if he were President he would not want his nominees rebuffed for ideological reasons, either. Obama's mentor at Harvard, Laurence Tribe, had testified against Robert Bork during the Reagan years and, in July, 1987, Edward Kennedy had insisted on the floor of the Senate that in "Robert Bork's America," women would be forced into "back-alley abortions," blacks would return to "segregated lunch counters," writers and artists would be "censored at the whim of the government," and "rogue police" making "midnight raids" could break into the homes of citizens. Was Roberts really Robert Bork's ideological twin? What good would it do to attack him? Perhaps, relying on the same rationale as he had when he voted for Rice, he should vote for Roberts. Eventually, Pete Rouse brought the discussion down to earth and into the realm of politics. He told Obama that he was not engaged in a moot-court exercise at Harvard Law School. There were real-life political implications to his decision. He told Obama that a vote in favor of the Roberts nomination could prove crippling among Democratic voters in a future Presidential primary.

As he had proved in Cambridge, Chicago, and Springfield, Obama could be shrewd when balancing the impulse of principle and the realities of politics and career. In a statement, he said that he had just spoken with Roberts the day before; he complimented him as "humble," "personally decent," and respectful of precedent in "ninety-five percent of the cases that come before the federal court." The problem, he said, came with the other five per cent, with cases involving affirmative action, reproductive decisions, and the rights of the disabled. Roberts, Obama said, told him that it was hard for him to talk about his values, except to say that he "doesn't like bullies" and views the law as a way of "evening out the playing field between the strong and the weak." In the end, Obama said that Roberts, in his work in the White House and the Solicitor General's Office, "seemed to have consistently sided with those who were dismissive of efforts to eradicate the remnants of racial discrimination." With "considerable reticence," he was going to vote against Roberts.

Obama's demurral hardly matched Kennedy's ferocious denunciation of Robert Bork; such rhetoric was not his style or his political way of being. The final tally was seventy-eight to twenty-two in favor of Roberts; nearly all the votes against Roberts came from blue-state Democrats. On similar grounds, Obama also voted against Samuel Alito, Bush's second nomination to the Supreme Court. In order "to send a signal" that the President "is not above the law," Obama also voted against Bush's nominee for director of the Central Intelligence Agency, General Michael Hayden.

Some combination of Obama's very real objections to Roberts's record and Rouse's hardheaded political logic had won the day. Obama was not reluctant to compliment his chief of staff for his prescience. "Pete's very good at looking around the corners of decisions and playing out the implications of them," Obama said, two years after the Roberts vote.

But the Roberts story did not end there. Some Democrats—Patrick

Leahy, Christopher Dodd, Carl Levin, Russ Feingold, and Patty Murray—had voted for Roberts, and, as a result, they were being excoriated on many left-leaning Web sites, including the popular collaborative blog Daily Kos. In his speech on the floor, Obama defended Leahy, especially, against these "broad-brush dogmatic attacks." He took the occasion of that fierce criticism of his colleagues to send a letter to Daily Kos that in many ways could be read as a kind of manifesto for his conciliatory temperament, which he clearly regarded as an essential element of his politics and of his appeal.

The letter was entitled "Tone, Truth, and the Democratic Party" and was posted on September 30, 2005.

After apologizing for failing to follow blogs "as regularly as I would like," Obama wrote that he wanted to address "friends and supporters":

There is one way, over the long haul, to guarantee the appointment of judges that are sensitive to issues of social justice, and that is to win the right to appoint them by recapturing the presidency and the Senate. And I don't believe we get there by vilifying good allies, with a lifetime record of battling for progressive causes, over one vote or position. I am convinced that, our mutual frustrations and strongly held beliefs notwithstanding, the strategy driving much of Democratic advocacy, and the tone of much of our rhetoric, is an impediment to creating a workable progressive majority in this country.

According to the storyline that drives many advocacy groups and Democratic activists—a storyline often reflected in comments on this blog—we are up against a sharply partisan, radically conservative, take-no-prisoners Republican party. They have beaten us twice by energizing their base with red meat rhetoric and single-minded devotion and discipline to their agenda. In order to beat them, it is necessary for Democrats to get some backbone, give as good as they get, brook no compromise, drive out Democrats who are interested in "appeasing" the right wing, and enforce a more clearly progressive agenda. The country, finally knowing what we stand for and seeing a sharp contrast, will rally to our side and thereby usher in a new progressive era.

I think this perspective misreads the American people. From traveling throughout Illinois and more recently around the country, I can tell you that Americans are suspicious of labels and suspicious of jargon. They don't think George Bush is mean-spirited or prejudiced, but have become aware that his administration is irresponsible and often incompetent. They don't think that corporations are inherently evil (a lot of them work in corporations), but they recognize that big business, unchecked, can fix the game to the detriment of working people and small entrepreneurs. They don't think America is an imperialist brute, but are angry that the case to invade Iraq was exaggerated, are worried that we have unnecessarily alienated existing and potential allies around the world, and are ashamed by events like those at Abu Ghraib, which violate our ideals as a country.

In a style of insistent reasonableness—the same tone that he employed the next year in his book *The Audacity of Hope*—Obama argued that most people saw the debate over the Roberts nomination through a "non-ideological" lens and that to argue in less than civil terms is to risk alienating most Americans and, worse, to endanger the creation of a progressive coalition. His rhetorical approach was to acknowledge the virtues of both sides, caution against moral equivalence, but insist on courtesy and respect. Obama insisted that civility need not come at the cost of rigor or principle. Some critics argued that Obama's emphasis on civility was a form of delicacy, an escape from rigor and principle. But Obama was convinced that his argument would resonate with voters weary of the yowling on cable news and the most profane battle scenes of the Web.

Obama asked Daily Kos readers to see that some Democrats (if not Obama himself) were concerned that a floor battle over Roberts would be "quixotic" and endanger the Party's attempt to win back the majority in the coming elections. In other words, there were valid reasons for liberal Democrats like Leahy to vote for Roberts. Similarly, Obama asked that the readers of Daily Kos not attack the motives of Richard Durbin or himself for failing to call for an immediate withdrawal from Iraq despite their early opposition to the invasion. Durbin, Obama said, "may be simply trying to figure out, as I am, how to ensure that U.S. troop withdrawals occur in such a way that we avoid all-out Iraqi civil war, chaos in the Middle East, and much more costly and deadly interventions down the road." In his letter, Obama aimed at assuring the readers of Daily Kos, and liberals in general, that they were his natural allies, but cautioned them against a rhetoric that alienates all but true believers. Without a broader coalition, progressives will not be able to overhaul health care, lift people out of poverty or "craft a foreign policy that meets the challenges of globalization or terrorism while avoiding isolationism and protecting civil liberties." The arguments for belligerent, unilateral foreign policy, the dismantling of a social safety net, and a politics of "theological absolutism" are relatively easy to make, Obama said. Liberalism is hard and demands nuance and exchange. Obama's argument was not for reflexive centrism or caving in to conservative opponents but, rather, for a flexibility of mind and tolerance in argument to gain liberal ends.

"This is more than just a matter of 'framing,' although clarity of language, thought, and heart are required," Obama wrote. "It's a matter of actually having faith in the American people's ability to hear a real and authentic debate about the issues that matter."

Afterward, Obama used a favorite phrase to describe the Roberts vote and his letter. He called it a "teachable moment." The letter was not, however, a wholly pedagogical gesture. Obama's desire was to position himself and the Party as being beyond the old arguments of the centrists of the Democratic Leadership Conference (a major influence in the Clinton Administration) and the "old-time-religion-Ted-Kennedy-die-hard types." The danger of the D.L.C., Obama said, was its impulse to "cut a deal no matter what the deal is," while the danger for traditional liberals was to be "unreflective" and "unwilling to experiment or update old programs to meet new challenges."

"And the way I would describe myself," Obama said, "is I think that my values are deeply rooted in the progressive tradition, the values of equal opportunity, civil rights, fighting for working families, a foreign policy that is mindful of human rights, a strong belief in civil liberties, wanting to be a good steward for the environment, a sense that the government has an important role to play, that opportunity is open to all people and that the powerful don't trample on the less powerful . . . I share all the aims of a Paul Wellstone or a Ted Kennedy when it comes to the end result. But I'm much more agnostic, much more flexible on how we achieve those ends."

Obama's desire for civility did not always succeed. Early in his second year in the Senate, in February, 2006, he had his first public run-in with a colleague. His adversary was the senior senator from Arizona, John McCain, and, by the decorous standards of the Senate, the incident was notably ugly.

In the wake of the arrest of Jack Abramoff, a lobbyist-conman who had worked with officials both in the Bush White House and on Capitol Hill, McCain organized a bipartisan group—seven Republicans and three Democrats—to work on reform of the rules governing lobbyists on the Hill. McCain thought that he'd got a commitment from Obama to work with his task force on the problem, but, when Obama sent him a note saying he had decided that a task force would delay action on the issue and, at the request of the Democratic leader, Harry Reid, he was joining a Democratic plan for reform, McCain was furious. Returning to Washington from a conference in Germany, he sent Obama an acid letter, accusing him of bad faith and callow ambition. McCain supported a bill that called on lobbyists to make public any gifts given to members of Congress; members of both the House and the Senate would have to wait two years, not one, to become a registered lobbyist. The Democratic version of the legislation, the Honest Leadership and Open Government Act, added more restrictions, banning meals and gifts from lobbyists. McCain, who was first elected to Congress in 1982 and had plenty of close relations with Democrats, thought that the freshman had been grandstanding and he let him know it:

> Dear Senator Obama:
>
> I would like to apologize to you for assuming that your private assurances to me regarding your desire to cooperate in our efforts to negotiate bipartisan lobbying reform legislation were sincere. When you approached me and insisted that despite your leadership's preference to use the issue to gain a political advantage in the 2006 elections, you were personally committed to achieving a result that would reflect credit on the entire Senate and offer the country a better example of political leadership, I concluded your professed concern for the institution and the public interest was genuine and admirable. Thank you for disabusing me of such notions with your letter to me dated February 2, 2006, which explained your decision to withdraw from our bipartisan discussions. I'm embarrassed to admit that after all these years in politics I failed to interpret your previous assurances as typical rhetorical gloss routinely used in politics to make self-interested partisan posturing appear more noble. Again, sorry for the confusion, but please be assured I won't make the same mistake again. . . .
>
> You commented in your letter about my "interest in creating a task force to further study" this issue, as if to suggest I support delaying the consideration of much-needed reforms rather than allowing the committees of jurisdiction to hold hearings on the matter. Nothing could be further from the truth. . . .
>
> As I explained in a recent letter to Senator Reid, and have publicly said many times, the American people do not see this as just a Republican problem or just a Democratic problem. They see it as yet

another run-of-the-mill Washington scandal, and they expect it will generate just another round of partisan gamesmanship and posturing. Senator Lieberman and I, and many other members of this body, hope to exceed the public's low expectations. . . .

As I noted, I initially believed you shared that goal. But I understand how important the opportunity to lead your party's effort to exploit this issue must seem to a freshman Senator, and I hold no hard feelings over your earlier disingenuousness. Again, I have been around long enough to appreciate that in politics the public interest isn't always a priority for every one of us. Good luck to you, Senator.

Sincerely,

John McCain

United States Senate

This seemed to be vintage McCain: he was known among his colleagues as much for his volcanic temper as for his intelligence and flashes of humor. In fact, the letter was drafted by his close aide, speechwriter, and alter ego, Mark Salter, who co-authored McCain's autobiography, *Faith of My Fathers*. The letter was meant to be both funny and stinging, a welcome-to-the-majors brushback pitch, to use McCain's words of instruction to Salter. "I obviously beaned him and wrote too sharp a response," Salter recalled. In no time at all the letter was e-mailed around Capitol Hill with a one-word subject line: "Wow."

Obama responded in a tone of polite bewilderment. He said he had "no idea what has prompted" McCain's two-page outburst and answered with a "Dear John" letter of artful restraint and righteous politesse:

During my short time in the U.S. Senate, one of the aspects about this institution that I have come to value most is the collegiality and the willingness to put aside partisan differences to work on issues that help the American people. . . . I confess that I have no idea what has prompted your response. But let me assure you that I am not interested in typical partisan rhetoric or posturing. The fact that you have now questioned my sincerity and my desire to put aside politics for the public interest is regrettable, but does not in any way diminish my deep respect for you nor my willingness to find a bipartisan solution to this problem.

After the epistolary exchange and a brief telephone conversation to cool things off, McCain told reporters, "We're moving on. We're still colleagues. We're still friends. I mean, this isn't war." When a reporter asked if he regretted the tone of his letter, however, McCain said, "Of course not."

Obama's words of reconciliation were similarly contingent. "The tone of the letter, I think, was a little over the top," he said. "But John McCain's been an American hero and has served here in Washington for twenty years, so if he wants to get cranky once in a while, that's his prerogative."

On the third and final day of the drama, Obama and McCain, who were both preparing to testify before the Senate Rules Committee, posed with their fists cocked at each other like a couple of publicity-hungry middleweights at a weigh-in. Before they testified, Obama said, "I'm particularly pleased to be sharing this panel with my pen pal, John McCain."

In June, 2006, Obama went a step further in trying to expand his own Party's political base. He accepted an invitation to speak from Jim Wallis, a white liberal evangelical Christian. Wallis's organization, known as the Sojourners, opposed the policies of the religious right and spoke out for social justice. Obama was among those in the Party who were eager to prove that the evangelical movement was far more diverse than the political class in Washington, New York, or Los Angeles believed, that religious Christians were as capable of independent thought and politics as any other seemingly cohesive voting bloc. Obama talked about his own church—Jeremiah Wright's Trinity United Church of Christ, on the South Side—and the way it viewed religious faith as commensurate with a belief in political liberation and compassion. Again, Obama asked his audience to step outside the accustomed barricades. He denounced both the intolerance of the religious right and the failure, often, of the secular left to respect the value of religious faith in the lives of others.

> What I am suggesting is this: secularists are wrong when they ask believers to leave their religion at the door before entering into the public square. Frederick Douglass, Abraham Lincoln, William Jennings Bryan, Dorothy Day, Martin Luther King—indeed, the majority of great reformers in American history—were not only motivated by faith but repeatedly used religious language to argue for their cause. So to say that men and women should not inject their "personal morality" into public-policy debates is a practical absurdity. Our law is by definition a codification of morality, much of it grounded in the Judeo-Christian tradition.

Moreover, if we progressives shed some of these biases, we might recognize some overlapping values that both religious and secular people share when it comes to the moral and material direction of our country. We might recognize that the call to sacrifice on behalf of the next generation, the need to think in terms of "thou" and not just "I," resonates in religious congregations all across the country. And we might realize that we have the ability to reach out to the evangelical community and engage millions of religious Americans in the larger project of American renewal.

Obama criticized leaders of the religious right, like Pat Robertson and Jerry Falwell, who had been at the forefront of the Reagan revolution, and those liberal secularists who are wary of any and all religious appeals. At the same time he paid tribute to preachers like Tony Campolo, Rick Warren, and T. D. Jakes, who had been active on issues like the genocide in Darfur, poverty, H.I.V./AIDS, and Third World–debt relief. It was a speech that recognized how ruinous was the divide between the Democratic Party and evangelicals. Obama was attempting to reconcile the constitutional requirement for separation of church and state with recognition of sincere religious impulse for the social good:

> The American people intuitively understand this, which is why the majority of Catholics practice birth control and some of those opposed to gay marriage nevertheless are opposed to a constitutional amendment to ban it. Religious leadership need not accept such wisdom in counseling their flocks, but they should recognize this wisdom in their politics.
>
> But a sense of proportion should also guide those who police the boundaries between church and state. Not every mention of God in public is a breach to the wall of separation—context matters. It is doubtful that children reciting the Pledge of Allegiance feel oppressed or brainwashed as a consequence of muttering the phrase "under God." I didn't. Having voluntary student prayer groups use school property to meet should not be a threat, any more than its use by the High School Republicans should threaten Democrats. And one can envision certain faith-based programs—targeting ex-offenders or substance abusers—that offer a uniquely powerful way of solving problems.
>
> So we all have some work to do here. But I am hopeful that we can bridge the gaps that exist and overcome the prejudices each of us

brings to this debate. And I have faith that millions of believing Americans want that to happen. No matter how religious they may or may not be, people are tired of seeing faith used as a tool of attack. They don't want faith used to belittle or to divide. They're tired of hearing folks deliver more screed than sermon. Because in the end that's not how they think about faith in their own lives.

One conceit of the Obama narrative, as told by his inner circle, is that the discussions about running for President did not come to the fore until the fall of 2006, with the publication of his second book, *The Audacity of Hope*, and the explosion of media interest that attended the publicity tour. Obama, the narrative continues, was moved less by the attention in the media (he was already accustomed to that) than by the crowds of ordinary people who came to get their book signed and pleaded with him to run. The emotional experience of hearing those pleas and stories of dissatisfaction and despair, at one venue after another, from coast to coast, hastened and intensified Obama's notion that there was, in the wake of the failed Bush Presidency, a hunger for integrity and newness, for change, that the presumed Democratic candidates, particularly Hillary Clinton, could never satisfy. Then, after long thought and intensive consultation, the Obama family went to Hawaii that Christmas, talked it through, and returned to Chicago unified in the decision to campaign. This was the story.

It's not a false narrative, but it is not a complete one, either. It's hard to say when Obama started thinking about running for President or what importance to attach to those "thoughts." Obama's sister, Maya, says that she and their mother used to tease him about running for President, if only to puncture his desire to win dinner-table debates. Many sources interviewed for this book and for countless other publications were eager to say that upon meeting Obama they knew, just *knew*, that he could be the first African-American President. Valerie Jarrett says that Obama "always" wanted to be President. And Obama himself has admitted that, when he arrived at Harvard and sized himself up against all the intelligent young men and women—a bracing encounter with a nascent ruling class—he felt that he could pursue high office. "I thought these will be the people who will be leading at some point," Obama recalled. "And, you know, I feel comfortable within this group, being able to lead."

Although Pete Rouse says he believed, initially, that Obama would not run until 2016, he saw the possibilities in the more immediate future. The first year had been one of establishing a sense of diligence in the Senate, of making no enemies. The second phase entailed raising Obama's profile, having him give speeches for fellow Democrats and extending favors, which would help him nationally should he want to run. On January 16, 2006, Rouse sent a memorandum to Obama saying, "It makes sense for you to consider now whether you want to use 2006 to position yourself to run in 2008 if a 'perfect storm' of personal and political factors emerges in 2007. . . . If making a run in 2008 is at all a possibility, no matter how remote, it makes sense to begin talking and making decisions about what you should be doing 'below the radar' in 2006 to maximize your ability to get in front of this wave should it emerge and should you and your family decide it is worth riding."

Events like the insurgency in Iraq and the revelations of torture in Abu Ghraib prison, the faltering economy, and the mismanagement of the rescue and reconstruction efforts on the Gulf Coast would make life very difficult for any Republican in 2008; what was more, although Hillary Clinton would enter a primary season bolstered by a well-financed, experienced campaign machine, she would be weighed down by the voters' overall weariness with familiar politicians. Clinton was far from a sure thing. Obama had to start considering the future, if only to think it through and come up with a coherent version of "not yet."

The Clintons had a vast network of operatives and fundraisers at their disposal—a machine developed over decades—while Obama had nothing like it. Still, the Clintons thought through the decision to run with no less deliberation than the Obamas did. "At the end of 2006, Hillary and Bill took a Caribbean vacation together and they were out on a boat together, nearly alone, and they swam to an island," one top Clinton aide recalled. "They sat on the beach and talked for about three hours and they talked about the pluses and minuses. Until then, they had set things up so there would be a turnkey campaign operation. She had to decide whether she wanted to go through the rigors of the campaign. And she loved the Senate. Finally he asked her, 'There is really one question to answer, and that's whether do you think you'd be the best person out there to be President?' After that, the staff got phone calls saying she's in. They set an announcement for January 20th.

"We were very confident, sometimes bordering on arrogant, and sometimes passing over the border," the aide went on. "At first, there was a low-grade worry about Obama, that's all. I remember hearing a phone call on the plane and Bill and Hillary were talking about Obama. And the tone of the conversation was of him reassuring her. Believe me, there were no phone calls reassuring her about Tom Vilsack or John Edwards. He was saying, 'If you sit around and worry about him, you'll be off your own game.'"

Part of Obama's calculation had to do with the job he already occupied. The truth was, David Axelrod told me, "Barack hated being a senator." Washington was a grander stage than Springfield, but the frustrations of being a rookie in a minority party were familiar. Obama could barely conceal his frustration with the torpid pace of the Senate. His aides could sense his frustration and so could his colleagues. "He was so bored being a senator," one Senate aide said. "It's picayune, it's small-ball everywhere. And he is restless. He was engaged with the big issues, like what to do about Iraq. What interested him was policy, strategy, not bills . . . His frustration was obvious to everyone in the office." An aide who was devoted to Obama nevertheless described how his offices at the Hart Building seemed "unlived in" and temporary, "as if he never really thought he would stay for long."

His friend and law colleague Judd Miner said, "The reality was that during his first two years in the U.S. Senate, I think, he was struggling; it wasn't nearly as stimulating as he expected. He felt there was very little opportunity to engage in meaningful dialogue, certainly with Republicans. The amount of time spent on creative or constructive policy debates was so limited. I remember one day he was really glowing when someone raised an issue about health care and he didn't know much about it. He discovered that the most valuable perk was that if you call someone, they call you back fast. He had contacted some people and got the names of five or six thinkers and got on the phone to hash it out. Lo and behold, all of them flew to Washington and spent the entire day with him." Similarly, he convened experts on everything from health care to voting rights, but those days, Obama was seeing, were the exception.

The one project that did engage Obama fully was work on *The Audacity of Hope*. He procrastinated for a long time and then, facing his deadline, wrote nearly a chapter a week. "This was not your average senator writing a book," one aide said. "His whole soul went into it, so it meant that there was less of him to go around elsewhere. In the office, he was distracted. He wasn't thrilled to be living the life of a senator, even on the best of days. The job was too small for him—not because he was arrogant but because his mind was on systemic change, not on votes.

"So he was punching the clock during the day and then coming alive at night to write the book," the aide went on. "The book was about a mortgage and cashing in on the success of the first book. And the book was a way to think through who he was and what he stood for. It was a culmination of thinking and refinement. He created a mechanism where he was chained to the mast and had to figure out who he was to meet a book deadline."

Obama also spent a lot of time now raising money for his political-action committee, Hopefund, and for his political colleagues. Eventually, Hopefund would become a bulwark for a Presidential campaign, accumulating money and a vast computerized list of contacts. As a fundraiser, Obama had uncommon capacities, especially for a Senate freshman. He could call on Steven Spielberg, David Geffen, Oprah Winfrey, and George Soros and ask for their support. Like a traditional pol, he spent hours making cajoling calls to potential donors, but, because of his celebrity, he could also do things quickly. On a single night, he drew a crowd of more than a thousand and raised a million dollars for the Arizona Democratic Party. With a single e-mail appeal, he raised eight hundred thousand dollars for Robert Byrd. When he went to Omaha, he won the glowing endorsement of Warren Buffett, one of the richest men in the world, and his daughter, Susie. Obama was completely at ease with financial barons like Buffett, and they, it seemed, saw something promising in him. "He has as much potential as anyone I've seen to have an important impact over his lifetime on the course that America takes," Buffett said of Obama.

In order to increase the sense of connection between himself and his donors, Obama, in late October, 2005, had invited a hundred people who had given at least twenty-five hundred dollars to Hopefund to a conference in Chicago to discuss policy and spend time together socially. Peter Bynoe, an African-American entrepreneur who helped build a new stadium for the Chicago White Sox and owned a chunk of the Denver Nuggets, thought Obama had become such a gifted fundraiser that he started calling him "Money." "When his name pops up on caller I.D. on my cell phone, I know it's going to cost a lot more than two cents a minute, but I'm compelled to take the call," Bynoe told one fund-raising audience. "I pride myself on saying no to politicians, but I can't say no to 'Money.'"

Ever since Obama's election to the Senate, his staff had been planning an official visit to Africa for him. They set the trip for August, 2006, after he completed the manuscript of *The Audacity of Hope* but before its publication. Obama could justify the trip—to Kenya, Djibouti, Chad, and South Africa—as an important fact-finding mission for a member of the

Senate Foreign Relations Committee and of the subcommittee on Africa. There were myriad issues for a legislator to discuss: H.I.V./AIDS, Darfur, extreme poverty, development, terrorism, the proliferation of conventional arms. It was hardly a cynical trip. Gibbs, Axelrod, Rouse, and Obama knew that the two-week journey would provoke an emotional reaction in Kenya and in the American press, not least among African-Americans who had not yet learned much about Obama. They did not realize the extent of the reaction: the huge crowds, people watching from balconies, children perched in the branches of trees.

Traveling with his wife and daughters and just two aides, Mark Lippert and Robert Gibbs, Obama visited a refugee camp in Chad to highlight the slaughter in Darfur; received a briefing from U.S. military officials at a base in Djibouti; and met with officials in South Africa. He made some policy pronouncements along the way, including a sharp denunciation of corruption and tribalism in Kenya that echoed his father's deepest political concerns and a critique of the South African leader, Thabo Mbeki, for his bewildering and dangerous beliefs about the source of AIDS. In Kenya, Obama made sure to travel beyond Nairobi. He visited Wajir, in the northeastern region of Kenya, near Somalia, which had experienced famine and drought. As a gesture of hospitality, the local Somali Kenyans took Obama to a camel auction and gave him the robes of a Somali elder. (During the 2008 Presidential campaign, right-wing Web sites published a photograph of Obama wearing the robes to suggest that he was, in fact, a Muslim.) Near Kisumu, where his father was born, he took an AIDS test to reduce the stigma of testing, which is especially prevalent among African men, and visited "Granny" at her modest concrete house in Kogelo.

"The happiest I've seen him, maybe, is when he saw his grandmother," Lippert said. "He truly has a relationship with her. You could see his reaction when he spotted her in a sea of people—it was so deep and genuine." Obama spent nearly two hours in his grandmother's house talking with relatives and eating a traditional stew. He also paid a visit to the raised, tile graves of his father and grandfather, who are buried near the house.

The extraordinary reception Obama received seemed to demonstrate the effect he could have in altering the battered image of America that had taken hold all over the world during the Bush Administration. The trip certainly reignited the media's infatuation. The networks ran clips, magazines had new pictures and cover stories, newspapers carried news of each event and venue—Obama's team was not disappointed.

. . .

Just a couple of weeks after returning from Africa, Obama accepted an invitation to speak at a venue that was very different from Kogelo. It was an invitation to appear at the Warren County Fairgrounds, in Indianola, Iowa. The occasion was Senator Tom Harkin's annual steak fry, at which more than three thousand people paid twenty-five dollars to eat fantastic quantities of food, stroll around the fairgrounds, and then settle on the grass or in lawn chairs to listen to a few speeches. The headliner in 2003 had been Bill Clinton and, in 2005, John Edwards. Obama had initially been reluctant to come to the event, but now he was willing to attract the attention and speculation.

To help guide Obama in Iowa, a trip that only the dense would fail to see as an exploratory mission for the 2008 caucuses, Pete Rouse called on a friend, Steve Hildebrand, who had run Al Gore's campaign in the state six years earlier, and had worked for Daschle, too. "I thought, let's have a little fun with this," Rouse said. "I wanted to create a little buzz." Much of the buzz was within the Clinton and Edwards camps; they, too, had hoped to hire Hildebrand. Harkin, a liberal who had taken a brief run at the Presidency in 1992, introduced his guest to the crowd by saying, "I really tried to get Bono this weekend. I settled for the second-biggest rock star in America."

Dressed in standard steak-fry garb for visiting Washingtonians— shirtsleeves and khaki pants—Obama was in good form. He began with his well-honed description of his family background (my mother is from Kansas, he said, "which is where I got this accent"), then he moved on to a description of the troubled state of the nation. If the country didn't change course soon the next generation would find life "a little bit meaner and a little bit poorer than the one we inherited from our parents." But he did not come to Iowa intent on attacking the President, or not personally.

"I don't think George Bush is a bad man," he said. "I think he's a patriotic person and I don't think that the people who work for him are stupid people. I think a lot of them are smart in their own way. I think that the problem is that they've got a different idea of America than the idea we've got."

In the simplest terms—terms that he had been rehearsing for a long time, terms that became the center of his stump speech in the months ahead—Obama provided a homey, deeply affecting vision of a liberal American idea:

> They believe in different things. They have a sense that in fact government is the problem, not the solution, and that if we just dismantle

government, piece by piece, if we break it up in tax cuts to the wealthy and if we just make sure that we privatize Social Security and we get rid of public schools and we make sure that we don't have police on the streets, we hire private security guards and we don't have public parks, we've got private parks and if we just break everything up, then in fact everybody's going to be better off—that in fact we don't have obligations to each other, that we're not in it together but instead you're on your own. That's the basic concept behind the ownership society. That's what George Bush and this Republican Congress have been arguing for the last six years. And it's a tempting idea because it doesn't require anything from each of us.

It's very easy for us to say that I'm going to think selfishly about myself, that I don't have to worry that forty-six million people don't have health insurance and I don't have to make any effort to deal with the fact that our children don't have any opportunities to go to college because student loans have been cut and I don't have to worry about the guy who just lost his job after working thirty years at a plant because his plant's moved down to Mexico or out to China, despite the fact that he has been producing profits on behalf of that company this whole time and that he's lost his health care and he's lost his pension as a consequence. I don't have to worry about those things.

But here's the problem. The problem is that idea won't work because despite the much-vaunted individual initiative and self-reliance that has been the essence of the American dream, the fact of the matter is that there has always been this other idea of America, this idea that says we have a stake in each other, that I am my brother's keeper, that I am my sister's keeper, that I've got obligations not just for myself, not just for my family but also for you, that every child is my child, that every senior citizen deserves protection. That simple notion is one that we understand in our churches and our synagogues and our mosques and we understand in our own families, in our blocks, in our own workplaces, but it also has to reflect itself in our government. You know, nobody here expects government to solve all our problems for us. We don't want government to solve our problems but what we do expect is that government can help. That government can make a difference in all of our lives and that is essentially the battle that we are going to be fighting in this election . . . a battle about what America is going to be.

Yet again, Obama was extending a hand to moderates, to voters who saw a black senator from Chicago and required complex forms of reassurance. In phrase after phrase, Obama emitted signals about religion, the economy, race, and much else, saying, in essence, Even if you don't agree with me on everything, I will listen to you, you are heard. It was the rhetoric, once more, of moderate liberalism and inclusion.

What besides Obama's skills as a speaker and politician could have given him and his circle of aides the idea that he could run for President, and run not foremost as a black candidate, but as a candidate with a chance to win? Millions of whites, Hispanics, and even African-Americans were not going to be easily convinced that Obama, or the country, was ready for this. What beyond the generally adoring press coverage and standing ovations provided a foundation for a Presidential candidacy?

First, there was the mood of the electorate, which was increasingly frustrated with, even despairing of, its leadership. "George Bush was instrumental in the rise of Barack Obama," Cornell Belcher, one of Obama's pollsters, said. "Quite frankly, before George Bush, who so screwed things up, we could not have had a Barack Obama. After Bush's election there was talk of a permanent Republican majority. Their Party structure was that strong and was built on the sense that their values were more in line with the values of regular Americans. And that was tied to security: 'I trust your values, therefore I trust you to keep us safe.' But George Bush undermined the Republican brand and created an environment in which people were hungry for something fundamentally new. By 2006, 2007, the country was positioned for something that didn't look like what had come before. There was deep-seated anger and anxiety, a monumental drop-off in voters' trust in politics as usual. Hillary is brilliant, but for a lot of people she couldn't answer that call because of her history. Everything about Barack Obama—the very name!—spoke of change."

But how much had the country really changed? Obama's experience running for Senate had been essential to his team's core of optimism—an optimism not only about the candidate and his qualities but also about the country and its deepest emotions about race. Obama's victories in white suburbs and rural counties had convinced his circle that he had the capacity to run extremely well not only among African-Americans and white progressives; he could also win votes in areas of the country which had once been bastions of racial animosity.

Much of the empirical basis for Obama's confidence about his prospects rested on persuasive evidence of generational change. First of all, the country was growing much more diverse. The whitest part of the American population was the oldest. Among people over sixty-five, the population was around eighty-per-cent white; the population under twenty-five is about half white. And the white population, even among older and middle-aged people, was susceptible to change in their attitudes. In the nineteen-thirties, thirty-seven per cent of the American people told pollsters from Gallup that they would be willing to vote for an African-American for President; now the percentage was ninety-five per cent. Other polls had somewhat lower numbers, but the trend was clear. When Colin Powell flirted with running for President in 1996, polls showed that the number of people who would not vote for him based on race was negligible.

The Obama team watched with keen interest as Harold Ford, Jr., the House member from Tennessee and a friend of Obama's in the congressional Black Caucus, ran an incredibly tight race in 2006 for Senate against the Republican, Bob Corker. It had been unthinkable that an African-American could beat a white opponent in a statewide race in the South. Ford ended up losing by just three points, and the reasons had far less to do with race or ideology than with the fact that, not long before the vote, one of Ford's relatives was indicted. Ford, like Obama—like Artur Davis, in Alabama, or Cory Booker, in Newark, Deval Patrick, in Massachusetts, and Michael Nutter, in Philadelphia—was a Joshua generation politician. He had attended the University of Pennsylvania, not seminary or a historically black college. His rhetoric was not that of struggle, of opposition to white oppression, but rather of mainstream American politics. The electorate seemed welcoming.

The country was also changing in terms of class and education, factors that could also have an impact on an Obama candidacy. Ruy Teixeira of the Brookings Institution and Alan Abramowitz of Emory University studied demographic trends and saw a dramatic decline in the primacy of the traditionally defined white working class and the rise of what they call a "mass upper-middle class." Simply put, in 1940 three-quarters of adults twenty-five and over were high-school dropouts or never made it to high school at all. Decade after decade, education rates rose so that by 2007 more than half the population had at least some college education. Similarly, in 1940, about thirty-two per cent of employed Americans had white-collar jobs as managers, professionals, or in clerical or sales positions. By 2006, that percentage had nearly doubled; there were now nearly three times as many white-collar Americans as manual workers. What was more, many white working-class voters had not permanently and entirely abandoned the Democratic Party; many had grown despairing of a broken health-care system, a failing economy, and the seemingly endless war in

Iraq. Teixeira and Abramowitz did not discount the continuing impor-tance of white working-class votes, especially in states like Pennsylvania and Ohio, but their study was one of the best among many that made clear how much the country was changing.

In the fall of 2006, Mark Alexander, a professor of constitutional law at Seton Hall University, in New Jersey, wrote a memorandum about a potential Obama campaign for the Presidency. The five-page memo, which was titled "It Can Be Done," gave a positive assessment of Obama's chances based on a variety of shifts in the demographic and racial land-scape of the country. Alexander reviewed Obama's policy positions; the scale and organizational strength of the black church and historically black colleges; promising trends in the census and voter lists, particularly the huge number of unregistered black voters in Georgia, North Car-olina, Florida, and Virginia. Alexander knew Obama; his sister, Elizabeth, was a poet and had been a professor at the University of Chicago, where she got to know the Obamas. (Their father, Clifford Alexander, was coun-sel to Lyndon Johnson and Jimmy Carter's secretary of the Army.) Mark Alexander had first met Barack and Michelle at Elizabeth's wedding, in 1997; he held on to Barack's cell-phone number. He'd worked for a string of liberal Democrats: Howard Metzenbaum, Edward Kennedy, Bill Bradley, and, most recently, Cory Booker; in Obama, he saw someone who could win the ultimate political prize. When he called Obama in 2006, he told him, "You may believe my memo or you may not believe my memo. But don't run unless you really believe it can happen." Obama took Alexander's advice so seriously that he eventually made him his campaign-policy director.

Alexander and other analysts were right in thinking that the country had changed. The old electoral map of Southern strategies, a dominant, monolithic religious right, and other post-Voting-Rights-era obstacles for the Democrats was in flux. In addition to overwhelming dissatisfaction with the Bush Administration, the very nature of how most Americans understood basic issues like race was shifting in ways that could only be encouraging to Obama and his circle. Virginia had elected a black gover-nor, Doug Wilder, as long ago as 1990. The South was no longer mono-lithic. Mississippi was still at the bottom of the nation in education and it was nearly impossible for a black politician to run statewide. But Virginia and North Carolina, with their centers for high-tech jobs, had attracted educated workers who were ready to vote for black candidates.

Obama's team believed it was possible that race could be, on balance, an asset. Nearly a quarter of the Democratic primary vote is African-

American. In 1980, Jimmy Carter retained the Democratic nomination after a strong challenge from Edward Kennedy not least because Carter secured more of the black vote; in 2000, Al Gore defeated Bill Bradley largely because of Gore's popularity among black voters. The Clintons had long been popular among African-Americans, but Obama could capture that vote if he could prove that he was a serious, and not a symbolic, candidate.

Still, for an African-American, no matter how skilled, no matter how intelligent and popular, a run for the Presidency was a weighty thing to consider.

Despite the small number of African-Americans who, since Reconstruction, have held office in districts and states where blacks were not in a majority, there has always been talk—at times derisive or farcical; at times quixotic, even messianic—of a black President. As early as 1904, George Edwin Taylor, a newspaperman born in Arkansas, accepted the nomination of the all-black National Liberty Party, but even much later in the century the prospect of a black President was almost always a discussion held in the spirit of a dream.

"We'd wonder, How long?" Don Rose, Martin Luther King's press secretary in Chicago, recalled, in an echo of the old movement chant "How long? Not long!" In 1967, members of the National Conference for New Politics tried to persuade King to run on a national ticket with Benjamin Spock. Scores of American soldiers and Vietnamese were dying every day. King had made speeches at Riverside Church, in New York, and at other venues across the country, calling not simply for peace negotiations, as Robert Kennedy and Eugene McCarthy had, but for immediate withdrawal from a lost war. With eloquence, bravery, and cunning, King had led the most important social and political movement in the history of the United States, rallying countless blacks and whites to the cause of civil rights. Now there were people who, desperate about the antiwar movement's seeming inability to have a similar effect on government, saw King as a savior figure, the one man who, as President, would end the Vietnam conflict. "One emotional student told him not to rule it out, that it was a matter of life or death," Taylor Branch, the author of a three-volume biography of King, said. Vietnam and poverty, as well as race, would have been at the center of his agenda as a politician, and King thought about it for a while. But in the end he refused entreaties to run. He knew that he was unlikely to win and, more important, that he might undermine his role as a prophetic voice of protest if he joined the stream of conventional politics.

Since that time, a number of black men and women had run for President, but none with serious prospects of winning and a few for purely symbolic reasons: among them were the comedian and writer Dick Gregory and the Black Panther Party leader Eldridge Cleaver, in 1968; the Brooklyn congresswoman Shirley Chisholm, in 1972; King's follower Jesse Jackson, in 1984 and 1988; Dr. Lenora Fulani, a developmental psychologist, who, as the leader of the New Alliance Party, got on the ballot of all fifty states in 1988; Alan Keyes, in 1996 and 2000; and Al Sharpton and Carol Moseley Braun, in 2004.

Some of those candidacies produced concrete results. Chisholm, who ran under the slogan "Unbought and Unbossed," introduced the reality of a mainstream black candidate. At the Miami Beach convention that put George McGovern's name forward as the Democratic nominee, she had a hundred and fifty-one delegates; Chisholm saw herself as a trailblazer. "The United States was said not to be ready to elect a Catholic to the Presidency when Al Smith ran in the nineteen-twenties," she said. "But Smith's nomination may have helped pave the way for the successful campaign John F. Kennedy waged in 1960. Who can tell? What I hope most is that now there will be others who will feel themselves as capable of running for high political office as any wealthy, good-looking white male." Chisholm, who died in 2005, was also quick to remind people of a fact that would have interested Hillary Clinton; she said, "Of my two handicaps, being female put many more obstacles in my path than being black."

Jesse Jackson's two runs at the Presidency have largely receded from memory, eclipsed at times by his penchant for grandstanding, but he made a powerful mark. Jackson spoke of a multicultural "rainbow coalition," a rhetoric of unity, but even his most passionate supporters saw him as a man of the civil-rights generation, a politician who had begun his career in protest against white supremacy. "My constituency," he once said, "is the desperate, the damned, the disinherited, the disrespected, and the despised." Jackson was a wounded, fatherless man from Greenville, South Carolina, whose extraordinary energies and compassion, as well as his undeniable gift for black-church oratory, was sometimes overwhelmed by his vanity—a vanity that dismayed even Martin Luther King. And yet Jackson forged historical results. In two national races he won a total of fourteen primaries and caucuses and came in second in thirty-six, including in white states such as Maine and Minnesota.

Jackson, like King before him, and like Malcolm X in his speech "The

Ballot or the Bullet," reminded African-Americans of the enormous potential power of the black vote in American political life and pleaded for that potential to be used properly. At rallies in the South, Jackson made the case that Ronald Reagan had won in 1980 "by the margin of our non-participation." He had taken eight Southern states by a hundred and eighty-two thousand votes, "while three million blacks there were unregistered." Jackson was right. Increased black registration, bolstered by Jackson himself, helped bring a series of white Democrats into statewide office who had failed to win white majorities: Wyche Fowler, Jr., in Georgia; John Breaux, in Louisiana; Alan Cranston, in California; Terry Sanford, in North Carolina; and Richard Shelby, in Alabama.

The spectacle and passion of Jackson's speeches at the 1984 and 1988 Conventions was enough to alter the sense of what was politically possible. "Nothing will ever again be what it was before," James Baldwin said of Jackson's 1984 race. "It changes the way the boy on the street and the boy on Death Row and his mother and his father and his sweetheart and his sister think about themselves. It indicates that one is not entirely at the mercy of the assumptions of this Republic, of what they have said you are, that this is not necessarily who and what you are. And no one will ever forget this moment, no matter what happens now."

Richard Hatcher, an ally of Jackson's who, in 1967, was elected the first black mayor of Gary, Indiana, used a metaphor familiar to Barack Obama to describe his friend's accomplishment. Not only did Hatcher's language anticipate Obama's; he even anticipated a political figure like Obama and the emotional impact that he would have on the older generation. Jackson, Hatcher said, was "like Moses, he's been allowed to see the Promised Land but will never be able to get there himself. He cannot be Joshua, going on over with the people into Canaan. Ironically, that could be some person very different from Jesse, who, in what he represents and wants to do, will irritate fewer whites, will be more acceptable to them, because they will see him as more like themselves—'O.K., I think I can get past the color thing and vote for him, because I know in my heart that in his heart he's just like me. He's proven that.' . . . While Jesse has hastened the day when there will be a black President, Jesse himself will never become President. In a way, there's a sadness in that."

Before the country could realize an African-American in the Presidency, it seemed, popular culture helped conceive it—first as comedy, then as commonplace, providing, over time, a clue to the shifting yearnings and anxieties connected to race and the highest political office.

In a twenty-one-minute film called "Rufus Jones for President," directed, in 1933, by Roy Mack, Ethel Waters tells her young son, played by Sammy Davis, Jr., "You's goin' be President!"

"Me?"

"Sure. They has kings your age. I don't see no reason why they can't have Presidents. Besides, the book says anybody born here can be a President." And as Ethel Waters dreamily sings "Stay on Your Own Side of the Fence," she and the boy fall into a reverie in which they see his black political supporters carrying signs reading "Down with the Reds, Put in the Blacks" and "Vote Here for Rufus Jones, Two Pork Chops Every Time You Vote." Rufus is elected and promises that he will change the national anthem to "The Memphis Blues." Then Waters sings another song:

> There's no fields of cotton, pickin' cotton is taboo;
> We don't live in cabins like our old folks used to do:
> Our cabin is a penthouse now on St. Nicholas Avenue,
> Underneath a Harlem moon.
> Once we wore bandannas, now we wear Parisian hats,
> Once we went barefoot, now we're sporting shoes and spats,
> Once we were Republicans but now we're Democrats,
> Underneath a Harlem moon.

This sly, yet cringe-inducing ditty ends with young Rufus waking from his improbable dream of political success to the reality of his dismal surroundings and the smell of his mother's burning pork chops. In 1933, the idea of a young black boy dreaming of the Presidency was a form of tragic comedy.

In Irving Wallace's Johnson-era best-seller, *The Man*, Douglass Dilman, a black senator from the Midwest, becomes President through a freakish accident. The incumbent, the Vice-President, and the Speaker of the House all die. Dilman is full of self-doubt ("I am a black man, not yet qualified for human being, let alone for President"); he gets impeached and eventually wins acquittal by a single vote.

When, in the seventies, Richard Pryor was hosting a variety show on network television, he took on the subject as a comic flight: once a black man was in office, would he be loyal to his race or to his country? Elected the fortieth President of the United States, President Pryor opens his first press conference calmly and with only a hint of racial pride. Before long, though, he allows that he will consider appointing the Black Panther leader Huey Newton as director of the F.B.I. ("He knows the ins and outs of the F.B.I., if anybody knows") and intends to get more black quarterbacks and coaches into the N.F.L. It's the same gag about Black Power and white anxiety that's at the center of "Putney Swope," the 1969 Robert Downey, Sr., film in which a seemingly mild-mannered black advertising executive is accidentally elected to chair the board of a white-run firm, whereupon he throws out all but one token white, replaces them with black militants, and renames the firm Truth & Soul, Inc.

More and more, a black President was an ordinary sight—on the screen, at least. Morgan Freeman, as President Tom Beck, prepared the world for an all-destroying comet in the 1998 science-fiction film "Deep Impact"; in the television series "24," President David Palmer, played by Dennis Haysbert, fends off a nuclear attack—and after he is killed by a sniper his brother becomes President. In Hollywood's imaginings, a black President had become an incidental plot point, a casting choice.

Few politicians, no matter how young or self-aware, could have resisted the incessant encouragement, inquiry, flattery, and adulation that were now coming Obama's way. In Africa, he had been greeted day after day with rapt attention and ecstatic cheering. At the Harkin steak fry in Indianola, the testing ground for Presidential hopefuls, he had won an enthusiastic ovation and the plaudits of local and national columnists. And now, as he toured the country to promote *The Audacity of Hope*, his days began and ended with talk of a Presidential run. *The Audacity of Hope* was not nearly as introspective as *Dreams from My Father*. There were personal moments in it, but the book was purposefully, cautiously political. It was a shrewd candidate's book, tackling in moderately liberal terms the issues of domestic policy, foreign affairs, race, religion, and law. Like Obama's letter to Daily Kos and his speech before the evangelicals, it established a tone: cool, polite, insistent on refusing the mud and assaults of the cable shouters and Internet haters, intent on winning over everyone. For such a consistent Democrat, Obama wrote a book that seemed not so much to straddle the ideological divide as to embrace the entire landscape of political opinion all at once. Joe Klein, writing in *Time*, said he had toted up at least fifty instances in which Obama provided "excruciatingly judicious" on-the-one-hand, on-the-other-hand formulations. ("The tendency is so pronounced," Klein wrote, "that it almost seems an obsessive-compulsive tic.") And David Brooks, the conservative *Times* columnist, wrote, "He seems like the kind of guy who spends his first 15 minutes at a restaurant debating the relative merits of fish versus meat." And yet, Klein was not exasperated with Obama for long; his piece, like his coverage, was largely admiring. And Brooks wrote that Obama's deliberative nature was "surely the antidote" to the Bush Presidency; his column, which ran in mid-October, was headlined "Run, Barack, Run."

Some critics argued that by insisting on civility as an essential virtue in politics, Obama risked acting superior to politics itself. Obama's equanimity, his critics seemed to suggest, was a form of vanity, a lack of real conviction. The Democratic left wondered what it could make of a politician who expressed admiration for Ronald Reagan; internationalists and hawks wondered whether Obama, reacting to the disaster in Iraq, hadn't fashioned a liberal rationale for isolationism. *The Audacity of Hope* was an intelligent book but an elusive one. And yet many readers and potential voters embraced Obama, not least for his message of a new tone in political discourse. Timing was the crucial factor; the book came along just as the Bush Presidency—marked by an obstreperous partisanship, an obsession with secrecy and absolutism—was reaching its nadir.

More and more, it seemed obvious that the "perfect storm" that Rouse had talked about as a possibility in January, 2006, was now forming. There would be no incumbent or sitting Vice-President in the 2008 race. The Republicans were in a state of real collapse; not only was Bush himself profoundly unpopular, but the Party itself, which had instigated a prolonged conservative era beginning with Ronald Reagan's 1980 election, now seemed starved of ideas, save a tired insistence on tax-cutting free-market absolutism. Hillary Clinton was the putative frontrunner for the Democratic nomination, but her family legacy had ineradicable negatives that she would have to contend with. And here was Obama, a potential candidate with a slender political record but an appealing character and life story, clean hands on the issue of Iraq, and a rhetoric of change that was exciting liberal Democrats more than anyone since Robert Kennedy. Finally, there were the historical trends and polling numbers that indicated that an African-American—in particular, *this* African-American—could succeed in a national election.

The voices for caution in Obama's camp argued that the majority of the electorate would want him to pay his dues in the Senate and slowly accumulate more political credibility and experience. But that argument was fast losing its appeal. More and more, people who had known Obama since his Springfield days told him that such moments do not come along twice in the life of a politician. What would he gain by waiting? Would he really be in a better spot if Hillary Clinton won? When would a chance even half as propitious come again? Obama might end up regretting his own reluctance or hesitation for the rest of his life.

At a magazine convention in Phoenix on October 23, 2006, I interviewed Obama in front of an audience of hundreds of editors and publishers. The publicity tour for *The Audacity of Hope* was in full swing and he was groping his way toward running. In January, Obama had kept Pete Rouse's "perfect storm" memo to himself, and had told Tim Russert on NBC's "Meet the Press" that he would absolutely serve out his term in the Senate and not run for President; the day before my interview with him, he altered his tone, telling Russert that he had "thought about the possibility." While he hadn't made any decisions, the unmistakable and well-calibrated message was that he was in the water, waist-high. Obama came to Phoenix prepared to deal with the most obvious question—of experience.

"There's a hotel, I think it's the Capitol Hilton, in Washington. And downstairs, where there are a lot of banquet halls, there's a whole row of all the Presidents," he said. "You walk by the forty-three that have been there and you realize there are only about ten who you have any idea what they did. . . . I don't know what exactly makes somebody ready to be President. It's not clear that J.F.K. was 'ready' to be President, it's not clear that Harry Truman, when he was elevated, was 'ready.' And yet, somehow, some people respond and some people don't. My instinct is that people who are ready are folks who go into it understanding the gravity of their work, and are able to combine vision and judgment." Vision and judgment: down the line these would be terms of great use to Obama—the first to indicate a sense of intellect and youthful vigor, the second to underline his opposition to the war in Iraq.

What also seemed interesting about Obama that day was his capacity for straight talk on religion, a subject that Democrats had often handled as if it were a hand grenade with the pin out. Rare for a politician, he talked about the role of skepticism in his psychology and spiritual life. His own faith, he said, "admits doubt, and uncertainty, and mystery."

"It's not 'faith' if you are absolutely certain," he said, adding, "Evolution is more grounded in my experience than angels."

Obama's book tour was reminiscent of Colin Powell's experience when, in September, 1995, he was promoting his autobiography, *My American Journey*; he was constantly peppered with questions about running for the Republican nomination to face Bill Clinton in the general election. Like Obama, Powell was lauded as the political version of Oprah Winfrey—an iconic person of color readily accepted by audiences of all races. "It's a modern phenomenon," says Henry Louis Gates, Jr. "You heard it about Michael Jordan and Tiger Woods before his problems: 'Oh, he's not black. He's *famous*.' " For a *Time* cover story published in October,

2006, Joe Klein asked Obama about the comparisons. "Figures like Oprah, Tiger, Michael Jordan give people a shortcut to express their better instincts," Obama said. "You can be cynical about this. You can say, It's easy to love Oprah. It's harder to embrace the idea of putting more resources into opportunities for young black men—some of whom aren't so lovable. But I don't feel that way. I think it's healthy, a good instinct. I just don't want it to stop with Oprah. I'd rather say, If you feel good about me, there's a whole lot of young men out there who could be me if given the chance."

Throughout the autumn of 2006, Obama cast around for advice, and even took some old allies by surprise; it seemed they had barely adjusted to his fame beyond the South Side. He called Ivory Mitchell, the chairman of the Democratic organization in the Fourth Ward who had helped him win his seat in the State Senate just ten years earlier. "I was in the hospital for a knee replacement, just coming out of anesthesia, and my cell phone is ringing," Mitchell recalled. " 'Hey, Ivory, this is Barack. I think I want to run for President.' I was seven hours out of surgery and I said, 'Barack, we just sent you to the Senate!' "

In David Axelrod's Chicago office in the River North neighborhood, just after the November, 2006, midterm elections, Obama met with Axelrod, Gibbs, Jarrett, Rouse, Steve Hildebrand, the strategist David Plouffe, Obama's close friend Marty Nesbitt, and his scheduler and aide, Alyssa Mastromonaco. The office walls are covered with framed newspaper pages announcing the victories of Axelrod's many clients. Rouse had prepared a background memo that included questions like "Are you intimidated by the prospect of being leader of the free world?"

Which made Obama laugh.

"*Someone's* got to do it," he said.

In this and other early meetings that fall, Obama and his staff discussed all the obvious political ramifications. Was it really time? Was Obama prepared for the rigors of non-stop travel and scrutiny, the constant atmosphere of BlackBerry urgency, brushfires from early morning until late at night? Did he want to spend month after month in the first four primary states—Iowa, New Hampshire, Nevada, and South Carolina? Would he ever be able to catch up with Clinton, who was thirty points ahead, in terms of fund-raising and field organizations? Was Obama willing to endure the inhuman effort that a Presidential race demanded when the chance of winning was so remote? "We thought he could win," Plouffe said, "but it was a *small* possibility . . . Barack had never been through the crucible. He'd never had negative ads run against him. So, the question was, could he deal with the intense scrutiny and the attacks that would come. It was an open question. It was going to be grueling. You'll never be home, it's lonely, you're going to be a huge underdog. You've just come off this book tour where you got all this adulation and pretty soon you're going to be in Iowa talking to twenty people, and none of them are going to be for you."

The Democrats had just achieved a majority and so life in the Senate for Obama might become more satisfying, as it had when the Democrats took the State Senate in Illinois. At home, he talked with his wariest constituent: Michelle Obama. For a long time, Michelle had held their family together, taking care of the girls, working at the university, managing what needed doing as a political spouse. A run for the Presidency would mean two years of constant campaigning, of an absent husband and father, a brutal process of public exposure and unpredictable turns. Obama's books were best-sellers. The family was financially secure. Was this life so bad? Did they really want to endure the separations and risks of a Presidential race? As late as Thanksgiving, some members of Obama's inner circle would have put the odds against his running, despite his now public admission that he was thinking it through.

The public adulation was extraordinary. One afternoon Abner Mikva waited for Obama at a famous German restaurant in the Loop called the Berghoff, which was just around the corner from Obama's Chicago office. "He was just a few minutes late but he pulled up in his black S.U.V. He hadn't walked, and I teased him about it," Mikva recalled. "Barack said, 'If I had walked, I would have been an *hour* late.' As it was he couldn't even eat. So many people came to the table just wanting to shake his hand. He said, 'It's getting more and more like this all the time.' "

Mikva's friend Newton Minow had had similar experiences of Obamamania. Throughout the summer he had been wary of Obama's running so soon for the Presidency—until he turned on C-SPAN and watched Obama's speech in Indianola. "I said, by God, he is Jack Kennedy all over again." On October 26th, Minow published an op-ed article in the *Tribune* headlined "Why Obama Should Run for President."

Obama read the article and asked to meet with Minow and Mikva. The three men assembled at Minow's office downtown. Obama began by telling them that Michelle was extremely reluctant; they were both concerned that he would be away from his daughters for nearly two years if he ran.

"Between Abner and me, we have six daughters, and they've all turned out pretty well," Minow replied. "Mine are all lawyers, Ab's are a rabbi, a judge, a lawyer, and we learned that a father's biggest role was when they are teenagers."

Barack wrote down a few notes and said that he wanted to mention that to Michelle.

"Then Abner was tough on him on security," Minow said. "We told him that there was a strong likelihood that someone would take a shot at him. And he said, 'You sound like Michelle.' He didn't seem rattled by it, though. He seemed less concerned than we were."

Obama talked about his chances and said that, if he lost, at least he would learn a lot about the country and have a good shot at the Vice-Presidency.

Back in Washington, Obama's confidant in the Senate, Richard Durbin, argued that greater seniority in the Senate could prove a liability. The two modern senators who went directly to the Presidency, Warren Harding and John Kennedy, had done so after short careers in the Senate. John Kerry had spent a lot of his time in debate in 2004 defending the many controversial votes he inevitably racked up over two decades on Capitol Hill. "I said to him, 'Do you really think sticking around the Senate for four more years and casting a thousand more votes will make you more qualified for President?'" Durbin recalled. Tom Daschle, who gave up a chance to run for President and then lost his seat in the Senate, had become another of Obama's mentors, and at a long meal, Daschle told him that his lack of experience was an asset, not a drawback. "I argued that windows of opportunity for running for the Presidency close quickly," Daschle recalled. "He shouldn't assume, if he passes up this window, that there will be another." The longer he stayed in Washington, Daschle told Obama, the harder it would be to present himself as a candidate of change. Walter Mondale, Bob Dole, and Kerry were just a few of the senators who, as Presidential candidates, suffered from an image of institutional calcification; their experience was, for many voters, offset by years of stentorian debate and stultifying compromise. Even the Senate Majority Leader, Harry Reid of Nevada, privately told Obama that he should at least consider running. Reid, as a Democratic Party leader, could obviously not show his hand, but he, too, was worried about Hillary Clinton's negatives.

There were, however, admirers of Obama's who worried that, like a college athlete who jumps into the professional ranks before graduation, he could do himself irreparable damage. Harry Belafonte, who had been deeply engaged in the civil-rights movement while he was on the rise in show business, was in contact with Obama and he worried about him.

"Because I do see in him something so terribly precious and I see in him such a remarkable potential, I would rather think of him as a work in progress," Belafonte said. "We are prone to push people beyond their time. We are so eager to devour our young. I think Senator Obama is a force, and I think he needs to see a lot about this nation and he needs to go to a lot of places. We've seen so many others who have come to high places and have failed so miserably. I think he could be our exception to the rule."

In November of 2006, at the offices of a Washington law firm, Obama held one of a series of secret brainstorming sessions about his chances. His friends and advisers asked if he could overcome the charge of inexperience. Could he challenge the Clinton machine? After the meeting had gone on for a while, Broderick Johnson, a prominent Washington lawyer and lobbyist, asked, "What about race?"

Obama replied, "I believe America is ready," and little more was said on the subject. Obama could not run a campaign like Jesse Jackson's, which had relied heavily on a black base; instead, he would aim at a notionally limitless coalition organized around a center-left politics.

At around the same time, Obama had a telephone conversation with one of his African-American fundraisers. The fundraiser told Obama that he wasn't sure it was the right time, that Obama was vulnerable on the question of experience, that he had never run a state office or a large business. Obama answered that if experience necessarily led to good judgment then Donald Rumsfeld and Dick Cheney would be supreme. "But look where that got us," he said.

The two men talked some more—about the Clintons, about the Republicans, and, most of all, about the barriers that Obama would face. Finally, the fundraiser said, "It's funny you call. I've taken my own plebiscite and there is an interesting divide."

Obama cut him off and said, "Yeah, yeah, I know. The white folks want me to run. And the black folks think I'm going to get killed."

That was it, exactly. The donor, who was older than Obama, had keen memories of the assassinations of Medgar Evers and Martin Luther King. When King was shot in Memphis, Obama was six years old and living in Indonesia. The older man felt that there was an emotional and temporal divide. "If you are brought up in that experience and heard the things you've heard, then the idea of a black guy running for President was a little scary," he admitted later. As both a candidate and then as President, Obama would make jokes about "getting shot" in order to put friends and visitors at ease; he and Michelle had made their peace with this new reality and were determined not to feel its weight.

Finally, Obama concluded that while he was not yet committed to running, it wasn't worthwhile to be consumed in speculation about the readiness, or not, of the American people for a black President. "If they're not ready now," he said more than once, "they won't be ready in my lifetime."

Mike Strautmanis, who had first met the Obamas when he was a paralegal at Sidley Austin, where Michelle was working, had become chief counsel in the Senate. Even though he was younger than many of the black political advisers and fundraisers talking to Obama and expressing their anxieties, he, too, felt angry at times with the white liberals for pushing so hard. "They weren't seeing the United States and remembering its history clearly enough for what it was," he said. In his most pessimistic moments, Strautmanis believed that "once again their ideals would lead to something terrible, and it was my friend who was going to pay the price."

And yet it calmed him to watch Obama sort through his options. "I remember a meeting in November, 2006," he recalled. "I'd heard from Pete Rouse how Barack and Michelle were going through this process, the questions they were asking. I realized that Barack had been thinking about this for a very long time. He'd been thinking about the political moment we're in for at least ten years. He was testing, seeing how all the pieces fit together. Would the pieces be there? The money? The ability to create a national political organization and a loyal team? And the pieces meant nothing unless you understood the political moment and how to meet it. He had a very sophisticated view of that. He'd been making a detailed, layered analysis of national politics for a long time."

Obama's view, Valerie Jarrett said, was that "he would not lose because he's black, and, therefore, let's not dwell on the fact that he's black. Because if you dwell on it, and you make race an issue within the campaign, then it will become an issue." Jarrett, who was personally closer to the Obamas than anyone in his political circle, said that once they had been assured of the professionalism of the Secret Service, their anxieties eased. "I can't let that paralyze me," Obama said.

"There were so many opportunities for him to be afraid along this path and to turn back," Jarrett recalled. "You know, when you were talking about the brothers saying, don't run because you might lose? They weren't worried about him. They were worried about themselves. They didn't want to be embarrassed."

Around Thanksgiving of 2006, John Rogers and others in Obama's circle went to see "Bobby," a film written and directed by Emilio Estevez. The film was set in the Ambassador Hotel in Los Angeles, where Robert Kennedy and many of his supporters were staying at the time of the 1968 California Democratic primary. These were what turned out to be the last hours of Kennedy's life. What moved Rogers and his friends was not the bloody climax of the film, but, rather, the way that the film's many ordinary characters—a retired doorman, a soldier, a beautician, a black kitchen worker, two Mexican busboys, the campaign donors, and the long-haired volunteers—were swept up in the promise of Kennedy's campaign, the way that they represented a multi-ethnic coalition. The film suggested, once more, R.F.K.'s campaign in 1968 as a model of idealism. In the wake of emotional events like the Africa trip and his meetings with crowds of people during his cross-country book tour, Obama and his circle were arriving at the conclusion that he could run and, if things broke the right way, win the Presidency.

"We were talking about this sense of passion and energy and love for Bobby and he was experiencing it in his life," Rogers recalled. "It's a rare thing to generate that kind of passion. You could just tell that it clearly affected him, what he was experiencing on the road. People were pushing him. I had had the sense he was going to push it off for the next time but when I met with him that November, December in the office here, you could sense that he was pretty well there. He was taking it really seriously and he was going to go to Hawaii and think about it. But reading body language, I had the strong feeling that he was going to move at warp speed."

Rogers, who had played basketball with Michelle's brother, Craig, at Princeton, had been a big supporter of Bill Bradley's political career. He told Obama that one of Bradley's problems was that he had waited too long to make his run; that, by the time he did, his moment had passed. Rogers also described watching Hillary Clinton, who had been in Chicago to speak at the Economic Club downtown. It was a dull spectacle that gave him hope. "There wasn't a chuckle or smile in the hour," he said. "It was drab, facts and figures and numbers and policy points. And I thought Hillary wouldn't capture the imagination of the American people."

On November 28, 2006, David Axelrod wrote Obama a tough-minded memorandum to force the issue. The memo asserted that Obama, because of his youth and non-partisan image, was the ideal antidote to the Bush Presidency: "You are uniquely suited for these times. No one among the potential candidates within our party is as well positioned to rekindle our lost idealism as Americans and pick up the mantle of change. No one better represents a new generation of leadership, more focused on practical solutions to today's challenges than old dogmas of the left and right. That is why your Convention speech resonated so beautifully. And it remains the touchstone for our campaign moving forward." Hillary Clinton's strategy, he said, will be "to suggest that she has the beef, while we offer only sizzle." She would, however, have a difficult task "escaping the well-formulated perception of her among swing voters as a left-wing ideologue." Axelrod did not discount John Edwards. He had worked for Edwards in his 2004 Presidential campaign—an experience that ended unhappily when, among other factors, Edwards's wife, Elizabeth, lost faith in him and helped to push him off the team. Edwards was ahead in Iowa, but, Axelrod said, that was because he was a "relentless campaigner and debater."

Echoing the advice of Durbin and Daschle, Axelrod counseled against waiting for a moment when Obama was more seasoned: "You will never be hotter than you are right now." A longer voting record could hang "from your neck like the anchor from the Lusitania."

There was no getting around the difficulties. "This is more than an unpleasant inconvenience. It goes to your willingness and ability to put up with something you have never experienced on a sustained basis: criticism. At the risk of triggering the very reaction that concerns me, I don't know if you are Muhammad Ali or Floyd Patterson when it comes to taking a punch. You care far too much [about] what is written and said about you. You don't relish combat when it becomes personal and nasty. When the largely irrelevant Alan Keyes attacked you, you flinched."

It was a shrewd memo, one written not only by a cunning political consultant attuned to the political moment but also by a friend who had the capacity to provoke Obama, purposively, preventatively. He made sure to finish on a note of idealistic purpose. "All of this," Axelrod wrote, "may be worth enduring for the chance to change the world."

Not long afterward, Obama was speaking with the Reverend Alvin Love, from the Lilydale First Baptist Church, on the South Side, an old friend from his organizing days. The two men were talking about Obama's decision when, finally, Love said, "You know, my father always said you have to strike when the iron is hot."

Obama laughed. "The iron can't get any hotter," he said.

Finally, Rogers and Jarrett, as well as wealthy allies like Penny Pritzker, thought that his growing appeal could be leveraged to raise enough money to make him a serious candidate. Pritzker, who had first met the Obamas in the mid-nineties when Craig Robinson coached her child in a summer Y.M.C.A. basketball league, became Obama's national finance chairman; her brother Jay did the same for Hillary Clinton. "I knew Barack would be able to raise the money," Rogers said. "He was always very disciplined about making his calls and building the relationships. Barack was the Michael Jordan of the political world. Jordan came into the

N.B.A. as a gifted player, but he worked at getting better. Barack had all the skills but he also worked at getting better and better. He knew how to organize a team."

In mid-December, Obama told his inner circle that he had moved "past the fifty-fifty mark," but he wanted to spend the holidays in Hawaii with his family and think it through to the end. The day before he left, he even told David Plouffe that he was "ninety per cent certain that I am running" and would give the "final green light" when he got back. Plouffe's concern was that the normalcy and fun of the trip with his family would awaken Obama to the many pleasures of private life that he would be giving up.

Obama's sister, Maya Soetoro-Ng, had been teasing Obama about running for President for years. At Christmas in 2005, she bought some "Obama '08" T-shirts from one of the draft movements and put them under the Christmas tree. Obama had just laughed and rolled his eyes. By Christmas of 2006, she said, "It felt less funny. It felt like people had been waiting for him." In Hawaii, as their daughters played in the sand, the Obamas talked through their last concerns—security, the loss of privacy, the effect on Malia and Sasha.

When Obama came home after the New Year, he said, "Well, I've decided to do it, but I want to go home just this one last weekend to make sure I don't have buyer's remorse." He did not. He was sure. Late at night, on January 6th, Obama called Plouffe and said, "It's a go. You can start hiring some core people quietly but swear them to secrecy."

On January 21, 2007, Obama attended the National Football Conference championship game between the Chicago Bears and the New Orleans Saints, at Soldier Field, in Chicago. Invited to the suite of Linda Johnson Rice, the chairman and C.E.O. of *Ebony*, Obama mingled with other guests, including Marc Morial, the president of the National Urban League and the former mayor of New Orleans. Obama admitted that he was moving toward a run for President—by then it was an open secret; on January 16th, two years after his swearing-in at the Senate, he had filed the necessary papers for an exploratory committee—and, when Morial asked him what his plan was, Obama said that he had to win the caucus in Iowa, an almost entirely white state.

"If I do that," he said, "I'm credible."

Chapter Thirteen

The Sleeping Giant

"Race isn't rocket science," one of Barack Obama's friends and law professors, Christopher Edley, used to say. "It's *harder*." In Obama's campaign for the Presidency, the most persistent of all American problems was a matter of intricate complexity from the first day.

February 10, 2007, was announcement day, in Springfield: what most people remember of that sunny, frigid afternoon is the young candidate in his dark overcoat speaking before the backdrop of the Old State Capitol where Lincoln began his 1858 Senate campaign, a crowd of thousands in the cold, shuffling tightly to keep warm, puffs of vapor rising as they cheered. Admitting to a "certain audacity" in his candidacy, Obama placed himself at the head of a "new generation" during a period of crisis, foreign, domestic, and environmental. He implicitly compared the national mission to that faced by the greatest leaders the country has known:

> The genius of our founders is that they designed a system of government that can be changed. And we should take heart, because we've changed this country before. In the face of tyranny, a band of patriots brought an Empire to its knees. In the face of secession, we unified a nation and set the captives free. In the face of Depression, we put people back to work and lifted millions out of poverty. We welcomed immigrants to our shores, we opened railroads to the West, we landed a man on the moon, and we heard a King's call to let justice roll down like waters, and righteousness like a mighty stream.

It was a typically eloquent performance, but what was hidden, what was left unsaid, was the anxiety of race—not "a King's" call but the continuing enigma of race. Obama was the first African-American running for the Presidency with any chance of winning, and it would have been naïve to think that race would fail to insinuate itself into the campaign somewhere along the line. What remains of our story is not the 2008 campaign in its every aspect but rather the story of race in the campaign—a story that was immediately evident on day one.

In planning his announcement speech, Obama had originally wanted Jeremiah Wright, his longtime friend and pastor, to deliver the invocation. A couple of days before the event, however, Obama's aides learned about a forthcoming article in *Rolling Stone* called "Destiny's Child," in which Wright was described as "a sprawling, profane bear of a preacher," given to "Afrocentric Bible readings." The article, written by a respected young journalist, Benjamin Wallace-Wells, was extremely positive, yet it quoted Wright saying, "Racism is how this country was founded and how this country is still run! . . . We are deeply involved in the importing of drugs, the exporting of guns and the training of professional KILLERS. . . . We believe in white supremacy and black inferiority and believe it more than we believe in God. . . . We conducted radiation experiments on our own people. . . . We care nothing about human life if the ends justify the means! . . . And. And. *And!* GAWD! Has GOT! To be SICK! OF THIS SHIT!"

Wallace-Wells's use of neo–Tom Wolfe punctuation to render the propulsive style of Wright's preaching was not much of an exaggeration. In writing about Wright's importance in Obama's life, Wallace-Wells concluded, "This is as openly radical a background as any significant American political figure has ever emerged from, as much Malcolm X as Martin Luther King, Jr." Wallace-Wells pointed out that Wright was hardly an "incidental" figure in Obama's life, that Obama himself had described how he "affirmed" his faith in Wright's church and often used his pastor as a "sounding board."

The obvious worry was that voters would assume that Wright's politics and outrage were a mirror of Obama's "true" positions and feelings. Would the campaign have to begin with countless, and perhaps futile, explanations of the role and style of the black church? Would the most promising black candidate for President in American history be derailed by the sermons of Jeremiah Wright? Obama's aides, particularly David Axelrod, were sufficiently alarmed to think that putting Wright up onstage with the candidate on the day of his announcement could kill the candidacy at the moment of its launch. "This is a fucking disaster," he said to Plouffe and Gibbs. "If Wright goes up on that stage, that's the story. Our announcement will be an asterisk. The Clinton campaign will insure it."

Axelrod, Gibbs, and Plouffe called Obama and appealed to him to talk to Wright. Obama, reluctantly, agreed.

On February 9th, Wright was at Amherst College, in Massachusetts, to attend an interfaith celebration of the life and work of Dr. King. Wright was looking forward to the evening; there was to be a dinner for the Jewish Sabbath and an interfaith service at which he would preach. Early that afternoon, Wright says, he got a call from Obama telling him, "I'm just warning you, because tomorrow, before you say your prayer, we don't want you to say anything that's going to upset anybody in Iowa, because we're leaving there to go to Iowa. Don't want to upset those Iowa farmers. Talk about my experience as a community organizer. I bring different factors to the table. Got it?" A couple of hours later, David Axelrod called Wright and repeated the message: please avoid anything controversial, stick to the script.

Wright thought that was the end of it, but at about four-thirty Obama called again. This time he told Wright, "*Rolling Stone* has got ahold of one of your sermons, and, you know, you can kind of go over the top at times." He said to Wright that his sermons were sometimes "kind of rough." As Obama spoke, Wright was trying to figure out what was going on. Then Obama made things plain: "So it's the feeling of our people that perhaps you'd better not be out in the spotlight, because they will make you the focus, and not my announcement. Now, Michelle and I still want you to have prayer with us. Can you still come and have prayer, before we go up?"

Wright agreed to stand down from giving the public invocation and to come to Springfield anyway to be with the Obamas. Wright is a prideful man. From almost nothing he had built a church and, over time, attracted thousands of parishioners. This was to be a year of reckoning and triumph; he was, at the age of sixty-six, planning to retire. But now the most famous member of his flock was putting distance between them for reasons he could not yet fathom. Wright says that he wasn't angry—not yet, anyway. He would do whatever Obama asked. Obama had said that he still wanted to represent Trinity at the announcement and asked Wright whether he would object to his calling on the Reverend Otis Moss III, the young minister who was going to replace Wright, to give the invocation.

"We want you to pray with us privately," Obama said, "but can he do the part?"

"Certainly," Wright said. "I'm going to give you his private number, so you can reach him."

According to Wright, he gave Obama the number and hung up, still trying to figure out what sermon *Rolling Stone* had quoted.

Wright immediately called Reverend Moss, and told him, "I just want you to know, I gave away your private number." He explained why and said Obama would call him soon.

Moss replied that, in fact, one of Obama's top aides had already called and made the request.

"They're trying to drive a wedge between us is what I feel," Moss said. "I'm not going to do that."

Wright was now starting to get angry. "Well, I don't know why he would call," he told Moss. "I hadn't given my permission yet."

Moss said that he barely knew Obama and would rather not give the invocation if it was going to cause a problem with Wright. "I don't feel comfortable with that," he said.

By this time, Wright was agitated. He called two of his four grown daughters, Janet Moore and Jeri Wright, and his wife, Ramah, and said, "Don't look for me on television tomorrow. I'm not doing the invocation."

That night in Amherst, after the Sabbath dinner, Wright delivered a thirty-five-minute sermon at Johnson Chapel that began with the first verses of the Book of Joshua. Wright never mentioned Obama directly and seemed unfazed by what had happened earlier. He described how in the text the Israelites, after forty years of wandering in the desert and the death of Moses, were "standing on the precipice of change" and new leadership. The generation that had been wandering in the desert, he said, had no direct memory of slavery or the battles that came after. They had become divided and forgetful of their history. In a way that was familiar to his parishioners in Chicago, Wright glided in and out of the Biblical text, tying it to the contemporary scene. He said that Dr. King, the great Moses figure, was not the plaster saint of popular memory but, rather, a rebellious minister who opposed "the maniacal ménage à trois" of militarism, capitalism, and racism. He lambasted the U.S. government for lying about the war in Iraq and a population that insisted on living in "fantasyland"— "on the corner of Fiction Avenue and Wishful Thinking Boulevard." At the pulpit, Wright betrayed no distress, saying, "I enjoyed the Shabbat shalom dinner with no hot sauce." His sermon was spirited and fluent, a variation on one that he had given many times before. In his performance, there was not a hint of bad feeling.

After the service, Wright drove to Boston, where he slept for three hours. He took an early flight to Chicago and then flew on to Springfield for the announcement speech. At the Old State Capitol, he was led to a holding area with the Secret Service, Richard Durbin, and the Obama family. Wright embraced Michelle Obama and led the family in prayer.

When they were finished, Obama went up to the stage and announced his candidacy. During the speech, Wright stood near Michelle.

By the time Wright got back to Chicago, word had begun to spread of how he had been asked to step aside. Jeri Wright told Al Sharpton. Otis Moss III told his father, one of the best-known civil-rights-era ministers. Bad feelings started to brew on all sides. A few days later, Obama spoke with Wright and his daughter Jeri.

"Do you know what it's like to feel that you've been put down by your own church?" he said.

"Do *you* know what it feels like to have your friend calling Pastor Moss before you got the number from Daddy?" Jeri Wright replied. Jeri also told Obama that his aide had "disrespected" her father.

Obama said that he had meant no disrespect and didn't know that the aide had called Moss before clearing it with the Reverend Wright.

"I know you didn't," Jeri Wright said, according to her father. "But you've got people around you who are doing stuff you don't know about. And, as a matter of fact, you never even heard the sermon that's being printed."

Jeremiah Wright finally determined that the sermon quoted in *Rolling Stone* had been delivered fourteen years earlier in Washington when the Reverend Bernard Richardson was installed as dean of the chapel at Howard University. Wright says that at that event he wanted to challenge Richardson to lead a prophetic, rather than a priestly, ministry at Howard, "like it was when I was there in '68." He challenged Richardson to be more like the righteous prophet Amos and less like Amaziah, "the priest of the government," more like Dr. King than like Billy Graham. In the full text of Wright's 1993 Howard sermon, he starts out by saying that he wants to "paraphrase" a talk by Tony Campolo, a well-known white pastor who is opposed to same-sex marriage and abortion but generally left-wing. Campolo, who ministered to Bill Clinton in the wake of the Monica Lewinsky scandal, is known for his ability to shake his listeners out of a comfortable piety. In one sermon he says, "I have three things I'd like to say today. First, while you were sleeping last night, thirty-thousand kids died of starvation or diseases related to malnutrition. Second, most of you don't give a shit. What's worse is that you're more upset with the fact that I said 'shit' than the fact that thirty-thousand kids died last night." Wright had been reading the text of a fiery sermon that Campolo had given to a gathering of white Southern Baptists in which he delineated the continuing inequities and tragedies in so many African-American lives. At the end of the litany, Campolo expressed his outrage at white America. Wright recalled, "And then he says at the end, and we continue to worship in our sanctuaries every week, completely oblivious of these facts. 'And God has got to be sick of this shit.' "

Wright's sermon at Howard was a kind of extended quotation of Campolo. That fact was not included in the *Rolling Stone* article. And yet the reporter had accurately captured the spirit of Wright's sermon. The full excerpt has Wright angrily reeling off a list of ten outrages, ranging from the undeniable (early U.S. support of apartheid, inequities in the health-care system) to the arguable and the absurd. Wright said in that sermon that the U.S. had practiced "unquestioning" support of Zionism and had accused anyone who supported Palestinian rights of anti-Semitism. Most disturbingly, he repeated the familiar conspiracy theory that the U.S. government had "created" the AIDS virus.

And so, on the day of Obama's announcement, poisonous seeds had been planted; the *Rolling Stone* article, one would have guessed, would surely inspire a footrace among media outlets and opposition researchers to comb through all of Wright's sermons of the past thirty-five years. The incident also planted a seed of resentment in Wright, an accomplished, sometimes arrogant man who had always seen himself as a trusted mentor to Barack Obama, but who now, in the year of his retirement, would be judged by people and a range of media that, for the most part, were unlettered in the history, complexity, and rhetorical styles of the black church.

The Wright incident was not the only racial controversy being played out on the day of Obama's announcement. Tavis Smiley, one of the most influential African-Americans in television and radio, was angry with Obama because he had scheduled his announcement for that day in Springfield rather than attending Smiley's annual State of the Black Union conference, in Hampton, Virginia, and, perhaps even making the historic news there.

Cornel West, one of the leading black intellectuals at the event and Smiley's close friend and mentor, had great respect for Wright—"I would take a bullet for Jeremiah Wright"—and warned against jumping too soon on the Obama bandwagon. West, a professor of philosophy and religion at Princeton, was born in Tulsa and grew up in Sacramento. A religious Christian and a democratic socialist, he lectures in a style that melds the classroom and the black church. Beyond his academic work, he is a self-described scholar-bluesman, who is on the road with a frequency that challenges B. B. King. When Smiley called on West to speak, West took aim. "Look, Obama is a very decent, brilliant, charismatic brother," he said. "There's no doubt about that. The problem is, is that he's got folk who are talking to him who warrant our distrust. Precisely because we know that him going to Springfield the same day Brother Tavis has set this up for a whole year—we already know then that him coming out there is not fundamentally about us. It's about somebody else. He's got large numbers of white brothers and sisters who have fears and anxieties. He's got to speak to them in such a way that he holds us at arm's length enough to say he loves us, but doesn't get too close to scare them. So he's walking this tightrope, you see what I mean?"

"I want to know, how deep is your love for the people?" West continued. "What kind of courage have you manifested and the stances that you have and what are you willing to sacrifice for? That's the fundamental question. I don't care what color you are. You can't take black people for granted just 'cause you're black."

Another speaker, Lerone Bennett, Jr., a historian and, for many years, the executive editor of *Ebony*, criticized Obama for announcing his candidacy in Springfield—a platform bound to draw favorable parallels with Lincoln. Bennett's view of Lincoln was almost completely negative, and he drew attention to Lincoln's written and spoken comments on the supposed inferiority of the black man, his support for recolonizing blacks, and his unsentimental attitude toward the slavery issue. Bennett's one-sided view of Lincoln is hardly the consensus view among historians, even on the left—he ignores the political pressures on Lincoln and his contradictory statements about slavery—but he drew applause from an audience that was frustrated with Obama.

Smiley, for his part, told the crowd that Obama had called him on the eve of the conference and said he was sorry that he couldn't come. But the crowd mainly seemed unimpressed, as did Smiley himself.

The one intellectual on the stage in Hampton who defended Obama was Charles Ogletree, who had taught both Barack and Michelle at Harvard Law School. He said he could vouch for Obama's intelligence and good intentions and reminded the crowd that Obama had sponsored a racial-profiling law in the Illinois state legislature and had opposed the war in Iraq well before the invasion. "He's young, he's inexperienced, and the one thing we know from the Scripture is that we fall down, but we get up," Ogletree said. "He might have fallen down today, but we have to be there, with love and appreciation, and say, 'Barack, get up, clean yourself up, we are here for you if you understand who you are.'"

"I was the only one who spoke in defense of him," Ogletree recalled later. "Afterward, Cornel came over to me and said, 'Tree, I didn't know he was your boy! I need to meet him!' "

All these statements won applause in Hampton, but inside the Obama campaign and beyond, they seemed strangely parochial, grandiose, and self-defeating. Even Ogletree, Obama's defender, appeared to condescend to Obama by suggesting that the candidate had "fallen down" by making his announcement a national affair. Obama was so upset by the incident that he talked with his aides about gathering several dozen African-American intellectuals and celebrities to talk about racial issues. His aides were more cautious, saying that such a meeting would attract a lot of press and put race too far forward for a campaign that was determined to be universal in its appeal. Instead, the campaign formed an informal—and not terribly meaningful—advisory council on race that included Cornel West and Charles Ogletree. This was a deft, Johnsonian move whose purpose was to keep as many voices inside the tent as possible. As in the 2004 Senate race, Obama was starting from way behind, even among African-Americans, but Axelrod and Plouffe were counting on his quickly capturing the vast majority of black primary voters in order to narrow the gap between him and Hillary Clinton.

The most persuasive instrument that Obama had for calming the situation was his own voice. At Ogletree's urging, he made a series of telephone calls to West, Smiley, Al Sharpton, and others, and, patiently listening to their concerns, tried to convince them that they were united but had very different, if equally important, roles to play. He told them that they were free to press their ideas and agendas, but he was running for President. Once in office, he could accomplish a great deal. First, though, he had to win. Obama was respectful, telling them that they were speaking out in the tradition of protest, the prophetic tradition, but that as a politician he could not always afford the same liberties.

The situation with Tavis Smiley and Cornel West was especially delicate. Smiley had a large black audience but also a lot of crossover appeal. Smiley, born in Gulfport, Mississippi, grew up in extremely modest circumstances, and, as a young man, he interned for Tom Bradley, the first black mayor of Los Angeles. Beginning in 1996, Smiley had been a commentator on Tom Joyner's popular radio show, and, four years later, he organized the first State of the Black Union meetings. In 2006, he published a best-selling book of political essays, *The Covenant with Black America*, that featured a kind of action plan to better the lives of African-Americans. Smiley, like West, was concerned that Obama was too much of a centrist or, as they put it, "neoliberal." If he was going to get widespread black support, they insisted, he had to show far greater interest in trans-formational political change. Smiley says that he "reveled" in Obama's potential as a black President, "but I didn't want him to sell his soul, sur-render his soul, or lose his soul in the process of getting there." The ques-tion, Smiley says, was, "Are you going to be a truth-teller or a power-grabber? . . . If Obama won't lead the country in a conversation about race matters, who will? If you have that conversation only when he's forced to and have a media that is complicit, a media that makes it seem like we live in a post-racial America and with a conservative media that says we should stop all the grievances, well, this is kind of like Alice in Wonderland."

Obama's conversations with Smiley and West were not always smooth, but they were successful. West recalled, "First thing he said was, 'Well, Brother West, you're much more progressive on these things than I am. We're not going to agree on everything.' I said, 'Of course! My only thing is—you be true to yourself, I'll be true to myself.' That's all I ask. Then he went in and talked about what King meant, what that legacy meant, how he'd been shaped by it, and so forth. And it was a genuine opening. That's why I could discern a certain decency. I said, 'Brother, I will be a critical supporter. I'll be a *Socratic* supporter.' "

Some African-Americans, even friends in the academy, criticized West and Smiley for being presumptuous, high-minded, ignorant of main-stream political realities, and potentially damaging to Obama's campaign. But, with time, the two sides came to understand one another. West agreed to campaign for Obama across the country, and Smiley was a sup-portive, if critical, voice for Obama on television. Later that year, at a fundraiser at the Apollo Theater, Cornel West introduced Obama with unbridled enthusiasm and Obama returned the flattery, calling West, who had made his life difficult, "a genius" and "an oracle."

Even for an experienced national politician, the process of learning how to run for President, how to balance advice and all the contrary voices bombarding you, isn't easy. And Obama was not experienced. Soon after announcing his candidacy, he read Doris Kearns Goodwin's book on Lin-coln, *Team of Rivals.* The book sold swiftly late in the campaign, because Obama said that he had admired it and because of what it suggested about Lincoln's way of assembling an effectively contentious cabinet, but, now, in the spring of 2007, Obama was still far behind Clinton in the polls. He called Goodwin and said, brightly, "We have to talk." They discussed, above all, the temperamental qualities that Obama admired in Lincoln: his ability to endure defeat and acknowledge error, his capacity to manage his emotions in the heat of the moment, to resist showing anger or dressing down a subordinate in public.

A couple of months after the call, the writer and her husband, Richard Goodwin, who worked in both the Kennedy and the Johnson White House, visited Obama at his Senate office. "The most interesting thing he said was 'I have no desire to be one of those Presidents who are just on the list, you see their pictures lined up on the wall,' " Goodwin recalled. "He said, 'I really want to be a President who makes a difference.' There was the sense that he wanted to be big. He didn't want to be Millard Fillmore or Franklin Pierce."

Goodwin had started out a supporter of Hillary Clinton's; she was steadily won over not merely by Obama's attentions but by his temperament and the way his campaign echoed, for her, the popular spirit and hope of the civil-rights movement. Richard Goodwin helped to write Johnson's pivotal speech after Bloody Sunday, in Selma, on the Voting Rights Act.

Nevertheless, Goodwin said that Obama would have been foolish to make too strong a biographical comparison with Lincoln. "Obama, despite being black in a white world and negotiating the complications of race, never had to feel what Lincoln did. Lincoln was dirt poor and could never go to college. He had all of twelve months of schooling in his life," she said. "Lincoln's father kept pulling him out of school to work the farm, and, when he was in debt, he made his boy work on other farms. Lincoln studied the law on his own at night. Then, there were the deaths. He loses his mother at nine, his sister, and so many more. Death stalked him. Lincoln was drawn to poetry about people who could not realize their talents. Obama would never have had to worry like that. The tragic sense doesn't seem to be there."

Obama and his circle of advisers hoped to carry out their Presidential campaign with only infrequent references to race. He occasionally spoke out on policy issues like incarceration rates and affirmative action but, unlike Jesse Jackson, whose campaigns were rooted in a sense of racial identity, the Obama team was not eager to put ethnicity at the center of the campaign. As he was making his first trips to Iowa, Obama thought about giving a major address on race. He was advised against it. "He would talk about a race speech in planning meetings and people would go, 'Yeah, yeah, yeah, we'll get to that,' " Obama's chief speechwriter,

Jonathan Favreau, recalled. "They didn't say it was a bad idea, exactly, but it was like, 'Yeah, we'll get to that,' and then forget about it. It got pushed off. I think there was some angst. It's politics. We were a very different campaign but on any campaign there is a traditional pull away from anything risky. He's a black candidate with a real shot—why have him take the risk?"

"He was itching to give it," Valerie Jarrett said. "But I think that the consensus around him was, don't wake up a sleeping giant. We've never had a politician who could have that conversation with the American people in a way that didn't polarize."

Don Rose, the Chicago political strategist who was close to David Axelrod, said that the Obama campaign set out trying to deal with race the way his client Jane Byrne dealt with gender in her campaign for mayor, in 1979. "We never once said anything about her being a woman," Rose said. "I had her dress as plainly as possible. She had bad hair, which had been dyed and dried over a lifetime, and she sometimes had it fixed twice a day. We had her wear a dowdy wig to look as plain as possible. We discouraged feminist organizations from endorsing her. I didn't want the issue of her being a woman to come up in the least. We knew that women who would identify with her, the gender-centric vote, would come our way without anyone raising it. You don't have to highlight what's already obvious."

It was not by accident that Jackson, Sharpton, and other potentially polarizing figures were seen so rarely on platforms with Obama during the campaign. "The rule was: no radioactive blacks," Rose said. "Harold Ford, fine. Jesse Jackson, Jr., fine. But Jesse, Sr., and Al Sharpton, better not." Rose noted that Obama referred to race in his stump speeches infrequently. "When Barack was using that line about how he didn't look like all the other Presidents on American currency, his numbers went down," Rose said. "He got whacked and the campaign noticed. You don't raise it, that's the axiom, and you let it work. The less said, the better."

The Obama campaign took polls on figures like Sharpton and could see that their presence on the campaign trail would be counterproductive. In Iowa, for example, Sharpton had a sixty-per-cent negative rating, and so when he declared that he was coming to the state to campaign in the final days of the caucus race, possibly to endorse Obama, they got the message to him, asking him, politely, to please not bother.

The near absence of Jackson and Sharpton on the campaign was so conspicuous that "Saturday Night Live" lampooned it. In a short animated film, a savvy Obama meets with Jackson for "secret strategy sessions," but only in a broom closet. Obama dispatches Jackson to faraway, imaginary African countries—Lower Zambuta and Bophuthatswana—for "important" missions. He sends Sharpton on a similarly absurd mission, and, when Sharpton returns, he asks gravely, "Al . . . how was East Paraguay?"

"Well, it turns out there is no East Paraguay," Sharpton says. "That set me back a month."

In the history of American politics, race has been, in Valerie Jarrett's term, the sleeping giant. The political scientist Tali Mendelberg, in her 2001 book, *The Race Card*, notes that the white-supremacist resistance to black men and women as political actors, as voters or candidates, began the moment that the slaves were freed. Just after Lincoln announced the Emancipation Proclamation, the Democratic Party of Ohio added to its slogan "The Constitution as it is, the Union as it was" the phrase "and the Niggers where they are." When blacks first started running for office, after the Civil War, white Southerners routinely deployed against them all the tropes of the racial grotesque: hyper-sexuality, drunkenness, criminality, idleness, ignorance. It was the Presidential campaign of 1864 in which the parties made their first explicit racial appeals. Speakers at the Democratic Convention mocked "flat-nosed, woolly-headed, long-heeled, cursed of God and damned of man descendants of Africa."

In 1868, Georges Clemenceau, a French journalist who later became prime minister, observed the Democratic Party Convention and reported, "Any Democrat who did not manage to hint that the negro is a degenerate gorilla would be considered lacking in enthusiasm." At that Convention, the Democrats nominated Horatio Seymour, a two-time governor of New York, to run with Francis P. Blair, Jr., a Missouri senator and former Union general, against Ulysses S. Grant. The Seymour-Blair ticket's appeal was thoroughly racist. One of its campaign badges read, "Our Motto: This Is a White Man's Country; Let White Men Rule." Democratic Party–controlled newspapers ran stories of the rape of white women and girls by black men, and Blair berated the Republican Party for yielding the South to "a semi-barbarous race of blacks who are worshippers of fetishes and polygamists."

The speeches, campaign posters, and party newspapers of Reconstruction and Jim Crow were filled with similarly explicit racist appeals that reflected the viciousness of the era. In the United States between 1890 and 1920, there were more lynchings than state-sanctioned executions. James Thomas Heflin, a U.S. senator from Alabama in the nineteen-twenties known as Cotton Tom, said, "The white race is the superior race, the king race, the climax and crowning glory of the four races of black, yellow, red, and white. The South's doctrine of white supremacy is right and it is fast becoming the doctrine of the American Republic."

The period between 1930 and 1960 was a racial battleground, not least within the ranks of the Democratic Party. Southern politicians, like Theodore Bilbo of Mississippi, continued to make appeals that were not only racist but incitements to murder: "You and I know what's the best way to keep the nigger from voting. You do it the night before the election. I don't have to tell you any more than that. Red-blooded men know what I mean." During a Senate hearing in 1946, Mississippi's James O. Eastland felt perfectly free to declare, "I know that the white race is a superior race. It has ruled the world. It has given us civilization. It is responsible for all the progress on earth." After the passage of a civil-rights plank at the 1948 Democratic Convention, at which Harry Truman was nominated, the entire Mississippi delegation and half of the Alabama delegation walked out and helped form a splinter party, the Dixiecrats; soon, they put forward Strom Thurmond, of South Carolina, to run for the White House.

Mendelberg writes that, as society changed, racial appeals gradually shifted from the explicit to the implicit. It took Lyndon Johnson, a white Southerner steeped in racial conflict and schooled in the Senate by the Georgian segregationist Richard Russell, to gather strength from the civil-rights movement and issue an explicit warning against racial appeals in American elections. "All they ever hear at election time is 'Negro, Negro, Negro!'" Johnson said in 1964, at a fund-raising dinner in New Orleans. He predicted that passage of the Civil Rights Act would cost the national Democratic Party the South for at least a generation, but explicit racist demagoguery was replaced by appeals that were more cleverly coded. George Wallace dropped slogans like "Segregation today, segregation forever" and called on his followers to awaken to the threat of a "liberal-Socialistic-Communist design to destroy local government in America."

In 1968, the Republican nominee, Richard Nixon, and his running mate, Spiro Agnew of Maryland, used the code of "law and order" to insure themselves of a solid white voting bloc in the South. Nixon, who was completely aware of the signals that he was sending, was first drawn to Agnew when the former Maryland governor denounced moderate black leaders for failing to "stand up" to militants. After filming a commercial about law and order in the schools during the campaign, Nixon said, "Yep, this hits it right on the nose. . . . It's all about law and order and the damn Negro–Puerto Rican groups out there."

As late as the nineteen-eighties, the Republican Party's two leading figures, Ronald Reagan and George H. W. Bush, made unmistakable, if implicit, racial appeals during their campaigns. On August 3, 1980, Reagan launched his general election campaign with a speech at the Neshoba County Fair, in Philadelphia, Mississippi, the town where three civil-rights workers—James Chaney, Andrew Goodman, and Michael Schwerner— were murdered by white supremacists during the 1964 voter-registration drives known as Freedom Summer. By delivering a speech in Philadelphia emphasizing his support of "state's rights," Reagan was making, at best, an insensitive and knowing appeal to George Wallace Democrats—an attempt to broaden what Nixon called the "Southern strategy."

In the 1988 Presidential campaign, in which Bush ran against Massachusetts Governor Michael Dukakis, he and his campaign manager, Lee Atwater, repeatedly seized on the case of William Horton, a murderer who was released on a furlough by Governor Dukakis while serving a life sentence. During the furlough, Horton committed an armed robbery and rape. Bush supporters ran commercials showing Horton, an African-American, as the threatening side of Democratic policy. (The commercial called him Willie Horton.) Bush pressed the Horton case with such passion that, Atwater said, "by the time this election is over, Willie Horton will be a household name." Bush's media consultant, Roger Ailes, who later became the president of the Fox News Channel, cracked, "The only question is whether we depict Willie Horton with a knife in his hand or without it."

It was hard to believe that Hillary Clinton would indulge in racial appeals of any kind. One of her dearest memories as a high-school student was going to hear Dr. King speak. She worked closely with civil-rights-era figures like Marian Wright Edelman and Vernon Jordan, attracted support from leading black politicians, and relied for advice on Maggie Williams, Minyon Moore, Cheryl Mills, and other black political operatives. The Clintons—Bill, especially—were at ease in black churches and black civic organizations and as a political family they were immensely popular in the African-American community. No group was more forgiving of Bill Clinton during his impeachment saga than African-Americans. In 2008, Hillary Clinton's aides were hoping that she would be able to hold on to around half the African-American vote in the primaries and then sweep it up almost entirely in a general election campaign.

From the start, the leading strategist in her campaign urged her to emphasize Obama's otherness. On December 21, 2006, Mark Penn— a pollster, public-relations executive, and longtime strategist for the

Clintons—distributed a memorandum on "launch strategy." The goal, he wrote, was to elect the "fwp"—the first woman President—despite a "relatively hostile media" eager to anoint "someone 'new' who can be their own." A resentful attitude toward the press was a longstanding fact of life in Clinton circles dating back to the days of the 1992 campaign—and not without reason. The wounds of Filegate, Travelgate, Whitewater, the impeachment, and much else persisted as a fact of psychological life. Even in retirement, the former President, as he worked mainly on his charitable foundation, the Clinton Global Initiative, sometimes let loose his rage at the press and other old enemies; a stray comment or mild question could set him off and Clinton's face would redden, his carotid artery engorge, as he re-engaged old arguments with his antagonists. His wife's election campaign represented a chance for redemption. Would Obama stand in the way of that chance?

Mark Penn wrote that he saw Obama as a "serious challenge" and counseled a cool head: "Research his flaws, hold our powder, see if he fades or does not run. Attacking him directly would backfire. His weakness is that if voters think about him five minutes they get that he was just a state senator and that he would be trounced by the big Republicans." His support came from a "Brie and cheese set" that "drives fund-raising and élite press but does not drive the vote. Kerry beat Dean. Gore easily defeated Bradley."

Three months later, on March 19, 2007, both Obama and Clinton were in the race, and Penn wrote another memo that distinguished between the two candidates primarily on the basis of class: "We are the candidate of people with needs. We win women, lower classes, and Democrats (about 3 to 1 in our favor). Obama wins men, upper class, and independents (about 2 to 1 in his favor)." Penn called on Clinton to be the champion of "the invisible Americans" and attempted to establish an iconic distinction between Obama and Clinton: "He may be the J.F.K. in the race, but you are the Bobby." In this dichotomy, J.F.K. represented an entitled, intelligent, élite, cool politician, R.F.K. a man of privilege who had come to identify most closely with the dispossessed—the whites of Appalachia, the Hispanic immigrants of Southern California, Texas, and Florida, the blacks of the inner city. Obama, too, had spoken of the inspiration of R.F.K.'s 1968 Presidential campaign and the coalitions that it had created before his death, but Penn seemed convinced that Hillary Clinton could best summon that romantic, yet tragic, past.

Penn's memo did not necessarily represent the strategy and psychology of the candidate herself. Clinton's campaign was, in fact, top-heavy with veteran advisers—Harold Ickes, Mandy Grunwald, Howard Wolfson, Patti Solis Doyle—and they generally loathed Penn, seeing him as cynical, pompous, and profoundly mistaken. To them, he was forever the associate of Dick Morris, the centrist operative who left the Clinton circle in disgrace, in 1996, after the tabloids published reports of his involvement with a prostitute. Ickes, who had been an activist in Mississippi during Freedom Summer, Solis Doyle, the daughter of Mexican immigrants, and others counseled greater caution than Penn, particularly on the question of race, and felt that his memos encouraged the candidate to go far beyond the bounds of brass-knuckle campaigning. Penn made no secret of the fact that he was more conservative than the rest of Hillary's team; what he resented was his need to win consensus from advisers who, he felt, were constantly undermining him.

"It's clear that they resisted a lot of his more sinister suggestions," David Plouffe recalled. Nevertheless, Penn's memo accurately reflected the resentful attitude toward Obama that reporters were noticing in Hillary Clinton's camp both before and during the campaign. Clinton and key advisers felt that Obama was an inexperienced, unschooled upstart, a novice with a talent for public speaking (as long as he was within range of a teleprompter). Obama, they believed, was relying almost solely on his speech-making abilities and the historically glamorous prospect of becoming the first black President.

In the March 19th memo, Penn suggested that the Clinton campaign target Obama's "lack of American roots." Using that supposed rootlessness, they could cast his candidacy as something fit only for the distant future. "All of these articles about his boyhood in Indonesia and his life in Hawaii are geared towards showing his background is diverse, multicultural and putting that in a new light," he wrote. "Save it for 2050."

"It also exposes a very strong weakness for him—his roots in basic American values and culture are at best limited," Penn's memo continued. "I cannot imagine America electing a President during a time of war who is not at his center fundamentally American in his thinking and in his values. He told the people of N.H. yesterday he has a Kansas accent because his mother was from there. His mother lived in many states as far as we can tell—but this is an example of the nonsense he uses to cover this up."

Penn counseled Clinton on how the campaign could "give some life" to these notions "without turning negative":

Every speech should contain the line you were born in the middle of America to the middle class in the middle of the last century. And talk about the basic bargain as about the deeply American values you grew up with, learned as a child and that drive you today. Values of fairness, compassion, responsibility, giving back.

Let's explicitly own "American" in our programs, the speeches and the values. He doesn't. Make this a new American Century, the American Strategic Energy fund. Let's use our logo to make some flags we can give out. Let's add flag symbols to the backgrounds.

We are never going to say anything about his background—we have to show the value of ours when it comes to making decisions, understanding the needs of most Americans—the invisible Americans.

"The invisible Americans" sounded a great deal like Nixon's "silent majority." Penn's strategy was to cast Obama as the candidate of the élite, a "phony," a neophyte, and an outsider—not quite as American as Hillary Clinton. Long after the race, Penn said to me that the memo "was not in any way, shape, or form meant to have any racial overtones. It was about the notion that [Obama's] childhood in Indonesia somehow better qualified him to manage international affairs—a fact he had repeatedly touted on the campaign trail."

Within the campaign, there was debate about Penn's tactics and an overall reluctance to highlight Obama's "otherness." But what could be expected of Bill Clinton, who had recovered from quadruple bypass surgery and was planning to campaign? Clinton had grown up in segregated Arkansas, comfortable in his relationships with black men and women. At Yale Law School he often made a point of sitting at the "black table" in the dining hall. Clinton's first adversary as a politician was James (Justice Jim) Johnson, a Klan-supported Democrat turned Republican who ran twice for governor and once for the Senate; Johnson was to the right of Orval Faubus, the infamous segregationist. As President, Clinton defended affirmative action, appointed African-Americans to his Cabinet, awarded Medals of Honor to black veterans whose heroism had been ignored, and apologized for the horrific Tuskegee syphilis experiment conducted on hundreds of black sharecroppers from 1932 to 1972. He delivered a number of speeches admired by the black leadership in Congress and cultivated friendships with leading civil-rights veterans like John Lewis, Andrew Young, and John Hope Franklin.

And yet Clinton was a politician to the core, a brilliant one, and sometimes a cynical one. Winning came first. During the 1992 campaign, in the midst of the Gennifer Flowers controversy and under attack as a Democrat "soft on crime," he flew to Arkansas and, to bolster his law-and-order bona fides, presided over the execution of a mentally handicapped black prisoner named Ricky Ray Rector, who, eleven years earlier, had killed a police officer. Then, attempting suicide, Rector shot himself in the head, in effect giving himself a lobotomy. The same year, Clinton accepted an invitation to speak at Jesse Jackson's Rainbow Coalition, in Washington, D.C., and then used the occasion to criticize the hip-hop performer Sister Souljah for a foolish comment she had made about black violence. ("If black people kill black people every day, why not have a week and kill white people?") With his host sitting nearby, Clinton compared Sister Souljah to the former Klansman David Duke and criticized Jackson for allowing her to be a member of his organization. It was a performance that infuriated Jackson but appealed to Reagan Democrats—as Clinton undoubtedly intended. "I can maybe work with him, but I know now who he is, what he is," Jackson said of Clinton at the time. "There's *nothin'* he won't do. He's immune to shame. Move past all the nice posturing and get really down there in him, you find absolutely nothing . . . nothing but an appetite." Eventually, Jackson forgave him.

In 1997, President Clinton initiated a "conversation" on race, led by John Hope Franklin, but it was a pallid, ceremonial affair, which disillusioned some black critics. "The initiative displayed the parochial, shallow self-servingness that besmirches all too much of Clinton's talk about race relations," the Harvard Law School professor Randall Kennedy wrote. "Portrayed as an effort at dialogue, the President's conversation was from the beginning a tightly scripted monologue that regurgitated familiar nostrums while avoiding discussing real problems." Compared with commissions on race under Harry Truman in 1946 and Lyndon Johnson in 1967, Kennedy said, Clinton's effort was "laughable."

In the long months before the Iowa caucuses and the New Hampshire primary, a generational drama played out among some of the most important figures in the civil-rights generation—a drama that reflected the dilemma of many ordinary African-Americans who were faced with a choice between Hillary Clinton and Obama.

Some made their choice without hesitation. Vernon Jordan, an attorney who had been president of the National Urban League, and who became a close adviser and friend of the Clintons, had given an early fundraiser for Obama's Senate campaign. But, before Obama announced for the Presidency, Jordan invited him to his house for dinner and told him, "Barack, I am an old Negro who believes that to everything there is a season—and I don't think this is your season. . . . If you do run, as I think you will, I will be with Hillary. I am too old to trade friendship for race. But, if you win, I will be with you."

Andrew Young, one of Martin Luther King's close advisers and, later, a mayor, a congressman, and Ambassador to the United Nations, was far less subtle about his loyalties. Speaking on television in December, 2007, Young said that he wanted Obama to be President—but only "in 2016." In a strange ramble for such a serious man, Young warned about Obama's lack of "maturity" and the need for a "protective network."

"It's like somebody wanting to be the next Martin Luther King," Young said. "They say, I wouldn't wish that on a friend of mine. Martin's home got bombed the first year, they took all his money the second year, and sued him for income-tax evasion. He got stabbed the third year. The fourth year, he came to Atlanta to try to escape from Alabama. They locked him up for picketing . . . and put him in a straitjacket, and took him from Atlanta to Reedsville before there were expressways. . . . Leadership requires suffering, and I would like to see Barack's children get a little older, see, because they're going to pick on them."

Young even went on about Bill Clinton's racial bona fides as a reason to vote for Hillary. "Bill is every bit as black as Barack," he said. "He's probably gone out with more black women than Barack. I'm clowning, but, when they went to Nelson Mandela's inauguration, they had a whole planeload of black folk who went down there. After the inauguration, there was a party. And Clinton was the one that said, 'Let's start a soul-train line.' All these middle class, bougie folk looked around, 'A soul-train line?' And Bill did the moonwalk in the soul train. . . . And Hillary pulled her skirt up above her knees, and she got down and went through too. . . . You look at Barack's campaign, and, first of all, I've talked to people in Chicago, and they don't know anybody around him. To put a brother in there by himself is to set him up for crucifixion."

Young eventually apologized, but his rhetorical flight did betray some commonly held anxieties about Obama—anxieties not only about his inexperience but also about his safety and about his authenticity as an African-American. Yet again in the life of Barack Obama, there were the old questions: Was he black enough? Was he ready? Was he tough enough?

Among all the living heroes of civil rights, the figure whom Obama admired most was John Lewis. At first, Lewis had signaled broadly to Obama that he would support him. Even though Obama had come to Washington only in January, 2005, the two men had formed a bond. That year, Obama went to Atlanta to speak at Lewis's sixty-fifth-birthday party.

Lewis was astonished by Obama's post-Boston appeal. "We walked the streets of Atlanta together and blacks and whites were asking him to run for President," Lewis recalled. "When we got to the restaurant, the waiters and waitresses were asking him to run. And when I introduced him that night I said, 'One day this man will be the President of the United States.'"

At the Selma speech in March, 2007, Obama felt confident that Lewis would be for him, but through the summer and into the early autumn, the Clintons kept appealing to Lewis on the basis of their long shared history.

"I've known Bill Clinton for so long—it was more than friendship, it was like a brotherly relationship. . . . And when Hillary would come to Georgia to speak, she would say, 'When I grow up I want to be like John Lewis,'" Lewis says. Lewis's bond with the Clinton family deepened at their worst moment. In August, 1998, after Bill Clinton went on television to admit to his relationship with Monica Lewinsky—an unprecedented humiliation—Lewis invited him to Union Chapel, on Martha's Vineyard, to commemorate the thirty-fifth anniversary of the March on Washington. "He didn't want to come, but I convinced him," Lewis recalled. "And, when the time came, I got up to introduce him and said, 'Mr. President, I was with you in the beginning and I will be with you in the end.' We both cried. . . . How could I abandon a friend like that?"

In October, 2007, Lewis finally came down on the side of the Clintons—there was just too much history to overlook. Lewis is one of the most principled figures in government, but there were also political considerations. Lewis represents the Atlanta area, a majority-black district, and Obama was not yet as well known or as popular as the Clintons among his constituents. "They didn't know him (a), and (b), they thought it was a long shot," Jesse Jackson said. "Black voters are comparatively conservative and practical." In 1984, Jackson had also struggled to get support from African-Americans who didn't think he had a chance.

For John Lewis, it was an agonizing time. Even before the Iowa caucuses, he was beginning to realize that Obama's candidacy was becoming increasingly serious and that his constituents were shifting away from Clinton. "If I had gone maybe with my gut," he said, "I probably would have gone with Obama from the outset."

The dilemma was plain. "These were people who knew Bill and Hillary and thought well of them and couldn't quite believe that this young guy with a foreign name had a chance to get elected," the civil-rights activist Julian Bond said. "After two Jackson campaigns, after Al Sharpton's campaign, after Shirley Chisholm, it seemed that these symbolic races hadn't delivered much. The promise had been that these candidates would extract some kind of benefits from the winners and the black cause would be advanced. That turned out to be less true than they had hoped."

Some civil-rights leaders did side with Obama early. The Reverend Joseph Lowery, a co-founder of the Southern Christian Leadership Conference and a leader of the 1965 march from Selma to Montgomery, told an audience in Atlanta in January, 2007, that "a slave mentality" still haunted those African-Americans who had counseled Obama to wait his turn. He compared those who discouraged Obama to the white ministers who told Martin Luther King, a half century ago, that the time was not ripe for civil dissent. "Martin said the people who were saying 'later' were really saying 'never,' " Lowery said. "The time to do right is always right now." A resident of John Lewis's district, Lowery signed on immediately with the Obama campaign.

When Lowery heard the news about Lewis's decision, he was just relieved he wasn't a politician. "John wasn't a civil-rights leader anymore, he was a politician, he had relationships and entanglements," Lowery said. "I told the Clintons that if Hillary got the nomination, I would support her, but, in the meantime, I felt Obama was destined to shake up the system."

Not that every black political or cultural leader was so understanding. The director Spike Lee, whose films include "Do the Right Thing" and a biopic of Malcolm X, was brutally dismissive of those who wavered. "These old black politicians say, 'Ooh, Massuh Clinton was good to us, massuh hired a lot of us, massuh was good!' Hoo!" he said. "Charlie Rangel, David Dinkins—they have to understand this is a new day. People ain't feelin' that stuff. It's like a tide, and the people who get in the way are just gonna get swept out into the ocean."

Similarly, not everyone in the Obama campaign was quite as forgiving of older black leaders like Lewis as the candidate himself. "Movements are led by the young," the pollster Cornell Belcher said, "and it was comical that the same people who were in their twenties during the civil-rights movement and demanded a seat at the table were now telling Barack Obama it wasn't his time."

Jesse Jackson, who also sided early with Obama, is an American character of emotional complexity, glaring weaknesses, and, far more than he is ordinarily given credit for, immense importance in the political advance of African-American politicians, including Barack Obama.

Jackson's flaws—his conceits, his neediness—are so well known that he is readily dismissed by those who do not bother to understand him.

George H. W. Bush once called him a "Chicago hustler." Even Martin Luther King, who, in Selma, brought Jackson close, raged against Jackson's need to thrust himself forward. Mario Cuomo, however, may have been right to say that when the definitive history of the 1984 election was finally written, "the longest chapter will be on Jackson."

"The man didn't have two cents," Cuomo said. "He didn't have one television or radio ad. And look at what he did." What Jackson did was to run the most serious Presidential campaign ever conducted by an African-American—a feat that he repeated in 1988. Even the Chicagoans in Obama's circle who are most dismissive of Jackson admit that he opened the door for them to the White House. Roger Wilkins worked for Jackson in 1984, he said, not because he thought he could win but, rather, to give the country a "civics lesson that there are black people in this country smart enough to be President of the United States."

Obama might have been wary of Jackson's presence in the campaign, but he could not escape his influence. In 2007 and 2008, when Obama quoted from King's speeches—quoted them with the same sense of reverence as a jazz musician quoting a passage in Armstrong or Coltrane—this was something fresh and affecting for younger voters. But it was hardly new. "When you are unkind to the homeless, disparaging them as derelicts, you on treacherous moral ground, Mr. Bush," Jackson said in the 1988 campaign. "'Cause there is another power. 'The moral arc of the universe is long, but it bends toward justice.' Those who cannot defend themselves, they got a silent partner, they got . . . got *another* power. And when you, when you attack liberals, good-hearted folks, lovers of civil liberties, Mr. Bush—Mr. Bush, watch out! You tamperin' with another power!" Jackson had a distinctively different style from Obama, but the sources of their inspiration converged.

Jackson did not intend merely to quote the prophetic voice of King for political purposes; he spoke in that voice because it was his own. Jackson pushed issues that were not always permissible in mainstream politics in 1984 and 1988, including Palestinian rights and opposition to South African apartheid. He received so many death threats that he often wore a bulletproof vest when he gave a speech.

Jackson did not have access to places like Punahou, Columbia, and Harvard. He was born and reared in segregated Greenville, South Carolina, a textile-mill town. His family had Cherokee and Irish blood. "We are a hybrid people," he said. "We are of African roots, with a little Irish, German, Indian. We are made up of America's many waters. Which makes us a new people, a true American people."

Jackson's father abandoned him before he was born, though he continued to live nearby. "I never slept under the same roof with my natural father one night in my life," Jackson has said. When he spoke on the campaign trail, he would talk about his deprived upbringing as the unassailable mark of his authenticity, the basis of his relationship to the poor and dispossessed. "You know, people'd always ask why is Jesse Jackson running for the White House," he would say. "They never seen the house I'm running from. Three rooms, tin-top roof, no hot or cold running water, slop jar by the bed, bathroom in the backyard in the wintertime. Wood over the windows, wallpaper put up not for decoration but to keep the wind out . . . In ways, it seems like a century ago . . . Yet I remain connected to all this. By continuing to live in those experiences here, you have high-octane gas in your tank—keep those experiences flowing through your soul, it gives you authenticity." When Jesse was a boy, Marshall Frady writes in his biography of Jackson, people still talked about the lynching of an epileptic black youth named Willie Earl; that murder was the subject of Rebecca West's classic essay "Opera in Greenville."

As a child in Greenville, Jackson was mocked by his schoolmates without mercy. "Jesse ain't got no daddy," they chanted. "Jesse ain't got no daddy." It was a Dickensian world of hurt transported to the segregated American South. "That's why I have always been able to identify with those the rest of society labels as bastards, as outcasts and moral refuse," he told Marshall Frady. "I know people saying you're nothing and nobody and can never be anything. I understand when you have no real last name. I understand. Because our very genes cry out for confirmation."

Greenville was a small town in those days and young Jesse would stealthily follow his father around town, spying on him, all the while wondering why he was denied his love. When he came to Greenville to give his first sermon as a preacher in his mother's church, both Charles Jackson, his mother's husband, and Noah Robinson, his birth father, were there, sitting in the front. For several minutes he just stood there in silence, tears streaming down his cheeks, looking down at his stepfather and the father who had disowned him.

In his twenties, Jackson became such a loyal acolyte of Martin Luther King, Jr., that he almost named his first son, who was born in 1965, Selma. When he was arrested and briefly imprisoned at demonstrations in Greensboro, North Carolina, he wrote, in imitation of King, "Letter from a Greensboro Jail."

Jackson's ambition was equal to his passion. In Selma, in 1965, when he was just twenty-four, he quickly made himself known around Brown

Chapel; he pushed his way to the front of marches. Unasked, he would give speeches from the steps of the church that imitated King's language and cadences, offending Andrew Young and other King lieutenants. "Jesse wanted to *be* Martin," Ralph Abernathy recalled.

Jackson alienated some of his civil-rights comrades when, in the days after Dr. King's assassination, he wore a shirt smeared with King's blood, a sign both of his grief and of his inheritance. Within days of King's death, he was wondering aloud whether he would now become the leader of the black freedom struggle. Jackson ascended rapidly in the world of African-American politics, making the cover of *Time* in 1970, but he also cemented his reputation, in some quarters, as a self-interested publicity hound, forever inserting himself into every high-profile domestic funeral and foreign negotiation. In 1983, Harold Washington did everything he could to avoid a too close association with Jackson during his campaign for City Hall. On victory night Washington was irritated when Jackson tried to hoist his arm in victory.

It was Harold Washington's triumph, however, that helped give Jackson the idea that he could run for President in 1984. And the pictures of him campaigning in the nearly all-white communities of Iowa forever altered the imagery of American politics. "They'd never seen a black man in the cornfields before," Jackson said. One night, Jackson was talking with some older farmers in Iowa and they told him that they had heard him speak, and liked him, but "we're not quite there yet. But don't give up on us."

In 1984, Jackson won nearly a fifth of all votes cast in the Democratic primaries and won South Carolina, Louisiana, and Washington, D.C.; in 1988, he won nine states and Washington, D.C. Two decades later, the children of those Iowa farmers had come along even further. They'd been brought up in schools where they learned about the civil-rights movement. They'd been brought up watching black and white athletes competing together. They pinned up posters of black athletes and musicians. Their popular culture was, in large measure, African-American popular culture. America was hardly the post-racial paradise imagined in some fantastical press accounts, but things had changed, and Jackson's candidacies in 1984 and 1988 had been essential in preparing the ground.

"My father's generation came out of World War II when returning black soldiers didn't have the same rights on the military bases that lots of German P.O.W.s had," Jackson says. "Barack once told me that when he was at Columbia as a student, he saw me debate Walter Mondale and Gary Hart there"—in March, 1984—"and he said he watched this and thought,

This thing can happen." Jackson said that "the whole idea" of his Presidential campaign was "to plant seeds."

Mainline politicians, black and white, criticized Jackson for his ego and his presumption, but his Convention speeches were anthologized alongside those of William Jennings Bryan and Mario Cuomo, and he got credit both for registering two million African-American voters and for changing the sense of the possible.

The first time Jackson ever heard of Obama was in his kitchen when his children were talking about Obama's efforts in Project Vote. Of course, he knew Michelle Obama from her childhood friendship with his daughter Santita. In the 2000 congressional campaign, Jackson had supported his old comrade Bobby Rush, but four years later during the Senate run, he was for Obama. The two men were never close—Jackson's pride and Obama's desire to be a different kind of leader prevented that—but at the East Bank Club, the downtown gym and hitching post for the Chicago élite, Jackson and Obama had occasionally talked about politics, and Obama sometimes spoke at Jackson's Saturday-morning meetings at Operation PUSH.

Jackson supported Obama in his run for the White House but he also understood why John Lewis, Andrew Young, and many other black politicians of his generation supported Hillary at first. "They had relationships," he said. "They'd known Hillary longer, they'd known Bill longer. No more, no less. And they believed Hillary would win. They thought they were betting on a winning horse. It was not anti-Obama. They didn't even know who he was, really. He'd never worked with us and dealt with blackness in Mississippi. She'd been with Marian Wright Edelman, working in legal-defense work. Hillary had a track record. Whatever his work was as a community organizer and all that, it's not as long and deep as Hillary's. She worked in the Arkansas Delta, the Mississippi Delta, and then eight years in the White House, and the work in Africa—I mean, there's a long list of accomplishments, and some people, as Vernon Jordan has said, do not switch horses without a reason that is compelling."

Nevertheless, once the Presidential campaign began, Jackson was not hesitant to show his displeasure with Obama when, in his judgment, he failed to speak out on racial issues. During a prolonged and ugly racial conflict at a school in the small town of Jena, Louisiana, Obama did not join a march—and Jackson let him hear about it. "If I were a candidate, I'd be all over Jena," Jackson said at the time. According to a South Carolina paper, Jackson thought that Obama, in his restraint, was "acting like he's white." Looking back, Jackson says he felt that Jena was an emblematic case in a country where there are over two million prisoners, nearly half of them black. "I thought it was the moment to send a statement about a change in criminal justice," he says. "Barack apparently did not want to be openly identified with that. But one can disagree with one's friends without jumping off a bridge. It wasn't no deal-breaker."

Barack Obama does not easily betray his emotions, but he was deeply disappointed that black leaders did not rally to him in greater numbers. John Lewis's decision to side with Hillary, in particular, felt like a stab in the back, he confided to aides. But in Iowa he was engaged in a much more immediate project—proving himself capable of winning white votes. "If Barack doesn't win Iowa, it's just a dream," Michelle said, in September, 2007. As Obama campaigned in the state and his remarkably devoted and well-organized network of young campaign workers outpaced their rivals, his appeal was looking less like Jesse Jackson's in 1984 and more like Gary Hart's. His most active support came from what strategists call "better-educated, upper-status whites," mainly college-educated, younger people who appreciated his outspoken opposition to the invasion of Iraq when he was still a state senator.

Oprah Winfrey endorsed Obama—the first time she had ever endorsed a Presidential candidate—and started to campaign in the early primary states. She threw him a dinner at her estate in Montecito, California, and invited Stevie Wonder, Tyler Perry, Quincy Jones, and other members of the black élite in show business, finance, and academia. Where Oprah Winfrey helped most, however, was with ordinary people. Her appeal transcended race, reaching huge numbers of middle-class, lower-middle-class, and working-class women, white and black.

With the Iowa caucuses getting closer, one could sense the panic in the Clinton ranks. Bill Clinton went on the "Charlie Rose Show" on December 14th and tried to plant the idea that Obama's election would be an enormous risk. "I mean, when is the last time we elected a President based on one year of service in the Senate before he started running?" Clinton said. "When I was a governor and young and thought I was the best politician in the Democratic Party, I didn't run the first time"—a reference to the 1988 campaign. "I knew in my bones I shouldn't run. I was a good enough politician to win, but I didn't think I was ready to be President." Inside the Clinton campaign, one former adviser said, "they were beyond furious"; they were convinced that the press was enamored of Obama and the narrative of an African-American candidate beating an entrenched machine. "Bill, especially, had to confront mortality," the former aide said. "They had once been young and romantic, but it's hard for a machine to be romantic. Their coverage had been good until November, December, 2007, but when it turned, it turned hard."

The Obama-Clinton race was historic for reasons of both race and gender, but, while Obama was able to adopt the language, cadences, imagery, and memories of the civil-rights movement and graft it onto his campaign, giving it the sense of something larger, a movement, Clinton never did the same with the struggle for women's rights. Clinton herself resisted it. Some inside the Clinton campaign later admitted that they were late to see the potency of Obama and race, and to realize the cost of their failure to connect the fight for women's rights to Clinton's candidacy and, thereby, enhance its power.

"We were just too late with gender," one of her senior aides said. "Also, in the minds of so many people, especially the press and the cognoscenti, Hillary had this hard, tough, anything-goes political ethos. She was branded that way, and that diminished her cachet and luster as the first real woman candidate for President. People saw something tawdry in her brass-knuckle political sense. She was battered and tarnished coming out of the White House years. She was the wicked witch. It is a cliché by now, but political toughness in a man is not criticized the way it is in a woman."

On January 3, 2008, Obama won the Iowa caucuses in commanding fashion. Hillary Clinton came in third behind John Edwards. The opening strains of Obama's victory speech that night were emblematic of the way that he treated race throughout the campaign. Amid the cheering in Des Moines, he began:

> You know, they said this day would never come. They said our sights were set too high. They said this country was too divided, too disillusioned to ever come together around a common purpose. But on this January night, at this defining moment in history, you have done what the cynics said we couldn't do. . . . We are one people. And our time for change has come!

An astonishing set of rhetorical gestures: Obama called on the familiar cadences and syntax of the black church, echoing Jesse Jackson's more overt lines: "Hands that picked cotton can now pick presidents: Our time has come!" He gestured toward what everyone was thinking about—the launching of a campaign that could lead to the first African-American President. Jon Favreau, Obama's speechwriter, said that the two of them were immersed in all of King's rhetoric, in the two Lincoln inaugurals, and in Robert Kennedy's 1968 campaign speeches. The opening of the Iowa speech—"they said this day would never come"—deliberately echoed King, but it was not explicitly racial; it was a way of intensifying a universalist purpose with a specific, historical ring. "I knew that it would have multiple meanings to multiple people," Favreau said.

Obama went on, "This was the moment when we tore down barriers that have divided us for too long. When we rallied people of all"—wait for it—"parties and ages." The displacement was deft and effective. The listener knew that he meant racial barriers—we could *feel* it—but the invocation was more powerful for being unspoken. The key pronoun was always "we," or "us." The historical fight for equal rights came only at the end of a peroration on national purpose:

> Hope is what led a band of colonists to rise up against an empire; what led the greatest of generations to free a continent and heal a nation; what led young women and young men to sit at lunch counters and brave fire hoses and march through Selma and Montgomery for freedom's cause. Hope—hope is what led me here today.

In Obama's speech the civil-rights struggle was recast in terms not of national guilt but of national progress: the rise of the Joshua generation, black and white, red and yellow. The black freedom struggle became, in Obama's terms, an *American* freedom struggle.

African-Americans watched Obama's victory speech in Des Moines with a sense of wonder. By winning Iowa and performing that night with such eloquence and force, Obama had proved that he had a chance, and now the black vote started to migrate steadily in his direction. A coalition of antiwar whites and blacks—perhaps something even wider than that—was now conceivable.

The tableau of Obama's victory-night speech, the television picture of him standing there with his family, also had a deep emotional impact. "Iowa was amazing," said Cliff Kelley, a leading host on WVON, the black talk-radio station in Chicago that had promoted Obama so heavily in recent years. "When Barack came out onstage with his wife and two gorgeous daughters, all of them looking like they were out of central casting, there were only five black people there in the room. Them and me." Until that moment, how many African-Americans—how many Americans—allowed themselves to believe that a black President was possible? Had the world really changed that much?

"It was only after Iowa, that they began to say, Oh my Lord, this could happen," Julian Bond said. "With Iowa you saw Obama could get white votes in the whitest of states. That made it all seem possible."

Iowa crushed Hillary Clinton's dream of an unstoppable juggernaut and endangered her candidacy. The New Hampshire primary was to take place five days later, and she was trailing in the state. But when she pulled out a victory there, both sides recognized that they were in for a long campaign.

Once more Jeremiah Wright came along to complicate things for Barack Obama. The Nevada caucus was to be held on January 19th, and, just before, Wright declared that the idea that the Clintons had been a friend to African-Americans when they were in the White House was preposterous. Bill Clinton, he said, "did the same thing to us that he did to Monica Lewinsky."

Once more Obama was forced to distance himself from his minister. "As I've told Reverend Wright, personal attacks such as this have no place in this campaign or our politics," he said in a statement. "That doesn't distract from my affection for Reverend Wright or appreciation for the good works he's done."

Chapter Fourteen

In the Racial Funhouse

In October, 2000, Anton Gunn, a community organizer in South Carolina and a former offensive lineman for the University of South Carolina Gamecocks, traveled to Arlington National Cemetery to bury his younger brother Cherone. A twenty-two-year-old Navy signalman, Cherone Gunn was among the seventeen crewmen of the U.S.S. Cole who were killed when Al Qaeda attacked the ship in the port of Aden, in Yemen. Cherone's father, Louge, a career Navy officer, and his mother, Mona, an elementary-school principal, wept as Anton knelt over his brother's flag-draped coffin and spoke softly to it, as if to someone half asleep. "I told him that I loved him," he said later, "and that I was going to miss him."

Even before his brother was killed, Anton Gunn had felt the urge to public service. After graduating from U.S.C., he worked for a variety of community groups around the state whose programs were aimed at helping poor families. In 2002, Gunn heard from one of his organizer friends about a guy named Obama, a former organizer in Chicago, who was running for statewide office in Illinois. He thought little of it. "The guy's name sounded foreign to me," Gunn says. "And I had no idea he was black."

Two years later, Gunn went to his local church to hear Obama speak in support of Inez Tenenbaum, a former teacher who was running for the Senate against a right-wing Republican, Jim DeMint. Tenenbaum lost the race but Gunn never forgot Obama.

By January, 2007, with Obama now a senator and preparing to announce his candidacy for President, Gunn was sold. On a trip to Washington, D.C., he bought a copy of *The Audacity of Hope* at the airport; he was so engrossed in the book that he failed to hear the boarding announcement and missed his flight. He resolved to help Obama in any way he could. First, he tried a blunt approach reminiscent of his days as a pile-driving blocker for the Gamecocks. He called Obama's office in Washington and informed aides that Obama was going to lose the South Carolina primary if he lacked the services of Anton Gunn. The response, at first, was silence.

Gunn then tried calling the Chicago office of Obama's nascent campaign. He left a similar message on the answering machine: "I may not know a lot about politics, but I know South Carolina. South Carolina is an early primary state. If you want to run for President, you need to have me involved."

That day, Obama himself called Gunn, expressing interest and saying that he was going to have Steve Hildebrand, the deputy national campaign director, get in touch. A few weeks later, Gunn went to Washington to talk with Hildebrand, who was planning the strategy for the early primary states, and David Plouffe, the campaign manager. They discussed Gunn's ideas for grassroots organizing in South Carolina. Plouffe, the most important figure in the development of Obama's campaign organization, knew something about working with black candidates; he had helped Axelrod run Deval Patrick's successful 2006 gubernatorial run in Massachusetts. But Gunn had special experience to offer, especially in the subtle racial politics of South Carolina. Gunn described how, as a neophyte, he had run for the state legislature, in 2006, in the majority-white, Republican stronghold of Richland and Kershaw Counties, which had never elected an African-American. He lost by only two hundred and ninety-eight votes.

At the time, the Obama campaign was still a minimalist operation. It had just a few people starting to work in Iowa and precisely no one in South Carolina, whose primary, on January 26, 2008, followed the Iowa caucuses by just twenty-three days. The Obama team hired Gunn as its South Carolina political director—its first employee in the state. During the next few weeks, Gunn began to set up a proper office. The Obama team also hired Stacey Brayboy, an experienced campaigner and aide on Capitol Hill, as state director, and Jeremy Bird, a Midwestern labor advocate and divinity student, as field director. Brayboy and Gunn are black; Bird is white. Together they built a structure based on community-organizing principles.

The Clinton campaign set up a fairly traditional organization in South Carolina, with an emphasis on acquiring the endorsements of local civic and religious leaders and handing out "walking around money" to them to help hire canvassers and poll watchers. At first, the Obama campaign tried to match the Clinton organization at this game. It offered a five-thousand-dollar-per-month fee to Darrell Jackson, a state senator who was the pastor of a church in Columbia with more than ten thousand congregants, and his public-relations firm to help turn out the vote. Reverend Jackson, who had gained a reputation for being able to get thousands of people to the polls, earned three times that amount in 2004, when he worked for John Edwards in the state. He finally accepted a competing offer from the Clinton campaign and, according to the *Wall Street Journal*, earned a hundred and thirty-five thousand dollars between February, 2007, and September, 2007.

With the backing of the Chicago headquarters, Gunn, Brayboy, and Bird decided to rely more on the grassroots-organizing style of their candidate. They knew that South Carolina was different from Iowa, where the caucus-goers are motivated civic activists. South Carolina is a primary state, and African-Americans form a large core of the potential Democratic Party vote. Obama's team wanted to register and reach African-Americans who had never gone to the polls before. In order to emphasize the campaign's universalist message, they also intended to make serious gains among white voters.

The campaign team quickly discovered that many African-Americans in South Carolina not only didn't know Obama's political positions but they had no idea who he was—or even that he was black. Those same voters knew a great deal about the Clintons and, in the main, admired them. To reach black voters, the Obama team had volunteers make repeated calls on churches, barbershops, and beauty salons, handing out a poster with a picture of Obama getting his hair cut in a South Carolina barbershop. If they were lucky, they won the endorsement of the proprietor, who would thereafter wear an Obama button. At churches, they targeted not the pastor, necessarily, but the informal community leaders. "Sometimes we'd rather have 'Miss Mary,' the woman everybody talks to, supporting us than the pastor himself," Anton Gunn said. They organized gospel concerts in Charleston and Florence where the only price of admission was to provide an address or e-mail contact. "We captured six or seven thousand people that way," Gunn said.

Early in the campaign, Gunn called the campaign offices in Chicago and said that the buttons and bumper stickers they were getting were inadequate. "We told David Plouffe, 'You can't keep giving out these buttons—they don't mean anything to anyone,' " Gunn said. " 'Design a button with his picture on it and say "Obama for President" so people can see this is a *black* man named Obama running for President.' " Gunn was a hip-hop fan, and he knew how performers marketed themselves by pass-

ing out free mix tapes and posters on the street. Gunn informed headquarters that the campaign had to give away, not sell, "chum," the term of
art for T-shirts, stickers, leaflets, and buttons. The campaign responded
with new campaign literature that featured pictures of Obama: some with
him and his family, some with him preaching in a church. New volunteers,
like novice organizers, got rigorous training and guidance, and passed out
the new chum at churches, fish fries, beauty salons, barbershops, ball
games, public-housing projects, medical clinics, and political rallies.

Long before the Iowa caucuses, Obama's campaign drew young volunteers who were willing to uproot and devote themselves to a long-shot
candidacy. In South Carolina, one of those volunteers was a twenty-three-
year-old woman from Venice, Florida, named Ashley Baia. Ashley Baia
was white. She moved to Horry County, South Carolina, in June, 2007,
and for the next six months campaigned in the beauty salons and barbershops of Florence and Myrtle Beach. For months, whites spurned her,
sometimes saying bluntly that they would "never vote for a nigger"; blacks
frequently told her that they wouldn't vote for Obama because they feared
that something would happen to him or because he "didn't have a chance."
Baia joined the campaign, she told her friends, because she saw in Obama
someone who understood the problems of the sick and the poor. She had
firsthand experience of those problems. When she was nine, her mother,
Marie, was diagnosed with uterine cancer. Marie lost her job and her
health insurance and she and her two daughters fell into bankruptcy. To
make her mother feel better about their meager dinners, Ashley told her
that she really did love relish sandwiches. Marie worked jobs—sometimes
two or three jobs at a time—that did not provide health insurance and
all the while, she did not know if she was going to have to leave her daughters to fend for themselves. "I didn't know if I was going to live or die," she
said later. She did secretarial work, waited on tables, delivered newspapers
in the middle of the night. To stretch out her prescriptions, she cut her
pills in half. "All those nights I thought she didn't hear me cry, she did,"
Marie said.

After a year, Marie began to recover and Ashley became a political idealist. When she was a student at the University of South Florida–
Sarasota/Manatee, she canvassed for John Kerry, and, two years later, she
became the vice-president of the Florida College Democrats. In May,
2007, after finishing school, she went to work for Obama in South Carolina recruiting voters and volunteers. The organizers and volunteers in
South Carolina and elsewhere called on the techniques of community
organizing, not least to strengthen the bonds among them. Obama had

interviewed church and community leaders about their "stories"; the volunteers told their own stories to each other at roundtable sessions. At one such session, in the late fall, with Valerie Jarrett present, Ashley described how her mother's suffering and the government's incapacity—or unwillingness—to do much for her had led her to politics. She wanted to "help the millions of other children in the country who want and need to help their parents, too." As Ashley spoke, Jarrett was in tears and was unable to give her own speech. Instead, she asked people to give the reasons that they had come to work for Obama.

"A lot of people talked about health care or some other issues," Ashley Baia recalled. "Then it came the turn of an older black man, a retired man, whom I'd been calling on over and over. He'd been very reluctant, though, to support Obama." The old man said that after having been visited by Baia so many times he had a simple reason for supporting Obama.

"I'm here because of Ashley," he said.

Valerie Jarrett was so touched by the encounter that she told Obama about it. He was so moved that he started thinking of that "moment of recognition," as he called it, that alliance between a poor white girl and an older black man, as emblematic of his own hopes for the campaign. For Obama, the stars were lining up in ways both big and small. He thought that he might use Ashley's story one day, perhaps in a speech.

In mid-October, 2007, with the South Carolina primary three months away, the New York *Times* ran a story that reflected the anxieties of many African-Americans in the state, particularly women. Clara Vereen, a sixty-one-year-old hair-stylist in the small town of Loris, said, "I've got enough black in me to want somebody black to be our President." But, she continued, "I fear that they just would kill him, that he wouldn't even have a chance." Miss Clara, as her friends called her, was considering not voting for Obama just to protect him. "We always love Hillary because we love her husband."

Black women made up twenty-nine per cent of the Democratic primary electorate in South Carolina, and they were not the only ones who felt as torn as Clara Vareen did. Obama made frequent trips to the state, and not only to black counties and neighborhoods. In June, 2007, he traveled to Greenville—the home base for Jim DeMint and Lindsey Graham—and thirty-five hundred people, blacks and whites, turned out.

In early November, Obama was in South Carolina and gave speeches at two different N.A.A.C.P. dinners in a single night. He also gave a speech in the town of Manning, on the steps of the Clarendon County Courthouse, the site of a desegregation case that became part of the Brown v. Board of Education decision. Clarendon is one of the poorest counties in the state. Manning sits along a strip of Interstate 95 so destitute that it is called the Corridor of Shame. Ernest Finney, the first black State Supreme Court justice in South Carolina since Reconstruction, introduced Obama, saying that he had dreamed of a black President when he was growing up in the segregated South, and now one "could be on the edge of winning."

From the staff in South Carolina, Obama had been hearing about the reluctance among some African-Americans to vote for him because of his youth and relative inexperience or because they feared for his safety. The level of threat was such that the Secret Service provided protection for Obama in May, 2007, sooner than for any other candidate except Hillary Clinton, who, as a former First Lady, had a detail with her from the start. In Manning, Obama had to respond to these anxieties, and, in the car, on the way to the speech, he kept fiddling with the text. When he arrived, he spoke directly to black voters:

> I've heard some folks say, "Yeah, he talks good. We like his wife. He's got some pretty children. But you know we're just not sure that America is ready for an African-American President." Y'all heard that before. You've heard the same voices you heard fifty years ago. "Maybe it's not time yet, maybe we need to wait. America is not ready." So I just want y'all to be clear: I would not be running if I were not confident I was going to win.
>
> I'm not interested in second place. I'm not running to be Vice-President. I'm not running to be secretary of something or other. I'm a United States senator already. Everybody already knows me. I already sold a lot of books. I don't need to run for President to get on television or on the radio. I've been on "Oprah." I'm running to be President of the United States of America. . . .
>
> So the brothers and sisters out there telling folks I can't win, don't defeat ourselves. Get that out of your mind that you can't do something. I don't believe in you can't do something. Yes, we can do something. What kind of message are we sending to our children, you can't do something?

This was the richest accent and the most direct form of rhetoric that Obama could summon. The speech was widely covered, but it still did not quite do the job; it did not completely erase the fears. "People were still talking about how the last time someone was as good as Barack was Bobby Kennedy or his brother John, and we saw what happened to them," Anton Gunn said. "There was general fear."

As the attacks on Obama began to accumulate on the Internet and cable television—attacks that tried to portray him as foreign, as a Muslim, as a covert radical in a business suit—the candidate summoned a vernacular that would not have worked in the cornfields and diners of Iowa. Speaking to a largely African-American crowd in Sumter, Obama rebuffed an e-mail barrage claiming that he was Muslim. "Don't let people turn you around because they're just making stuff up. That's what they do. They try to bamboozle you, hoodwink you." Similar lines are spoken by Malcolm X, in Spike Lee's biopic. Played by Denzel Washington, Malcolm warns a gathering of blacks about being "bamboozled" by "the white man." ("I say, and I say it again, you been had. You been took. You been hoodwinked. Bamboozled. Led astray. Run amuck. This is what he does.") Obama's spokesman, Robert Gibbs, solemnly informed the press that he didn't really know if the candidate knew the language was inspired by Lee's film about Malcolm X, but it was impossible to believe that he didn't.

Obama had still not wiped away all resistance to his candidacy. Anton Gunn admitted with some trepidation that in South Carolina it would help Obama if African-American voters saw that he had not married a white or a light-skinned black woman. "Like it or not, that stuff matters to people here," he said. ("I don't think Obama could have been elected President if he had married a white woman," Melissa Harris-Lacewell, a political scientist at Princeton who regularly attended Obama's church when she lived in Chicago, said. "Had he married a white woman, he would have signaled that he had chosen whiteness, a consistent visual reminder that he was not on the African-American side. Michelle anchored him. Part of what we as African-Americans like about Barack is the visual image of him in the White House, and it would have been stunningly different without Michelle and those brown-skinned girls.")

The campaign decided to send Michelle Obama to South Carolina to speak a few days before Thanksgiving. The site they chose was Orangeburg, a town of thirteen thousand that, from the start of the civil-rights movement, had been the scene of school desegregation battles, hunger strikes, protest marches, commercial boycotts, and, in February, 1968, a violent confrontation between police and demonstrators from South Carolina State University, a nearby black college who were protesting at a segregated bowling alley. The police fired into the crowd, killing three protesters and injuring twenty-eight; the incident is known as "the Orangeburg Massacre." The campaign scheduled the speech on the campus of South Carolina State.

Michelle Obama began by describing a meeting with Coretta Scott King, who died in 2006. "What I remember most was that she told me not to be afraid because God was with us, Barack and me, and that she would always keep us in her prayers," she said. She recounted all that Coretta Scott King had suffered, and reeled off the names of her heroic predecessors: Sojourner Truth, Harriet Tubman, Fannie Lou Hamer, Rosa Parks, Dorothy Height, Shirley Chisholm, C. Delores Tucker, Mary McLeod Bethune. "These were all women who cast aside the voices of doubt and fear that said, 'Wait,' 'You can't do that,' 'It's not your turn,' 'The timing isn't right,' 'The country just isn't ready.' "

Michelle Obama made countless appearances on the campaign trail, but the Orangeburg speech was her Joshua-generation speech—a pivotal direct address to the African-American community. The campaign, in general, had been so careful not to overdo the theme of race for fear of putting off white voters; this speech was one of the exceptional moments. Michelle Obama was sure to pay tribute to the generation of the past—"I am standing on their shoulders today"—before asking for the confidence and the support of the voters. She made plain her family history. She was like them. She was descended from slaves who lived in the state. Her grandfather was from Georgetown, South Carolina. She had the love of her parents, teachers, and pastors, but she also recalled the voices of classmates "who thought a black girl with a book was acting white." She had learned to put aside "that gnawing sense of self-doubt that is common within all of us." She described her path from the South Side of Chicago to Harvard Law School, but quickly showed that she was aware that "too many little black girls" don't have the chances that she did. These were girls who were routinely held back by poverty, unsafe and inadequate schools, crime, and racism. Her husband, she said, "is running to be the President who finally lifts up the poor and forgotten in all corners of this country." He should be President "not because of the color of his skin, it is because of the quality and consistency of his character"—an echo of King's "content of their character." Finally, she addressed the fears that so many black South Carolinians had expressed to Obama's earnest young volunteers—the fear that he was not ready, the fears for his life:

Now, I know folks talk in the barbershops and beauty salons, and I've heard some folks say, "That Barack, he seems like a nice guy, but I'm not sure America's ready for a black President." Well, all I can say is we've heard those voices before. Voices that say, "Maybe we should wait," and "No, you can't do it." "You're not ready"—"You're not experienced." Voices that focus on what might go wrong, rather than what's possible. And I understand it. I know where it comes from, this sense of doubt and fear about what the future holds. That veil of impossibility that keeps us down and keeps our children down, that keeps us waiting and hoping for a turn that may never come. . . .

And I want to talk not just about fear but about love. Because I know it's also about love. I know people care about Barack and our family. I know people want to protect us and themselves from disappointment, failure. I know people are proud of us. I know that people understand that Barack is special. You don't see this kind of man often.

I equate it to that aunt or that grandmother that bought all that new furniture—spent her life savings on it and then what does she do? She puts plastic on it to protect it. That plastic gets yellow and scratches up your leg and it's hot and sticky. But see grandma is just trying to protect that furniture—the problem is that she doesn't get the full enjoyment, the benefit, from the furniture because she's trying to protect it. I think folks just want to protect us from the possibility of being let down—not by us but by the world as it is. The world, they fear, is not ready for a decent man like Barack. Sometimes it seems better not to try at all than to try and fail.

We have to remember that these complicated emotions are what folks who marched in the civil-rights movement had to overcome all those decades ago. It's what so many of us have struggled to overcome in our own lives. And it's what we're going to have to overcome as a community if we want to lift ourselves up. We're going to have to dig deep into our souls, confront our own self-doubt, and recognize that our destiny is in our hands, that our future is what we make of it. So let's build the future we all know is possible. Let's prove to our children that they really can reach for their dreams. Let's show them that America is ready for Barack Obama. Right now. . . .

I want you to dream of that day—the day Barack Obama is sworn in as President. Imagine our family on that inaugural platform. America will look at itself differently. The world will look at America differently.

The message, conveyed in language far more emotionally raw than her husband ever allowed himself, was unmistakable. Just as Coretta King had no fear and, finally, no regrets, Michelle Obama had no fears—or at least no fears that held her back from supporting her husband. Her message was homey and direct. *He will be O.K. He wants what you want. Now is the time. And he can win.* Michelle Obama appeared before larger audiences—her speech at the Democratic Convention in Denver reached many millions of people, not a few thousand—but she never gave a more direct racial appeal. In Orangeburg, she asked black men and women to focus on the intersection of emotion and historical imagination; that was the sweet spot of her speech and the campaign was banking on it to work.

In the days before the primary, the voters of South Carolina did not provide much clarity in the polls. The black leadership in the state was still divided. One state senator, Robert Ford, a civil-rights veteran who had worked for King during the Poor People's Campaign, told a reporter that Obama's chances of getting the nomination were "slim," and that if he were to head the Democratic ticket "we'd lose the House and the Senate and the governors and everything. . . . I'm a gambling man. I love Obama, but I'm not going to kill myself." Ford stayed with Hillary. The situation among white voters seemed even more in doubt.

On January 20, 2008, a week before the South Carolina primary, Obama went to Atlanta to speak in honor of Martin Luther King's birthday at Ebenezer Baptist. The speech was reminiscent of the speech in Selma and several thereafter—until the end, when he told the story of Ashley Baia and the elderly black man in Horry County who said that he had been won over by her:

> By itself, that single moment of recognition between that young white girl and that old black man is not enough to change a country. By itself, it is not enough to give health care to the sick, or jobs to the jobless, or education to our children. But it is where we begin. It is why I believe that the walls in that room began to crack and shake at that moment.
>
> And if they can shake in that room, then they can shake in Atlanta. And if they can shake in Atlanta, they can shake in the state of Georgia. And if they can shake in Georgia, they can shake all across America. And if enough of our voices join together, if we see each other in each other's eyes, we can bring those walls tumbling down. The walls of Jericho can finally come tumbling down.

Once more, the story and the cadences of the civil-rights movement were extended to meet the story of the Obama campaign—and all in a resonant place. With time, Obama's confidence regarding the black vote and the question of authenticity increased. When, in a South Carolina debate, a reporter asked him, "Do you think Bill Clinton was our first black President?" Obama smiled and risked playing the role of a wry arbiter of blackness. Suddenly, he was no longer the cautious candidate but a man unafraid to parade his ethnic pride. "I would have to investigate more of Bill's dancing abilities," Obama said, "before I accurately judge whether he was, in fact, a brother."

In the same debate, a brutal encounter that took place on Martin Luther King Day at the Palace Theater, in Myrtle Beach, Hillary Clinton tried to emphasize her own presence in the Presidential race as a triumph of the civil-rights movement. "I'm reminded of one of my heroes, Frederick Douglass," she said, "who had on the masthead of his newspaper in upstate New York, *The North Star*, that right has no sex and truth no color. And that is really the profound message of Dr. King."

The Myrtle Beach debate was the nastiest of the entire campaign, with the candidates exchanging barbs over Obama's relationship with the "slum landlord" Tony Rezko and Clinton's advocacy as a corporate lawyer for Walmart. It was such a charged evening that as Clinton walked off the stage, she told her team, "I'm sorry, but he was such an asshole." Obama told Jarrett, "I probably went a little too far but she did, too."

After months of underestimating Obama's campaign, the Clintons now recognized the threat. "We were running against a very talented man," one of their top aides said. "In South Carolina, we didn't understand what to do. After we lost Iowa, the African-American vote was draining out of us so fast, like there was a hole at the bottom of the swimming pool, and you could just watch the tracking polls and see it evaporate. In New Hampshire we had won, even though we'd been down as much as sixteen points. It was unbelievable. We were so unprepared to win that we had to throw Howard"—Howard Wolfson, Clinton's communications director—"on TV, unshaven. The press decided that because we won by three [points] and the polls had shown her down eight, there was something back in play called the Bradley effect. Reporters were convinced that had to be the explanation. It undermined, it delegitimized, our win, and now it was out there, a new element being discussed coming into South Carolina, where so much of the Democratic vote is black."

On January 26th, Obama far exceeded expectations in South Carolina, winning overwhelmingly. In a three-way race with Clinton and John Edwards, he took fifty-five per cent overall to Clinton's twenty-seven.

Obama lost only two of the state's forty-six counties. Edwards, who came from neighboring North Carolina, drew a weak eighteen per cent of the vote and, four days later, withdrew from the race. Obama won eighty per cent of the African-American vote, and he continued to win at least that for the rest of the campaign. In a three-way race, Obama also won a quarter of the white vote; he even came in first with white voters under the age of forty. It was the calculus of the 2004 Illinois Democratic primary campaign taking shape on the Presidential level—a near sweep of the black vote combined with a healthy percentage of white progressives and some centrists.

"South Carolina was incredibly emotional," Cassandra Butts, Obama's longtime friend and aide, recalled. "Sitting in the boiler room and watching the returns, we realized that we had done exactly what we needed to do. Afterward there was the victory rally and people were chanting 'Race Doesn't Matter! Race Doesn't Matter!' Intellectually, I know that isn't the case, but these people were so moved by this candidate that they were willing to suspend disbelief."

African-American leaders now started to reconsider their loyalties as their constituents abandoned the Clintons. "I had an executive session with myself," John Lewis said. His constituents in Atlanta were behind Obama, and Lewis, for the first time in many years, was facing possible opposition in what had long been a safe district. He sensed that Obama was leading a campaign that was an electoral echo of the movement that had shaped his own life. Politically and emotionally, he was left with no option. He phoned Bill and Hillary Clinton to tell them that he loved them but that he was going with Barack Obama. "I realized that I was on the wrong side of history," Lewis said.

Until South Carolina, the Clintons thought that their history and relationships would assure them of a large percentage—even half—of the African-American vote. "Our whites on the staff, like Harold Ickes, had tons of experience with race," one Clinton adviser said. "Ickes had lost a kidney when he was beaten by whites at a civil-rights demonstration in Louisiana and had worked for Jesse Jackson. So when the time came that we lost John Lewis, Ickes said that it was like a kick in the nuts. He said, 'I can't believe this is happening.' But the Clintons understood that John Lewis had to move."

The South Carolina primary also revealed something about the Obama campaign. Although it was run mainly by a very tight circle of aides—David Plouffe, David Axelrod, Robert Gibbs, and other white men—there was a diversity of opinion at work that gave the campaign greater versatility. Valerie Jarrett, Cornell Belcher, Cassandra Butts, and, on a local level, people like Anton Gunn and Stacey Brayboy were able to shape tactics.

"I don't think there was ever a Presidential campaign before with a lot of people who looked like me," the pollster Cornell Belcher, said. "I wasn't sitting at just the smaller table dealing with the black shit. There was a lot of back-and-forth conversation about these subtle racial issues—a lot of conference calls, for instance, about Orangeburg. We had to really deal with the fact that there were African-Americans, older ones, who remember people dying. We had to win their confidence."

The conventional wisdom was that Iowa was the key: once blacks in South Carolina saw that whites would vote for Obama, they believed he had a real chance to win. Anton Gunn and Cornell Belcher, however, were among those who thought that there were limits to that analysis. "To say that Iowa broke it open and made black people support him is close to being racist," Belcher said. "Obama's numbers popped *everywhere* after Iowa. It wasn't just that his black numbers popped, it was everywhere."

Obama's increasing success as a national candidate, Belcher went on, was based on the fact that Obama was judged as an individual. "Because of who he is, he was inoculated from the stereotypes, the idea that somehow African-Americans don't share your values or are more morally loose or less intelligent," he said. "There were things about Barack, whether it was his family or his educational credentials, that made him able to individuate himself. What were the X factors? Does a biracial family heritage figure in? His Ivy League education? The image of a strong family man speaking out about personal responsibility?

"South Carolina was revealing," Belcher continued. "So much unfolded there about where we are, racially and culturally. Obama didn't start off winning black people in America or in South Carolina. That took effort. What went down was that he became an authentic, credible voice in the African-American community to such an extent that he wasn't just winning black voters; he was blowing Hillary away. She didn't break fifteen per cent of the African-American vote. He completely dominated a core Democratic constituency. No one could compete with him in North Carolina, Louisiana, Virginia, Mississippi, or Alabama. Think about if Hillary could have won twenty, twenty-five per cent of the black vote in Alabama, Mississippi, Georgia—it's a different race."

The nomination battle between Obama and Clinton lasted for four and a half more months. After the breakthrough victory in South Carolina,

Obama won a dramatic endorsement from Edward and Caroline Kennedy, but he emerged from Super Tuesday, on February 5th, with a projected lead of just fourteen delegates—a virtual dead heat. What Obama had done, however, was to prove that Clinton was not inevitable and that her campaign was weak, unfocused, and disorganized. It was absolutely impossible to overstate the friction inside the Clinton campaign, its resentment of the press, the sense of wounded pride. For the rest of the race, Obama never relinquished his lead, and, despite the fury in her ranks, Clinton was tenacious and, arguably, she defeated Obama in the majority of their debates. At one campaign event, Obama told an old Chicago friend, "Do I have to drive a stake through her heart? She just will not die!"

No small part of the drama of this seeming hundred years war was the racial dynamic, those not infrequent moments when a candidate or a surrogate said something that could be interpreted as a racial appeal. One early sign that the 2008 race would feature this subtext came when Joseph Biden, an early candidate for the nomination, said, in January, 2007, that Obama was the "first mainstream African-American [candidate], who is articulate and bright and clean and a nice-looking guy." Anyone who knew Biden assumed that he was being his usual self: syntactically undisciplined and oblivious of the resonance of terms like "articulate" and "clean." But, unlike older black leaders, including Jackson and Sharpton, who condemned Biden for the remark, Obama was initially unfazed. He brushed it off, saying that Biden "didn't intend to offend" anyone; "I have no problem with Joe Biden." Obama wanted to appear to be the opposite of hypersensitive—*I'm not the guy who sees racism everywhere*—but, when the criticism of Biden continued, he issued a statement that Biden's comments "obviously were historically inaccurate."

The mood among Obama's aides was less forgiving when one of Clinton's campaign co-chairmen in New Hampshire, Bill Shaheen, told the Washington *Post* that Obama would come under extra scrutiny from the Republicans for his use of drugs as a youth: "It'll be 'When was the last time? Did you ever give drugs to anyone? Did you sell them to anyone?' " Shaheen's comment echoed one of David Axelrod's memos to Obama, but in this context it seemed like a poisonous insinuation. At first Hillary Clinton was delighted with the statement and urged her aides to amplify it, but then when her campaign realized that it was playing terribly in the press, Shaheen apologized and resigned. Clinton herself met with Obama on the tarmac at Reagan Airport, in Washington, D.C., to apologize—a meeting that quickly turned sour when the two started exchanging recriminations.

In the course of the campaign, the slights (real or imagined, depending on the listener) began to mount. There was Robert Johnson, the African-

American media mogul and Hillary supporter, saying that while the Clintons were working hard for blacks and the public good, "Barack Obama was doing something in the neighborhood—and I won't say what he was doing, but he said it in his book." The reference, of course, was to Obama's self-described drug use as a young man.

There was Hillary Clinton saying, in January, "Dr. King's dream began to be realized when President Lyndon Johnson passed the Civil Rights Act of 1964. It took a President to get it done." To a Hillary supporter, she was merely stating the historical fact: King rallied public opposition to racism, but to change policy in Washington required Johnson and the power of the Presidency. To some Obama supporters, however, Clinton was slighting the heroism, the struggle, and the suffering of the movement. "The perception was that she was discounting the prophetic voice, diminishing the role that Martin Luther King played—and by extension diminishing Barack and his ability," Cassandra Butts said. "This goes to the critique of Barack as a lightweight, that he wasn't the hard worker that Senator Clinton was. It wasn't in isolation." In a conference call with reporters, Obama said that Clinton "made an unfortunate remark, an ill-advised remark."

The day before the New Hampshire primary, with polls promising a victory for Obama, Bill Clinton had told an audience, "This whole thing is the biggest fairy tale I've ever seen." To those who heard or read the line in isolation, Clinton seemed to be referring to Obama himself as a "fairy tale," an enchantment boosted by a smitten press. What he was saying, however, was something quite different—it was that Obama's opposition to the war was a "fairy tale." The Clintons kept hammering home the message that after Obama became a senator, his votes and his rhetoric on Iraq were much the same as Hillary Clinton's. This, too, was arguably true—and echoed one of Mark Penn's themes—but it was not racial. Clinton also referred to Obama as a "kid," a throwaway moment of condescension that some Obama supporters, like the prominent Harvard sociologist Orlando Patterson, cited as another term "for being uppity, it's a way of saying 'Who is he?'" Donna Brazile, who had been a campaign aide to President Clinton in 1992 and 1996, said, "I will tell you, as an African-American, I find his tone and his words to be very depressing."

When it seemed that Obama was going to win in South Carolina, Bill Clinton, who had campaigned hard in the state, remarked to reporters, "Jesse Jackson won South Carolina twice, in '84 and '88. And he ran a good campaign and Senator Obama has run a good campaign here. He's run a good campaign everywhere." To many in the Obama campaign, it seemed that Clinton was trying to yoke Jackson and Obama together as black candidates running implausible, can't-win campaigns.

"I don't think there was a racial strategy behind it, but I think it was delivered trying to diminish the win," David Plouffe said. Jackson himself saw nothing racist in Clinton's remarks, and, later that year, Clinton, while he was traveling in Africa, made clear his resentment of commentators who said that such remarks had hurt his wife's campaign.

"Do you personally have any regrets about what you did campaigning for your wife?" the ABC correspondent Kate Snow asked Clinton.

"Yes, but not the ones you think," he said. "And it would be counter-productive for me to talk about it. There are things that I wish I had urged her to do, things I wish I had said, things I wish I hadn't said. But I am not a racist, I never made a racist comment. And I didn't attack [Obama] personally.

"The South Carolina thing," Clinton continued, "was twisted for deliberate effect by people who weren't for Hillary. It was O.K. with me, but, you know, these people don't have an office in Harlem. They haven't lived the life I have lived."

Mark Penn, the most senior of Hillary's aides, says, "The Clintons had been like heroes in the African-American community. They had never done anything in their lives that would have allowed their comments to be misconstrued. And the treatment of the Clintons by the press was funda-mentally unfair."

And yet, another close aide to the Clinton campaign said, "Bill Clinton sometimes forgets he's a former President and he behaves like a history teacher, and he'll say something that is historically true but rings the wrong way coming from him. We were not sensitive enough. Remember, we were exhausted. All we were hearing from the press was how much we sucked, how Obama was heading a change movement, how our crowds were smaller than his—and this pisses you off, it beats you down. In eight days, you go from having no conversation about race at all to having it be a huge subject. You don't quite feel it happening because of everything else going on. It's the fog of war. You are like a frog in boiling water. You don't quite sense the life being drained out of you until it's too late."

Some of Clinton's friends watched what was happening with a mixture of dismay and sympathy. "All through the Bush years, black America and liberal America really loved Bill Clinton," one longtime friend said. "Bill could go out and, without a speech in his hand, be brilliant on so many topics. But I think after Obama showed up it was really hard on him not to be the cool guy anymore, not to be the smart guy, or the liberal guy or the black guy."

Bill Clinton's frustration was so deep, and his lack of discipline so strik-ing, that he told a Philadelphia radio station, "I think they played the race card on me." And later, when he was asked about the remark, he denied having said it.

The Obama people knew that their best political move was to step back and watch. Meanwhile, on black radio stations, one could hear African-American voters saying that they were dismayed with the Clintons, that they were now crossing over to Obama. "Until Bill Clinton's comments in South Carolina, there were still a lot of black people who weren't convinced Barack could succeed and we were still hearing that old 'Is he black enough?' stuff," said Mona Sutphen, a former aide in the Clinton administration, who became a foreign policy adviser for Obama and ended up as deputy chief of staff in the Obama White House. "When Clinton linked him to Jesse, ironically, he *made* him black enough. . . . The dustup turned black folks off. You can't out-black a black man, was the common refrain. If you try to go down that road, it's going to be a disaster."

In the wake of Super Tuesday, Sean Wilentz, a historian at Princeton and a Clinton supporter, wrote an angry article in *The New Republic* saying that reporters' adoration of Obama, together with their notion of the Clintons as sleazy and power-hungry, had allowed them to take innocuous remarks and turn them into racial appeals. "To a large degree," Wilentz wrote, "the campaign's strategists turned the primary and caucus race to their advantage when they deliberately, falsely, and successfully portrayed Clinton and her campaign as unscrupulous race-baiters." Wilentz called such tactics "the most outrageous deployment of racial politics since the Willie Horton ad campaign in 1988 and the most insidious since Ronald Reagan kicked off his 1980 campaign in Philadelphia, Mississippi, praising states' rights." Wilentz even compared Bill Clinton's situation to that of Coleman Silk, the tragic hero of Philip Roth's novel *The Human Stain*. Silk, a light-skinned black man who is a professor of classics and who has passed for white all his life, is ruined when, preposterously, he is accused of making racist remarks in his classroom during a period of hyper-vigilant political correctness on campus. Wilentz was not part of the campaign, but he certainly reflected the feelings of the Clintons, who thought that Obama and his advisers were expertly exploiting the charges of race for their political benefit. At the same time, however, Hillary wished her husband would tone down his attacks; they were not helping her. The problem was, she could not bear to confront him herself.

Not long after Wilentz's article appeared, Geraldine Ferraro, the Democratic Vice-Presidential candidate in 1984, told the *Daily Breeze*, a newspaper in Torrance, California, "If Obama was a white man, he would not be in this position. And if he was a woman of any color, he would not be in this position. He happens to be very lucky to be who he is. And the country is caught up in the concept." A week later, after Ferraro had been heavily criticized and the Clinton campaign failed to embrace her remarks, she told the New York *Times*, "I am livid at this thing. Any time you say anything to anybody about the Obama campaign, it immediately becomes a racist attack."

Privately, Hillary Clinton was deeply frustrated by these eruptions. They were distractions and did her no good. "Her reaction to the President's Jesse Jackson comment in South Carolina was 'Oh no!' " one aide recalled. "She loves him, but she knows what kind of game this is. She remembers that when she said that thing, in 1992, about staying home and baking chocolate-chip cookies, you get burned. That's the environment. And these blips, these moments—people believed that we were engineering them, that we were trying to paint Obama as the 'black candidate.' "

Hillary Clinton had not adopted Mark Penn's advice to isolate Obama as a "foreign" candidate. The comment of hers that smacked most of rank desperation, however, came in May, 2008, before the Kentucky and West Virginia ballots. "I have a much broader base to build a winning coalition on," she told *USA Today*. She cited an article and polling information in the Associated Press "that found how Senator Obama's support among working, hardworking Americans, white Americans, is weakening again, and how the, you know, whites in both states who had not completed college were supporting me. There's a pattern emerging here." Again, the statement was literally true—white working-class Democratic voters mainly favored her—but the phrasing was so maladroit (to be charitable) and the racial sensitivities so heightened, that Clinton came in for another round of criticism. This time, she was the culprit, not her husband. Charles Rangel, the New York congressman, who was one of her leading black supporters, told the New York *Daily News*, "I can't believe Senator Clinton would say anything that dumb."

Mona Sutphen, who became deputy chief of staff for Obama, was among those in Obama's camp who were beginning to see that race was helping far more than it was hurting his candidacy. "The diversity of Barack's background, not that he was African-American per se, was essential," she said. "He was doing well in the places where the electorate was younger, and, the younger the electorate is, the browner it is, the more diverse. He sums up, he *is*, the embodiment of American diversity. In the end, that played really well for him."

· · ·

With time, political campaigns tend to be viewed through the triumphalist prism of the winner. Obama's campaign is of such historical importance that it is easy to forget just how close the race actually was. Obama was far from an inevitability. We tend to forget that, if Hillary Clinton had won the Presidency, she, too, would have broken a historical barrier. What's more, Clinton was arguably on the receiving end of more condescension ("You're likable enough, Hillary") and bigoted remarks in the media and on the Internet; along the way, she was compared to everything from a "hellish housewife" to a castrating Lorena Bobbitt.

One afternoon, months after the election was over and the emotions of the campaign had cooled, a veteran Clinton aide told me about the way he and his colleagues—and the Clintons themselves—had experienced their run against Barack Obama:

> We knew we were walking in a racial minefield—the "racial funhouse," the President called it. It would now be an issue that, no matter what our history, we were white and they were black. By the way, Obama didn't seem to want this, either. But the racial arbiters, it seemed to us, were mainly Northeastern liberals, who had very little contact with African-Americans in their lives—the press.
>
> The conversations we were having in the campaign were chaotic, confused. Everything was turned on its head, everything was distorted and flipped and skewed. Some people inside thought we should address it. More thought that no, this was never supposed to be part of the campaign. We lived and died by the presumption that we were geniuses, that everything we did and everything that happened was by design and was brilliant. Remember, for sixteen years the Clintons were the big dogs of the Democratic Party. We knew how to win. Who else did? But the Obama campaign was running a Clinton operation— but better than us, cooler, more disciplined. Believe me, the Obama people pushed every bit as much opposition research stuff at the press as we did, but their reputation in the press was that they were . . . *nice*. We had the reputation of "the War Room," the tough guys. And, if you are a jewel thief and walk into a jewelry store, all eyes are going to be on you. If you are perceived to be making a false move, you get arrested.
>
> We still believed that we'd get the benefit of the doubt, that these two people, with their history in civil rights, with a largely African-American management team, were not running a race-baiting campaign. The conventional wisdom, though, was that we were. In the same way that Barack didn't want to be the black candidate, Hillary

didn't want to be the female candidate. She made an emotional speech at Wellesley but we got kicked for it, for playing the woman card!

Both campaigns discovered an old political reality: that exquisite interpretation is a constant in Presidential campaigns—especially when race and gender are such enormous factors. Politics becomes a spectacle of exhausted candidates and their exhausted aides trying to calibrate their words and, no matter what their talents, they cannot hope to be received in some ideal way that assumes their good intentions. The crosscurrents of competition, calculation, malice, frenetic communication, and indiscipline practically guarantee an atmosphere of ongoing crisis, mistrust, and mutual rage. Never mind that the amount of truly intentional malevolence on either side during the 2008 Democratic primary race was, in the light of many earlier campaigns, minimal. This spectacle is a large part of what is called, in the cliché of the time, the "narrative" of politics. Indeed, both Obama and Clinton usually went out of their way *not* to accent their sense of injury as a means to win sympathy and votes.

"We did a video," a Clinton aide recalled, "called 'The Politics of Pile-On,' which made her seem like the victim, and she was so mad about that. She said, 'I've spent a long time convincing moderate Republicans and conservative Democrats that I am capable of being a commander-in-chief, I've kicked the shit out of the boys on defense and security issues in these debates, and now you want me to be the victim?' *Vogue* wanted to do a story by Julia Reed with pictures by Annie Leibovitz. Even though *Vogue* had done a spectacular rehab job, a cover, after Monica, and probably the most flattering pictures ever taken of Hillary, she said, 'After spending years getting people to take me seriously as a commander-in-chief, a glamorous photo shoot in *Vogue* doesn't strike me right.' "

In the end, Clinton's aides realized that their campaign was less agile and cohesive, less romantic than Obama's. Their theme of reliability was the wrong one for the time. "Early on, there was an idea to make her a change candidate, too, and it was even suggested that we'd get a million women to give twenty-five dollars apiece. But by the time we thought to do it, it was decided that it would look desperate," one of her aides said. "We never pivoted successfully from 'strength and experience' to a sense of the person. People always just assumed Hillary was power-hungry, an in-fighter, robotic, and we never got across the sense of her as a devoted public servant. She was badly served by us. We never made her a three-dimensional person, a person with a rich history. We began with the most famous woman in the world and we didn't do enough with it."

Clinton's aides, like Clinton herself, came to respect the way Obama had played the game they thought that they had mastered above all others—Democratic Party politics. But, despite that respect, the Clintons and their advisers felt an overpowering sense of grievance and resentment, as if the rules of the contest had been written in Obama's favor.

"Throughout the whole campaign, it felt like we were playing as the visiting team at Soldier Field in Chicago," one aide said. "Every time they did something, the place went wild. Every time we won something, there was silence. Obama was *new* and he was hopeful and he projected change. And he had a better narrative. Of course, we thought the narrative was full of shit. We didn't understand why his politically calculating chameleon nature was never discussed. We were said to be the chameleons, but he changed his *life* depending on who he was talking to. He melded himself according to what the situation was."

Chapter Fifteen

The Book of Jeremiah

On March 13, 2008, nine days after Obama lost the Ohio and Texas primaries to Clinton, ABC's "World News Tonight" broadcast video clips of Jeremiah Wright preaching at Trinity United Church of Christ. This was more than a year after Wright had been quoted in *Rolling Stone* and he was asked not to give the invocation at Obama's announcement speech, in Springfield. Shockingly, neither the Obama campaign nor the Clinton campaign had bothered to do the obvious—dig deeply into recordings of Reverend Wright's sermons, many of which were on sale in the church gift shop. It was a ludicrous oversight. "It's not like we ignored it completely, but what we didn't do is to have people like me say, 'I want to watch all of the tapes,'" David Plouffe recalled. "I didn't do that. Ax didn't do that. . . . We live in a visual world. The moments in the campaign that really exploded were those that were on video. We failed the candidate in that regard." If a network had found the sermons on the eve of the Iowa caucuses or another early pivotal moment, Obama might have been knocked out of the race in a single stroke.

Brian Ross, the ABC journalist who put together the report, had been asked by the producers of "Good Morning America" to look into Jeremiah Wright. The job was not especially urgent, Ross felt, but, in mid-February, after a request for an interview was turned down by Wright, he and a couple of assistants went online and, for about five hundred dollars, ordered twenty-nine hours of Wright's sermons on DVD.

"The Clinton people pushed opposition research but not about Wright," Ross recalled. "We started watching these sermons. They were entertaining enough, but they were endless. It was a low-priority project. But then we started seeing things that were of interest." One day, while he was doing a couple of other things, Ross glanced up at the video of Wright giving a fiery sermon about 9/11. "I thought, Oh, gee. This is something,"

Ross said. "It had been background noise. What I had really been looking for was a panning shot of Obama in the congregation. Given the efficiency of the Obama operation and how the *Tribune* and Lynn Sweet at the *Sun-Times* worked, I figured someone had already gone down this road."

Once he had assembled the clips of Wright, Ross called one of Obama's spokesmen, Bill Burton. The campaign told Ross about Wright's career in the military, about his importance on the South Side and as a national figure in the black church, but said little about the sermons. Ross and his producer started to prepare a report, including the excerpts from Wright's sermons and some footage of congregants at Trinity praising him.

The clip on the ABC broadcast that had first caught Ross's attention came from a sermon called "The Day of Jerusalem's Fall," delivered on September 16, 2001—the first Sunday after the Al Qaeda attacks on Manhattan and Washington. "We bombed Hiroshima. We bombed Nagasaki. And we nuked far more than the thousands in New York and the Pentagon—and we never batted an eye!" Wright shouted angrily. "We have supported state terrorism against the Palestinians and black South Africans and now we are indignant because the stuff we have done overseas is now brought right back into our own front yards. America's chickens! Are coming home! To roost!" The last formulation would have been known to anyone in that church; it was a direct quotation of what Malcolm X said a week after the assassination of John F. Kennedy, the remark that led Elijah Muhammad to suspend Malcolm from the Nation of Islam. Malcolm X also charged the U.S. government with complicity in the murders of Medgar Evers, Patrice Lumumba, and four black girls in a church bombing in Birmingham, Alabama.

Viewers also saw Wright condemning "the U.S. of K.K.K. A.," castigating Condoleezza Rice for her "Cond-amnesia," and saying, "No, no, no! Not God bless America. God *damn* America" in a sermon delivered on April 13, 2003, called "Confusing God and Government."

"When it came to treating her citizens of African descent fairly, America failed," Wright said. "She put them in chains. The government put them in slave quarters, put them on auction blocks, put them in cotton fields, put them in inferior schools, put them in substandard housing, put them in scientific experiments, put them in the lowest-paying jobs, put them outside the equal protection of the law, kept them out of their racist bastions of higher education and locked them into positions of hopelessness and helplessness. The government gives [young black men] drugs, builds bigger prisons, passes a three-strike law and then wants us to sing

'God Bless America.' No, no, no! Not God Bless America. God *damn* America—that's in the Bible—for killing innocent people. God *damn* America for treating her citizens as less than human." In this case, Wright claimed to me, he was quoting not only Biblical injunctions against murder but also William James, who wrote in a letter, "God damn the U.S. for its vile conduct in the Philippine Isles."

The ABC report also showed Wright endorsing an ugly conspiracy theory: "The government lied about inventing the H.I.V. virus as a means of genocide against people of color."

Within hours, the clips of Wright's sermons were all over the airwaves and the Internet. The day after, the Obama campaign removed Wright from the largely ceremonial African-American Religious Leadership Committee.

Fox played the clips in a constant cycle and the tabloid New York *Post* called Wright "Obama's Minister of Hate." But it was not just the right-wing media and Web sites that were attacking Wright. Some liberal and left-wing black journalists were also deeply critical, finding the 9/11 speech heartless and the conspiracy mongering outrageous. Bob Herbert, in the New York *Times*, called him a "loony preacher"; Patricia Williams, in *The Nation*, called him a "crazy ex-minister."

Clinton's operatives had done a cursory review of Wright as early as September, 2007, but the campaign, led by Hillary Clinton herself, decided that pursuing the story too aggressively and attempting to push it to the media was a foolhardy tactic. At first, in their overconfidence, they felt they didn't need to take Obama seriously enough to warrant a risky opposition-research strategy. Then, as Obama's campaign became a greater threat, the Clinton people thought that pushing the story could backfire. If it ever got out that they were behind a leak, they believed, the campaign could be branded as racist. In retrospect, some aides regretted their lack of focus on Wright.

"There was a school of thought in our campaign that felt it was hard to believe that Senator Obama, who was long associated with that church and pastor, didn't know about Wright's statements," one senior campaign adviser said. "It strained credulity. By contrast, the Obama campaign was very adroit at turning such attacks against him around and saying that they were racially motivated." Ruefully, Hillary Clinton wondered aloud what the public reaction would have been if her pastor in Little Rock had made similar statements. The sense of persecution, the sense of a slanted press and a tilted playing field, deepened in her camp. Some aides held out hope that rumors of a tape showing Michelle Obama castigating "whitey" would save the campaign. The tape did not exist. The atmosphere of dark frenzy and frustration was so deep that the Clinton team fastened onto any notion that the Obamas were anti-white or were subtly dealing the race card.

"If Jeremiah Wright had dropped in January, it would have been over," another Clinton aide said. "We sent someone up to Chicago to check it out but we found too little to make anything of it. The ABC stuff was not from us. With Wright, we sensed blood in the water—those of us whose job it is to sense blood in the water—but Hillary refused to let us go after it more. She didn't want it to go away, mind you, and she was really troubled by what Wright said and the whole relationship between him and Obama, but she knew that if we touched it too explicitly it would turn to poison."

In fact, the report did have a toxic effect on the Obama campaign and threatened to kill it. T. Denean Sharpley-Whiting, a professor of African-American studies at Vanderbilt, wrote astutely about the threat of Wright's rhetoric for the Obama campaign. "Wright's homiletics had the effect of coloring Obama in a bit too darkly; his damning of American racism and genocides at home and abroad diminished Obama's averred gift of 'second sight' into both black and white worlds, marred his claim to authenticity and a new politics," she wrote. "Jeremiah's jeremiads imperiled the currency of the 'O' brand of politics, one that shunned partisan political attacks as well as dicing up the electorate into so many factions." This might have been putting it too fancily. More bluntly, the sermons associated Obama with an angry radicalism that could potentially alienate countless voters—and not only white voters.

There was, Wright's friends and supporters contended, a context for "God damn America" and for his most radical rhetoric. Wright saw himself as—and Obama understood him to be—an inheritor of a tradition of protest from the pulpit, not an accommodationist, and hardly a politician. His Sunday-morning sermons were meant to rouse, to accuse, and to help people shake free of their apathy and dejection. Wright's faults were obvious—his outsized ego and his pride, his tendency to mistake conspiracy theory for reality, his unwillingness ever to find fault in leaders like Louis Farrakhan or Muammar Qaddafi—but at his best he was part of a tradition well known to millions of churchgoing African-Americans. Certainly, his devotion to his community was immense. He poured enormous energy and resources into education and into helping single mothers, addicts, alcoholics, and the homeless. But that would never be explained adequately on cable television. The Obama campaign knew that voters would see those videotapes and be encouraged to wonder about the candidate's associations and allegiances. Underneath Obama's cool yet embracing demeanor, was he a cartoon version of Wright, full of condemnation and resentment? Damage control, in the form of sound bites and surrogate interviews, would not work.

As Obama's political career grew more intense and his children got a little older, he and Michelle did not spend quite as much time at Trinity as they had when they were first together. Sometimes, on Sundays, Obama might go to Trinity, but he also went to other churches, for political reasons, or skipped church entirely. Nevertheless, he had certainly sat through enough radical sermons by Wright—and without protest—so that it would be folly to start trying to make fine distinctions. He knew that that sort of hairsplitting would mean nothing, not after he had repeatedly, in his book and in public remarks, praised Wright as a minister and a personal adviser. As recently as January, 2007, he had been quoted in the Chicago *Tribune* saying, "What I value most about Pastor Wright is not his day-to-day political advice. He's much more of a sounding board for me to make sure that I am speaking as truthfully about what I believe as possible and that I'm not losing myself in some of the hype and hoopla and stress that's involved in national politics."

Obama's aides were not deluded, either. For months, they had tried to keep race in the background of the campaign, but they realized that Wright's sermons intensified it in the worst way possible and could even bring down Obama's candidacy. Jon Favreau, the lead speechwriter, learned the news about Wright and felt sick. Favreau channel-surfed for a while, and when he hit on the Wright clips, he thought, Oh, Jesus, this is going to be bad. The campaign put out a statement distancing Obama from the sermons but it was obvious that a more concerted effort was needed.

On Friday, the day after the ABC broadcast, Obama called David Axelrod and said that he wanted to give a speech on race. He had been thinking about it for months and had been talked out of it by the staff. Now it was an absolute necessity. In the meantime, though, he could not cancel a pair of trying appointments: he was scheduled to meet with the editorial boards of both the *Tribune* and the *Sun-Times* to talk about, and distance himself from, the developer Tony Rezko, who had been his friend and early campaign contributor and was now under indictment. At the *Tribune* session, Obama admitted that it had been "boneheaded" of him to go in on a deal with Rezko to buy his house when Rezko was so clearly mired in corruption. At the same session, Obama claimed that he hadn't been in church during the "offensive" sermons that had been excerpted on the air, and would have objected "fiercely" if he had been. Neither explanation was especially winning. The Wright situation was only going to fester.

"On Saturday morning we had ten people on a strategy conference call," Favreau said. "Axelrod said I should get started on something and I was like, no, I couldn't do it without [Obama]. But he was campaigning till ten-thirty that night. I went to the office and I was so panicked. I brainstormed and met Ax there. We talked about what might be in the speech. And Ax said what he always says: 'He'll come up with the right thing and we'll have it.' Barack called me at home at ten, ten-thirty. I said, 'How are you?' and he was, like, 'You know, I've had better days, but, this is what you deal with when you run for President. I should be able to tell people this and explain what happened and say what I believe. And if it goes right it could be a teaching moment.' He said, 'I have thoughts, and I will tell them to you stream of consciousness and you type and you come up with a draft.' Well, his stream of consciousness was pretty much a first draft. It was more than he had ever given me before for a speech. He is known as an inspiring writer, but the lawyer in him was there, too. First this, then that: the logic of the speech was all there. And we talked about the ending, the story we told him about Ashley and the relish sandwiches. He had used it already at Ebenezer, Dr. King's church. We went back and forth on it, and we decided that even though he had used it before, it was too perfect. I worked all day Sunday on the structure, adding lines. At six, he e-mailed me and said he was going to put the girls to bed, he would send me something at eight. He was up until two or three and told me Monday that he made good progress and needed one more night and e-mailed it to me. He sent the speech to me, Valerie, Ax, Gibbs, and Plouffe. He said, 'Favs, if you have rhetorical or grammar stuff, O.K., but the rest of you, no substantial changes. This is what I want.' I had no idea how it was going to play, but I had never been so proud to be on this campaign."

On Tuesday, March 18th, Obama delivered his speech, "A More Perfect Union," at the National Constitution Center, in Philadelphia, on a stage adorned by a row of American flags. At stake was the candidacy of a man who, until this moment, had had an excellent chance to become the first African-American President.

African-American history is distinguished, in no small part, by a history of African-American rhetoric—speeches given at essential moments. In 1852, Frederick Douglass gave his Fourth of July speech at Corinthian Hall, in Rochester, New York, and his mood was one of defiance, an insistence that the majority population see the injustice staring it in the face: "What, to the American slave, is your Fourth of July? I answer; a day that reveals to him, more than all other days in the year, the gross injustice and cruelty to which he is the constant victim." Obama, who used to speak so admiringly of Douglass's rhetoric in his classes at the University of Chicago, could not now speak in the key of outrage. His tone had to be one of unity and embrace; he had to speak to, and reach, everyone—otherwise, his run for the Presidency was, quite possibly, at an end.

To begin, Obama called once more on his own biography as a form of authority in addressing the problem of race: "I am the son of a black man from Kenya and a white woman from Kansas. . . . I've gone to some of the best schools in America and lived in one of the world's poorest nations. I am married to a black American who carries within her the blood of slaves and slaveowners—an inheritance we pass on to our two precious daughters. I have brothers, sisters, nieces, nephews, uncles, and cousins, of every race and every hue." He gave his credentials. Now his capacity as a cultural linguist, a man who had lived in both worlds, white and black, and can speak to those worlds without a foreign accent, was to be tested.

After repeating his condemnation of Reverend Wright's sermons "in unequivocal terms," Obama tried to broaden the country's understanding of Wright's activities as pastor of the Trinity United Church of Christ: Wright was a former Marine, he reminded the huge television audience, who had built a large and passionate ministry that represented "the doctor and the welfare mom, the model student and the former gangbanger." Obama disagreed with Wright's most inflammatory, indefensible remarks, which represented "a profoundly distorted view of this country." In his view, despair, the Biblically unforgivable sin, was at the heart of Wright's mistake. And it was a generational despair, the rage of an older man who failed to account for the way the racial situation had changed, at least to some degree, in America. Wright's "profound mistake," Obama said, was that "he spoke as if our society was static, as if no progress had been made." This is a gesture that the philosopher Richard Rorty discussed in his 1998 book, *Achieving Our Country* (the title comes from a phrase of James Baldwin's). The idea is that there is hope and inspiration to be found in the American past, not merely shame, and that hope is located in the evidence of our capacity to mobilize political and social movements to overcome grave injustice. Wright sees a static condition of outrageous oppression, while Obama sees one of progress and promise. He signals to the national audience that Wright is entangled in his own anger, though he refuses to condemn him outright:

I can no more disown him than I can disown the black community. I can no more disown him than I can my white grandmother—a woman who helped raise me, a woman who sacrificed again and again for me, a woman who loves me as much as she loves anything in this world, but a woman who once confessed her fear of black men who passed her by on the street, and who on more than one occasion has uttered racial or ethnic stereotypes that made me cringe. These people are a part of me. And they are a part of America, this country that I love.

Obama was engaged in a high-stakes rhetorical balancing act. He empathized not only with his embittered preacher but also with the embittered white workers who have seen "their jobs shipped overseas or their pension dumped after a lifetime of labor" and cannot understand why their children might be bused across town or why a person of color has a leg up through affirmative action "because of an injustice that they themselves never committed." Obama indicated to all sides that he heard them, that he "got it." He spoke as a kind of racial Everyman. A white Southerner, even Bill Clinton, could not dare to do that in a speech on race, and Jesse Jackson, whose tradition had been more about the rhetoric of grievances and recompense, never would have chosen to. Obama's ability to negotiate among the sharply disparate perspectives of his fellow citizens was at the heart of his political impulse and his success. Perhaps when people spoke of Obama's "distance," they meant just this capacity to inhabit different points of view—a mastery that sometimes seemed more anthropological than political. Obama said that black anger about past and present wrongs was counterproductive, even a form of post-traumatic stress; he also pointed to the way that American politics had been shaped since the Nixon era by the exploitation of white anger in the South and elsewhere.

Finally, the speech was about the "unfinished" character of the American experiment and the need for unity—racial, religious, and generational—to fight injustice and move forward. To close the speech, he relied once more on the story of Ashley Baia, her trials as a girl, her idealism, and her unlikely recruitment of an elderly African-American to the campaign. ("I'm here because of Ashley.") That "moment of recognition," Obama said, "is where our union grows stronger. And as so many generations have come to realize over the course of the two hundred and twenty-one years since a band of patriots signed that document in Philadelphia, that is where the perfection begins."

Obama's speech won praise in the leading newspapers (the New York *Times* editorial called it a "Profile in Courage"; the Washington *Post* labeled it "an extraordinary moment of truth-telling"). The right wing's response was equally unvaried: Rush Limbaugh sneeringly compared Obama to Rodney King; Newt Gingrich called it "intellectually, fundamentally, dishonest"; and many more, from Fred Barnes to Karl Rove and Joe Scarborough, adopted the trope that Obama had "thrown his grandmother under a bus."

Henry Louis Gates, Jr., told me the speech not only rescued the Obama candidacy, it made him think of Obama as a "post-modern Frederick Douglass":

> For anthropologists, the mythical "trickster" figure reconciles two irreconcilable natures through mediation, like an animal joined with a man. Frederick Douglass is the figure of mediation in nineteenth-century American literature; he, the mulatto, mediates between white and black, slave and free, between "animal" and "man." Obama, as mulatto, as reconciler, self-consciously performs the same function in our time, remarkably self-consciously. And the comparisons don't stop there: they both launched their careers with speeches and their first books were autobiographies. They spoke and wrote themselves into being: tall, elegant, eloquent figures of mediation, conciliation, and compromise. Douglass launched his career as a radical no-holds-barred combatant against slavery. As he aged, however, he grew more conservative. He certainly believed in the basic class structure of American capitalism; and he believed in a natural aristocracy and that he was a member of it—just like Obama.
>
> The only thing radical about Obama is that he wanted to be the first black President. In the race speech, he was performing the very opposite of "radical." He distanced himself, quite deftly, from radical black nationalism and embraced cosmopolitanism. He is certainly proud of his ethnic heritage, but in the manner of a "bourgeois nationalist" (as Eldridge Cleaver liked to say), the kind of person who hangs a Romare Bearden print on the wall and owns the complete Coltrane, but he doesn't want to be confined or defined entirely by his or her blackness. When he juxtaposes, rhetorically, his white grandmother with Jeremiah Wright as two examples of the wrong approach to race, he is doing this to show that he is our ultimate figure of mediation, standing tall above quarrels that most of us assume to be irreconcilable. And he does this for a larger political purpose. Like Douglass, he is a very gifted rhetorician; form and content are inextricably political for Barack Obama, from start to finish.

Further to the left, Cornel West, whom Obama had called an "oracle," was privately irritated with the speech, thinking that it was politically effective but "intellectually thin." He was especially angry that Obama had equated the oppression of blacks with white resentment. "I can understand that, the white moderates need that nice little massage and so on, but it has nothing to do with the truth, at all," West said many months later. "Do they have grounds for being upset? Absolutely. There have been excesses of affirmative action and so forth and so on, but Jim Crow de facto is still in place. . . . Who are the major victims of that? Poor, disproportionately, black and brown and red. You got to tell the truth, Barack. Don't trot out this shit with this coded stuff." But even West, who had promised Obama that he would be a "critical supporter," held his fire in public. "It was a very delicate moment," he said.

The speech was overall a success in the polls. Obama enhanced his stature while achieving the more immediate aim of putting distance between himself and his pastor. "The speech helped stanch a real frenzy," Axelrod said. "Barack turned a moment of great vulnerability into a moment of triumph. He said, 'I may lose, but I will have done something valuable.' He was utterly calm while everyone was freaking out. He said, 'Either they will accept it or they won't and I won't be President.' It was probably the most important moment of the whole campaign."

As important as the message was the tone of the messenger. Obama's personality served him well. The civil-rights-era activist Bob Moses, one of Obama's heroes, said, "His confidence in himself—and his peacefulness with himself—came through in a way that can't be faked. You are under too much pressure to actually adopt a persona. You can't do it under that pressure and not have it blown away. People said he couldn't afford to be the angry black candidate, but the point is that he is not angry. If he were angry, it would have come out." Indeed, in the sixties Moses, leading voter-registration drives in Mississippi, was known for those same qualities—his intelligence and his even temper.

Studs Terkel, who compiled oral histories about race and the Depression and was, at ninety-six, a Chicago institution, recalled the Philadelphia speech just a week before he died, in October, 2008, telling me that Obama's political calm under pressure reminded him of Gene Tunney, the heavyweight champion of the mid-nineteen-twenties, who used craft, more than brawn, to defeat Jack Dempsey. "The guys on the street, the mechanics and shoe clerks, saw Tunney as an intellectual, but he won," Terkel said. "Obama is like that. He's one cool fighter."

The speech in Philadelphia did more than change the subject. It not only gave a context to the Jeremiah Wright affair—at least, for those who were willing to be persuaded—but also positioned Obama himself as a historical advance, the focal point of a new era, embracing America itself for all its tribes, for all its historical enmities and possibilities. In effect, it congratulated the country for getting behind him. Wright, Jesse Jackson—they were leaders of the old vanguard. Obama would lead the new vanguard, the Joshua generation.

"He leaned in, and that's always kind of his tendency: if you see something coming at you, lean in," Valerie Jarrett said. She would have preferred that he not have had to give the speech, but, she said, "The American people listened more carefully, because we were in the midst of a crisis. I think if he'd given that same speech earlier, we probably wouldn't have had every single news outlet cover it and talk about it for the following five news cycles."

The crisis had not come at the worst time: the next primaries were not until April 22nd, in Pennsylvania (Hillary was favored to win), and May 6th, in Indiana and North Carolina. The speech stabilized Obama's standing in the polls.

It did not, however, stabilize the mood of Jeremiah Wright. Wright had known all along that his relationship with Obama would, at best, be tested by the campaign. But he deeply resented what had happened to him, to his family, and to his church. The media, he complained, had reduced his decades of sermons and work for social justice to an ugly caricature, portraying him as an "anti-American, radical, homo-loving, liberal-whatever minister that [Obama] sat under for twenty years." His e-mail was clogged with obscene and abusive messages. His office received death threats. The church received bomb threats. Police cars had to be parked outside the church, his house, his daughters' houses.

When Obama gave his speech in Philadelphia, Wright was with his wife, five children, son-in-law, and three grandchildren on a long-planned Caribbean cruise—a "cruise from hell," he called it. For the entire trip, cable news was looping reports about Wright. "Many of the white passengers on the boat were livid with me, saying ugly things to me and around me," Wright said after the election. " 'You're unpatriotic, you oughta go back to Africa.' " Some people at the dining table next to Wright's asked to be moved. "I started staying in my cabin most of the time," Wright recalled, "except for dinner at night with my family, because to be out was going to invite comments that I didn't want my grandkids to hear." When the ship docked in Puerto Rico, Wright picked up a copy of the New York *Times* in which Maureen Dowd called him, indelibly, a "wackadoodle."

Wright was not at all shocked by Obama's speech, saying that it was what he had to do, as a politician, to stay in the race. But the idea that Obama was not "disowning" him was disingenuous. "You already did disown me," Wright said as if Obama were in the room. "And you're being forced into saying things that I would not say—but I'm not running for public office."

Obama, Wright said, sent him a text message wishing him a happy Easter. That hardly eased his upset with the speech, and its denunciation of his sermons. "I said to him, as soon as I got back, 'Not only haven't you heard the sermon, Barack, you're responding to news clips being looped on television,' " Wright said, recalling an hour-long private meeting with Obama at Wright's house. "You didn't read the sermon, that's certainly been in print since 2001. And it seems to me that the *Harvard Law Review* editor would at least read a sermon before he makes a pronouncement about it." Wright says that Obama apologized: "He said, 'You're right, I hadn't read the sermon, or heard it. And I was wrong.' But, I said, 'You're apologizing in my living room. You're busting me out internationally— over something you had not heard or read.' "

Wright's presumption was that his meanings had been radically distorted by the clips of his sermons that appeared on ABC and in the rest of the media, that somehow Obama and everyone else, if they only read or heard the full version, would share his wisdom. The truth is that while those sermons were, of course, more nuanced than any five-second excerpt could represent, Wright's rhetoric and his ferocious tone, on the subject of 9/11 and much else, were not something that the Obama campaign would put in a commercial.

According to Wright, Obama said he would greatly prefer that Wright stay at home and keep quiet through the rest of the campaign rather than continue to preach in Chicago and on the road. "He said, 'You know what your problem is, is you've got to tell the truth,' " Wright said. "I said, 'That's a good problem for me to have.' That's a good problem for all preachers to have. . . . He said, 'It's going to get worse if you go out there. It's really going to get worse.' And he was so right."

At around the same time, Wright said, he was getting messages from Joshua DuBois, a Pentecostal minister and the Obama campaign's religious affairs director, and from other aides and supporters, asking him not to preach and give interviews until after the election. One Obama supporter—"a close friend of Barack's," Wright claimed—even offered to send Wright money if he would only be quiet. Wright refused. He was retired now and needed to earn a living and help support grandchildren in college. "Where's the money going to come from?" he said. "I'm just going to be quiet until November the fifth? I'm not supposed to say a word? What do I tell these people who have invited me to preach? All of these dates between April and November? So, no, I didn't cancel engagements, and I didn't cancel what I was supposed to be doing."

Wright was simply not going to apologize for what he said were "snippets" taken out of proper context, and he resented deeply the media's "attempts to use me as a weapon of mass destruction."

"I'm not running for office," he said. "I don't have to win. I don't have to compromise in terms of trying to appease this faction to get their vote."

Any notion that the Jeremiah Wright affair had settled down died on April 28, 2008, when he accepted an invitation to speak at the National Press Club in Washington. Three nights before, in an interview with Bill Moyers on PBS, he had been calm and reasoned; a speech in Detroit was harsher, but got little attention. Wright was in Washington for the annual Samuel DeWitt Proctor Conference, a gathering of leaders of the black church. Before taking the stage at the National Press Club, he stood in a circle holding hands with six or seven close friends and colleagues, including Cornel West and the Reverend James Forbes, Jr., the pastor of Riverside Church in New York. Forbes prayed that Wright would perform well and keep his cool.

Wright began with a prepared speech about the history, thought, and diverse strands of the black church—the long history stretching from Africa to slavery, from Jim Crow to the present day. He talked about the prophetic tradition, with its roots in the book of Isaiah, the voices of protest during slavery and segregation and the black-liberation theology of James Cone. After completing his survey, Wright talked about his own church's tradition of protest against apartheid and other instances of injustice, as well as its support of programs for victims of H.I.V./AIDS, drug addicts and alcoholics, and troubled young people.

When Wright finished, Donna Leinwand, a reporter for *USA Today* and the vice-president of the National Press Club, had the unenviable task of reading to him written questions from the audience. The first question she read was about Wright's post-9/11 line that "America's chickens are coming home to roost."

"Have you heard the whole sermon?" Wright said.

Leinwand, of course, had not asked the question so much as relayed it, but Wright used her as his foil. When she asked a question about his patriotism, Wright, not without some justification, began to unwind:

"I served six years in the military. Does that make me patriotic? How many years did Cheney serve?"

Wright's demeanor began to change: he became more combative, more sarcastic, and started to perform in the broadest sense, clowning, rolling his eyes, preening for his friends and the camera. Applause rolled in from his colleagues and friends, including a number of ministers, the former Washington mayor Marion Barry, and Malik Zulu Shabazz, of the New Black Panther Party. Cornel West, for one, thought that Wright had begun well but now was starting to "disintegrate."

Asked about Louis Farrakhan, Wright said, "Louis Farrakhan is not my enemy. He did not put me in chains, he did not put me in slavery, and he didn't make me this color."

More and more, Wright played to his supporters and mugged for the camera. The calm he had displayed with Moyers was gone; he clearly felt that the questions were unworthy and foolish and he answered in kind. When he was asked about the notion that the H.I.V. virus was invented as a weapon to be employed against people of color, Wright didn't deny it. Instead, he recommended *Emerging Viruses,* a self-published book by a conspiracy theorist and former dentist named Leonard G. Horowitz, who suggests that H.I.V. originated as a biological-weapons project. "Based on this Tuskegee experiment and based on what has happened to Africans in this country," he said, "I believe our government is capable of doing anything."

From the Obama campaign's point of view, Wright's performance at the National Press Club was catastrophic. It was broadcast live and in full; there could be no complaints that Wright had been reduced to edited "snippets." Wright said that he was "playing the dozens" with people who had somehow shown him no respect, and yet it was obvious that his tone of contempt and mockery would do Obama no good. Wright, at this point, did not seem to care.

"We both know that if Senator Obama did not say what he said he would never get elected," Wright said at the Press Club. "Politicians say what they say and do what they do based on electability, based on sound bites, based on polls. . . . I do what pastors do, he does what politicians do. I'm not running for office." Then, as if to add an acid punctuation to his performance, he joked that maybe he would be Vice-President.

. . .

Obama had been campaigning in North Carolina when Wright appeared at the National Press Club. After being briefed, but without having seen the tape, Obama made a statement about Wright—"He does not speak for me"—at the Wilmington airport. Late that night, he watched Wright on cable television and realized that it had been even worse than Valerie Jarrett and other aides had suggested. Obama was devastated and felt a deep sense of betrayal.

"I don't know if we could have designed something as destructive" as Wright's appearance at the National Press Club, David Plouffe recalled. "It was like living in a 'Saturday Night Live' parody. I remember I was on the phone with Obama, describing what had happened, and we were both just very quiet. It was hard to believe that this was happening. It was emotionally very difficult for him."

As usual, Plouffe had taken the late-night call from Obama in the bathroom so that he wouldn't wake his wife. Finally, after a long, agonized conversation, Obama said that he would speak out. "I know what I need to say," he said. "You guys don't worry about it."

The next day, in Winston-Salem, Obama followed a town hall meeting with a pointed press conference. Looking stricken and grave, he said that Wright had offered a "different vision of America"—one that he did not share. He pronounced himself "outraged" by his pastor and his "divisive and destructive" comments, adding that they did not accurately represent the black church, much less his campaign. "And if Reverend Wright thinks that that's political posturing, as he put it, then he doesn't know me very well," Obama said. "And based on his remarks yesterday, well, I may not know him as well as I thought, either."

Lost in the furor was a clear picture of Jeremiah Wright himself. Intelligent yet given to conspiracy thinking, devoted yet erratic, he was many things at once: ambitious, compassionate, volatile, egocentric. Here was a man who had been at a pinnacle of his South Side domain. He was preparing for a triumphant retirement, handing over the leadership of a church that he had built from eighty-seven congregants to six thousand, just as his most famous parishioner was, quite possibly, headed toward the White House. He had done a great deal for a great many. Now he was demonized on television, with reporters asking him rude questions, strangers insulting him and harassing his family; and now, too, Obama was through with him. Wright's pride did not allow him to be silent until the end of the campaign; he did not think that he should have to. What had he ever done to Barack Obama except advise him, teach him, embolden his soul? That was how he saw it, anyway. Wright was wounded and weary. ("I'm a *tired* bastard," he said.) He knew well that he would forever be known for those moments on television, not for his good works. There was no way out of such a hole. And he could not help it if his view of Obama fluctuated from the tender to the furious, from the proud to the patronizing.

"Your children mess up, your children make mistakes, your children listen to bad advice—you don't stop loving your children," Wright told me. "Barack was like a son to me. I'm not going to stop loving him. I think he listened to the wrong people and made some bad choices. . . . As I said, he may have disowned me; I didn't disown him, and I won't disown him, because I love him. I still love him. I love him like I love my kids."

But the humiliation was deep. Northwestern University rescinded an honorary degree. Some speaking invitations were withdrawn. Wright said that the media hounded his youngest child at her senior prom and again when she moved into her dormitory at Howard University. "That's one of the reasons there's still the rawness and the pain," he said.

And yet he continued to make strange, sometimes hate-filled statements and speeches. Speaking at an N.A.A.C.P. dinner, Wright gave a pseudo-scientific disquisition on the genetic differences between African-American "right-brain" and European "left-brain" learning styles. At the point where he started talking about the different ways black people and white people clap their hands, their varying rhythmic capacities, it became possible to see a once-respected pastor coming undone. Interviewed by Cliff Kelley on WVON after the election, Wright revealed the depths of his hurt and resentment. He talked not only about the sins of the mass media but also recounted the names of the hip-hop artists and comedians who had criticized him. His hurt was palpable. "You've not only dissed me . . . you have urinated on my tradition," Wright said. "You've urinated on my parents, my grandparents, and our whole faith tradition. I feel like Ralph Ellison's Invisible Man."

During the primary debates, Obama had said that under the right conditions he would talk to any foreign leader—Ahmadinejad, Kim Jong Il— "but he can't talk to me," Wright said ruefully to Kelley. Even though Wright said that he had not disowned Obama, he now felt free to mock him. One of Obama's assets in the race had been his comfort in the church; now his pastor criticized him for his lack of devotion. "He doesn't have a church," he said. "He has a health club he goes to every morning, but he doesn't have a church he goes to every week. He's sort of church-less. He's taking care of his body."

Wright never seemed to get over his wounds, and, when he failed to watch himself, which was increasingly often, he said hateful things. As late as June, 2009, he bitterly told a newspaper in Virginia, the *Daily Press*, "Them Jews ain't going to let him talk to me. I told my baby daughter that he'll talk to me in five years when he's a lame duck, or in eight years when he's out of office." He also said that Jewish voters and "the AIPAC" vote were "controlling" Obama; they were persuading him not to send delegations to a conference on racism in Geneva because "they would not let him talk to someone who calls a spade what it is." With these flourishes, Wright made it a great deal more difficult to see, or care about, the complexity of his drama. His subsequent half-apologies betrayed only his regret that he had not used more euphemistic language. His parishioners, for the most part, would not stop loving him, they would not forget all the good he had done, but the rest of the world moved on.

For a few weeks after Wright's National Press Club appearance, Obama worried about the campaign's survival. He joked with his aides that he could always make speeches for money—he'd make as much as Bill Clinton!—and he could keep hanging around with his friends from the campaign. The gallows humor was understandable. The polls in North Carolina and, especially, Indiana, were not promising. Would Wright's behavior, his unwillingness to swallow his pride and stay quiet, be the end of the Obama campaign?

In the end, however, Obama won North Carolina by fourteen points, and he lost Indiana by just two points. The race for the Democratic nomination remained close to the end, but Obama never fell behind. That night, on NBC, Tim Russert declared, "We know who the Democratic nominee is going to be, and no one is going to dispute it." George Stephanopoulos, on ABC, and Bob Schieffer, on CBS, soon followed suit. Because Obama had proved his resiliency through the Wright affair and the balloting in North Carolina, the decisive super-delegates started to commit themselves to voting for him at the Convention. For a while, Hillary Clinton ignored reality and soldiered on.

In mid-June, Obama went to his friend Arthur Brazier's church, on the South Side, the Apostolic Church of God, and delivered a Father's Day speech. Thematically, Obama was repeating himself. Speaking both as a politician and as the child of a fatherless household, he had talked many times to audiences and journalists about the importance of family, responsibility, and fatherhood.

African-Americans, in general, welcome such sermons, and Obama was well received at Brazier's church, but, to some black intellectuals and activists, Obama was patronizing his audiences and minimizing the themes of institutionalized racism. The critique of Obama on this subject was similar to the critique of the comic Bill Cosby, who for many years had angered some black intellectuals with his lectures on black self-empowerment, families, fatherhood, and self-discipline. Michael Eric Dyson wrote in *Time* that while Obama had cited a Chris Rock comedy routine about black men expecting praise for things like staying out of jail, "Rock's humor is so effective because he is just as hard on whites as on blacks. That's a part of the routine Obama has not yet adopted." The novelist Ishmael Reed pointed out that the polls now showed Obama with a fifteen-point lead over the presumptive Republican nominee, John McCain. "It's obvious by now that Barack Obama is treating black Americans like one treats a demented uncle, brought out from his room to be ridiculed and scolded before company from time to time," Reed wrote, adding that the Father's Day speech was "meant to show white conservative males," who had failed to vote for him in the primaries, "that he wouldn't cater to 'special interest' groups, blacks in this case."

Glenn Loury, a prominent black economist, who grew up in Chicago, said, "It wasn't that he was wrong or off base, nor was it a washing of dirty linen in public, but I thought that he was talking over the audience to the rest of the country and using the fact of his 'courage' to say these things to convey to the rest of the country that he shares our values despite the doubts we might have had about him."

On July 6th, Jesse Jackson, who had been fairly quiet during the long campaign, was preparing to appear on Fox television when an open mike recorded him criticizing Obama for his "faith-based" speech on Father's Day at Apostolic. Speaking softly to another guest, Jackson also said that Obama had been "talking down to black people." He made a slicing gesture with his hand and said, "I wanna cut his nuts out."

What seemed to irritate Jackson and many others was the potential for a double discourse, the way that Obama's rhetoric was being overheard by white audiences that might understand it not as brotherly sympathy but, rather, as lofty reproach. "Barack would go to various groups and spell out public policy," Jackson told me. "He'd go to Latino groups and the conversation would be about the road to citizenship and immigration policy. He'd go to women and talk about women's rights, Roe v. Wade. But he'd gone to several black groups talking about responsibility, which is an important virtue that should be broadly applied, but, given our crisis, we need government policy, too. African-Americans are No. 1 in voting for him, because he excited people, but we're also No. 1 in infant mortality, No. 1 in shortness of life expectancy, No. 1 in homicide victims."

Fox played the tape on the air, and Jackson came in for a few days of comprehensive bashing. The ritual played itself out: Jackson apologized. This, in turn, allowed Obama to accept the apology. Jackson looked petty and jealous. Obama looked magnanimous. Once more, a distance between the two men was established.

"I was shocked by the language, but I knew Jesse had the feeling that Obama played to white Americans by criticizing black Americans, for not doing enough to help ourselves," Julian Bond said. "Whether he intended it, I don't know, but I am sure Jesse provided Obama that sort of Sister Souljah moment."

Even many of Obama's early critics acquired a grudging respect for his cool strategic sense, his tactical agility. Tavis Smiley, who went on attacking Obama for "pivoting" on issues like gun control and the death penalty and who absorbed enormous criticism for doing so, was among those who now saw the promise in him. Throughout the campaign, Smiley, like his mentor Cornel West, kept in touch with Obama. "Each time Obama and I talked during the campaign, maybe a half-dozen times on the phone," he said, "we aired our positions and differences, but it always ended with him saying, 'Tavis, I gotta do what I gotta do and I respect the fact that you have to do what you have to.' We confirm our love for each other and then we hang up." Obama did not, and could not, represent the prophetic tradition: he was not Frederick Douglass or Bishop Turner, Dr. King or Malcolm X. He could borrow their language, he could take inspiration from their examples, but he was a pragmatist, a politician. To change anything, he needed to win. The romancing of Tavis Smiley was a small part of that effort.

The acrimony inside the Clinton campaign never eased. The enmity between the chief strategist, Mark Penn, and Harold Ickes was only the most vividly bitter relationship in a thoroughly dysfunctional organization. Ickes, a liberal with a decades-long relationship with the Clintons, resented Penn for his centrist politics and big-business ties and viewed him as incompetent; Penn was convinced that Ickes contributed only back-biting and rancor to the campaign. At one point in the campaign, Hillary Clinton had presided over a regular strategy meeting at her house on Embassy Row, on Whitehaven Street, in Washington. Around fifteen senior advisers were seated at a long table, with Clinton at the head, Penn at her side. Toward the end of the meeting, she said with frustration, "O.K., then, what's my message?"

The question seemed shocking to some in the room, but Penn forged ahead, rambling on about "Right from Day One" and other rubrics of the campaign. No one else had much to offer.

"Suddenly, Hillary got this sad, faraway look," one of the advisers recalled. "And she said, almost plaintively, 'Well, when you figure it out, someone give me a call.' She felt let down, betrayed, and there was good reason for her to feel that way. But she hired every fucking one of us, and it was one of the weakest political staffs I've ever seen." Throughout the campaign, Clinton expressed frustration with each of her leading aides, and had to fire her campaign manager, Patti Solis Doyle, but the adviser was right—she had chosen every one of them.

By June, 2008, the long battle between Clinton and Obama was over. Clinton, for her part, tried, fitfully at first, to reconcile herself to reality and move forward—possibly at the side of her antagonist. In some private meetings, however, she revealed her lingering sense of injury. Both her campaign and her husband had failed to perform with any consistency. She was angry with the press, which, she felt, had valorized Obama and punished her for their own weariness with the Clinton saga since 1992 and for every misstep in the campaign, real or perceived. She even made clear to some people that her team had early knowledge of Jeremiah Wright's sermons and Obama's extraordinarily close relationship with the preacher. What if *she* had had such a friendship? What would the press have said about her? And yet, she said with some bitterness, she got no credit for holding back. Only her husband's sense of umbrage was greater.

Sometimes Hillary Clinton's anger could quiet a room with its intensity, but as the weeks passed that sense of outrage turned to a desire to survive in the new order. It was no secret to Clinton that she was being considered for Vice-President or a top Cabinet position.

It took a while longer, however, for the top aides on both sides to cool down. "The Obama people were so angry at us, they thought that we had gone too far, that there had been race-baiting," one Clinton aide said. "I thought that enmity would last a really long time. I was angry and so were a lot of other people about how we were treated. There was no sense immediately afterward of 'Good game, well played.' No, it was 'We really took those fuckers *down*. We retired the Clintons to the trash heap of history.'

"Bill Clinton and Michelle Obama took a lot longer to get over it," the aide continued. "They are protective, competitive spouses, and for them to get over these compounding slights wasn't easy. Michelle clearly had a generalized feeling by the end of the campaign that we had run a race-baiting campaign. I don't think Obama himself did—or not nearly as much."

David Plouffe, Obama's campaign manager, admitted that he had been furious, in the latter stages of the primaries, that Clinton seemed to live in an "alternate universe" in which she still thought victory possible. Plouffe continued to be resentful long after the contest was over. "I'm a warrior, so it was hard for me to put down the sword," he said.

The relatively relaxed period of the summer of 2008 allowed that enmity to exhaust itself, and, by late August, when the Democratic Party gathered in Denver for its Convention, a sense of comity, be it sincere or forced, was in place. The Clintons both gave conciliatory, supportive speeches in favor of the nominee and Obama was free to concentrate on kicking off his national campaign against John McCain and the Republicans.

On the afternoon of August 28th Obama was rehearsing his acceptance speech in a modest meeting room on the nineteenth floor of the Westin Tabor Center, the hotel where he was staying in Denver. In a few hours, he was to appear under the lights at Mile High Stadium. Obama has always preferred to work in the nest of a very small circle of aides and now his audience was three: his political strategist, David Axelrod; the speechwriter, Jon Favreau; and a teleprompter operator. The rehearsal was mainly an exercise in comfort, in making sure that there were no syntactical hurdles left in the text, no barriers to clarity. Obama was never spirited in rehearsal, but he wanted to make sure he had a firm grasp of the rhythm of the sentences, so that when he looked at the teleprompter he would be like a well-rehearsed musician glancing at the score.

As a piece of rhetoric, the Convention speech was more of a ramble and a litany than what Obama usually favored; the text carried the burden of presenting a bill of particulars, a case, as Favreau put it, "of why yes to Obama and no to John McCain." Obama could not just inspire; he had to answer detailed questions of policy and difference. Late in the speech, however, the rhetoric shifted to the historical uplift and significance of the campaign. In the rehearsal session, Obama came to a passage paying homage to the March on Washington, forty-five years earlier to the day, when tens of thousands of people gathered near the Lincoln Memorial to "hear a young preacher from Georgia speak of his dream." Obama chose not to mention Martin Luther King, Jr., by name in the text, and, later, some black intellectuals would say that he had done so for fear of appearing "too black," of emphasizing race in front of a national audience. And yet even as he rehearsed the passage, there was a catch in Obama's voice and he stopped. He couldn't get past the phrase "forty-five years ago."

"I gotta take a minute," Obama told his aides.

He excused himself and took a short, calming walk around the room. "This is really hitting me," he said. "I haven't really thought about this before really deeply. It just hit me. I guess this is a pretty big deal."

His eyes filling with tears, Obama went to the bathroom to blow his nose. Favreau thought that the only time he had ever seen or heard of Obama being this emotional was back in Iowa when he addressed a group of young volunteers who were caucusing for the first time. Axelrod agreed. "Usually, he is so composed," he said, "but he needed the time."

"It's funny, I think all of us go through this," Favreau recalled. "We've gone through this whole campaign and, contrary to what anyone might think, we don't think of the history much, because it's a crazy environment and you're going twenty-four hours a day, seven days a week. And so there are very few moments—and I think it's the same with Barack—when he stops and thinks, 'I could be the first African-American elected President.' "

Obama returned to the room and practiced the paragraph a couple more times to make sure he could get through it without interruption. Although the passage did not mention King by name, the references were unmistakable.

Early in the evening, before the motorcade left for the stadium, Obama called Favreau in his room to go over some stray detail in the speech about science policy.

"I'm just being nervous, aren't I?" Obama asked him.

Sometime after five, Obama left the hotel in a motorcade. The drive lasted about fifteen minutes and all he could see through the window was faces, crowds, signs, people ten deep cheering and yelling, and the roar grew louder as he pulled into the stadium to deliver his acceptance speech to eighty thousand people and a television audience of more than thirty-eight million Americans.

Part Five

Your door is shut against my tightened face,
And I am sharp as steel with discontent;
But I possess the courage and the grace
To bear my anger proudly and unbent.
—Claude McKay, "The White House" (1922)

This world is white no longer, and it will never be white again.
—James Baldwin, *Notes of a Native Son*

Chapter Sixteen

"How Long? Not Long"

In the traditional rhythm of American presidential politics, the general-election drama begins after the Democratic and Republican Conventions and the Labor Day weekend. But that nicety was abandoned by both parties long ago. John McCain and his spokesmen spent much of the summer sniping at their putative opponent, laying the groundwork for a campaign that questioned, again and again, the worth and credentials of Barack Obama. Is he ready? Is he trustworthy? What has he ever done?

From the start, McCain salted legitimate contention with dubious insinuation. On October 6th, at a rally in Albuquerque, after suggesting that his opponent had taken "illegal foreign funds from *Palestinian* donors," McCain asked, "Who is the *real* Barack Obama?" When his aides charged—falsely—that Obama had willfully "snubbed" wounded American veterans at a base in Germany while making his triumphant summer visit to Europe, they stood their ground even after the charge had been disproved. They told a reporter for the Washington *Post* that they were intent on creating a "narrative" about Obama's supposed "indifference toward the military"—just the sort of meme, they thought, that would work for McCain, who had been shot down and wounded in Vietnam and spent nearly six years in a North Vietnamese prison camp. Obama, one McCain ad said, "made time to go to the gym" in Europe but not to visit the wounded from Iraq and Afghanistan in a German hospital.

When Obama told the St. Petersburg *Times* that McCain was trying to "scare" voters because "I don't look like I came out of central casting when it comes to Presidential candidates," McCain, affecting startled offense, charged reverse racism. "His comments were clearly the race card," McCain said. And yet as McCain spoke, his hesitant speech and body language betrayed his own ambivalence. McCain's most painful memory from the 2000 Presidential campaign was of the Bush machine smearing him and his family during the South Carolina primary; pro-Bush operatives used robo-calls and flyers to spread rumors that McCain had fathered a black child out of wedlock and that he had been a traitor in Vietnam. After McCain lost that race, he told his supporters that he wanted the Presidency "in the best way—not the worst way," and that he would never "dishonor the nation I love or myself by letting ambition overcome principle. Never. Never. Never." Now, in 2008, it seemed obvious that McCain felt distaste, or worse, for what he himself was doing in the name of electoral advantage. He paused uncomfortably and then seemed to sputter when he talked about Obama's supposed dealing of the race card. His moral resolve had receded in the face of ambition, and the internal struggle was both pitiful and visible.

The story is not simple. McCain did tell his advisers that it would be wrong and counterproductive to try to use Jeremiah Wright against Obama. But his instructions were circumscribed. Conservative surrogates of all kinds, ranging from right-wing authors to McCain's own Vice-Presidential nominee were only too pleased to do the dirty work—the sort of work that McCain had denounced eight years before.

In the summer weeks leading up to the Conventions, the No. 1 New York *Times* nonfiction best-seller was a scurrilous exercise called *The Obama Nation*. The author was Jerome R. Corsi, who, in the previous election cycle, had won a measure of fame as the co-writer of a highly effective piece of hardcover anti-Kerry propaganda called *Unfit for Command: Swift Boat Veterans Speak Out Against John Kerry*. In Vietnam, Kerry had won a Bronze Star, a Silver Star, and three Purple Hearts before coming home to speak out against the war in Congress and in the media, and yet the book managed to discredit him for many voters as a military fraud. Meanwhile, George W. Bush, who avoided Vietnam, sat back and watched the results add up in his electoral column.

Corsi, by any fair accounting, was a bigot, a liar, and a conspiracy theorist. Online, he had called Hillary Clinton a "fat hog" and "a lesbo," branded Islam "a worthless, dangerous Satanic religion," denounced Pope John Paul II as a "senile" apologist for "boy buggering," and charged that the World Trade Center towers had actually been destroyed by means other than hijacked airplanes. *The Obama Nation* was the kind of pernicious, unhinged production that was once the specialty of the John Birch Society. Such books, however, long ago went mainstream and insinuated themselves into the blogosphere and cable television where, of course, Corsi was a frequent guest. In a tendentious pseudo-scholarly tone, he marshaled clippings and bogus evidence to "prove" that Obama was a corrupt, unpatriotic, foreign-born, drug-dealing, Muslim-mentored non-Christian socialist élitist, who plagiarized his speeches, lied about his past, and found his closest associates among dangerous former Communists and terrorists. Corsi's subtitle was "Leftist Politics and the Cult of Personality." Corsi advertised the fact that he had a doctorate in political science from Harvard—his byline is "Jerome R. Corsi, Ph.D."—and so he must have known that the phrase "cult of personality" was not something from "Entertainment Tonight"; it was the phrase that Nikita Khrushchev had used to denounce Stalin for the purges and for the murder of millions of Soviet citizens.

Corsi was not a basement-dwelling marginal. He had mainstream backing. His publisher was Threshold Editions, a conservative imprint of Simon & Schuster whose chief editor was Mary Matalin, a Bush-family confidante and a former aide to Dick Cheney; Matalin had also been chief of staff to Lee Atwater when he ran the Republican National Committee.

Corsi was not alone in his efforts to reduce Obama to an alien figure with a shadowy background and pernicious intentions. Similar descriptions and "evidence" were everywhere on right-wing Web sites, talk shows, and news shows, particularly on Fox. Opinion polls showed that an alarming percentage of the American public believed at least some of it, particularly the idea that Obama was lying about his religion.

The Obama campaign countered the myths and lies on its Web site with a running feature called "Fight the Smears." But the corrosive effect of these untruths on public opinion was impossible to ignore. In mid-July, during the pre-Convention lull in the campaign, *The New Yorker* published a cover parodying the libels against Obama with the aim of making them ridiculous; the cover image, by Barry Blitt, showed the Obamas in the Oval Office with an American flag crisping in the fireplace, a portrait of Osama bin Laden on the mantel, Michelle dressed as a sixties-era militant, and Obama as a turbaned Muslim. For years, Blitt had been drawing covers mocking the Bush Administration—he and the magazine itself were clearly unsympathetic to the conservative right—but the Obama campaign declared that the cover was in "bad taste" and thousands of people wrote to the magazine, and to me, its editor, in protest. Most of the people who wrote expressed the opinion that while they, of course, understood the intent of the image, they were worried that it could inflame the bigoted sentiments of others and hurt Obama.

In early October, Sean Hannity broadcast a multipart series on Fox called "Obama & Friends: A History of Radicalism." Like Corsi, Hannity played an extended game of guilt by association and drive-by character assassination, suggesting that Obama was connected to Louis Farrakhan; a supporter of socialist revolution in the mode of Hugo Chávez; and close to Rashid Khalidi, a distinguished professor of Middle Eastern politics whom Hannity characterized as "an allegedly former member of a terror organization." In all, Hannity concluded, "Obama's list of friends reads like a history of radicalism."

By the fall of 2008, the leaders of the McCain campaign harbored the sense that they were playing in an unfair contest. They felt both wounded and self-righteously furious that McCain no longer won plaudits, as he had in 2000, for candor, wry amiability, and intellectual suppleness. Like Bill and Hillary Clinton, McCain thought of Obama as a talented speaker but a callow politician, serenely entitled, lucky beyond measure.

McCain's appeal and his sense of himself were based on the values of honor, self-sacrifice, and service. "It is your character, and your character alone, that will make your life happy or unhappy," he wrote in one of his best-selling collaborations with his senior aide, Mark Salter. The many Democrats, moderates, and journalists who had expressed admiration for him in 2000 pointed both to his unquestionable valor and sacrifice in Vietnam and to his willingness to fight his own party on tobacco, tax cuts for the wealthy, campaign finance, secret "earmarks" for local pork projects, and other issues. In those days, he was so independent that he entertained the idea of leaving the Republican Party. After losing to Bush, McCain flirted with a variety of fates: joining the Democrats, creating a third party modeled on Theodore Roosevelt's Bull Moose Party, and, in 2004, joining his friend John Kerry on the Democratic ticket. He remained a Republican.

But now the McCain people found to their chagrin that they no longer possessed the non-ideological glamour that had once had columnists aching to ride on McCain's bus, the Straight Talk Express, and that led the novelist David Foster Wallace to write a long admiring profile of McCain as an "anti-candidate" in *Rolling Stone.* Why had Obama monopolized the affections of the press corps? McCain's people asked. What sacrifices had Obama ever made? When had he ever risked the displeasure of his own Party, much less his own ambitions? They saw Obama as the ultimate Ivy League yuppie meritocrat—young, talented, effete, impertinent, unbruised, untested, and undeservedly self-possessed. Where were the scars? It was a familiar generational dynamic with the added element of race.

Mark Salter claimed that the press was enamored of Obama because of an urge to participate in the historic narrative of the rise of an African-American President; as a result, he said, it forgave or ignored his every fault and exaggerated McCain's. Salter was especially insistent on telling reporters about McCain's right-mindedness on race. He reminded reporters about how McCain had campaigned in Memphis in a driving rain to address a black audience. The message was: Even if I am not your candidate, if I win, I will be your President. Outside the Lorraine Motel, where Dr. King was slain in 1968, McCain told voters that he had made a mistake twenty-five years earlier when he voted against making King's birthday a national holiday.

"We went to great lengths to avoid pushing the rumors about Obama or trying to scare people, but McCain didn't get an ounce of fucking credit for it," Salter said. "The press was smitten with a candidate and was determined to see him win. Where were the investigative pieces? We must have had fifty. Where was the press on Obama or Axelrod? There was nothing! My personal view is that reporters had to rationalize a dislike for McCain that they hadn't had before. They had to conjure it."

As early as 2006, when McCain accepted an invitation to speak at Jerry Falwell's Liberty University, he made it plain that he was no longer looking to run a maverick campaign. In 2000, McCain had called Falwell one of the "agents of intolerance," but now he was assembling a Republican majority and needed the votes of the Christian right.

Jon Stewart, the host of "The Daily Show," had said in 2000 that he would have voted for McCain had he won the Republican nomination, but now he invited him on the show and said that the speech at Liberty University "strikes me as something you wouldn't ordinarily do. Are you going into crazy base world?"

McCain paused, smiled, and said sheepishly, "I'm afraid so."

McCain's sense of injury was even less easy to credit when he nominated Sarah Palin to be his running mate and dispatched her to be an assault-weapon-in-chief. At rallies, Palin raised the specter of one of Corsi's main arguments proving Obama's supposed radicalism—his "relationship" with the former Weatherman Bill Ayers. "Our opponent," she said, "is someone who sees America as imperfect enough to pal around with terrorists who targeted their own country."

It was a brilliantly ominous formulation. Ayers went unnamed, allowing the listener to wonder who exactly these plural "terrorists" were. The phrase "targeted their own country" sounded like some sort of link with domestic sleeper agents.

Palin was not alone in the effort. McCain himself asked that Obama come clean about his closeness to a "washed-up terrorist." He also questioned his opponent's patriotism, saying that Obama would prefer to "lose a war in order to win a political campaign."

Ayers wasn't the only weapon in the arsenal. McCain, using the same kind of robo-calls that had been deployed against him eight years earlier in South Carolina, promoted the message that Obama had urged doctors not to treat "babies born alive after surviving attempted abortions." McCain not only hired consultants in the Karl Rove circle; he embraced the universe of the Bush Administration—precisely when it was in the process of imploding. The spectacle of McCain's confusion, his courtship of right-wing evangelists, free-market absolutists, and other conservatives new to his world would have been pitiable had it not been so dangerous.

After Palin started linking Obama to "terrorists" and McCain, too, did his own part to rub the magic lantern with speeches and television ads, the crowds at rallies began shouting "Terrorist!" and "Murderer!" and "Off with his head!" These were isolated outbursts, yet they so rattled McCain that he finally had to declare that Obama was, in fact, an honorable man. When a woman asking a question at a town-hall meeting informed McCain that Obama was an "Arab," McCain finally interrupted her, saying, "No, ma'am. He's a decent family man." (As if this were the opposite of "Arab.") At a rally in Lakeville, Minnesota, McCain said, "I will respect him, and I want everyone to be respectful." McCain's supporters rewarded him with boos. If McCain ever thought that he could take a middle road, asserting that he was firmly against slanderous appeals but also delegating Palin to rouse the worst suspicions among "the base," he was now disabused of that illusion.

McCain quickly became used to the criticism of countless commentators and some former military and political allies, but one attack truly hurt. In *Why Courage Matters* (2004), McCain and Salter had written about the bravery and patriotism of John Lewis, in Selma in 1965, and at many other civil-rights demonstrations. Now, a month before the election, Lewis issued a harsh statement saying that McCain and Palin were "sowing the seeds of hatred and division":

During another period, in the not too distant past, there was a governor of the state of Alabama named George Wallace who also became a Presidential candidate. George Wallace never threw a bomb. He never fired a gun, but he created the climate and the conditions that encouraged vicious attacks against innocent Americans who were simply trying to exercise their constitutional rights. Because of this atmosphere of hate, four little girls were killed on Sunday morning when a church was bombed in Birmingham, Alabama.

Lewis warned that McCain and Palin were "playing with fire, and if they are not careful, that fire will consume us all." McCain issued a statement saying that Lewis's attack was "brazen and baseless," but it was clear to everyone on his campaign bus that he was deeply disturbed by the incident.

Ayers, for his part, had avoided reporters ever since his name first started appearing in the press during the campaign. Now in his sixties, he was unrepentant about his past in the Weather Underground, justifying his support for violence as a response to the slaughter in Vietnam. While Ayers had, for decades, been living an ordinary life as an educator, he had said reprehensible things as a young man. In 1974, for instance, he had dedicated a revolutionary manifesto called "Prairie Fire" to a range of radicals, including Harriet Tubman—but had also added the name of Robert Kennedy's assassin, Sirhan Sirhan. Much of the Chicago academic establishment now showed its support for Ayers—even Richard M. Daley commended him for his good works in education—but Palin and the McCain campaign knew that by linking Obama to Ayers they could cast doubt on Obama's loyalties, his character, and his past. Obama was never remotely a radical; as a student, lawyer, professor, and politician he had always been a gradualist—liberal in spirit, cautious in nature. Obama was disingenuous when he described Ayers merely as "a guy who lives in my neighborhood," but the idea that they were ever close friends or shared political ideas was preposterous.

"I think my relationship with Obama was probably like that of thousands of others in Chicago and, like millions and millions of others, I wished I knew him better," Ayers said, when my colleague Peter Slevin and I talked to him at his house on Election Day. Ayers said that while he wasn't bothered by the many threats—"and I'm not complaining"—the calls and e-mails he received had been "pretty intense." "I got two threats in one day on the Internet," he said, referring to an incident that took place the previous summer when he was sitting in his office at the University of Illinois-Chicago, where he has taught education for two decades. "The first one said that there was a posse coming to shoot me, and the second said that they were going to kidnap me and water-board me." During the general-election campaign, Ayers's alderman, Toni Preckwinkle, called him to say the threats were so serious that she would have police squad cars patrol by his house periodically. When he spoke at Millersville University, in Pennsylvania, he was told that there had been threats against him, and police with bomb-sniffing dogs patrolled outside the hall.

Ayers seemed unfazed by what he called "the Swiftboating" process of the 2008 campaign. "It's all guilt by association," he said. "They made me into a cartoon character—they threw me up onstage just to pummel me. I felt from the beginning that the Obama campaign had to run the Obama campaign and I have to run my life." Ayers said that once his name became part of the campaign maelstrom he never had any contact with the Obama circle. "That's not my world," he said.

One endorsement that the Obama campaign did want was that of General Colin Powell. Just as the Kennedy-family endorsement was a boon during the primary campaign, an endorsement from Powell would help among centrist Republicans and independents. Powell had left the Bush Administration, in 2005, after serving as Secretary of State, and had revealed his political hand discreetly since then, sometimes through background interviews with favored journalists, sometimes through former aides. But in the past year he had been unable to avoid mention of the Presidential race. When Obama was deciding whether to run, Powell had met with him and assured him that the country was ready to vote for a black President. Powell watched the campaign closely and, in June, in the space of a week, met with both Obama and John McCain. "I told them the concerns I had with each of their campaigns," Powell recalled, "and I told them what I liked about them. I said, 'I'm going to be watching.' "

In 1995, with his reputation burnished by the first Gulf War, and long before it was tarnished by the second, Powell had been uniquely positioned to become the first African-American President. His reputation as a soldier and as an adviser to Presidents had been, for millions of Americans, unimpeachable, and his life story, as he described it in his autobiography, *My American Journey*, was no less appealing, if less tortured, than Obama's in *Dreams from My Father*. Powell put himself forward in the old-fashioned way: the man of accomplishment "who just happens to be black."

For a few weeks, as his book sat atop the best-seller lists, Powell discussed a run for the 1996 Republican nomination with his family and his inner circle of aides and friends. Bill Clinton, a popular President, was running for a second term, but Clinton, political tacticians believed, lacked Powell's particular strengths: his maturity, his solidity in foreign affairs. In a center-right country, the scenario went, Powell could beat the incumbent. But there were considerations that went beyond polls. "Some in my family, in my circle of acquaintances, were concerned that, as a black person running for office, you're probably at greater personal risk than you might be if you were a white person," Powell told me. "But I've been at risk many times in my life, and I've been shot at, even."

Powell thought about the question for a few weeks and then, he said, he realized, "What are you doing? This is not you. It had nothing to do with race. It had to do with who I am, a professional soldier, who really has no instinct or gut passion for political life. The determining factor was I never woke up a single morning saying, 'Gee, I want to go to Iowa.' It was that simple. So the race thing was there, and I would've been the first prominent African-American candidate, but the reality is that the whole family, but especially me, had to look in the mirror and say, 'Is this what you really think you would be good at? And do you really want to do it?' And the answer was no."

Powell saw the campaign unfold over the summer of 2008, and, increasingly, he was dismayed by the ugly rhetoric on the Republican side. "It wasn't just John," Powell said. "Frankly, very often it wasn't John; it was some sheriff in Florida introducing—I can't remember who the guy was introducing, whether it was Governor Palin or John—who said, 'Barack *Hussein* Obama.' That's all code words. I know what he's saying: 'He's a Muslim, and he's black.' "

Finally, just two weeks before Election Day, Powell chose to accept a standing invitation from NBC and Tom Brokaw. He appeared on "Meet the Press," on Sunday morning, October 19th.

Powell prepared thoroughly for the appearance. Clearly, Brokaw knew what was coming; he had only to ask the obvious question and sit back. Powell, for his part, had suffered politically. He felt that Bush and Cheney had used him to sell the invasion of Iraq; that he had gone to the United Nations to speak out on Iraqi military capability equipped, as it turned out, with bogus intelligence. With a keen sense of how to deal, publicly and not, with the Washington press, Powell had, for decades, been a master of his own image—his fingerprints were all over Bob Woodward's books going back to the Administration of George H. W. Bush—but now he knew that he had to repair his reputation. His appearance on "Meet the Press" was a matter not only of expressing a preference but of making a comeback in the public eye. In his long, perfectly formed answer—more a soliloquy than a reply—Powell was careful not to alienate Republicans or insult McCain, but was also clear about the future:

On the Republican side over the last seven weeks, the approach of the Republican Party and Mr. McCain has become narrower and narrower. Mr. Obama, at the same time, has given us a more inclusive, broader reach into the needs and aspirations of our people. He's crossing lines—ethnic lines, racial lines, generational lines. He's thinking about, all villages have values, all towns have values, not just small towns have values.

Powell even questioned why surrogates for the Republican Party were trying to exploit the Ayers "issue," such as it was:

Why do we have these robo-calls going on around the country trying to suggest that because of this very, very limited relationship that Senator Obama has had with Mr. Ayers, somehow, Mr. Obama is tainted? What they're trying to do is connect him to some kind of terrorist feelings. And I think that's inappropriate. . . .

So, when I look at all of this and I think back to my Army career, we've got two individuals. Either one of them could be a good President. But which is the President that we need now? Which is the individual that serves the needs of the nation for the next period of time? And I come to the conclusion that because of his ability to inspire, because of the inclusive nature of his campaign, because he is reaching out all across America, because of who he is and his rhetorical abilities—and we have to take that into account, as well as his substance; he has both style and substance—he has met the standard of being a successful President, being an exceptional President. I think he is a transformational figure. He is a new generation coming into the world, onto the world stage, onto the American stage. And for that reason I'll be voting for Senator Barack Obama.

Colin Powell's endorsement of Barack Obama was, for some Republicans, like Kenneth Duberstein, Ronald Reagan's last chief of staff, "the *Good Housekeeping* seal of approval." In the days that followed, the calls, letters, and e-mails that Powell received were mostly positive. The Pakistanis in his local supermarket appreciated what he had to say about the use of "Arab" or "Muslim" as a pejorative. Some critics said that his endorsement of Obama was an act of "disloyalty and dishonor." Rush Limbaugh was only the loudest of the right-wing voices who denounced him. Limbaugh felt no compunction about saying that Powell's only reason for endorsing Obama was race.

Powell received some racist letters, but they were generally unsigned and had no return address. "I've faced this in just about everything I've ever done in my public life," he said to me. "It's there in America, and it can't be denied that there are people like this."

Powell said that Obama had run a completely new kind of campaign when it came to race. "Shirley [Chisholm] was a wonderful woman, and I admire Jesse [Jackson] and all of my other friends in the black community," he said, "but I think Obama should not be just—well, 'They were black, and he's black, therefore they're his predecessors.'

"Here's the difference in a nutshell, and it's an expression that I've used throughout my career—first black national-security adviser, first black chairman of the Joint Chiefs, first black Secretary of State. What Obama did—he's run as an American who is black, not as a black American. There's a difference. People would say to me, 'Gee, it's great to be the black Secretary of State,' and I would blink and laugh and say, 'Is there a white one somewhere? I am the Secretary of State, who happens to be black.' Make sure you understand where you put that descriptor, because it makes a difference. And I faced that throughout my career. You know, 'You're the best black lieutenant I've ever seen.' 'Thank you very much, sir, but I want to be the best lieutenant you've ever seen, not the best black lieutenant you've ever seen.' Obama has not shrunk from his heritage, his culture, his background, and the fact that he's black, as other blacks have. He ran honestly on the basis of who he is and what he is and his background, which is a fascinating background, but he didn't run just to appeal to black people or to say a black person could do it. He's running as an American."

Powell's "happens to be black" terminology was not quite in synch with how Obama saw his campaign, but, like Obama, he rejected the notion that victory would signal the rise of a "post-racial" period in American history. "No!" he said. "It just means that we have moved farther along the continuum that the Founding Fathers laid out for us two hundred and thirty-odd years ago. With each passing year, with each passing generation, with each passing figure, we move closer and closer to what America can be. But, no matter what happens in the case of Senator Obama, there are still a lot of black kids who don't see that dream there for them."

Not long before Election Day, as the American financial system reached a state of such extreme crisis that there was talk of a second Great

Depression, Obama's lead over McCain widened. McCain had not been able to distance himself effectively from the Bush Presidency, and his confused performance during the financial crisis, his muddled and fleeting proposal that the Presidential campaign be suspended to allow all parties to concentrate on remedies for the banking disaster, was now hurting him further. Moreover, in the debates Obama had performed evenly, soberly, consistently, while, at times, McCain reinforced the cartoon of himself as obstreperous and too old for the job. Nearly all the polls showed Obama winning the debates, and that too helped bolster his growing lead.

There was also little doubt that one large non-voting constituency favored Obama: the rest of the world. In a poll conducted by the BBC World Service in twenty-two countries, respondents preferred Obama to McCain by a four-to-one margin. Nearly half the respondents said that if Obama became President it would "fundamentally change" their perception of the United States.

With Obama now ahead in the polls, I visited New Orleans, the ruined landscape that will forever be associated with the Bush Presidency. The last time I was there the city had been underwater. This was not the scene of heavy campaigning. Obama had pledged to run a fifty-state strategy, but even his enormous war chest would not pay for futility. The state went for Bush in 2000 and 2004 and was headed for McCain in 2008. Nevertheless, African-Americans in New Orleans—in Treme, in Mid-City, in the Lower Ninth—watched Obama's campaign obsessively. They listened to Tom Joyner, on WYLD; Michael Baisden, on KMEZ; Jamie Foxx, on Sirius. On Canal Street, vendors sold the same Obama T-shirts that I'd seen on 125th Street, in Harlem. The most popular paired Obama and Martin Luther King. Kids who would normally wear oversized throwback sports jerseys now wore Obama paraphernalia instead. There were Obama signs in the windows of barbershops, seafood and po'boy joints, and people's homes.

One night, I went out for a beer with Wendell Pierce, a New Orleanian who made his name as an actor playing the homicide cop Bunk Moreland on "The Wire," Obama's favorite television show. Pierce is in his mid-forties. His parents' neighborhood, Pontchartrain Park, was destroyed by Katrina, and he had spent months trying to redevelop the area. Pierce picked me up on Canal Street; he is built like a fireplug and has a double-bass voice. We drove to Bullet's, a working-class bar on A. P. Tureaud Avenue, in the Seventh Ward. There we met Mike Dauphin, a Vietnam veteran, who sat at our table for a long time talking about his childhood in Jim Crow New Orleans, riding in the back of the bus and going to segregated schools and working at American Can and U.S. Steel.

When Katrina came, he was sheltered first at a hospice and then, with thousands of others, at the Convention Center, downtown, "where we had almost no water or food for five days." He could hardly wait to vote, and he was talking in the same terms as many older people around town: "I never dreamed in my lifetime that I would see a black man as President of the United States. I was a kid growing up under Jim Crow. We couldn't drink out of the same water faucet—but now it seems that America has changed."

In African-American neighborhoods, that was the nearly unanimous feeling—a refrain of relief, anticipatory celebration. Yet you also heard from many people a great wariness, a defense against white self-congratulation or the impression that somehow Obama's election would automatically transform the conditions of New Orleans and the country. In Treme, a neighborhood adjacent to the French Quarter and, arguably, the oldest black community in the country, I met Jerome Smith, a veteran of the Freedom Rides in Alabama and Mississippi. These days, Smith was running youth programs at Treme Community Center. On a sunny fall afternoon, we sat on the steps of a former funeral home on St. Claude Avenue that was now operating as the Backstreet Cultural Museum, an apartment-size collection of artifacts from the black bands that played Mardi Gras and second-line parades.

"Obama winning the Presidency breaks a historical rhythm, but it does not mean everything," Smith said. "His minister did not lie when he said that the controlling power in this country was rich white men. Rich white men were responsible for slavery. They are responsible for unbreakable levels of poverty for African-Americans. Look at this bailout today, which is all about us bailing out rich white men. And there are thousands of children from this city who have gone missing from New Orleans. Who will speak for them? Obama?

"Obama is the recipient of something, but he did not stand in the Senate after he was elected and say that there is a significant *absence* in this chamber, that he was the only African-American and this is wrong. He is no Martin Luther King, he is no Fannie Lou Hamer"—who helped found the Mississippi Freedom Democratic Party, in 1964. "He is a man who can be accommodated by America, but he is not my hero, because a politician, by nature, has to surrender. Where the problems that afflict African-Americans are concerned, Obama can't go for broke. And the white people—good, decent white people—who vote for him just can't understand. They don't have to walk through the same misery as our children do."

Smith was angry but, as an activist contemplating a mainstream leader, not misguided. It was inevitable that euphoria would fade. And what would remain is a litany of disasters: cresting worldwide recession, wars in Iraq and Afghanistan, a rickety, unjust health-care system, melting polar ice caps, nuclear proliferation in the Middle East and South Asia—to say nothing of the crisis that comes from out of nowhere. In 2008, the new President was going to inherit a web of crises, almost too many to imagine.

Colin Powell said that, after a prolonged period in which American prestige abroad has dwindled, Obama would enjoy a "honeymoon period," especially abroad, which would give him an opportunity to "move forward on a number of foreign-policy fronts.

"That is also something that will perish or diminish over time, as he faces problems and crises," Powell continued. "If the excitement of the first black President is great, it'll diminish if he doesn't do something about the economy, or the economy worsens, or if we suddenly find ourselves in a crisis. . . . The next President will be challenged, and how the President responds to that challenge will be more important than what his race happens to be at that moment. But, for the initial period of an Obama Presidency, there will be an excitement, an electricity around the world that he can use."

As Election Day neared, the world of John McCain and his circle became increasingly bitter. The Obama campaign, which had forgone its promise to limit spending and instead refused public monies in order to accept unlimited donations, was outspending McCain by an estimated five hundred million dollars. With the economy continuing to shrivel and McCain seeming more and more unnerved by the crisis, moderates gravitated to Obama in swing states like Virginia, North Carolina, Indiana, and Colorado. Odds of an Obama victory were gaining fast. McCain could not help but see Obama as someone absurdly fortunate, a man possessed of such self-assurance, even hauteur, that he seemed to be "trying to get the country to prove something to him and not vice-versa," as Salter put it. "For Obama, if the country showed the good sense to elect him, it will have shown itself worthy of the promise it once had because I represent the fulfillment of that promise. The insinuation was that if you don't have the guts to change or become better, then you vote for John McCain. A vote for John McCain was not to show the proper courage; he's old, doesn't know how to use a computer."

Privately, McCain's aides knew that they had done themselves enormous injury by nominating Sarah Palin. She had proved herself so wildly undereducated in the affairs of the country and the world, so willing to say or do anything as long as she attracted attention, that it made McCain look weak and, worse, cynical. Like Rudy Giuliani, she disgraced herself by mocking Obama for working for the poor as a community organizer. It is unclear that another Vice-Presidential nominee would have helped McCain avoid losing—not in the midst of an economic free-fall with a weak, unpopular Republican President in the White House—but she did help him lose ingloriously. She behaved erratically, heedlessly, and McCain did nothing to stop her. By giving himself over to her rhetoric, by failing to put an end to the sort of smears she reveled in, McCain had forfeited some part of what he valued most in himself—his sense of honor.

Mark Salter and other McCain lieutenants felt that they had never been given a chance, that they were victims of a "meta-narrative" pushed by the press, especially by reporters old enough to have a memory of the civil-rights movement. In their frustrated view, these reporters attached themselves to the Obama campaign as an act of personal mission. "A lot of them, like me, never served in the military," Salter said. "Civil rights was a great struggle, and now they could all do their bit."

Salter felt that he and McCain's other principal aides had never been able to set aside their differences and get it together to present him as an equally compelling candidate, a man who had lost his way when he was young and then found it through public service and military sacrifice, someone who was so committed to his country and his fellow soldiers that he refused repeated offers from the North Vietnamese to be released before his comrades. "We could have done a better job for a guy who was good to us," Salter said.

For everyone involved in the campaign, it would forever be impossible to recapture the sense of what it was like to be in the midst of the prolonged battle. Salter's sense of injury, which reflected McCain's, was profound. "The truth is, all that will be remembered of the campaign is that America's original sin was finally expunged," Salter said. "That's all. In history, that's all. The real McCain will be lost to history. He's got years ahead of him, but he is lost to history. The narrative is the narrative, completely untrue and unfair, but he is the old guy who ran a derogatory campaign and can't remember how many houses he had."

Barack Obama won the election with fifty-three per cent of the popular vote to McCain's forty-six per cent. He won by more than nine and a half million votes and took three hundred and sixty-five electoral votes of a total five hundred and thirty-eight. Turnout was the highest since 1968. African-American turnout rose a full two per cent and was crucial to Obama in winning unlikely states like North Carolina and Virginia. Obama won every region of the country by double digits except the South, where McCain led by nine points. Nationally, Obama did not win the white vote—McCain won it fifty-five per cent to forty-three—but the country was becoming increasingly diverse and non-white. One of the breakthroughs of the election was to reinforce the demographic and psychological reality that the United States was, in the twenty-first century, a different place.

For weeks before the voting, commentators and voters wondered if Obama's poll numbers would collapse in the voting booth, if white voters would privately turn against him in significant numbers. In other words, they worried about the "Bradley effect," which holds that many white voters who tell pollsters that they would vote for a black candidate—like Los Angeles mayor Tom Bradley—do otherwise when they are actually in the voting booth. This happened repeatedly in the nineteen-eighties and earlier, but the Obama campaign had taken heart from more recent campaigns, like Harold Ford's Senate race in Tennessee, where voters seemed unaffected by the old trend. It turned out, in fact, that many white voters, acting on economic issues, were completely prepared to turn to Obama. Most famously, in Fishtown, Pennsylvania, a depressed white suburb of Philadelphia, some openly racist voters told a pollster that they were undecided. Suddenly, there was talk of a "Fishtown effect" that would replace the Bradley effect. As David Bositis, an expert on racial voting patterns, put it, the Bradley effect was a force when "Santa Claus powered his sleigh with coal. It's no longer germane to American society." There was even talk of a "Palmer effect" or a "Huxtable effect"—a nod to the normalizing influence on whites of pop-culture African-Americans like President David Palmer, the black President on "24," or Bill Cosby's sitcom about an appealing African-American family that was, in its time, the most popular program on the air.

On Election Night, there were street celebrations all over the country: in Harlem and on the South Side, on college campuses and in town squares. There were celebrations in world capitals and around a makeshift video screen in Obama's ancestral village, in western Kenya.

The weather in Chicago was sunny and cool. Gold and russet leaves skittered with the wind along the streets in Hyde Park. While Obama waited out the results at his house on South Greenwood Avenue, and, later, at a hotel suite downtown, the whole city seemed alive to the coming party. By nightfall, along Michigan Avenue, huge crowds headed in one direction—toward Grant Park. The votes were not in, but there was no reason to believe that Obama could lose. People were singing, listening to street musicians, buying up stacks of Obama "chum": T-shirts, buttons, posters. Jay-Z and Nas and other hip-hop performers who had supported Obama and written lyrics about him played from speakers all along the avenue.

The crowd in Grant Park was vast—a hundred and twenty-five thousand people, all of them happy in the cool night. A blue stage was assembled with a long row of American flags set behind the speaker's lectern. All night, as the votes came in, I could think of only a few comparable days or nights in my life as a reporter: running along the streets of East Berlin, in 1989, as the first anti-Communist demonstrations broke out; not long after, sitting in the Magic Lantern Theater, in Prague, when Václav Havel and Alexander Dubček toasted the resignation of the ruling Politburo and the end of Communist rule in Czechoslovakia; the late August evening along the Moscow River in 1991 when the K.G.B.-led coup collapsed and Mikhail Gorbachev was returned from captivity on the Black Sea. There were fireworks, too, that night in Moscow, singing, the waving of flags by people who had been wary of waving one. In Berlin, Prague, and Moscow, there was a sense of historical emancipation and grand promises, of a country being returned to its people. In Chicago, the history was not the same. A regime had not fallen. The color line had not been erased or even transcended, but a historical bridge had been crossed.

At one point, after Obama's victory had been announced, the crowd in Grant Park recited the Pledge of Allegiance. Derrick Z. Jackson, an African-American and a veteran reporter for the Boston *Globe*, wrote, "I have never heard such a multicultural throng recite the pledge with such determined enunciation, expelling it from the heart in a treble soaring to the skies and a bass drumming through the soil to vibrate my feet. The treble and bass met in my spine, where 'liberty and justice for all' evoked neither clank of chains nor cackle of cruelty, but a warm tickle of Jeffersonian slave-owning irony: Justice cannot sleep forever."

"The analogy I have for this is when Jackie Robinson broke into the majors," the journalist and civil-rights lawyer Roger Wilkins said. "From the time Branch Rickey signed him, I was just consumed. I couldn't think of anything else. What I discovered as I got older is what a real change

Jackie made in people's attitudes—partly because he was a superb player, but also because he was an extraordinary man, who had the guts to hold his passion in. I had conversations for years with people who told me they had changed within. I think Barack Obama has the brains, the drive, the discipline, the toughness, and the cool to make a success of his Presidency, despite the mess he is being handed by the people who were there before. I've already seen white people responding to him during the campaign. My neighbor in our building is a widow born and raised on the Eastern Shore of Maryland, which was very racist. She had an Obama sticker on her door. So I asked her, 'Ann, why are you doing this, so deeply engaged.' She looked at me and said, 'Because I want to feel good about my country.' There are a lot of white people who haven't thought about this a lot or never had somebody teach them about race and here is this guy, Obama, and he doesn't have to make big racial speeches every day. All he has to do is be a good President. These are still hideous numbers about poverty and prisons and education in America—grotesque disparities. He can't wave a magic wand and make it all go away. These things are deep in our national D.N.A."

After the Electoral College count tipped past 270, the decisive number, the Obamas—Barack, Michelle, Malia, and Sasha—walked out on the Grant Park stage. What broke out is what can best be described as well-mannered pandemonium: crying, flag-waving, the embracing of friends and strangers. In his concession speech, McCain paid gracious tribute to the moment. The cameras captured Jesse Jackson standing alone, tears streaming down his face. The cynical interpretation was that they were crocodile tears, fakery, tears of regret that he wasn't the one on the stage. When I had the chance later to ask Jackson about the moment, he said that he had been thinking that night of Emmett Till, of Rosa Parks, of Martin Luther King at the Lincoln Memorial, the march in Selma. "And in my own head I saw the funerals," he said. "I wish Dr. King and Malcolm could have been there for, like, just thirty seconds, just to see what they got killed about. That's when I began to well up and cried. Think about the martyrs: Fannie Lou Hamer, if she could have just been there for just a minute." He thought of a trip to Europe where people were telling him that Obama could never win. "It was all converged in my consciousness, both the journey to get there and the joy of the moment. I was in awe. I could see Dr. King putting on his shoes in Selma, getting ready to march, and Jim Farmer, and John Lewis—all of them. These were the people who made this day happen."

When the cheering finally quieted down, Obama gave a brisk and

moving speech, one of thanks, unification, and promise. And, as he had so
many times before, he called on a personal story to embody the sense of
the moment, the emotions in the air. Earlier in the campaign it had been
Ashley Baia, a young volunteer in South Carolina. Now it was Ann Nixon
Cooper, who, at the age of a hundred and six, had just voted for him in
Atlanta. Cooper was the grandmother of Lawrence Bobo, a sociologist at
Harvard and one of the most prominent African-American academics in
the country. Bobo's scholarly work centered on the complexities and
changes in racial attitudes among whites and blacks. The Obama campaign had called Bobo's grandmother and said that he might mention her
in the speech—campaign aides had seen her interviewed on CNN—
but the family had no idea that the President-elect would take her life to
show the passage from suffering to suffrage and then the moment of his
ascension:

> She was born just a generation past slavery; a time when there were no
> cars on the road or planes in the sky; when someone like her couldn't
> vote for two reasons—because she was a woman and because of the
> color of her skin. And tonight I think about all that she's seen through-
> out her century in America—the heartache and the hope; the struggle
> and the progress; the times we were told that we can't, and the people
> who pressed on with that American creed: Yes, we can.
>
> At a time when women's voices were silenced and their hopes dis-
> missed, she lived to see them stand up and speak out and reach for the
> ballot. Yes, we can.
>
> When there was despair in the Dust Bowl and depression across the
> land, she saw a nation conquer fear itself with a New Deal, new jobs,
> and a new sense of common purpose. Yes, we can.
>
> When the bombs fell on our harbor and tyranny threatened the
> world, she was there to witness a generation rise to greatness and a
> democracy was saved. Yes, we can.
>
> She was there for the buses in Montgomery, the hoses in Birming-
> ham, a bridge in Selma, and a preacher from Atlanta who told a people
> that "We Shall Overcome." Yes, we can.
>
> A man touched down on the moon, a wall came down in Berlin, a
> world was connected by our own science and imagination. And this
> year, in this election, she touched her finger to a screen, and cast her
> vote, because after a hundred and six years in America, through the best
> of times and the darkest of hours, she knows how America can change.
>
> Yes, we can.

On a night of triumph, Obama's tone was not triumphal, it was not ringing; his tone was grave. Having cast himself in Selma twenty months earlier as one who stood on the "shoulders of giants," as the leader of the Joshua generation, he hardly had to mention race. It was the thing always present, the thing so rarely named. He had simultaneously celebrated identity and eased it into the background. Ann Nixon Cooper was an emblem not only of her race, but of her nation.

"Change has come to America," Obama declared, and, in a park best remembered until now as the place where, forty summers ago, police did outrageous battle with antiwar protesters, everyone knew that change had come, and that—how long? *too* long—it was about damned time.

Chapter Seventeen

To the White House

Two centuries before Barack Obama ran for President, slaves built the White House. They quarried stone in Virginia, made nails and baked bricks in Georgetown. West Africans by heritage, they had no last names or carried the names of their masters. The records tell us that they went by "Tom," "Peter," "Ben," "Harry," "Daniel," and so on. Three slaves at the White House construction site were on loan from its architect, an Irishman from Charleston named James Hoban. One of his slaves was designated "Negro Peter." Hoban designed the President's mansion to look like Leinster House, in Dublin, but there are echoes, too, of a Southern plantation house. Sometimes, the slaves were given the equivalent of a dollar a day, but nearly all of their wages were passed along to their owners. Working alongside free blacks and white European laborers, the slaves helped build Washington along the designs of Pierre-Charles L'Enfant and the architects of Europe. They built the Capitol dome. They cleared the woods and dug up the stumps near the Potomac. They drained swamps. And, not far from the building site of the White House, auctioneers from the Virginia-based firm of Franklin & Armfield sold new slaves. Cash changed hands as frightened young blacks, held in pens, shackled, dressed in rags, stared out at their new masters. Soon they would be boarded on steamships and sent to Natchez, Charleston, Mobile, and New Orleans.

There were many reasons that the founding generation finally voted to move the capital south to Washington. One was the requirements of construction, another the politics of slavery in the North. "Can one imagine a succession of twelve slaveholder presidents if the capital had remained in Philadelphia?" Garry Wills writes in his study of Jefferson, *Negro President.* "The southerners got what they wanted, a seat of government where slavery would be taken for granted, where it would not need perpetual apology, excuse, or palliation, where the most honored men in the nation were not to be criticized because they practiced and defended and gave privilege to the holding of slaves."

At the end of the eighteenth century, hundreds of slaves were working on federal buildings in the new capital. "To the Southern-born, the district now presented the reassuringly familiar panorama of a plantation work site," the historian Fergus M. Bordewich writes, "with white overseers directing black workmen grubbing stumps, hauling timber, dragging sledges, digging foundations, toting baskets of stone, bushels of lime, and kegs of nails, chiseling stone, stirring mortar, and tending brick kilns. Wherever buildings were under construction, including the Capitol and the President's House, teams of enslaved sawyers in broad-brimmed hats could be seen sweating at their work in the sawpits beneath cascades of sawdust, slicing logs into boards, with the rhythmic, angled, backbreaking strokes of a six-foot blade."

Construction had begun on the White House in 1792, and, by 1798, around ninety black men were working at the site and on the Capitol. On a given day, about five or six slaves were out sick, laid up in a makeshift clinic. The commissioners employed one Dr. May to care for them. They spent fifty cents a day on treatment.

Twelve Presidents owned slaves, eight of them while in office. John and Abigail Adams, the first inhabitants of the White House, were, by the standards of the day, abolitionists, and, at the White House, they kept only two servants, a white farm couple. Their idealism was rewarded by the many guests who mocked their food, their housekeeping, and their hospitality. Thomas Jefferson brought to the White House members of his considerable household staff, including a few slaves. James and Dolley Madison brought more. The most famous of Madison's slaves was his "body servant," Paul Jennings, who was born on Madison's estate, in Montpelier, Virginia. Jennings's father was an English trader, his mother a slave. At the White House, Jennings was in constant contact with the President and became the executive mansion's first tell-all memoirist, leaving behind a short manuscript titled "A Colored Man's Reminiscences of James Madison." He was a young man when he served Madison and saw the British attack the White House. Jennings recalled Dolley Madison grabbing what valuables she could and stuffing them in her reticule before fleeing the White House; he recalled the "rabble" that raided the mansion soon afterward and "stole lots of silver and whatever they could lay their hands on." Although Jennings was, like jewelry or a horse, Madison's property, a commodity, he wrote with tender and forgiving affection for the President. "Mr. Madison, I think, was one of the best men that ever lived," he wrote, and went on:

> I never saw him in a passion, and never knew him to strike a slave, although he had over one hundred; neither would he allow an overseer to do it. Whenever any slaves were reported as stealing or "cutting up" badly, he would send for them and admonish them privately, and never mortify them before others. They generally served him very faithfully. . . .
>
> He often told the story, that one day riding home from court with old Tom Barbour (father of Governor Barbour), they met a colored man who took off his hat. Mr. M. raised his, to the surprise of old Tom; to whom Mr. M. replied, "I never allow a Negro to excel me in politeness."

Jennings was a loyal servant, who stayed with Madison in his retirement, deteriorating health, and, finally, his death. As in so many slave manuscripts, the narrator asserts his own selfhood, his dignity, through the power of loyalty and his sympathy for the "family" that owns him:

> I was always with Mr. Madison till he died, and shaved him every other day for sixteen years. For six months before his death, he was unable to walk, and spent most of his time reclined on a couch; but his mind was bright, and with his numerous visitors he talked with as much animation and strength of voice as I ever heard him in his best days. I was present when he died. That morning Sukey brought him his breakfast, as usual. He could not swallow. His niece, Mrs. Willis, said, "What is the matter, Uncle James?" "Nothing more than a change of mind, my dear."
>
> His head instantly dropped, and he ceased breathing as quietly as the snuff of a candle goes out. He was about eighty-four years old, and was followed to the grave by an immense procession of white and colored people.

Jennings died in 1874, when he was seventy-five. In his lifetime, he took part in an abolitionist plot to free slaves on a Washington schooner, worked for Daniel Webster (from whom he bought his freedom), and, toward the end of his life, served in the Department of the Interior.

Nearly all of the hundreds of slaves who followed Jennings in service at the White House worked in livery and died in anonymity. They wrote no memoirs and left barely a trace in the archives. Andrew Jackson brought his slaves to Washington, D.C., from his estate in Tennessee but little is known about the "body servant" who shared his bedroom in the White House. We do know that James Polk bought slaves even while President, paying, on July 20, 1846, a total of $1,436 for "Hartwell & his wife & her child nine years old." In the eighteen-fifties, slaves were eliminated from the White House staff not because of any doubts about the morality of chattel slavery, but, rather, because James Buchanan thought that white British servants would better preserve his daily privacy.

Abraham and Mary Todd Lincoln had no slaves in the White House. Their servants were either from their household in Illinois or white Europeans inherited from the previous Administration. They did, however, employ a black dressmaker, a *modiste*, named Lizzy—Elizabeth Keckley—who was born a slave in Dinwiddie Courthouse, Virginia, near Petersburg. No black man or woman, not even Paul Jennings, ever knew such intimacy with a First Family, and what is most remarkable about Keckley is that she left behind a memoir called *Behind the Scenes, or, Thirty Years a Slave, and Four Years in the White House*, which, in its way, stands with the slave narratives and memoirs that make up the core of early African-American literature. Like Sojourner Truth, Harriet Jacobs, and other slaves who gained their freedom and became the authors of narratives of their lives, Keckley wrote to assert her literacy, her history, her status as a thinking, feeling being. She was not as profound a memoirist as Harriet Jacobs, or Booker T. Washington, or W. E. B. DuBois, but her view of the world was unlike any other. Her testimony came from the living quarters of the White House, from within the confidence and embrace of the Lincoln family.

Keckley's mother was a slave named Agnes. Her father was her mother's master, an Army colonel named Armistead Burwell. Elizabeth learned her father's identity many years later when her mother was on her deathbed. As a child of four, she started working in the Burwell household. Keckley called slavery a "cruel custom" by which "I was robbed of my dearest right" and yet, much like Jennings before her, she displayed an understanding of the predicament of the slave master that, to us, seems shockingly sympathetic. She expresses an empathy for her owners—owners who did not hesitate to torture her—simply because they, too, had been born into the social and economic system of slavery.

Considering the cruelties Keckley endured, her equanimity seems beyond the capacities of a saint. When she was living in Hillsboro, North Carolina, where Burwell was in charge of a Presbyterian church, a Mr. Bingham ran the school and often visited the parsonage. One day, without evident reason Bingham demanded that she lower her dress to receive a whipping. Keckley relates that she feared most for her sense of modesty. She was, she tells us, eighteen "and fully developed." Bingham binds her hands, tears her dress, and picks up a rawhide, "the instrument of torture":

> I can feel the torture now—the terrible, excruciating agony of those moments. I did not scream; I was too proud to let my tormentor know what I was suffering.

Even in this unnervingly balanced narrative—a narrative without the hint of rebellion or abolitionist fervor—there is no doubting the extent of the slave master's depravity. Some slaves, Keckley reports, preferred to die rather than suffer any longer. When her uncle makes an absent-minded mistake on the farm, losing a pair of plow lines, he so fears the result, the thrashing and humiliation that will surely be his, that he hangs himself from a willow tree "rather than meet the displeasure of his master."

The dominion of the slave master was limitless. The slave enjoyed no private realm, no right of family or sexual protection. For four years, Keckley worked in North Carolina for a man named Alexander Kirkland, who raped her at his whim. The resulting pregnancy "brought me suffering and deep mortification" and the unbearable thought that she was bearing a son who could not possibly escape the fate of his mother and every other slave.

Keckley understood well the outrageous hypocrisy of her masters, "who preached the love of Heaven, who glorified the precepts and examples of Christ, who expounded the Holy Scriptures Sabbath after Sabbath from the pulpit," and yet treated her with no more regard than a dog. And still, like Booker T. Washington in his memoirs a half-century later, Keckley writes of slavery as a "school" in which she learned her humanity.

Eventually, she made her way to St. Louis and, by 1855, had bought her freedom. She married but refused to have any more children—"I could not bear the thought of . . . adding one single recruit to the millions bound to hopeless servitude." Instead, she developed her skills as a seamstress and moved on to Washington, D.C., where she developed a business as a dressmaker; she came to work for the wives of Robert E. Lee and Jefferson Davis and admitted to a "great desire to work for the ladies of the White House."

On the day of Lincoln's first inauguration, Keckley was summoned to Willard's Hotel for a private interview with Mary Lincoln. Mrs. Lincoln had spilled coffee on the dress she was going to wear that evening after the swearing-in ceremonies; the stain, Keckley realized, had "rendered it necessary that she should have a new one for the occasion." Keckley set to work on a dress for the new First Lady. While she worked, the Lincolns talked amiably.

"You seem to be in a poetical mood to-night," said his wife.

"Yes, mother, these are poetical times" was his pleasant reply. "I declare, you look charming in that dress. Mrs. Keckley has met with great success."

Then, Keckley recalls, "Mrs. Lincoln took the President's arm, and with smiling face led the train below. I was surprised at her grace and composure. I had heard so much, in current and malicious report, of her low life, of her ignorance and vulgarity, that I expected to see her embarrassed on this occasion. Report, I soon saw, was wrong. No queen, accustomed to the usages of royalty all her life, could have comported herself with more calmness and dignity than did the wife of the President."

The Lincolns allowed Lizzy a remarkable intimacy with the household. She seems to have been in the living quarters much more frequently than dressmaking would have required. "I consider you my best living friend," Mrs. Lincoln later wrote to her. On the evening of a White House reception, she was in Mrs. Lincoln's bedroom attending to her hair and dress ("White satin, trimmed with black lace") while eleven-year-old Willie lay ill. His parents were terribly worried and considered canceling the reception, but the doctor told them that there was no immediate cause for alarm. The Lincolns went downstairs, and Keckley, sitting in the sickroom with Willie, could hear the "rich notes" of the Marine Band in the apartments below—the "subdued murmurs, like the wild, faint sobbing of far-off spirits." Mrs. Lincoln came upstairs several times to check on Willie. The boy's fever grew worse through the night. Days later, his condition became grave, and then he died. Almost immediately, the Lincolns summoned Keckley to the White House to deal with the gruesome and heartbreaking details: "I assisted in washing him and dressing him, and then laid him on the bed, when Mr. Lincoln came in. I never saw a man so bowed down with grief. He came to the bed, lifted the cover from the face of his child, gazed at it long and earnestly, murmuring, 'My poor boy, he was too good for this earth. God has called him home.' "

Keckley describes Lincoln sobbing as he spoke, his head buried in his hands, his tall frame "convulsed with emotion." She watches, crying. "His grief unnerved him, and made him a weak, passive child. I did not dream that his rugged nature could be so moved. I shall never forget those solemn moments—genius and greatness weeping over love's idol lost."

Mrs. Lincoln was even more overcome than her husband. And in a scene of gothic strangeness, Keckley recalls how, "in one of her paroxysms of grief, the President kindly bent over his wife, took her by the arm and gently led her to the window. With a stately, solemn gesture, he pointed to the lunatic asylum.

"Mother, do you see that large white building on the hill yonder? Try and control your grief, or it will drive you mad and we may have to send you there."

Elizabeth had a kind of access to the private lives of the Lincolns denied to many of his aides and friends. There is no end to the disturbing proximity of their relationship—the closeness between master and servant, the contradictory moral universe that allowed even the greatest leader in his nation's history to consider repatriating blacks to Africa, considering them the physical and mental inferior of the white man, and yet trust a woman born a slave as an intimate and a witness.

When Lincoln was shot at Ford's Theatre and died, on April 15, 1865, Keckley was summoned to the White House. First, she was taken to a darkened room where Mrs. Lincoln was "tossing uneasily about upon a bed" and then to the Guest's Room where the President lay in state: "When I crossed the threshold of the room, I could not help recalling the day on which I had seen little Willie lying in his coffin where the body of his father now lay." Cabinet members were there. Dignitaries milled around. "They made room for me, and, approaching the body, I lifted the white cloth from the white face of the man that I had worshipped as an idol—looked upon as a demi-god."

After paying her respects to Lincoln, she returned to her charge, to carry out the duties that she knew were expected of her: "I shall never forget the scene—the wails of a broken heart, the unearthly shrieks, the terrible convulsions, the wild, tempestuous outbursts of grief from the soul. I bathed Mrs. Lincoln's head with cold water, and soothed the terrible tornado as best I could."

The tragedy of Elizabeth Keckley was that a serious person—a woman who not only served the First Lady, but ran a successful business, created a freed-people's relief society in Washington, and even played a small role in bringing both Frederick Douglass and Sojourner Truth to the White House for conversations with President Lincoln—was met with such vicious mockery when, in 1868, she published her memoir.

Just the year before, Mrs. Lincoln, living in a modest Chicago hotel and desperate for money, had arranged to meet Keckley in New York to ask her to help sell her old gowns and jewelry. Disdained by many whites as an imperious provincial, Mrs. Lincoln could rely on her as on no one else. But after the book appeared, Elizabeth Keckley was branded a "traitorous eavesdropper" in the press. A burlesque was produced entitled " 'Behind the Seams,' by a Nigger Woman who took in work from Mrs. Lincoln and Mrs. Davis." She had violated the codes of her era and threw a sense of fear into the slave-owning and servant-possessing classes. "Where will it end?" one reviewer said. "What family of eminence that employs a negro is safe from such desecration?" Mrs. Lincoln denounced the book and "the coloured historian." She cut off the seamstress she had once called her "best and kindest friend."

In a letter to the New York *Citizen*, Elizabeth Keckley asked if she was being denounced because "my skin is dark?" Was she not free to speak and write as a free woman? Toward the end of her life, she worked at Wilberforce University in Ohio, heading its Domestic Science Department. She died, in 1907, at the age of eighty-nine in Washington, D.C. She was a resident of the National Home for Destitute Colored Women and Children.

If Elizabeth Keckley was the most intimate African-American observer of the Lincoln White House, Frederick Douglass was surely its most important black visitor. Douglass had few illusions about Lincoln, realizing that the President had committed the North to civil war with the Confederacy to bring the South back into the Union with slavery in place. It was only as the war progressed that Lincoln came to see the untenable nature of fighting a slave power without attacking slavery itself. Lincoln came from Illinois, where racist feeling was strong and intact, and, as a political creature, he could not easily ignore the ingrained power of that prejudice. He needed to retain the loyalty of the border states of Maryland, Missouri, Delaware, and Kentucky, all of which were crucial to military strategy against the Confederacy and opposed any anti-slavery rhetoric from Washington.

Douglass, like so many other Americans, black and white, tried to make sense of the contradictory nature of Lincoln's statements and actions when it came to slavery and the history of black men and women in America. "To become President," Richard Hofstadter writes in *The American Political Tradition*, "Lincoln had to talk more radically on occasion than he actually felt; to be an effective President he was compelled to act more conservatively than he wanted." Lincoln had to cope with the extremes of violent racists, both in the North and the South, and the abolitionist tendency among a small, liberal intelligentsia. As a calculating politician, he could not act the revolutionary; he could not outpace the abolitionists. If Lincoln grew, the abolitionist Wendell Phillips said, "it was because we have watered him." For Lincoln, the Union came first. As he wrote to Horace Greeley, "If I could save the Union without freeing any slave, I would do it; and if I could do it by freeing all the slaves, I would do it." It was only late in 1862 that Lincoln determined that military necessity demanded that he put forward a proclamation of emancipation. But he neither denounced slavery as a moral travesty nor liberated the slaves in states loyal to the Union. The Emancipation Proclamation was the cagiest of historical acts. The resulting document, Hofstadter notes, "had all the moral grandeur of a bill of lading."

Even in August, 1863, nearly a year after Emancipation, Douglass remained deeply distrustful of Lincoln, calling him a "genuine representative of American prejudice"—and with reason. In the early summer, there were draft riots in New York. White protesters, many of them of Irish ancestry, were furious that they were made to fight for the rights of "niggers," as they invariably put it, and hundreds of men rampaged through the city, torching black-owned houses and charities and lynching blacks from city lampposts. It took four days for Union troops to quell the rioting. In the end, there were a hundred dead and hundreds more injured. To Douglass's dismay, Lincoln so feared any further insurrection from whites angry at conscription that he refused to declare martial law or even prosecute the rioters. Nor could Douglass countenance Lincoln's earlier support for separation of the races. The President had raised hundreds of thousands of dollars to colonize American blacks abroad. He signed a contract with a firm called the Chiriqui Improvement Company to repatriate five hundred freed slaves to Panama. He urged them to move abroad and work in the coal mines. "Your race are suffering, in my judgment, the greatest wrong inflicted on any people," he told a group of blacks from the District at a White House reception. "But even when you cease to be slaves, you are yet far removed from being placed on an equality with the white race."

Lincoln's plan to send former slaves to Central America stalled—blacks were not interested in going, and the countries involved showed no sign of wanting them—but it was plain to Douglass that the President, despite his signature on the Emancipation documents and his evident moral probity, did not consider the Negro equal in his capacities to the white man.

Douglass had been working to recruit black soldiers for Union regiments. For him, there was no greater immediate cause and no greater sign of equal rights. The rolls of the Massachusetts Fifty-fourth Volunteers, the first black regiment from a free state, were filled thanks largely to his efforts. And yet black soldiers in the Union Army were paid a pittance, half, at best, what their white counterparts received, and, if captured by Confederate forces, they were routinely tortured, imprisoned, or made to work as slaves—all with barely a word of protest from the Lincoln White House.

Douglass, who was now forty-five years old and, in the abolitionist ranks, a comrade of William Lloyd Garrison, had come to Washington to appeal to the President. How he would reach him he did not know. He traveled for several days on sleeper trains from his home in Rochester, New York, alighting, filthy with soot, at the B&O Station on New Jersey Avenue, near the Capitol. It was August 10, 1863, a shatteringly hot morning. Washington had long been a city of slaves and slave auctions, but now the capital was home to eleven thousand freedmen. They were a marked, even dominant, presence in the city that summer, many of them walking the streets dirty, poorly dressed, jobless, as a large proportion of the moneyed white population and much of the government had fled the city to the countryside to avoid Washington's swampy heat and the many diseases—diphtheria, typhoid, and measles—that had become so common there.

Douglass had no appointment at the White House. His only hope of gaining access lay in a letter of introduction from a wealthy Boston abolitionist named George Stearns, a connection to an anti-slavery senator from Kansas named Samuel Pomeroy, and the national renown he had won for his anti-slavery speeches and editorials and for the first of three autobiographies, *Narrative of the Life of Frederick Douglass, an American Slave*.

In middle age, Douglass had a distinctive physical presence: he was smartly dressed, confident in his bearing, and wore his hair in a graying nimbus. As one of his biographers, John Stauffer, writes, above Douglass's right eye "a streak of white shot out from his scalp, tincturing the symmetry until it diffused into gray at the back of his head."

Washington in the mid-nineteenth century was not the capital of an imperial power; it was small and sleepy; its habits of appointment were extraordinarily casual. Douglass set off on foot for the highest American offices. Accompanied by Senator Pomeroy, he called on the Secretary of War, Edwin Stanton, at the War Department, where his petition for higher pay and better treatment of black soldiers met with unclear results. In Douglass's mind, Stanton was full of disdain for him. His glance, Douglass recalled, said, "Well, what do you want? I have no time to waste upon you or anybody else, and I shall waste none. Speak quick, or I shall leave you." And yet by the end of the session, Stanton had offered Douglass a job as an "assistant adjutant" to the Army to help recruit troops in the South. As Douglass went from one government office to the next that morning, from the War Department to the Department of the Interior, his persistence and his eloquence gained him an ever-longer roster of signatures on his "letter of safe passage."

With his letter in hand, Douglass walked with Pomeroy to the White House. The two men expected to have to wait many hours, even days, to see the President, and yet, just moments after Douglass's calling card was relayed to the inner offices of the White House, an assistant came to bring him to Lincoln. This flash of credibility and access did not come without incidental insult. As Douglass went up the stairs, he heard someone mutter, "Yes, damn it, I knew they would let the nigger through."

Writing many years later in his third and final autobiography, *Life and Times of Frederick Douglass,* Douglass brushed past the accustomed libel—the sort he had been hearing all his life—and concentrated on the astonishing encounter he was about to experience: "I was an ex-slave, identified with a despised race, and yet I was to meet the most exalted person in this great republic." Douglass encountered a shambling, homely man, six feet four in height, surrounded by scurrying aides and piles of documents:

> Long lines of care were already deeply written on Mr. Lincoln's brow, and his strong face, full of earnestness, lighted up as soon as my name was mentioned. As I approached and was introduced to him he arose and extended his hand, and bade me welcome. I at once felt myself in the presence of an honest man—one whom I could love, honor, and trust without reserve or doubt. Proceeding to tell him who I was and what I was doing, he promptly, but kindly, stopped me, saying, "I know who you are, Mr. Douglass; Mr. Seward has told me all about you. Sit down. I am glad to see you."

Douglass laid out his list of complaints about the unequal payment and treatment of black Union recruits. Lincoln listened intently and, to Douglass's satisfaction, with sincere concentration. There was none of Stanton's disdain or impatience. ("I was never in any way reminded of my humble origin, or my unpopular color.") Douglass was impressed by Lincoln's evident ease, his naturalness with a black man, something that was not always the case even with the white abolitionists of Douglass's acquaintance. Lincoln hardly satisfied Douglass's political demands, however, insisting that the mere enlistment of black men into the Union Army "was a serious offense to popular prejudice." Lincoln said that black men "ought to be willing to enter the service upon any condition" and accept lower pay and inferior treatment as a "necessary concession." Lincoln, Douglass discovered, was foremost a politician, careful not to get ahead of his white majority in his treatment of a race that he himself still regarded as inferior. Douglass soon conceded to himself that the radicals, the abolitionists, still had a role to play after Emancipation. He could not rely on even a relatively enlightened President to blaze the trail of political equality.

Finally, at the end of the meeting, Douglass told Lincoln that Secretary Stanton had offered him the task of recruiting freed blacks in the South. Lincoln took from him the pass admitting him into the executive mansion and wrote, "I concur. A. Lincoln. Aug. 10, 1863."

Douglass left Washington for home "in the full belief that the true course to the black man's freedom and citizenship was over the battlefield, and that my business was to get every black man I could into the Union armies." Two of Douglass's sons were already fighting with Union regiments. The father would help add to the contingent.

Douglass waited at home for his official papers of commission. Week followed week. The papers did not arrive. It was never clear if he had been forgotten in the fog of the capital's bureaucracy or if he had been deliberately seduced, mollified, and then ignored. It seemed of little consequence to him at the time that the most important aspect of his meeting with Abraham Lincoln was the very fact that it had occurred—a black man had entered the White House to petition and counsel the President of the United States.

In the decades that followed, such meetings took place only occasionally. As late as four decades after Lincoln's assassination, Grover Cleveland quashed any rumors that he had met with a Negro at the White House, proudly declaring, "It just so happens that I have never in my official position, either when sleeping or waking, alive or dead, on my head or on my heels, dined, lunched, or supped, or invited to a wedding reception, any colored man, woman, or child." And in 1904, after Theodore Roosevelt had met at the White House with Booker T. Washington, Senator Benjamin Tillman, of South Carolina, remarked, "Now that Roosevelt has eaten with that nigger Washington, we shall have to kill a thousand niggers to get them back to their places."

In the days before Barack Obama was inaugurated, he received a series of intelligence briefings about a potential terrorist plot to take place on the day of the ceremonies in Washington. More than a million people were expected to gather on the Mall. Bush Administration officials and intelligence analysts, working in consultation with Obama's national security team, reviewed a series of top secret reports that Somali extremists were planning to cross the Canadian border and detonate explosives in the crowd while the nation watched. During a gathering in the Situation Room that included Condoleezza Rice, Stephen Hadley, and Robert Gates, Hillary Clinton, Obama's designated Secretary of State, said, "Is the Secret Service going to whisk him off the podium so the American people see their incoming President disappear in the middle of the inaugural address? I don't think so." Obama decided to go forward with the ceremony, but it was determined that Robert Gates, who was remaining as Secretary of Defense, would stay away from the ceremony. If the absolute worst happened, a catastrophe on the steps of the Capitol, Gates would be in line to assume the Presidency.

As Obama emerged into the noonday light on January 20, 2009, to receive the oath of office, his mood was somber. "You know, the actual moment of being sworn in and speaking to the crowd is one that can't be separated from all the stuff that had gone on the days before," he told me later. "So, us traveling from Pennsylvania on a train and seeing the crowds, and then the wonderful concert in front of the Lincoln Memorial, and the service activities that Michelle and I did in the days prior to the inauguration—all that, I think, spoke to a sense of hopefulness and possibility that was expressed on inauguration day, which was very powerful to me. I have to tell you that you feel a little disembodied from it. Never during that week did I somehow feel that this was a celebration of me and my accomplishments. I felt very much that it was a celebration of America and how far we had traveled. And that people were reaffirming our capacity to overcome all the old wounds and old divisions, but also new wounds and new divisions. And in that sense, you know, I was along for the ride. And it was a wonderful spirit. It's interesting, though, that when I hear stories from people who participated in it, in some ways their experiences were more powerful, because they talked about getting on the trains very early in the mornings, and it's packed, and it's festive, and they're people from all different walks of life. Having that lens to see the inauguration would have been special."

Despite everything going on in his mind at the moment he walked through the door, Obama said he was not anxious or frightened. "I wasn't scared," he said. "I think at that point I had a pretty firm grasp on what the moment required. . . . There is no doubt that between Election Day and my first night in the White House, there is an escalating sense of responsibility that comes over you, a certain soberness about all that the office entails. That's especially true after having gone through a month and a half of briefings in which you realize that the economy's on the verge of collapse. But it's interesting: I do think that two years of campaigning under some pretty high-pressure situations in a perverse way does prepare you for the pressures involved in the office, because you're used to being on the high-wire, you're used to people scrutinizing you, you're used to—in some ways—a lot of folks depending on you. This is just at a different level. It's not politics, it's governance, so there's an added weight there. But it didn't feel—there was not a moment where I suddenly said, Whoa, what have I gotten myself into?"

After absorbing the blast of cold and the thudding roar from the Mall, Obama glanced to his right. He spotted on the steps, a few feet away, John Lewis—squat, bald, hatless—the eleven-term representative of Georgia's Fifth Congressional District and the only one of the speakers at the 1963 March on Washington still alive. Obama bent to embrace him.

"Congratulations, Mr. President," Lewis whispered in his ear.

Obama smiled at the sound of that and said, "Thank you, John. I'll need your prayers."

"You'll have them, Mr. President. That, and all my support."

At the March on Washington, King's speech was the most eloquent, John Lewis's the most radical. Lewis was just twenty-three at the time, the leader of SNCC. In the original draft of his speech, his demand for racial justice and "serious revolution" was so fearless that, in the last minutes before the program began, Dr. King, Bayard Rustin, Roy Wilkins, and other movement organizers negotiated with him to remove any phrases that might offend the Kennedy Administration. Lewis planned to say, "We will march through the South, through the heart of Dixie, the way Sherman did. We shall pursue our own 'scorched earth' policy and burn Jim Crow to the ground—nonviolently. We shall fragment the South into a thousand pieces and put them back together in the image of democracy." He had to lose the bit about Sherman's army, but the rest of the text, capped by its final warning—"We will not be patient!"—left no doubt about Lewis or about the audacious generation that he represented.

Two years later, in Selma, Lewis led the march at the Edmund Pettus Bridge straight into a blockade set up by Alabama state troopers. The first nightstick wielded in anger landed on his skull. At the White House that night, Lyndon Johnson watched it all on television and deepened his resolve to push the Voting Rights Act. The day before Obama's inaugura-tion, which came just after what would have been King's eightieth birthday, Lewis told me at his office, in the Cannon House Office Building, "Barack Obama is what comes at the end of that bridge in Selma."

Inaugural weekend had been "bewildering" to John Lewis. "It is almost too much, too emotional," he said. Preaching at the Shiloh Baptist Church on Ninth Street N.W., Lewis had told parishioners that he would have thought that only a "crazy" person would predict the election of an African-American President in his lifetime, but now he was sure that the masses on the Mall would be joined by the "saints and angels": by Harriet Tubman and Carter G. Woodson, Marcus Garvey and W. E. B. DuBois, Nat Turner and Frederick Douglass, John Brown and Sojourner Truth.

For hours, Lewis greeted constituents at his office and handed out inaugural tickets. When he shook people's hands, he could feel that they were still freezing from the hours they had spent in long lines outside. He offered them coffee, hot chocolate, sandwiches, and donuts. After a while, he set off to visit the Mall, moving, it seemed, in a daze of unreality. He could scarcely believe the size of the crowds gathering so early—especially the great numbers of African-Americans, young and old, many of them from distant places.

As Lewis walked around the Mall, greeting people, posing for hundreds of photographs, a young man introduced himself as the police chief of Rock Hill, South Carolina. Lewis smiled incredulously. "Imagine that," he said. "I was beaten near to death at the Rock Hill Greyhound bus terminal during the Freedom Rides in 1961. Now the police chief is black."

One teenage boy sweetly asked, "Mr. Lewis, my mama says you marched with Dr. King. Is that true?" Like an old fighter who is not displeased to recount tales of ancient battle, Lewis nodded and said, well, yes he had, and perhaps for the five-thousandth time he sketched the journey from Selma to Montgomery.

"Barack was born long after he could experience or understand the movement," Lewis said, heading back to the Capitol. "He had to move *toward* it in his own time, but it is so clear that he digested it, the spirit and the language of the movement. The way he made it his own reminds me of a trip I made to South Africa in March, 1994, before the post-apartheid elections. We met with a few leaders of the African National Congress—young people—and despite their age they knew everything about the late fifties and sixties in the American South, the birth of the civil-rights movement. They were using the same rhetoric, they had the same emotional force. One young South African actor got up and recited a poem by a black slave woman from Georgia! And that is the way it is with Barack. He has absorbed the lessons and spirit of the civil-rights movement. But, at the same time, he doesn't have the scars of the movement. He has not been knocked around as much by the past."

Obama's promise to shut down Guantánamo, to outlaw torture and begin reversing immediately some of the most egregious policies of the Bush era, to start the march toward universal health care and end the long war in Iraq, gave Lewis hope that the idealism of "the movement" had finally come to the White House. In these inaugural days, it was hard for him—for anyone—to acknowledge that governing would be far different from campaigning, a switch from poetry to prose, from celebration and adulation to battle and compromise, even defeat. Obama's popularity would plummet soon enough. One of the qualities that he valued most in himself—the capacity for pragmatic conciliation—would inevitably run up against a range of opponents and forces that resisted his charms. A supremely self-confident politician whose first closely contested ballot was the Iowa caucus, who was four years out of the Illinois legislature, would be tested beyond description. He would soon encounter his own limitations, and the public would see the gulf between romance and accomplishment. But for a few days at least, John Lewis and millions of others cherished the moment of promise.

"People have been afraid to hope again, to believe again," Lewis said. "We have lost great leaders: John F. Kennedy, Martin, Robert Kennedy. And so people might have questioned whether or not to place their full faith in a symbol and a leader. The danger of disappointment is immense, the problems are so big. None of them can be solved in a day or a year. And that's the way it was with the civil-rights movement. This is the struggle of a lifetime. We play our part and fulfill our role."

For the inaugural ceremony, Obama had invited Rick Warren to give the invocation, a gesture to mainstream evangelicals, but surely the most moving performance on the podium, besides Obama's own somber address, was the final benediction. A few weeks before the ceremony, Obama had called the Reverend Joseph Lowery, Dr. King's comrade in the Southern Christian Leadership Conference, who was now eighty-seven years old. Obama left a message and asked him to call him on his cell phone. Lowery had campaigned with Obama in Iowa and Georgia. He had introduced him in Selma with his speech about all the "good crazy" things going on in the country. He had been with Obama from the start. Lowery returned the call, saying, "I am looking for the fellow who is going to be the forty-fourth President."

"Well, I believe that would be me, Brother Lowery," Obama replied.

When Obama asked him to do the benediction on January 20th, Lowery said, "Let me check my calendar." Then, after a long pause, he said, "Hmmm, I do believe I am free that day." The news spread quickly and some of Lowery's friends questioned why Rick Warren had been given the honor of giving the invocation.

"Don't worry," he answered them. "This way I get the last word."

Lowery sat near the Supreme Court justices. He thought that the justices in their robes looked like elders in a church choir. ("Are you going to sing?" he asked the Chief Justice. John Roberts smiled and said, "God forbid." Then Lowery poked Clarence Thomas in the ribs and said, "When are you gonna retire and come home to Georgia?")

When his turn came to speak, Lowery stepped slowly to the microphone and, as he looked out at the vast crowd, he could see the monuments, blurry in the distance. For a second or two, he was overwhelmed by a powerful thought, a kind of hallucination: "When you have eighty-seven-year-old eyes, there is always a haze. But the eyes of my soul at that moment could see the Lincoln Memorial and the ears of my soul could hear Martin's voice on the steps of the Lincoln Memorial summoning the nation to move out of the low land of race and color to the higher ground of the content of our character. And I thought the nation had finally responded to the summons, nearly forty-six years later, by inaugurating a black man as the forty-fourth President of the United States."

Lowery gathered himself and then, in a worn growly whisper, he began his benediction with James Weldon Johnson's "Lift Every Voice and Sing." The principal of a segregated school in Jacksonville, Florida, Johnson wrote the poem in 1900 to celebrate Lincoln's birthday. By the nineteen-twenties, the hymn, with music written by Johnson's brother, was known as the Negro national anthem and was sung in black churches and schools as a form of protest against Jim Crow and as a sign of faith in a higher American ideal. Johnson spoke of the "exquisite anguish" that he felt whenever he heard the lines "sung by Negro children." Now Lowery, standing a few feet from the first African-American President, read the final verse:

God of our weary years,
God of our silent tears,
Thou who has brought us thus far along the way,
Thou who has by Thy might led us into the light,
Keep us forever in the path, we pray.
Lest our feet stray from the places, our God, where we met Thee,
Lest, our hearts drunk with the wine of the world, we forget Thee;

Shadowed beneath Thy hand,
May we forever stand,
True to thee oh God, and
True to our native land.

The weather was bitter cold. For months Lowery had been suffering from severe back and leg pain. His voice was not as strong as it was in Selma when he helped ignite Obama's campaign in Brown Chapel, but he had come prepared with a prayer crafted to the historical moment. In closing, he was both sly and full of feeling, refusing self-satisfaction or sentimentality:

> Lord, in the memory of all the saints, who from their labors rest, and in the joy of a new beginning, we ask you to help us work for that day when black will not be asked to get back, when brown can stick around, when yellow will be mellow, when the red man can get ahead, man, and when white will embrace what is right.

Obama, who had bowed his head in prayer, broke into a broad smile. Lowery said he was improvising on the familiar Sunday-school song "Jesus Loves the Little Children," but the language he was playing with was really an old saying taken up by, among others, Big Bill Broonzy in "Black, Brown, and White," a blues lament about the Jim Crow South. The riff seemed to almost everyone a gesture both joyful and wary, a celebration of historic progress and a reminder that the day of post-racial America had yet to come. Lowery, one of the titans of the Moses generation, had paid obeisance to the fallen "saints," and then had all the millions who were watching say amen. Three times we all said amen. An incredible moment, and yet some commentators, including Rush Limbaugh and Glenn Beck, two of Obama's most hysterical antagonists, could see only anti-white malice in Lowery's words. "Even at the inauguration of a black President," Beck said, "it seems white America is being called racist." Lowery, though, was unfazed. "The only second thought I have," he said, "is that, with more than a million people there, I didn't find a way to take up an offering."

The ceremony was over. On the east front of the Capitol, George W. Bush's helicopter rose into the air, hovered a moment, and headed for Andrews Air Force Base and the flight home to Texas. People began waving derisively and singing, "Nah, nah, nah, nah, hey, hey, goodbye!" Then they cheered as the new President and his guests left the grandstand.

Obama had kept a wall of heroes at the Hart Senate Office Building down the street: a portrait of Gandhi at his spinning wheel; Thurgood Marshall in his judicial robes; Nelson Mandela reclining in a gold armchair, his cane at his side; Martin Luther King, Jr., at the microphone; Alexander Gardner's photograph of a war-weary Lincoln. Obama also displayed a framed cover of *Life* magazine from March, 1965; it showed a long line of demonstrators, led by John Lewis, about to confront the Alabama state troopers at the Edmund Pettus Bridge. Lewis had signed and framed the cover and had given it to Obama as a gift. Now, at the luncheon following the swearing-in ceremony, Lewis approached Obama with a sheet of paper and, to mark the occasion, he asked him to sign it. The forty-fourth President of the United States wrote, "Because of you, John. Barack Obama."

Epilogue

One year after the 2008 election it was fair to wonder whether the most profound moment of the Obama era would be its first. Obama himself had said at a press conference, in March, 2009, that the "justifiable pride" the country had taken in electing the first black President had "lasted about a day." This did not seem to concern him much. "Right now," he said, "the American people are judging me exactly the way I should be judged"—on performance. And yet by the time the year was over, his visions of post-partisan comity had given way to the reality of prolonged battle with congressional Republicans and conservative Democrats. In the 2008 election, Obama had won some unlikely states, including Virginia, North Carolina, and Colorado. Now, for many Americans, including independents who had voted for Obama, the sense of dissatisfaction ran deep. In Massachusetts, a Republican of slender gifts named Scott Brown was elected to replace the late Edward Kennedy in the Senate. Obama moved quickly to put his campaign manager, David Plouffe, in charge of the Democratic effort in the 2010 midterm elections, but that was hardly a guarantee that the Party would avoid a disaster like the 1994 midterms.

After Scott Brown's win, Barry Blitt, the *New Yorker* artist who had drawn the controversial cover called "The Politics of Fear," drew another—a four-paneled cover that showed Obama walking on water in radiant dawn light. But, as he draws closer to the viewer, he loses his miraculous footing and plunges into the drink. The morning that issue of the magazine was on the newsstands, I got a call from Eric Lesser, David Axelrod's assistant, saying that Axelrod and Obama were laughing about the cover: could I send a framed copy signed by Barry Blitt to the President? A couple of days later, Obama told some correspondents about his amusement; their meeting was off the record but it quickly leaked. I couldn't help thinking that while Obama might actually have thought the drawing was amusing, he was also eager to broadcast his own sense of humor and the idea that he had never believed in his own hype.

It was hard to imagine that any President would have remained popular for long in a time of terrible unemployment, record deficits, and political rancor. During the transition period, Obama learned more about the depth of the economic crisis. "Things were plummeting. The skies were darkening," Axelrod told me. "All the economic data pointed to the likelihood of a deep, deep recession. This was not the way we wanted to start the Presidency. I remember talking to Obama and saying, 'It would be fun to start this without a recession and two wars to deal with.' And he said, 'Yes, but if we didn't have that, we wouldn't be here in the first place.' " The terror threat on the day of the inauguration, Axelrod said, "was a raw initiation into the responsibilities of the Presidency."

Some of Obama's achievements during his first year in office were related to what did *not* happen. Thanks to government interventions, neither the banking system nor the automobile industry collapsed. By most accounts, the country had not only avoided a depression, it was, slowly, fitfully, and unequally, emerging from recession. And yet the reality of ten-per-cent unemployment and the galling spectacle of investment bankers' coming to Capitol Hill to justify their gaudy bonuses prevented any sense of gratitude or celebration. There were other achievements. Obama appointed Sonia Sotomayor, the first Hispanic justice on the Supreme Court. He liberalized national science policy. He set a firm timetable to withdraw American troops from Iraq. He moved against discriminatory policies toward homosexuals in the military. Despite the pleas of some of his advisers, Obama also began his term by calling on Congress to overhaul the health-care system; he got further in that effort than any President in a half-century, but he lost momentum when Brown won his seat in the Senate. At the same time, there were policies sure to dismay those Obama voters who, despite the evidence accumulated during his relatively brief career as a state and U.S. senator, believed he would forgo the habit of compromise. His failure to follow through on a promise to close Guantánamo within a year; his dismissal of his chief counsel, Gregory Craig; and many other decisions did little to encourage the left. The Democratic left probably did not imagine that arguably the most influential member of the Obama cabinet would be a Republican fixture of the capital, Secretary of Defense Robert Gates.

Surely the most absurd moment of Obama's first year in office came not long after he committed more than thirty thousand new troops to Afghanistan. On October 9, 2009, Robert Gibbs woke the President with a call at around six in the morning to tell him that there had been an announcement in Oslo: Obama, after less than nine months in office, had been awarded the Nobel Prize for Peace. The President's reaction was a more elongated and colorful version of "Shut up."

"It was not helpful to us politically," Obama told me in an interview at the Oval Office in mid-January, 2010. "Although Axelrod and I joke about it, the one thing we didn't anticipate this year was having to apologize for having won the Nobel Peace Prize."

Obama's acceptance speech in Oslo brought to mind his 2002 antiwar speech on Federal Plaza, in Chicago. Neither was the statement of a pacifist and, as such, neither wholly pleased its audience. Obama could admire King, but he could never be him. He was not the leader of a movement; he was a politician, a commander-in-chief.

"The speeches are of a piece, and they reflect my fundamental view of the issues of war and peace, which is that we have to recognize that this is a dangerous world and that there are people who will do terrible things and have to be fought," Obama said. "But we also have to recognize that in fighting against those things, there's the possibility that we ourselves engage in terrible things. And so, trying to maintain that balance of the tragic recognition that war is sometimes necessary but never anything less than tragic and never worthy of glorification is, I think, one of the best attributes of America's own character. That's why I celebrate Lincoln. That's why I think we survived the Civil War—because we had a leader of such wisdom and depth that there was no triumphalism on his part at the end, or at all."

One lesson that Obama seemed to internalize early in his term was that there was no percentage in talking about race when it was not on his terms. In July, 2009, at the very end of a press conference on domestic policy, Obama was asked about an incident in Cambridge, Massachusetts, in which a police officer handcuffed and arrested a Harvard professor and pioneer in African-American studies, Henry Louis Gates, Jr., in his own home after a neighbor reported that someone might have been breaking into the house.

Obama, who had worked on racial-profiling issues during his years in the Illinois state legislature and was even pulled aside for an extra search at Logan Airport after his triumphant speech at the 2004 Democratic Convention, waded in. "Now, I don't know, not having been there and not seeing all the facts, what role race played in that, but I think it's fair to say, number one, any of us would be pretty angry," Obama told the reporters. "Number two, that the Cambridge police acted stupidly in arresting somebody when there was already proof that they were in their own home. And, number three, what I think we know, separate and apart from this incident, is that there is a long history in this country of African-Americans and Latinos being stopped by law enforcement disproportionately. And that's just a fact."

In the coming days, Obama was criticized for sins ranging from a disrespect for the police to mouthing off without knowing both sides of the story. Although he was a great deal more right than wrong in his defense of Gates, Obama and his advisers regretted the furor, not least because it raised a sensitive subject precisely when he was trying to push an ambitious political agenda in an era of bitterly partisan political rhetoric. You got the feeling that the White House staff would have preferred to talk about anything—Bill Ayers, Tony Rezko, *anything*—other than Professor Gates and Sergeant James Crowley. Obama tried to resolve the affair with a "beer summit" at the White House, but in the months to come, at some of the conservative Tea Party rallies around the country and elsewhere, there were signs of persistent resentment about the incident and, more worrying, about the spectacle of a black President's speaking out honestly, even emotionally, about race in general. The angriest of the Tea Party demonstrators usually avoided overtly racist language; instead they spoke of "taking our country back."

Obama was extremely cautious in talking about the racial component of the opposition to him. Certainly it was not the dominant strain of opposition, but it was a presence. "America evolves, and sometimes those evolutions are painful," Obama told me. "People don't progress in a straight line. Countries don't progress in a straight line. So there's enormous excitement and interest around the election of an African-American President. It's inevitable that there's going to be some backlash, potentially, to what that means—not in a crudely racist way, necessarily. But it signifies change, in the same way that immigration signifies change, in the same way that a shift from a manufacturing-based economy to a service-based economy signifies change, in the same way that the Internet signifies change and terrorism signifies change. And so I think that nobody should have ever been under the illusion—certainly I wasn't, and I was very explicit about this when I campaigned—that by virtue of my election, suddenly race problems would be solved or conversely that the American people would want to spend all their time talking about race. I think it signifies progress, but the progress preceded the election. The progress facilitated the election. The progress has to do with the day-to-day interactions of people who are working together and going to church together and teaching their kids to treat everybody equally and fairly. All those little interactions that are taking place across the country add up to a more just, more tolerant, society. But that's an ongoing process. It's one that requires each of us, every day, to try to expand our sense of understanding. And there are going to be folks who don't want to promote that understanding because they're afraid of the future. They don't like that evolution. They think, in some fashion, that it will disadvantage them or, in some sense, diminishes the past. I tend to be fairly forgiving about the anxiety that people feel about change because I think, if you're human, you recognize that in yourself."

In matters of décor, Obama altered the Oval Office only slightly. The Resolute desk, a gift from Queen Victoria to Rutherford B. Hayes, is still there; an antique grandfather clock still ticks the seconds, an unnervingly loud reminder to the occupant that his stay is brief. Obama, however, made one striking change. He returned a bust of Winston Churchill by the sculptor Jacob Epstein to the British government, which had lent it to George W. Bush as a gesture of solidarity after the attacks of September 11, 2001, and replaced it with busts of Abraham Lincoln and Martin Luther King, Jr. For Obama, the black freedom struggle defines not just the African-American experience, but the American experience itself.

"I am a direct beneficiary of their sacrifice and their effort—my entire generation is," he said. "There is a certain awe that I continue to hold when I consider the courage, tenacity, and audacity of the civil-rights leaders of that time. They were so young. That's what always amazes me. King was twenty-six when Montgomery starts. At the height of his fame and influence, he's in his mid-thirties. I mean, he's a kid. And that was true for all these leaders. So, part of what I was trying to communicate in Selma"—in March, 2007—"was this sense that the battles they fought were so much more difficult, fraught with so many risks, that it would be foolish to compare me running for the Senate, or for that matter the Presidency, to them risking their lives in a highly uncertain and dangerous situation." Obama disavowed the comparison between their struggles and his political campaigns, saying, "They are related only in the sense that at the core of the civil-rights movement, even in the midst of anger, despair, Black Power, Stokely Carmichael, Huey Newton, all that stuff, there is a voice that is best captured by King, which is that we as African-Americans are American, and that our story is America's story, and that by perfecting our rights we perfect the Union—which is a very optimistic story, in the end."

When there are no television cameras around, Obama speaks even more deliberately than usual. I could hear the grandfather clock ticking during his long pauses. Outside his door, a flock of advisers was accumulating. There was little over a week left before the State of the Union address.

"It's fundamentally different from the story that many minority groups go through in other countries," Obama said finally. "There's no equivalent, if you think about it, in many other countries—that sense that through the deliverance of the least of these, the society as a whole is transformed for the better. And, in that sense, what I was trying to communicate is: we didn't quite get there, but that journey continues."

Debts and Sources

The sentimental narrative of Barack Obama is that his election in 2008 was the end, somehow, of the most painful of all American struggles. Nothing has ended, of course, and questions of race—cultural, legal, penal, educational, social—remain despite all the evident promise and progress since the civil-rights movement. De-facto segregation, for example, persists in countless neighborhoods and schools, and Chicago, Obama's chosen city, is rated the most segregated city in America. And yet his election had undeniable historical meaning. It is preposterously early for definitive, scholarly biographies. My hope was to write a piece of biographical journalism that, through interviews with his contemporaries and certain historical actors, examined Obama's life before his Presidency and some of the currents that helped to form him.

In this effort, I had the help of two extraordinary people: Katherine Stirling and Christopher Jennings. I am grateful to them both for their care, intelligence, and hard work.

Katherine Stirling carried out innumerable tasks, all necessary to a work of this sort: setting up interviews, running down contacts and source materials, and transcribing interviews. She also read the manuscript and made enormously helpful suggestions all along the way.

Chris Jennings checked the manuscript and saved me from missteps of fact, large and small—a complicated job for a long magazine piece, an immeasurably more difficult one when the author has a maddening tendency to revise a book-length manuscript until the final bell.

I want to express my thanks to my sources, the great majority of whom spoke to me on the record. While it is often problematic for friends, family members, colleagues, rivals, enemies, and acquaintances of a sitting President to talk freely to a reporter, I was gratified to discover that so many people were willing to do so and did not insist on diving automatically into the waters of deep background. These sources are quoted liberally throughout the text. There were, of course, some sources, particularly in government and in the Presidential campaign, who did ask to speak anonymously. Where I have quoted or relied on published interviews, articles, and books, I have provided the source information in the endnotes.

My gratitude for interviews to: Neil Abercrombie; Mark Alexander; Susan Arterian; Gha-is Askia; Eli Attie; Loretta Augustine-Herron; David Axelrod; William Ayers; Ashley Baia; Michael Baron; Cornell Belcher; Derrick Bell; Brad Berenson; Jeff Berkowitz; Mary Bernstein; Timuel Black; Robert Blackwell, Jr.; Rod Blagojevich; Mark Blumenthal; Philip Boerner; Roger Boesche; Julian Bond; John Bonifaz; Caroline Boss; Susan Botkin; Maxine Box; Bishop Arthur Brazier; Marvin Bressler; David Brooks; Rosellen Brown; Will Burns; Jill Burton-Dascher; Cassandra Butts.

Mary Beth Cahill; Geoffrey Canada; Paul Carpenter; Bob Casey; Jim Cauley; Lou Celi; Hasan Chandoo; Bill Clinton; James Clyburn; David William Cohen; Steve Coll; Susan Coll; Jack Corrigan; John Corrigan; Jeffrey Cox; Allison Davis; Jarvis DeBerry; Alice Dewey; David Dinkins; Alan and Lois Dobry; Gary and Kendra Duncan; Anita Dunn; Christopher Edley, Jr.; Joella Edwards; Pal Eldredge; Lolis Elie; David Ellen; Richard Epstein; Virginia Dashner Ewalt.

Jonathan Favreau; Andrew Feldstein; Henry Ferris; Thomas L. Friedman; Greg Galluzzo; Marshall Ganz; Tom Geoghegan; Pete Giangreco; Mack Gilkeson; Robin Givhan; David Goldberg; Lawrence Goldyn; Mariko Gordon; Kent Goss; Anton Gunn; Wahid Hamid; Melissa Harris-Lacewell; Carol Anne Harwell; Lisa Hay; George Haywood; Rickey Hendon; Eileen Hershenov; Louis Hook; Patrick Hughes; Blair Hull; Charlayne Hunter-Gault; Dennis Hutchinson.

Lisa Jack; Jesse Jackson, Sr.; Denny Jacobs; T. D. Jakes; Valerie Jarrett; Benjamin Jealous; Emil Jones, Jr.; Ben Joravsky; Vernon Jordan; Elena Kagan; Dan Kahan; John Kass; Marilyn Katz; Jerry Kellman; Cliff Kelley; Randall Kennedy; Al Kindle; Michael Klonsky; Mike Kruglik; Eric Kusunoki.

Cathy Lazere; John Lewis; Kimberly Lightford; Terry Link; Anne Marie Lipinski; Mark Lippert; Ronald Loui; Alvin Love; Joseph Lowery; Kenneth Mack; Chris MacLachlin; Susan Mboya; Salil Mehra; David Mendell; Margot Mifflin; Abner Mikva; Judson Miner; Martha Minow; Newton Minow; Ivory Mitchell; Eric Moore; Pat Moore; Mark Morial; Bob Moses; Salim Muwakkil.

Martin Nesbitt; Eric Newhall; Sandy Newman; Salim al Nurridin; Martha Nussbaum; Barack Obama; Philip Ochieng; Charles Ogletree;

Frederick Okatcha; Bruce Orenstein; Peter Osnos; Olara Otunnu; John Owens; Mansasseh Oyucho; Clarence Page; Edward (Buzz) Palmer; Marylyn Prosser Pauley; Charles Payne; Mark Penn; Tony Peterson; Earl Martin Phalen; Wendell Pierce; David Plouffe; Jeremiah Posedel; Richard Posner; Colin Powell; Toni Preckwinkle; John Presta; Francine Pummel.

Linda Randle; Kwame Raoul; Vicky Rideout; Rebecca Rivera; Byron Rodriguez; John Rogers; Donald Rose; Brian Ross; Pete Rouse; Bobby Rush; Mark Salter; Bettylu Saltzman; Chris Sautter; John Schmidt; Bobby Seale; Al Sharpton; Michael Sheehan; Dan Shomon; Sephira Shuttlesworth; Tavis Smiley; Jerome Smith; Rik Smith; Maya Soetoro-Ng; Daniel Sokol; Bronwen Solyon; Aaron Sorkin; Christine Spurell (Lee); Robert Starks; Iona Stenhouse; Geoffrey Stone; Ken Sulzer; Mona Sutphen.

Larry Tavares; Elizabeth Taylor; Studs Terkel; Don Terry; Laurence Tribe; Donne Trotter; Scott Turow; Roberto Mangabeira Unger; C. T. Vivian; Nicholas von Hoffman; Chip Wall; Maria Warren; Dawna Weatherly-Williams; Lois Weisberg; Cora Weiss; Cornel West; Robin West; Jim Wichterman; David B. Wilkins; Roger Wilkins; Jeremiah Wright; Quentin Young; Fareed Zakaria; Andrew (Pake) Zane; Eric Zorn; Mary Zurbuchen; Hank De Zutter.

I also would like to thank the scholars with whom I consulted during my reporting on matters ranging from Hawaiian history to the black church. Some are also quoted in the text. They include Danielle Allen; William Andrews; Mahzarin Banaji; Lawrence Bobo; David Bositis; Taylor Branch; Adam Cohen; David William Cohen; Gavan Daws; Michael Dawson; Alice Dewey; Caroline Elkins; Eric Foner; Henry Louis Gates, Jr.; Eddie Glaude, Jr.; Doris Kearns Goodwin; William J. Grimshaw; Lani Guinier; Jill Lepore; David Levering Lewis; Glenn Loury; John McWhorter; Tali Mendelberg; Orlando Patterson; Jonathan Reider; Dick Simpson; Werner Sollors; Robert Stepto; Elizabeth Taylor; Ronald Walters; Sean Wilentz; and William Julius Wilson.

Anyone who writes about Barack Obama's life owes a debt to the many reporters and writers who have covered him. Two standout reporters, David Mendell and Jeff Zeleny, both former Chicago *Tribune* staff writers, have provided, with their countless stories, a wealth of invaluable information. I also have reason to be grateful to Kim Barker, David Jackson, John Kass, Ray Long, Evan Osnos, Clarence Page, Kirsten Scharnberg, Don Terry, Jim Warren, and Eric Zorn of the Chicago *Tribune*; Scott Fornek, the late Steve Neal, Lynn Sweet, and Laura Washington of the Chicago *Sun-Times;* Hank De Zutter, Ben Joravsky, and Ted Kleine of the Chicago *Reader;* David Bernstein, David Brooks, Carol Felsenthal, and Grant Pick of *Chicago* magazine; Matt Bai, Jo Becker, Christopher Drew, Jodi Kantor, Serge F. Kovaleski, Janny Scott, and Jeff Zeleny (encore) of the New York *Times;* Edmund Sanders of the Los Angeles *Times;* Jackie Calmes of the *Wall Street Journal;* my colleagues Lauren Collins, William Finnegan, David Grann, Ryan Lizza, and Larissa MacFarquhar of *The New Yorker;* John Heilemann of *New York;* Zadie Smith and Garry Wills of the *New York Review of Books;* Salim Muwakkil of *In These Times;* Todd Purdum of *Vanity Fair;* Scott Helman, Sasha Issenberg, Sally Jacobs, Derrick Z. Jackson, Michael Levenson, and Jonathan Saltzman of the Boston *Globe;* Joshua Green and Andrew Sullivan of *The Atlantic;* Joe Klein and Amanda Ripley of *Time;* Jonathan Alter, Jon Meacham, Richard Wolffe, and Fareed Zakaria of *Newsweek;* Michelle Cottle, Franklin Foer, Ryan Lizza, and Noam Scheiber of *The New Republic;* Eric Alterman and Ta-Nehisi Coates of *The Nation;* Benjamin Wallace-Wells of *Rolling Stone;* Ben Smith of *Politico;* Dan Balz, Robin Givhan, David Maraniss, Kevin Merida, Liza Mundy, and Peter Slevin of the Washington *Post;* and Nancy Benac of the Associated Press. The coverage of Barack Obama and the 2008 campaign by National Public Radio (particularly by Michele Norris), Slate, Real Clear Politics, The Root, Salon, and many other Web sites proved extremely useful. No student of Barack Obama and South Side politics can do without the Chicago *Defender,* the Hyde Park *Herald,* or the broadcasts of WVON.

To ask friends to read a book-length manuscript, or some portion of it, and to ask them for their thoughts, arguments, and corrections is to ask an enormous favor. I am grateful to those who did just that: Richard Brody, Ta-Nehisi Coates, Henry Finder, Jeffrey Frank, Ann Goldstein, Hendrik Hertzberg, Nicholas Lemann, George Packer, Peter Slevin, and Dorothy Wickenden. Thanks to Whitney Johnson for helping me with the photographs. I am especially grateful to my colleagues and friends at *The New Yorker* and to Si Newhouse, who has supported the magazine with consistency, determination, and grace.

My thanks to Knopf's commander-in-chief, Sonny Mehta, who took me in and led me to my wonderful editor, Dan Frank. Thanks, as well, to Chip Kidd, Katherine Hourigan, Lydia Buechler, Pat Johnson, Tony Chirico, Karen Mugler, George Wen, Kate Norris, and Paul Bogaards, at

Knopf. My agent, Kathy Robbins, has watched out for me for many years, and so has my friend and assistant Brenda Phipps. I would also like to thank Eric Lewis, Michael Specter, Pam McCarthy, Lisa Hughes, Wendy Belzberg, Strauss Zelnick, Robert Glick, and Alexa Cassanos, as well as Barbara Remnick, Richard, Will, and Talia Remnick, Lisa Fernandez, the Feins in their multitude, and Pat Burnett and Deta McDaniel.

Finally, love and gratitude to my patient and loving family—Esther, Alex, Noah, and Natasha—and we all, in turn, extend our thanks to those who have helped Natasha over the years. My sons, Alex and Noah, were deeply encouraging. This book is dedicated to Esther Fein. For me, there is no life without her.

Notes

Prologue: The Joshua Generation

4   Selma, Ralph Abernathy: Abernathy, *And the Walls Came Tumbling Down*, p. 297.

5   On January 2: Garrow, *Bearing the Cross*, p. 372.

6   As a boy, he wanted to leave: Halberstam, *The Children*, p. 240.

6   "There was something magical": Lewis and D'Orso, *Walking with the Wind*, p. 25.

6   In 1955, Lewis listened: Ibid., p. 45.

6   Some of the deepest: Ibid., p. 269.

7   He knew Jim Clark: Ibid., p. 316.

7   In early February, 1965: Ibid., p. 324.

7   Now, in early February: Garrow, *Bearing the Cross*, p. 386.

8   Lewis gave a handwritten: Lewis and D'Orso, *Walking with the Wind*, p. 326.

8   "Would a fiction writer": Martin Luther King, Jr., New York *Times*, March 14, 1965.

8   At the funeral, in Brown Chapel: Branch, *At Canaan's Edge*, p. 24.

9   Bevel had been beaten: Ibid., p. 13.

9   When Governor Wallace: Lewis and D'Orso, *Walking with the Wind*, p. 330.

9   He tells it best: Ibid., p. 338.

9   "There facing us at the bottom": Ibid.

10 Lewis remembered the terrible: Ibid., p. 340.

11 Dozens of demonstrators: Ibid., p. 344.

11 That night, at around 9 P.M.: Branch, *At Canaan's Edge*, 56.

12 As Robert Caro makes clear: Caro, *The Path to Power*, p. 166.

12 "At times, history and fate": "Nation: A Meeting of History and Fate," *Time*, March 26, 1965.

12 Watching Johnson that night: Garrow, *Bearing the Cross*, p. 408.

13 "I know you are asking today": Martin Luther King, Jr., Montgomery, Alabama, March 25, 1965.

14 "The Negro potential for": King, *Why We Can't Wait*, p. 139.

14 The syndicated black radio host: Wickham, *Bill Clinton and Black America*, p. 24.

14 Writing in *The New Yorker*: Toni Morrison, "Comment," *The New Yorker*, October 5, 1998.

14 In January, according to: Michael A. Fletcher, Washington *Post*, January 25, 2007.

15 "Just because you are our color": Leslie Fulbright, San Francisco *Chronicle*, February 19, 2007.

15 Artur Davis, an African-American congressman: "World News Sunday," ABC, March 4, 2007.

15 When Bill Clinton read the comparative accounts: David Remnick, "The Wanderer," *The New Yorker*, September 18, 2006.

15 "After all the hard work": Hilary Clinton, First Baptist Church, Selma, Alabama, March 4, 2007.

17 "When Harriet Tubman would run": Joseph Lowery, Brown Chapel, Selma, Alabama, March 4, 2007.

18 Obama's speech in Selma: Barack Obama, Brown Chapel, Selma, Alabama, March 4, 2007.

19 In *Moses, Man of the Mountain*: Hurston, *Moses, Man of the Mountain*, p. 180.

19 King asserted his role: King, *Why We Can't Wait*, p. 60.

19 "I just want to do God's will": Martin Luther King, Jr., Mason Temple, Memphis, Tennessee, April 3, 1968.

19 And to universalize his message: Barack Obama, Brown Chapel, Selma, Alabama, March 4, 2007.

22 After Hurricane Katrina: John M. Broder, New York *Times*, September 5, 2005.

23 At his announcement speech in Springfield: Barack Obama, Springfield, Illinois, February 10, 2007.

25 popped a piece of Nicorette: Jason Horowitz, New York *Observer*, March 12, 2007.

Chapter One: A Complex Fate

29 It is an ordinary day, 1951: "Kenya: Ready or Not," *Time*, March 7, 1960.

29 At Holy Ghost College: Ibid.

30 He thought about studying for the priesthood: Mboya, *Freedom and After*, p. 10.

30 "Is *nobody* here?": "Kenya: Ready or Not," *Time*, March 7, 1960.

30 When Tom was still living: Ibid.

30 "Madam," he says: Ibid.

30 In 1955, when he was twenty-five: Ibid.

31 "Too often during the nationalist struggle": Mboya, *Freedom and After*, p. 141.

31 Mboya tried to persuade the British: Albert G. Sims, "Africans Beat on Our College Doors," *Harpers*, April, 1961.

32 In 1958, as Mboya was developing: Ibid.

32 Albert Sims, a former State Department: Ibid.

32 For six weeks, he gave as many: Shachtman, *Airlift to America*, p. 76.

32 He obtained promises: Ibid, p. 107.

33 Factually and poetically: Michael Dobbs, Washington *Post*, March 30, 2008.

33 A Nixon ally, Senator Hugh Scott: Ibid.

34 When Obama was running: Mendell, *Obama: From Promise to Power*, p. 39.

34 He was impatient with village life: Obama, *Dreams from My Father*, p. 397.

34 A "domestic servant's pocket register": Ibid., p. 425.

35 "Wow, that guy was *mean!*": Ibid., p. 369.

35 "He did not like the way": Ben Macintyre and Paul Orengoh, *The Times* of London, December 3, 2008.

36 "During the Emergency": Mboya, *Freedom and After*, p. 42.

37 "Questions like the number of oaths": Elkins, *Imperial Reckoning*, p. 68.

37 "The small conductor was either": Ibid., p. 258.

38 According to an interview: Ben Macintyre and Paul Orengoh, *The Times* of London, December 3, 2008.

39 "He had difficulty walking": Obama, *Dreams from My Father*, p. 418.

39 "When the pupils were naughty": Xan Rice, *The Guardian*, June 6, 2008.

39 "He asked to dance with me": John Oywa, *The Standard*, November 11, 2008.

40 "There was so much excitement": Edmund Sanders, Los Angeles *Times*, July 17, 2008.

41 "We've got this guy": Alan Jackson, *The Times* of London, June 6, 2008.

41 "He's like a fictional character": Bill Flanagan, *The Times* of London, April 6, 2009.

41 And as a genealogist: http://www.wargs.com/political/obama.html.

42 Kansas was the "dab-smack": Obama, *Dreams from My Father*, p. 13.

42 "Part of me settling in Chicago": Toby Harnden, *Daily Telegraph*, August 23, 2008.

42 In his memoir, Obama alludes: Obama, *Dreams from My Father*, p. 14. Benac's article tells the entire story of Dunham's military career.

43 "They read the Bible": Ibid.

44 "He was really gung-ho": Nancy Benac, *Associated Press*, June 5, 2009.

44 "Sgt. Dunham has been doing a good job": Ibid.

45 When Stanley Dunham came home: Obama, *Dreams from My Father*, p. 15.

46 In their first year in Seattle: Jonathan Martin, Seattle *Times*, April 8, 2008.

46 Ann's friends jokingly dubbed: Ibid.

47 The Dunhams sometimes attended: Tim Jones, Chicago *Tribune*, March 27, 2007.

47 "The changing time was impressing itself": "Investigations: Out of a Man's Past," *Time*, April 11, 1955.

48 "Let's rise on our hind legs": Ibid.

49 The local press took a keen interest: David Maraniss, Washington *Post*, August 22, 2008.

49 When a Honolulu paper published: Sally Jacobs, Boston *Globe*, September 21, 2008.

50 "When I first came here": David Maraniss, Washington *Post*, August 22, 2008.

53 One day Obama asked her to meet him: Obama, *Dreams from My Father*, p. 127.

53 She "was that girl with the movie": Ibid.

53 Kezia told a Kenyan reporter: John Oywa, *The Standard*, November 11, 2008.

54 Toward the end of her life: Mendell, *Obama: From Promise to Power*, p. 29.

55 "She was very much of the early": Amanda Ripley, "The Story of Barack Obama's Mother," *Time*, April 9, 2008.

55 "What can you say": Jodi Kantor, New York *Times*, January 21, 2009.

55 For him, the choice was easy: Obama, *Dreams from My Father*, p. 126.

57 To survive, Lolo's mother: Ibid., p. 42.

58 The Soetoros lived in a crowded: Paul Watson, Los Angeles *Times*, March 15, 2007.

59 "You never know": Obama, *Dreams from My Father*, p. 31.

59 In Hawaii, he had seemed liberated: Obama, *Dreams from My Father*, p. 43.

60 One friend, Julia Suryakusuma: Michael Sheridan and Sarah Baxter, *Sunday Times*, January 28, 2007.

60 "At first, everybody felt it was weird": Paul Watson, Los Angeles *Times*, March 15, 2007.

60 one of his teachers at St. Francis: Paul Watson, Los Angeles *Times*, March 15, 2007.

60 Cecilia Sugini Hananto: Kirsten Scharnberg and Kim Barker, Chicago *Tribune*, March 25, 2007.

61 "In the Muslim school": Obama, *Dreams from My Father*, p. 154.

62 Obama, Jr., has called his father: Jon Meacham, "On His Own," *Newsweek*, September 1, 2008.

62 Philip Ochieng, a prominent Luo journalist: Philip Ochieng, *Daily Nation*, October 11, 2008.

63 When Barack, Jr., visited Nairobi: Edmund Sanders, Los Angeles *Times*, July 17, 2008.

63 But there was more to it: Keith B. Richburg, Washington *Post*, November 5, 2009.

63 Little more than a year: Barack H. Obama, Sr., "Problems Facing Our Socialism," *East Africa Journal*, July, 1965.

63 As an ideologist of Kenyan independence: Goldsworthy, *Tom Mboya: The Man Kenya Wanted to Forget*, p. 55.

64 It poses the central question: Barack H. Obama, Sr., "Problems Facing Our Socialism," *East Africa Journal*, July, 1965.

64 "One need not be a Kenyan": Ibid.

65 "To that extent, he was naïve": Edmund Sanders, Los Angeles *Times*, July 17, 2008.

66 "Barack never really recovered": Ibid.

66 Walgio Orwa, a professor: Ibid.

66 According to Njenga's lawyer: Billy Muiruri, *Daily Nation*, July 3, 2009.

67 "I was with Tom only last week.": Joe Ombuor, *The Standard*, April 11, 2008.

68 He declared that Odinga's party: "Kenya: We Will Crush You," *Time*, November 7, 1969.

68 "He would pass out on the doorstep": Edmund Sanders, Los Angeles *Times*, July 17, 2008.

68 He complained to Okoda: John Oywa and George Olwenya, *The Standard*, November 15, 2008.

68 In his sober moments: Ibid.

Chapter Two: Surface and Undertow

71 Years later, she confided: Obama, *Dreams from My Father*, p. 57.

71 The waiting list was long: Ibid., p. 58.

72 The novelist Allegra Goodman: Allegra Goodman, "Rainbow Warrior," *The New Republic*, February 13, 2008.

72 "Would you prefer": Obama, *Dreams from My Father*, p. 59.

73 "One of the challenges": Barack Obama, Punahou School, Honolulu, Hawaii, December 2004.

73 In truth, he knew little: Obama, *Dreams from My Father*, p. 63.

74 He was fragile—oddly cautious: Ibid., p 65.

74 "We all stood accused": Ibid., p. 68.

74 He remembers that the next day: Ibid, p 69.

74 To the contrary: Ibid., p. 70.

75 "We all gathered as a group": Ramos, *Our Friend Barry*, p. 15.

76 "On the mainland": Ibid., p. 38.

77 He took part in high-school goofs: Ibid., p. 81.

78 Constance Ramos, whose background: Ibid., p. 13.

78 "The lovely tropical home": Allegra Goodman, "Rainbow Warrior," *The New Republic*, February 13, 2008.

79 "When I started reading": Ramos, *Our Friend Barry*, p. 70.

80 When he started making trouble: Kirsten Scharnberg and Kim Barker, *Chicago Tribune*, March 25, 2007.

82 "I remember her feeling saddened": Wolffe, *Renegade*, p. 150.

82 "Some of the problems of adolescent rebellion": David Mendell, Chicago *Tribune*, October 22, 2004.

82 "When I think about my mother": Amanda Ripley, "The Story of Barack Obama's Mother," *Time*, April 9, 2008.

83 "I didn't feel [her absence]": Ibid.

85 She had a capacity to get: Dunham, *Surviving Against the Odds*, p. xxi.

88 "She wasn't ideological": Amanda Ripley, "The Story of Barack Obama's Mother," *Time*, April 9, 2008.

89 "He became the kind of person": Andra Wisnu, Jakarta *Post*, November 14, 2008.

91 "He didn't know who he was": Jodi Kantor, New York *Times*, June 1, 2007.

91 "Basketball was a good way for me": Todd Purdum, "Raising Obama," *Vanity Fair*, March 2008.

92 "It was good to get a few props": Austin Murphy, "Obama Discusses His Hoops Memories at Punahou High," *Sports Illustrated*, May 21, 2008.

92 In 1999, Obama, writing: Barack Obama, Punahou *Bulletin*, 1999.

92 Exhausted in his attempt: Obama, *Dreams from My Father*, p. 93.

93 In what may be the most famous: Ibid.

93 "It was Hawaii in the seventies": Toby Harnden, *Daily Telegraph*, August 21, 2009.

93 "I'm sure if my mother": Todd Purdum, "Raising Obama," *Vanity Fair*, March 2008.

93 In a letter from Indonesia: Kirsten Scharnberg and Kim Barker, Chicago *Tribune*, March 25, 2007.

93 Obama admits, "I probably": Austin Murphy, "Obama Discusses His Hoops Memories at Punahou High," *Sports Illustrated*, May 21, 2008.

93 "Junkie. Pothead": Obama, *Dreams from My Father*, p. 93.

94 "At best, these things were a refuge": Ibid., p. 85.

94 Like Stanley, Frank Marshall Davis: Davis, *Livin' the Blues*, p. 3.

94 In his memoir, *Livin' the Blues*: Ibid., p. 7.

95 In 1948, Paul Robeson came to Hawaii: Honolulu *Star-Bulletin*, March 22, 1948.

95 "I am not too fond": Davis, *Livin' the Blues*, p. xv.

95 Some of his "fellow freedom fighters": Ibid., p. 311.

96 "Virtually from the start": Ibid., p. 312.

96 "A preacher's daughter": Obama, *Dreams from My Father*, p. 90.

97 "He's basically a good man": Ibid.

Chapter Three: Nobody Knows My Name

100 As he put it, "The more": Ibid., p. 100.

100 "I smoke like this because I want": Scott Helman, Boston *Globe*, August 25, 2008.

101 "Moment: Freshman year at Oxy": Phil Boerner's Diary, March 15, 1983.

101 There were very few black students: Sue Paterno, *The Occidental*, February 1, 1991.

101 "And you could count the black faculty": Ibid.

101 The college's weekly newspaper: *The Occidental*, January 1981.

105 "I want to get into public service": Adam Goldman and Robert Tanner, Associated Press, May 15, 2008.

107 During the Presidential campaign: Kerry Eleveld, *The Advocate*, April 2008.

109 It was, as Margot Mifflin recalled: Margot Mifflin, New York *Times*, January 18, 2009.

110 Obama was to open the rally: Obama, *Dreams from My Father*, p. 106.

110 Ngubeni, who, as a student in South Africa: Anthony Russo, *The Occidental*, February 20, 1981.

110 "After the rally, a pair of folk singers": Margot Mifflin, New York *Times*, January 18, 2009.

111 "I was on the outside again": Obama, *Dreams from My Father*, p. 107.

111 "I was concerned with urban issues": Linda Matchan, Boston *Globe*, February 15, 1990.

113 "When I transferred, I decided": Shira Boss-Bicak, *Columbia College Today*, January 2005.

113 Obama often fasted on Sundays: Obama, *Dreams from My Father*, p. 120.

114 "We didn't have a chance in hell": Adam Goldman and Robert Tanner, Associated Press, May 15, 2008.

115 Many years later, as a way of warding off the press: Ibid.

115 On the night of November 24, 1982: Jon Meacham, "On His Own," *Newsweek*, September 1, 2008.

115 "He couldn't cope," said Obama's sister: *Senator Obama Goes to Africa*, directed by Bob Hercules, 2007.

115 "At the time of his death": Obama, *Dreams from My Father*, p. 5.

116 In March, 1983: Barack Obama, "Breaking the War Mentality," *Sundial*, March 10, 1983.

117 In his early twenties: Obama, *Dreams from My Father*, p. 134.

117 "That was my idea of organizing": Ibid.

119 He had a young idealist's disdain: Ibid., p. 136.

119 "I said he needed to realize": Sasha Issenberg, Boston *Globe*, August 6, 2008.

121 In early 1985: Obama, *The Audacity of Hope*, p. 42.

122 "It embodied the notion": Ibid.

Chapter Four: Black Metropolis

125 In June and July: Bernstein, *A Woman in Charge*, p. 54.

125 Then, as a pro-Rockefeller volunteer: Ibid., p. 55.

125 Finally, she spent a few weeks: Ibid., p. 56.

125 "People were crushed and demoralized": Saul Alinksy interview, *Playboy*, March 1972.

126 He arranged sit-ins: Ibid.

126 Such an endorsement: Ibid.

126 "Shit," Alinsky said: Ibid.

127 In 1964, he threatened Mayor Daley: Ibid.

127 And when Alinsky was working: Ibid.

127 When an interviewer asked: Ibid.

127 "Right now they're frozen": Ibid.

128 At sixteen, Alinsky himself: Ibid.

128 "I was their one-man student body": Ibid.

129 In the late nineteen-fifties: Ibid.

130 She wrote of Alinsky: Hillary Rodham Clinton, "There Is Only the Fight," senior thesis, Wellesley College, p. 6.

130 "In spite of his being featured": Ibid., p. 74.

130 "Keeping in mind that": Ibid., appendix.

130 In the endnotes: Ibid.

143 African-Americans have lived: Drake and Cayton, *Black Metropolis*, p. 31.

143 Until the Civil War: Cohen and Taylor, *American Pharaoh*, p. 30.

144 "Turn a deaf ear to everybody": Drake and Cayton, *Black Metropolis*, p. 59.

144 John (Mushmouth) Johnson: Travis, *An Autobiography of Black Politics*, p. 38.

144 Still, many whites in Chicago: Drake and Cayton, *Black Metropolis*, p. 64.

145 One of the major white real-estate: Travis, *An Autobiography of Black Politics*, p. 66.

145 The August 2nd issue: Hofstadter and Wallace, *American Violence*, p. 246.

145 That summer, the Jamaican-born poet: McKay, *The Complete Poems*, p. 177.

146 "Every colored man who moves": *The Property Owner's Journal*, January 1, 1920.

146 During his political races: Drake and Cayton, *Black Metropolis*, p. 347.

147 And, in 1960: Cohen and Taylor, *American Pharaoh*, p. 95.

148 Richard Wright, who had come North: Drake and Cayton, *Black Metropolis*, p. xvii.

148 When, in 1951: Lemann, *The Promised Land*, p. 74.

149 Furious with City Hall's assault: Ibid. p. 77.

149 Studs Terkel once said of Daley: Rakove, *Don't Make No Waves . . . Don't Back No Losers*, p. 16.

150 When a young man from South Carolina: Lemann, *The Promised Land*, p. 91.

150 "Whenever I would raise a point": Travis, *An Autobiography of Black Politics*, p. 236.

150 Despres recalls Holman once telling Daley: Ibid.

150 "A good legitimate Negro": Ibid., p. 318.

151 At a downtown rally in 1965: Ibid., p. 341.

152 At first, King's associate: Hampton and Fayer, *Voices of Freedom*, p. 302.

152 Dorothy Tillman, who came to town: Travis, *An Autobiography of Black Politics*, p. 346.

152 "If anything they were more zealous": Abernathy, *And the Walls Came Tumbling Down*, p. 373.

152 "I have never seen such hopelessness": Travis, *An Autobiography of Black Politics*, p. 347.

153 "Yes, we are tired": Martin Luther King, Jr., Soldier Field, Chicago, Illinois, July 10, 1966.

154 "I've never seen anything like it": Travis, *An Autobiography of Black Politics*, p. 386.

154 "I'd never seen whites like these": Hampton and Fayer, *Voices of Freedom*, p. 312.

154 "Like Herod, Richard Daley was a fox": Abernathy, *And the Walls Came Tumbling Down*, p. 395.

154 Chicago, David Halberstam wrote: David Halberstam, "Notes From the Bottom of the Mountain," *Harpers*, June 1968.

155 At a press conference: Cohen and Taylor, *American Pharaoh*, p. 455.

155 When King came to Chicago: Garrow, *Bearing the Cross*, p. 444.

155 Metcalfe asked Daley: R. W. Apple, Jr., New York *Times*, May 10, 1972.

155 "What Daley did was smother King": Chicago *Sun-Times*, January 19, 1986.

156 "I'm sick and tired": Travis, *An Autobiography of Black Politics*, p. 572.

157 The ad said that the black church: Ibid., p. 582.

157 When Washington won the nomination: "This American Life," # 376, Chicago Public Radio, March 13, 2009.

158 On the streets of white ethnic neighborhoods: Levinsohn, *Harold Washington*, p. 200.

158 The Chicago *Tribune* endorsed Harold Washington: Leanita McClain, Washington *Post*, July 24, 1983.

158 Haskel Levy, an aide to Bernard Epton: "This American Life," # 376, Chicago Public Radio, March 13, 2009.

158 "I am not ashamed of being white!": Travis, *An Autobiography of Black Politics*, p. 602.

159 A young reporter for the *Tribune*: Rivlin, *Fire on the Prairie*, p. 191.

159 When asked on a radio call-in show: "This American Life," # 84, Chicago Public Radio, November 9, 2007.

160 At his victory celebration: Travis, *An Autobiography of Black Politics*, p. 610.

160 "He never became what I would consider": "This American Life," # 84, Chicago Public Radio, November 9, 2007.

162 One winter morning: Knoepfle, *After Alinsky*, p. 36.

164 The menace of the place: Obama, *Dreams from My Father*, p. 165.

165 Allen interviewed residents: Martha Allen, Chicago *Reporter*, 15, no. 6 (June 1986).

167 Obama wrote that the trip: Obama, *Dreams from My Father*, p. 242.

167 Walter Jacobson did a report: Martha Allen, Chicago *Reporter*, 15, no. 7 (July 1986).

170 In a sermon that deeply affected Obama: Wright, *What Makes You So Strong?*, p. 97.

170 "When I was growing up": Ibid., p. 28.

171 At first, he told Roger Wilkins: Roger Wilkins, "Frontline," PBS, June 16, 1987.

171 After enduring the humiliations: Cone, *Black Theology and Black Power*, p. 32.

172 In an America that continued: Ibid.

172 Blackness, for Cone: Ibid., p. 37.

172 By way of explanation: Ibid., p. 13.

172 The spirituals, Cone writes: Ibid., p. 100

172 In *The Negro Church*: Frazier, *The Negro Church in America*, p. 149.

173 For instance, to explain: Jeremiah Wright, N.A.A.C.P. Benefit, Detroit, Michigan, April 27, 2008.

175 "Some people say": Obama, *Dreams from My Father*, p. 283.

175 In 1981, a committee at Trinity: www.tucc.org.

176 When conservative critics suggested: Manya A. Brachear and Bob Secter, Chicago *Tribune*, February 6, 2007.

177 On November 25, 1987: Obama, *Dreams from My Father*, p. 287.

177 In many ways, Obama revered Washington: Ibid., p. 288.

179 Just after he left his job as an organizer: Knoepfle, *After Alinsky*, p. 36.

179 "We tend to think of organizing": Ibid., p. 133.

179 "They are not necessarily": Ibid., p. 134.

180 To disdain politics, he told the panel: Ibid., p. 133.

Chapter Five: Ambition

182 "I would learn about interest rates": Obama, *Dreams from My Father*, p. 276.

183 Obama said that Harvard Law School: Elise O'Shaughnessy, "Harvard Law Reviewed," *Vanity Fair*, June 1990.

187 When Derrick Bell: Fox Butterfield, New York *Times*, May 21, 1990.

188 "We felt as if we had the hardest": Noam Scheiber, "Crimson Tide," *The New Republic*, February 4, 2009.

188 Obama lived much as he had: Michael Levenson and Jonathan Saltzman, Boston *Globe*, January 28, 2007.

189 Beyond the "boot camp": Turow, *One L*, p. 300.

189 "If anybody had walked by": Michael Levenson and Jonathan Saltzman, Boston *Globe*, January 28, 2007.

189 A group would go together: Ibid.

189 "In law school, we had a seminar": Larissa MacFarquhar, "The Conciliator," *The New Yorker*, May 7, 2007.

190 Ian Macneil, the visiting contracts professor: Paul Hutcheon, *Sunday Herald*, June 8, 2008.

193 Not a few of his colleagues were shocked: Stewart Yerton, "Midas Touch in the Ivory Tower: The Croesus of Cambridge," *American Lawyer* 16, no. 3 (1994).

196 In May, 1915, *The Crisis*: Kluger, *Simple Justice*, p. 105.

197 "Charles Houston became": Ibid., p. 106.

197 Houston was committed to purpose: McNeil, *Groundwork*, p. 84.

197 As Houston's biographer Genna Rae McNeil: Ibid., p. 7.

198 After the great victory in Brown: Lisa Krause, "Charles Houston: The Man Who Killed Jim Crow," *National Geographic*, February 7, 2001.

198 In 1991, Obama filmed: http://www.youtube.com/watch?v=L489QHEQa_4.

198 Frankfurter once said: Kerlow, *Poisoned Ivy*, p. 20.

199 Obama nearly botched his bid: Michael Levenson and Jonathan Saltzman, Boston *Globe*, January 28, 2007.

200 "Honestly, we were just very polarized": Christine Spurell interview, "Frontline," PBS, October 14, 2008.

200 Robinson, like everyone at the firm: Michelle Obama interview with Suzanne Malveaux, CNN, January 1, 2009.

201 "He sounded too good to be true": Mendell, *Obama: From Promise to Power*, p. 93.

201 To her surprise: Michelle Obama interview with Suzanne Malveaux, CNN, January 1, 2009.

201 Besides, she and Obama were two: Mendell, *Obama: From Promise to Power*, p. 94.

201 "Man, she is hot!": Carol Felsenthal, "The Making of a First Lady," *Chicago Magazine*, February 2009.

201 They also had their first kiss: Barack Obama, "My First Date with Michelle," *O, The Oprah Magazine*, February 2007.

201 "Probably by the end of that date": Michelle Obama interview with Suzanne Malveaux, CNN, January 1, 2009.

202 "When you grow up as a black kid": Peter Slevin, *Princeton Alumni Weekly*, February 18, 2009.

203 "It was my secret shame": Mundy, *Michelle*, p. 67.

203 "My experiences at Princeton": Michelle Robinson, "Princeton-Educated Blacks and the Black Community," undergraduate thesis, Princeton University, p. 2.

205 When they were first: Liza Mundy, Washington *Post*, August 12, 2007.

205 Obama, for his part: Ibid.

206 "Most of my peers at the *Law Review*": Ibid.

207 "Before I could say a word, another black student": Tammerlin Drummond, Los Angeles *Times*, March 19, 1990.

207 Interviewed for the New York *Times*: Fox Butterfield, New York *Times*, February 6, 1990.

208 Obama gave many interviews: Jodi Kantor, New York *Times*, January 28, 2007.

208 Nearly all the articles: Ryan Lizza, "Making It," *The New Yorker*, July 21, 2008.

208 Obama told the Boston *Globe:* Linda Matchan, Boston *Globe,* February 15, 1990.

210 She argued that goals of tolerance: Jeffrey Ressner and Ben Smith, *Politico,* June 23, 2008.

212 Bell wrote, in "Serving Two Masters": Derrick Bell, "Serving Two Masters," *Yale Law Journal,* 1976.

212 "Black people will never gain": Bell, *Faces at the Bottom of the Well,* p. 12.

213 On April 9, 1990: Letter from Derrick Bell to Robert Clark, April 9, 1990.

213 apologetic for failing to realize: Ibid.

214 Dressed in khakis and a light-blue dress shirt: "Frontline," PBS, January 19, 2009.

214 "One of the luxuries of going": Tammerlin Drummond, Los Angeles *Times,* March 19, 1990.

215 Obama wrote to the *Record:* Barack Obama, *Harvard Law Record* 91, no. 7 (November 16, 1990).

216 "I have no way of knowing": *Journal of Blacks in Higher Education,* no. 30 (Winter 2000–2001).

216 In the annual parody issue: Jodi Kantor, New York *Times,* January 28, 2007.

217 At Harvard, Obama secretly: Obama, *Dreams from My Father,* p. 437.

218 "Well, no, actually": Janny Scott interview, "Frontline," PBS, October 14, 2008.

Chapter Six: A Narrative of Ascent

220 "He spent a lot of time": James L. Merriner, "Friends of O," *Chicago Magazine,* June 2008.

222 "Today, we see hundreds": Vernon Jarrett, Chicago *Sun-Times,* July 11, 1992.

223 In an interview with the Chicago *Reader:* Interview, Chicago *Reader,* March 17, 2000.

224 *Crain's Chicago Business:* "Forty Under Forty," *Crain's Chicago Business,* September 27, 1993.

225 When a reporter who was writing: Gretchen Reynolds, "Vote of Confidence," *Chicago Magazine,* January 1993.

226 "All my life, I have been stitching together": Mariana Cook, "A Couple in Chicago," *The New Yorker,* January 19, 2009.

227 Her associate Jay Acton: Robert Draper, "Barack Obama's Work in Progress," *GQ,* November 2009.

227 After his wedding and honeymoon: Ibid.

228 In a preface to the 2004: Obama, *Dreams from My Father,* p. ix.

229 There are more than six thousand: Gates, *The Classic Slave Narratives,* p. ix.

229 "Deprived of access to literacy": Gates, *Bearing Witness,* p. 4.

230 He reads histories by Will Durant: Malcolm X, *The Autobiography of Malcolm X,* p. 178.

230 In *Soul on Ice:* Cleaver, *Soul on Ice,* p. 31.

230 Claude Brown told an audience: Gates, *Bearing Witness,* p. 4.

230 Even Sammy Davis, Jr.: Davis, *Yes I Can,* p. 63.

230 "Barack is who he says he is": Wolffe, *Renegade,* p. 156.

231 He signals his awareness: Obama, *Dreams from My Father,* p. xvi.

231 While the book is based on his journals: Ibid., p. xvii.

231 W. E. B. DuBois set a standard: Du Bois, *The Autobiography of W. E. B. Du Bois,* p. 12.

231 When the young Frederick Douglass: Douglass, *Autobiographies,* p. 60.

232 "Of my ancestry": Washington, *Up from Slavery*, p. 1.

232 Obama's reading of black memoirists: Obama, *Dreams from My Father*, p. 85.

232 "His repeated acts of self-creation": Ibid., p. 86.

232 Obama was disturbed: Ibid.

233 "We're all black to the white man": Malcolm X, *Autobiography of Malcolm X*, p. 206.

233 Obama, who has been raised: Obama, *Dreams from My Father*, p. 286.

234 As Obama writes: Obama, *Dreams from My Father*, p. xvi.

235 Veteran residents of the building: Jennifer 8 Lee, New York *Times*, January 30, 2008.

235 Obama places himself: Obama, *Dreams from My Father*, p. 3.

236 His "kindred spirit": Ibid., p. 5.

236 As he is cooking his eggs: Ibid.

236 When Obama writes a new preface: Ibid., p. xi.

237 When he is writing about: Ibid., p. 18.

237 His mother, Ann: Ibid., p. 20.

237 "Racism was part of that past": Ibid., p. 21.

237 Obama is also wise to Hawaii: Ibid., p. 23.

238 In Chapter 2, he recalls a day: Ibid., p. 28.

238 During the Presidential campaign: Kirsten Scharnberg and Kim Barker, Chicago *Tribune*, March 25, 2007.

239 The scene cannot help: Malcolm X, *The Autobiography of Malcolm X*, p. 54.

239 "My mother's confidence": Obama, *Dreams from My Father*, p. 50.

240 When they would talk: Ibid., p. 80.

240 Poignantly, Obama: Ibid., p. xv.

240 "We were in goddamned Hawaii": Ibid., p. 82.

240 "As it was, I learned to slip": Ibid.

240 Chapter 5, which covers: Ibid., p. 92.

241 He is reminded again: Ibid., p. 99.

241 The role model who shocks: Ibid., p. 104.

242 "Then, as if the sight": Ibid., p. 178.

243 "I tried to imagine": Ibid., p. 183.

243 but he worries: Ibid., p. 203.

244 In New York, he tells us: Ibid., p. 210.

244 As he sits in the pews: Ibid., p. 294.

245 He is a "Westerner": Ibid., p. 301.

245 On the road between Madrid: Ibid., p. 303.

246 "For the first time in my life": Ibid., p. 305.

246 "All of this while a steady procession": Ibid., p. 311.

246 When she tells a story: Ibid., p. 215.

246 "I felt as if my world": Ibid., p. 220.

247 Sitting with his relatives: Ibid., p. 318.

247 "It was a savage scene": Ibid., p. 356.

247 Would a British officer: Ibid., p. 368.

248 "First there was Miwiru": Ibid., p. 394.

248 Onyango, Sarah tells him: Ibid., p. 398.

248 Soon, the white man's presence: Ibid.

249 "This was it, I thought to myself": Ibid., p. 427.

249 "Standing before the two graves": Ibid.

249 "For a long time I sat": Ibid., p. 429.

249 A history teacher named Rukia Odero: Ibid., p. 433.

249 In the words of the Declaration of Independence: Ibid., p. 437.

250 "To a happy ending": Ibid., p. 442.

250 At Eso Won Books: Robert Draper, "Barack Obama's Work in Progress," *GQ*, November 2009.

251 His biographer Edmund Morris: Morris, *The Rise of Theodore Roosevelt*, p. xxxiii.

252 "Motives of delicacy": Marshall, *The Life of George Washington, Volume 2*, p. 136.

252 "People went by, and he took no account": Howells, *The Lives and Speeches of Abraham Lincoln and Hannibal Hamlin*, p. 31.

253 "American campaign biographies": Jill Lepore, "Bound for Glory," *The New Yorker*, October 20, 2008.

253 Obama himself admitted: Janny Scott, New York *Times*, May 18, 2008.

253 For instance, Cashill wrote: Jack Cashill, *American Thinker*, June 28, 2009.

254 A writer for the *National Review*'s popular blog: Andy McCarthy, *The Corner*, October 11, 2008.

254 Writing elevated a slave from non-being: Andrews, *African-American Autobiography*, p. 9.

255 In Frederick Douglass's narrative: Douglass, *Autobiographies*, p. 217.

255 "Mr. Douglass has very properly": Ibid., p. 7.

Chapter Seven: Somebody Nobody Sent

257 "So he tested these truths": Bellow, *Dean's December*, p. 165.

260 He appeared in court: Abdon Pallasch, Chicago *Sun-Times*, December 17, 2007.

260 "I was one of the better writers": Ibid.

261 A number of progressive groups: Ibid.

264 When, during the Presidential campaign: Jodi Kantor, New York *Times*, July 30, 2008.

266 During the Presidential campaign: Larissa MacFarquhar, "The Conciliator," *The New Yorker*, May 7, 2007.

267 In his memoir, *Livin' the Blues*: Davis, *Livin' the Blues*, p. 332.

270 In 1990, one of Rezko's vice-presidents: Tim Novak, Chicago *Sun-Times*, April 23, 2007.

270 Obama did not do much real-estate work: Ibid.

271 The work was so dull: Don Terry, Chicago *Tribune Magazine*, July 27, 2008.

272 In July, 1991: Jonathan Becker, "Barack's Rock," *Vogue*, October 2008.

272 "She is made for you": Ibid.

275 Savage had also referred to Ron Brown: Christopher Drew and Ray Gibson, Chicago *Tribune*, August 14, 1994.

276 Now, as he watched his brief career: William Safire, New York *Times*, October 2, 1994.

276 Admitting that he made "mistakes": "Larry King Live," CNN, September 1, 1995.

277 "I married you because you're cute": Jodi Kantor, New York *Times*, November 1, 2009.

277 "I wasn't a proponent of politics": Scott Helman, Boston *Globe*, October 12, 2007.

278 Alan Dobry, a former Democratic: David Jackson and Ray Long, Chicago *Tribune*, April 4, 2007.

278 "I hadn't publicly announced": Ibid.

278 Palmer doesn't dispute that: Ibid.

278 "I'm absolutely certain": Ibid.

279 "Pray for Mel Reynolds": Kevin Knapp, Hyde Park *Herald*, July 5, 1995.

279 In the last paragraph: Ibid.

279 He received his first campaign contributions: Tim Novak, Chicago *Sun-Times*, April 23, 2007.

281 In 2005, long before Obama: warrenpeacemuse.blogspot.com.

282 One African-American politician: Hank De Zutter, "What Makes Obama Run," *The Chicago Reader*, December 8, 1995.

282 "Now all of this may be": Ibid.

282 On September 19, 1995: Monice Mitchell, Hyde Park *Herald*, October 4, 1995.

282 "In this room, Harold Washington": Ibid.

284 "What I saw was a powerful demonstration": Hank de Zutter, *The Chicago Reader*, December 8, 1995.

286 The Hyde Park *Herald* reported: Kevin Knapp, Hyde Park *Herald*, October 25, 1995.

289 The *Defender* reported: Ryan Lizza, "Making It," *The New Yorker*, July 21, 2008.

289 Writing in the *Defender:* Ibid.

290 That day, Obama told the *Tribune:* Thomas Hardy, Chicago *Tribune*, December 19, 1995.

290 This is a routine, and often effective: David Jackson and Ray Long, Chicago *Tribune*, April 4, 2007.

291 "To my mind, we were just abiding": Ibid.

291 "If you can get 'em, get 'em": Ibid.

292 "It was very awkward": Ibid.

293 "He was a classic charismatic leader": Hank De Zutter, "What Makes Obama Run," *The Chicago Reader*, December 8, 1995.

294 In a tone of rueful apology: Ibid.

295 "In Chicago, for instance": Adolph Reed, Jr., "The Curse of Community," *Village Voice*, January 16, 1996.

296 "It's probably a terrible thing to say": Editorial, Chicago *Tribune*, December 6, 2002.

296 The minute he took over: Ibid.

301 One Republican, Bill Brady: Rick Pearson and Ray Long, Chicago *Tribune*, May 3, 2007.

301 He said, "When it turned out": Ibid.

303 Trotter called Obama "the knight": Ibid.

303 In the spring of 1997: Barack Obama, Hyde Park *Herald*, April 16, 1997.

303 In other columns, he wrote about: Barack Obama, Hyde Park *Herald*, February 19, 1997; June 18, 1997; September 10, 1997; December 31, 1997.

304 During a debate, in Springfield: Ryan Lizza, "Making It," *The New Yorker*, July 21, 2008.

Chapter Eight: Black Enough

307 Their brand of black nationalism: Hampton and Fayer, *Voices of Freedom*, p. 353.

308 The Panthers adopted the uniform: Ibid., p. 351.

308 "The purpose of this counterintelligence endeavor": Ibid., p. 511.

310 "We'd go through political orientation": Ibid., p. 523.

311 "Chairman, chairman, wake up!": Ibid., p. 534.

311 The police held a press conference: Cohen and Taylor, *American Pharaoh*, p. 501.

311 "You see this man?": Frady, *Jesse*, p. 261.

311 Rush claimed that: Cohen and Taylor, *American Pharaoh*, p. 502.

311 The columnist Mike Royko: Ibid.

312 Bobby Rush said, "Hampton": Philip Caputo, Chicago *Tribune*, December 10, 1969.

312 The service ended with the singing: Ibid.

312 A few weeks later: Hampton and Fayer, *Voices of Freedom*, p. 538.

312 At a speech to Chicago college students: Scott Stewart, Chicago *Sun-Times*, February 21, 1999.

313 Soon after entering Congress: Scott Stewart, Chicago *Sun-Times*, February 21, 1999.

315 "The First Congressional District": Ted Kleine, "Is Bobby Rush in Trouble," *The Chicago Reader*, March 17, 2000.

319 Obama, Kappy Scates joked: Ben Calhoun, Chicago Public Radio, August 8, 2008.

319 The early poll showed Rush: Michael Weisskopf, "Obama: How He Learned to Win," *Time*, May 8, 2008.

319 That summer, Steve Neal: Steve Neal, Chicago *Sun-Times*, August 1, 1999.

320 "I'm not part of some longstanding": Greg Downs, Hyde Park *Herald*, September 29, 1999.

320 "Our responsibility—*my* responsibility": John McCormick and Peter Annin, "A Father's Anguished Journey," *Newsweek*, November 29, 1999.

320 "I know my faith is being tested": Ted Kleine, "Is Bobby Rush In Trouble," *The Chicago Reader*, March 17, 2000.

321 "I believe that this glorification": Ibid.

321 "What a bunch of gutless sheep": Editorial, Chicago *Tribune*, December 21, 1999.

321 In one of his columns: Barack Obama, Hyde Park *Herald*, January 12, 2000.

322 They were a "random-ass mix": Ryan Lizza, "Making It," *The New Yorker*, July 21, 2008.

325 They pointed to campaign contributions: Ted Kleine, "Is Bobby Rush in Trouble," *The Chicago Reader*, March 17, 2000.

326 "Less than halfway into the campaign": Obama, *The Audacity of Hope*, p. 106.

326 Inevitably, he began his speeches: Ted Kleine, "Is Bobby Rush in Trouble," *The Chicago Reader*, March 17, 2000.

327 "Eight years ago": Editorial, Chicago *Tribune*, March 6, 2000.

327 Obama began the day: Presta, *Mr. and Mrs. Grassroots*, p. 63.

327 On March 16th: Ibid., p. 57.

327 Ted Kleine's article: Ted Kleine, "Is Bobby Rush in Trouble," *The Chicago Reader*, March 17, 2000.

328 Obama jumped in: Ibid.

329 "MAN'S VOICE: Oh, man": Don Gonyea, "Morning Edition," National Public Radio, September 19, 2007.

330 He taped a thirty-second radio commercial: Steve Neal, Chicago *Sun-Times*, March 12, 2000.

331 The night of his defeat: Curtis Lawrence, Chicago *Sun-Times*, March 22, 2000.

331 "I've got to make assessments": Ryan Lizza, "Making It," *The New Yorker*, July 21, 2008.

331 Long after the loss: Obama, *The Audacity of Hope*, p. 107.

331 In addition to the professional anxieties: Michael Weisskopf, "Obama: How He Learned to Win," *Time*, May 8, 2008.

331 Obama began to wonder: Obama, *The Audacity of Hope*, p. 4.

332 "My hope was that": Scott Helman, Boston *Globe*, October 12, 2007.

332 "I found myself subjected": Obama, *The Audacity of Hope*, p. 340.

332 Dan Shomon told a reporter: Carol Felsenthal, *Chicago Magazine*, February 2009.

333 "For God's sake, Barack": Scott Helman, Boston *Globe*, October 12, 2007.

Chapter Nine: The Wilderness Campaign

334 When Obama arrived at the airport: Obama, *The Audacity of Hope*, p. 354.

336 For fourteen months: Chuck Neubauer and Tom Hamburger, Los Angeles *Times*, April 27, 2008.

336 When Barack called in from the road: Carol Felsenthal, "The Making of a First Lady," *Chicago Magazine*, February 2009.

337 On September 19, 2001: Hyde Park *Herald*, September 19, 2001.

338 "Suddenly Adelstein's interest": Mendell, *Obama: From Promise to Power*, p. 150.

339 Writing in the *Herald:* Barack Obama, Hyde Park *Herald*, February 20, 2002.

339 "He explained to me": Hendon, *Black Enough/White Enough*, p. 31.

340 As Hendon recalls it: Ibid., p. 32.

340 In Hendon's self-dramatizing version of the incident: Hendon, *Black Enough/White Enough*, p. 30.

340 In *Black Enough/White Enough*: Ibid., p. 33.

341 "I barely knew where the law library": Ray Long and Christi Parsons, Chicago *Tribune*, October 25, 2006.

341 Rahm Emanuel, who was then: Ryan Lizza, "Making It," *The New Yorker*, July 21, 2008.

341 Blagojevich's campaign adviser: Jake Tapper, ABCNews.com, December 9, 2008.

341 Appearing in June, 2002: "Public Affairs with Jeff Berkowitz," June 27, 2002.

342 With the 2002 elections: Jo Becker and Christopher Drew, New York *Times*, May 11, 2008.

343 On September 12th: George W. Bush, United Nations, New York, September 12, 2002.

345 The *Tribune* reporter at the rally: Bill Glauber, Chicago *Tribune*, October 3, 2002.

346 "This is a rally to stop a war": Ibid.

347 Carl Davidson, one of the rally's: Jo Becker and Christopher Drew, New York *Times*, May 11, 2008.

348 "There was nothing about that speech": Don Gonyea, "Morning Edition," National Public Radio, March 25, 2008.

349 "He said to me, he said": Todd Purdum, "Raising Obama," *Vanity Fair*, March 2008.

350 "I had reservations": Editorial, Chicago *Tribune*, May 9, 2003.

351 "Driving while black": Barack Obama, Hyde Park *Herald*, July 23, 2003.

351 "The original presentation of the bill": Scott Helman, Boston *Globe*, September 23, 2007.

352 In 2005, in the midst of a series: Fran Spielman, Chicago *Sun-Times*, August 5, 2005.

352 In January, 2007: Fran Spielman, Chicago *Sun-Times*, January 22, 2007.

353 In October, 2002: David Mendell, Chicago *Tribune*, October 22, 2004.

354 When they pulled over: Ibid.

Chapter Ten: Reconstruction

355 As Eric Foner, the leading historian: Eric Foner, *The Nation*, October 15, 2008.

356 The Raleigh *News and Observer*: Dray, *Capitol Men*, p. 410.

356 "This, Mr. Chairman": Ibid., p. 351.

357 "Our bases overlapped so much": Liza Mundy, Washington *Post*, August 12, 2007.

358 Not long after the breakfast: Mendell, *Obama: From Promise to Power*, p. 155.

358 "The big issue around the Senate for me": Ibid., p. 152.

359 Eric Zorn, an influential liberal: Eric Zorn, Chicago *Tribune*, January 18, 2003.

360 At the press conference: Rick Pearson and John Chase, Chicago *Tribune*, January 22, 2003.

361 "The fact that I conjugate my verbs": Jennifer Senior, "Dreaming of Obama," *New York Magazine*, September 24, 2006.

362 "A little old lady said to me": Jodi Enda, *American Prospect*, February 2006.

364 In one fantastical column: David Axelrod, Hyde Park *Herald*, May 8, 1974.

365 "I've been a Chicago police officer": Robert Kaiser, Washington *Post*, May 2, 2008.

367 Maria Pappas, the Cook County treasurer: David Mendell, Chicago *Tribune*, December 7, 2003.

368 When Joshua Green: Joshua Green, "Gambling Man," *The Atlantic*, January/February 2004.

371 "We are technologically illiterate": Presta, *Mr. and Mrs. Grassroots*, p. 116.

373 The *Tribune*'s lead writer covering: David Mendell, Chicago *Tribune*, February 10, 2004.

373 "I don't begrudge extraordinarily": Andrew Herrmann and Scott Fornek, Chicago *Sun-Times*, February 22, 2004.

373 Laura Washington, a columnist: Laura Washington, Chicago *Sun-Times*, February 16, 2004.

375 One of the candidates: David Mendell and Molly Parker, Chicago *Tribune*, February 24, 2004.

375 "The fact of the matter is": Ibid.

375 "We debated whether to frame it": Scott Fornek, Chicago *Sun-Times*, March 5, 2004.

375 The documents revealed: David Mendell, Chicago *Tribune*, February, 28, 2004.

376 The papers described multiple: Frank Main, Chicago *Sun-Times*, February 28, 2004.

376 Hull informed the *Tribune*: David Mendell, Chicago *Tribune*, February, 28, 2004.

376 "It is my total reputation": Ibid.

379 Steven Rogers, a businessman: Christopher Drew and Mike McIntire, New York *Times*, April 3, 2007.

379 At the start of the campaign: Michael Weisskopf, "Obama: How He Learned to Win," *Time*, May 8, 2008.

381 Eric Zorn, the *Tribune* columnist: Eriz Zorn, Chicago *Tribune*, March 18, 2004.

381 When, just after 7 p.m., the call came: Ibid.

381 As the television news crews filed in: Ibid.

381 "I think it's fair to say": Scott Fornek and Robert Herguth, Chicago *Sun-Times*, March 17, 2004.

382 On primary night he told the crowd: David Mendell, Chicago *Tribune*, March 18, 2004.

382 "I have an unusual name": Monica Davey, New York *Times*, March 18, 2004.

382 As Obama and Durbin were driving: Barack Obama, N.A.A.C.P., Detroit, Michigan, May 2, 2005.

Chapter Eleven: A Righteous Wind

387 As Kerry watched Obama speak: Jill Zuckman and David Mendell, Chicago *Tribune*, July 15, 2004.

387 In a Profile published in *The New Yorker:* William Finnegan, "The Candidate," *The New Yorker,* May 31, 2004.

388 Jan Schakowsky, a Democratic congresswoman: Ibid.

389 "I made clear to Respondent": Associated Press, June 22, 2004.

389 Ryan said in the filing: John Chase and Liam Ford, Chicago *Tribune*, June 22, 2004.

390 "I've tried to make it clear": Mendell, *Obama: From Promise to Power,* p. 264.

390 Later, Obama would lower his head: Ibid.

390 "In the Senate race in Illinois": Jay Leno, "The Tonight Show," NBC, June 22, 2004.

390 "A lot of people were saying": John Chase and Liam Ford, Chicago *Tribune*, June 22, 2004.

391 "Jack is a good man": Debbie Howlett, *USA Today,* June 22, 2004.

391 Ryan also found support: William Saletan, Slate.com, June 23, 2004.

391 "I consider him an honest man": Stephen Kinzer, New York *Times*, June 23, 2004.

391 On June 25th, Ryan complied: Rahul Sangwan, *The Dartmouth Independent,* October 4, 2004.

391 "What happened to him": John Chase and Liam Ford, Chicago *Tribune*, June 22, 2004.

392 Obama was riding from Springfield: Obama, *The Audacity of Hope,* p. 354.

392 Sometimes, in order to get away: Eli Saslow, Washington *Post*, August 25, 2008.

392 Obama faxed his first draft to Axelrod: David Bernstein, "The Speech," *Chicago Magazine*, June 2007.

395 "I love to body surf": Christopher Wills, Associated Press, July 26, 2004.

395 When he was asked about: John Kass, Chicago *Tribune*, July 27, 2004.

395 Apologizing, he said: David Mendell, Chicago *Tribune*, July 28, 2004.

396 "That fucker is trying": David Bernstein, "The Speech," *Chicago Magazine*, June 2007.

396 As crowds milled around: Ibid.

400 "I thought that was one of the most": Mary Mitchell, Chicago *Sun-Times*, July 29, 2004.

401 Richard Daley . . . acknowledged: Scott Fornek, Chicago *Sun-Times*, July 29, 2004.

401 Even Bobby Rush: Michael Sneed, Chicago *Sun-Times*, July 30, 2004.

401 "A superstar is born": Clarence Page, Chicago *Tribune*, August 1, 2004.

402 The *Sun-Times* printed: Dave McKinney, Chicago *Sun-Times*, August 4, 2004.

404 "This is all so, well, interesting.": David Mendell, Chicago *Tribune*, August 2, 2004.

405 On a hot evening in mid-August: Liam Ford and David Mendell, Chicago *Tribune*, August 13, 2004.

406 In his announcement speech: Editorial, Chicago *Tribune*, August 16, 2004.

406 One *Tribune* editorial: Ibid.

406 But at times: Scott Fornek, Chicago *Sun-Times*, November 1, 2004.

406 As he spread his arms: Liam Ford and John Chase, Chicago *Tribune*, October 22, 2004.

407 "That's why I have a pastor": Ibid.

407 "At the hard points": Ibid.

407 On one occasion: Obama, *The Audacity of Hope*, p. 211.

407 In late October: Editorial, Chicago *Tribune*, October 24, 2004.

407 According to Bill Daley: James L. Merriner, "Making Peace," *Chicago Magazine*, June, 2008.

409 Of the many articles written: Don Terry, Chicago *Tribune Magazine*, October 24, 2004.

410 He was equally disturbed: Noam Scheiber, "Race Against History," *The New Republic*, May 31, 2004.

412 On Halloween night: Alan Keyes, Spirit of God Fellowship Church, Chicago, October 31, 2004.

412 As the cameras followed: Alison Neumer, Chicago *Tribune*, November 3, 2004.

412 "Thank you, Illinois!": Scott Fornek, Chicago *Sun-Times*, November 3, 2004.

Chapter Twelve: A Slight Madness

415 "If you don't have enough": ABC News, November 1, 2007.

415 "Are you going to try": Jeff Zeleny, New York *Times*, December 24, 2006.

418 "I am not running for President": David Mendell, Chicago *Tribune*, November 4, 2004.

418 Obama got especially irritated: Scott Fornek, Chicago *Sun-Times*, November 4, 2004.

418 "It's going to be important": Ibid.

419 "I don't think we're trying to dampen": David Mendell, Chicago *Tribune*, November 4, 2004.

419 On ABC's daytime show: Rudolph Bush, Chicago *Tribune*, November 23, 2004.

419 On Letterman's show: "The Late Show," CBS, November 26, 2004.

420 Adopting a tone: Lynn Sweet, Chicago *Sun-Times*, December 6, 2004.

420 She was inspired to re-issue: Janny Scott, New York *Times*, May 18, 2008.

421 Woodward once called him: Ibid.

421 Although Peter Osnos: Peter Osnos, *The Century Foundation: News and Commentary*, October 30, 2006.

424 He met with Obama: Wolffe, *Renegade*, p. 38.

424 "I know what I'm good at": Pete Rouse interview, "Frontline," PBS, July 11, 2008.

425 Obama told Rouse: Ibid.

425 He planned to help Obama: Ibid.

425 Oprah Winfrey declared: Jeff Zeleny, Chicago *Tribune*, March 20, 2005.

425 At times, Obama's celebrity: Ibid.

425 One of the first books: Jeff Zeleny and Kate Zernike, New York *Times*, March 9, 2008.

426 Nevertheless, Obama told: Jeff Zeleny, Chicago *Tribune*, March 20, 2005.

426 "All of us are a mixture": Ibid.

426 When Obama paid a visit: Ibid.

427 At the swearing-in ceremony: Ibid.

427 "Over the next six years": Ibid.

427 During Rice's confirmation hearings: Ben Wallace-Wells, "Destiny's Child," *Rolling Stone*, February 22, 2007.

428 Faced with the prospect: Jeff Zeleny, Chicago *Tribune*, September 23, 2005.

428 "So we enter into the building": Barack Obama, Council on Foreign Relations, Washington, D.C., November 1, 2005.

429 Three months after: Barack Obama and Richard Lugar, Washington *Post*, December 3, 2005.

432 Then, appearing on ABC's: "This Week with George Stephanopoulos," ABC, September 11, 2005.

432 In an interview with the *Tribune*: Jeff Zeleny, Chicago *Tribune*, September 12, 2005.

433 "The burden is on us": Ibid.

434 Eventually, Pete Rouse: Perry Bacon, Jr., Washington *Post*, August 27, 2007.

434 "Pete's very good": Ibid.

435 The letter was entitled: Daily Kos, September 30, 2005.

437 Afterward, Obama used: Jodi Enda, "Great Expectations," *The American Prospect*, January 16, 2006.

437 "And the way I would describe": Ibid.

438 Returning to Washington: Jeff Zeleny, Chicago *Tribune*, February 7, 2006.

439 "I obviously beaned him": Mark Salter interview, "Frontline," PBS, May 30, 2008.

440 "The tone of the letter": Jeff Zeleny, Chicago *Tribune*, February 8, 2006.

440 Before they testified: Jeff Zeleny, Chicago *Tribune*, February 9, 2006.

440 "What I am suggesting is this": Barack Obama, Washington, D.C., June 28, 2006.

442 Valerie Jarrett says: Larissa MacFarquhar, "The Conciliator," *The New Yorker*, May 7, 2007.

442 "I thought these will be": "World News Tonight," ABC, November 1, 2007.

443 On January 16, 2006: Balz and Johnson, *The Battle for America 2008*, p. 26.

445 "He has as much potential": Jeff Zeleny, Chicago *Tribune*, November 20, 2005.

445 "When his name pops up": Ibid.

447 "I thought, let's have a little fun": Perry Bacon, Jr., Washington *Post*, August 27, 2007.

447 "I don't think George Bush": Barack Obama, Harkin Steak Fry, Indianola, Iowa, September 17, 2006.

450 Ruy Teixeira of the Brookings: Alan Abramowitz and Ruy Teixeira, "The Decline of the White Working Class and the Rise of a Mass Upper Middle Class," Brookings Working Paper, April 2008.

451 When he called Obama: Bob Gilbert, "The President Prediction," *Seton Hall Magazine*, March 31, 2009.

453 "The United States was said": Chisholm, *The Good Fight*, p. 162.

453 Chisholm, who died in 2005: Chisholm, *Unbought and Unbossed*, p. xii.

453 "My constituency": Jesse Jackson, Democratic National Convention, San Francisco, July 17, 1984.

454 At rallies in the South: Frady, *Jesse*, p. 306.

454 "Nothing will ever again": Ibid., p. 370.

454 Jackson, Hatcher said: Ibid., p. 417.

455 The incumbent, the Vice-President: Wallace, *The Man*, p. 251.

456 Joe Klein, writing in *Time*: Joe Klein, "The Fresh Face," *Time*, October 15, 2006.

456 And David Brooks: David Brooks, New York *Times*, October 19, 2006.

458 In January, Obama had kept: "Meet the Press," NBC, October 22, 2006.

458 For a *Time* cover story: Joe Klein, "The Fresh Face," *Time*, October 15, 2006.

459 In David Axelrod's Chicago office: Balz and Johnson, *The Battle for America*, p. 28.

461 "I said to him, 'Do you really think' ": Jill Zuckman, Chicago *Tribune*, October 18, 2006.

461 Tom Daschle, who gave up a chance: Tom Daschle interview, "Frontline," PBS, June 10, 2008.

462 "Because I do see in him": Jeff Zeleny, Chicago *Tribune*, December 25, 2005.

464 On November 28, 2006: Balz and Johnson, *The Battle for America 2008*, p. 29.

465 Echoing the advice of Durbin: Ibid., p. 30.

466 In mid-December, Obama: Pete Rouse interview, "Frontline," PBS, July 11, 2008.

466 When Obama came home: Ibid.

466 Late at night, on January 6th: Plouffe, *The Audacity to Win*, p. 27.

Chapter Thirteen: The Sleeping Giant

467 "The genius of our founders": Barack Obama, Springfield, Illinois, February 10, 2007.

468 A couple of days before: Ben Wallace-Wells, "Destiny's Child," *Rolling Stone*, February 22, 2007.

468 "This is a fucking disaster": Plouffe, *The Audacity to Win*, p. 40.

473 "Look, Obama is a very decent": Cornel West, State of the Black Union, Hampton, Virginia, February 10, 2007.

473 "He's young, he's inexperienced": Charles Ogletree, State of the Black Union, Hampton, Virginia, February 10, 2007.

477 The Obama campaign took polls: Plouffe, *The Audacity to Win*, p. 124.

477 The near absence of Jackson: "Saturday Night Live," NBC, March 2, 2008.

478 Just after Lincoln: Mendelberg, *The Race Card*, p. 36.

478 Speakers at the Democratic Convention: Ibid., p. 39.

478 In 1868, Georges Clemenceau: Ibid., p. 43.

478 One of its campaign badges: Ibid., p. 45.

478 Democratic Party–controlled newspapers: Ibid., p. 47.

478 In the United States between 1890: Ibid., p. 58.

478 James Thomas Heflin: Branch, *Parting the Waters*, p. 51.

479 Southern politicians, like Theodore Bilbo: Mendelberg, *The Race Card*, p. 71.

479 During a Senate hearing in 1946: Ibid.

479 George Wallace dropped: Ibid., p. 91.

479 After filming a commercial: Ibid., p. 97.

480 Bush pressed the Horton case: Ibid., p. 142.

480 Bush's media consultant: Ibid.

480 On December 21, 2006: Joshua Green, "The Hillary Clinton Memos," *The Atlantic*, August 11, 2008.

481 Three months later: Ibid.

484 "I can maybe work with him": Frady, *Jesse*, p. 493.

484 "The initiative displayed the parochial": Randall Kennedy, "The Triumph of Robust Tokenism," *The Atlantic*, February 2001.

485 Speaking on television in December: "Newsmakers Live," December 2007.

487 The Reverend Joseph Lowery: Paige Bowers, "A Civil Rights Divide Over Obama," *Time*, January 31, 2008.

487 "These old black politicians": Logan Hill, "How I Made It: Spike Lee on 'Do the Right Thing,' " *New York Magazine*, April 7, 2008.

488 George H. W. Bush once called him: Frady, *Jesse*, p. 5.

488 Mario Cuomo, however: Ibid., p. 14.

488 "When you are unkind to the homeless": Ibid., p. 48.

488 "We are a hybrid people": Ibid., p. 76.

489 "I never slept under": Ibid.

489 "You know, people'd always ask": Ibid., p. 82.

489 When Jesse was a boy: Ibid., p. 97.

489 "Jesse ain't got no daddy": Ibid., p. 86.

489 When he came to Greenville: Ibid., p. 91.

490 "Jesse wanted to *be* Martin": Ibid., p. 209.

491 "If I were a candidate": Andrew Sullivan, "Goodbye to All That: Why Obama Matters," *The Atlantic*, December 2007.

491 According to a South Carolina paper: Ibid.

492 "If Barack doesn't win Iowa": Mike Glover, Associated Press, September 27, 2007.

492 Bill Clinton went: "The Charlie Rose Show," PBS, December 14, 2007.

493 "You know, they said": Barack Obama, Des Moines, Iowa, January 3, 2008.

493 An astonishing set of rhetorical gestures: Frady, *Jesse*, p. 306.

495 Bill Clinton, he said: Michael Hill, Baltimore *Sun*, January 16, 2008.

Chapter Fourteen: In the Racial Funhouse

496 "I told him that I loved him": Steve Vogel, Washington *Post*, October 21, 2000.

497 It offered a five-thousand-dollar-per-month: Christopher Cooper, Corey Dade, and Valerie Bauerlein, *Wall Street Journal*, January 23, 2008.

498 He finally accepted a competing offer: Ibid.

499 "I didn't know if I was going to live": Eric Ernst, (Sarasota, Florida) *Herald Tribune*, October 15, 2008.

499 "All those nights I thought": Ibid.

500 She wanted to "help": Barack Obama, National Constitution Center, Philadelphia, March 18, 2008.

500 In mid-October, 2007: Katherine Q. Seelye, New York *Times*, October 14, 2007.

501 "I've heard some folks say": Barack Obama, Manning, South Carolina, November 2, 2007.

502 "Don't let people turn you around": Ben Smith, *Politico*, January 27, 2008.

503 "What I remember most": Michelle Obama, Orangeburg, South Carolina, November 20, 2007.

505 One state senator: Jim Davenport, Associated Press, February 13, 2007.

505 "By itself, that single moment": Barack Obama, Ebenezer Baptist Church, Atlanta, Georgia, January 20, 2008.

506 When, in a South Carolina debate: CNN Democratic Debate, Myrtle Beach, South Carolina, January 21, 2008.

506 In the same debate, Clinton: Ibid.

506 It was such a charged evening: Heilemann and Halperin, *Game Change*, p. 206.

509 One early sign that the 2008 race: Jason Horowitz, New York *Observer*, February 4, 2007.

509 He brushed it off: CNN.com, January 31, 2007.

509 Obama wanted to appear: Ibid.

509 The mood among Obama's aides: Anne E. Kornblut, Washington *Post*, December 13, 2007.

509 There was Robert Johnson: CNN, January 13, 2008.

510 There was Hillary Clinton: Editorial, New York *Times*, January 9, 2008.

510 The day before the New Hampshire primary: Abdon M. Pallasch, Chicago *Sun-Times*, January 9, 2008.

510 Donna Brazile, who had been: Ben Smith, *Politico*, January 11, 2008.

510 When it seemed that Obama: Steve Kornacki, New York *Observer*, January 26, 2008.

511 "Do you personally have any": ABC News, July 4, 2008.

511 Bill Clinton's frustration was so deep: CNN, April 22, 2008.

512 In the wake of Super Tuesday: Sean Wilentz, "Race Man," *The New Republic*, February 27, 2008.

512 Not long after Wilentz's article: Katherine Q. Seelye and Julie Bosman, New York *Times*, March 12, 2008.

513 The comment of hers: Kathy Kiely and Jill Lawrence, *USA Today*, May 8, 2008.

513 Charles Rangel: Richard Sisk and David Saltonstall, New York *Daily News*, May 9, 2008.

Chapter Fifteen: The Book of Jeremiah

519 Fox played the clips: Editorial, New York *Post*, March 14, 2008.

519 Bob Herbert, in the New York *Times*: Bob Herbert, New York *Times*, April 3, 2008.

519 Patricia Williams, in *The Nation*: Patricia Williams, "Let Them Eat Waffles," *The Nation*, May 1, 2008.

520 "Wright's homiletics had the effect": Sharpley-Whiting, *The Speech*, p. 7.

521 As recently as January, 2007: Manya A. Brachear, Chicago *Tribune*, January 21, 2007.

521 At the *Tribune* session: Editorial, Chicago *Tribune*, March 16, 2008.

523 To begin, Obama called: Barack Obama, National Constitution Center, Philadelphia, March 18, 2008.

523 "I can no more disown him": Ibid.

524 Obama's speech won: Editorial, New York *Times*, March 19, 2008; editorial, Washington *Post*, March 19, 2008.

525 The right wing's response: "Fox News," March 18, 2008.

530 "Have you heard the whole sermon": Jeremiah Wright, National Press Club, Washington, D.C., April 28, 2008.

532 Speaking at an N.A.A.C.P. dinner: Jeremiah Wright, N.A.A.C.P., Detroit, Michigan, April 27, 2008.

532 Interviewed by Cliff Kelley: "The Cliff Kelley Show," WVON, November 25, 2008.

532 "He doesn't have a church": Ibid.

533 As late as June, 2009: David Squires, *Daily Press*, June 10, 2009.

533 He joked with his aides: Wolffe, *Renegade*, p. 184.

533 That night, on NBC: NBC, May 6, 2008.

534 Michael Eric Dyson: Michael Eric Dyson, "Obama's Rebuke of Absentee Black Fathers," *Time*, June 19, 2008.

534 The novelist Ishmael Reed: Ishmael Reed, *CounterPunch*, June 24, 2008.

534 On July 6th, Jesse Jackson: "The O'Reilly Factor," Fox News, July 6, 2008.

Chapter Sixteen: "How Long? Not Long"

539 "Your door is shut": McKay, *The Complete Poems*, p. 148.

541 When his aides charged: Michael Shear and Dan Balz, Washington *Post*, July 30, 2008.

541 When Obama told the St. Petersburg *Times:* Adam C. Smith, St. Petersburg *Times*, August 2, 2008.

541 "His comments were clearly": CNN, August 3, 2008.

542 After McCain lost: John McCain, Charleston, South Carolina, February 19, 2000.

543 In early October: "Hannity's America," Fox News, October 5, 2008.

544 "It is your character": McCain, *Character Is Destiny*, p. xi.

545 In 2000, McCain had called: Brian Knowlton, New York *Times*, February 29, 2000.

545 Jon Stewart, the host: David Grann, "The Fall," *The New Yorker*, November 17, 2008.

545 "Our opponent," she said: CNN, October 4, 2008.

546 McCain, using the same: David Grann, "The Fall," *The New Yorker*, November 17, 2008.

546 Now, a month before the election: *Politico*, October 11, 2008.

547 McCain issued a statement: David Grann, "The Fall," *The New Yorker*, November 17, 2008.

547 Obama was disingenuous: Democratic Debate, National Constitution Center, Philadelphia, April 16, 2008.

550 "On the Republican side": "Meet the Press," NBC, October 19, 2008.

552 In a poll conducted by the BBC: BBC News, September 10, 2008.

554 The Obama campaign: Jonathan D. Salant, "Bloomberg News," December 27, 2008.

557 Derrick Z. Jackson: Derrick Z. Jackson, Boston *Globe*, November 22, 2008.

559 She was born: Barack Obama, Grant Park, Chicago, November 5, 2008.

Chapter Seventeen: To the White House

561 The records tell us: White House Historical Association, www.whitehousehistory.org.

561 Three slaves at the White House: Ibid.

561 "Can one imagine": Wills, *Negro President*, p. 213.

562 "To the Southern-born": Bordewich, *Washington: The Making of the American Capital*, p. 191.

562 On a given day: Robert J. Kapsch, "Building Liberty's Capital: Black Labor and the New Federal City," *American Visions*, February-March 1995.

562 Jennings recalled Dolley: Jennings, *A Colored Man's Reminiscences of James Madison*, p. 12.

563 "I never saw him in a passion": Ibid., p. 17.

563 "I was always with Mr. Madison": Ibid., p. 20.

564 We do know that James Polk: William Seale, "Upstairs and Downstairs: The 19th Century White House," *American Visions*, February-March 1995.

564 Keckley called slavery: Keckley, *Behind the Scenes*, p. 3.
565 She was, she tells us: Ibid., p. 14.
565 When her uncle: Ibid., p. 12.
565 The resulting pregnancy: Ibid., p. 16.
565 Keckley understood well: Ibid., p. 15.
565 She married but refused: Ibid., p. 20.
565 Instead, she developed her skills: Ibid., p. 34.
566 Mrs. Lincoln had spilled coffee: Ibid., p. 35.
566 "You seem to be": Ibid., p. 39.
566 On the evening: Ibid., p. 45.
566 Almost immediately: Ibid., p. 46.
566 Keckley describes Lincoln: Ibid.
567 And in a scene of gothic strangeness: Ibid., p. 47.
567 First, she was taken: Ibid., p. 83.
567 "They made room for me": Ibid., p. 84.
567 After paying her respects: Ibid.
568 But after the book appeared: Carolyn Sorisio, "Unmasking the Genteel Performer: Elizabeth Keckley's Behind the Scenes and the Politics of Public Wrath," *African American Review* 34, no. 1 (2000).
568 "Where will it end?": Fleischner, *Mrs. Lincoln and Mrs. Keckly*, p. 317.
568 In a letter to the New York *Citizen*: Ibid., p. 318.
568 "To become President": Hofstadter, *The American Political Tradition*, p. 164.
569 If Lincoln grew: Ibid., p. 165.
569 As he wrote to Horace Greeley: Ibid., p. 169.
569 The resulting document: Ibid.
569 Even in August: Stauffer, *Giants: The Parallel Lives of Frederick Douglass and Abraham Lincoln*, p. 17.
569 "Your race are suffering": Ibid.
570 As one of his biographers: Ibid., p. 6.
570 His glance, Douglass recalled: Douglass, *Autobiographies*, p. 787.
571 As Douglass went up the stairs: Stauffer, *Giants: The Parallel Lives of Frederick Douglass and Abraham Lincoln*, p. 19.
571 Writing many years later: Douglass, *Autobiographies*, p. 785.
571 "Long lines of care": Ibid.
571 Lincoln hardly satisfied: Ibid., p. 786.
572 Douglass left Washington: Ibid., p. 798.
572 As late as four decades after: New York *Times*, April 12, 1904.
572 And in 1904: McNeil, *Groundwork: Charles Hamilton Houston and the Struggle for Civil Rights*, p. xvi.
572 In the days before Barack Obama was inaugurated: Peter Baker, "Obama's War Over Terror," *The New York Times Magazine*, January 17, 2010.
577 Johnson spoke of: Johnson, *James Weldon Johnson: The Complete Poems*, p. 109.
577 "God of our weary years": Joseph Lowery, Inaugural Benediction, Washington, D.C., January 20, 2009.
578 "Even at the inauguration": Fox News, January 20, 2009.

Bibliography

Abernathy, Ralph David. *And the Walls Came Tumbling Down: An Autobiography.* New York: Harper Collins, 1991.

Alinsky, Saul D. *John L. Lewis: An Unauthorized Biography.* New York: G.P. Putnam's Sons, 1949.

———. *Rules for Radicals.* New York: Random House, 1971.

Anderson, David. *Histories of the Hanged: The Dirty War in Kenya and the End of Empire.* New York: W.W. Norton, 2005.

Andrews, William, L. *To Tell a Free Story: The First Century of Afro-American Autobiography, 1760–1865.* Chicago: University of Illinois Press, 1986.

———, ed. *African-American Autobiography: A Collection of Critical Essays.* Englewood Cliffs, N.J.: Prentice Hall, 1993.

Andrews, William, and Henry Louis Gates, Jr., eds. *Slave Narratives.* New York: The Library of America, 2000.

Appiah, Kwame Anthony. *Cosmopolitanism: Ethics in a World of Strangers.* New York: W.W. Norton, 2006.

Asim, Jabari. *What Obama Means.* New York: William Morrow, 2009.

Baker, Houston A., Jr. *Long Black Song: Essays in Black American Literature and Culture.* Charlottesville: University of Virginia Press, 1972.

Baldwin, James. *Collected Essays.* New York: The Library of America, 1998.

Balz, Dan, and Haynes Johnson. *The Battle for America 2008: The Story of an Extraordinary Election.* New York: Viking, 2009.

Bell, Derrick. *Faces at the Bottom of the Well: The Permanence of Racism.* New York: Basic Books, 1993.

———. *Confronting Authority: Reflections of an Ardent Protester.* Boston: Beacon Press, 1994.

———. *The Derrick Bell Reader.* Edited by Richard Delgado and Jean Steancic. New York: New York University Press, 1995.

Bernstein, Carl. *A Woman in Charge: The Life of Hillary Rodham Clinton.* New York: Alfred A. Knopf, 2007.

Biles, Roger. *Richard J. Daley: Politics, Race, and the Governing of Chicago.* DeKalb: Northern Illinois University Press, 1995.

Black, Timuel D., Jr. *Bridges of Memory: Chicago's First Wave of Black Migration.* Evanston: Northwestern University Press, 2003.

———. *Bridges of Memory: Chicago's Second Generation of Black Migration.* Evanston: Northwestern University Press, 2007.

Bordewich, Fergus. *Washington: The Making of the American Capital.* New York: Amistad, 2008.

Branch, Taylor. *Parting the Waters: America in the King Years, 1954–1963.* New York: Simon & Schuster, 1988.

———. *Pillar of Fire: America in the King Years, 1963–1965.* New York: Simon & Schuster, 1998.

———. *At Canaan's Edge: America in the King Years: 1965–1968.* New York: Simon & Schuster, 2006.

Breitman, George, ed. *Malcolm X Speaks: Selected Speeches and Statements*. New York: Grove Press, 1990.

Brown, Claude. *Manchild in the Promised Land*. New York: Macmillan, 1965.

Caro, Robert. *The Path to Power: The Years of Lyndon Johnson*. New York: Alfred A. Knopf, 1981.

———. *Master of the Senate: The Years of Lyndon Johnson*. New York: Alfred A. Knopf, 2002.

Carson, Clayborne, et al., eds. *The Eyes on the Prize Civil Rights Reader*. New York: Penguin, 1991.

Casper, Scott E. *Constructing American Lives: Biography and Culture in Nineteenth-Century America*. Chapel Hill: University of North Carolina Press, 1999.

Chisholm, Shirley. *Unbought and Unbossed*. Boston: Houghton Mifflin, 1970.

———. *The Good Fight*. New York: HarperCollins, 1973.

Cleaver, Eldridge. *Soul on Ice*. New York: Delta, 1968.

Clinton, Bill. *My Life*. New York: Alfred A. Knopf, 2004.

Clinton, Hillary. *Living History*. New York: Simon & Schuster, 2003.

Cohen, Adam, and Elizabeth Taylor. *American Pharaoh: Mayor Richard J. Daley—His Battle for Chicago and the Nation*. New York: Little, Brown, 2000.

Cone, James H. *A Black Theology of Liberation*. Maryknoll, N.Y.: Orbis Books, 1990 (Twentieth Anniversary Edition with responses).

———. *Martin & Malcolm & America: A Dream or Nightmare*. Maryknoll, N.Y.: Orbis Books, 1991.

———. *Black Theology and Black Power*. Maryknoll, N.Y.: Orbis, 2008.

Corsi, Jerome R. *The Obama Nation: Leftist Politics and the Cult of Personality*. New York: Threshold Editions, 2008.

Davis, Frank Marshall. *Livin' the Blues: Memoirs of a Black Journalist and Poet*. Madison: University of Wisconsin Press, 2003.

Davis, Sammy, Jr., and Burt Boyar. *Yes I Can: The Story of Sammy Davis, Jr.* New York: Farrar, Strauss & Giroux, 1965.

Daws, Gavan. *Shoal of Time: A History of the Hawaiian Islands*. Honolulu: University of Hawaii Press, 1968.

Dawson, Michael. *Black Visions: The Roots of Contemporary African-American Political Ideologies*. Chicago: University of Chicago Press, 2001.

Despres, Leon M., with Kenan Heise. *Challenging the Daley Machine: A Chicago Alderman's Memoir*. Evanston, Ill.: Northwestern University Press, 2005.

DeYoung, Karen. *Soldier: The Life of Colin Powell*. New York: Alfred A. Knopf, 2006.

Douglass, Frederick. *Autobiographies*. New York: The Library of America, 1994.

Drake, St. Claire, and Horace R. Cayton. *Black Metropolis: A Study of Negro Life in a Northern City*. Chicago: University of Chicago Press, 1993.

Dray, Philip. *Capitol Men: The Epic Story of Reconstruction Through the Lives of the First Black Congressmen*. New York: Houghton Mifflin, 2008.

Du Bois, W. E. B. *The Autobiography of W. E. B. Du Bois*. New York: International Publishers, 1968.

Du Bois, W. E. B. *The Suppression of the African Slave-Trade; The Souls of Black Folk; Dusk of Dawn; Essays and Articles*. New York: The Library of America, 1986.

Dunham, S. Ann. *Surviving Against the Odds: Village Industry in Indonesia*. Durham, N.C.: Duke University Press, 2009.

Dunier, Mitchell. *Slim's Table: Race, Respectability, and Masculinity*. Chicago: University of Chicago Press, 1992.

Dyson, Michael Eric. *April 4, 1968: Martin Luther King, Jr.'s Death and How It Changed America.* New York: Basic Books, 2008.

Ehrenhalt, Alan. *The Lost City: Discovering the Forgotten Virtues of Community in the Chicago of the 1950s.* New York: Basic Books, 1995.

Elkins, Caroline. *Imperial Reckoning: The Untold Story of Britain's Gulag in Kenya.* New York: Henry Holt, 2005.

Ellison, Ralph. *Invisible Man.* New York: Random House, 1952.

———. *The Collected Essays of Ralph Ellison.* New York: Modern Library, 1995.

Fleischner, Jennifer. *Mrs. Lincoln and Mrs. Keckly: The Remarkable Story of the Friendship Between a First Lady and a Former Slave.* New York: Broadway Books, 2003.

Foner, Eric. *Reconstruction: America's Unfinished Revolution, 1863–1877.* New York: Harper Perennial, 2002.

Frady, Marshall. *Jesse: The Life and Pilgrimage of Jesse Jackson.* New York: Random House, 1996.

Frazier, E. Franklin. *The Negro Church in America.* New York: Schocken Books, 1974. (This edition of Frazier's 1964 book also includes C. Eric Lincoln's volume *The Black Church Since Frazier.*)

Freddoso, David. *The Case Against Barack Obama: The Unlikely Rise and Unexamined Agenda of the Media's Favorite Candidate.* Washington, D.C.: Regnery, 2008.

Frederickson, George M. *Racism: A Short History.* Princeton, N.J.: Princeton University Press, 2002.

Fremon, David. *Chicago Politics, Ward by Ward.* Bloomington: Indiana University Press, 1988.

Garrow, David J. *Protest at Selma: Martin Luther King, Jr., and the Voting Rights Act of 1965.* New Haven: Yale University Press, 1980.

———. *Bearing the Cross: Martin Luther King, Jr., and the Southern Christian Leadership Conference.* New York: William Morrow, 1986.

Gates, Henry Louis, Jr. *Bearing Witness: Selections from African-American Autobiography in the Twentieth Century.* New York: Pantheon, 1991.

———. *Thirteen Ways of Looking at a Black Man.* New York: Random House, 1997.

———, ed. *The Classic Slave Narratives.* New York: Mentor, 1987.

Gates, Henry Louis, Jr., and Cornel West. *The Future of the Race.* New York: Alfred A. Knopf, 1996.

Glaberman, Stu, and Jerry Burris. *The Dream Begins: How Hawaii Shaped Barack Obama.* Honolulu: Watermark Publishing, 2009.

Goldsworthy, David. *Tom Mboya: The Man Kenya Wanted to Forget.* Nairobi: Heinemann Educational Books, Ltd., 1982.

Griffin, John Howard. *Black Like Me.* New York: Signet, 1962.

Grimshaw, William J. *Bitter Fruit: Black Politics and the Chicago Machine, 1931–1991.* Chicago: University of Chicago Press, 1992.

Grossman, James R., Ann Durkin Keating, and Janice L. Reiff, eds. *The Encyclopedia of Chicago.* Chicago: University of Chicago Press, 2004.

Guzman, Richard R., ed. *Black Writing from Chicago.* Carbondale: Southern Illinois University Press, 2006.

Haas, Jeffrey. *The Assassination of Fred Hampton.* Chicago: Lawrence Hill Books, 2009.

Haas, Michael, ed. *Multicultural Hawaii: The Fabric of a Multiethnic Society.* New York: Garland, 1998.

Halberstam, David. *The Children.* New York: Ballantine Books, 1999.

Hampton, Henry, and Steve Fayer. *Voices of Freedom: An Oral History of the Civil Rights Movements from the 1950s through the 1980s.* New York: Bantam, 1991.

Hansen, Drew D. *The Dream: Martin Luther King, Jr., and the Speech That Inspired a Nation*. New York: Ecco, 2003.

Heale, M. J. *The Presidential Quest: Candidates and Images in American Political Culture, 1787–1852*. London and New York: Longman, 1982.

Heilemann, John, and Mark Halperin. *Game Change: Obama and the Clintons, McCain and Palin, and the Race of a Lifetime*. New York: Harper, 2010.

Hendon, Rickey. *Black Enough/White Enough: The Obama Dilemma*. Chicago: Third World Press, 2009.

Hirsch, Arnold R. *Making the Second Ghetto: Race and Housing in Chicago, 1940–1960*. Cambridge: Cambridge University Press, 1983.

Hofstadter, Richard. *The American Political Tradition*. New York: Alfred A. Knopf, 1948.

Hofstadter, Richard, and Michael Wallace, eds. *American Violence: A Documentary History*. New York: Alfred A. Knopf, 1970.

Hopkins, Dwight N. *Introducing Black Theology of Liberation*. Maryknoll, N.Y.: Orbis Books, 1999.

———, ed. *Black Faith and Public Talk: Critical Essays on James H. Cone's Black Theology and Black Power*. Waco: Baylor University Press, 2006.

Horwitt, Sanford D. *Let Them Call Me Rebel: Saul Alinsky, His Life and Legacy*. New York: Vintage, 1992.

Horwitz, Tony. *Confederates in the Attic: Dispatches from the Unfinished Civil War*. New York: Vintage, 1999.

Howells, William Dean. *The Lives and Speeches of Abraham Lincoln and Hannibal Hamlin*. New York: W.A. Townsend & Co., 1860.

Hughes, Langston. *The Big Sea: An Autobiography*. New York: Alfred A. Knopf, 1940.

Hurston, Zora Neale. *Moses, Man of the Mountain*. New York: HarperCollins, 1939.

———. *Novels and Stories*. New York: The Library of America, 1995.

Jacobs, Ron. *Obamaland: Who Is Barack Obama?* Honolulu: Booklines Hawaii, Ltd., 2009.

Jennings, Paul. *A Colored Man's Reminiscences of James Madison*. Cornell University Library Digital Collections, 2000.

Johnson, James Weldon. *The Complete Poems*. New York: Penguin, 2000.

———. *The Autobiography of an Ex-Colored Man*. New York: The Library of America, 2004.

Keckley, Elizabeth. *Behind the Scenes: or, Thirty Years a Slave, and Four Years in the White House*. New York: Penguin, 2005.

Kerlow, Eleanor. *Poisoned Ivy: How Ego, Ideology, and Power Politics Almost Ruined Harvard Law School*. New York: St. Martin's Press, 1994.

King, Martin Luther, Jr. *A Testament of Hope: The Essential Writings and Speeches of Martin Luther King, Jr.* Edited by James M. Washington. New York: HarperCollins, 1991.

———. *Why We Can't Wait*. New York: Signet Classics, 2000.

Kluger, Richard. *Simple Justice*. New York: Alfred A. Knopf, 1975.

Knoepfle, Peg, ed. *After Alinsky: Community Organizing in Illinois*. Springfield: Illinois Issues, 1990.

Lemann, Nicholas. *The Promised Land: The Great Black Migration and How It Changed America*. New York: Alfred A. Knopf, 1991.

Levinsohn, Florence Hamlish. *Harold Washington: A Political Biography*. Chicago: Chicago Review Press, 1983.

Lewis, David Levering. *W. E. B. Du Bois: Biography of a Race, 1868–1919*. New York: Henry Holt, 1993.

Lewis, John, and Michael D'Orso. *Walking with the Wind: A Memoir of the Movement*. New York: Harvest Books, 1999.

Lincoln, C. Eric, and Lawrence H. Mamiya. *The Black Church in the African-American Experience*. Durham, N.C.: Duke University Press, 1990.

Malcolm X., with Alex Haley. *The Autobiography of Malcolm X*. New York: Ballantine Books, 1965.

Maraniss, David. *First in His Class: A Biography of Bill Clinton*. New York: Simon & Schuster, 1995.

Marshall, John. *The Life of George Washington, Volume 2*. Philadelphia: Crissy & Markley, 1848.

Mboya, Tom. *The Challenge of Nationhood*. London: Andre Deutsch, 1970.

———. *Freedom and After*. Nairobi, Kenya: Heinemann, 1986.

McCain, John, with Mark Salter. *Faith of My Fathers*. New York: Random House, 1999.

———. *Worth the Fighting For: The Education of an American Maverick, and the Heroes Who Inspired Him*. New York: Random House, 2002.

———. *Character Is Destiny*. New York: Random House, 2005.

McKay, Claude. *The Complete Poems*. Urbana and Chicago: University of Illinois Press, 2004.

McNeil, Genna Rae. *Groundwork: Charles Hamilton Houston and the Struggle for Civil Rights*. Philadelphia: University of Pennsylvania Press, 1983.

Mendelberg, Tali. *The Race Card: Campaign Strategy, Implicit Messages, and the Norm of Equality*. Princeton: Princeton University Press, 2001.

Mendell, David. *Obama: From Promise to Power*. New York: Amistad, 2007.

Morris, Edmund. *The Rise of Theodore Roosevelt*. New York: Coward, McCann & Geoghan, 1979.

Moses, Wilson Jeremiah. *Creative Conflict in African-American Thought*. Cambridge: Cambridge University Press, 2004.

Mundy, Liza. *Michelle: A Biography*. New York: Simon & Schuster, 2009.

Murray, Albert. *The Omni-Americans: Black Experience & American Culture*. New York: Da Capo Press, 1970.

Murunga, Goodwin R., and Shadrack W. Nasong'o, eds. *Kenya: The Struggle for Democracy*. Dakar: Codesria, 2007.

Muwakkil, Salim. *Harold! Photographs from the Harold Washington Years*. Evanston, Ill.: Northwestern University Press, 2007.

Obama, Barack. *Dreams from My Father: A Story of Race and Inheritance*. New York: Three Rivers Press, 1995.

———. *The Audacity of Hope: Thoughts on Reclaiming the American Dream*. New York: Crown, 2006.

Okamura, Jonathan Y. *Ethnicity and Inequality in Hawaii*. Philadelphia: Temple University Press, 2008.

Philpott, Thomas Lee. *The Slum and the Ghetto: Immigrants, Blacks, and Reformers in Chicago, 1880–1930*. New York: Oxford University Press, 1978.

Plouffe, David. *The Audacity to Win*. New York: Viking, 2009.

Powell, Colin, with Joseph Persico. *My American Journey*. New York: Ballantine, 1995.

Presta, John. *Mr. and Mrs. Grassroots: How Barack Obama, Two Bookstore Owners, and 300 Volunteers Did It*. Paoli, Pa.: The Elevator Group, 2009.

Rakove, Milton. *Don't Make No Waves . . . Don't Back No Losers.* Bloomington: Indiana University Press, 1975.

———. *We Don't Want Nobody Nobody Sent: An Oral History of the Daley Years.* Bloomington: Indiana University Press, 1979.

Ramos, Constance F. *Our Friend Barry: Classmates' Recollections of Barack Obama and Punahou School.* Lulu.com, 2008.

Reed, Adolph L., Jr. *The Jesse Jackson Phenomenon.* New Haven: Yale University Press, 1986.

Reporting Civil Rights, Volumes One and Two. New York: The Library of America, 2003.

Rieder, Jonathan. *The Word of the Lord Is Upon Me: The Righteous Performance of Martin Luther King, Jr.* Cambridge, Mass.: Belknap Press, 2008.

Rivlin, Gary. *Fire on the Prairie: Chicago's Harold Washington and the Politics of Race.* New York: Henry Holt, 1992.

Royko, Mike. *Boss: Richard J. Daley of Chicago.* New York: Plume, 1971.

Shachtman, Tom. *Airlift to America: How Barack Obama, Sr., John F. Kennedy, and 800 East African Students Changed Their World and Ours.* New York: St. Martin's Press, 2009.

Sharpley-Whiting, T. Denean, ed. *The Speech: Race and Barack Obama's "A More Perfect Union."* New York: Bloomsbury, 2009.

Sollors, Werner. *Neither Black Nor White Yet Both.* Cambridge: Harvard University Press, 1997.

———, ed. *An Anthology of Interracial Literature: Black-White Contacts in the Old World and the New.* New York: New York University Press, 2004.

Stauffer, John. *Giants: The Parallel Lives of Frederick Douglass and Abraham Lincoln.* New York: Twelve, 2008.

Steele, Shelby. *A Bound Man: Why We Are Excited About Obama and Why He Can't Win.* New York: Free Press, 2008.

Stepto, Robert B. *From Behind the Veil: A Study of Afro-American Narrative.* Chicago: University of Illinois Press, 1991.

Street, Paul. *Barack Obama and the Future of American Politics.* Boulder: Paradigm, 2009.

Sugrue, Paul. *Sweet Land of Liberty: The Forgotten Struggle for Civil Rights in the North.* New York: Random House, 2008.

Sundquist, Eric J. *King's Dream.* New Haven & London: Yale University Press, 2009.

Swain, Carol M., *Black Faces, Black Interests: The Representation of African Americans in Congress.* Lanham: University Press of America, 2006.

Teixeira, Ruy, ed. *Red, Blue & Purple: The Future of Election Demographics.* Washington D.C.: Brookings, 2008.

Thomas, Evan. *Robert Kennedy: His Life.* New York: Simon & Schuster, 2000.

———. *A Long Time Coming: The Inspiring, Combative 2008 Campaign and the Historic Election of Barack Obama.* New York: PublicAffairs, 2009.

Todd, Chuck, and Sheldon Gawiser. *How Barack Obama Won: A State-by-State Guide to the Historic 2008 Presidential Election.* New York: Vintage, 2009.

Toomer, Jean. *Cane.* New York: Boni and Liveright, 1923.

Travis, Dempsey J. *An Autobiography of Black Chicago.* Chicago: Urban Research Press, 1981

———. *An Autobiography of Black Politics.* Chicago: Urban Research Press, 1987.

———. *Harold: The People's Mayor.* Chicago: Urban Research Press, 1989.

Turow, Scott. *One L: The Turbulent True Story of a First Year at Harvard Law School*. New York: Farrar, Straus & Giroux, 1977.

Wallace, Irving. *The Man*. New York: Fawcett, 1967.

Walters, Ronald. *Black Presidential Politics in America: A Strategic Approach*. Albany: State University of New York Press, 1988.

Washington, Booker T. *Up from Slavery*. Oxford: Oxford University Press, 1995.

Wickham, DeWayne. *Bill Clinton and Black America*. New York: Ballantine Books, 2002.

Wilentz, Sean. *The Age of Reagan: A History, 1974–2008*. New York: Harper Collins, 2008.

Wilkins, Roger. *A Man's Life: An Autobiography*. Woodbridge: Ox Bow Press, 1991.

Williams, Erma Brooks. *Political Empowerment of Illinois' African-American State Lawmakers from 1877 to 2005*. Lanham, Md.: University Press of America, 2008.

Williams, Juan. *Eyes on the Prize: America's Civil Rights Years, 1954–1965*. New York: Viking Penguin, 1987.

Wills, Garry. *Negro President: Jefferson and the Slave Power*. New York: Houghton Mifflin, 2003.

Wilson, William Julius. *The Declining Significance of Race*. Chicago: University of Chicago Press, 1980.

Wolffe, Richard. *Renegade: The Making of a President*. New York: Crown, 2009.

Wood, Forrest G. *Black Scare: The Racist Response to Emancipation and Reconstruction*. Berkeley: University of California Press, 1968.

Wright, Jeremiah A., Jr. *What Makes You So Strong?* Valley Forge, Pa.: Judson Press, 1993.

———. *Africans Who Shaped Our Faith*. Chicago: Urban Ministries, 1995.

Wright, Richard. *Black Boy (American Hunger)* and *The Outsider*. New York: Library of America, 1991.

Index

Abacha, Sani, 356
Abbott, Robert S., 144, 319
ABC, 511, 533
    Bloody Sunday reported by, 11
    Wright reported by, 517–19, 520
Abercrombie, Neil, 51, 52, 53, 54, 56,
    65, 71
Abernathy, Ralph, 152, 312, 490
Abner, Willoughby, 150
abolitionists, 143, 255, 269, 571
abortion, 406, 433, 434, 471, 546
Abortion: The Clash of Absolutes (Tribe),
    193
Abramoff, Jack, 437
Abramowitz, Alan, 450–1
Abu Ghraib, 411, 443
Abyssinian Baptist Church, 113
Achieving Our Country (Rorty), 523
Ackerman, Sam and Martha, 283
A.C.L.U. liberals, 187
ACORN, *see* Association of Community
    Organizations for Reform Now
Acton, Jay, 227
Adams, Abigail, 562
Adams, Charles, 171
Adams, John, 562
Adams, Romanzo, 50
Addams, Jane, 156
Adelstein, Eric, 338
Adi, Zulfan, 60
Advocate, 107
affirmative action, 71, 187, 191, 211,
    214, 215–16, 262, 263, 399, 434,
    476, 483, 526
Afghanistan, Soviet invasion of, 99,
    105
Afghanistan War, 541, 554, 582
A.F.L.-C.I.O., 370, 387
Africa, 431, 518
    colonialism in, 247–8
African-American Religious Leadership
    Committee, 519
African-Americans
    American readiness for presidency of,
        449, 452–6, 462, 486, 490, 504, 553
    autobiographies of, 13, 228–30, 231–3,
        235

in Chicago, 143–60, 162, 343
in Congress, 355, 356–7
at Harvard Law, 187, 191, 197, 198,
    200, 205, 207–8
higher education and, 98–9
Kerry not embraced by, 395
political power of, 14
poverty among, 284
preaching styles of, 18, 23–4
at Princeton, 202–4
in prison, 284, 307, 492
in Reconstruction, 355–6
in run for presidency, 452–4
and 2008 presidential campaign,
    13–14, 467–78, 480–7, 492–5,
    498–506, 507, 508, 556
unemployment among, 284, 285,
    307
on university faculties, 212–14
as war veterans, 164
see also race
African-American Students
    Foundation, 32
African Methodist Episcopal Church,
    5
African National Congress, 575
Afro-American Patrolmen's League, 268,
    311
Afrocentrism, 173
Agnew, Spiro, 479
Ahmadinejad, Mahmoud, 532
AIDS, *see* H.I.V./AIDS
Aid to Dependent Children, 176
Ailes, Roger, 480
Alabama state troopers, 9–11
Alda, Alan, 423
Alexander, Clifford, 451
Alexander, Elizabeth, 451
Alexander, Mark, 451
Ali, Muhammad, 142, 270, 286, 410
Alinsky, Saul, 121, 125–6, 127–30, 133,
    151, 156, 162, 163, 164, 174
    BHO's critique of, 179–80
Alito, Samuel, 187, 434
Allen, Martha, 165, 167
Alliance for Progress, 431
Al Qaeda, 338, 347